THE GREAT PURGE TRIAL

mum of information and to guide the interested reader to the significant literature dealing with events and issues discussed at the trial. Wherever possible, an English translation of the original source has been cited. In a few instances, the biographical notes are limited by the fact that the defendants in question were minor Party functionaries whose careers were not officially described in the usual biographical sources prior to the trial.

The unorthodox spelling of Russian names used in the Soviet translation presents a problem. The solution here has been to deviate from the original in the annotations and to utilize the most common English form (e.g., Piatakov, rather than Pyatakov) in each case. This should eliminate uncertainties for the reader who wishes to consult the standard literature in English.

The co-editor, who prepared the annotations, would like to express appreciation to Mrs. Jean Steinberg of Frederick A. Praeger, Inc., and to Mrs. Janet Zagoria for allowing him to examine and to cite parts of the forthcoming *Bolsheviks and Bureaucrats* (Essays by Boris I. Nicolaevsky) to be published later in 1965. Also to Seweryn Bialer, who kindly furnished additional information which has made the biographical notes on the defendants more complete.

The author of the Introduction has been privileged to talk over several pertinent questions with Boris Nicolaevsky, and is very grateful to him for sharing his unique wealth of memory and insight into Soviet history. He owes much to suggestions and critical comment from his co-editor. He has benefited from discussions with Donald Lammers, François Bourricaud and others among the fellows for 1964-1965 at the Center for Advanced Study in the Behavioral Sciences. He wishes, in addition, to thank the Center of International Studies of Princeton University for assistance.

ROBERT C. TUCKER
STEPHEN F. COHEN

VIII

THE GREAT PURGE TRIAL

Edited, and with notes, by

ROBERT C. TUCKER and **STEPHEN F. COHEN**

With an introduction by **ROBERT C. TUCKER**

GROSSET & DUNLAP

PUBLISHERS

NEW YORK

Preface

It was Howard Fertig, editor of the Universal Library series, who first suggested to us the need for a new edition of the verbatim report of the 1938 Moscow Trial. On reflection it became clear that this record of the most important of the purge trials of Stalin's time should be made available to a wide public because it continues to have great relevance to basic political and intellectual problems of our age — in particular, the problem of totalitarianism.

This is a difficult as well as rewarding document. Consequently, in preparing an American edition of it we have attempted to provide the general reader with some of the essential equipment for reading it with critical understanding: biographical notes, annotations, a suggested list of readings, and an introductory essay. The aim of the Introduction is both to interpret the 1938 trial in its historical setting and to re-examine, in the light of significant new data made public since Stalin's death, the meaning of the Moscow trials and the Great Purge of which they were an integral part. An effort to assess the validity of some earlier Western thinking on these problems has necessarily entered into this task.

This edition of the verbatim report is based on the official Soviet translation published in several languages in 1938. For reasons of space, and to make possible the inclusion of explanatory notes, biographical information about the defendants, and a list of readings, it has been necessary to omit three sessions. The deletions, however, do not constitute a major abridgment of the substance of the proceedings. The testimony given at these three sessions was devoted largely to medical evidence concerning the alleged murders of Gorky, Kuibyshev, Menzhinsky, and Peshkov. Similar testimony appears in other sessions, most notably in the evening session of March 8. Moreover, each of the omitted sessions is briefly recounted and the summaries appear in their proper sequence.

The annotations, biographical notes, and suggested list of readings are designed for the non-specialist. They seek only to furnish a mini-

Introduction

STALIN, BUKHARIN, AND HISTORY AS CONSPIRACY

By ROBERT C. TUCKER

> BUKHARIN: *It must be said for the sake of historical exactitude. . . .*
>
> VYSHINSKY: *Don't trouble to speak for history, accused Bukharin. History will itself record what will be interesting for history.*
>
> FROM THE TRIAL

1.

The court, like every human institution, is corruptible. Under certain conditions it comes to be employed for ends extraneous and alien to its proper primary purpose, which is to promote justice through the determination of guilt or innocence by the open examining and arguing of evidence. History has witnessed many examples of this misuse of the court in the form of political trials, in which governments exploit the courtroom for such aims as the defamation and defeat of their political opponents. A sub-category of the political trial is the show trial. Here the court proceedings become literally a dramatic performance in which not only the judge and the prosecutor but also the defendant or defendants play prearranged parts just as actors do on the stage. The crux of the show trial is the confession. The defendant plays the leading part by confessing in vivid detail to heinous crimes allegedly committed by himself and others as part of a great conspiracy. Such spectacles have antecedents going back to the medieval witchcraft trials in which the accused confessed to riding on broomsticks at night and passing through keyholes for their evil purposes. In our time totalitarian regimes have adopted and perfected the show trial. Indeed, the propensity to stage these political dramas in the courtroom is one of the telltale symptoms of that still imperfectly understood phenomenon of the modern age called "totalitarianism."

Political trials have taken place throughout the history of Soviet Russia, from Lenin's time to the present. The show trial, however, is one of the special hallmarks of the Stalin era and of Stalinism. It began with the Shakhty case, in which a number of Soviet and foreign engineers who had worked in the Donets coal basin confessed to participating in a conspiracy to commit crimes of industrial sabotage, or "wrecking," on orders from abroad. This show trial was staged in 1928, the year of Stalin's emergence into ascendancy in the post-Lenin regime. Others soon followed: the trial of Professor Ramzin and the "Industrial Party" in 1930, the Menshevik trial in 1931, and the Metro-Vickers case in 1933. But all these were mere curtain-raisers for the series of major show trials during Stalin's Great Purge of the Communist Party in 1936-1938. Then, after World War II, which brought a respite in this business, show trials were resumed on Stalin's orders and under the direction of Stalin's agents in a number of countries of Eastern Europe which had come under Soviet domination. And when Stalin died in March 1953, he was in the midst of preparations for one more great and macabre show trial in Russia — the trial of a group of Kremlin doctors, most of them Jewish, on charges of conspiracy to commit medical murder of Soviet leaders on instructions from the Anglo-American intelligence services. This project may have been Stalin's own undoing, for it seems quite possible that he was put out of the way in order to prevent the doctors' trial — and the new party purge that would have accompanied it — from taking place. Since his death there have been no more show trials in the Soviet Union.

The three big purge trials staged in Moscow in 1936-1938 and widely known abroad simply as the "Moscow trials" hold a special place in this history. Whereas non-Party specialists, so-called "bourgeois remnants," had figured prominently in the earlier show trials, now the cast of the accused contained many of the great names of Bolshevism. In the prisoners' dock were most of the surviving leaders of the Bolshevik Old Guard, former People's Commissars in the Soviet government, former Soviet ambassadors who had served in major world capitals like Berlin and London, and, finally, a few obscure N.K.V.D. agents whose function in the trials was to assist the prosecution in special ways by blackening the principal accused. To see more clearly to what extent the Bolshevik Old Guard was on trial, it may be useful to recall that when Lenin, towards the end of his life, considered the problem of choosing a successor in a letter that became known in the Party as his "Testament," he mentioned the names of six prominent party figures: Trotsky, Stalin, Zinoviev, Kamenev, Bukharin, and Piatakov. One only — Stalin — was ruled out, for Lenin in a postscript to this letter directed the Party leadership to remove him from the post of General Secretary because of grave character defects that could, he said, prove of decisive significance. The other five, four in person and one in absentia, were leading defendants in the Moscow trials. Zinoviev and Kamenev headed the lists of sixteen accused in the trial of the "Trotskyite-Zinovievite Terrorist Centre" in August 1936. Piatakov, along with Karl Radek, former Secretary of the Communist International, were the leading names in the group of seventeen accused in the case of the "Anti-Soviet Trotskyite Centre" in January 1937. Bukharin, along with Alexei Rykov, Lenin's successor as Chairman of the Council of People's Commissars, led the list of twenty-one defendants in the trial of the "Anti-Soviet Bloc of Rights and Trotskyites" in March 1938. And Trotsky, although not physically present in the dock, was being tried in absentia. In fact he was the arch-criminal of Bolshevik political history according to the picture of events that unfolded in the course of the three Moscow trials. In passing sentence in the second trial, the court directed that he and his son be arrested and tried if apprehended on Soviet territory. This was an esoterically phrased death sentence and was carried out by the agent of Stalin who assassinated Trotsky in Mexico in 1940.

The 1938 trial of the twenty-one, the transcript of which is presented here in slightly abbreviated form, has good claim to be considered "the great purge trial." Here the series of show trials staged during the Great Purge reached its climax. The major accusatory themes introduced in the earlier purge trials were restated and brought together with new charges, one of them being that Marshal Tukhachevsky and fellow Soviet military leaders who were executed in June 1937 after a secret trial, had headed a "military conspiratorial organization" linked with the larger conspiracy of which Bukharin and others had allegedly been ringleaders. The summing-up speech of the prosecutor, Vyshinsky, in the 1938 trial is the classic presentation of the ideology of the Moscow purge trials in its full-blown development, and the trial itself may justly be regarded as the supreme production in the Stalin genre of political show trial. It was likewise, as I shall argue below, the scene of an encounter between Vyshinsky and the chief defendant, Nikolai Bukharin, who endeavored by a technique of indirection to transform his trial into an anti-trial, an indictment and conviction of his accuser, Stalin.

The problem of the Moscow trials, and of this one in particular, takes on still greater interest at present owing to the post-Stalin Soviet disclosures concerning the Great Purge and the purge trials. De-Stalinization has meant, in no small part, a process of exoneration and rehabilitation — posthumous in very many cases — of purge victims. In this process much significant information has been brought to light. Khrushchev's secret report on Stalin to the Twentieth Party Congress in 1956, although not published inside the Soviet Union to this day, was nevertheless the fountainhead of an official Soviet literature about the purges that went on accumulating during the years of Khrushchev's ascendancy and has continued to flow even after his fall from power in October 1964. Although it still leaves many questions unsolved or incompletely answered, this body of Soviet material provides a basis not only for a fresh look at the trials and purges themselves but also for a critical re-examination of the ideas and assumptions underlying the voluminous Western literature on this subject, most of which was produced in the Stalin era.

A crucially important point that emerges from the post-Stalin Soviet revelations about the Great Purge is that Stalin personally conceived, initiated, and directed the entire process, including the planning, preparation, and actual conduct of the purge trials. It is true that testimony to the same effect had reached us from other sources much earlier. Stalin had been pictured as director-general of the purges and trials by high-ranking Soviet police officials with firsthand knowledge of the situation who escaped to the West at the time and published their stories.[1] However, this view of the matter, with all its profound implications, somehow failed to make the requisite deep impression upon the Western mind. Nor was it understood by the Soviet public and intelligentsia, who had no access to such sources of information. In memoirs published long after Stalin's death the writer Ilya Ehrenburg recalls what went on in the minds of Soviet

---

[1] See in particular W. G. Krivitsky: *In Stalin's Secret Service* (New York: Harper, 1939) and Alexander Orlov: *The Secret History of Stalin's Crimes* (New York: Random House, 1953).

intellectuals during the Great Purge: "We thought (perhaps we wanted to think) that Stalin knew nothing about the senseless violence committed against the Communists, against the Soviet intelligentsia. Meyerhold said: 'They conceal it from Stalin.' One night . . . I met Boris Pasternak in Lavrushensky lane; he waved his arms about as he stood between the snowdrifts: 'If only someone would tell Stalin about it.' "[2] Many purge victims reasoned similarly. Some addressed anguished appeals to Stalin from N.K.V.D. cells, protesting their innocence. General Yakir, one of those arrested in 1937 in the Tukhachevsky case, is said to have shouted at the moment he was shot: "Long live the Party, long live Stalin!" Khrushchev, who related this story at the Twenty-Second Party Congress in 1961, explains: "He thought that enemies had infiltrated the organs of the People's Commissariat of Internal Affairs."[3] Among some political prisoners in concentration camps this belief took the form of a theory that fascists had wormed their way into positions of power under Stalin. Another widely held belief was that the events of the time were the work of the N.K.V.D. chief, Yezhov; in fact, the climax of the Great Purge in 1937-1938 became known in Russia as the *Yezhovshchina,* or "time of Yezhov."

In reality it was the time of Stalin. The picture given earlier in the accounts of N.K.V.D. defectors such as Krivitsky and Orlov has been fully and convincingly confirmed by official Soviet sources of the post-Stalin period. The man whom many believed to be incompletely informed about the Great Purge was in fact running it. The man to whom some appealed for justice over the head of the N.K.V.D. was in fact directing all its activity. In his secret report to the Twentieth Party Congress, Khrushchev tells, for example, how Yezhov would send to Stalin for his approval lists of persons in N.K.V.D. custody with proposed sentences indicated upon them. "In 1937-1938," he says, "383 such lists containing the names of many thousands of Party, Soviet, Komsomol, Army and economic workers were sent to Stalin. He approved these lists."[4] He tells us further that Stalin rather than Yezhov made all the decisions concerning arrests of high party leaders, many of whom were arrested without

---

[2] *Memoirs: 1921-1941,* translated by T. Shebunina in collaboration with Y. Kapp (Cleveland and New York: World Publishing Co., 1963), pp. 426-427.

[3] *Documents of the Twenty-second Congress of the CPSU* (New York: Crosscurrents Press, 1961), Vol. I, p. 228.

[4] This and all further references to Khrushchev's secret report are based on the text as originally printed in *The New York Times* for June 5, 1956 and reprinted in *The Crimes of the Stalin Era* (New York: The New Leader, 1956), with annotations by Boris I. Nicolaevsky.

the prosecutor's knowledge. "In such a situation," Khrushchev goes on, "there is no need for any sanction, for what sort of a sanction could there be when Stalin decided everything? He was the chief prosecutor in these cases. Stalin not only agreed to, but on his own initiative issued, arrest orders." Naturally, Stalin could not have engineered the Great Purge without the zealous and capable assistance of many others, among whom his police chiefs, Yagoda and Yezhov, deserve special mention. But these men as well as their subordinates were essentially Stalin's accomplices and tools, not independent figures acting in their own right. Thus Yagoda, who had assisted Stalin in preparing the 1936 trial, was then removed (to become a defendant himself in the 1938 trial) and replaced by Yezhov, who in turn was eliminated after serving as Stalin's right-hand man at the height of the reign of terror.

Why did so many Russians, including some high-ranking victims of the purge, fail to understand that Stalin was the moving spirit and director of the whole business? Ehrenburg probably gives part of the answer when he speaks of their wish to believe otherwise. We must also take account of the traditional Russian habit of absolving the Tsar of personal responsibility for flagrant injustices, which were thought to be the work of evil ministers who kept the Tsar in ignorance of the people's sufferings. But a further and crucial part of the explanation is that Stalin contrived to hold himself aloof and in the background so that people would not understand his true role in the events of the time. His activity as stage manager of these events was carried on behind the scenes and was known only to a few, most of whom perished before the end. Even in the fateful Central Committee session of March 3-5, 1937, during which Stalin's two speeches were signals for intensification of the Great Purge as it entered the final period, he carefully posed as a force for moderation by cautioning in conclusion against "a heartless attitude toward people" and castigating unnamed Party leaders who were expelling Party members with reckless abandon and "think it a mere bagatelle to expel thousands and tens of thousands of people from the Party."[5] By such means Stalin successfully carried out one of the greatest acts of deliberate deception in modern political history. That is, he contrived to make the time of Stalin go down in Russian history as the "time of Yezhov."

As we re-examine the problem of the Moscow show trials, then, it is essential to bear in mind that these were basically one-man shows of which Stalin himself was organizer, chief producer, and

---

[5] Joseph Stalin: *Mastering Bolshevism* (New York: New Century Publishers, 1946), p. 45.

stage manager as well as an appreciative spectator from a darkened room at the rear of the Hall of Columns, where the trials were held. Vyshinsky spoke for the prosecution, but we must understand that he spoke with the voice of Stalin. Although he did not claim personal authorship, Stalin was the chief playwright of the case of the "Anti-Soviet Bloc of Rights and Trotskyites" and the other cases enacted in the show trials.

2.

"We have internal enemies. We have external enemies. This, comrades, must not be forgotten for a single moment." This was Stalin's "general conclusion" in a major speech of April 1928 on the state of the Soviet Union. It flowed from his analysis of the Shakhty case, which he described as an economic counter-revolution plotted by bourgeois experts who "banded together in a secret group and were receiving money for sabotage purposes from former owners now living abroad and from counter-revolutionary anti-Soviet capitalist organizations in the West."[6] Here, in embryo, was the ideology of the later purge trials as elaborated by Vyshinsky with the assistance of the confessing defendants. Here was the *Weltanschauung* of those trials.

The world of the Moscow trials is one of long-drawn-out conspiratorial cold war waged for the purpose of destroying the Soviet state and the Revolution it embodies. It is a world dominated by the machinations of external and especially internal "enemies" who are diabolically cunning as well as totally vicious and evil. Abroad they may at times operate in the open, although their chief arm is the secretly functioning intelligence services of the major powers. But inside the Soviet Union they do all their nefarious work by stealthy and devious means, practicing deception as their primary technique of political warfare. They wear "masks" of loyal citizens and prominent party and government leaders until they are finally exposed as persons who, in the words of Vyshinsky's summing-up speech in the Bukharin trial, "spent the whole of their lives behind masks . . . " And these internal enemies are no less a deadly danger to the Soviet state for the fact that they represent, in actual numbers, only a small minority of the total population. For, as Stalin explained in the March 1937 Central Committee meeting, "it does not at all need a big number of people to do harm and to cause damage . . . Thousands of people are required to build a big railway bridge, but a few people

---

6 J. V. Stalin: *Works* (Moscow: Foreign Language Publishing House, 1954), Vol. XI, p. 57.

are sufficient to blow it up. Tens and hundreds of such examples could be quoted. Consequently, we must not comfort ourselves with the fact that we are many, while they, the Trotskyite wreckers, are few."[7]

In this same speech Stalin represented the above-mentioned world-view as being "what Leninism teaches us," and Vyshinsky echoed the point in the 1938 summing-up speech. Though Stalin, in all probability, seriously believed this, he was mistaken. Lenin had provided a foundation for this world-view in his concept of an international class war between a "socialism" embodied in the Soviet Republic and a "capitalism" dominant in the rest of the world, which represented therefore a hostile "capitalist encirclement." But Stalin filled these old Leninist concepts with a new, distinctively Stalinist content, which found expression in the materials of the Moscow purge trials. The chief distinctive feature was the quite un-Leninist emphasis upon *conspiracy* as the hallmark of the present epoch. Although it did not exclude underhanded methods, the original Bolshevik or Leninist ideology did not view the international class war as a conflict being waged by essentially conspiratorial means. Nor did it see this conflict as centering in the hostile activities of masked enemies operating inside Soviet society. In Stalinism the Leninist notion of an international class war turns into the notion of a conspiratorial cold war against the Soviet Union. The final and finished expression of this conspiratorial interpretation of contemporary history is to be found in the pages of the trial transcript here presented.

As we examine it we must bear in mind that the history of Lenin's party from its founding early in the century to the end of the 1920's was characterized by factional struggles and opposition movements supporting programs of Party policy that were at times openly debated. Shortly following the Bolshevik Revolution of 1917, for example, Bukharin, one of the outstanding leaders and theoreticians of the Party, headed a "Left Communist" opposition that favored revolutionary war as against Lenin's policy of accepting the annexationist peace dictated by the German government to Trotsky at Brest-Litovsk. Other opposition movements rose and fell in the Party during the turbulent first years of its rule, and factionalism flourished in spite of the formal prohibition of it in the resolution on Party unity adopted by the Tenth Party Congress in 1921. With Lenin's death the Party's inner conflicts intensified. In the mid-1920's the Trotskyite or "Left Opposition," joined in 1926 by Stalin's former allies

---

[7] *Mastering Bolshevism,* pp. 26-27.

Zinoviev and Kamenev, vainly opposed its program of rapid industrialization and "permanent revolution" to the platform of "socialism in one country." Though the latter became identified with Stalin, it originated with a group of "Right Communists" headed by Bukharin, who had now shifted to a moderate position, Alexei Rykov, and the trade-union leader Mikhail Tomsky. To these men "socialism in one country" meant a program of gradual industrialization without forcible measures to collectivize the Russian peasantry, continual alleviation of the harsher aspects of the dictatorship, and in foreign affairs a tendency to de-emphasize the policy of fomenting revolution in Europe in favor of efforts to cement diplomatic ties with and secure economic credits from the Western democracies.[8] Having taken over the slogan of "socialism in one country" from this source and used it with signal success against the Left Opposition, Stalin subsequently gave it an interpretation very different from that of the right-wing leaders, whose position was stigmatized at the end of the 1920's as the "Right Opposition." To Stalin "socialism in one country" meant a strengthening of the dictatorship and an orientation of the nation's economy towards preparation for total war. This was to be achieved through breakneck industrialization, emphasizing heavy industry and arms production, and exploitation of peasant labor by means of coercive collectivization. Stalin's program went into effect during the First Five-Year Plan (1928-1933) at ghastly cost to the country in strain, dislocation, privation, sacrifice, and suffering.

The right-wing leaders were opposed in principle to this Stalinist "general line" and fought it as hard and as long as they could. Bukharin, their foremost theorist and the soul of the Right Opposition, bore the brunt of the fight. In the course of it he made a move to secure support from Stalin's old left-wing opponents Zinoviev and Kamenev. On July 11, 1928, in an interview with Kamenev later published abroad by the Trotskyites, Bukharin said that his group considered Stalin's line fatal to the Revolution. Stalin, he said, was leading the country to famine, ruin, and a police regime with his program of exacting "tribute" from the peasantry for forced industrialization, and was ideologically justifying this line with an argument of "idiotic illiteracy" to the effect that resistance and therewith internal

---

[8] For an account of the Right Opposition see Robert V. Daniels: *The Conscience of the Revolution: Communist Opposition in Soviet Russia* (Cambridge: Harvard University Press, 1960), Chapter 13. A full-scale treatment of the development of the views of the right-wing group in the 1920's will be presented in a forthcoming study by Stephen F. Cohen: *Bukharin and the Politics of Right Communism: 1923-1929.*

class conflict must grow as socialism grows. After comparing Stalin with Genghis Khan, Bukharin said that conditions were ripening in the Central Committee for dismissing Stalin but were not yet fully ripe. Meanwhile Stalin, who was at bottom interested only in power, was determined to strangle the opposition. "Stalin knows only vengeance," Bukharin declared. "We must remember his theory of sweet revenge." This was a reference to something that Stalin had said one summer night in 1923 to Kamenev and Dzerzhinsky: "To choose one's victim, to prepare one's plans minutely, to slake an implacable vengeance, and then to go to bed . . . There is nothing sweeter in the world."[9] Publication of this interview proved extremely damaging to Bukharin and the Right Opposition.

At the beginning of 1929 he was still editor of *Pravda,* and he made a final open attempt to oppose Stalin's course in an article on "Lenin's Political Testament" published in *Pravda* on January 21, the fifth anniversary of Lenin's death. He argued carefully and convincingly here that the essence of Lenin's final position was that the building of a socialist system in Russia should be achieved through a long process of *"peaceful organization and cultural work"* (Lenin's words, italics by Bukharin) and specifically without coercion of the peasantry. In short, it was Lenin's political testament, according to Bukharin's reading, that socialism could and should be built without an intensified class struggle in Soviet society and without such a violent "third revolution" as was plainly implicit in the Stalin program. In the following month matters came to a head in a stormy session of the Politburo during which the right-wing leaders attacked Stalin for one-man decisions and argued that his collectivization program was leading to what Bukharin called "military-feudal exploitation of the peasants."[10] From this point on the Right Opposition went down to defeat. Later in 1929 Bukharin was expelled from the Politburo and dismissed from his positions as editor of *Pravda* and member of the Executive Committee of the Comintern. Rykov was dismissed as Premier and Tomsky was removed from leadership of the trade unions. The three right-wing leaders publicly renounced their "deviation" in November, and open opposition came to an end. Earlier that year, it will be recalled, Trotsky had been deported from the country.

---

[9] Boris Souvarine, *Stalin: A Critical Survey of Bolshevism* (New York: Alliance Book Corporation, 1939), pp. 482-485.

[10] For an account of this meeting, see Leonard Schapiro: *The Communist Party of the Soviet Union.* (New York: Random House, 1959), p. 373.

Though open opposition ceased, Bukharin, an exceedingly adroit thinker and talented writer, continued on occasion to convey criticism of Stalin by a technique of indirection, or double-talk, that was known, among the older revolutionists who had developed it under Tsarist censorship conditions, as "Aesopian language." Thus in a *Pravda* article of March 7, 1930, which was ostensibly a long polemic against the papacy in general and Pope Pius in particular for his newly published encyclical on communism, Bukharin skillfully conveyed that "popes" meant Stalin and his followers, "Jesuit order" the Stalinist N.K.V.D., "heresy" the opposition viewpoint, and so on. Of special political significance was a passage that he quoted here from a book on Church history, saying: "If they (the popes, N. Bukharin) kill the soul, then why have they a right to call themselves the successors of Christ? Where is the similarity of their institutions? Christ, speaking to Peter, once said: Feed my sheep! But what do the popes do? Do they not lead the Christians, *completely pillaged by papal plundering, to starvation? Do they not fleece their sheep continually, and cut into their flesh whilst shearing them?"* (Italics by Bukharin.) The "Aesopian" message here was that Stalin, who was pillaging the peasantry and leading the people to starvation with the catastrophic forced collectivization campaign then in progress, had thereby turned against the true heritage of Bolshevism as embodied in Lenin's political testament. That others in the party shared this view of the events of the time is shown by the clandestine circulation of the so-called "Riutin platform," in which a former follower of Bukharin bitterly assailed Stalin for his policies and called for his removal. By the time of the Seventeenth Party Congress in 1934, however, the situation in the country had eased. Such prominent former oppositionists as Bukharin, Rykov, Zinoviev, Kamenev, Piatakov, and Radek appeared on the platform to emphasize their approval of the general line and pay tribute to Stalin's leadership in carrying it out. Bukharin, though demoted from full to candidate membership in the Party Central Committee after the Congress, was appointed editor of *Izvestia,* a position he held until his arrest early in 1937.

Meanwhile there was one last episode of opposition to Stalin on the part of Bukharin. In the first of the great show trials, the Zinoviev-Kamenev trial of August 1936, several defendants named Bukharin, Rykov, and Tomsky (the last-named committed suicide at this time) as co-participants in the criminal activities to which they confessed. A press campaign of vilification of the former right-wing leaders ensued, and in early September a meeting was reportedly called in the Central Committee to consider their expulsion from the party.[11] Presenting Stalin's case against them, Yezhov at this meeting moved for the expulsion of Bukharin and Rykov on the ground that they, along with Trotsky, Zinoviev, and Kamenev, had been involved since 1918 in a "monstrous conspiracy" in the course of which they had become agents of the Gestapo and were even now plotting, in concert with the Trotskyites, a *coup d'état*. Replying in his own defense, Bukharin agreed that a monstrous conspiracy was being carried out against the Party and state in the Soviet Union. But its leaders, he declared, were Stalin and Yezhov, who were plotting and acting to change the Bolshevik Party regime inherited from Lenin into an N.K.V.D. regime in which Stalin would enjoy unlimited personal power. He contended that the elimination of himself and Rykov was a necessary part of this conspiratorial plan and that what was now being decided, therefore, was not the "Bukharin question" but the fate of the country. Stalin's supporters in the Politburo supported the Yezhov motion in the ensuing discussion; others did not. When the vote was taken, the motion was supported by less than a third of the Central Committee members present. Stalin indicated his acceptance of the adverse decision, and a statement was published in *Pravda* on September 10 announcing that the case against Bukharin and Rykov was being closed because investigation had not established judicial bases for legal proceedings against them. Stalin meanwhile went on maneuvering. The Tukhachevsky military group, whose representatives in the Central Committee had supported the pro-Bukharin majority, were arrested and executed in June 1937. In 1937-1938, according to data in Khrushchev's secret report, 98 members and candidates of the Central Committee, or 70 per cent of the total, were arrested and shot. It seems very likely that the physical liquidation of the overwhelming majority of this highest ruling body in the Soviet system was connected at least in part with the events just recounted. In any event, the way was now cleared for the. trial of Bukharin and Rykov, which opened in March 1938.

---

[11] There was no official announcement of this meeting. An account appears in Uralov (pseudonym of Abdurakhman Avtorkhanov, a Party official and historian then living in the U.S.S.R.): *The Reign of Stalin* (London: Bodley Head, 1953), pp. 43-47. Most Western specialists accept this account as on the whole trustworthy, although there is some dispute about the particulars, e.g., whether the reported meeting was a full plenary session as reported by Avtorkhanov or a more informal meeting of high-ranking persons within the Central Committee.

The case developed in this trial was an elaboration of the "monstrous conspiracy" charge made against Bukharin and Rykov in the reported secret Party meeting in 1936. It pictured the erstwhile Left and Right oppositions as two interconnected prongs of a conspiracy of many years standing to destroy the Revolution and the Lenin-Stalin regime. It was held that in 1918 Bukharin and his group of Left Communists and Trotsky and his group had plotted to frustrate the Brest-Litovsk peace, overthrow the Soviet government, arrest and murder Lenin and Stalin, and form a new government. Bukharin had helped inspire the terrorist attempt on Lenin's life by Dora Kaplan in August 1918. Trotsky had entered the service of the German intelligence in 1921. Bukharin and Rykov had long been connected with foreign intelligence services through accomplices, and Krestinsky, Rosengoltz, and Rakovsky had been agents of foreign powers since the early 1920's. Both Trotskyite and Right oppositions had from the start been subversive movements motivated by criminal anti-Soviet aims rather than genuine oppositionist convictions. In 1932-1933, when the futility of further open opposition activity was clear, they had formed, on instructions of foreign intelligence services, a conspiratorial group called "Bloc of Rights and Trotskyites," on behalf of which Trotsky had negotiated an agreement with Nazi Germany looking to the overthrow of the Soviet government and the defeat and dismemberment of the U.S.S.R. in a coming war. The conspirators also had entered into a secret agreement with Japan under which she would render armed assistance in overthrowing the Soviet government and later be recompensed with the Maritime Region in the Soviet Far East. In preparation for functioning as a fifth column and opening the front in time of war, the conspiracy had engaged in espionage, wrecking activities, incitement of peasant risings, and the planning or execution of terrorist acts against Soviet leaders. The wrecking activities, aimed both at undermining the economy and at stirring up anti-Soviet feeling which would hamper the defense effort in time of war, included deliberate mismanagement of the ruble and state savings banks by Finance Commissar Grinko, deliberate infecting of pigs with the plague through the efforts of Agriculture Commissar Chernov, and the mixing of glass and nails into butter by arrangement of the head of the consumer cooperatives, Zelensky. The terrorist acts had included the assassination of the Leningrad Party leader Sergei Kirov in 1934, and the medical murder of two other prominent Party leaders, Kuibyshev and Menzhinsky, and of Maxim Gorky and his son. The medical murders had been committed by well-known Soviet doctors on orders of the N.K.V.D. chief, Yagoda, who had made a deep study of the history of murder by poisoning and had planned, among other crimes, to murder Yezhov by poisoning the air in his office with mercury dissolved in an acid. Another and key unfulfilled aim of the conspirators had been the murder of Stalin.

How true or false was this conspiratorial view of Soviet history? It contained some sheer fabrications, such as the allegations about the espionage connections of the accused and their collaboration with Nazi Germany and Japan. But not everything falls in this category. Some actual facts have been mentioned in the foregoing summary, and many more appear in the voluminous trial proceedings themselves. There was, as we have seen, a real history of opposition activity, a "Riutin platform," a 1928 anti-Stalin talk between Bukharin and Kamenev, and so on. Krestinsky, who was Soviet ambassador in Berlin in the 1920's, undoubtedly had conversations with German military men. Bukharin did, as mentioned in his testimony and final statement, have meetings in Paris early in 1936 with the well-known scholar and Menshevik leader Boris Nicolaevsky. Some criminal acts mentioned in the trial actually occurred. Dora Kaplan did make an attempt on Lenin's life, Sergei Kirov was in fact assassinated, and it may be, although this is not definitely confirmed, that Gorky was murdered by poisoning. It is true that Yagoda, a one-time pharmacist, was knowledgeable in the history of murder by poisoning. Some peasant outbreaks did occur in the early 1930's and there was great loss of livestock then. Some savings banks were mismanaged, timber-floating operations were disorganized, the supply of school exercise books was in places interrupted, the sowing of vegetables was misplanned, and there were various goods shortages — facts which are mentioned in the trial — and these and like situations did create much popular discontent. It may even be that nails and glass had in places turned up in Soviet butter.

On the other hand, these real facts and incidents are all falsified in the manner in which they were presented at the trial. For they did not occur as elements in a vast anti-Soviet conspiracy. Thus Bukharin's opposition to Lenin over Brest-Litovsk harbored no anti-Lenin conspiratorial designs, and nothing in the world was more foreign to his makeup than a desire to harm Lenin. Although he came to loathe Stalin and wished it were possible to unseat him from power, he had not been involved in a terrorist plot to accomplish this. He met with Nicolaevsky in Paris in 1936 not for conspiratorial anti-Soviet purposes but in order to negotiate, on behalf of the Communist Party, for purchase of the Marx-Engels archives from the German Social Democratic Party. The peasant disturbances were a reaction to forced collectivization, not a product of right-wing plotting, and livestock was lost in great numbers because peasants slaughtered their animals in resistance to collectivization. The shortages, disruptions of supply, and general disorganization in the land were generated by Stalin's convulsive "third revolution" rather than by deliberate "wrecking" activity in connection with a conspiracy. Finally, the murder of Kirov was not organized by the accused but rather, it very strongly appears, by Stalin, who sought thereby both to remove a potential rival and to create a pretext for launching the Great Purge.

What unfolds before us in the trial, then, is a gigantic texture of fantasy into which bits and pieces of falsified real history have been woven along with outright fiction. It forms an elaborate unified system in the sense that everything hangs together in a coherent, logical, and internally self-consistent whole. The master theme running through it all and giving it a dramatic unity is the great anti-Soviet conspiracy. It furnishes the motivation and therewith the explanation for hundreds of events and incidents spoken of in the trial, many of which really happened. Now this scheme bears a definite and, as I shall suggest further on, understandable resemblance to textbook descriptions of a paranoid delusional system. Authorities describe a paranoid system as an intricate, schematized, and logically elaborated structure with a "central delusional theme" involving a hostile plot of which the person concerned is an intended victim. The plot is ascribed to a "paranoid pseudo-community," which is "an imaginary organization, composed of real and imagined persons, whom the patient represents as united for the purpose of carrying out some action upon him."[12]

That the conspiratorial master theme in the case of the "Anti-Soviet Bloc of Rights and Trotskyites" was fictional is no longer subject to dispute. The great anti-Soviet conspiracy around which the

---

[12] Norman Cameron: "Paranoid Conditions and Paranoia," in *American Handbook of Psychiatry* (New York: Basic Books, 1959), p. 519. Dr. Cameron adds that the malevolent pseudo-community may be conceived as a gang of international spies, a secret police force, or a racial or religious group. The official handbook of the American Psychiatric Association describes paranoia as "characterized by an intricate, complex, and slowly developing paranoid system, often logically elaborated after a false interpretation of an actual occurrence," and adds: "The paranoid system is particularly isolated from much of the normal stream of consciousness, without hallucinations and with relative intactness and preservation of the remainder of the personality, in spite of a chronic and prolonged course" (*Mental Disorders*: American Psychiatric Association, Washington, D. C.: 1952, p. 28).

whole case is organized was quite imaginary. The "Bloc of Rights and Trotskyites" never existed as an organized conspiratorial group seeking to undermine the Soviet state and overthrow the Stalin government. As Bukharin correctly mentioned in his final statement, "the accused in this dock are not a group" and insofar as the "Bloc" actually existed it did so as a venture in back-stage opposition politics undertaken at the time of his conversation with Kamenev in 1928. Since that was prior to Hitler's rise to power, he went on, the group could not possibly have been formed on instruction of fascist intelligence services. That is, the basic conspiracy charge, relating to the alleged dealings of the accused with the Axis governments, was false. Bukharin's denial on this key point has been fully borne out. Had there been any foundation at all for the charge that the accused collaborated with the Nazis and Japanese, the captured archives of the defeated Axis powers and the memories of their surviving leaders should have furnished evidence of this collaboration. But they have not.[13]

The non-existence of the great counter-revolutionary conspiracy has been admitted by the Soviet regime since Stalin's death. A special commission of inquiry appointed by the Party Central Committee to look into the events of 1937-1938 found "nothing tangible" at the bottom of the treason charges brought against so many thousands of Party members at that time. This was reported by Khrushchev in his secret speech to the Twentieth Party Congress. He says here that "when the cases of some of these so-called 'spies' and 'saboteurs' were examined, it was found that all their cases were fabricated." And further: "Many thousands of honest and innocent Communists have died as a result of this monstrous falsification of such 'cases.'" To illustrate the methods by which N.K.V.D. officials "manufactured various fictitious 'anti-Soviet centers' and 'blocs'" and "fabricated 'anti-Soviet plots,'" he cites the case of a survivor, one Rozenblum, who told the commission how, after being subjected to terrible torture, he was brought before the N.K.V.D. investigator Zakovsky. The latter

---

[13] On this point Isaac Deutscher writes: "Among all the documents of the Nuremberg trial of the Nazi leaders not a single one contains as much as a hint at the alleged Nazi fifth column in the Soviet Government and army. Could there be a more eloquent refutation of the purge trials than that amazing gap in the otherwise abundant evidence of Hitler's preparations for the war?" (*Stalin: A Political Biography*, New York: Vintage Books, 1960, p. 379 n.). Deutscher does suggest, however, that Marshal Tukhachevsky and his military associates were planning a *coup d'état* against Stalin, entirely on their own. It must be said that no evidence has appeared to support this hypothesis.

informed him that the N.K.V.D. would work out the legend for his case: " 'You yourself,' said Zakovsky, 'will not need to invent anything. The N.K.V.D. will prepare for you a ready outline for every branch of the center; you will have to study it carefully and remember well all questions and answers which the Court might ask. This case will be ready in four-five months, or perhaps a half year. During all this time you will be preparing yourself . . . Your future will depend on how the trial goes and on its results.' " This description, incidentally, accords with the accounts of surviving victims of the purge who found their way to the West and published stories of their experiences.

If the cases of so many thousands of "honest and innocent Communists" were fabricated, if mythical "anti-Soviet centers," "blocs," and "plots" were invented in full detail by expert N.K.V.D. political playwrights for acting out by prisoners in trials, then obviously the central super-conspiracy, with which all the lesser conspiratorial centers around the country were alleged to be linked, was similarly a fabrication. The Soviet regime has admitted this, although unfortunately it has not yet done so in a wholly unambiguous and comprehensive manner. Marshal Tukhachevsky and his fellow officers of the "military conspiratorial group" mentioned in the Bukharin trial are now declared to have been entirely innocent, patriotic Soviet citizens and devoted Party members done to death on trumped-up treason charges. As of this writing (December 1964) several of the defendants in the Bukharin trial, including Krestinsky, Grinko, and Ikramov, have been similarly rehabilitated, which of course shatters the entire case, since their testimony interlocks at so many points with that of the other defendants. These others, particularly Bukharin and Rykov, have not yet been restored to places of honor in the history of the Party. It is notable, however, that the criminal conspiracy charges against Bukharin and Rykov have already been dismissed publicly. Speaking at a conference of Soviet historians late in 1962, P. N. Pospelov, director of the Institute of Marxism-Leninism, declared that "neither Bukharin nor Rykov of course were spies or terrorists."[14]

Since the Moscow trials a voluminous literature has grown up in the West on the question of why the defendants confessed. Certain points regarding the motives of Bukharin, who seems to have been something of a special case, will be made below. Here I should

---

[14] *Vsesoiuznoe soveshchanie o merakh uluchsheniia podgotovki nauchno-pedagogicheskikh kadrov po istoricheskim naukam* (Moscow, 1964), p. 298.

like simply to point out that Soviet post-Stalin disclosures corroborate earlier reports by N.K.V.D. defectors and purge victims who later escaped to the West that torture and extreme pressure, including threats of doing harm to loved ones, were employed. In the secret report to the Twentieth Congress Khrushchev cites a coded telegram sent out by Stalin to the heads of N.K.V.D. organizations and other officials on January 20, 1939, saying that methods of "physical pressure" in N.K.V.D. practice, which had been permissible from 1937 on, should continue to be applied "obligatorily" to "known and obstinate enemies of the people as a method both justifiable and appropriate." Khrushchev states further: "Confessions of guilt of many arrested and charged with enemy activity were gained with the help of cruel and inhuman tortures." This statement is borne out by testimony from a variety of sources. The defendants confessed because they were forced to.

3.

The Moscow trials understandably aroused enormous interest in the West. In the discussion that started then and went on for a good many years, two questions were asked most insistently and discussed at greatest length: Were they guilty? Why did they confess? Inside Russia, on the other hand, attention focused upon a different question: Why the trials, and why the Great Purge as a whole? Ehrenburg recalls in his memoirs: "I realized that people were being accused of crimes which they had not and could not have committed, and I asked myself and others: why, what for? No one could give me an answer. We were completely at sea."[15] According to Beck and Godin, two purge victims who lived to write a book about it, the "enemies of the people" were asking the very same questions during their interrogation period and afterwards in the camps: "There was no question that excited the prisoners so much as that which the reader must already have asked himself time and again. 'Why? What for?' The question was endlessly argued. . . . The words 'Why? What for?' were to be found scratched with smuggled bits of broken glass on the inside walls of the 'black raven,' and the coaches of the prison trains. 'Why? What for?.' "[16]

These Russians were asking the real main question, and it is one that scholars need to reopen in the light of the new information and better perspective that we now possess on the events of the time.

---

[15] *Op. cit.*, p. 426.
[16] F. Beck and W. Godin: *Russian Purge and the Extraction of Confession* (New York: Viking Press, 1951), p. 215.

One of the tendencies in Western writings has been to answer it by reference to postulated functional needs of the Soviet system as a form of "totalitarianism." Periodical blood purges, accompanied by such events as the Moscow show trials, have been viewed as a necessity or deep-lying tendency of totalitarianism *as a system*. This way of thinking is based upon an image of totalitarianism, in whatever form, as a fundamentally impersonal phenomenon, a system in which virtually all, including the highest functionaries of the state, are essentially cogs in a machine. Miss Hannah Arendt, whose important writings on totalitarianism have been one of the sources of this image, has suggested, for example, that blood purges such as those of the Stalin era, quite unlike the Party purges in the early years of the Russian Revolution, served as an "instrument of permanent instability."[17] Such instability, in turn, is treated as a functional requisite of totalitarianism as a system.

A different approach seems to be suggested by all that we now know. First, the phenomena in question were not at all functional necessities of the Soviet system. On the contrary, the system would have been better off and far more equipped to meet the coming test of total war had there been no Great Purge, which was, in effect, a great wrecking operation in Soviet society. We have testimony from the lips of no less an authority than Khrushchev that the Soviet order, far from requiring the Great Purge, was hard put to survive it. "Only because our party has at its disposal such great moral-political strength," he says in the secret report, "was it possible to survive the difficult events in 1937-1938 and to educate new cadres. There is, however, no doubt that our march forward toward socialism and toward the preparation of the country's defense would have been much more successful were it not for the tremendous loss of cadres suffered as a result of the baseless and false mass repressions in 1937-1938." We do not yet have any official Soviet statistics on the total losses resulting from the Great Purge, but it has been credibly estimated that around nine million persons were arrested during it.[18] And it

---

[17] *The Origins of Totalitarianism* (New York: Harcourt, Brace, 1951), p. 376 n. For an elaborated interpretation of the Stalinist purge in terms of postulated functional needs of the Soviet system, see Zbigniew K. Brzezinski: *The Permanent Purge: Politics in Soviet Totalitarianism* (Cambridge: Harvard University Press, 1956), esp. Chapters 5 and 10.

[18] For the computations underlying the estimate of nine million, see Alexander Weissberg *The Accused* (New York: Simon and Schuster, 1951), pp. 318-325. Boris Nicolaevsky has estimated that from five to eight million persons were victims of the Great Purge. The number of those who were executed at the time has been estimated by a high Yugoslav Communist source at three million (V. Dedijer: *Tito*, New York: Simon and Schuster, 1953, p. 106).

must be borne in mind that the great majority of these victims were from the Party and non-Party governing strata of Soviet society, including professional people of all kinds and technicians.

Secondly, a great lesson to be learned from a study of the events of that time is that our theory of totalitarianism has unduly neglected the personal factor. It has not taken account, or sufficient account, of the role of the dictator and his personality in determining the conduct of the regime, the dynamics of totalitarianism itself, in such truly totalitarian situations as Germany under Hitler and Russia in the time of Stalin. Not the needs of the Soviet system but Stalin's own needs, both political and psychological, underlay the events of 1937-1938 in Russia. Not only was he, as noted earlier, the prime mover and director of those events; they occurred basically because he relentlessly willed them and was skillful enough to make others do his bidding, just as the "final solution" was perpetrated in Nazi Germany in the last analysis because Hitler fanatically desired to destroy European Jewry and succeeded in imposing his will upon the totalitarian machine of state. Of course, the Great Purge, once it started, acquired a self-propelling momentum of its own as a result, largely, of the N.K.V.D. system of forced denunciation under which each arrested person was coerced not only to admit participating in a non-existent conspiracy but also to name those who had recruited him into the imaginary conspiratorial center and those whom he himself had recruited. This helps to explain the probably unanticipated extent of the holocaust in Soviet society. But the key causal role was Stalin's. And his determination to force through the Great Purge and the trials was dictated by powerful motives that were peculiarly his own and not widely shared in the Soviet ruling elite. A full analysis of them is beyond the scope of this essay, but I will comment on three principal facets of the motivation.

We are here particularly concerned with the purge trials. But the reasons for staging them must be seen in the context of the motives for the total purge, in which thousands were executed or sent to camps by administrative order for every one who was placed on trial in public. For the purge trials had, in the first place, a political symbolic function, which was to provide a rationale for the purge, to make publicly meaningful the campaign of arrests that was going on night after night. The underlying assumption of the Great Purge was that treason was abroad in the land, especially among Party members, and that it had to be cleaned out and exterminated on the massive scale that this treason itself had assumed. The three great Moscow show trials and a

number of lesser local trials held at this time were designed to dramatize this idea, to show the existence, enormity, and scope of the purported treasonable activity, which had — it was thus made to appear —
been organized and directed by men at the pinnacle of the Party and
state as well as their counterparts at the provincial level. Accordingly,
the question of Stalin's motives is first of all the question of what he
wanted to achieve by the purge as a whole.

A large part of the answer is that he wanted to achieve an unre-
stricted personal dictatorship with a totality of power that he did not
yet possess in 1934. By the late 1920's he had become the acknowl-
edged supreme leader of the Party and state. In the Bolshevik political
tradition, however, this did not make him an absolute autocrat like the
Russian Tsars, for no such position had been institutionalized in
Lenin's one-party system. He could not dictate his will to the ruling
elite at the level of the Politburo and Central Committee without fear
of being contradicted. He could not count — as Lenin before him
could not — on automatic acceptance of his policy designs without
critical debate and opposition in the inner councils of the Party. And
there are indications, as we have seen, that such debate and occasional
opposition continued even in the early 1930's. The prime internal political purpose of the Great Purge from Stalin's point of view was to end all
this, to eliminate the Bolshevik habits of criticism and opposition as
well as the men who personified these habits, and to create for himself an autocracy as absolute as any that ever existed. To purge those
Party members who had opposed him in the past was not enough for
this purpose. Given the intricate system of patronage that prevailed
at all levels in the Party and state bureaucracy, the purge of a major
figure logically entailed the purge of his patronage group of associates
and retainers, many of whom had lesser patronage groups of their
own, and so on. Lack of objective incriminating facts about an individual was no obstacle to unmasking him, since he could be accused
of *potential* oppositionism. Thus many of the purge victims were
staunch Stalinists with no taint of real oppositionism in their records;
their tragedies were caused by often quite accidental career associa-
tions. The outcome of the whole process was a veritable circulation
of the Soviet elite. Total subservience to Stalin was now established
as the first requirement for survival and political advancement.
Emerging from the events of 1936-1938 as a personal dictator
in what was now a truly totalitarian system of power, Stalin had
achieved the internal political purpose of the Great Purge.

But this political purpose was connected with psychological needs.

Stalin has been called, and with good foundation, a technician of power. It would be a mistake, though, to see him as only that. He was not a cold-blooded cynic who viewed his villainy as villainy and accepted it as such. In making himself an absolute autocrat at so sickening a price in blood and misery, he thought he was serving the interests of the Party he was purging and the country he was terrorizing. We have evidence for the view that in engineering the events of 1936-1938 he really believed himself to be cleansing the Soviet land of treason. Some of it comes from Khrushchev, who says in the secret report: "Stalin was a very distrustful man, sickly suspicious; we know this from our work with him. He could look at a man and say: 'Why are your eyes so shifty today' or 'Why are you turning so much today and avoiding to look at me in the eyes?' The sickly suspicion created in him a general distrust even toward eminent party workers whom he had known for years. Everywhere and in everything he saw 'enemies,' 'two-facers' and 'spies.'" This description of a personality of pronounced paranoid tendency is supported by further testimony from a variety of sources, both Soviet and non-Soviet.

By what mechanism of thinking did Stalin apprehend "enemies," "two-facers," and "spies" all around him when, as we know, there was no real anti-Soviet conspiracy afoot? An essential part of the answer is that he regarded opposition to or criticism of himself — and there had been a great deal of both in the history of the Party — as evidence of profound malevolence and treasonable tendencies. Khrushchev points to this mechanism when he says in the secret report that the category "enemy of the people" was applied to "those who in any way disagreed with Stalin" as well as to "those who were only suspected of hostile intent" or "had bad reputations" (that is, politically). Stalin's tendency to identify oppositionism with treason was linked with his inability to tolerate the thought that oppositional or simply critical attitudes towards him could have any real basis in imperfections of his mind and character or in flaws in his leadership, and policies. Given this inhibition, which was rooted in his need to see himself as the perfect leader "of genius" (*genial'ny*, the term constantly used of him in Russia in his later lifetime), it followed logically that any opposition, whether open or merely a subtle suggestion of a critical attitude, must be a sign of hidden hostile designs and must stem from an enmity all the more deep and dangerous in that it was often concealed behind an appearance ("mask") of loyalty and friendliness. In short, it was evidence of probable participation in a criminal conspiracy or, at the very least, of an intention to participate in one. According to this logic, which is similar to if not actually paranoid logic,[19] the Party and country in the early 1930's, when Stalin began planning the Great Purge, were crawling with traitors.

The purge trials are constructed around this paranoid-like logic. The reader will note that a great deal of the discourse between Vyshinsky and the defendants proceeds on the tacit understanding that an imputation of criminal conspiracy may be made on the basis of oppositional acts or attitudes. This idea defines the rules of the trial game, or "rules of translation" as they have been called.[20] A whole table of equivalences was accepted in which, for example, anti-Stalin = "counter-revolutionary," oppositional activity = "treason," anti-Stalin grouping = "conspiratorial terrorist center," anti-Stalin political orientation = "orientation on terrorism," etc., the general formula being that any opposing or criticizing of Stalin or his policies = "counter-revolutionary terrorism." In the 1937 trial Piatakov alluded to this system of equivalences when, in agreeing that he had given a certain man orders to make connections with German intelligence, he added that he had done this only in a "more algebraical formulation" — by having a talk with the man in an oppositional vein.[21] Similar allusions are made by Bukharin and

---

[19] Speaking of paranoid delusions, Dr. Otto Fenichel writes that "the hatred is never projected at random but is felt usually in connection with something that has a basis in reality. Patients with persecutory ideas are extremely sensitive to criticism and use the awareness of actual insignificant criticisms as the reality basis for their delusions. This basis has, of course, to be extremely exaggerated and distorted in order to be made available for this purpose. Just as the 'monsters' in a dream may represent an 'amoeba' from daily life, so the monster of a paranoid delusion may be a misapprehended real microbe" (*The Psychoanalytic Theory of Neurosis,* New York, Norton, 1945, p. 428). Elsewhere we read that the paranoid individual "is constantly looking for hidden meanings in the statements and activities of those about him" (R. M. Dorcus and G. W. Schaffer: *Textbook of Abnormal Psychology,* Baltimore: Williams and Wilkins, 1950, p. 438).

[20] N. Leites and E. Bernaut: *Ritual of Liquidation: The Case of the Moscow Trials* (Glencoe: The Free Press, 1954), p. 111. These writers express here the view that the defendants "accepted" these rules of translation because (1) they shared a contemptuous belief that the masses can only understand a simple and extreme story, and (2) they had come to feel that the fables they agreed to tell were in some special sense true. I believe, on the contrary, that their acceptance of the rules of translation was strictly a forced acceptance, and that they did not consider the fables true even in some special sense.

[21] *The Case of the Anti-Soviet Trotskyite Center* (Moscow: People's Commissariat of Justice of the U.S.S.R., 1937), pp. 188-189. Vyshinsky replied at this point: "I know what you mean by algebra, but I must now deal not with algebra but with facts."

others in the 1938 trial. The trials are thus in large part intricate exercises in the ferreting out of sinister terroristic *hidden meanings* in activities of the chief defendants which consisted mostly of critical or oppositional talk, especially about Stalin. The great counter-revolutionary conspiracy itself represents, as it were, the highly systematized sum total of all these hidden meanings, treated as true; it is the premise on which all of Stalin's most ominous suspicions about what was going on behind his back would have been well founded.

What I am arguing, then, is that the "algebra" of the Moscow trials was a reflection of the general way in which their organizer's mind actually worked. It is all the more understandable according to this view that Stalin, as has been reported, played a leading part in devising the legends for the trials. It need not be supposed that he believed them altogether literally. But they must have appeared to him as being true in principle and false, if at all, only in being embellishments on reality itself — embellishments, moreover, in which he could legitimately take a certain artistic pride. The implication is that the trials served not alone the above-mentioned political symbolic function of rationalizing the Great Purge but, at the same time, the psychological symbolic function of rationalizing Stalin's own paranoid tendency. The world of the Great Purge and the purge trials, peopled by multitudes of masked enemies conspiring to destroy Stalin's regime and Stalin himself, was Stalin's own mental world. Under his guidance the N.K.V.D., assisted by Vyshinsky and others, was confirming the reality of it and making it appear still more concretely and convincingly real by arresting huge numbers of Soviet citizens, compelling them to *confess* that they had been masked enemies and putting on show trials in which leading former oppositionists and others publicly proclaimed themselves guilty of high treason. Accordingly, we may view the trials as vehicles for the acting out of something similar to a paranoid delusional system complete with central theme (the great conspiracy) and malevolent pseudo-community ("Bloc of Rights and Trotskyites," etc.). In this regard the verbatim report here presented is a document out of the history of human psychopathology.

But there was much political method in this psychopathology. As indicated earlier, the thesis that the politics of the purge were psychological politics is in no way inconsistent with the view that practical political ends were pursued. Something has been said already about the internal political ends. But an interpretation of the trials must also take account of their external political purpose, their connection with Stalin's foreign policy.

4.

A widely shared opinion sees the Great Purge as an attempt to prepare the Party and the country for the coming test of total war by consolidating the home front in advance. The trials themselves, with their charges that the accused were plotting to act as a fifth column in a war with the fascist powers, invited such an interpretation. Probably not many informed people followed the former U.S. ambassador in Moscow, Joseph Davies, in taking the position (in his wartime book *Mission to Moscow*) that the treason charges had been factually true. But Western opinion has tended to accept the general idea that Stalin's major concern was to assure a solid internal situation in the face of the threat of German invasion. According to a sophisticated version of it that has been expounded by Isaac Deutscher in his influential biography of Stalin, the point of the purge trials was to forestall any disruption of the future war effort, and Stalin's leadership of it, by eliminating those leaders with a record of political dissent who might be inclined to unseat him in a crisis. According to Deutscher, "His reasoning probably developed along the following lines: they may want to overthrow me in a crisis — I shall charge them with having already made the attempt. They certainly believe themselves to be better fitted for the conduct of war, which is absurd. A change of government may weaken Russia's fighting capacity; and if they succeed, they may be compelled to sign a truce with Hitler, and perhaps even agree to a cession of territory as we once did at Brest-Litovsk. I shall accuse them of having entered already into a treacherous alliance with Germany (and Japan) and ceded Soviet territory to those states."[22]

During and after World War II Stalin probably liked to view the events of 1936-1938 in retrospect as part of his preparation of Russia for the coming great conflict with Hitler. But the idea that this was his motive at the time he planned and directed those events appears unsound. First, the Great Purge, as has been remarked above, was in effect a great wrecking operation in Soviet society. Stalin himself must have been aware that the onslaught upon the Soviet managerial elite was not calculated to make the Soviet system and economy better able to withstand the test of war. He must have realized too that the preparedness and morale of the army would

[22] *Stalin: A Political Biography*, pp. 377-378.

scarcely be furthered by the purging of 35,000 officers (the estimated number of those affected) along with the high command headed by the immensely able Tukhachevsky. This military purge itself accounts in considerable measure for the Red Army's poor performance during most of the Finnish war and its staggering setbacks in 1941-1942; and those effects were easily predictable. Next, Stalin, for all his pathological suspiciousness, was shrewd and discerning enough to realize that in a national crisis brought on by a Nazi invasion of Russia, even his worst old Party enemies would rally instantly and unreservedly around the war effort and his personal leadership of it. For these old Bolshevik leaders, and the Tukhachevsky group, were anti-fascist Communists. Finally, the view that the Great Purge and the trials were preparation for a coming conflict with Hitler collides with evidence that Stalin at this time was *not in fact preparing for conflict with Hitler but for collaboration with him.* He was preparing the diplomacy of the Soviet-Nazi pact that was finally concluded, on Stalin's initiative, in August 1939. And insofar as the politics of the purge and the trials were externally oriented, they were, as I shall now try to show, a preparation for the active alliance of the two dictators which was thereby inaugurated.

It is a mistake to look upon the diplomacy of the pact with Hitler as the only possible course the Soviet government could have followed at the end of the 1930's. Nor was it a course that the Bolshevik leaders as a group could find politically compelling and psychologically acceptable, as Stalin did. For though there were strong resemblances between communism and fascism as institutional structures, the revolutionary intellectuals of the Bolshevik Old Guard, most of them Russian or Jewish by origin, felt that their aims and values if not their institutions were fundamentally different from those of the German Nazis. The one among them who voiced this feeling most effectively, the intellectual leader of Bolshevik anti-fascism, was Bukharin. His speech at the Seventeenth Party Congress early in 1934 was notable not only for his tribute to Stalin's policy and leadership but also for the impassioned warning and outcry against Hitlerism with which he concluded. Quoting the Nazi poet who had said, "Every time I hear the word 'culture' I reach for my Browning," he eloquently portrayed Hitlerism's cult of blood and violence, and foresaw for the Soviet Union an unavoidable collision with this irrational force: "This is what stands before us, and these are the ones whom we shall have to face, comrades, in all those stupendous historical battles that history has laid on our shoulders."[23] This part of the speech reportedly made a strong impression upon the assembly. After the Congress Bukharin became not only editor of *Izvestia* but also a member of the commission set up in February 1935 to draft a new Soviet constitution, which was to show by its humanistic and democratic features the chasm that separated the Soviet order from fascism. There is reason to believe, moreover, that he was one of the leading drafters of this document.

Stalin's speech at the Seventeenth Congress reflected a very different line toward Hitler's Germany. He cautioned the Germans against thinking that the U.S.S.R. was now orienting itself toward France and Poland because fascism had come to power in Germany. "Of course, we are far from enthusiastic about the fascist regime in Germany," he said. "But fascism is beside the point, if only because fascism in Italy, for example, has not kept the U.S.S.R. from establishing the best of relations with that country." Stalin went on to indicate clearly that a *rapprochement* with Berlin was not to be excluded, if Soviet interests would be served thereby and if, within Hitler's government, a pro-Soviet tendency should prevail over an anti-Soviet one.[24] If an anti-Hitler diplomacy was implicit in Bukharin's speech, the diplomacy of the 1939 pact was prefigured in Stalin's; and the divergence between them reflected a real division of tendencies in the Soviet leadership that was ended only by the Great Purge. According to Krivitsky, Stalin's inclination to make a deal with Hitler was strengthened by the latter's successful blood purge of Captain Roehm and his group on the night of June 30, 1934, an event that Stalin construed as evidence of the consolidation of Hitler's regime. But for some time Hitler showed no receptiveness to feelers from the East. In these circumstances Stalin was content to go along with the politics of the anti-fascist Popular Front and the diplomacy of collective security which Foreign Commissar Litvinov pursued vigorously in the middle 1930's.[25] If in the eyes of the anti-fascist Communists the Litvinov foreign-policy line was a correct political orientation, from Stalin's point of view it had at least the virtue of placing pressure on a reluctant Hitler to respond to his advances.

---

[23] *XVII S'ezd vsesoiuznoi kommunisticheskoi partii (b). Stenograficheskii otchet* (Moscow, 1934), pp. 128-129.

[24] *Ibid.*, pp. 13-14.

[25] *In Stalin's Secret Service*, pp. 1-4. For a detailed and convincing argument that the Soviet leadership until the Great Purge was divided over the main lines of its foreign policy, with Stalin and Bukharin as exponents of the two main opposing positions, see Robert M. Slusser: "The Role of the Foreign Ministry," in Ivo J. Lederer, (ed.): *Russian Foreign Policy: Essays in Historical Perspective* (New Haven: Yale University Press, 1962).

Hitler's unopposed occupation of the Rhineland in March 1936 hardened Stalin's resolve to make a deal with Germany if possible, and this in turn spurred his efforts to proceed with the full-scale internal purge towards which he had long been moving for other reasons. It is notable in this connection that Party members (both Soviet and foreign) who could be suspected of being genuinely anti-fascist Communists were particularly hard hit *as a class* by the mass repressions of 1936-1938.[26] It was not simply that these people, including the great majority of Old Bolshevik leaders, would have found it very hard to stomach a treaty with the Nazis. To understand Stalin's special motive for getting rid of them, we must remember that he visualized the coming pact with Hitler as more than merely a way of securing temporary safety from invasion and buying time for further defense preparation. What he contemplated, as his alliance with Hitler in 1939-1941 showed in retrospect, was a kind of Moscow-Berlin axis, an active collaboration of the two dictatorships for territorial expansion, the division of spheres of influence in Eastern Europe, the Balkans, and even the Middle East. Now the Old Bolsheviks and other Party members who shared their outlook were revolutionaries, not old-fashioned Russian imperialists. They could have gone along, if reluctantly, with a simple non-aggression arrangement with Berlin. But a policy of outright imperialistic aggression in collaboration with Nazi Germany would have been extremely repugnant to very many of them, as Stalin knew. Nor could the Polish Communist Party (which was simply dissolved in · the Great Purge) be expected to acquiesce supinely in a new partition of Poland between Russia and Germany. Consequently, to get a fully free hand for the diplomacy of the Soviet-Nazi alliance, Stalin needed to eliminate or expel thousands of foreign as well as Soviet Communists and to achieve in external as well as internal policy the absolute autocracy that, as we have seen, only the Great Purge brought him.

That this was his plan must have become clear to Bukharin upon his ill-fated return to Moscow from Paris in early April 1936, and in his final months of circumscribed freedom he did what he could to resist. His last signed editorial article appeared in *Izvestia* on July 6, 1936, under the title "Routes of History" and with a sub-

---

[26] "We even met prisoners who had been prophesying the Hitler pact since 1938, simply on the basis of the categories that had been arrested" (Beck and Godin: *op. cit.,* p. 234).

title ("Thoughts Aloud") that alerted the knowing reader, by its very unusualness in the Soviet press, to expect something significant. Starting with lavish praise of the "Stalin Constitution" that had by then been drafted and submitted for nation-wide public discussion, Bukharin expounded the theme that "real history" had not proceeded in our time along the routes previously predicted. Certain "false prophets" (by subtle allusion Stalin is indicated to have been foremost among them) had failed, for example, to foresee that fascism would emerge as the greatest international problem. Now it is a "paradox of history," the article goes on, that though the masses are regarded by the fascist ideologues as *Untermenschen,* the rulers in order to retain control must deceive the people by creating an illusion of being with and for the masses. In actuality, whereas socialism raises the mass, enriches the content of personality, and elevates the intellectual functions, fascism "creates a depersonalized mass, with blind discipline, with a cult of Jesuitical obedience, with suppression of the intellectual functions." Thus deception is the essence of fascism: "An intricate network of decorative deceit (in words and deeds) is the extraordinarily essential characteristic of fascist regimes of all kinds and complexions." And while the deceitful fascist elite allows that its people own the means of production only "spiritually," for its own part it means to own "cannon," "airplanes," and "lands in the east of Europe" not in a "spiritual" sense only, but materially. But this deception must sooner or later come to light: "Its perpetrators have it in mind to gain for themselves an historical respite by sending everything into the yawning abyss of war. However, this is a game of winner take all in which they will lose everything."

This most audacious and desperate of Bukharin's essays in anti-Stalin Aesopian polemics[27] may be translated as follows: Do not take the Stalin Constitution and its democratic phraseology seriously. It is only a decorative façade of political deceit behind which Stalin

---

[27] The Aesopian message was very probably intended for the Western world as well as for Soviet and foreign communist circles. In this connection we have Bukharin's own word for it that he consciously endeavored to communicate messages to the outside world by the use of veiled language in press articles. In one of his meetings with Boris Nicolaevsky in Paris in early 1936, Bukharin said that his unsigned editorial articles in *Izvestia* written after the murder of Kirov had contained various passages in which he had tried to reveal by indirection the substance of issues then under debate behind the scenes in higher Party circles. I am indebted to Mr. Nicolaevsky for his permission to reveal this here.

is moving to create, by means of a huge blood purge, a new Soviet regime of fascist complexion which will be a denial of the Marxist ideals of the Russian Revolution. It will be a totally despotic regime based on police terror and suppression of the Party leadership and the intelligentsia ("intellectual functions"). Stalin is seeking by these means to pave the way for an alliance with the German fascists which will precipitate a second world war in which he expects to remain at least temporarily uninvolved while we build cannon and airplanes and assimilate Eastern European territories that we will occupy under the deal. But the whole plan will lead only to disaster. Why Bukharin thought Stalin's plan would lead to disaster was explained shortly after in another editorial, which was unsigned but bore indications (for example, the characteristic touch of quoting from Shelley's "Masque of Anarchy") of Bukharin's personal authorship. "It would be unforgivable blindness," it said, "not to see that it is the land of Soviets that attracts the most savage hatred of the unbridled adventurists." It was folly, in other words, to suppose that Hitler could be deflected for long from attacking the U.S.S.R. The editorial also made an emotional appeal to the British ruling circles to take a firm stand against the Nazis. Picturing Lords Lothian, Londonderry, and others as "fawning on Hitler," it recalled the war dead of 1914-1918 and asked: "How are the sons of England sleeping in Flanders fields?" This editorial, entitled "War and Peace," appeared in *Izvestia* on August 1. Later that month the trial of the sixteen began, and with it the public denunciations of Bukharin.[28]

For Stalin the purge trials had a foreign-policy motive beyond those just discussed. He wanted to use them as a means of communicating to Hitler the seriousness of his interest in a collaborative arrangement, and simultaneously as a way of softening the shock that a Stalin-Hitler pact would inevitably cause in Russia and especially in the world Communist movement. These motives may seem implausible in view of the fact that negotiating a deal with the Nazis was presented, particularly in the 1937 and 1938 trials, as one of the most heinous acts of treason on the part of the accused. Did this

---

[28] To say that the Western world failed to decipher Bukharin's messages and grasp the meaning of developments afoot in Russia at that time would be putting it kindly. Hugo Dewar describes, for example, as follows the reaction of *The Times* of London in 1936 and 1937: "The trials, it thought, reflected the triumph of Stalin's 'nationalist' policy over that of the revolutionary diehards. The conservative forces, with the overwhelming support of the nation, had now demonstrably gained the day" ("How They Saw the Moscow Trials," *Survey*, April, 1962, p. 94).

not impart a strongly anti-fascist coloring to these trials? Superficially it did, but let us take a closer look. The men in Berlin well knew that the charges of treasonable dealings with Nazi Germany were baseless. But if negotiating with the Nazis was not their real crime, was it, in Stalin's eyes, a crime at all? If the German Embassy in Moscow followed the 1938 trial closely, it must have noted that the defendant Bessonov, who had been counselor of the Soviet Embassy in Berlin at the start of the Nazi era, pleaded guilty in the very first session to receiving and acting on orders from Deputy Foreign Commissar Krestinsky and also from Trotsky to obstruct a "normalization of relations between the Soviet Union and Germany." This charge, repeated later in the trial, carried the significant implication that the anti-Stalin Communist opposition had been standing in the way of developing fruitful diplomatic relations between the Soviet and Nazi governments. Moreover, the Germans could not but know that many of the principal trial defendants, above all Bukharin, had been foremost among the anti-fascist Communists, and that a sizable proportion were Jews. Putting all this together, the fascist leaders could very reasonably infer from the trials that Stalin was seriously getting ready to do business with them. Evidence that the trials were so interpreted is to be found in a foreign-affairs commentary printed in the Italian fascist paper *Popolo d'Italia* on March 5, 1938. Reacting to the Bukharin trial then taking place in Moscow, the commentary asked whether "in view of the catastrophe of Lenin's system, Stalin could secretly have become a fascist." In any event, it went on: "Stalin is doing a notable service to fascism by mowing down in large armfuls his enemies who have been reduced to impotence." The commentator was Benito Mussolini.

The trials had, finally, the function of softening in advance the shock that the treaty of alliance with Hitler would administer to Soviet and world Communist opinion. This function was served, in particular, by the charges against the Trotskyite and Right Oppositions of negotiating a deal with the Nazis. In developing these charges in the trials, much was made of the theme that such prominent anti-Stalinist Communists as Trotsky and Bukharin were not only prepared to have dealings with the Nazis but were themselves pro-fascist. Thus the defendant Ivanov pictures himself and Bukharin as having, politically speaking, "arrived directly at fascism," and Vyshinsky, in the summing-up speech, says of Bukharin: "Like a true watchdog of fascism, he barked joyfully expressing his admiration for German fascism." This smearing of the accused as both fascist in mentality and bent on collaborating with the Nazis was preparation for *Stalin's* collaboration with them — in the sense that it undermined the whole idea that communism stood for anti-fascism, and spiked in advance the thought (which certainly would have occurred to many in Russia and the Communist movement) that the Old Bolsheviks, unlike Stalin, would have avoided the Soviet-Nazi pact *on anti-fascist principle.* In short, it paradoxically tended, if not to establish in advance the political respectability of Stalin's plan for the pact with Hitler, at least to diminish its disreputability. In these terms the trials were saying: If the anti-Stalin Communists were ready and willing to bargain with the Nazis for *anti*-Soviet purposes of defeating and dismembering the U.S.S.R., what is so bad about striking a bargain with Berlin that will *serve* Soviet interests by expanding our territorial possessions and keeping us out of war while the Germans and the West fight it out? To a considerable extent the trials fulfilled this devious design. For while the pact of August 1939 came as a shock to the international Communist movement, which suffered significant defections as a result of the disgust many felt at this turn of events, the shock would have been all the greater and more damaging to the movement and to Stalin had he not, by means of the purge trials, compromised the notion that no Communists, and no Old Bolsheviks in particular, would have friendly dealings with the Nazis.

5.

The conduct of Bukharin at his trial has long fascinated the Western mind. Rubashov, the Old Bolshevik hero of Arthur Koestler's well-known novel about the purge trials, *Darkness at Noon,* appears to have been drawn, at least in part, upon the model of Bukharin. In 1947 the French philosopher M. Merleau-Ponty published a small book, *Humanisme et Terreur,* which was devoted largely to a critique of what the author called Koestler's "Rubashov-Bukharin" and to an interpretation along different lines of Bukharin's decision to confess. Others too have contributed to this literature, and no examination of the great purge trial would be complete without an effort to solve the problem of Bukharin's motivation. What I should like to do here is to outline some of the evidence for an interpretation of it that relies in part on what is called "Kremlinology," that is, the analysis of Soviet political processes as reflected in eṣoteric communication or veiled controversy in published Soviet materials.

For it seems to me that in one of its many aspects the verbatim report is a kind of laboratory for the study of Soviet politics by the Kremlinological method.

We must recognize, to begin with, that Bukharin agreed to participate in the trial only under some kind of duress. There were others, such as Yenukidze and Karakhan, who refused to do this and went to their death without public trial. Bukharin himself hints at his resistance. He was under arrest for well over a year before the trial, and says in his final statement: "For three months I refused to say anything." To have resisted pressure for so long was in itself a remarkable feat. For as Bukharin put it in an Aesopian passage of his final statement, speaking of his confession: "But here we also have the internal demolition of the forces of counter-revolution. And one must be a Trotsky not to lay down one's arms." This was a way of saying: Stalin and his men have ways of demolishing a person's resistance by playing upon his innermost feelings, ways that hardly anyone can resist unless he is a Trotsky, that is, unless he is living in Mexico or somewhere else outside the reach of the N.K.V.D. What were the feelings in question? We have no evidence that physical torture was used in Bukharin's case, or that a deal was struck to spare his life if he cooperated, for he made it rather clear in the trial that he expected no mercy for himself. The lives of others, however, do appear to have been at stake. What was reportedly used as the chief means of coercing Bukharin into agreement to go on trial was the threat to retaliate against his young wife and little boy if he should refuse.[29] This was an all but irresistible form of pressure to which Stalin had also resorted in other cases, notably Kamenev's.

It is very likely, however, that in the case of Bukharin, as in some others involving former leaders of the Party, Stalin and his men also made use of certain blandishments, including the invitation to play the trial role as a "last service" to the Party and the Revolutionary cause. As a person whose whole life had been bound up with the Party and the Revolution, Bukharin could hardly have been insensitive to such an approach. Perhaps on this account the theory of the "last service" figures prominently in the Western literature

---

[29] Orlov: *The Secret History of Stalin's Crimes,* pp. 280-281. I am again indebted to Mr. Nicolaevsky for pointing out to me in this connection that the three principal defendants in the 1938 trial, Bukharin, Rykov, and Krestinsky, all had children with whom they were very close, whereas Yenukidze and Karkhan, both of whom would have been in Stalin's eyes logical candidates for major roles as defendants in this trial, did not. These two men were executed in 1937 without public trial.

about Bukharin on trial. In *Darkness at Noon,* for example, the Stalinist investigator Gletkin appeals to Rubashov-Bukharin to render a final service to the Party by going on trial and thereby helping to consolidate the country behind the Stalin regime in the face of an imminent danger of war, and Rubashov performs this service, although with deepening doubt of the moral validity of the Revolutionary cause to which he had devoted his life and was now sacrificing it. Merleau-Ponty, on the other hand, in effect makes out Bukharin to be a man who dialectically arrived on his own at Gletkin's kind of reasoning. On this view Bukharin, though not guilty of the counter-revolutionary crimes with which he was charged, nevertheless sees in his dialectician's mind that he *was* guilty, since oppositionism in any form was tantamount to treason under the precarious conditions of existence of the Soviet state in the 1930's. Thus Merleau-Ponty ascribes to Bukharin an acceptance in principle of that peculiar Stalinist algebraic formula according to which any opposing of Stalin = "counter-revolutionary terrorism."

If we suppose (as seems reasonable) that Bukharin's consent to take part in the trial represented in some sense a deliberate political choice as well as a bowing to coercion, then the idea that he wanted to render a last service to his cause is highly plausible. But the versions of the theory just mentioned, and others similar to them, encounter certain objections. First, we have reason to doubt that the Moscow trials were in fact a means of preparing the country to withstand the test of war. Bukharin, moreover, certainly saw them as a means of preparing for the Soviet-Nazi alliance, and it is unimaginable that he could have brought himself to a decision to take part in the show trial in order to help Stalin pave the way for his pact with Hitler. Furthermore, the theory of the last service in its conventional forms would lead us to expect Bukharin to play his part in the show trial in active cooperation with the prosecutor or at any rate in a spirit of resignation. But this he did not do. He did make a point of admitting and even underlining the enormity of his guilt; and this is a salient fact that our interpretation must account for. But at the same time we have a mass of textual evidence and eyewitness testimony to the effect that there was a play within the play of the show trial, and that the inner play was a real contest between Bukharin and Vyshinsky.

During the trial Bukharin, even though he had to speak in broad conformity with a script prepared in advance to suit his accusers, fought constantly. Thus he intervened on occasion to impugn by a single question the credibility of a defendant who had testified against him (see, for example, his question to Ivanov in the morning session of March 3), and at one point he directly described two of the defendants, Ivanov and Sharangovich, as police agents ("agents provocateurs"). He pleaded guilty to "the sum total of crimes committed by this counter-revolutionary organization," but thereupon suggested that not only did he not take part in but he even lacked knowledge of "any particular act" involved. He denied, as we have seen, that the defendants constituted a conspiratorial group in the sense of the trial indictment. He disclaimed all knowledge of his alleged connections with the German fascists, denied ever having spoken of opening the front in time of war, rejected the charge of plotting the assassination of Lenin, Stalin, and Sverdlov in 1918, failed to recall ever having directed anyone to engage in wrecking activities, categorically denied all connection with foreign intelligence services as well as any complicity in the assassination of Kirov, Gorky, and his son, and so on. During Vyshinsky's summing-up speech, which preceded his own, he was observed furiously taking notes. His own final statement was so little pleasing to Stalin that it was not, like the preceding parts of the verbatim record, printed in full in the next day's *Pravda* but only briefly summarized. And foreign observers present at the trial were profoundly impressed· by his fighting demeanor. According to the *New York Times* correspondent, "Mr. Bukharin alone, who all too obviously in his last words fully expected to die, was manly, proud and almost defiant. He is the first of the fifty-four men who have faced the court in the last three public treason trials who has not abased himself in the last hours of the trial."[30] Fitzroy MacLean, who attended the trial as an official representative of the British Embassy in Moscow and later wrote a vivid account of it, pictures Bukharin, in giving his final statement, as standing there "frail and defiant," admitting in principle the justice of the case against him and then proceeding "to tear it to bits, while Vyshinsky, powerless to intervene, sat uneasily in his place, looking embarrassed and yawning ostentatiously."[31]

That Bukharin was putting up a fight is clear enough, but what was he fighting for? It is evident that he was not fighting in any real sense to defend himself or to save his life, since any small chance of saving his life would only have been erased by the very fact that he

[30] *The New York Times,* March 13, 1938.

[31] *Escape to Adventure* (Boston: Little, Brown, 1950), p. 74.

put up this fight. I suggest, therefore, that his aim in the contest was offensive rather than defensive. Not to defend himself but to convict his accuser was the purpose. That he would have *wanted* to do this, if he could, is quite clear from evidence already cited in these pages. He had long before begun to view Stalin as a coarse bungling political leader who was ideologically illiterate on crucial points and was leading Lenin's party and the Bolshevik Revolution to ruination out of a monstrous appetite for personal power. Before his arrest he had even pictured Stalin as engaged in transforming Soviet communism into a Soviet form of fascism, and he had attempted to warn the Party and the world that Stalin was scheming to make common cause with Hitler in a great and ill-starred political gamble that would bring on World War II and destroy the Soviet Union. By no stretch of political imagination could he now identify Stalin's regime with historic Bolshevism or see Stalin himself as other than anti-Bolshevik. Is it not clear, then, that for Bukharin a last service to the Party and the Revolution could consist only of a last denunciation of Stalin for betraying and ruining both? That such an idea would occur to him was all the more likely, moreover, in view of a certain tradition in the Russian revolutionary movement before 1917 — the tradition of turning trials into anti-trials. The crux of this maneuver was that a revolutionist on trial for attempting to overthrow the existing order would seek to turn the tables upon his accusers and place them on trial before the court of public opinion and history. He would do this by foregoing a speech of defense and delivering instead a revolutionary oration, a denunciation of his accusers, their motives, their policies, and their social order.

Now there was no possibility for Bukharin to deliver such an oration in one of Stalin's show trials. Nor would the course followed by Krestinsky meet the needs of the anti-trial strategy. In the initial session Krestinsky publicly retracted his pre-trial confession, intimating that he had confessed under duress. But this gesture availed him nothing, for a little later on in the trial, after unknown events transpired behind the scenes, he retracted his retraction and from then on played his part unresisting. Bukharin must have been fully aware of the futility of such a course. Nevertheless, he appears to have found and put into practice a method of achieving his purpose. It required, first of all, simply a decision to go on trial — something that he in any event was being coerced to do. Secondly, it required the pursuit of certain tactics during the trial which I shall comment upon presently. Stalin was insisting that he appear as chief defendant in the trial. Well and good. He would do so, and try to save his family by complying with that basic and irreducible demand. But he would do so in his own way, speaking his lines according to the Stalin-Vyshinsky script but at the same time saying between these lines whatever he could say to make *his* point. Stalin, knowing Bukharin well, undoubtedly realized that he would do this. But he evidently thought it a tolerable price to pay for the great success of persuading Bukharin to go on trial and confess himself guilty of counter-revolutionary conspiracy. And he probably assumed that Vyshinsky and Ulrich, with the help of many of the trial defendants who would in effect be prosecution witnesses in the guise of defendants, would together manage to hold Bukharin in check.

Bukharin thus has a twofold objective in the trial — to comply with Stalin by confessing and at the same time to turn the tables on him. He wants to make it two trials in one. He himself tells us this in a brilliant display of Aesopian language in his final statement. Taking up the theme of the puzzlement that Western European and American intellectuals were showing over the Moscow trials and particularly over the confessions, Bukharin stresses that he has retained his "clarity of mind" and he dismisses fanciful hypotheses that would explain the confessions as based on hypnotism or a mysterious "Slavic soul" or a Dostoyevskyan psychology of self-abasement, etc. He says further that "the first thing to be understood" is that he and any others like him ("the enemy") have "a divided, a dual mind." What he meant by this is indicated by further statements a little later on.[32] The trial, he says, has an aspect of confession, but this is not the crux of it: "The confession of the accused is not essential. The confession of the accused is a medieval principle of jurisprudence." Here Bukharin is saying between the lines that in one

---

[32] An important rule to bear in mind in translating Bukharin's Aesopian language in the trial is that a certain spacing is necessarily involved. He cannot, without being too obvious, present a whole sequence of his own points in any one passage, but must confine himself to saying one thing. So we must look for the sequence of his argument in a series of separate passages each of which contains some one component of it. A telltale sign of the presence of an Aesopian point in a given passage is a certain suggestion of incoherence or lack of full coherence at this place. A further presupposition of his mode of communicating is that symbols have multiple meanings. In one of its meanings a given symbol may belong to the logic of the show trial; in another, to that of the anti-trial. Thus "Trotsky" may, as in an instance mentioned above, mean "counter-revolutionary" in terms of the show trial and "person living abroad" in terms of the anti-trial. Bukharin refers in one place to "my terminology" in order to convey that he is using words in special ways of his own.

of its aspects this trial is a sort of medieval witchcraft trial, and that we should not take the confession *per se* seriously, since in such a trial the witch, as a matter of course, has to confess. And the other aspect? Bukharin communicates this point by way of observing that Lion Feuchtwanger's *Moscow 1937,* a little piece of pro-Stalinist apologetics for the trials that had been shown him in prison, did not get to the core of the matter, "when, as a matter of fact, everything is clear. *World history is a world court of judgement"* (my italics). The crucial message is contained in Hegel's dictum on world history as the world's court of justice. In its second aspect, Bukharin was saying, this trial is taking place before the bar of history.

If in the one aspect it was a trial of Bukharin, in the other it was obviously, in Bukharin's eyes, a trial of Stalin. On the basis of his pre-trial political past we can see that the crime for which he would have wanted, if possible, to condemn Stalin before the court of history was that of desecrating the memory of Lenin, betraying what the Revolution stood for, and crushing the Party. Since it would be out of the question to say such things openly in the courtroom, they would have to be conveyed by indirection. Now the essence of convicting someone of a crime is to demonstrate that he has committed it. In the present instance the task would be to demonstrate by indirection that Stalin was committing what in Bukharin's eyes was the supreme political crime — destroying Bolshevism. How could he accomplish this? One way, and under the circumstances the only way, was simply to go on public trial and thereby permit Stalin, his accuser, to convict himself symbolically of destroying Bolshevism by committing the judicial murder of *him*. What enabled Bukharin to accomplish this purpose by this means was his own stature in the Russian Communist movement. He himself was a symbol. If any surviving Old Bolshevik had special claim to represent the original Bolshevik heritage and the link with Lenin, who was the founder and moving spirit of Bolshevism, it was Bukharin. In the "Testament" Lenin himself had said of him: "Bukharin is not only the most valuable and biggest theoretician of the Party, but also may legitimately be considered the favorite of the whole Party." More than Trotsky, who had always been something of an independent quantity, more than Zinoviev and Kamenev, and unquestionably more than Stalin, who claimed the title, Bukharin had a basis to be considered "Lenin today." And though he had been bested by Stalin in the post-Lenin struggles in the Party, his prestige in the eyes of a generation of Party members was very great. Indeed, it was over the "Bukharin question," as we noted earlier, that Stalin appears to have encountered finally a real if belated attempt in the Party leadership to oppose his plans for the Great Purge.

Bukharin was thus in a position to dramatize by his own self-immolation in the show trial what Stalin was doing to Bolshevism. By undergoing the ordeal of defamation to which Stalin and Vyshinsky systematically subjected him all through the trial, by permitting and indeed inviting Vyshinsky to cover him with a torrent of vituperative abuse as "the acme of monstrous hypocrisy, perfidy, jesuitry and inhuman villainy," Bukharin was able not only to convict Stalin of putting Bolshevism on trial but to catch him, as it were, red-handed in the act and show him up before the world in the process. Unquestionably it cost him great agony to go through this experience of having his whole revolutionary past besmirched and being accused of what to him would be quite inconceivable acts such as conspiring to kill Lenin or to destroy the Soviet order. But he evidently decided upon it, in part, because it would be a meaningful political act in terms of all that he had set store by in his previous political life. And this is what I believe he was trying to communicate when he said in his final statement that in the face of "the absolutely black vacuity" confronting him, he wanted to die for something. In the next breath he said it would be something that would cost him the sacrifice of his revolutionary reputation and pride: "And at such moments, Citizens Judges, everything personal, all the personal incrustation, all the rancour, pride, and a number of other things, fall away, disappear."

But the anti-trial was much more than a passive act of self-sacrifice designed to dramatize by Bukharin's own fate that Stalin was condemning Bolshevism. There was an active effort on Bukharin's part to transform the trial into an anti-trial. The fight that he put up against Vyshinsky was entirely dedicated to this purpose, and his tactics all through the trial were precisely calculated to fit the needs of the anti-trial strategy. First of all, as mentioned earlier, he made a special effort to underline his own great guilt. Thus he accepted full responsibility for the mass of counter-revolutionary acts with which the "Bloc" was charged, although in doing so he insisted that this was *political* responsibility, that as a leader of the alleged conspiracy he was guilty for whatever acts were committed, either by himself or by others in carrying it out. Still more to the point, he repeated several times in the trial that he wished not to defend but to accuse himself. "I did not want to minimize my guilt, I wanted to aggravate it," he said in one place. "This is not my defence, it is my self-accusation," he said elsewhere. "I have not said a single word in my defence." All this was to say: My tactics in the anti-trial are tactics of self-accusation. By emphasizing in this manner how terribly guilty I, an Old Bolshevik leader, am in Stalin's eyes, I am showing implicitly how guilty *he* is of murderous attitudes and acts against the people who embody historic Bolshevism. Hence my tactics of self-accusation are my way of placing my accuser on trial for his crimes against our party.

This view that Bukharin was not trying to defend himself may seem to be contradicted by what was said earlier here about his denial of guilt under the specific criminal charges. But only in a surface sense was this a defensive move. Bukharin rejected the criminal charges not with a view to pleading innocent in the trial but rather with a view to making more clear where his real guilt lay — in the political field. For this purpose, of course, it was necessary to indicate that he was *not* guilty of certain things. Thus the denial of the criminal charges was an organic part of the whole strategy of exposing and convicting Stalin through his own self-accusation. Only if the public saw the accused Bukharin as a political man would it see that the accuser Stalin was destroying a political tendency, condemning Old Bolsheviks for their Bolshevism. Only in this event would it be clear that when, as Bukharin put it, "out of certain deviations monstrous conclusions are formed by the logic of the struggle," these monstrous conclusions and the paranoid-like logic that produced them were Stalin's.

So it was vital to Bukharin's whole case in the anti-trial to show that he had been a Bolshevik oppositionist in relation to Stalin and not, as Vyshinsky was trying very hard to show, a criminal element masquerading for long years as a Bolshevik revolutionary. The duel that rages between the two all through the great purge trial is thus one in which Vyshinsky argues that all Bukharin's purported political acts were really crimes and Bukharin maintains that all his alleged crimes were really political acts. If Bukharin came off remarkably well in this encounter, despite all the disadvantages of his situation compared with Vyshinsky's, one reason lay in the fact that his contention was true.

Contents

PREFACE VII

INTRODUCTION IX

MORNING SESSION, MARCH 2
Opening of the Trial 1
Indictment 5
Examination of the Accused Bessonov . . . 38

EVENING SESSION, MARCH 2
Examination of the Accused Grinko 67
Examination of the Accused Chernov . . . 88

MORNING SESSION, MARCH 3
Examination of the Accused Ivanov 110
Examination of the Accused Zubarev . . . 138

EVENING SESSION, MARCH 3
Examination of the Accused Krestinsky . . . 152
Examination of the Accused Rykov 158

SUMMARY OF MORNING SESSION, MARCH 4 . . . 200

EVENING SESSION, MARCH 4
Examination of the Accused Rosengoltz . . . 202
Second Examination of the Accused Krestinsky . 220
Examination of the Accused Rakovsky . . . 245

MORNING SESSION, MARCH 5
Examination of the Accused Rakovsky (resumed) 251
Examination of the Accused Zelensky . . . 272

EVENING SESSION, MARCH 5
Examination of the Accused Ikramov 297
Examination of the Accused Bukharin . . . 327

MORNING SESSION, MARCH 7
    Examination of the Accused Bukharin (resumed) 351
    Examination of the Witness Yakovleva . . 397

EVENING SESSION, MARCH 7
    Examination of the Witness Yakovleva (resumed) 411
    Examination of the Witness Ossinsky . . . 416
    Examination of the Witness Mantsev . . . 424
    Examination of the Witness Kamkov . . . 442
    Examination of the Witness Karelin . . . 454

SUMMARY OF MORNING SESSION, MARCH 8 . . . 471

EVENING SESSION, MARCH 8
    Examination of the Accused Bulanov . . . 473
    Examination of the Accused Yagoda . . . 489
    Examination of the Accused Kryuchkov . . 505

SUMMARY OF MORNING SESSION, MARCH 9 . . . 511

EVENING SESSION, MARCH 9
    Session *in camera* 513

MORNING SESSION, MARCH 11
    Speech for the Prosecution by A. Y. Vyshinsky,
    Procurator of the U.S.S.R. 514

EVENING SESSION, MARCH 11
    Speech for the Defence by I. D. Braude . . 587
    Speech for the Defence by N. V. Kommodov . 594
    Last Plea of the Accused Bessonov . . . 604
    Last Plea of the Accused Grinko 607
    Last Plea of the Accused Chernov 610

MORNING SESSION, MARCH 12
    Last Plea of the Accused Ivanov 615
    Last Plea of the Accused Krestinsky . . . 619
    Last Plea of the Accused Zubarev 625
    Last Plea of the Accused Rykov 626
    Last Plea of the Accused Sharangovich . . 630
    Last Plea of the Accused Khodjayev . . . 632
    Last Plea of the Accused Zelensky . . . 637
    Last Plea of the Accused Ikramov . . . 643
    Last Plea of the Accused Rakovsky . . . 647
    Last Plea of the Accused Rosengoltz . . . 653

EVENING SESSION, MARCH 12
    Last Plea of the Accused Bukharin 656
    Last Plea of the Accused Levin 668
    Last Plea of the Accused Bulanov 671
    Last Plea of the Accused Yagoda 673
    Last Plea of the Accused Kryuchkov 676
    Last Plea of the Accused Pletnev 676
    Last Plea of the Accused Kazakov 677
    Last Plea of the Accused Maximov-Dikovsky . 679
    The Verdict 681

NOTES 693

THE DEFENDANTS: BIOGRAPHICAL NOTES . . . 717

READINGS ON THE MOSCOW TRIALS
    AND THE PURGE ERA 723

THE GREAT PURGE TRIAL

MORNING SESSION, MARCH 2, 1938

COMMANDANT OF THE COURT: The Court is coming, please rise.

THE PRESIDENT: Be seated. I declare the session of the Military Collegium of the Supreme Court of the U.S.S.R. open.

The trial is of Nikolai Ivanovich BUKHARIN, Alexei Ivanovich RYKOV, Genrikh Grigorievich YAGODA, Nikolai Nikolayevich KRESTINSKY, Khristian Georgievich RAKOVSKY, Arkady Pavlovich ROSENGOLTZ, Vladimir Ivanovich IVANOV, Mikhail Alexandrovich CHERNOV, Grigori Fedorovich GRINKO, Isaac Abramovich ZELENSKY, Sergei Alexeyevich BESSONOV, Akmal IKRAMOV, Faizulla KHODJAYEV, Vasily Fomich SHARANGOVICH, Prokopy Timofeyevich ZUBAREV, Pavel Petrovich BULANOV, Lev Grigorievich LEVIN, Dmitry Dmitrievich PLETNEV, Ignaty Nikolayevich KAZAKOV, Venyamin Adamovich MAXIMOV, and Pyotr Petrovich KRYUCHKOV on charges of treason to the country, espionage, committing acts of diversion, terrorism, wrecking, undermining the military power of the U.S.S.R. and of provoking a military attack of foreign states upon the U.S.S.R., i.e., of crimes covered by Articles 58^{1a}, 58^2, 58^7, 58^8, 58^9 and 58^{11} of the Criminal Code of the R.S.F.S.R.[1]

Accused Bukharin, Nikolai Ivanovich, have you received a copy of the indictment?

BUKHARIN: Yes, I have.

THE PRESIDENT: Accused Rykov, Alexei Ivanovich, have you received a copy of the indictment?

RYKOV: Yes.

THE PRESIDENT: Accused Yagoda, Genrikh Grigorievich, have you received a copy of the indictment?

YAGODA: Yes.

THE PRESIDENT: Accused Krestinsky, Nikolai Nikolayevich, have you received a copy of the indictment?

KRESTINSKY: Yes.

THE PRESIDENT: Accused Rakovsky, Khristian Georgievich, have you received a copy of the indictment?

RAKOVSKY: I have.

THE PRESIDENT: Accused Rosengoltz, Arkady Pavlovich, have you received a copy of the indictment?

1

ROSENGOLTZ: Yes.

THE PRESIDENT: Accused Ivanov, Vladimir Ivanovich, have you received a copy of the indictment?

IVANOV: I have received a copy of the indictment.

THE PRESIDENT: Accused Chernov, Mikhail Alexandrovich, have you received a copy of the indictment?

CHERNOV: I have.

THE PRESIDENT: Accused Grinko, Grigori Fedorovich, have you received a copy of the indictment?

GRINKO: I have.

THE PRESIDENT: Accused Zelensky, Isaac Abramovich, have you received a copy of the indictment?

ZELENSKY: I have.

THE PRESIDENT: Accused Bessonov, Sergei Alexeyevich, have you received a copy of the indictment?

BESSONOV: I have.

THE PRESIDENT: Accused Ikramov, Akmal, have you received a copy of the indictment?

IKRAMOV: Yes.

THE PRESIDENT: Accused Khodjayev, Faizulla, have you received a copy of the indictment?

KHODJAYEV: I have.

THE PRESIDENT: Accused Sharangovich, Vasily Fomich, have you received a copy of the indictment?

SHARANGOVICH: I have.

THE PRESIDENT: Accused Zubarev, Prokopy Timofeyevich, have you received a copy of the indictment?

ZUBAREV: I have.

THE PRESIDENT: Accused Bulanov, Pavel Petrovich, have you received a copy of the indictment?

BULANOV: I have.

THE PRESIDENT: Accused Levin, Lev Grigorievich, have you received a copy of the indictment?

LEVIN: I have.

THE PRESIDENT: Accused Pletnev, Dmitry Dmitrievich, have you received a copy of the indictment?

PLETNEV: I have.

THE PRESIDENT: Accused Kazakov, Ignaty Nikolayevich, have you received a copy of the indictment?

KAZAKOV: I have.

THE PRESIDENT: Accused Maximov, Venyamin Adamovich, your real name is Dikovsky, Venyamin Adamovich, alias Abramovich?

MAXIMOV: Yes.

THE PRESIDENT: Have you received a copy of the indictment?

MAXIMOV: Yes.

THE PRESIDENT: Accused Kryuchkov, Pyotr Petrovich, have you received a copy of the indictment?

KRYUCHKOV: I have.

THE PRESIDENT: I announce the composition of the Court in this case: President—Army Military Jurist V. V. Ulrich, President of the Military Collegium of the Supreme Court of the U.S.S.R.; Members of the Court—Army Corps Military Jurist I. O. Matulevich, Vice-president of the Military Collegium; Divisional Military Jurist B. I. Yevlev; and Reserve Member of the Court—Brigade Military Jurist I. M. Zyryanov.

The prosecution is conducted by the Procurator of the U.S.S.R., A. Y. Vyshinsky.

The following are Defending Counsel: for accused Levin—Member of the Collegium of Defence Braude; for accused Pletnev and Kazakov—Member of the Collegium of Defence Kommodov; the other accused, asked, when the investigation was concluded, whether they needed Counsel for Defence, declined and said that they would defend themselves.

I repeat the question about defence:

Accused Bukharin, do you desire to have Counsel for Defence?

BUKHARIN: No.

THE PRESIDENT: Accused Rykov, do you desire to have Counsel for Defence?

RYKOV: No.

THE PRESIDENT: Accused Yagoda, do you desire to have Counsel for Defence?

YAGODA: No.

THE PRESIDENT: Accused Krestinsky, do you desire to have Counsel for Defence?

KRESTINSKY: No, I will defend myself.

THE PRESIDENT: Accused Rakovsky, do you desire to have Counsel for Defence?

RAKOVSKY: No.

THE PRESIDENT: Accused Rosengoltz, do you desire to have Counsel for Defence?

ROSENGOLTZ: No.

THE PRESIDENT: Accused Ivanov, do you desire to have Counsel for Defence?

IVANOV: No, I do not need Counsel, I do not intend to defend myself. I am here to bear full responsibility for my crimes.

THE PRESIDENT: Accused Chernov, do you desire to have Counsel for Defence?

CHERNOV: No.

THE PRESIDENT: Accused Grinko, do you desire to have Counsel for Defence?

3

GRINKO: No.

THE PRESIDENT: Accused Zelensky, do you desire to have Counsel for Defence?

ZELENSKY: No.

THE PRESIDENT: Accused Bessonov, do you desire to have Counsel for Defence?

BESSONOV: No.

THE PRESIDENT: Accused Ikramov, do you desire to have Counsel for Defence?

IKRAMOV: No.

THE PRESIDENT: Accused Khodjayev, do you desire to have Counsel for Defence?

KHODJAYEV: No.

THE PRESIDENT: Accused Sharangovich, do you desire to have Counsel for Defence?

SHARANGOVICH: No.

THE PRESIDENT: Accused Zubarev, do you desire to have Counsel for Defence?

ZUBAREV: No.

THE PRESIDENT: Accused Bulanov, do you desire to have Counsel for Defence?

BULANOV: No.

THE PRESIDENT: Accused Maximov, do you desire to have Counsel for Defence?

MAXIMOV: No.

THE PRESIDENT: Accused Kryuchkov, do you desire to have Counsel for Defence?

KRYUCHKOV: No.

THE PRESIDENT: I must explain to the accused who have declined Counsel for Defence that, in addition to their last pleas, they have the right to make speeches in defence.

I must explain to all the accused that they have the right to put questions to each other and to give explanations on any point in the Court investigation.

Comrade Procurator, have you any request to make in respect to the calling of supplementary witnesses in the case, or in respect to the inclusion of any supplementary documents in the case?

VYSHINSKY: Not so far, but in accordance with the Code of Criminal Procedure I have the right at any moment in the course of the Court proceedings to request that witnesses be called and that supplementary documents be included in the case. I ask that this right be reserved for me.

THE PRESIDENT: Certainly. Have Counsel for Defence any requests?[2]

COUNSEL FOR DEFENCE: (Reply in the negative.)

4

THE PRESIDENT: Have the accused any statement to make in respect to the calling of witnesses or inclusion of documents? No. We will now hear the indictment.

(The Secretary of the Court reads the indictment.)

INDICTMENT

in the case of N. I. BUKHARIN, A. I. RYKOV, G. G. YAGODA, N. N. KRESTINSKY, K. G. RAKOVSKY, A. P. ROSENGOLTZ, V. I. IVANOV, M. A. CHERNOV, G. F. GRINKO, I. A. ZELENSKY, S. A. BESSONOV, A. IKRAMOV, F. KHODJAYEV, V. F. SHARANGOVICH, P. T. ZUBAREV, P. P. BULANOV, L. G. LEVIN, D. D. PLETNEV, I. N. KAZAKOV, V. A. MAXIMOV-DIKOVSKY and P. P. KRYUCHKOV, accused of having on the instructions of the intelligence services of foreign states hostile to the Soviet Union formed a conspiratorial group named the "bloc of Rights and Trotskyites" with the object of espionage on behalf of foreign states, wrecking, diversionist and terrorist activities, undermining the military power of the U.S.S.R., provoking a military attack by these states on the U.S.S.R., dismembering the U.S.S.R. and severing from it the Ukraine, Byelorussia, the Central Asiatic Republics, Georgia, Armenia, Azerbaijan and the Maritime Region of the Far East for the benefit of the aforementioned foreign states, and lastly, with the object of overthrowing the Socialist social and state system existing in the U.S.S.R. and of restoring capitalism, of restoring the power of the bourgeoisie.

The investigation instituted by the organs of the People's Commissariat of Internal Affairs has established that on the instructions of the intelligence services of foreign states hostile to the U.S.S.R. the accused in the present case organized a conspiratorial group named the "bloc of Rights and Trotskyites," the object of which was to overthrow the Socialist social and state system existing in the U.S.S.R., to restore capitalism and the power of the bourgeoisie in the U.S.S.R., to dismember the U.S.S.R. and to sever from it for the benefit of the aforementioned states the Ukraine, Byelorussia, the Central Asiatic Republics, Georgia, Armenia, Azerbaijan and the Maritime Region.

The investigation has established that the "bloc of Rights and Trotskyites" united within its ranks underground anti-Soviet groups of Trotskyites, Rights, Zinovievites,[3] Mensheviks, Socialist-Revolutionaries[4] and bourgeois nationalists of the Ukraine, Byelorussia, Georgia, Armenia, Azerbaijan and the Central Asiatic Republics, which is corroborated by the materials not only of the present investigation, but also by the materials of the trials which have taken place in various parts of the U.S.S.R., and, in particular, the trial of the group of military conspirators—TUKHACHEVSKY

5

and others[5]-who were convicted by a Special Session of the Supreme Court of the U.S.S.R. on June 11, 1937, and of the trial of the Georgian bourgeois nationalist group of MDIVANI,[6] OKUDJAVA and others, who were convicted by the Supreme Court of the Georgian Soviet Socialist Republic on July 9, 1937.

Lacking all support within the U.S.S.R., the members of the "bloc of Rights and Trotskyites" in their struggle against the Socialist social and state system existing in the U.S.S.R. and for seizing power placed all their hopes exclusively upon the armed assistance of foreign aggressors, who promised the conspirators this assistance on the condition that the U.S.S.R. was to be dismembered and that the Ukraine, the Maritime Region, Byelorussia, the Central Asiatic Republics, Georgia, Armenia and Azerbaijan were to be severed from the U.S.S.R.

This agreement between the "bloc of Rights and Trotskyites" and the representatives of the aforementioned foreign states was facilitated by the fact that many of the leading participants of this conspiracy had long been agents of foreign intelligence services and had for many years carried on espionage activities on behalf of these intelligence services.

This applies first of all to one of the inspirers of the conspiracy, enemy of the people TROTSKY. His connection with the Gestapo was exhaustively proved at the trials of the Trotskyite-Zinovievite Terrorist Centre in August 1936, and of the Anti-Soviet Trotskyite Centre in January 1937.[7]

However, the materials in the possession of the investigating authorities in the present case establish that the connections between enemy of the people TROTSKY and the German political police and the intelligence services of other countries were established at a much earlier date. The investigation has definitely established that TROTSKY has been connected with the German intelligence service since 1921, and with the British Intelligence Service since 1926.

As far as the accused in the present case are concerned, a considerable number of them, on their own confession, have been espionage agents of foreign intelligence services for a long period of time.

Thus, the accused N. N. KRESTINSKY, on the direct instructions of enemy of the people TROTSKY, entered into treasonable connections with the German intelligence service in 1921.

The accused A. P. ROSENGOLTZ, one of the leaders of the Trotskyite underground organization, began his espionage work for the German General Staff in 1923, and for the British Intelligence Service in 1926.

The accused K. G. RAKOVSKY, one of L. Trotsky's most inti-

6

mate and particularly trusted men, has been an agent of the British Intelligence Service since 1924, and of the Japanese intelligence service since 1934.

The accused M. A. CHERNOV began his espionage work on behalf of Germany in 1928, when he established connections with the German intelligence service on the initiative and with the assistance of the notorious émigré Menshevik DAN.[8]

The accused V. F. SHARANGOVICH was enlisted by the Polish intelligence service and was sent on espionage work to the U.S.S.R. in 1921.

The accused G. F. GRINKO became a spy of the German and Polish intelligence services in 1932.

The leaders of the "bloc of Rights and Trotskyites," including RYKOV, BUKHARIN and others accused in the present case, were fully informed of the espionage connections of their accomplices and did everything to encourage the expansion of these espionage connections.

All this sufficiently explains why these gentlemen, being in the service of foreign intelligence services, so readily agreed to the dismemberment of the U.S.S.R. and to the severance of whole regions and republics from it for the benefit of foreign states.

Agreement between the "bloc of Rights and Trotskyites" and foreign intelligence services was also facilitated by the fact that several of the conspirators accused in the present case had been provocateurs and agents of the tsarist secret police.

Having wormed their way into responsible posts in the Soviet state, these provocateurs, however, never ceased to fear the exposure of the crimes they had committed against the working class, against the cause of Socialism. Constantly in fear of exposure, these participants in the conspiracy saw their only hope of safety in the overthrow of the Soviet power, in the destruction of the Soviet system and in the restoration of the power of the landlords and capitalists, in whose interests they had sold themselves to the tsarist secret police, and under whose rule alone they could feel safe.

Thus, the accused I. A. ZELENSKY had been an agent of the Samara Gendarme Administration since 1911. From that time onwards ZELENSKY, under the pseudonyms of "Ochkasty" and "Salaf," systematically informed the Gendarme Administration about the activities of the Samara Bolshevik organization, for which he received a regular monthly monetary remuneration.

The accused IVANOV began his provocateur activities in 1911, when he was enlisted for this purpose by the Tula Secret Police and became an agent of the secret police under the pseudonym of "Samarin."

The accused ZUBAREV was enlisted by the tsarist police in 1908 and worked for them under the pseudonyms of "Vasily," "Palin," and "Prokhor."

As the investigation has established, for the purpose of achieving their criminal object of overthrowing the Soviet government, of seizing power and restoring capitalism in the U.S.S.R., the conspirators, on the direct instructions of the foreign intelligence services, carried on extensive espionage work on behalf of these intelligence services, organized and carried on wrecking and diversion activities with the object of bringing about the defeat of the U.S.S.R. in the forthcoming attack upon the U.S.S.R. by the fascist aggressors, did their utmost to provoke the acceleration of this attack of the fascist aggressors, and also organized and carried out a number of terrorist acts against the leaders of the Party and the government and prominent Soviet public men.

I. ESPIONAGE AGAINST THE SOVIET STATE AND TREASON TO THE COUNTRY

The investigation has established that the majority of the leaders of the "bloc of Rights and Trotskyites" accused in the present case carried on their criminal activities on the direct instructions of TROTSKY and in accordance with plans which were widely conceived and elaborated by the General Staffs of certain foreign states.

Agent of the German intelligence service, prominent Trotskyite, the accused KRESTINSKY, while under examination at the office of the Procurator of the U.S.S.R. on December 2, 1937, stated:

> "I established espionage connections with the Germans on the direct instructions of TROTSKY, who instructed me to start negotiations on this matter with General SEECKT. . . ."
>
> (Vol. III, p. 102.)[9]

As regards the circumstances under which connections between the Trotskyite organization and the German intelligence service were established, the accused KRESTINSKY testified that in the winter of 1921 he carried on negotiations with General SEECKT, Commander-in-Chief of the German Reichswehr, with a view to receiving from the Reichswehr funds for the purpose of carrying on Trotskyite underground work in exchange for espionage materials which the Trotskyites were to supply the German intelligence service.

On this matter the accused KRESTINSKY testified as follows:

8

". . . TROTSKY instructed me on my arrival in Berlin to start negotiations on this matter with General SEECKT. This instruction of TROTSKY'S I carried out. . . ."

(Vol. III, p. 14 reverse.)

Dealing with his own treasonable activities and with those of his accomplices, the accused KRESTINSKY testified as follows:

"We came to an agreement with Generals SEECKT and HASSE to the effect that we would help the Reichswehr to create a number of espionage bases on the territory of the U.S.S.R. by permitting the unhindered entry of spies sent by the Reichswehr, and that we would supply the Reichswehr with espionage materials, i.e., to put it plainly, that we would be German spies. In return for this the Reichswehr undertook to pay us 250,000 marks per annum as a subsidy for counter-revolutionary Trotskyite work. . . ."

(Vol. III, p. 102.)

"The monetary subsidy was paid in regular instalments several times a year, mostly in Moscow, but sometimes in Berlin. . . .

"If for some reason the money was not paid in Moscow, I received it in Berlin myself directly from SEECKT; and I used to take it to Moscow myself and hand it to TROTSKY."

(Vol. III, p. 15.)

Another prominent Trotskyite, one of the leaders of the anti-Soviet Trotskyite underground organization and an active participant in the conspiracy, the accused ROSENGOLTZ, who is charged with espionage, during the investigation corroborated the fact that TROTSKY had entered into an agreement with the Reichswehr and testified as follows:

"My espionage activities began as far back as 1923, when, on TROTSKY'S instructions, I handed various secret information to the Commander-in-Chief of the Reichswehr, SEECKT, and to the Chief of the German General Staff, HASSE. Subsequently, direct connections with me were established by the ——— Ambassador in the U.S.S.R., Mr. N, to whom I periodically gave information of an espionage character. After Mr. N's departure I continued my espionage connections with the new Ambassador, Mr. N." (Vol. VI, p. 131 reverse.)

After the fascist coup in Germany, the espionage activities of the Trotskyites assumed a still wider and sharply expressed defeatist character.

The accused BESSONOV, who on his own confession took an active part in the secret negotiations between the Trotskyites and the German fascist, mainly military, circles, on the matter of jointly fighting the U.S.S.R., not only personally negotiated for support for the anti-Soviet conspiracy with DAITZ, ROSENBERG'S closest colleague in the foreign affairs department of the fascist party, but was kept informed of the meetings and negotiations between L. TROTSKY and HESS, NIEDERMEIER and Professor HAUSHOFER, with whom L. TROTSKY reached an agreement on the terms mentioned by PYATAKOV at the trial of the Anti-Soviet Trotskyite Centre.

The accused BESSONOV testified:

> ". . . As is evident from these terms . . . the main emphasis in the underground work of the Trotskyites was placed on undermining, espionage, diversion and terrorist acts in the U.S.S.R." (Vol. XI, p. 106.)

The existence of an agreement between L. TROTSKY and the Trotskyite organization in the U.S.S.R., on the one hand, and the fascist circles, on the other, and the carrying on in the U.S.S.R. of undermining defeatist activities on the instructions of the German intelligence service was admitted during the investigation by other accused in the present case.

However, the defeatist activities of the Trotskyite hirelings were not limited merely to connections with German fascism. In conjunction with other participants in the anti-Soviet conspiracy, in conformity with L. TROTSKY'S line, they orientated themselves also on another fascist aggressor—Japan.

The factual side of the treasonable connections of the anti-Soviet conspirators with the Japanese intelligence service is presented in the materials of the investigation in the following way.

As was testified by the accused KRESTINSKY, at a meeting he had with L. TROTSKY in Meran in October 1933, TROTSKY urged the necessity of establishing closer connections with the Japanese intelligence service.

KRESTINSKY conveyed TROTSKY'S instructions to PYATAKOV and other leaders of the conspiracy, who through the medium of the accused RAKOVSKY and other participants in the conspiracy entered into treasonable connections with representatives of Japan, the latter undertaking to render the conspiracy armed assistance in overthrowing the Soviet government, in exchange for which the conspirators promised to surrender the Soviet Maritime Region to Japan.

As has been established by the investigation, the accused RAKOVSKY, in view of his departure for Japan in the summer of 1934, received from PYATAKOV instructions to the effect that it was

10

"... necessary at the same time to increase activities abroad in the sense of establishing contact with governments hostile to the U.S.S.R. .... necessary to make efforts to take advantage of the visit to Tokyo and probably —— will take the necessary steps in this direction."[10]   (Vol. IV, p. 194.)

The accused RAKOVSKY carried out this instruction, and while in Tokyo did indeed enter into criminal connections with —— circles.

On this matter the accused RAKOVSKY testified as follows:

"All these circumstances had as their logical and practical consequence the fact that I ... when I was in Tokyo became a direct spy-agent of ——, being enlisted for this purpose, on the instructions of ——, by Mr. N, a most influential political figure in capitalist-feudal Japan, and one of her biggest plutocrats."   (Vol. IV, p. 186.)

The aforementioned accused RAKOVSKY, speaking of the connections of enemy of the people L. TROTSKY with the British Intelligence Service, testified as follows:

"I knew that TROTSKY has been an agent of the Intelligence Service since the end of 1926. TROTSKY himself informed me of it."   (Vol. IV, p. 363.)

The groups of bourgeois nationalists which belonged to the "bloc of Rights and Trotskyites" were also very closely connected with foreign intelligence services.

Thus, the accused GRINKO, who was an agent of the German and Polish intelligence services, in dealing with the anti-Soviet activities of the Ukrainian national-fascist organization of which he was one of the leaders, testified as follows:

"... In 1930, we in our organization discussed the necessity of coming to an agreement with Poland about obtaining military assistance for an insurrection in the Ukraine against the Soviet government. As a result of these negotiations with Poland an agreement was reached and the Polish General Staff increased the quantity of arms and the number of diversionists and PETLIURA emissaries sent to the Ukraine."
          (Vol. IX, p. 18.)

And he said further:

"At the end of 1932 I, in connection with my nationalist activities, entered into treasonable connections with Mr. N. We met in my office, where Mr. N used to come to see me on business concerning a German concession.

"In the latter half of 1933 Mr. N told me plainly that the

11

German fascists wanted to co-operate with the Ukrainian nationalists on the Ukrainian question. I expressed to Mr. N my readiness to co-operate. Subsequently, during 1933 and 1934, I met Mr. N several times, and before his departure from the U.S.S.R. he put me in touch with Mr. N, with whom I continued my treasonable connections."

(Vol. IX, p. 286 reverse.)

Another participant in the anti-Soviet conspiracy, and one of the leaders of the nationalist organization in Uzbekistan, the accused IKRAMOV, testified as follows:

"The question constantly arose before us of orientating ourselves upon one of the strong European states, which would render us direct assistance at the outbreak of the armed struggle against the Soviet power. . . ."

(Vol. XII, pp. 59-60.)

". . . Some of the members of the counter-revolutionary organization were of the opinion that England was the most likely country in regard to helping us, as she was a powerful country and could render us sufficiently effective assistance in the direct armed struggle. . . ."   (Vol. XII, p. 60.)

The accused SHARANGOVICH, agent of the Polish intelligence service and one of the leaders of the anti-Soviet organization of Byelorussian national-fascists, has admitted that this organization pursued its undermining activities not only on the instructions of the Rights and the "bloc of Rights and Trotskyites," but also on the instructions of the Polish intelligence service.

On this matter the accused SHARANGOVICH testified as follows:

"By this time (1933) all differences between the Rights, the Trotskyites and the national-fascists had been ironed out. We all set ourselves the same task, the task of fighting the Soviet government by every possible method, including terrorism, diversion and wrecking. The ultimate object of all three organizations operating in the territory of the national republic was to sever Byelorussia from the Soviet Union and to create an 'independent' buffer state, which undoubtedly would have been entirely in the hands of Poland and Germany. . . ."   (Vol. XIV, p. 27.)

And he said further:

"Notwithstanding the fact that the instructions we received came from Moscow, from the centre of the Rights and Trotskyites, on the one hand, and from Warsaw, from Polish

12

—— circles, on the other, there was no difference between them, they were exactly the same, and we were carrying them out."

(Vol. XIV, p. 31.)

The accused RYKOV fully corroborated the existence of treasonable connections between the Rights and fascist Poland in the following testimony:

"...A group of members of the Right organization, in conformity with the instructions of the centre of the Rights and my personal instructions, with the object of achieving our conspiratorial, treasonable plans, established connection with fascist Poland, and with the Polish intelligence service in particular."　　　　　　　　　　　　　　　　(Vol. I, p. 118.)

Speaking further of the plans to sever Byelorussia from the U.S.S.R., the accused RYKOV testified as follows:

"The general formula on which we then agreed was that in the negotiations with the Poles ... we would agree to the severance of the Byelorussian Soviet Republic from the U.S.S.R. and to the formation of an 'independent' Byelorussia as a Polish protectorate. . . ."　　　　　　　　(Vol. I, p. 119.)

As has been established by the investigation, the whole of the criminal activities of the anti-Soviet group of Rights which belonged to the "bloc of Rights and Trotskyites" proves that the Rights were agents of foreign General Staffs equally with the other participants in this conspiracy.

Some of the Rights directly, and others through the medium of· their accomplices, were also connected with the intelligence services of foreign states, on whose assistance alone they counted in their fight against the Soviet government.

The accused BUKHARIN was aware of the negotiations carried on between L. TROTSKY and the German fascists and, like L. TROTSKY, made preparations for the defeat of the U.S.S.R. and for the severance of the Ukraine, Byelorussia, the Maritime Region, Georgia, Armenia, Azerbaijan and the Central Asiatic Republics from the U.S.S.R.

This has been fully admitted by the accused BUKHARIN, who testified as follows:

"At the time TROTSKY was negotiating with the German fascists and promising them territorial concessions, we Rights were already in a bloc with the Trotskyites. RADEK told me that TROTSKY considered that the main chance of the bloc coming into power depended upon the defeat of the U.S.S.R. in a war with Germany and Japan and that he

13

proposed after this defeat to surrender the Ukraine to Germany and the Far East to Japan. RADEK told me this in 1934. . . ." (Vol. V, p. 107.)

On this matter the accused F. KHODJAYEV testified as follows during the investigation:

"BUKHARIN urged that Uzbekistan and Turkmenia should be severed from the U.S.S.R. and should exist as protectorates of Japan and Germany; but it would be impossible to ignore England, and it was therefore necessary to establish connection with the English. The most feasible proposal was a British protectorate, and that is why stress was laid on England." (Vol. XIII, pp. 89-89 reverse.)

The testimony of the accused F. KHODJAYEV is fully corroborated by other materials of the investigation, which fully expose the defeatist line of the "bloc of Rights and Trotskyites."

Thus, on this point the accused RYKOV testified as follows:

"As for our defeatist position, BUKHARIN fully agreed with it and expressed himself in its favour even more strongly than we did. In particular, it was he who proposed and formulated the idea of opening the front to the Germans in the event of war." (Vol. I, p. 152.)

Characterizing his own attitude towards this question, the accused RYKOV testified as follows:

"Like the other members of the Rights' centre, I was aware of the treasonable negotiations that were being carried on between the representatives of our counter-revolutionary organization and the German fascists, whose assistance we sought. Naturally, this assistance was dependent upon our making concessions to the German fascists, and to this we agreed." (Vol. I, p. 151 reverse.)

Such were the espionage and defeatist activities of the "bloc of Rights and Trotskyites" of these traitors who sold Soviet state secrets to foreign intelligence services, who traded in the freedom of the peoples of the U.S.S.R., in the independence and inviolability of the workers' and peasants' Socialist states.

In pursuit of their criminal designs, the anti-Soviet conspirators, on the direct instructions of foreign fascist intelligence services, organized a wide network of diversionist and wrecking nests in a number of industrial, transport, agricultural and distributing enterprises in various republics, territories and regions of the Soviet Union.

Entering into an agreement with the fascist circles treacherously to open our fronts to the armies of these fascist states in the event of war, the participants in the Right and Trotskyite conspiracy prepared to undermine the material and technical base of the Red Army—the defence industry.

By preparing for a number of destructive and diversionist activities, the conspirators counted in the event of war on blowing up and destroying the decisive defence enterprises in our Socialist fatherland. They also made preparations to wreck troop-trains, causing great loss of life.

They set themselves the task of paralysing the whole economic life of the country, of paralysing the food and munition supplies of the army.

The investigation has established that the conspirators actually carried out a number of diversionist and wrecking acts of this kind in various branches of national economy.

As has been established by the investigation, that hireling of foreign intelligence services, enemy of the people TROTSKY, in a number of his letters and personal instructions to the leading participants in the anti-Soviet conspiracy in the U.S.S.R., demanded the intensification of wrecking and diversionist activities in the Soviet Union.

The accused KRESTINSKY, a leading participant in the conspiracy, testified that in 1933, in Meran, L. TROTSKY told him personally that

"... it would be easier for him, TROTSKY, to negotiate with the Germans if he could tell them that really serious work was being carried on in the way of diversionist and wrecking activities and preparation for terrorism."

(Vol. III, pp. 54-55.)

The investigation has established that a number of diversionist acts committed in the Far Eastern Territory were planned and carried out by the participants in this anti-Soviet conspiracy on the direct instructions of the Japanese intelligence service and of enemy of the people L. TROTSKY. Thus, on the instructions of the Japanese intelligence service they organized the wreck of a military freight train at Volochayevka Station, and the wreck of train No. 501 on the Khor-Dormidontovka section, in which 21 persons were killed and 45 injured. In conformity with the same Japanese instructions, acts of diversion were committed in pits No. 10 and 20 in Suchan. (Vol. XLV, pp. 1-14.)

Detailed testimony on similar instructions emanating from L. TROTSKY has been given by the accused ROSENGOLTZ, who stated the following:

"In addition to instructions I received from TROTSKY through KRESTINSKY and SEDOV to carry on wrecking acti-

15

vities in the sphere of foreign trade with the object of rendering direct assistance to Germany and Japan, the character of my wrecking activities was also determined by instructions I received from the —— Ambassadors in the U.S.S.R., Mr. N and Mr. N, connections with whom played an important part in this matter, as I had to be guided in my work by their definite instructions.

"After I had established contact with TUKHACHEVSKY and RYKOV, I informed the former through KRESTINSKY, and the latter I myself informed, of TROTSKY'S instructions regarding wrecking activities, and both approved of the work I had done.

"As the result of all this, wrecking activities in foreign trade proceeded mainly along the following three lines: first—economic assistance to Germany and Japan at the expense of the U.S.S.R.; second—causing economic loss and damage to the U.S.S.R.; third—causing political damage to the U.S.S.R." (Vol. VI, p. 49.)

On the instructions of the "bloc of Rights and Trotskyites" the accused SHARANGOVICH carried on extensive wrecking activities in agriculture and industry in the Byelorussian Soviet Socialist Republic.

On this matter the accused SHARANGOVICH testified as follows:

"For the purpose of putting our wrecking designs into effect we created in the local districts a network of wrecking and diversionist groups. . . . All of us, from the leaders of the organization down to the rank-and-file members, were national-fascists and carried on activities against the Soviet government for severing Byelorussia from the U.S.S.R., sticking at nothing in our efforts. . . ." (Vol. XIV, p. 40.)

The accused CHERNOV, who for a number of years has been connected with the German intelligence service as one of its secret agents in the U.S.S.R., also took active advantage of the high official position he occupied in the U.S.S.R. to organize, on the instructions of the German intelligence service, a number of diversionist and wrecking acts in the sphere of agriculture.

The accused CHERNOV, a German spy, giving testimony on his criminal connections with the German spy SCHEFFER, the correspondent of the "Berliner Tageblatt," and on his wrecking activities in the sphere of agriculture, stated the following:

"When I went to work at the Committee of Agricultural Stocks SCHEFFER conveyed to me the instructions of the Germans

16

to carry on wrecking activities in the sphere of operations of the Committee of Agricultural Stocks, particularly in regard to mobilization reserves.

"The wrecking instructions I received from the intelligence service coincided with those which I, as a member of the Right organization, had received from RYKOV. All the more ready was I, therefore, to carry them out."

(Vol. VIII, pp. 98 reverse, 25.)

In respect to this, CHERNOV testified as follows:

"In 1934 I met RYKOV at his country house and he gave me instructions to carry on wrecking activities on a wide scale in the sphere of agriculture. I carried out these instructions and pursued wrecking and undermining activities fairly actively." (Vol. VIII, p. 93.)

The investigation has revealed considerable undermining wrecking activities in the sphere of agriculture also in Uzbekistan, where the nationalist organizations, which, through their leaders, the accused IKRAMOV and KHODJAYEV, were in alliance with the centre of the anti-Soviet conspiracy, operated.

The accused FAIZULLA KHODJAYEV, one of the leaders of this nationalist organization, testified as follows:

"We did not confine ourselves only to preparing cadres for our armed struggle against the Soviet power; we were already actively working with the object of undermining the power of the U.S.S.R." (Vol. XIII, p. 66.)

The extensive application of wrecking measures in Uzbekistan was also fully corroborated by the accused IKRAMOV, who testified that the "bloc of Rights and Trotskyites" had set him the following tasks:

"...a) to make extensive preparations in Uzbekistan for armed insurrection, to be started simultaneously with the beginning of intervention;

"b) vigorously to carry on wrecking and diversionist operations in all branches of the national economy with a view to their consequences rousing among the toilers discontent with the Soviet power and thus creating favourable ground for the organization of armed insurrection at the proper moment."

"In addition to this," the accused IKRAMOV stated, "the object of our wrecking activities was to hinder the strengthening of the defence of the U.S.S.R." (Vol. XII, pp. 95-96.)

Wrecking activities in agriculture as well as in a number of other branches of the national economy and Socialist construction were also carried on by other accused in the present case.

Thus, the accused GRINKO pursued wrecking activities in the sphere of finance.

The accused GRINKO testified as follows:

"The main object of undermining work in the People's Commissariat of Finance was the following: to weaken the Soviet ruble, to weaken the financial power of the U.S.S.R., to dislocate the economy and thus rouse among the population discontent with the financial policy of the Soviet power, discontent over taxes, discontent with the bad savings banks service, delays in paying wages, etc., which were to result in wide, organized discontent with the Soviet power and were to help the conspirators to recruit adherents and to develop insurrectionary activities." (Vol. IX, p. 79.)

The accused ZELENSKY and the group of wreckers he organized in the Centrosoyuz and the co-operative societies caused confusion in the planning of such goods as sugar, butter, eggs, makhorka, etc., deliberately held up the shipment of goods to the rural districts, utterly confused accounts, which facilitated the robbery and squandering of state funds with impunity, and encouraged the cheating and robbery of consumers.[11]

Speaking of the wrecking system of accounting of goods and money he introduced in the Centrosoyuz, the accused ZELENSKY testified as follows:

"Under these circumstances the thief remained unpunished, while, owing to the complicated system of accounting, the honest worker got muddled up and was immediately accused of embezzlement." (Vol. X, p. 56.)

Treasonable wrecking activities on a considerable scale were also carried on by the now exposed agent of foreign intelligence services, the accused ROSENGOLTZ.

Concerning his treasonable activities in this sphere, the accused ROSENGOLTZ testified as follows:

"In so far as TROTSKY had an agreement with Germany and Japan, of which I had been informed (both during the negotiations—at my meeting with Sedov in 1933; and of the agreement that had been reached—at my meeting with him in 1934), I received corresponding instructions from TROTSKY, and my wrecking activities in the sphere of foreign trade served the same purpose."[12] (Vol. VI, p. 48.)

Simultaneously with the organization of active diversionist and wrecking activities, the conspirators, on the orders of the fascist intelligence services, set themselves the task of rousing an insurrectionary bandit movement in our country with the object

18

of organizing an armed rising of their insurrectionary anti-Soviet gangs in the rear of the Red Army on the outbreak of intervention against the U.S.S.R.

The accused RYKOV testified as follows:

"We took the course of the violent overthrow of the leadership of the Party and the Soviet power, and we decided to secure this overthrow by organizing kulak risings." [13]
(Vol. I, p. 150 reverse.)

The investigation has established that the kulak insurrectionary armed risings that were being organized to take place in the rear of the Red Army were part and parcel of the plans and calculations of the fascist states which were preparing to attack the U.S.S.R.; and that the Right and Trotskyite conspirators were preparing to rise at the signal of the General Staffs of the fascist countries.

Pursuing the instructions of the fascist intelligence services, the participants in the conspiracy collected insurrectionary bandit cadres, preparing them for an active armed rising in the Far East, the North Caucasus and other places in the Soviet Union, particularly in Uzbekistan.

On this matter the accused KHODJAYEV testified as follows:

"The main object of the practical work of our organizations was to prepare active anti-Soviet cadres and to train them in the spirit of struggle against the U.S.S.R. We accustomed the members of the organization to the idea that the fight against the Soviet power would assume acute forms and would lead to armed conflicts. That is why we devoted attention to the preparation of the fighting forces of our organization." (Vol. XIII, p. 66.)

The organizers of insurrectionary bandit cadres relied only on the remnants of the old counter-revolutionary elements, expecting to reinforce their insurrectionary reserves with the remnants of the Basmachis [14] and White Guards, [15] who were to be smuggled into the Soviet Union from abroad, and with criminal bandits, inmates of prison camps, etc.

Speaking of the insurrectionary bandit activities of the bourgeois nationalist organization headed by him in Uzbekistan, the accused IKRAMOV testified:

"We preserved the necessary cadres, which in future were to be utilized for an armed struggle against the Soviet power. These cadres consisted chiefly of remnants of the kulaks, priests and former Basmachis. We instructed the members of our organization holding leading district posts to preserve these cadres. Furthermore, we assumed that in case of armed action the remnants of the Basmachi bands which at one time had had to retreat across the frontier would return to Soviet territory." (Vol. XII, p. 56.)

The materials of the investigation and the personal testimony of the accused BUKHARIN, ZUBAREV, ZELENSKY and others establish the fact that they had engaged in the active training of insurrectionary cadres, attempting to cover as many districts of the Soviet Union as possible, and that, with the purpose of enlarging the insurrectionary base to the maximum, the leaders of the conspiracy had established contact with an illegal Socialist-Revolutionary organization.

Thus, the accused BUKHARIN testified:

"The establishment of connections with the Socialist-Revolutionaries dates back to the period when the organization of the Rights placed its stakes on kulak risings. In view of the fact that the Rights had embarked on the organization of such risings, the necessity arose of establishing connections with the Socialist-Revolutionaries, who had their roots in the kulak strata in the countryside.

"... I personally established connections through SEM-YONOV with the underground Central Committee of the Socialist-Revolutionaries within the Soviet Union, and through CHLENOV with the foreign Central Committee of the Socialist-Revolutionaries in Paris." (Vol. V, pp. 90-91.)

Such is the chain of shameful villainies perpetrated by the "bloc of Rights and Trotskyites," which for many years carried on its treasonable activities in the interests of foreign states hostile to the U.S.S.R.

II. MURDER OF SOVIET PUBLIC MEN—S. M. KIROV, V. R. MENZHINSKY, V. V. KUIBYSHEV AND A. M. GORKY[16] PLOT AGAINST V. I. LENIN IN 1918

Entertaining no hope of the overthrow of the Soviet system by means of espionage, wrecking, diversion, and kulak risings, the Right and Trotskyite conspirators, possessed with rage and hatred for the U.S.S.R., proceeded to make preparations for and to commit terrorist acts against leaders of the government and the C.P.S.U.

The investigation has established the fact that by direct agreement with the Japanese and German intelligence services, and upon the instructions of enemy of the people L. TROTSKY, the "bloc of Rights and Trotskyites" engineered and committed a number of terrorist acts against some of the finest people of our country.

20

The accused RYKOV explained the motives for the adoption of terrorist methods by the "bloc of Rights and Trotskyites" as follows:

> "In view of the illegal and conspiratorial character of the counter-revolutionary organization of the Rights, the absence of any kind of mass basis for its counter-revolutionary activities, and the absence of all hope of arriving at power in any other way, the adoption of terrorist methods and a 'palace coup d'état,' in the opinion of the Centre, held out some prospects."　　　　　　　　　　　　　　(Vol. I, p. 50.)

The accused BUKHARIN, who in the course of the investigation admitted that the "bloc of Rights and Trotskyites" had already adopted terrorist methods in 1932, testified as follows:

> "In 1932, too, during a meeting and conversation I had with PYATAKOV, I learnt from him of his meeting with L. SEDOV and his receipt through SEDOV of direct instructions from TROTSKY to adopt terrorist methods against leaders of the Party and the Soviet government. I must also confess that it was then that we virtually consented to an agreement with terrorists, and my conversation with PYATAKOV was an agreement to co-ordinate with TROTSKY our actions directed towards the forcible overthrow of the leadership of the Party and the Soviet government."
> 　　　　　　　　　　　　(Vol. V, p. 105 reverse.)

The terrorist activities of the conspirators were closely connected with the whole of their defeatist work, which is borne out, for example, by the following testimony of the accused IVANOV:

> "Speaking of terrorism, BUKHARIN said that the 'liquidation,' as he expressed it, of the leaders of the Party and the Soviet government . . . would be very important for our accession to power and would facilitate the defeat of the U.S.S.R. in war."　　　　　　　　　(Vol. VII, p. 81.)

In pursuance of the decisions taken in this connection, the conspiratorial bloc widely developed the organization of terrorist groups and the practical preparations for the perpetration of terrorist acts against leaders of the C.P.S.U.[17] and the Soviet government.

This is what the accused RYKOV testified in this connection:

> "By that time we had already adopted the path of terrorism as one of the methods of combating the Soviet government. . . . This position of ours took the form of quite definite activity on our part, and in particular on my part, in preparing terrorist acts against members of the Political Bureau,

leaders of the Party and the government, and, first and foremost, against STALIN, MOLOTOV, KAGANOVICH and VOROSHILOV.[18] In 1934 I had already given instructions to have the automobiles of leaders of the Party and the government watched by the ARTEMENKO terrorist group I had formed." (Vol. I, pp. 150 reverse, 151.)

Speaking of the proposal of the Socialist-Revolutionary SEMYONOV to organize a terrorist group, the accused BUKHARIN testified:

"I want to tell the truth and declare that this proposal was reported by me to a meeting of the centre, and we decided to charge SEMYONOV with the organization of terrorist groups." (Vol. V, p. 106 reverse.)

The investigation has established that the vile assassination of S. M. KIROV committed by the Leningrad Trotskyite-Zinovievite terrorist centre on December 1, 1934, was also committed in pursuance of a decision of the "bloc of Rights and Trotskyites," members of which are being charged in the present case.

The investigation has established that one, of the participants in this vile murder was the accused YAGODA, who testified as follows:

"That preparations for the assassination of S. M. KIROV were being made in accordance with a decision of the conspiratorial centre, I had previously learnt from YENUKIDZE.[19] YENUKIDZE told me not to hinder the organization of this terrorist act, and I agreed. With this purpose I summoned ZAPOROZHETZ [20] from Leningrad and instructed him not to hinder the terrorist act that was being prepared against S. M. KIROV." (Vol. II, p. 209.)

This was confirmed by ZAPOROZHETZ and YENUKIDZE during the investigation.

The villainous terrorist activities of the Right and Trotskyite traitors and conspirators were not confined to the assassination of S. M. KIROV.

As the investigation of the present case has established, A. M. GORKY, V. R. MENZHINSKY and V. V. KUIBYSHEV fell victims to terrorist acts committed on the instructions of the Joint Centre of the "bloc of Rights and Trotskyites."

As to the reasons which induced the Right and Trotskyite conspirators to commit the unparalleled and monstrous murder of A. M. GORKY, the accused YAGODA testified:

"For a long time the Joint Centre of the Right and Trotskyite organization had endeavoured to influence GORKY and

22

make him sever his close connections with STALIN. For this purpose KAMENEV,[21] TOMSKY [22] and a number of others were attached to GORKY. But no real results were achieved. GORKY remained faithful to STALIN and was an ardent supporter and advocate of his line. As the overthrow of the STALIN leadership and the seizure of power by the Rights and Trotsky-ites was being considered seriously, the centre could not ignore the exceptional influence of GORKY within the country and his prestige abroad. If GORKY remained alive he would raise his voice in protest against us. That we could not allow. Having become convinced that GORKY could not be severed from STALIN, the Joint Centre, therefore, had to decide to do away with GORKY." (Vol. II, p. 200.)

The testimony of the accused YAGODA was fully corrobora-ted by the accused RYKOV, who, when interrogated by the Pro-curator of the U.S.S.R. on January 10, 1938, testified:

"I know that TROTSKY, through his representatives in the contact centre, did his utmost to fan animosity against GORKY. This is naturally to be explained by the fact that TROTSKY was well aware that GORKY considered him a scoundrel and adventurer. On the other hand, the close friend-ship of GORKY for STALIN was generally known, and the fact that he was an inflexible political supporter of STALIN aroused the animosity of our organization against him."
(Vol. I, p. 166 reverse.)

To this the accused RYKOV added:

"In 1935 I had a conversation with YENUKIDZE, who bluntly told me that the Trotskyite-Zinovievite part of the bloc insisted on eliminating the political activities of GORKY and would stop at nothing to attain this end. This conversation made it clear to me that the question of doing away with GORKY by terrorist methods might also arise."
(Vol. I, pp. 166 reverse, 167.)

This was also corroborated by the accused BUKHARIN, who testified that in the beginning of 1935 TOMSKY had told him that:

". . . The Trotskyite part of the Joint Centre of the bloc had proposed to organize a hostile act against A. M. GORKY because he was a supporter of STALIN'S policy."
(Vol. V, p. 119 reverse.)

In this connection the accused BUKHARIN explained that he does not preclude the possibility that it was the physical removal of GORKY that was then contemplated. That preparations

23

for the physical removal of M. GORKY were contemplated is shown by the testimony of the accused BESSONOV, who was personally given a "line" to this effect directly by L. TROTSKY when he met the latter at the end of July 1934.

The accused BESSONOV testified that at this meeting L. TROTSKY, having declared that

" '... it would be unpardonable squeamishness if we did not at once proceed to the systematic physical removal of STALIN and of all his immediate colleagues,' said:

" 'M. GORKY is very intimate with STALIN. He plays an exceptional role in winning sympathy for the U.S.S.R. among the democratic opinion of the world and especially of Western Europe. GORKY is very popular as a close friend of STALIN'S and as a vehicle of the general line of the Party. Our former supporters among the intelligentsia are leaving us very largely under the influence of GORKY. From this I draw the conclusion that GORKY must be put out of the way. Convey this instruction to PYATAKOV in the most categorical form: GORKY must be physically exterminated at all costs.' " (Vol. XI, pp. 74-75.)

It was in accordance with this instruction of enemy of the people L. TROTSKY that the "bloc of Rights and Trotskyites" adopted its monstrous decision to murder A. M. GORKY.

"The execution of this decision was entrusted to me," the accused YAGODA testified.

The accused YAGODA enlisted the accused in this case Dr. L. G. LEVIN, former family doctor of A. M. GORKY, Professor D. D. PLETNEV, P. P. KRYUCHKOV, A. M. GORKY'S secretary, and P. P. BULANOV, YAGODA'S own secretary, as the immediate perpetrators of this villainous plan.

The accused BULANOV, one of the organizers of this crime, testified:

"Professor PLETNEV, Dr. LEVIN and GORKY'S secretary, KRYUCHKOV, took a direct part in the killing of A. M. GORKY. I, for instance, personally witnessed how YAGODA frequently summoned KRYUCHKOV and advised him to cause GORKY to catch a chill, to make him fall ill in one way or another. YAGODA stressed the point that the condition of GORKY'S lungs was such that any illness caused by a cold would increase the chances of his death. The rest would be done by PLETNEV and LEVIN, who had suitable instructions on this score." (Vol. XVI, p. 72.)

The accused PLETNEV, who took a direct part in the murder of A. M. GORKY and V. V. KUIBYSHEV, testified:

"YAGODA told me that I must help him to secure the physical removal of certain political leaders of the country. He bluntly proposed that I should take advantage of my position as physician to V. V. KUIBYSHEV and A. M. GORKY to hasten their death by wrong methods of treatment. I attempted to refuse, but in the end was forced to consent. After this, YAGODA informed me that my accomplice would be Dr. LEVIN, and, in the case of A. M. GORKY, the latter's secretary, P. P. KRYUCHKOV, as well.

"Having accepted this gruesome commission from YAGODA, I, in conjunction with Dr. LEVIN, drew up a plan for the killing of A. M. GORKY and V. V. KUIBYSHEV.

"I must confess that my anti-Soviet sentiments played a part in my consent to this crime. Until my arrest I concealed these anti-Soviet sentiments in every way, playing a game of duplicity and claiming to be a Soviet supporter."

(Vol. XVIII, pp. 72-73.)

This was corroborated by the accused LEVIN, who testified:

"I confess that by deliberately adopting a wrong method of treatment and prescribing medicines unsuited to the given illness, I, together with my accomplices, and in agreement with YAGODA, was responsible for the untimely death of MAXIM GORKY and KUIBYSHEV." (Vol. XVII, p. 10.)

During the course of the investigation, the accused LEVIN and PLETNEV gave detailed testimony as to the way they actually arranged the killing of A. M. GORKY and V. V. KUIBYSHEV.

The investigation has established that the accused MAXIMOV, V. V. KUIBYSHEV'S secretary, took an active part in bringing about the death of V. V. KUIBYSHEV. MAXIMOV testified as follows:

"I consented to this crime as a member of the counter-revolutionary organization of the Rights, which I had joined in 1928.

"YAGODA also knew that I belonged to the counter-revolutionary organization and was present during one of my conversations with YENUKIDZE, when we drew up the plan for doing away with KUIBYSHEV."

(Vol. XX, p. 45 reverse.)

V. R. MENZHINSKY, Chairman of the O.G.P.U.,[23] was also murdered by the accused Dr. LEVIN and Dr. KAZAKOV on the direct instructions of YAGODA.

Interrogated by the Procurator of the U.S.S.R. on February 4, 1938, the accused KAZAKOV testified:

25

"YAGODA told me that MENZHINSKY liked and trusted me and that therefore Dr. LEVIN and I could succeed in doing away with MENZHINSKY. YAGODA gave me the following instructions: I was to work out with Dr. LEVIN a method of treatment for V. R. MENZHINSKY that would hasten his death and end his life as soon as possible. . . ."

(Vol. XIX, p. 51 reverse.)

Continuing to relate his conversation with the accused YAGODA in which the latter spoke of the necessity of hastening the death of V. R. MENZHINSKY, the accused KAZAKOV testified:

"After this conversation with YAGODA, LEVIN and I drew up a method of treatment for V. R. MENZHINSKY which in reality totally undermined his strength and determined the rapid onset of death. Thus LEVIN and I actually murdered V. R. MENZHINSKY in this way.

"I gave Dr. LEVIN a mixture of lysates I had composed, which, in conjunction with alkaloids, led to the desired result, namely, the virtual murder of MENZHINSKY."

(Vol. XIX, p. 51 reverse.)

This was fully corroborated by the accused L. G. LEVIN and P. P. BULANOV.

The accused L. G. LEVIN confirmed that, having received instructions from the accused YAGODA to hasten the death of V. R. MENZHINSKY, he, LEVIN, decided to enlist Dr. KAZAKOV in this crime.

The accused LEVIN testified:

"I said that this could be done best of all by KAZAKOV, as he used medicines which he himself prepared without control in his own laboratory, and what he injected he alone knew.

"After preliminary and preparatory talks with KAZAKOV, I conveyed to him the instructions I had received from YAGODA. He hesitated very much at first, fearing that the crime might be discovered, but in the end he consented. I did not ask what he used, all the more since he usually kept his medicines secret, but I knew that he had wide opportunities in this respect.

"V. R. MENZHINSKY'S death occurred suddenly during sleep from paralysis of the heart, on the eve of the death of MAXIM PESHKOV (A. M. GORKY'S son), if I am not mistaken. I had no doubt that this was KAZAKOV'S work."

(Vol. XVII, pp. 54-55.)

On the subject of the murder of V. R. MENZHINSKY, the accused BULANOV testified:

"YAGODA had long ago conceived the idea of physically removing MENZHINSKY. He several times in my presence expressed dissatisfaction that MENZHINSKY continued to live and to occupy the post of head of the O.G.P.U. Then he said outright that MENZHINSKY must be put out of the way. It was difficult to arrange the job through Dr. LEVIN, because MENZHINSKY did not like LEVIN and refused to be treated by him. I then suggested to YAGODA to 'fix up' some other doctor for MENZHINSKY. This was done. With the assistance of Dr. LEVIN, MENZHINSKY was 'fixed up' with Dr. KAZAKOV, who did the job, or, to put it plainly, hastened MENZHINSKY'S death by deliberately employing a wrong method of treatment." (Vol. XVI, p. 75.)

Apart from the murder of A. M. GORKY and V. V. KUIBY-SHEV, the accused LEVIN and KRYUCHKOV, on direct instructions of the accused YAGODA, in 1934 killed M. A. PESHKOV, the son of A. M. GORKY, in a similar way.

In this connection, the accused LEVIN testified:

"I confess my guilt in the murder of Maxim and want to say here that I did it on the direct demand of YAGODA. I did not have the courage to refuse, and I became a murderer."
(Vol. XVII, p. 138 reverse.)

The accused KRYUCHKOV, who took an active part in the crimes organized by YAGODA, testified:

"In these crimes I was guided by the directions of certain members of the anti-Soviet organization of the Rights, in particular by the directions of YAGODA. It was from YA-GODA that I received instructions forcibly to do away with Maxim PESHKOV, and then Alexei Maximovich GORKY.
"In addition to myself, YAGODA enlisted for the commission of these crimes the physicians LEVIN and VINOGRA-DOV and Professor PLETNEV." (Vol. XXI, p. 16.)

The accused YAGODA, confirming that M. A. PESHKOV was murdered on his instructions, testified:

"In May 1934, with the help of KRYUCHKOV, Max (M. A. PESHKOV) contracted double pneumonia, and the physicians LEVIN, VINOGRADOV and PLETNEV treated him in such a way as to bring about his death." (Vol. II, p. 193.)

After being removed from his post as People's Commissar of Internal Affairs of the U.S.S.R., the accused YAGODA also took measures to murder Comrade N. I. YEZHOV,[24] People's Commissar of Internal Affairs of the U.S.S.R.

In his testimony, the accused YAGODA explained the motives which induced him to hasten a terrorist act against N. I. YEZHOV as follows:

> "My removal from my post in the People's Commissariat of Internal Affairs and the appointment of YEZHOV in my place meant the complete collapse of our conspiracy, because it would be impossible to prevent the routing of the cadres of the anti-Soviet organization. YEZHOV would dig up everything. YEZHOV had to be put out of the way. This was the only decision I could come to, and I began to make energetic preparations to put it into effect...." (Vol. II, pp. 141-42.)

YAGODA attempted to carry out his plan through his accomplices, a prominent part being played by the accused BULANOV.

The accused YAGODA and the accused BULANOV confessed that it was proposed to accomplish the murder of Comrade N. I. YEZHOV by means of a poison specially prepared for the purpose:

> "When YAGODA was removed from the People's Commissariat of Internal Affairs," the accused BULANOV testified, "he gave me and his personal agent, SAVOLAINEN, direct instructions to poison YEZHOV." (Vol. XVI, p. 27.)

Describing in detail the methods by which the accused YAGODA tried to murder Comrade N. I. YEZHOV, the accused BULANOV testified that he (BULANOV) himself prepared the mixture of drugs intended for the poisoning of Comrade YEZHOV.

Interrogated in the Office of the Procurator of the U.S.S.R., the accused YAGODA fully admitted having committed this crime, testifying:

> "Yes, I must admit that I made preparations for the perpetration of this crime. I made preparations for the murder of YEZHOV as a man who was dangerous to the counter-revolutionary plot and who might expose our counter-revolutionary organization." (Vol. II, p. 209.)

Thus the investigating authorities consider it established beyond all doubt that the leading members of the "bloc of Rights and Trotskyites," against whom criminal proceedings are being brought in this case, committed terrorist acts against S. M. KIROV, V. R. MENZHINSKY, V. V. KUIBYSHEV, A. M. GORKY and M. A. PESHKOV and made preparations for a number of other terrorist acts which they had no time to carry out.

The murder of Soviet public men completed the circle of heinous state crimes by which this band of contemptible apostates of

28

our country, provocateurs of the tsarist secret police and hirelings of foreign intelligence services, who were selling our land and liberty to foreign capitalists, strove to carry out a fascist plan for the overthrow of the Soviet system and the restoration of capitalism in our country.

As has now been brought to light, neither in the case of the Trotskyites nor in the case of the Rights were these monstrous crimes fortuitous.

The investigation has established that as far back as 1918, directly after the October Revolution, at the time of the conclusion of the Peace of Brest-Litovsk, BUKHARIN and his group of so-called "Left Communists," and TROTSKY and his group, together with the "Left" Socialist-Revolutionaries, hatched a plot against V. I. LENIN, the head of the Soviet government.[25]

As the materials of the investigation show, BUKHARIN and other conspirators aimed at frustrating the Brest-Litovsk Peace, overthrowing the Soviet government, arresting and murdering V. I. LENIN, J. V. STALIN and J. M. SVERDLOV,[26] and forming a new government consisting of Bukharinites—who as a blind at that time called themselves "Left Communists"—of Trotskyites and of "Left" Socialist-Revolutionaries.

Questioned in the Office of the Procurator of the U.S.S.R. on February 19 and 20, 1938, V. A. KARELIN, former member of the Central Committee of the Party of "Left" Socialist-Revolutionaries, gave the following testimony regarding the conspiratorial activities of the Socialist-Revolutionaries and Bukharinites in 1918:

> "Final agreement with the 'Left Communists' in the struggle against the Soviet government headed by LENIN, STALIN and SVERDLOV was reached by us after the Seventh Congress of the Communist Party.
> "On the instructions of the Central Committee of the 'Left' Socialist-Revolutionaries, the negotiations with the 'Left Communists' were conducted by KAMKOV, PROSHYAN, and myself." [27]　　　　　　　　　(Vol. XLIV, p. 86.)

Speaking of the character of these negotiations and the part played by the accused N. I. BUKHARIN, V. A. KARELIN further testified as follows:

> "BUKHARIN proposed that we should not stop at the arrest of the government but bring about the physical extermination of the leaders of the Soviet power, and in the first place of LENIN and STALIN." 　　(Vol. XLIV, p. 38.)

29

This was corroborated by other persons who were examined as witnesses in the present case.

B. D. KAMKOV, one of the former leaders of the Central Committee of the "Left" Socialist-Revolutionary Party, testified:

"I personally had a conversation with BUKHARIN in which he said roughly the following: 'The struggle within our Party against LENIN'S position on the Brest-Litovsk Peace is assuming acute forms. Within our ranks the question is being discussed of creating a new government consisting of "Left" Socialist-Revolutionaries and "Left Communists."'' BUKHARIN mentioned PYATAKOV as a possible candidate for leader of the new government, and stated that the idea was to bring about the change of government by arresting its members, headed by LENIN.

"Further negotiations with BUKHARIN were conducted by KARELIN and PROSHYAN. By the end of March a final agreement was reached between the 'Left Communists' and the 'Left' Socialist-Revolutionaries on the following points: 1) that in the struggle against the Bolsheviks and the Soviet government the 'Left Communists' were to render organizational and political assistance to the 'Left' Socialist-Revolutionaries; 2) that by joint action of the 'Left' Socialist-Revolutionaries and 'Left Communists,' LENIN'S government was to be overthrown and a new government formed, consisting of 'Left Communists' and 'Left' Socialist-Revolutionaries.

"After this, the 'Left' Socialist-Revolutionaries organized the assassination of MIRBACH and the July revolt.[28] The 'Left Communists' were fully aware of the preparations being made for the assassination of MIRBACH and for the July revolt."

(Vol. XLIV, p. 92 reverse.)

Questioned in the capacity of witnesses in the Office of the Procurator of the U.S.S.R. on February 19, 1938, V. N. YAKOVLEVA, V. V. OSSINSKY and V. N. MANTSEV, former leaders and active members of the group of "Left Communists," fully corroborated that in 1918 a plot was hatched, on the initiative of the accused BUKHARIN, by the bloc of "Left Communists" and "Left" Socialist-Revolutionaries against V. I. LENIN as head of the Soviet government:[29]

Thus, V. N. YAKOVLEVA testified:

"BUKHARIN expressed to me the idea that the political struggle was assuming ever more acute forms and that matters could not be confined to the mere political formulation of lack of confidence in the Central Committee of the Party. BUKHARIN declared that a change of leadership was inevitable, and that in this connection the question was being discussed of arresting LENIN, STALIN and SVERDLOV, and even of their physical extermination. . . ."

(Vol. XLIV, p. 77.)

In this connection V. V. OSSINSKY testified as follows:

"It was with N. I. BUKHARIN that I principally talked about our measures for the overthrow of LENIN'S government. . . . Approximately in May (or at the end of April) 1918 I had a talk with BUKHARIN when I asked him to what extent the information I had about his designs to arrest the LENIN government was correct.

"BUKHARIN did not deny that he had such designs."

(Vol. XLIV, p. 54.)

Speaking further about these "measures," V. V. OSSINSKY testified:

"I learned about the bloc of the 'Left Communists' with the 'Left' Socialist-Revolutionaries from YAKOVLEVA and then from BUKHARIN. I also learned from them that in March or April 1918 BUKHARIN proposed at the bureau (of the Moscow region) that LENIN, STALIN and SVERDLOV should be arrested. BUKHARIN further stressed the point that he was of the opinion that after the arrest of the government, LENIN, STALIN and SVERDLOV should be physically exterminated." (Vol. XLIV, p. 88 reverse.)

Similar testimony was given by V. N. MANTSEV when questioned in the Office of the Procurator of the U.S.S.R. on February 20, 1938:

"I confirm that a bloc was formed between the 'Left Communists' and 'Left' Socialist-Revolutionaries.

"I confirm that roughly in March or April, at a close meeting of the bureau, BUKHARIN made a report in which he uttered a number of slanderous statements against the Soviet government and proposed to organize the overthrow of the Soviet power and the arrest of LENIN, STALIN and SVERDLOV, with the purpose of physically exterminating them." (Vol. XLIV, p. 82.)

Speaking of the role of L. TROTSKY in the plot against V. I. LENIN in 1918, the accused BUKHARIN testified:

"At that time the idea again arose of a coup and the arrest of LENIN, STALIN and SVERDLOV as the dominant figures in the Party and Soviet leadership. This time it arose on the initiative of TROTSKY, to whom the proposal of the

31

'Left' Socialist-Revolutionaries apparently became known—through PYATAKOV, I presume." (Vol. V, p. 124.)

Interrogated during the preliminary investigation, V. N. YAKOVLEVA testified:

"TROTSKY considered that the political struggle had only just begun, that it might assume the most aggressive forms, that against LENIN'S position on the question of peace the 'Left Communists' would have the support of the 'Left' Socialist-Revolutionaries and other parties, that preparations must be made for a change of government and the arrest of its leaders, headed by LENIN and STALIN. TROTSKY considered that in so acute a period of the revolution, if the struggle were to develop, matters might not be confined only to the arrest of the leaders, and that the arrests would logically and inevitably lead to the question of their physical removal." (Vol. XLIV, p. 78.)

Interrogated in the preliminary investigation, V. N. MANTSEV, one of the leaders of the group of "Left Communists," testified:

"Several days after my conversation with YAKOVLEVA, TROTSKY asked me to come and see him. I had a long talk with him at his home, during which TROTSKY developed at length the idea that LENIN and STALIN must be assassinated." (Vol. XLIV, p. 84.)

The investigating authorities now possess irrefutable evidence proving that the villainous attempt on the life of V. I. LENIN committed on August 30, 1918, by the Socialist-Revolutionary terrorist F. KAPLAN was a direct result of the realization of the criminal plans of the "Left Communists," headed by N. I. BUKHARIN, and of their accomplices, the "Left" and Right Socialist-Revolutionaries, and was initiated by the accused BUKHARIN.

Questioned in the Office of the Procurator of the U.S.S.R. on February 19, 1938, V. A. KARELIN testified:

"I must also confess to the gravest crime, namely, the participation of the 'Left' Socialist-Revolutionaries and the 'Left Communists' in the organization of the attempt on the life of LENIN. This fact has been concealed from the Soviet people for twenty years. The fact was concealed that we, in conjunction with the Right Socialist-Revolutionaries, on the insistence of BUKHARIN, attempted to murder LENIN. The trial of the Right Socialist-Revolutionaries did not disclose the real circumstances of this crime and did not reveal the part played in it by the 'Left' Socialist-Revolutionaries and the 'Left Communists.' [30]

"After the July revolt, the Central Committee of the 'Left' Socialist-Revolutionaries decided to adopt terrorist methods in the struggle against the Soviet government.

"It should be mentioned that even after the revolt PROSH-YAN had meetings with BUKHARIN, who bluntly put before him the question of the physical extermination of LENIN. More precisely, the question of committing a terrorist act against LENIN was raised by BUKHARIN in the second half of July 1918. PROSHYAN reported this to us members of the Central Committee of the 'Left' Socialist-Revolutionaries.

"Such a demand by the 'Left Communists' played a great part in hastening the terrorist act against LENIN committed by the Central Committee of the Right Socialist-Revolutionaries."   (Vol. XLIV, pp. 86-87.)

This was also corroborated by V. V. OSSINSKY, who, when interrogated on February 19, 1938, testified as follows:

"At the end of 1918 STUKOV,[31] who together with BUKHA-RIN was connected with the Socialist-Revolutionaries, told me that the shot fired at LENIN by the Right Socialist-Revolutionary KAPLAN was the result not only of the instructions of the leadership of the Right Socialist-Revolutionaries, but also of measures that had been outlined by the bloc of 'Left Communists' with the Socialist-Revolutionaries aiming at the physical extermination of LENIN, STALIN and SVERDLOV."   (Vol. XLIV, p. 89.)

At confrontations in the Office of the Procurator of the U.S.S.R. of the accused BUKHARIN with the witnesses V. V. OSSINSKY, V. N. YAKOVLEVA, V. N. MANTSEV, V. A. KARELIN and B. D. KAMKOV, these witnesses fully confirmed their testimony as set forth above.

Under the weight of the evidence, the accused BUKHARIN admitted a number of criminal facts and testified:

"I must admit that we had direct contact with the 'Left' Socialist-Revolutionaries, whose platform was the forcible overthrow of the Soviet government, headed by LENIN, STALIN and SVERDLOV, to be followed by the arrest of LENIN, STALIN and SVERDLOV and the setting up of a new government consisting of 'Left Communists' and 'Left' Socialist-Revolutionaries...."   (Vol. V, p. 122 reverse.)

The facts now established regarding the crimes committed by the accused BUKHARIN and enemy of the people TROTSKY in 1918 against the Soviet state and its leaders, V. I. LENIN, J. V. STALIN and J. M. SVERDLOV, throw a vivid light on the whole subsequent criminal counter-revolutionary activity of the gang of

BUKHARIN and TROTSKY, which is now charged with the gravest state crimes committed on the direct instructions of fascist intelligence services during the period 1921-1937.

DEFINITION OF THE CHARGE

The investigating authorities consider it established:

1) that in 1932-33, on the instructions of intelligence services of foreign states hostile to the U.S.S.R., a conspiratorial group named the "bloc of Rights and Trotskyites" was formed by the accused in the present case with the object of espionage on behalf of foreign states, wrecking, diversionist and terrorist activities, undermining the military power of the U.S.S.R., provoking a military attack by these states on the U.S.S.R., working for the defeat of the U.S.S.R., dismembering the U.S.S.R. and severing from it the Ukraine, Byelorussia, the Central Asiatic Republics, Georgia, Armenia, Azerbaijan and the Maritime Region of the Far East for the benefit of the aforementioned foreign states, and, lastly, with the object of overthrowing the Socialist social and state system existing in the U.S.S.R. and of restoring capitalism and the power of the bourgeoisie in the U.S.S.R.;

2) that the "bloc of Rights and Trotskyites" entered into relations with certain foreign states with the purpose of receiving armed assistance from them for the accomplishment of its criminal designs;

3) that the "bloc of Rights and Trotskyites" systematically engaged in espionage on behalf of these states, supplying foreign intelligence services with highly important state secret information;

4) that the "bloc of Rights and Trotskyites" systematically performed wrecking and diversionist acts in various branches of Socialist construction (industry, agriculture, railways, in the sphere of finance, municipal development, etc.);

5) that the "bloc of Rights and Trotskyites" organized a number of terrorist acts against leaders of the C.P.S.U. and the Soviet government and perpetrated terrorist acts against S. M. KIROV, V. R. MENZHINSKY, V. V. KUIBYSHEV and A. M. GORKY.

All the accused stand convicted both by the testimony of witnesses and by the documents and material evidence in the files and have fully admitted that they are guilty of the charges preferred against them.

On the aforementioned grounds the following persons:

1) BUKHARIN, Nikolai Ivanovich, born 1888;
2) RYKOV, Alexei Ivanovich, born 1881;
3) YAGODA, Genrikh Grigorievich, born 1891;
4) KRESTINSKY, Nikolai Nikolayevich, born 1883;
5) RAKOVSKY, Khristian Georgievich, born 1873;
6) ROSENGOLTZ, Arkady Pavlovich, born 1889;

7) IVANOV, Vladimir Ivanovich, born 1893;
8) CHERNOV, Mikhail Alexandrovich, born 1891;
9) GRINKO, Grigori Fedorovich, born 1890;
10) ZELENSKY, Isaac Abramovich, born 1890;
11) BESSONOV, Sergei Alexeyevich, born 1892;
12) IKRAMOV, Akmal, born 1898;
13) KHODJAYEV, Faizulla, born 1896;
14) SHARANGOVICH, Vasily Fomich, born 1897;
15) ZUBAREV, Prokopy Timofeyevich, born 1886;
16) BULANOV, Pavel Petrovich, born 1895;
17) LEVIN, Lev Grigorievich, born 1870;
18) PLETNEV, Dmitry Dmitrievich, born 1872;
19) KAZAKOV, Ignaty Nikolayevich, born 1891;
20) MAXIMOV-DIKOVSKY, Venyamin Adamovich (Abramovich), born 1900;
21) KRYUCHKOV, Pyotr Petrovich, born 1889
—are accused of having, as active participants in an anti-Soviet conspiracy, committed the gravest state crimes enumerated in paragraphs 1-5 of the Definition of the Charge, i. e., crimes covered by Articles 58^{1a}, 58^2, 58^7, 58^8, 58^9, and 58^{11} of the Criminal Code of the R.S.F.S.R., and the accused IVANOV, ZELENSKY and ZUBAREV, in addition, of crimes covered by Article 58^{13} of the Criminal Code of the R.S.F.S.R.

On the aforesaid grounds all the above-mentioned accused are subject to trial by the Military Collegium of the Supreme Court of the U.S.S.R.

The cases of V. V. OSSINSKY, V. N. YAKOVLEVA, V. N. MANTSEV, V. A. KARELIN, B. D. KAMKOV, I. N. STUKOV, E. V. ARTEMENKO, I. V. ZAPOROZHETZ, I. M. SAVOLAINEN, G. I. SEMYONOV and S. B. CHLENOV have been made the subject of separate proceedings. [32]

Proceedings against Dr. A. I. VINOGRADOV have been terminated owing to his death.

The case of A. S. YENUKIDZE was tried by the Military Collegium of the Supreme Court of the U.S.S.R. on December 15, 1937.

The present indictment was drawn up in Moscow on February 23, 1938.

A. VYSHINSKY

Procurator of the U.S.S.R.

* * *

35

THE PRESIDENT: Accused Bukharin, do you plead guilty to the charges brought against you?

BUKHARIN· Yes, I plead guilty to the charges brought against me.

THE PRESIDENT: Accused Rykov, do you plead guilty to the charges brought against you?

RYKOV: Yes, I do.

THE PRESIDENT: Accused Yagoda, do you plead guilty to the charges brought against you?

YAGODA: Yes, I do.

THE PRESIDENT: Accused Krestinsky, do you plead guilty to the charges brought against you?

KRESTINSKY: I plead not guilty. I am not a Trotskyite. I was never a member of the bloc of Rights and Trotskyites, of whose existence I was not aware. Nor have I committed any of the crimes with which I personally am charged, in particular I plead not guilty to the charge of having had connections with the German intelligence service.

THE PRESIDENT: Do you corroborate the confession you made at the preliminary investigation?

KRESTINSKY: Yes, at the preliminary investigation I confessed, but I have never been a Trotskyite.

THE PRESIDENT: I repeat the question, do you plead guilty?

KRESTINSKY: Before my arrest I was a member of the Communist Party of the Soviet Union (Bolsheviks) and I remain one now.

THE PRESIDENT: Do you plead guilty to the charge of participating in espionage activities and of participating in terrorist activities?

KRESTINSKY: I have never been a Trotskyite, I have never belonged to the bloc of Rights and Trotskyites and have not committed a single crime.

THE PRESIDENT: Accused Rakovsky, do you plead guilty to the charges brought against you?

RAKOVSKY: Yes, I do.

THE PRESIDENT: Accused Rosengoltz, do you plead guilty to the charges brought against you?

ROSENGOLTZ: Yes, I do.

THE PRESIDENT: Accused Ivanov, do you plead guilty to the charges brought against you?

IVANOV: Yes, I do.

THE PRESIDENT: Accused Chernov, do you plead guilty to the charges brought against you?

CHERNOV: I do.

THE PRESIDENT: Accused Grinko, do you plead guilty to the charges brought against you?

GRINKO: Yes, I do.

THE PRESIDENT: Accused Zelensky, do you plead guilty to the charges brought against you?

ZELENSKY: Yes, I plead guilty to the charge of belonging to the organization of the Rights, I plead guilty to the charge of having participated in wrecking activities, which I carried out on the instructions of the Rights' centre, I plead guilty to having put on the staff of the Centrosoyuz alien and rebel cadres, I plead guilty to the charge of having served in the tsarist secret police.

THE PRESIDENT: Accused Bessonov, do you plead guilty to the charges brought against you?

BESSONOV: Yes, I do.

THE PRESIDENT: Accused Ikramov, do you plead guilty to the charges brought against you?

IKRAMOV: Yes, I do.

THE PRESIDENT: Accused Khodjayev, do you plead guilty to the charges brought against you?

KHODJAYEV: Yes, I do.

THE PRESIDENT: Accused Sharangovich, do you plead guilty to the charges brought against you?

SHARANGOVICH: Yes, wholly and entirely guilty.

THE PRESIDENT: Accused Zubarev, do you plead guilty to the charges brought against you?

ZUBAREV: Yes, I do.

THE PRESIDENT: Accused Bulanov, do you plead guilty to the charges brought against you?

BULANOV: Yes, I do.

THE PRESIDENT: Accused Levin, do you plead guilty to the charges brought against you?

LEVIN: Yes, I do.

THE PRESIDENT: Accused Pletnev, do you plead guilty to the charges brought against you?

PLETNEV: Yes, I do.

THE PRESIDENT: Accused Kazakov, do you plead guilty to the charges brought against you?

KAZAKOV: Yes, I do.

THE PRESIDENT: Accused Maximov, do you plead guilty to the charges brought against you?

MAXIMOV: Yes, I do.

THE PRESIDENT: Accused Kryuchkov, do you plead guilty to the charges brought against you?

KRYUCHKOV: Yes, I do.

THE PRESIDENT: Adjournment for 20 minutes.

* * *

COMMANDANT OF THE COURT: The Court is coming, please rise.

THE PRESIDENT: The session is resumed. Comrade Procurator, have you any proposals to make concerning the procedure of the Court investigation?

VYSHINSKY: Yes, I have. I would ask that the following procedure be adopted for the Court investigation: that we start with the examination of the accused Bessonov. Then I would ask to examine Grinko, Chernov, Ivanov, Krestinsky, Zubarev, Rykov, Sharangovich, Khodjayev, Zelensky, Ikramov, Rakovsky, Rosengoltz, and then Bukharin, Levin, Bulanov, Yagoda, Pletnev, Kryuchkov, Kazakov, and lastly Maximov.

THE PRESIDENT: Have Counsel for Defence any objection to the proposed procedure?

COUNSEL FOR DEFENCE BRAUDE: No.

THE PRESIDENT: Have the accused any objection to the procedure of the Court investigation as proposed by the Procurator?

THE ACCUSED: (Reply in the negative.)

THE PRESIDENT: Before proceeding to examine the accused I consider it necessary to warn the parties and the accused that the omissions that were made in reading the indictment must be taken into account during the course of the Court investigation.

Accused Bessonov, do you corroborate the testimony you made during the preliminary investigation?

BESSONOV: Yes, I do.

THE PRESIDENT: Comrade Procurator, have you any questions to put to the accused Bessonov?

VYSHINSKY: Yes, I have.

Accused Bessonov, tell the Court briefly, in a few words, your biography.

BESSONOV: I was born in 1892 in the town of Kirzhach, Vladimir Gubernia. I studied at the Vladimir Divinity School and at the Ecclesiastical Seminary, then I was sent abroad.

VYSHINSKY: Did you finish your studies at the Ecclesiastical Seminary?

BESSONOV: No, I did not. I was twice expelled.

VYSHINSKY: How is it that you went to study at an Ecclesiastical Seminary?

BESSONOV: My father was a verger, and this explains why I went to the Divinity School and then to the Ecclesiastical Seminary.

VYSHINSKY: Who sent you abroad?

BESSONOV: The Moscow patron Shakhov, in 1912.

VYSHINSKY: In 1912?

BESSONOV: Then I returned to Russia to take my diploma.

I was deported to Vologda Gubernia because I belonged to a Socialist-Revolutionary organization.

VYSHINSKY: You joined the Socialist-Revolutionary Party in 1912?

BESSONOV: Yes.

VYSHINSKY: And how long did you remain in that party?

BESSONOV: Until 1918.

VYSHINSKY: Hence, the October Revolution found you in the ranks of the Socialist-Revolutionaries?

BESSONOV: Yes.

VYSHINSKY: What was your attitude towards the October Revolution?

BESSONOV: Socialist-Revolutionary.

VYSHINSKY: That is?

BESSONOV: Together with the other Socialist-Revolutionaries I did not accept the October Revolution. In August 1918 I broke with the Socialist-Revolutionaries, and in October 1918 I officially announced this.

VYSHINSKY: But up to 1918?

BESSONOV: Up to 1918 I agreed wholly and entirely with the line of the Socialist-Revolutionary Party, except for the war period, when I was a defeatist.

VYSHINSKY: At that period what was your attitude towards the October Revolution, the Communist Party? Friendly or hostile?

BESSONOV: Hostile.

VYSHINSKY: How did your hostility express itself?

BESSONOV: On the instructions of the Vologda City and Regional Committees of the Socialist-Revolutionary Party I spoke at meetings, explaining and defending the position of the Socialist-Revolutionaries on the October Revolution and on current events. The last public speech I made was on the Brest-Litovsk Peace.

VYSHINSKY: What did you say in that speech?

BESSONOV: I was sharply opposed to the signing of the Brest Peace.

VYSHINSKY: In 1919?

BESSONOV: In 1919 I stood wholly and entirely on the platform of supporting the Soviet government, I joined the Red Army as a volunteer.

VYSHINSKY: When did you join the Communist Party?

BESSONOV: In 1920, in May.

VYSHINSKY: When did you take the path of Trotskyite activities?

BESSONOV: I would ask permission to relate this in greater detail.

VYSHINSKY: That is a matter for the Court.

THE PRESIDENT: Relate only the main facts.

BESSONOV: My Trotskyite activities began in 1931, in Berlin.

VYSHINSKY: Under what circumstances?

BESSONOV: In 1931 I was working in the Berlin Trade Representation of the U.S.S.R. and was director of the Commercial Policy Department. In the course of the negotiations which the Soviet government was conducting in 1931 with the German industrialists concerning the matter of credits, I was one of the most active figures in the negotiations. This brought me into close contact with Pyatakov, who drew me into the Trotskyite organization.

VYSHINSKY: What was the nature of your underground Trotskyite activities at that time?

BESSONOV: The main task that Pyatakov set before me at that time, apart from my participating in the negotiations with the German industrialists—negotiations which, of course, deserve to be dealt with in somewhat greater detail later on—the main task that Pyatakov set before me was to establish constant and regular connections with Trotsky.

VYSHINSKY: Why did Pyatakov make you the proposal to organize these connections?

BESSONOV: As far as I understand, Pyatakov had had connections with Trotsky before that. But these connections were of an irregular character and suffered from a number of defects. But circumstances demanded of Pyatakov and of the whole Trotskyite organization the establishment of regular constant connections that would enable the receipt of Trotsky's instructions and information about the activities of the Trotskyites in the U.S.S.R. to be constant. This was the principal motive that led to the formation in Berlin of a permanent liaison point which functioned right up to my departure from Berlin in February last year.

VYSHINSKY: But why did the choice fall upon you?

BESSONOV: I was one of the most, I would say, firmly established persons on the staff of the Berlin Trade Representation.

VYSHINSKY: What post did you occupy there?

BESSONOV: I occupied the post of member of the Soviet Trade Representation.

VYSHINSKY: Of the Berlin Trade Representation?

BESSONOV: Yes, of the Berlin Trade Representation, which was then the most central trade representation, through which trade negotiations were conducted with ten European countries. This work required very long experience and, quite naturally, there was a definite opinion that under these circumstances I probably would remain and stay in Berlin longest.

VYSHINSKY: Hence your official position was a very convenient one for carrying out the duties of liaison man?

BESSONOV: Quite so.

VYSHINSKY: Did you agree to play this role?

40

BESSONOV: Yes, I did.

VYSHINSKY: Why?

BESSONOV: I have already said that Pyatakov drew me into the Trotskyite organization. . . .

VYSHINSKY: Hence, you agreed as a Trotskyite?

BESSONOV: Pyatakov drew me into the Trotskyite organization, consequently, I thereby undertook certain obligations towards that organization. When instructions were given me, in particular, to organize connections with Trotsky, I carried out those instructions.

VYSHINSKY: At that time were you aware that the Trotskyite organization, under the leadership of Pyatakov, as Trotsky's representative in the U.S.S.R., and under Trotsky's own leadership, was already carrying on definite plotting conspiratorial undermining work?

BESSONOV: Yes.

VYSHINSKY: How did you become aware of this, and under what circumstances?

BESSONOV: Pyatakov, during one of his emphatic talks with me about this subject, described to me the state of the opposition in the U.S.S.R. Besides, he described the situation in the U.S.S.R. in entirely false and slanderous colours. The picture he described was sufficiently expressive to influence me in a definite way. Moreover, Pyatakov himself, as a personality, could not but impress me. Of the people with whom life had brought me in touch up to that time he seemed to be best informed about European affairs, and he impressed me as a business leader.

I began to listen to Pyatakov with considerably greater attention than I had done under other circumstances. I, like many other employees abroad, had become widely familiar with foreign—under our Soviet conditions illegal—literature, in particular, with the bulletin published by Trotsky.[33] And finally, when Pyatakov came to organize me—to enlist me—he presented to me a picture of the state of the opposition forces in the U.S.S.R. First of all he mentioned the fact that the Trotskyites and Zinovievites had united on a common platform. Then he went on to say that steps had been taken, contact had been established with the Rights, steps which promised to be very successful. He spoke about the actual discontent which existed among broad strata of the illegal united Trotskyite-Zinovievite organizations, into which it was proposed also to draw the Rights, with whom contact was actually established. Pyatakov rather emphatically said that it was a matter of changing the leadership.

VYSHINSKY: You then learnt from what Pyatakov said that a definite organization existed?

41

BESSONOV: Yes.

VYSHINSKY: Under whose leadership was this organization operating?

BESSONOV: Pyatakov did not in the least conceal the fact that the organization was entirely guided by Trotsky's instructions.

VYSHINSKY: What specifically did Pyatakov tell you about the Rights, and whom did he mention?

BESSONOV: Pyatakov said that steps were being taken to establish organizational contact with the Rights.

VYSHINSKY: Concretely, with whom?

BESSONOV: With Bukharin, Rykov and Tomsky.

VYSHINSKY: And the latter—Bukharin, Rykov and Tomsky—did they take any steps in this direction?

BESSONOV: Up to 1931 I had not heard any talk about this.

VYSHINSKY: But had there been any talk about it?

BESSONOV: In 1932 Pyatakov spoke about it, without, it is true, dealing with it in detail.

VYSHINSKY: What did he say?

BESSONOV: In 1932 Pyatakov said that contact had been established.

VYSHINSKY: Hence, in 1932 the task of making such contact had been carried out?

BESSONOV: Yes.

VYSHINSKY: Under what circumstances?

BESSONOV: In 1932 I met Pyatakov several times. He stayed in Germany a very long time in connection with the trade negotiations. I saw him very often, and during one of his conversations with me he told me about it.

VYSHINSKY: In short, that the Trotskyite group had been organized under the leadership of its centre, that the Zinovievites had joined it, and that at that period, as far as you know, negotiations were going on with the Bukharinites?

BESSONOV: Yes.

VYSHINSKY: Permit me to ask Bukharin.

THE PRESIDENT: You may.

VYSHINSKY: Accused Bukharin, can you corroborate Bessonov's evidence that at that period your group was negotiating with the Zinovievite organization about your work?

BUKHARIN: In my testimony during the preliminary examination I stated in detail that attempts at establishing contact between the Rights and the Zinovievites, and later on also the Trotskyites, had been made even before that. [34]

VYSHINSKY: You—accused Bukharin, and also Rykov and Tomsky—were carrying on negotiations with Pyatakov and other Trotskyites concerning united operations against the Soviet power?

42

BUKHARIN: Yes.

VYSHINSKY: You corroborate this?

BUKHARIN: Yes, I do.

VYSHINSKY (to Bessonov): Continue your explanation.

BESSONOV: Pyatakov put before me the task of organizing systematic and constant connections with Trotsky.

VYSHINSKY: What did you do definitely in this respect?

BESSONOV: After several talks with him on this subject (this was in the beginning of May 1931), and on his advice, I, with a letter of recommendation from Pyatakov, found Trotsky's son, Sedov, in Berlin, and through him conveyed Pyatakov's first letter to Trotsky.

VYSHINSKY: Tell us, where, when, at what time and under what circumstances did you hand him the letter?

BESSONOV: Sedov was then the centre of attention of the German, I would say, gutter press, because before that something had happened to his sister—Trotsky's daughter—as a result of which the German press wrote a great deal about Trotsky, about his children, and in particular about Sedov, who at that time was studying at the Berlin Polytechnicum.[35] It was not difficult for me to find Sedov, just as it was not difficult to find any person in Berlin, as I had very many connections in Berlin. I could have established contact with Sedov in any way, but on Pyatakov's advice, not to advertise the matter, I used an address which he gave in a Berlin daily newspaper. . . .

VYSHINSKY: . . . And at this address?

BESSONOV: . . . And at this address, at the end of May 1931, with Pyatakov's letter of recommendation, I found Sedov and had a brief conversation with him.

VYSHINSKY: Had Sedov known you before that?

BESSONOV: No, he had not.

VYSHINSKY: You were quite a new person to him?

BESSONOV: Yes, I was.

VYSHINSKY: Then why did Sedov agree to discuss this subject with a person who was a stranger to him?

BESSONOV: I gave him Pyatakov's letter—that was enough.

VYSHINSKY: And after that?

BESSONOV: After that he talked with me rather in detail about the question of organizing this correspondence. He at once said that it was not a matter of one or two letters that one could take for delivery, but of establishing systematic connections.

VYSHINSKY: What was the upshot of your conversation with Sedov?

BESSONOV: He thought that it was necessary, if we were going to set ourselves the task of establishing permanent connections, to appoint a special person who was less prominent than he,

Sedov. After some time, having met Sedov in a manner previously agreed upon, at one of the railway stations in Berlin, I handed him Pyatakov's letter to Trotsky, which Trotsky received, and to which in a relatively short time a reply was received. At the same time I handed over the first sum of money which Pyatakov had given me.

VYSHINSKY: What money?

BESSONOV: He had given me 2,000 marks to hand over to Sedov specially for the purpose of covering expenses connected with the sending of the first letters.

VYSHINSKY: What money was this?

BESSONOV: I don't know. Pyatakov had rather large sums at his disposal.

VYSHINSKY: What sums were these; did they belong to him personally?

BESSONOV: I don't think they belonged to Pyatakov.

VYSHINSKY: Whose were they, then?

BESSONOV: It was money that belonged to the Soviet state, placed at the disposal of Pyatakov as Chairman of the Negotiations Committee. . . .

VYSHINSKY: For what purpose?

BESSONOV: I think it was placed at his disposal for what are called entertainment expenses.

VYSHINSKY: That is, expenses connected with his official duties?

BESSONOV: Yes, of course. But this money was used for the purpose of organizing the first connections with Trotsky.

VYSHINSKY: How would you qualify this, considering the present situation, in the language of the Criminal Code? How can this utilization of other people's money for criminal purposes be qualified?

BESSONOV: (No reply.)

VYSHINSKY: Perhaps I can help you?

BESSONOV: I think you can do it better than I. What coming from me just now may sound insincere and unconvincing will sound real if it comes from you.

VYSHINSKY: It follows then that Pyatakov stole government money? He stole this money and sent it for the purpose of helping the Trotskyite organization?

BESSONOV: Yes, that is quite true.

VYSHINSKY: And you helped him to do this?

BESSONOV: Yes.

VYSHINSKY: He stole the money and you helped him by conveying from Pyatakov 2,000 marks which belonged to the Soviet state?

BESSONOV: Yes, that is so, but money transactions with Sedov ended with this, because, as far as I remember, at that period no more than three letters were sent and received through Sedov.

VYSHINSKY: Did money transactions with the Trotskyites end entirely with this?

BESSONOV: I prefer to deal with this later, because I have to mention a number of facts on this question. I must say that, of course, money transactions with the Trotskyites did not end with this.

VYSHINSKY: They continued?

BESSONOV: I would not say that there was direct financing with Soviet money. . . .

VYSHINSKY: But what took place?

BESSONOV: But what took place was the utilization of the situation in Germany at the time and of a Soviet official position for the purpose of receiving considerable funds for illegal Trotskyite work. There can be no doubt about that.

VYSHINSKY: The financing of the Trotskyite organization at the expense of the interests of the Soviet state continued?

BESSONOV: Certainly.

VYSHINSKY: Continue.

BESSONOV: At my first meeting with Sedov he raised the question of appointing a special person for permanent connections with Trotsky.

VYSHINSKY: Was that on Sedov's initiative?

BESSONOV: Yes. I told Pyatakov about it. He thought it was quite right and soon after (this was in the beginning of July, or at the end of June, 1931) he introduced me to engineer Reich, who at that time was working in the Iron and Steel Department of the Berlin Trade Representation, a man who knew Europe very well, in particular the European iron and steel industry, had lived in different countries and spoke several European languages.

VYSHINSKY: But principally?

BESSONOV: Principally, he had been a Trotskyite since 1923.

VYSHINSKY: Until that moment you had not known him?

BESSONOV: Until that moment I had not known him.

VYSHINSKY: Not at all?

BESSONOV: Not at all.

VYSHINSKY: And you had not met him?

BESSONOV: I had seen him now and again in the corridors of the Trade Representation.

VYSHINSKY: Since you had seen him in the Trade Representation you must have known him.

BESSONOV: I did not know his name.

VYSHINSKY: Very well, but you knew him by sight? You

45

knew that there was a man named Reich, but you were not acquainted with him?

BESSONOV: That is so, until I was introduced to him. . . .

VYSHINSKY: Did you know Reich before Pyatakov introduced him to you as a Trotskyite?

BESSONOV: As a member of the staff of the Trade Representation.

VYSHINSKY: He was not a new man to you?

BESSONOV: No.

VYSHINSKY: Only you did not know that he was connected with Trotsky?

BESSONOV: No.

VYSHINSKY: And it was Pyatakov who connected you with him as a Trotskyite?

BESSONOV: Yes.

VYSHINSKY: And when did Reich become Johannson?

BESSONOV: Reich said that the technique of connections was a very simple, uncomplicated matter; true, it required a fairly large amount of money and considerable modesty on the part of the man who was serving as the connection. But for a member of the staff of the Soviet Trade Representation, who travelled everywhere with a Soviet passport, it was a rather difficult matter, because at every frontier he attracted special attention, and because of this it was necessary to find another man who could do this connection work in such a way as to be able to come and go across the frontier without rousing suspicion.

When this was reported to Pyatakov he said that there was no sense in looking for a foreigner for this purpose, and that Reich could be made a foreigner. And indeed, Reich did become a foreigner, that is to say, in 1931, I think it was in December, Reich succeeded, not without the aid of the Trotskyites, in transforming himself into Karl Johannson.

VYSHINSKY: With the aid of the Trotskyites?

BESSONOV: Yes, with the aid of the Trotskyites.

VYSHINSKY: With the aid of the Trotskyites he obtained a passport?

BESSONOV: I know that obtaining a passport means bribing officials. I do not exclude the possibility that this took place with the financial assistance of the Trotskyites, because Pyatakov told me that it would cost a certain amount of money.

VYSHINSKY: The Trotskyites obtained the passport?

BESSONOV: They obtained the passport of a naturalized Danish citizen.

VYSHINSKY: But all this was a fake, as a matter of fact he is not a Dane, had never been to Denmark before that.

BESSONOV: He had never been to Denmark.

VYSHINSKY: What sort of a naturalization was it if he had never been to Denmark?

BESSONOV: The passport was an official one, a real one.

VYSHINSKY: But actually?

BESSONOV: Actually there was a double citizenship. At the end of 1931, or the beginning of 1932, Reich, while a Soviet citizen and a member of the staff of the Trade Representation, thanks to the assistance of the Trotskyites and money, became a Danish citizen. In the spring of 1932 he was commissioned to go to Moscow, but he did not return to Moscow and became a deserter. And from that time I knew him as Johannson, who served as liaison man between me and Trotsky.

VYSHINSKY: Reich became a Dane and a deserter. He was a double.

BESSONOV: For some period of time he had two citizenships, of which one—Soviet citizenship—was open, and the Danish citizenship was secret.

VYSHINSKY: Which citizenship was open?

BESSONOV: The Soviet citizenship, but the Danish citizenship was secret.

VYSHINSKY: Hence this was a swindle, and in addition, desertion, and when a Soviet citizen becomes a deserter it is treason, he thereby betrays his country.

BESSONOV: Certainly.

VYSHINSKY: You knew about this and helped it, is that right?

BESSONOV: Quite right.

VYSHINSKY: Did this Reich play an important role as a liaison man in Trotskyite affairs?

BESSONOV: Undoubtedly, he played an important role. I know that Reich carried out commissions for Trotsky in a number of other countries. I want to speak only about what I know.

VYSHINSKY: We are not interested in what you surmise, but in what you know.

BESSONOV: His work consisted of systematically bringing and taking correspondence. Secondly, he arranged meetings with Trotsky or Sedov whenever that was necessary.

VYSHINSKY: Meetings with you?

BESSONOV: I have in mind the meeting with Pyatakov in 1932. Then I have in mind the meeting between Krestinsky and Trotsky which took place in October 1933.

VYSHINSKY: Hence in October 1933, with Reich's assistance, a meeting was arranged between Krestinsky and Trotsky?

BESSONOV: Yes, a meeting was arranged between Krestinsky and Trotsky.

VYSHINSKY: How did you know that Reich arranged this meeting?

BESSONOV: Except for Pyatakov and myself, nobody knew of Reich's existence.

VYSHINSKY: But did Krestinsky know of Reich's existence?

BESSONOV: Probably he knew.

VYSHINSKY: Why do you suppose this?

BESSONOV: Krestinsky had worked in Berlin as Ambassador.

VYSHINSKY: Reich visited the Embassy in his official capacity, did he not?

BESSONOV: Certainly.

VYSHINSKY: How did this Reich arrange the meeting between Krestinsky and Trotsky?

BESSONOV: I cannot tell the Court what the technical arrangements for this meeting really were, for I do not know.

VYSHINSKY: But what can you tell?

BESSONOV: When Krestinsky, in the late summer of 1933, came to Germany for a cure, he stayed for a long time in Berlin. He had two conversations with me which could be characterized as conversations between members of the Trotskyite organization. The first conversation was about the arrangements for the meeting between Trotsky and Krestinsky.

VYSHINSKY: Who desired this meeting, Trotsky or Krestinsky?

BESSONOV: Krestinsky. It must be said that this was not an easy task at that time. At that time Trotsky to a certain degree had become the centre of European attention, a great deal was being written about him in the newspapers, and it was not easy under those circumstances to arrange a meeting with him. I had no doubt that Johannson had wide connections and could arrange this matter without difficulty. I asked him to come to Berlin, and shortly afterwards he returned and reported that the meeting could take place in October 1933.

VYSHINSKY: When?

BESSONOV: In October 1933.

VYSHINSKY: Hence you helped Krestinsky to arrange a meeting with Trotsky?

BESSONOV: Krestinsky knew that I had arranged the matter, but how I had arranged it, Krestinsky did not know.

VYSHINSKY: The technical side?

BESSONOV: Yes, the technical side.

VYSHINSKY: Hence, we may establish the following facts: the first is that Krestinsky travelled through Berlin.

BESSONOV: I think that was in September, or the end of August, 1933.

VYSHINSKY: Where was he going?

48

BESSONOV: To Kissingen.

VYSHINSKY: What for?·

BESSONOV: To take a cure. He stopped at the Trade Representation and I had a talk with him. Twice we talked on Trotskyite subjects.

VYSHINSKY: And he says that he was never a Trotskyite. Perhaps he censured the Trotskyites? You heard him say here that he was not a Trotskyite. Is that right or wrong?

BESSONOV: (Smiles.)

VYSHINSKY: Why are you smiling?

BESSONOV: I am smiling because the reason why I am standing here is that Nikolai Nikolayevich Krestinsky named me the liaison man with Trotsky. Besides him and Pyatakov nobody knew about this. And if Krestinsky had not spoken to me about this in December 1933 I would not be in the dock now.

VYSHINSKY: So you think that you are obliged to him for this? Permit me to ask the accused Krestinsky.

Accused Krestinsky, did you really travel to Kissingen in 1933, in August or September?

KRESTINSKY: In the beginning of September.

VYSHINSKY: Do you confirm this fact?

KRESTINSKY: I do.

VYSHINSKY: Did you see Bessonov?

KRESTINSKY: Yes.

VYSHINSKY: Did you talk to him?

KRESTINSKY: Yes.

VYSHINSKY: What about? The weather?

KRESTINSKY: He was counsellor to the Embassy in Berlin. At that time he was acting as chargé d'affaires. He informed me about the political situation in Germany, about the frame of mind of the fascist party, which at that time was in power, and about their program and attitude towards the U.S.S.R.

VYSHINSKY: And about Trotskyite affairs?

KRESTINSKY: We did not talk about them. I was not a Trotskyite.

VYSHINSKY: You never talked about them?

KRESTINSKY: Never.

VYSHINSKY: That means that Bessonov is not telling the truth, and that you are telling the truth. Do you always tell the truth?

KRESTINSKY: No.

VYSHINSKY: Not always. Accused Krestinsky, you and I will have to examine serious matters and there is no need to get excited. Consequently, Bessonov is not telling the truth?

KRESTINSKY: No.

VYSHINSKY: But you too do not always tell the truth. Is that not so?

KRESTINSKY: I did not always tell the truth during the investigation.

VYSHINSKY: But at other times you always tell the truth?

KRESTINSKY: The truth.

VYSHINSKY: Why this lack of respect for the investigation, why during the investigation did you tell untruths? Explain.

KRESTINSKY: (No reply.)

VYSHINSKY: I hear no reply. I have no further questions. Accused Bessonov, when did your conversations with Krestinsky about Trotskyite affairs take place?

BESSONOV: The conversation in Berlin was not the first, but the second.

VYSHINSKY: And where did the first take place?

BESSONOV: The first took place in Moscow in May 1933.

VYSHINSKY: Under what circumstances? When did you speak to Krestinsky about Trotskyite affairs in Moscow, and what exactly did you talk about?

BESSONOV: After I returned to Moscow from England with the whole trade organization, I was appointed counsellor to the Soviet Embassy in Germany. Before assuming that post I had a long conversation with Pyatakov and Krestinsky.

VYSHINSKY: I am not interested in Pyatakov just now; I am interested in Krestinsky. Where did you talk to him?

BESSONOV: In Krestinsky's office in the People's Commissariat of Foreign Affairs.

VYSHINSKY: Was it about Trotskyite matters?

BESSONOV: Yes, Krestinsky told me that in accordance with a talk he had with Pyatakov, and on the latter's recommendation, he deemed it necessary to talk to me absolutely frankly about the tasks that confronted me in Berlin. He said that he had already spoken to the Germans about my appointment, the Moscow Germans—referring to the German Embassy in Moscow.

THE PRESIDENT: Accused Bessonov, you have not forgotten the warning I gave at the beginning of the hearing?

BESSONOV: What I want to say will probably in no way reflect on the honour of any Embassy. He said that Germany was pleased with my appointment because I had worked for a long time in Germany, knew Germany well and they knew me, and from that standpoint they were pleased that they would have a man they knew. The real meaning of this remark, of course, was what Pyatakov had very vividly formulated several times earlier and what Krestinsky had told me before, namely, that my work in Germany during 1931-32 had undoubtedly earned me, as a member of the Trotskyite organization, definite popularity and sympathy among certain circles of German industrialists and partly of German military men, a popularity which should now be utilized for new purposes. Krestinsky formulated these purposes as follows.

VYSHINSKY: Briefly, because I think that Krestinsky will himself talk about these purposes later.

BESSONOV: To formulate quite briefly Krestinsky's ideas and the commission I received from him, it was that I, in my capacity of counsellor to the Berlin Embassy, must first and foremost devote my energies to hampering and if possible preventing the normalization of relations between the Soviet Union and Germany along the usual, normal diplomatic lines.

VYSHINSKY: Accused Krestinsky, do you recall such "diplomatic" conversations with Bessonov?

KRESTINSKY: No, we never had such conversations.

VYSHINSKY: Were there no diplomatic conversations at all?

KRESTINSKY: I did not quite catch what Bessonov said just now. You can't hear well from here.

VYSHINSKY: But you are sitting quite close to him.

KRESTINSKY: From the back here you can't hear very well what Bessonov is saying.

VYSHINSKY: Allow me to request you, Comrade President, to have Krestinsky sit nearer to Bessonov so that he might hear him better. Otherwise I am afraid that at the most important moments Krestinsky's hearing will fail him.

(Krestinsky seats himself nearer to Bessonov.)

VYSHINSKY: I request Bessonov specially for Krestinsky's benefit to repeat what he said; and I would ask Krestinsky to listen carefully, to keep his ears open.

BESSONOV: I repeat, the commission which I at that time received from Krestinsky was that in my post of counsellor to the Berlin Embassy of the U.S.S.R., where I, of course, enjoyed definite opportunities for the accomplishment of this commission, I was by every means open to me—naturally observing all due diplomatic decorum—to hamper, hinder and prevent the normalization of relations between the Soviet Union and Germany along normal diplomatic lines, and in this way to compel the Germans to seek for illegal, non-diplomatic, secret, clandestine means of arriving at an agreement with the Trotskyite organization.

VYSHINSKY: Did you hear that?

KRESTINSKY: Yes.

VYSHINSKY: Did you have any conversations with Bessonov in May 1933?

KRESTINSKY: I had conversations with Bessonov before he left for Berlin.

51

VYSHINSKY: You had. Do you remember what they were about?

KRESTINSKY: I do not remember the details.

VYSHINSKY: You do not remember the details, but Bessonov does.

KRESTINSKY: There was not a word said about the Trotskyite stand.

VYSHINSKY: Did you say what he was to do abroad, or did you not?

KRESTINSKY: Of course I did.

VYSHINSKY: You did say what he was to do?

KRESTINSKY: Yes.

VYSHINSKY: What was he to do?

KRESTINSKY: He was to try to create normal relations as far as possible.

VYSHINSKY: As far as possible. But if it was impossible?

KRESTINSKY: If he did not succeed, it would be another matter. But he was to try.

VYSHINSKY: Accused Bessonov, is what Krestinsky says true?

BESSONOV: Absolutely untrue. What is more, during this conversation Krestinsky gave me detailed organizational instructions how I was to communicate with him in the future. Apart from the official letters which the Embassy in Germany exchanges with the People's Commissariat of Foreign Affairs, I was to maintain correspondence with Krestinsky. And if in this correspondence Krestinsky were to say that his view on current questions of Soviet-German relations was such-and-such, and that he advised waiting for official instructions on this question, that would mean that I was to act in accordance with his "personal" point of view, irrespective of what the official instructions might be.

And, finally, Krestinsky referred me to Stern, his immediate subordinate along Trotskyite lines and along official lines, so that I might get addresses for the establishment of connections with Trotsky.

VYSHINSKY: You hear that Bessonov speaks in fairly great detail about your conversations, which are far from bearing the character you attribute to them. What about it?

KRESTINSKY: There were no such conversations, although during the confrontation which took place in January I admitted part of the conversation.

VYSHINSKY: At the confrontation with Bessonov you admitted this part?

KRESTINSKY: Yes.

VYSHINSKY: So there was such a conversation?

KRESTINSKY: No.

VYSHINSKY: So what Bessonov says must be understood the other way round?

KRESTINSKY: Not always.

VYSHINSKY: But what about your admission?

KRESTINSKY: During the investigation I gave false testimony several times.

VYSHINSKY: You said: "I did not formally belong to the Trotskyite centre." Is that true or not?

KRESTINSKY: I did not belong to it at all.

VYSHINSKY: You say that formally you did not belong. What is true and what is not true here? Perhaps it is all true, or it is all untrue, or only half of it is true? What percentage, how many grams of it are true?

KRESTINSKY: I did not belong to the Trotskyite centre because I was not a Trotskyite.

VYSHINSKY: You were not a Trotskyite?

KRESTINSKY: No.

VYSHINSKY: Never?

KRESTINSKY: Yes, I was a Trotskyite until 1927.

THE PRESIDENT: At the beginning of the trial you said in reply to my question that you had never been a Trotskyite. That is what you said.

KRESTINSKY: I said that I am not a Trotskyite.

VYSHINSKY: And so you were a Trotskyite until 1927?

KRESTINSKY: I was.

VYSHINSKY: And when did you stop being a Trotskyite in 1927?

KRESTINSKY: Just before the Fifteenth Party Congress.[36]

VYSHINSKY: Recall the date.

KRESTINSKY: I date my rupture with Trotsky and Trotskyism from November 27, 1927, when, through Serebryakov,[37] who had returned from America and was in Moscow, I sent Trotsky a sharp letter containing sharp criticism. . . .

VYSHINSKY: That letter is not in the records. We have another letter—your letter to Trotsky.

KRESTINSKY: The letter I am referring to is in the possession of the Court investigator, because it was taken from me during the search, and I request this letter to be attached to the records.

VYSHINSKY: The records contain a letter dated July 11, 1927, taken from you during the search.

KRESTINSKY: But there is another letter of November 27. . . .

VYSHINSKY: There is no such letter.

KRESTINSKY: That cannot be. . . .

VYSHINSKY: We are just now conducting the Court investigation, and you yourself said that during the preliminary investigation you did not always tell the truth. You said during the preliminary investigation that you did not formally belong to the centre. That means that during the preliminary investigation you admitted that in general you were, actually speaking, a member of the Trotskyite centre. Did you admit this during the preliminary investigation?

KRESTINSKY: No, I did not.

VYSHINSKY: In your testimony (pp. 9 and 10) you said: "Formally I did not belong. . . ." This can be taken as meaning that you did belong, but not formally. Is that so?

KRESTINSKY: I did not belong to the Trotskyite centre at all.

VYSHINSKY: That means that you testified falsely?

KRESTINSKY: I have already stated that this testimony of mine does not conform to the facts.

VYSHINSKY: When I interrogated you during the preliminary investigation, were you telling me the truth?

KRESTINSKY: No.

VYSHINSKY: Why did you tell untruths? Did I ask you to tell untruths?

KRESTINSKY: No.

VYSHINSKY: Did I ask you to tell the truth?

KRESTINSKY: You did.

VYSHINSKY: Why, when I asked you to tell the truth, did you nevertheless tell untruths, compel the investigator to write them down, and then sign it? Why?

KRESTINSKY: At the preliminary investigation, before I was questioned by you, I had given false testimony.

VYSHINSKY: . . . And then you stuck to it.

KRESTINSKY: . . . And then I stuck to it, because from personal experience I had arrived at the conviction that before the trial, if there was to be one, I would not succeed in refuting my testimony.

VYSHINSKY: And do you think that you have succeeded in refuting it now?

KRESTINSKY: No, that is not the important thing. The important thing is that I declare that I do not admit myself to be a Trotskyite. I am not a Trotskyite.

VYSHINSKY: You stated that you were on a special conspiratorial footing. What does this "special conspiratorial footing" mean?

KRESTINSKY: Well, you know. . . .

VYSHINSKY: Don't make me a witness in this case. I am asking you, what does "special conspiratorial footing" mean?

KRESTINSKY: That was said in my testimony. . . .

VYSHINSKY: You do not want to answer my questions.

KRESTINSKY: This phrase about my being on a special con-

54

spiratorial footing is contained in my testimony of June 5 or 9, which is false from beginning to end.

VYSHINSKY: That is not what I am asking you, and I therefore request you not to be in a hurry with your answers. I am asking you what a "special conspiratorial footing" means.

KRESTINSKY: It does not correspond to the facts.

VYSHINSKY: We shall elucidate that later. I want to know the meaning of the statement that you are on a special conspiratorial footing.

KRESTINSKY: If it corresponded to the facts, it would mean that I, while really being a Trotskyite, take every precaution to conceal my adherence to Trotskyism.

VYSHINSKY: Excellent, but in order to conceal your Trotskyism you must deny it.

KRESTINSKY: Yes.

VYSHINSKY: Just now you are declaring that you are not a Trotskyite. Is it not in order to conceal that you are a Trotskyite?

KRESTINSKY (after a pause): No, I declare that I am not a Trotskyite.

VYSHINSKY (to the Court): May I question the accused Rosengoltz? Accused Rosengoltz, did you hear this dialogue?

ROSENGOLTZ: Yes.

VYSHINSKY: Do you take it that Krestinsky was a Trotskyite?

ROSENGOLTZ: He is a Trotskyite.

VYSHINSKY: Accused Krestinsky, I ask you to listen, because you will be saying that you did not hear.

KRESTINSKY: I don't feel well.

VYSHINSKY: If the accused declares that he doesn't feel well, I have no right to question him.

KRESTINSKY: I have only to take a pill and I shall be able to continue.

VYSHINSKY: Do you request not to be questioned for the present?

KRESTINSKY: For a few minutes.

VYSHINSKY: Can you listen when I question others?

KRESTINSKY: Yes.

VYSHINSKY: Accused Rosengoltz, what grounds have you for testifying that Krestinsky is a Trotskyite, and that consequently he is not telling the truth here?

ROSENGOLTZ: It is borne out by the conversations I had with him as a Trotskyite.

VYSHINSKY: When did these conversations take place?

ROSENGOLTZ: They took place from 1929 onwards.

VYSHINSKY: Until what year?

ROSENGOLTZ: Until quite recently.

55

VYSHINSKY: That is?

ROSENGOLTZ: Until 1937.

VYSHINSKY: And so you say that these conversations went on from 1929 to 1937? For eight years you "conversed" with him as a Trotskyite? Do I understand you rightly?

ROSENGOLTZ: Yes.

VYSHINSKY: Accused Grinko, what do you know about Krestinsky as a Trotskyite?

GRINKO: I know.

VYSHINSKY: What do you know?

GRINKO: In my conspiratorial work I had connections with Krestinsky as a conspirator, as a Trotskyite, as a member of the Right-Trotskyite, conspiratorial centre, on very important questions about which I shall have to give testimony.

VYSHINSKY: Can you tell us briefly what questions? Questions of supporting the Soviet power or of combating it?

GRINKO: Questions of combating the Soviet power, of establishing connections with foreign states hostile to the Soviet power.

VYSHINSKY: And do you know whether Krestinsky was connected with other foreign intelligence services?

GRINKO: He helped me to establish connections with one of the foreign intelligence services.

VYSHINSKY: So Krestinsky helped you to establish connections with a foreign intelligence service. Do you hear that, accused Krestinsky? Is it true?

KRESTINSKY: No.

VYSHINSKY: Yet you testified that it was true.

KRESTINSKY: That I helped Grinko to establish connections?

VYSHINSKY: More than that, that you yourself were the agent of a foreign intelligence service.

GRINKO: There is another fact I would like to mention. It is that I helped Krestinsky, as former Assistant People's Commissar of Foreign Affairs, to utilize the valuta funds which had accumulated abroad from exchange differences, and which he needed to finance the Trotskyites.[38]

VYSHINSKY: Tell us, please, was there an occasion when Krestinsky asked you not to audit the valuta fund?

GRINKO: That is what I am referring to.

VYSHINSKY: Accused Krestinsky, did you have a valuta fund?

KRESTINSKY: I did.

VYSHINSKY: Did you ask Grinko, former People's Commissar of Finance, not to audit that fund?

KRESTINSKY: I did not.

VYSHINSKY: Did he audit it?

KRESTINSKY: He did not personally, but his staff did.

56

VYSHINSKY: Accused Grinko, did you audit it?

GRINKO: No.

VYSHINSKY: Here Grinko says he did not. Did you audit it?

KRESTINSKY: No, I did not audit it.

VYSHINSKY: Who did audit it?

KRESTINSKY: The staff of the People's Commissariat of Finance.

VYSHINSKY: Name those who did.

KRESTINSKY: I know that an audit was conducted every year.

VYSHINSKY: Who personally, on the instructions of Grinko, former People's Commissar of Finance, audited your fund?

KRESTINSKY: Officials of the People's Commissariat of Finance in charge of valuta matters.

VYSHINSKY: Who?

KRESTINSKY: There was Kagan and Martenson. Each year, when the estimates were discussed, the expenditure for the previous year was checked.

VYSHINSKY: Grinko, is that true?

GRINKO: No, it is not. Krestinsky is not referring to what I am talking about. Of course, when the official valuta estimates of the People's Commissariat of Foreign Affairs were examined for any given year, the expenditure in the previous year was checked. I am not talking about these estimates; what I am talking about is that owing to fluctuations in exchange rates in various countries funds accumulated in the hands of the People's Commissariat of Foreign Affairs arising out of exchange differences.

VYSHINSKY: Is that correct?

KRESTINSKY: Nothing accumulated in the hands of the People's Commissariat of Foreign Affairs, but funds were formed in the hands of individual Embassies.

VYSHINSKY: So they did accumulate?

KRESTINSKY: No, they did not accumulate. We would remit less valuta.

VYSHINSKY: And so what Grinko says is correct?

KRESTINSKY: No, he is giving a wrong picture. The position is as follows. A certain sum was assigned. If the Embassy exchanged the valuta at the official rate it would receive a bigger sum for it; if it exchanged it at the unofficial rate less money would have to be remitted. We remitted less money, and the rest remained with Grinko.

VYSHINSKY: Did you ask Grinko, as former People's Commissar of Finance, not to audit your valuta fund?

KRESTINSKY: I did not.

VYSHINSKY: And what do you say, Grinko?

GRINKO: I affirm that he did ask, and that I acceded to his request.

57

VYSHINSKY: Let us now pass to Bessonov. What was that meeting in Meran? Who met whom?

BESSONOV: I have testified that at the beginning of September 1933, when passing through Berlin, Krestinsky asked me to arrange a meeting for him with Trotsky. After first discussing where this meeting should be arranged, we both came to the unanimous conclusion that it could not be arranged in France or in Germany. Krestinsky then proposed a place of meeting in Italy, in the former Austrian and now Italian health resort of Meran in the Tyrol. I summoned Johannson, who was the man to arrange this meeting, gave him the necessary instructions and some time later received information from him that in spite of the difficulties Trotsky could travel to Meran. I then learned from Johannson that the meeting between Krestinsky and Trotsky had taken place. Nikolai Nikolayevich had assumed that I would come there at the same time. But I could not, and so I was not present at the meeting and know about it from the accounts of Nikolai Nikolayevich himself and Johannson, who arranged the meeting.

VYSHINSKY: Accused Krestinsky, were you in Meran?

KRESTINSKY: Yes.

VYSHINSKY: In what year?

KRESTINSKY: In 1933, in October.

VYSHINSKY: So you were there then, as Bessonov says?

KRESTINSKY: That is correct.

VYSHINSKY: Correct? Is the place correct?

KRESTINSKY: It is.

VYSHINSKY: Is the month correct?

KRESTINSKY: It is.

VYSHINSKY: Is the day correct?

KRESTINSKY: It is. I was there to take the cure and did not see any of the Trotskyites.

VYSHINSKY: With whom did you spend this Nachkur?

KRESTINSKY: I was there with my wife and did not see any of the Trotskyites.

VYSHINSKY: That means that Bessonov is wrong and you are speaking the truth?

KRESTINSKY: Yes, he is wrong. He is repeating my testimony, which is untrue.

VYSHINSKY: When we interrogated you at the preliminary investigation, what did you say on this score?

KRESTINSKY: In giving testimony I did not refute any of my previous testimony, which I deliberately confirmed.

VYSHINSKY: You deliberately confirmed it. You were misleading the Procurator. Is that so, or not?

KRESTINSKY: No.

VYSHINSKY: Why did you have to mislead me?

KRESTINSKY: I simply considered that if I were to say what I am saying today—that it was not in accordance with the facts—my declaration would not reach the leaders of the Party and the government.[39]

VYSHINSKY: But you signed the protocol?

KRESTINSKY: I did.

VYSHINSKY: You remember that I directly asked you whether you had any declarations or complaints to make against the investigator. Was that not so?

KRESTINSKY: It was.

VYSHINSKY: Did you answer me?

KRESTINSKY: Yes.

VYSHINSKY: Did I ask whether you had any complaints, or not?

KRESTINSKY: Yes, and I answered that I had no complaints.

VYSHINSKY: If you were asked whether you had complaints, you should have answered that you had.

KRESTINSKY: I had in the sense that I did not speak voluntarily.

VYSHINSKY: I shall read the reply which you gave the investigator Sheinin to the question put. Krestinsky's reply (p. 103): "I have no complaints to make against the investigator."

KRESTINSKY: I confirm that.

VYSHINSKY: You confirm it?

KRESTINSKY: I do.

VYSHINSKY: I have no more questions. I have a question to ask Bessonov.

Accused Bessonov, why do you mention facts which Krestinsky denies and contradicts?

BESSONOV: I do not know any other facts.

VYSHINSKY: Perhaps you are mixing things up? Perhaps it was not Krestinsky but somebody else?

BESSONOV: No, I had a number of other talks with Krestinsky.

VYSHINSKY: Tell us, were your relations with Krestinsky at that period good, friendly, or bad?

BESSONOV: I would not say that my relations with Krestinsky were very good, but all the same I would say that they were just good.

VYSHINSKY: May I ask the accused Krestinsky?

Accused Krestinsky, what are your relations with Bessonov like, good or bad?

KRESTINSKY: Good.

VYSHINSKY: Allow me to ask Rosengoltz.

Accused Rosengoltz, what were your relations with Krestinsky like? Good?

ROSENGOLTZ: I never had any differences with him.

VYSHINSKY: In what sphere?

ROSENGOLTZ: Not in any sphere. There was complete agreement in all spheres.

VYSHINSKY: Including the sphere of underground work.

Allow me to ask Krestinsky.

Accused Krestinsky, what were your relations with Rosengoltz like?

KRESTINSKY: Our relations were not bad. We had differences on questions of foreign policy.

VYSHINSKY: Were your relations with Rosengoltz good or bad?

KRESTINSKY: Not bad.

VYSHINSKY: Not bad, that means good?

KRESTINSKY: Yes.

VYSHINSKY: What were your relations with Grinko like?

Allow me to ask the accused Grinko.

Accused Grinko, what were your relations with Krestinsky like?

GRINKO: I consider that they were good.

VYSHINSKY: And what do you consider, accused Krestinsky?

KRESTINSKY: They were good.

VYSHINSKY: Accused Krestinsky, here are three men on good terms with you who say what is not true?

KRESTINSKY: Yes.

VYSHINSKY: Let us continue the interrogation of Bessonov.

Accused Bessonov, what were your subsequent conversations with Krestinsky about?

BESSONOV: In 1933 I had another conversation with him about the situation that had arisen in German industrial circles in connection with a certain dropping off of Soviet orders in Germany. I said that a certain disappointment existed among German industrialists with the course of development of Soviet-German economic relations. In this connection Krestinsky, even more sharply than in May, stressed that it was my duty to make it clear to the German industrialists that there could be no serious and important relations with the Soviet Union as long as the present leadership was in power in the Soviet Union. The more German industrial and military circles became disillusioned as to the possibility of normalizing relations with the Soviet Union, even diplomatic relations, the more readily and the more resolutely would they make for an agreement with the groups that were fighting the Soviet power. He stated that the task was a very difficult one, but after all, he said, you are a diplomat. It is true that at that time I was a young diplomat, but the task he assigned me I carried out.

When Krestinsky was passing through Berlin he spoke of the soundings that Rosenberg, the leader of the Foreign Affairs Department of the National-Socialist Party of Germany, had at that time made in our circles on the question of a possible secret agreement between the National-Socialists in Germany and the Russian Trotskyites, in particular and especially on the question of a raw material base for Germany, and in this connection on the question of the Ukraine. These soundings became known to me through Krestinsky. Krestinsky summoned me on the day of his departure for Kissingen. He was very agitated by this news, and asked my advice as to what should be done. And in this connection he emphasized that the soundings made by Rosenberg referred to the presence of Krestinsky in Berlin. Krestinsky's real character was fairly well known to Rosenberg and to other German public men. This news therefore had a quite definite political meaning. In this connection Krestinsky asked me to hasten his meeting with Trotsky, because he considered it expedient to receive instructions on this important question. Thus you have the three conversations, or the three main themes which developed during Nikolai Nikolayevich Krestinsky's stay in Berlin in September 1933. I did not see him on his return from Meran. I only saw him the following year, when actually there was nothing particularly new he could tell me about his conversation with Trotsky; nevertheless, I learnt that the conversation in the main amounted to an approbation of the line which had apparently been laid down earlier and of which Nikolai Nikolayevich had spoken to me in general outline when I was leaving for Berlin in May 1933, that is, a few months before this. And in addition to all the points about which I have already spoken, and which I learnt from Pyatakov, there was also the point that he, Nikolai Nikolayevich Krestinsky, and some other, whom he referred to as "we," were sounding the ground and establishing definite contact with military circles in the Soviet Union. And in this connection he mentioned the names of Tukhachevsky and Uborevich,[10] which later, as he himself informed me, was confirmed in Meran.

Another point in this Meran meeting which I know about, and which is also nothing but a development of the tactics which formerly existed and which were outlined during concrete negotiations in 1931, was the achievement of a special agreement of the opposition groups in the Soviet Union in the struggle for power, an agreement with foreign states which might help them in this matter. This agreement was to be with the National-Socialist Party of Germany, not as it is officially expressed, but in different circles, which I do not think it necessary to dwell upon specially just now, because it would lead me very far from the question you have put.

I repeat that as a development of these tactics there was in the Meran discussions between Nikolai Nikolayevich Krestinsky and Trotsky, a line which in its first version was a most

61

precise and clear formulation of defeatist tactics, although as a matter of fact, and this is what I said even at the confrontation with Krestinsky, essentially it was in effect defeatist tactics already when he was concluding the trade agreement which was being carried out when he was Ambassador in Germany, and these defeatist tactics were pursued by Pyatakov during the economic negotiations and were now being laid down as the basic tactics.

Many of the points in the talks between Krestinsky and Trotsky in Meran I learnt from Krestinsky himself. Johannson's information confirmed the meeting, and as far as I understood from my talks with Johannson, the meeting took place in Meran in the Hotel Meranhof—I do not remember its exact name. It should not be forgotten that this was in October, during what is known as the grape season in Meran, and that at this time it is made easy for people to travel to Meran for the grape season and back again. And I fully concede that Trotsky might well have managed to do this, although at that time it was extremely difficult for Trotsky to disappear from France.

VYSHINSKY: Tell us about your Trotskyite underground activities in the period immediately following this.

BESSONOV: I should like to finish what I have to say about the organization of the liaison point. The liaison point was organized in 1931 and existed until 1937, and, as the Berlin liaison point, disappeared when I left Berlin for the Soviet Union in February 1937.

During this period a large number of letters had been received from and sent to Trotsky. I cannot just now remember how many, but at any rate it was a matter of six or seven letters of instruction in both directions a year. In addition there were a number of letters that were sent through the diplomatic mails. Moreover, there were letters sent through the diplomatic mails written on foreign letter-heads, chiefly of German and Belgian firms, which conveyed most urgent information written in business language. It was the purpose of this liaison point to arrange personal meetings. Johannson was the man who made the trip to Oslo with Pyatakov, and whose name he refrained from mentioning when he testified before the Military Collegium in January 1937.

VYSHINSKY: From whom did you learn that Johannson organized Pyatakov's trip and meeting with Trotsky in Oslo?

BESSONOV: From Pyatakov and Johannson themselves.

VYSHINSKY: From Pyatakov and Johannson themselves. Go on.

BESSONOV: Finally, in 1932 I knew there had been a meeting with Sedov. I did not consider it possible to mention this subject while speaking on the significance of this Berlin liaison point in a number of meetings; but I will not talk about it because I do not know it. I might also mention that with and by Johannson's help contact was organized and the conditions for a preliminary agreement arranged between the Trotskyites and the Trudovaya Krestyanskaya Partia, headed by Maslov, who was in Prague. I can give more detailed testimony on this point, because I took a direct part in these negotiations.

VYSHINSKY: Tell us about the meeting with Trotsky in Paris in 1934. What exactly did Trotsky instruct you to do, and what exactly did you do in fulfilment of these instructions?

BESSONOV: I received a short letter through Johannson, a note from Trotsky, in which he wrote about arranging a meeting with one of the Trotskyites in Germany to inform him about the events of June 30 in Germany. I was the only person who could go. At the end of July 1934 I arrived in Paris by the day train and also left by the day train. The whole talk took place in a hotel at which Johannson always stayed. Trotsky said that he knew me very well from Pyatakov's letters and from Krestinsky's accounts.

VYSHINSKY: What did you and Trotsky say about your underground Trotskyite tasks?

BESSONOV: He imposed on his followers working in the diplomatic field the task of adopting the line of sabotaging official agreements in order to stimulate the interest of the Germans in unofficial agreements with opposition groups. "They will come to us yet," said Trotsky, referring to Hess and Rosenberg. He said that we must not be squeamish in this matter, and that we might be ensured real and important help from Hess and Rosenberg. He said we must not stop short at consenting to big cessions of territory.

VYSHINSKY: which exactly?

BESSONOV: We shall consent to the cession of the Ukraine, Trotsky said. Bear that in mind in your work and in your negotiations with the Germans, and I shall also write about it to Pyatakov and Krestinsky. He then dealt with questions connected with the work of the Trotskyite organizations in the Soviet Union and particularly stressed the fact that under conditions when an inevitable war was brewing the only possible way in which the Trotskyites could come to power was by the defeat of the Soviet Union in that war.

He then dwelt on the methods of work of the Trotskyite organizations in the Soviet Union, particularly emphasizing the necessity of resorting to the most extreme terrorist methods of struggle. At this point he mentioned the words which are contained in the indictment and which were read out here today, namely, that it would be unpardonable squeamishness were we, his followers in the Soviet Union, not to proceed now to the direct extermination and removal of Stalin and all his immediate followers.

Quite unexpectedly, he dwelt in this connection on Maxim Gorky, saying that the part played by Maxim Gorky was extremely exceptional in view of his influence not only in the Soviet Union, but above all abroad. He referred to Gorky's extremely close friendship with Stalin and said that Maxim Gorky's utterances were most definitely driving away from Trotsky many of his followers among the European intelligentsia and bringing them closer to the position of the leadership of the Party. And in this connection he had arrived at the conclusion, which he openly expressed to me, that Gorky must be removed, mentioning those words which were quoted here about the necessity of physically exterminating Gorky at all costs. Such were his instructions.

VYSHINSKY: Did you transmit them?

BESSONOV: Yes. Shortly after this, in the autumn of 1934, I was in Moscow and gave a detailed account of this conversation to Pyatakov.

VYSHINSKY: Go on.

BESSONOV: That, actually speaking, is all I can say about my meeting with Trotsky in 1934.

VYSHINSKY: After 1934 did you have any meetings or conversations with leaders of the underground Trotskyite organization?

BESSONOV: Yes, I met Pyatakov every year until the year of his arrest. I did not see him any more in the autumn of 1936. Every time I came to Moscow I met Nikolai Nikolayevich Krestinsky, and in particular I met him in the autumn of 1936 after Pyatakov's arrest.

VYSHINSKY: What did you talk about after Pyatakov's arrest?

BESSONOV: At the very end of September, or in the early part of October 1936, I met Krestinsky in Moscow. Krestinsky in a state of great agitation told me that the affairs of the Trotskyite centre were in a very bad way, that there had been a number of exposures, that Pyatakov, Radek and a number of others had been arrested, that his own arrest was not out of the question, and that he asked me, on my return to Berlin, immediately to send written information on the subject to Trotsky. He said that, in the event of his arrest, all the organizational contacts would have to be transferred to Karakhan, although he had no idea how exactly this was to be done. He asked me even to repeat it twice to show whether I understood him when he said that the situation of the Trotskyites in the Soviet Union in the autumn of 1936 must be regarded as extremely serious and that the agreement reached by the Trotskyites with the German National-Socialist Party on the possibility of hastening war, which would facilitate the coming to power of the Trotskyites, must be expedited at all costs.

On arriving in Berlin I reported this in detail to Trotsky and received to my letter a reply from him, which I transmitted to Krestinsky. Then, this was in December 1936 or perhaps in the early part of January 1937—more exactly in December 1936— I received another letter from Krestinsky for Trotsky, which I read but did not fully understand because it was written in cryptic language.

VYSHINSKY: By whom was this letter written, to whom, and when?

BESSONOV: This letter was written in December 1936 by Krestinsky to Trotsky, and was transmitted by me.

VYSHINSKY: You transmitted it?

BESSONOV: I transmitted it through Johannson in December 1936.

VYSHINSKY: On your arrival in Berlin?

BESSONOV: Yes, on my arrival in Berlin.

VYSHINSKY: You transmitted it through Johannson?

BESSONOV: Yes, through Johannson. And within a few days I received a reply from Trotsky.

VYSHINSKY: Did you acquaint yourself with this material?

BESSONOV: No, I do not know the reply.

VYSHINSKY: And are you acquainted with Krestinsky's letter?

BESSONOV: I read Krestinsky's letter because it was addressed to me. But I can only give a general impression because the letter was written in very vague language known only to Krestinsky and Trotsky, but not quite clear to me.

VYSHINSKY: What did you make of it?

BESSONOV: It said that the situation was such that the Trotskyites could not wait until the Germans got moving, and therefore they asked for permission to act before war broke out, before the Germans attacked, with the help of the centre which they had organized. What this centre was I can't say, because it was difficult to decipher the contents of this letter.

VYSHINSKY: What more would you like to add to your testimony, or have you completed your explanations?

BESSONOV: In reply to the last question asked, namely, who took the greatest part and with whom were the most systematic connections maintained, I must say that it was with Pyatakov, whom I regarded as my immediate chief along Trotskyite lines, and with whom I had meetings until the last time in December 1935, when he told me about his visit to Trotsky.

VYSHINSKY: Who were your immediate chiefs along Trotskyite lines?

BESSONOV: Only three men, with whom I communicated and who knew about my work—Pyatakov, Krestinsky, and Trotsky. Rosengoltz knew that I was a participant of the Trotskyite organization. In the autumn of 1931, when I was connected with

65

the German negotiations, mutual relations were established between Arkady Pavlovich Rosengoltz and myself such as could exist only between members of the Trotskyite organization. Moreover, Pyatakov recommended me to Rosengoltz as a member of the Trotskyite organization.

VYSHINSKY (to Rosengoltz): Accused Rosengoltz, did you know that Bessonov was a Trotskyite?

ROSENGOLTZ: No, I did not.

VYSHINSKY: Did not Pyatakov recommend him?

ROSENGOLTZ: I never talked to him on this subject.

VYSHINSKY: But did you know Bessonov was a Trotskyite?

ROSENGOLTZ: I knew it from Krestinsky.

VYSHINSKY: What did you learn from Krestinsky about Bessonov?

ROSENGOLTZ: I learnt that he was a Trotskyite and that he, Bessonov, helped Krestinsky in Trotskyite work.

VYSHINSKY: Who told you that?

ROSENGOLTZ: Krestinsky told me.

VYSHINSKY: Krestinsky personally?

ROSENGOLTZ: Yes, Krestinsky personally.

VYSHINSKY: Do you remember in what year it was?

ROSENGOLTZ: I cannot say exactly.

VYSHINSKY: Roughly, was it in 1933?

ROSENGOLTZ: Yes, roughly in that year.

VYSHINSKY: Under what circumstances did he tell you this and in what connection?

ROSENGOLTZ: He was telling me about the people in the People's Commissariat of Foreign Affairs who helped him in this work, and among them mentioned Bessonov.

VYSHINSKY: Accused Krestinsky, did you hear this testimony?

KRESTINSKY: I deny it.

VYSHINSKY: You deny it?

KRESTINSKY: I do.

VYSHINSKY: Absolutely?

KRESTINSKY: Absolutely.

VYSHINSKY: Of course.

KRESTINSKY: Of course.

VYSHINSKY. I have no further questions.

THE PRESIDENT: Adjournment for two hours.

[*Signed*] PRESIDENT: V. ULRICH

Army Military Jurist

*President of the Military Collegium of
the Supreme Court of the U.S.S.R.*

SECRETARY: A. BATNER

Military Jurist First Rank

EVENING SESSION, MARCH 2, 1938

COMMANDANT OF THE COURT: The Court is coming, please rise.

THE PRESIDENT: Be seated.

The session is resumed. Comrade Vyshinsky, have you any questions to put to Bessonov?

VYSHINSKY: Not to Bessonov.

THE PRESIDENT: Have the defence any questions to put to Bessonov?

COUNSEL FOR DEFENCE: (Reply in the negative.)

THE PRESIDENT: Have any of the accused questions to put to Bessonov? (Reply in the negative.)

We will proceed to the examination of the accused Grinko.

Accused Grinko, do you corroborate the testimony you gave at the preliminary investigation?

GRINKO: I corroborate it wholly and entirely.

THE PRESIDENT: What questions have you to put, Comrade Procurator?

VYSHINSKY: Accused Grinko, tell the Court about your criminal activities.

GRINKO: In order that the path by which I arrived at committing the enormous chain of crimes against the Soviet power and the country, at treason to the country, may be clear, I must recall that I joined the Communist Party as one of the Borotbists— the Ukrainian nationalist organization.[1] A large group of the leaders of the Borotbists: Shumsky, Poloz, Blakitny, I—Grinko —Lyubchenko, and others who merged with the Communist Party of the Ukraine, continued to adhere to and later intensified our bourgeois-nationalist position.

I can enumerate the main stages in the development of the nationalist, conspiratorial, counter-revolutionary work of this Borotbist nucleus.

The first stage was the period approximately of 1925-26. This is what is called the period of Shumsky-ism. Already at that time Shumsky-ism was in all essentials a program of severing the Ukraine from the U.S.S.R., a program of bourgeois-nationalist restoration in the Ukraine. Already at that time it was a sort of large-scale political reconnoitring by the nationalists,

67

a trial of strength, the demand to discredit Russian towns in the Ukraine, to discredit Russian cadres, etc.

Shumsky-ism was crushed politically and undermined organizationally.

The second stage...

VYSHINSKY: You must tell us more about this stage.

What steps did the Borotbist organization take in that period in the direction of foreign relations?

GRINKO: In that period no steps in this direction were taken. This applies to the second period.

VYSHINSKY: What years do you limit this period to?

GRINKO: 1925-26. All that was done in this period was that the connections between Shumsky and the capitalist elements of Western Ukraine were firmly established.

VYSHINSKY: Only with these elements?

GRINKO: Yes. But I know nothing about connections with the intelligence services and government circles of other states in that period.

VYSHINSKY: You did not maintain them?

GRINKO: No.

VYSHINSKY: The facts that you relate occurred in the period of 1926?

GRINKO: Yes.

VYSHINSKY: In your testimony you speak about reconnoitring. Was that nationalist reconnoitring?

GRINKO: The reconnoitring of the internal forces in the Ukraine which might support a nationalist action.

VYSHINSKY: Hence it was a trial of nationalist forces?

GRINKO: That is what I said.

VYSHINSKY: What year does the second period cover?

GRINKO: 1929-32.

VYSHINSKY: In the first period, was there any connection with the Rights?

GRINKO: There were no organizational connections with the Rights, but undoubtedly the fight which the Trotskyites and the Rights waged against the Party stimulated the nationalists. There were no organizational connections.

VYSHINSKY: Can we say that this was to a certain extent a self-contained nationalist organization?

GRINKO: Yes, but it had not yet taken definite shape.

VYSHINSKY: Did this organization come out on a wider arena?

GRINKO: It did, but in the next period.

VYSHINSKY: It did in the next period, from 1929-32 on. Will you please tell us about your line in foreign politics?

GRINKO: If the Court permits, I will deal with all my lines in foreign politics in a special section.

VYSHINSKY: As you please.

THE PRESIDENT: You may.

GRINKO: When this nationalist organization was smashed, only fragments of it remained. But about 1929 a nationalist organization revived again in Moscow, consisting of Shumsky, myself, Poloz, Maximovich, Solodub and a number of others. This organization approached its program and its tactics differently from the way it did in the first period. The relatively moderate position of the first period is to a certain extent to be explained by the ideas we then had, when the N.E.P. was at its height. We considered that the evolution of the N.E.P. in the direction we desired was not excluded. On the other hand, we did not see in Europe the forces in alliance with which we could advance more resolutely. In the second period the situation changed—this was the period of the wide Socialist offensive, when the positions of the capitalist elements in the country had been severely undermined, when the evolution of the N.E.P. towards capitalism was out of the question. Even the blind could see this. Then we gradually put out feelers for foreign political forces that could help us. In the second period the Ukrainian nationalist organization had entirely taken up the position of the Rights on general political questions, that is to say, the position of fighting industrialization and collectivization. Although the organization had no direct organizational connection with the Right organization in this period, I personally had contacts with a number of rather second-rate individuals in the Right camp.

VYSHINSKY: Did you have connections with Rykov at that time?

GRINKO: In that period I had no political connections with him. My connections with Rykov were established in a later period —the period when the national-fascist organization was created, with which I will deal later; this was in 1934-35. In this period the nationalist organization gave its members instructions to collect forces and wage an active struggle, mainly against collectivization, and even to go to the lengths of organizing insurrection. In this struggle we already had connections with certain circles in a certain state which is hostile to the Soviet Union. These allies of ours helped us. To assist the partisan struggle they intensified the smuggling of diversionists and Petliura emissaries, and arms, etc., into the Ukraine. This connection was maintained through Konar, through Kotsyubinsky. I don't know whether I ought to mention all these states here.

VYSHINSKY: No, mention them at the session to be held in camera.

THE PRESIDENT: And mention the names at the in camera session.

VYSHINSKY: Did you personally take part in organizing the smuggling of arms, etc.?

GRINKO: I was kept informed about the negotiations and gave my consent to them.

VYSHINSKY: Did you direct this business?

GRINKO: I did.

VYSHINSKY: Continue.

GRINKO: This period came to an end at the beginning of 1933 owing to the arrest of nearly the whole of this group. I was the only one not arrested. But I did not lay down my nationalist arms in my fight against the Soviet power. In this period my personal connections began with the fascist organizations abroad, with influential elements in the fascist organizations, and with certain government circles. The object of these connections was to establish contact for the purpose of preparing for the severance of the Ukraine from the U.S.S.R. and to organize the struggle against the Soviet power.

I will give the detailed facts and names at the in camera session. Here I will only say that these connections were established after a series of conversations I had with representatives of these hostile circles who occupied rather prominent official positions here in the U.S.S.R.

At the beginning of 1935 I heard from Lyubchenko about the creation in the Ukraine of a national-fascist organization, the object of which was to sever the Ukraine from the U.S.S.R., and which counted on receiving assistance in the shape of military intervention on the part of those forces and elements with whom I had already established personal contact at that time. The national-fascist organization also set itself the aim of uniting with the "bloc of Rights and Trotskyites," which had established contact with the military conspirators.

When I learnt about this organization I agreed to join it. I was commissioned to establish connections with the Right and Trotskyite centre and with government circles of certain states hostile to the Soviet power, and to help Lyubchenko to develop this work in the Ukraine.

At the time I joined it, the organization had already begun to crystallize itself as a national-socialist organization.

Lyubchenko told me about this organization's centre in the Ukraine, to which Lyubchenko, Poraiko and others belonged. He told me that at the centre the question was being discussed of the character of the party organization and the type of Ukrainian state to be established if the organization was successful. According to what Lyubchenko said the organization had taken the path of creating a centralized party after the type of the national-socialist party. In the event of success the organization intended to set up a bourgeois Ukrainian state after the type of the fascist state.

About this character of the organization I told a prominent member of the Right and Trotskyite conspiracy, Yakovlev.[3] In the Right and Trotskyite circles with whom I had occasion to speak, this tendency to transform our organization into a fascist type of organization undoubtedly existed.

How did I carry out the tasks that were entrusted to me by this national-fascist organization?

Firstly, connections with the Right and Trotskyite centre. I maintained these connections with Gamarnik,[4] Pyatakov and Rykov. I established connections with Gamarnik through Lyubchenko, who had connections with Yakir[5] and Gamarnik. Through Gamarnik I established connections with Pyatakov, and then with Rykov. Simultaneously I carried out tasks in foreign politics, in so far as Pyatakov and Gamarnik had told me that Trotsky had agreed to paying compensation at the expense of the Ukraine for the military assistance that we were to receive in our fight against the Soviet power.

Simultaneously with the establishment of connections with the "bloc of Rights and Trotskyites" I accelerated the establishment of connections with foreign forces through Krestinsky, with whom Pyatakov had connected me.

I established connections with Gamarnik, Pyatakov and Rykov about the end of 1935.

VYSHINSKY: Tell us about your connections with Rykov. What were these connections?

GRINKO: The connections were that the Ukrainian organization came under the command of the Right and Trotskyite centre.

VYSHINSKY: In what did it find expression?

GRINKO: It found expression firstly in that the Ukrainian organization received instructions from the Right and Trotskyite centre. I, as a member of this organization, received instructions...

VYSHINSKY: From whom did you receive instructions?

GRINKO: From Rykov.

VYSHINSKY: Whom else?

GRINKO: Mainly from Rykov.

VYSHINSKY: Very well. Proceed.

GRINKO: In 1935 and the beginning of 1936 I had, in the main, carried out the tasks entrusted to me by the Ukrainian organization. I had established connections with the Right and Trotskyite centre through Krestinsky and had established connections with fascist circles in a foreign state which accepted the point of view that we wanted. Through Krestinsky I conveyed the formula of our Ukrainian organization, and through him I received the reply that the forces concerned had accepted this formula. Having my old personal connections with fascist circles, I myself later on verified this fact and received confirmation.

VYSHINSKY: Permit me to dwell on this question. Hence, in 1935 you had already established connections with the Rights, as you state, in the person of the accused Rykov. Is that right?

GRINKO: Yes.

VYSHINSKY: With whom did you establish connections through Krestinsky?

GRINKO: With the fascist circles of a state hostile to the Soviet Union.

VYSHINSKY: With representatives of these circles? With representatives of fascist circles?

GRINKO: Yes.

VYSHINSKY: When was that?

GRINKO: At the end of 1935 and the beginning of 1936.

VYSHINSKY: But had you personally no connections with any fascist circles before 1935?

GRINKO: I had, from the end of 1932.

VYSHINSKY: Why did you have to resort to Krestinsky's assistance in 1935?

GRINKO: Because the Trotskyites had their line of connections in respect to the Ukraine. I considered that the official relations of this Ukrainian national-fascist organization should be established officially, through Krestinsky, so as to make sure that the same thing was being discussed, so as to avoid negotiations on one thing in one place and on another thing in another place.

VYSHINSKY: There was a certain amount of reinsurance here?

GRINKO: Yes, I really wanted to verify these connections with those I had personally.

VYSHINSKY: And you exposed Krestinsky?

GRINKO: No, I did not expose, I got confirmation. I had nothing exposing him.

VYSHINSKY: And not at this Court?

GRINKO: That is another matter.

VYSHINSKY: Have you exposed Krestinsky now?

GRINKO: Yes.

VYSHINSKY: Accused Krestinsky, did you hear this part of the evidence?

KRESTINSKY: Yes, I heard it. But I did not connect him with any fascists, I introduced him to business people.

VYSHINSKY: You did not connect, you "introduced"?

KRESTINSKY: Not to fascists.

72

VYSHINSKY: Then we need no names at the in camera session. Either you connected him or you did not connect him.

KRESTINSKY: I cannot tell you now.

VYSHINSKY: Of course, you deny it?

KRESTINSKY: I deny that I talked with fascists for Trotskyite purposes.

VYSHINSKY: You deny, but (to Grinko) you affirm. Perhaps, accused Grinko, you are confusing this with something else? Perhaps he introduced you to a pleasant gentleman, although a foreign gentleman, and you...

GRINKO: I think joking is out of place here.

VYSHINSKY: But that is how it works out.

GRINKO: I am surprised at what Krestinsky says.

VYSHINSKY: Can you, accused Grinko, say where the negotiations with Krestinsky took place?

GRINKO: I can say that they took place in my former office in the People's Commissariat of Finance.

VYSHINSKY (to Krestinsky): Did you visit Grinko in his office?

KRESTINSKY: I visited him quite often at different conferences.

VYSHINSKY: On financial affairs or the affairs of the People's Commissariat of Foreign Affairs?

KRESTINSKY: I visited him because I was appointed to some committee together with Grinko, a committee which dealt with the affairs of the People's Commissariat of Finance and of the People's Commissariat of Foreign Affairs.

VYSHINSKY: That was natural in your position.

GRINKO: I told Krestinsky that we held such-and-such a position, that Pyatakov had sent me, that I requested that this position be communicated and that I receive a reply. Krestinsky informed me that he had communicated this position and that this position had been accepted. And later on I myself, in the Grand Theatre, spoke with the person with whom Krestinsky had communicated.

VYSHINSKY: Will you be able to mention the names of these persons at the in camera session?

GRINKO: Of course.

VYSHINSKY: How do you explain the fact that Krestinsky is denying everything?

GRINKO: I cannot explain it.

VYSHINSKY: Besides this case, did you have any other talks with Krestinsky on questions concerning anti-Soviet activities?

GRINKO: There was the talk I mentioned at the morning session about utilizing valuta. I did not need much mediation as I had my own direct connections.

VYSHINSKY (to Rykov): Do you corroborate the part of the evidence in which Grinko refers to you?

RYKOV: Yes, I had two meetings with him. One at the end of 1935 and the other at the beginning of 1936.

VYSHINSKY: What was the nature of these meetings?

RYKOV: They were meetings of members of an illegal organization who were fighting the Party and the Soviet government.

VYSHINSKY: Did you have occasion to speak to Grinko about Krestinsky?

RYKOV: Not about Krestinsky. There was no need for me to speak about him because I knew without Grinko's telling me that Krestinsky was a Trotskyite. Similarly, Krestinsky knew that I was a member of the illegal organization.

VYSHINSKY: It follows then that Krestinsky is not telling the truth here and is trying to wriggle out of his connection with the Trotskyites?

RYKOV: Not only is he not telling the truth, but he wants to confuse the truth that has come out here.

VYSHINSKY: Accused Krestinsky, did you hear this?

KRESTINSKY: Yes, I heard it.

VYSHINSKY: Do you corroborate it?

KRESTINSKY: I do not corroborate that I am not telling the truth, and do not corroborate that I want to confuse the truth.

VYSHINSKY: I have a question to put to Krestinsky.

But you knew that Rykov was engaged in an underground struggle?

KRESTINSKY: No.

VYSHINSKY: You did not know?

KRESTINSKY: That is, I knew about it from the statements that were made at the Plenum of the Central Committee.

VYSHINSKY: Oh, only in that way?

KRESTINSKY: Only in that way.

VYSHINSKY: And what would you say, accused Rykov? How could he have learnt about the position you adhered to at that time?

RYKOV: In the first place, if at a Plenum of the Central Committee a statement is made about the illegal activities of a member of the Central Committee, that member of the Central Committee ceases to be a member of the Central Committee.

We had conversations on this subject, sufficiently frank conversations to know exactly who was speaking to whom. I think this was in 1932-33; I do not remember the exact date.

VYSHINSKY: Accused Rykov, do you corroborate that you knew that Krestinsky was a Trotskyite and a member of the bloc of Rights and Trotskyites?

RYKOV: That is, at that period such a complete bloc did not

exist, but that he was a member of the Trotskyite organization I knew.

VYSHINSKY: And he had conversations with you?

RYKOV: He conversed with me as a member of the illegal organization in the Party.

VYSHINSKY: You discussed matters of an illegal nature?

RYKOV: We discussed matters of an illegal nature.

VYSHINSKY: You assert that Krestinsky knew about your affairs in the illegal organization in the Party, but Krestinsky denies it; it follows then that Rykov is now not telling the truth and that you, accused Krestinsky, are telling the truth?

KRESTINSKY: I am telling the truth.

VYSHINSKY: And since when have you been telling the truth?

KRESTINSKY: On this matter?

VYSHINSKY: Yes.

KRESTINSKY: Today I am telling the truth.

THE PRESIDENT: Since 12 o'clock?

KRESTINSKY: Yes, in this Court.

VYSHINSKY: Very well, so it was with Rykov and Krestinsky. Proceed now, accused Grinko, and tell us please whether you knew that some of the others now in the dock were at that time members of your underground organization. Enumerate them.

GRINKO: I knew that Bukharin belonged to it.

VYSHINSKY: Accused Bukharin, do you corroborate this?

BUKHARIN: Yes, I do. I emphasize this because once I had a conversation with Grinko himself.

GRINKO: Yes, that is so.

VYSHINSKY: So Grinko is telling the truth?

BUKHARIN: Yes.

VYSHINSKY: You see, I am verifying this because Krestinsky says that the accused Grinko is wrong.

BUKHARIN: I added the correction simply in order to make things clear, because it is not that he might have known about my underground work from Rykov, but that I met Grinko personally.

GRINKO: That was later.

Then I learnt from Gamarnik about Rosengoltz's membership, and about his direct connections.

VYSHINSKY: Accused Rosengoltz, do you corroborate this?

ROSENGOLTZ: Yes.

VYSHINSKY: Proceed.

GRINKO: I knew about Zelensky's membership, and about his direct connections.

VYSHINSKY: Accused Zelensky, is the accused Grinko telling the truth?

ZELENSKY: The truth.

GRINKO: From Rykov I learnt that Yagoda belonged to this organization, but I had no direct connections with Yagoda.

VYSHINSKY (to the Court): Permit me to question Rykov. Accused Rykov, did you tell Grinko about this?

RYKOV: I do not remember exactly, but I cannot exclude such a fact.

VYSHINSKY: Hence, you told him about Yagoda's membership?

RYKOV: Yes.

VYSHINSKY (to the Court): Permit me to question Yagoda. Accused Yagoda, do you corroborate this?

YAGODA: Yes, as regards myself it is true, but that Grinko was a member I did not know.

VYSHINSKY: Permit me to question Krestinsky.

Accused Krestinsky, all the accused say that in regard to themselves the truth is being told; you say that it did not happen. Are you telling the truth?

KRESTINSKY: I am telling the truth.

VYSHINSKY: Today?

KRESTINSKY: Yes.

VYSHINSKY: Accused Grinko, continue your evidence.

GRINKO: Gradually extending my connections with the Right and Trotskyite centre, and having ascertained who belonged to it, I at the beginning of 1934 formed an opinion of what the "Right and Trotskyite centre" was.

From a number of conversations and connections, and the tasks I received from Rykov, Bukharin, Gamarnik, Rosengoltz, Yakovlev, Antipov, [6] Rudzutak, [7] Yagoda, Vareikis [8] and a number of other persons, it became clear to me that at that time the "Right and Trotskyite centre" based itself mainly on the military aid of aggressors. This was the common position of the Trotskyites, the Rights and the nationalist organizations, in particular of the Ukrainian nationalist organization. This meant undermining the power of defence of the Soviet Union, undermining activities in the army and in the defence industry, opening the front in the event of war and provoking this war; it meant extending connections with aggressive anti-Soviet elements abroad; it meant consenting to the dismemberment of the U.S.S.R. and compensating the aggressors at the expense of the border territories of the U.S.S.R.

In addition to this, the Right and Trotskyite centre had a plan to seize the Kremlin.

VYSHINSKY: What year was that?

GRINKO: This was discussed throughout the period of 1935-36. It was being discussed all the time. Perhaps even earlier. Terrorist inclinations, and not only terrorist inclinations but terrorist activities undoubtedly existed in the Right and Trot-skyite centre.

I know of two attempts to prepare terrorist acts which are not mentioned in the indictment, and which I must tell the Court.

VYSHINSKY: Tell us about the terrorist activities.

GRINKO: At that period terrorist activities were one of the main weapons in the common arsenal of struggle against the So-viet power.

VYSHINSKY: From whom did you learn this?

GRINKO: From Rykov, Yakovlev, Gamarnik and Pyatakov.

VYSHINSKY: And from the accused in the present case?

GRINKO: From Rykov I learnt that it was a terrorist organi-zation; when Rykov informed me of the character of this organi-zation he said that terrorism was included in the program.

VYSHINSKY (to Rykov): Accused Rykov, do you corroborate Grinko's evidence?

RYKOV: I do.

VYSHINSKY: Where did this terrorist line emanate from?

GRINKO: From Trotsky. I learnt this from Gamarnik.

VYSHINSKY: Tell us the concrete facts about preparations of terrorist acts that you personally know of.

GRINKO: I want to tell of two terrorist acts that were prepared but not carried out. These occurred in the last period, approxi-mately in the first half of 1937, which is connected with the be-ginning of the crushing of the conspiratorial organizations. After the trial of Pyatakov and the others, and particularly after the February-March Plenum of the Central Committee of the C.P.S.U. (Bolsheviks) in 1937, there was great consternation in the Right and Trotskyite centre. I was told about this at the time by Gamarnik, and he said that he had conferred with Rykov and Bukharin about this. It was then said that something extraor-dinary had to be done to shuffle the cards and to check the offensive that the Party and the People's Commissariat of Internal Affairs were then waging against the conspirators. After the February Plenum of the Central Committee a campaign was raised in the conspirators' circles against Yezhov, in whom the determination and unity of purpose of the Party to crush the conspirators was concentrated. In the Right and Trotskyite centre this campaign was waged along two lines: on the one hand, an attempt was made to discredit Yezhov and the work he was doing in the Party, to slander him. Also the question was bluntly raised of removing Yezhov as the man who was most dangerous to the conspirators.

VYSHINSKY: What does "removing" mean?

GRINKO: To remove means to kill.

VYSHINSKY: That is what you should have said.

GRINKO: I said "remove" because it had a double meaning: on the one hand to discredit Yezhov in the Party, to undermine his prestige, and on the other hand, to remove him physically.

VYSHINSKY: That I understand, but I was also interested to know what the word "remove" meant in the criminal sense.

GRINKO: To remove means to kill.

VYSHINSKY: And is that how you talked?

GRINKO: I had learnt from Gamarnik that Yakir and Gamarnik had instructed the Trotskyite Ozeryansky, who was then working in the People's Commissariat of Finance, to prepare a terrorist act against Yezhov.

VYSHINSKY: Ozeryansky was your immediate subordinate?

GRINKO: Yes.

VYSHINSKY: What was his position?

GRINKO: He was the Chief of the Department of Savings Banks.

VYSHINSKY: Did he belong to your organization?

GRINKO: Yes, he did. I learnt that from Gamarnik, but I had no direct connections with him in preparing the terrorist act.

VYSHINSKY: But in other counter-revolutionary matters?

GRINKO: I had connections with him in undermining activities in the People's Commissariat of Finance.

VYSHINSKY: Ozeryansky is a suitable man for this sort of crime, is he not?

GRINKO: He is a fighter, a former anarchist. . . .

VYSHINSKY: And a cut-throat?

GRINKO: He is capable of such things.

The second fact that I know, and which occurred in the same period, is the preparation by Bergavinov, from the Head Office of the Northern Sea Route, of a terrorist act against Stalin. This I also learnt from Gamarnik. Antipov and Yakovlev knew about this, and I heard it from Bergavinov himself, who told me that he had accepted Gamarnik's commission and that he was trying to carry it out.

One of the tasks set me by the Right and Trotskyite centre was to organize undermining activities in the People's Commissariat of Finance. I gave detailed testimony on this during the preliminary investigation. Here I will deal only with the main lines and moments of these undermining activities.

This task of the Right and Trotskyite centre was conveyed to me by Rykov, and in doing so he emphasized that the leadership of the centre, he and Bukharin, attached great importance to the development of undermining activities in the People's Commissariat of Finance in view of the special importance and political significance of money. At the same time he gave me Bukharin's formula: strike at the Soviet government with the Soviet ruble. This was conveyed to me by Rykov, and I also discussed it with Bukharin. It must be said that the Right and Trotskyite centre attached so much importance to this task that Rykov came to see me about it at the People's Commissariat of Finance and we jointly drew up a program of measures for it.

Wrecking activities were to be carried on in connection with those financial measures that are connected with the broad masses of the population: taxes, savings banks, loans, etc. The program was drawn up by Rykov and myself. The wrecking activities were developed through my Assistant Commissar, Levin, through Ozeryansky, through Chetverikov and several others.

For example, in regard to taxes. The distortions which found most striking expression in the Lepel case in Byelorussia were part of these undermining measures. And the reason why the exposure of the Lepel case was not turned sharply against the People's Commissariat of Finance at that time was that Yakovlev went there to expose this case, and he warded off the blow from the People's Commissariat of Finance.

In regard to savings banks, two measures were adopted: the reduction in the number of savings banks; and the other in connection with borrowing on state loan bonds. The reduced number of savings banks was not prepared for this wide measure, and as this operation was connected with a service affecting tens of millions of people, it caused irritation among broad masses of the population.

Considerable undermining work was carried out in the sphere of the state budget. This work was directed towards undermining budget finance discipline, loosening financial control and thereby creating possibilities for utilizing state funds at the centre and in the periphery, for the purposes of the conspiracy. All this work on the instructions given me by the Right and Trotskyite centre I carried out through a number of people working on the staff of the People's Commissariat of Finance.

The undermining activities were not limited to this, however. From the Right and Trotskyite centre I received instructions to utilize the finances for the purpose of assisting undermining activities in a number of other branches of the national economy. For example, the Right and Trotskyite centre drew up a rather big program of undermining activities in capital construction. Pyatakov, I think Bukharin, and I took part in drawing up this program. The object of this program was to slow down capital construction, to reduce the scale of capital construction and fully to apply Bukharin's "bottleneck" theory in capital construction, the more so that capital construction is important not only as a most important branch of the national economy but also is of enormous defence importance. [9]

I also participated in undermining activities in the sphere of agriculture by carrying out wrecking financial measures. Undermining activities in the sphere of agriculture were regarded by the Right and Trotskyite centre as a very important task.

Stalin had urged collectivization as the decisive means of overcoming the backwardness of agriculture. On the basis of the successes achieved in collectivization the task was set of achieving a harvest of 7-8 billion poods per annum. The Right and Trotskyite centre drew up a plan of undermining measures which, had they been successful, would at all events have delayed, if not prevented, the obtaining of harvests amounting to 7-8 billion poods. In particular, Rykov put the question in the following way: things must be so arranged that the collective farmer shall receive as little as possible for his workday. From the point of view of the political preparations for the anti-Soviet struggle, this was of enormous significance, the more so that the question of grain reserves is of enormous defence significance, which was also taken into consideration by the Right and Trotskyite centre when the program was drawn up.

In carrying out the wrecking measures and wrecking instructions in the financing of agriculture, no little assistance was rendered by Rudzutak, who was in charge of financial affairs in the Council of People's Commissars, and by Yakovlev.

I think I have said what is fundamental and most important about general political matters. Thus, I would like to say that here, before the Supreme Court of the Soviet Union, I must answer and do answer for a long chain of heinous crimes against the Soviet power, and for a most acute struggle against the Soviet power, firstly as one of the participants in the nationalist counter-revolutionary struggle in the Ukraine, which, after passing through a number of stages, degenerated into a national-fascist organization, of which I was one of the leaders, and as one of the members of the bloc of Rights and Trotskyites, who did not confine himself only to working in the national-fascist organization in the Ukraine but, having started with connections with the bloc of Rights and Trotskyites, was drawn by the latter into wider work in conspiratorial Right and Trotskyite activities; at the same time I answer for treason to the country and for those direct connections with influential circles in certain fascist states which were established for the purpose of fulfilling the tasks of the bloc of Rights and Trotskyites, of overthrowing the Soviet power and of severing from the U.S.S.R. a number of regions.

I plead guilty wholly and entirely, and I need not add that I do not in the least intend in my testimony to minimize my guilt.

THE PRESIDENT: Has anyone else any questions to put to the accused Grinko?

VYSHINSKY: I would like to clear up several questions.

Firstly, do you know, accused Grinko, about the wrecking activities of the bloc of Rights and Trotskyites in the sphere of supplying the population with articles of prime necessity—bread, etc.?

GRINKO: Along with wrecking activities in the sphere of capital construction and agriculture, the bloc of Rights and Trotskyites carried on quite extensive undermining activities in the sphere of trade turnover. In this sphere I had direct connections with Zelensky.

VYSHINSKY: Did you establish these connections directly with Zelensky on your own initiative, on his initiative, or on the instructions of other persons?

GRINKO: I find it hard to say, I cannot say definitely, but I think the connections were established without intermediaries, it was on my own initiative. There was an intervening link here. Gamarnik put me in touch with Zelensky's assistant, Mayorov, who connected me with him. But most likely I established connections with him myself. I will recall it later on and tell you exactly.

VYSHINSKY: What crimes were committed in this sphere?

GRINKO: In the sphere of trade turnover Zelensky and other wreckers in this sphere, for example Bolotin in the People's Commissariat of Internal Trade, carried on undermining activities, created a shortage of goods, goods difficulties in the country. This applies to provisions as well as to articles of prime necessity. For example, the proper territorial distribution of goods in conformity with the size of the harvest, with the purchasing capacity of the population, the prosperity of the population in the different regions is of enormous importance. Zelensky, on the instructions of the bloc of Rights and Trotskyites, sent huge quantities of goods to the districts where there was a poor harvest and smaller quantities of goods to the districts where there were good harvests, and this caused goods to remain on the shelves in some districts and a shortage of goods in others.

VYSHINSKY: How do you know that Zelensky did these things?

GRINKO: I know it from Zelensky himself; and with Rykov too we spoke of such measures as having been and being carried out expediently—from the point of view of the conspiratorial organization, of course.

VYSHINSKY: Hence, you personally knew it from Zelensky as well as from . . .

GRINKO: As well as from Rykov and Bolotin.

VYSHINSKY: So you assert this not groundlessly but you base it on hard facts.

GRINKO: Of course.

VYSHINSKY: Zelensky, did you hear this part of Grinko's evidence? What do you think about it?

ZELENSKY: Grinko is telling the truth.

VYSHINSKY: Accused Rykov, what do you say?

RYKOV: I must deny part of it. If it is about Zelensky, I did not say it.

VYSHINSKY: Not about Zelensky, but about the fact, about wrecking activities in trade turnover.

RYKOV: I did not speak to him about this in such detail. We spoke about wrecking in general; as for my drawing up a definite plan of wrecking in the People's Commissariat of Finance, that is not the case.

VYSHINSKY: What do you remember?

RYKOV: I remember that there was talk about overthrowing the Soviet government. I remember that just at that time the trial of wreckers was taking place in Siberia. At this trial wreckers were discovered, were caught. I said to Grinko that it was more difficult to catch wreckers in the sphere of finance.

VYSHINSKY: That was a theoretical conversation?

RYKOV: No, we talked like two men who recognized wrecking as one of the methods of counter-revolutionary activity.

VYSHINSKY: That is, you talked as two members of a wreckers' organization?

RYKOV: Yes.

VYSHINSKY: About wrecking which ought to be done in such-and-such a manner.

RYKOV: Yes, yes, there is no doubt about that.

VYSHINSKY: And you remember that?

RYKOV: Yes.

VYSHINSKY: But you do not remember the details of your conversation?

RYKOV: About drawing up a plan or program of wrecking in the People's Commissariat of Finance—that I do not remember.

VYSHINSKY: That in principle it was necessary to do wrecking, to affect the most acute problems?

RYKOV: No, I do not remember this.

VYSHINSKY: And you, Grinko, do you remember?

GRINKO: I will remind him. Rykov, you came to me in the People's Commissariat of Finance on the question of extending the network of village post offices (you were then People's Commissar of Post and Telegraph). After we had finished the, so to speak, legal part, you stayed on and we had a general political talk—about Ukrainian affairs, and about the connections between the Ukrainian underground organizations and the Right and Trotskyite centre. You then said that wrecking in the sphere of finance was lagging.

VYSHINSKY: You say that the accused Rykov spoke about the People's Commissariat of Finance lagging, but in what?

GRINKO: In wrecking activities.

VYSHINSKY: Rykov said that you were wrecking badly?

GRINKO: It was then that we agreed on the main lines along which the work was to be developed.

VYSHINSKY: Accused Rykov, do you corroborate this conversation with Grinko about wrecking?

RYKOV: I don't accept that. I deny it, but not because I want to minimize my guilt. I have done much worse things than this.

VYSHINSKY: But do you remember the conversation about wrecking?

RYKOV: Yes.

VYSHINSKY: And about it being difficult to catch people in this sphere. But you preferred to do wrecking where it was difficult to catch people, and not where it was easy to catch them?

RYKOV: A wrecker cannot always take this into consideration.

VYSHINSKY: Do you plead guilty to the charge of wrecking?

RYKOV: Yes.

VYSHINSKY: At all events you discussed wrecking with Grinko in respect to possible converging wrecking measures, that is to say, criminal deeds.

RYKOV: In respect to this measure being necessary and it being one of the necessary measures in the fight against the Soviet power.

VYSHINSKY: Hence, Grinko had a right to say that Rykov sufficiently instructed him as to the direction of wrecking.

RYKOV: Here we could not instruct each other because there was no disagreement between us.

VYSHINSKY: But in the sphere of the People's Commissariat of Finance, did Grinko need your instruction as a wrecker, or did he know what to do himself?

RYKOV: I will speak about this in my testimony. We had this talk at the beginning of 1936, but he enumerated a number of things which, if they had taken place, would have taken place much earlier. One could judge of the results by the budget, but the results of the budget were known after my arrest, that is, the 1937 budget.

VYSHINSKY: You do not accept the formula that was mentioned here—strike at the Soviet government with the Soviet ruble?

RYKOV: I did not say that.

VYSHINSKY: But that was the task that was set?

RYKOV: I remember what he said about the Clemenceau thesis.

VYSHINSKY: Did Clemenceau also want to strike anybody with the Soviet ruble?

RYKOV: At one time the Clemenceau thesis was known as the formulation of the desire for a change of government.

VYSHINSKY: That is understandable in regard to the Clemenceau thesis; but what relation has it to wrecking work in the sphere of the People's Commissariat of Finance?

RYKOV: It has no direct relation to wrecking work. It is one of the violent forms.[10]

VYSHINSKY: Grinko spoke here about the military group of traitors—Tukhachevsky and others, who some time ago were convicted by the Supreme Court. Do you corroborate the part of this evidence that concerns you?

RYKOV: I knew about Tukhachevsky's military group.

VYSHINSKY: What did you know?

RYKOV: This military group was organized independently of the bloc, independently of shades—Trotskyite or Bukharinite. The military group set itself the object of violently removing the government of the Union and, in particular, it took part in the preparations for a Kremlin coup.

VYSHINSKY: You were aware of that?

RYKOV: Yes.

VYSHINSKY: When did you learn of it?

RYKOV: I learnt of it from Tomsky in 1934.

VYSHINSKY: In 1934?

RYKOV: Probably.

VYSHINSKY: Does this part of Grinko's evidence correspond with the truth?

RYKOV: Yes.

VYSHINSKY: Accused Grinko, in regard to the harvest, what conversations did you have with Rykov? Make it more precise.

GRINKO: The talk I had with Rykov was to the effect that the "Right and Trotskyite centre" attached enormous importance to the development of undermining measures in the sphere of agriculture, which is emphasized by Rykov himself, that it was Bukharin's point of view, and followed from the following postulate: collectivization should result in the removal of the contradiction between the level of industrial development of the country and the level of development of agriculture, a removal which is absolutely necessary for the further rapid rate of Socialist construction. On the other hand, there was the enormous program of 7-8 billion poods of grain, which would solve the question of the prosperity of the rural districts and of removing the differences between town and country.[11] This program was making considerable progress, and this was of enormous importance from the point of view of the defence of the Soviet Union in respect to creating grain reserves.

Rykov said that he knew about the program of the "Right and Trotskyite centre," and that undermining work must be developed to the full.

VYSHINSKY: What interests me is the question, why Rykov found it necessary to talk to you on this question?

GRINKO: I told Rykov that when I had established the connections of the Ukrainian organizations we would inevitably have to take up all the principal political questions. We had an exchange of opinion which was informative. My wrecking work in the People's Commissariat of Finance was the next supplement to this general political connection. On the other hand, I at one time had worked in the People's Commissariat of Agriculture, had been Assistant People's Commissar, and I had personal connections. For agriculture, for the machine and tractor stations, for the collective farms, etc., the whole mechanism of finance is of enormous importance, and it was in this connection that Rykov spoke to me, related the undermining measures in agriculture and advised me what to do in this respect.

VYSHINSKY: Accused Grinko, did you have occasion to speak to Bukharin?

GRINKO: I had a short talk with Bukharin in the Kremlin about the principle basis of undermining measures in the sphere of finance, a talk about the hostility of the bloc of Rights and Trotskyites towards the Franco-Soviet Treaty.

VYSHINSKY: Did not Bukharin explain to you why he was dissatisfied with the Franco-Soviet Treaty? [12]

GRINKO: I will speak about that later. Then, as we were walking in the corridor we talked generally about whether wrecking was permissible as a method of political struggle, because it caused enormous economic loss; but he said that in so far as politics predominated in this case wrecking was permissible; on the other hand, the establishment of wider economic connections with the capitalist world would create possibilities for making good the loss caused by wrecking.

As for the Franco-Soviet Treaty, in the Right and Trotskyite centre (I had a talk with Rykov and with Bukharin about this) there was fairly widespread hostility to the Franco-Soviet Treaty because the Franco-Soviet Treaty was one of the stages in the peace policy of the Soviet power which removed or postponed the clash with the aggressor, the clash on which the bloc of Rights and Trotskyites had put their stake; the annulment of the Franco-Soviet Treaty for the purpose of unleashing opportunities for the aggressor was part of the program of the bloc of Rights and Trotskyites.

VYSHINSKY: Tell us in greater detail about the defeatist line of the bloc of Rights and Trotskyites.

GRINKO: The first talks I had with a number of the leading members of the bloc of Rights and Trotskyites showed me that the principal political stake—if we are to speak concretely and not in general—was put on the defeat of the Soviet Union in a war with an aggressor, on compensating the aggressor at the expense of the border territories of the Soviet Union, and on the overthrow of the Soviet government in the course of this. In addition, as I have already stated, I can recall, for example, that when I told Rykov some of the details connected with the sale of the Chinese Eastern Railway . [13]

VYSHINSKY: Don't forget that we shall have an in camera session of the Court.

GRINKO: I am not forgetting. We had an exchange of remarks as a result of which it was clear that this was the elimination of one of the causes of the possible war with Japan which had entered into the plans of the bloc of Rights and Trotskyites.

VYSHINSKY: Hence, the bloc of Rights and Trotskyites orientated themselves towards war.

GRINKO: Yes, towards war, towards the military defeat of the Soviet Union, and the assistance of the aggressor in seizing power.

VYSHINSKY: Orientation towards military defeat and the assistance of the aggressor in seizing power.

GRINKO: Yes.

VYSHINSKY: Apart from Rykov, did you work out the plans for these crimes with anyone else?

GRINKO: From among those participating in the present trial?

VYSHINSKY: Yes. From among those now in the dock.

GRINKO: From among the accused in the present case—I do not remember.

VYSHINSKY: And so you discussed this with Rykov?

GRINKO: Yes, with Rykov, and the Franco-Soviet Treaty with Bukharin.

VYSHINSKY: And Rosengoltz?

GRINKO: It was Gamarnik who put me in touch with Rosengoltz. This fact alone shows that this is connected with some of the military Trotskyite plans; but with Rosengoltz I discussed mainly the measures, the undermining activities, which he was carrying out in the sphere of foreign trade.

This is the economic aspect of the same defeatist position, in so far as Rosengoltz was carrying out measures for the purpose of helping the aggressor at the expense of the Soviet Union.

86

VYSHINSKY: In short, in Rosengoltz's criminal activities there were the same defeatist motives as in your activities?

GRINKO: They lay at the base of everything.

VYSHINSKY: So we can say that it is not only Rykov and Bukharin, but also Rosengoltz. I have one more question. Did you know about the Tukhachevsky plot, and if so, from whom?

GRINKO: From Gamarnik.

VYSHINSKY: And who of the participants in this trial, of the accused in the dock, besides Rykov, knew about this plot?

GRINKO: Rosengoltz knew.

VYSHINSKY: And who else?

GRINKO: From what Rykov said, Bukharin knew.

VYSHINSKY: And who else?

GRINKO: No one else. I did not have connections with them all. I think Yagoda knew. . . .

VYSHINSKY: You think, or did anybody tell you? Why do you think with such insight?

GRINKO: Because of the talks about Yagoda which I had with Rykov.

VYSHINSKY: Naturally, you are speaking very cautiously in order not to say too much.

GRINKO: Generally, Rykov spoke about Yagoda mostly in hints.

VYSHINSKY: Thus the people who were informed about the Tukhachevsky plot and about the connection between the bloc of Rights and Trotskyites with Tukhachevsky's conspiratorial group were, besides yourself, Rykov, Rosengoltz, Bukharin, and, you take it, Yagoda?

GRINKO: Yes, and a number of other people who are not now in the dock.

VYSHINSKY: I am referring to the people who are participants in the present trial.

I have no more questions.

GRINKO: I would like to say two words in conclusion.

THE PRESIDENT: You may.

GRINKO: I could and should qualify the testimony I gave at the preliminary investigation, on the one hand, as an exposure of myself, because this testimony was given after my arrest; but at the same time, in the process of giving this testimony, in the process of all that I felt in the course of the preliminary investigation, this testimony was also my repentance. I would like to emphasize in concluding my evidence that I answer here as one who is exposed, but at the same time I answer as a traitor to his country who has repented of his crimes.

THE PRESIDENT: Adjournment for 20 minutes.

*   *   *

87

COMMANDANT OF THE COURT: The Court is coming, please rise.

THE PRESIDENT (to Vyshinsky): Have you any more questions to put to the accused Grinko?

VYSHINSKY: No.

THE PRESIDENT: Have the defence any questions?

COUNSEL FOR DEFENCE: (Reply in the negative.)

THE PRESIDENT: Have the accused any questions?

THE ACCUSED: (Reply in the negative.)

THE PRESIDENT: Accused Chernov, do you corroborate the testimony you gave during examination in the course of the preliminary investigation?

CHERNOV: I corroborate it wholly and entirely.

THE PRESIDENT (to Vyshinsky): Do you desire to put any questions?

VYSHINSKY: Accused Chernov, briefly tell the Court your biography.

CHERNOV: I was born in 1891. For two years I studied at the Ecclesiastical Seminary. I entered the Moscow University, where I studied for about two years. Once I was arrested for revolutionary activities, but I was not imprisoned. In 1916 I joined the Menshevik Party and remained a Menshevik until January 1920, when I joined the Communist Party (Bolsheviks).

VYSHINSKY: That was formally?

CHERNOV: Yes.

VYSHINSKY: But actually?

CHERNOV: After joining the Communist Party (Bolsheviks) in January 1920, I up to 1927 honestly carried out all the duties the Party imposed upon me.

VYSHINSKY: Up to 1927?

CHERNOV: Yes. But I must frankly confess that I undoubtedly preserved my old Menshevik nature, and as soon as the Party passed from the restricting method to the method of an offensive against the kulak elements in the rural districts, this Menshevik nature immediately asserted itself.

VYSHINSKY: How did this find expression, in what way did the Menshevik nature assert itself?

CHERNOV: In the autumn of 1927 definite doubts began to arise in my mind about the correctness of the Party's general line.

VYSHINSKY: What did it lead to?

CHERNOV: I was at that time People's Commissar of Trade of the Ukraine and was in charge of grain collections. And grain was precisely the whetstone that served most to sharpen the resistance and struggle of the kulaks against the Soviet power. That autumn Vyacheslav Mikhailovich Molotov came to the Ukraine and put the question of grain collections to the Central Committee of the Ukraine, and to us who were working on grain collections, in an entirely new way. Before that the method on which grain collections were based was free purchase and sale. This suited my Menshevik nature. But now we were told to adopt extraordinary measures against the rich kulak upper stratum of the rural population. This was the beginning of the decisive offensive against the kulaks. I considered this wrong, and that it would lead to the ruin of agriculture and to a reduction in the marketable surplus of agricultural produce. And that is when my doubts began.

VYSHINSKY: And I am asking you—what did your doubts lead to?

CHERNOV: These doubts were fortified in 1928. In 1928 there was a bad harvest in the Ukraine, and I did not attribute this bad harvest to weather conditions, which were the real cause—there had been a bad winter and a bad spring that year in the Ukraine, which had ruined the crop—but considered that this bad harvest was an organic, and not an accidental phenomenon, caused by the adoption of extraordinary measures in the grain collections, inasmuch as these extraordinary measures, in my opinion, had killed in the peasants, including the middle peasants, all interest in the development of their farms, in the care of the crops, in the better cultivation of the soil, and so on. I did not keep these doubts, which had already become fortified in 1928, to myself, but expressed them to the people I worked with, and sought supporters of my views among them. [14]

VYSHINSKY: And did you find them?
CHERNOV: I did.
VYSHINSKY: Who were they?

CHERNOV: Goldin—he was chairman of the Ukrainian Grain Department; then there was Vasiliev, who worked in the Ukrainian Agricultural Co-operative Society, and a number of people with whom I then worked in the sphere of grain collections in the Ukraine. And, in addition, I found that similar views were held by people who were not directly connected with me in the sphere of grain collections, but who often conversed with me as the man that headed the grain-collection work and knew the situation in the country-side, and who also expressed their dissatisfaction with the rural policy of the Central Committee. Among them were Zatonsky, Poraiko, Grinko and a number of other persons, all of whom I cannot now recall.

VYSHINSKY: What year was that?
CHERNOV: That was in 1928.

VYSHINSKY: Were you a member of the illegal organization of the Rights in 1928?

CHERNOV: I consider that inasmuch as I expressed my views to those who held like opinions and who expressed dissatisfaction with the policy of the Party, that was already the beginning of the attempt to create such an organization in the Ukraine; but I consider that I formally joined the organization of the Rights after my first meeting with Rykov.

VYSHINSKY: You were drawn into this organization by Rykov?

CHERNOV: Yes, but I was already prepared for it.

VYSHINSKY: You found each other, in fact?

CHERNOV: Yes, you can put it that way. I met Rykov in the autumn of 1928.

At the request of Mikoyan,[15] People's Commissar of Trade of the U.S.S.R., I was to go to Mukhalatka, to the sanatorium in the Crimea where Mikoyan was spending his vacation, to report on my work as People's Commissar of Trade of the Ukraine. Alexei Ivanovich Rykov was there at the same time, as I had learnt, incidentally. Among those who shared my views, the idea was discussed that it would be a good thing if one of us were to see Rykov and to discuss with him the questions we had been talking about in the Ukraine, which I have just mentioned. I decided to take advantage of Rykov's stay in Mukhalatka, and we met. At our meeting I informed Rykov of the state of affairs in the Ukrainian villages, of the bad harvest in the Ukraine, and of the impoverishment which was to be observed in the Ukrainian villages. Rykov was particularly interested in the distortions of policy which were taking place, which had occurred in some instances in the grain-collection work, and I told him of these instances. Then, I recall, after I had given my information and had told of the individual instances of distortion, Rykov said: "You think that these are individual cases of stupidity on the part of the grain-collection apparatus? You are mistaken. It is a result of the policy of the Central Committee of the Party, which is leading to the ruin of the countryside and of agriculture."

VYSHINSKY: Well, and how did you react?

CHERNOV: I reacted to this by greater boldness in expressing to him the doubts of which I have just told the Court. Rykov explained to me the views of the Rights on this question: that is, not only on this question, but the views and program of the Rights, which were opposed to collectivization and to the industrialization of the country.

During this meeting I told Rykov that there were people who shared my views in the Ukraine. Rykov replied that all these people were known, that the majority of them were known to him and could be of great assistance to the cause of the Right organization. But, he said, you should not act on too broad lines just now and thus divulge your forces. The time for broad action has not yet arrived. You must know, he said, how the Central Committee demolished the Trotskyites, and if we were to disclose our forces already it would react unfavourably on our Right organization.

I thereupon said to Rykov that if I understood him rightly we must create a secret underground organization. This he confirmed, adding moreover that I, Chernov, was People's Commissar of Trade of the Ukraine and occupied a very important post. My task, he said, was to conduct my work in such a way as to incense the middle peasants by extending to them the repressive measures which the government had laid down for the kulaks. I was to accentuate the distortions of policy, to incense the middle peasants, to take special account of the national feelings of the Ukrainian population and to explain everywhere that these distortions were a result of the policy of Moscow; and in this way we would both create our cadres and at the same time rouse the peasants against the Soviet government and the Central Committee. In conclusion, Rykov and I agreed that when I came to Moscow I should come and see him and maintain contact with him for the purpose of co-ordinating the actions of the Right organization in the Ukraine.

VYSHINSKY: Accused Rykov, tell us, does this part of what Chernov says correspond with the facts?

RYKOV: I met Chernov and tried to convince him of the correctness of my counter-revolutionary activities at that time. I intended to make him my follower, but I found a ready-made follower in Chernov.

VYSHINSKY: You did not have to try very hard?

RYKOV: On the contrary, I did not have to try at all.

I cannot relate things with the detail he does. All that he says is essentially and fundamentally true, but as to the part in which he said that I was in favour of distortions, it seems to me he is wrong. In everything else he is right.[16]

VYSHINSKY: Well, let us speak about everything else.

Did Chernov really come to see you in 1928, and did he really put before you, as one of the leaders of the Right trend—let us put it that way—of that time, a number of questions of a political nature, and did you elucidate these questions from your standpoint, calculating on inducing him to join your group? Did you already at that time have a group of Rights acting on an underground footing?

RYKOV: No, not on an underground footing.

VYSHINSKY: But the group had already been formed?

91

RYKOV: Yes. It could only be a question of creating such a type of organizational kernel, semi-legal.

VYSHINSKY: And so there was a semi-legal group headed by you. And by who else? Bukharin and Tomsky? Is that right?

RYKOV: Yes, there was such a group.

VYSHINSKY: And you decided to draw Chernov into this group?

RYKOV: Yes, I found a supporter in Chernov. When I was in Mukhalatka in 1928, I did not know what Chernov's position was on this question, and I tried, so to speak, to convince him, to win him over. It was a surprise to me at the time to find a ready-made supporter in Chernov.

VYSHINSKY: You found a ready-made partner. And did you meet Chernov after that?

RYKOV: Yes.

VYSHINSKY: In what year?

RYKOV: Several months later, when he was about to go abroad.

VYSHINSKY: Accused Chernov, is this correct?

CHERNOV: No, I met him several times. I confirm that I met Rykov before leaving for abroad, but I would add that this was not the only meeting and that there were several other meetings, about which I can tell if the Court wishes.

VYSHINSKY: If it has any relation to the subject of the accusation. Meanwhile, accused Rykov, you may sit down.

CHERNOV: I once more affirm—Alexei Ivanovich has forgotten it apparently, but I remember it very well, and I remember how it was expressed. I cannot vouch for every word, but only for the contents and construction of Rykov's phrases: it was to the effect that I must organize my work in such a way as to accentuate the distortions of policy and thus incense the middle peasants, and that in my work as a member of the Right organization I was to take account of the nationalist sentiments of the Ukrainian population. That I remember very well.

VYSHINSKY: We can go into that later. The question at present is your conspiratorial connections with Rykov. Continue.

CHERNOV: The subsequent character of my activities was somewhat modified by the fact that I had previously counted on working in the Ukraine, but was then transferred to other work in Moscow.

I now pass to the next episode. At the end of 1928 I was about to go to Germany for a cure. Knowing that an old comrade of mine in the Menshevik organization was living in Germany, I decided to see him.

VYSHINSKY: Who was that?

92

CHERNOV: Kibrik, with whom I had corresponded until 1925, and who was living in Germany under another name.

Before leaving for Germany I decided to see Rykov in Moscow.

VYSHINSKY: Why did you go to Rykov?

CHERNOV: Because I had arranged with him that we were to co-ordinate our actions as members of the Right organization, and also to find out whether he had any commissions to give me in Germany.

VYSHINSKY: Commissions in relation to . . . underground work?

CHERNOV: I was not thinking of that.

VYSHINSKY: Commissions along what lines?

CHERNOV: Before my conversation with Rykov I did not know what the commissions would be.

VYSHINSKY: You just thought to yourself: I am going abroad, what commissions will there be—legal or illegal?

CHERNOV: I was not thinking of that.

VYSHINSKY: Whether there would be commissions along underground lines?

CHERNOV: In connection with the Right organization.

VYSHINSKY: In connection with the Right organization.

CHERNOV: I telephoned Rykov's secretary—Nesterov, I think it was—and told him that I was going abroad and that I wanted to speak to Rykov about foreign exchange matters, about the rise in foreign exchange, expecting that Rykov would understand me and receive me. I telephoned his secretary and did indeed get an appointment with Rykov.

During this meeting with Rykov I informed him about conditions in the Ukrainian countryside and how the grain collections were proceeding. I told him that I was leaving for Germany, and asked him if he had any commissions to give me. Knowing that I was an old Menshevik, Rykov asked me whether I could not get to see Dan while I was in Germany, establish connections with him and transmit a message from the Right centre. I told Rykov that I might be able to do this and that I thought that I might be assisted in this by my comrade in Menshevik work. This was Kibrik, of whom I have just spoken. Rykov then commissioned me to get in touch with Dan and to convey to him a message from the Right centre.

VYSHINSKY: What message?

CHERNOV: I forgot to say that Tomsky was present during my conversation with Rykov. The message was as follows: through the parties of the Second International to rouse the public opinion of capitalist countries against the Soviet government; through the leaders of the Second International to get the bourgeois governments to intensify the hostile attitude towards the Soviet

93

Union; to secure from the Second International and, through its leaders, from bourgeois governments, a pledge of support in the event of the seizure of power by the Rights in the country. I told Rykov that it would not be enough to convey only these messages to Dan. Dan would undoubtedly raise a number of questions about the strength of the Right organization and about what the Right organization would do after it came to power. To this Rykov replied: "You may assure Dan that we possess enough forces in the country to overthrow the existing government and to seize the power." He particularly stressed the point that we possessed these forces also among prominent and responsible military men. The second thing he mentioned was that I could declare to Dan that after the Rights came to power they would establish a government that would take into account the demands both of the Second International and of the bourgeois governments, and would consent to an arrangement with the bourgeois governments both on economic questions and, if necessary, on territorial questions. I distinctly remember that Tomsky, who was present during this conversation, stated that the anti-Soviet parties did not exist formally, but were actually working and striving for the overthrow of the Soviet power. He said that we must not only utilize them but also give them a share in the government of the state.

VYSHINSKY: Accused Rykov, did you see Chernov before he left for Berlin?

RYKOV: Yes.

VYSHINSKY: Did you speak to Chernov in Tomsky's presence, or in private?

RYKOV: In Tomsky's presence.

VYSHINSKY: Did you commission Chernov to get in touch with Dan in Berlin?

RYKOV: Yes.

VYSHINSKY: With what purpose?

RYKOV: As far as I can recall there were two: firstly, to get the foreign press to write about the situation in the countryside, the discontent of the peasants....

VYSHINSKY: Which press?

RYKOV: The foreign press.

VYSHINSKY: Which exactly?

RYKOV: I did not enumerate parties or newspapers; I had both the Socialist and bourgeois press in mind.

VYSHINSKY: And the Menshevik press?

RYKOV: Yes.

VYSHINSKY: Perhaps the "Sotsialistichesky Vestnik" especially. [17]

RYKOV: It, in particular.

VYSHINSKY: By the way, did you generally during this period contribute to the "Sotsialistichesky Vestnik," directly or through somebody else?

RYKOV: I had connections with the "Sotsialistichesky Vestnik" through Nikolayevsky.[18]

VYSHINSKY: You had connections with the "Sotsialistichesky Vestnik." That is to say, you were a contributor to the "Sotsialistichesky Vestnik."

RYKOV: I supplied it with material.

VYSHINSKY: That is being a contributor.

RYKOV: A contributor is one who writes.

VYSHINSKY: And you did not write, you only supplied material. You were a co-contributor.

RYKOV: That is a matter of words and style.

VYSHINSKY: But that is the idea. You had connections with the "Sotsialistichesky Vestnik" and supplied it with various kinds of material. What kind of material?

RYKOV: The material chiefly concerned the same question about which Chernov spoke, in the period 1928-30, in connection with the difficulties with the kulaks which the Party was at that time overcoming.

VYSHINSKY: This material was selected tendentiously?

RYKOV: Of course.

VYSHINSKY: Perhaps it was of a slanderous character?

RYKOV: Tendentious and slanderous, the one easily passes into the other.

VYSHINSKY: That is what I am asking. Did your material pass from the tendentious to the slanderous?

RYKOV: It is difficult to draw a line between these concepts.

VYSHINSKY: In a word, it was both.

RYKOV: In an acute question like this, everything tendentious is slanderous.

VYSHINSKY: What post did you hold at that time?

RYKOV: At that time I was Chairman of the Council of People's Commissars of the U.S.S.R. and of the R.S.F.S.R.

VYSHINSKY: And at the same time you were sending material of a slanderous character to the "Sotsialistichesky Vestnik"? Do I understand you correctly?

RYKOV: Quite correctly.

VYSHINSKY: A praiseworthy occupation!

RYKOV: If it were a praiseworthy occupation, it would not be my misfortune to be talking to you now.

VYSHINSKY: That is perfectly true.

RYKOV: Now about the second task. Chernov is very much rushing the events, because in this case the question of the seizure of power, which was before us and which I too had raised,

95

dates not to 1928 but to the beginning of 1930. I did not say this then, I could not have said it, because I spoke about it two or three years later, whereas at that time this question was not before us.

VYSHINSKY: Then let us ascertain what exactly you did say at that time. You talked about two purposes. The first purpose was to inform Dan about the internal situation in the U.S.S.R.

RYKOV: Yes, to endeavour through Dan to supply definite tendentious information about the state of affairs in the country-side and about the rural policy of the Party.

VYSHINSKY: That was one task. What was the other?

RYKOV: The second task was to secure support from the parties of the Second International for our position, the position we held on this question.

VYSHINSKY: Please explain.

RYKOV: Our position in 1928-29 was as follows: a struggle chiefly in legal forms, as expressed in Bukharin's utterances, in the fight against the Central Committee, and in utilizing the congresses of the trade unions; and we were only in the first stage of the formation of an illegal organization, which was beginning to be formed, but which was not yet the decisive factor in our struggle against the Central Committee.

VYSHINSKY: That I understand. But when you say that Chernov and Dan placed before the parties of the Second International the question of supporting your struggle, what are you referring to? In what forms was this struggle expressed, and in what way was the Second International to support you?

RYKOV: To get the public organizations of the bourgeois states to put such pressure on the Central Committee of the C.P.S.U. as to make it change its policy. In 1928 the possibility and hope of this had not been abandoned either by myself or by the other members of the organization.

VYSHINSKY: Consequently, these were the two tasks you had set yourselves and it was in connection with them that you gave your commission to Chernov?

RYKOV: Yes. And later he informed me, directly or through a third party—I do not quite remember just now—that he had fulfilled this commission.

VYSHINSKY: When were you informed of this?

RYKOV: It was after Chernov's return, about three or four months later.

VYSHINSKY: And in 1930 you had a special conversation with Chernov in which you raised the question of overthrowing the Soviet power?

RYKOV: I do not remember having such a conversation with

Chernov, but of course the possibility of such a conversation is not precluded.

VYSHINSKY: Since you set yourself such a task, of course this possibility was not precluded.

Accused Chernov, do you consider that what the accused Rykov has said here is true?

CHERNOV: I confirm it, but I consider that Rykov is telling only half the truth. He has not told the Court that he gave me a commission for Dan to speak not only about the assistance of the Socialist Parties belonging to the Second International, but also that Dan, through the leaders of the Second International, should get the bourgeois governments to intensify the hostile attitude to the Soviet Union.

VYSHINSKY: Is that how you understood Rykov's commission?

CHERNOV: Yes, that is how I understood it and that is how it really was.

VYSHINSKY: One is not much different from the other.

CHERNOV: It is not, but it is only half the truth.

VYSHINSKY: Accused Rykov, do you insist upon your testimony?

RYKOV: Yes, I do.

VYSHINSKY: So at that time you did not give these instructions in such a sharp form?

RYKOV: This question arose later.

VYSHINSKY: Consequently, you, accused Chernov, affirm that the chief task and the chief commission which the accused Rykov gave you consisted not so much in giving information as in arranging for assistance by imperialist states hostile to the U.S.S.R. —is that what you affirm?

CHERNOV: Yes, yes, I do.

VYSHINSKY: Did you subsequently speak to Rykov on similar subjects?

CHERNOV: Yes, I did. I shall speak about that later.

VYSHINSKY: Tell us about it now.

CHERNOV: When I returned from abroad I saw Rykov and told him how I had fulfilled the commission he had given me for Dan.

VYSHINSKY: Had you fulfilled that commission?

CHERNOV: I had. I went to see Dan and conveyed the commission from the Right centre. I did not receive a reply at once, because Dan said that he could not give it at once and would have to consult the leaders of the Second International. A few days later, at a second meeting, I received a favourable reply from Dan on all these questions.

VYSHINSKY: And did you inform Rykov of this?

97

CHERNOV: Yes, I did inform Rykov of this.

VYSHINSKY: Eye to eye?

CHERNOV: Yes.

VYSHINSKY: May I interrogate Rykov on this subject? Do you confirm this?

RYKOV: I have already said that on his return, I do not remember whether he did so personally or through a third party, he told me that he had fulfilled the commission.

VYSHINSKY: Accused Chernov, continue.

CHERNOV: I forgot to say that during this same meeting I was commissioned, not by Rykov but by Tomsky, to form a Right organization among my acquaintances, if there should happen to be such on the staff of the Trade Representation and the Embassy in Germany. This I also fulfilled upon my arrival in Germany, when I met Yanovitsky. I learnt from him that he had looked up Kibrik and knew his telephone number and address, and that I could get in touch with him. When I arrived in Berlin I telephoned Kibrik and we arranged to meet in the Bavarian Hall of the Vaterland Restaurant. It was there that the meeting with him took place. Kibrik and I were quite pleased to meet each other as old friends. In the course of the conversation I told him, as a good comrade, about my sentiments, my political sentiments, of course, and among other things told him that it was very necessary that I meet Dan, saying why I had to see him. Kibrik said that he could arrange the meeting.

VYSHINSKY: Did the meeting take place?

CHERNOV: Yes, I shall tell you everything in detail presently. We agreed that Kibrik should arrange my meeting with Dan in Königstein; I went there for a cure and the meeting took place in Königstein. Kibrik called for me and we went to the hotel where Dan was staying. There the meeting with Dan took place in private, because Kibrik left. I told Dan about the state of affairs in the Soviet Union, painted a gloomy picture of the position of agriculture in the Ukraine, and conveyed to him all the commissions I had received from the Right centre, as represented by Rykov.

Dan replied that he considered the proposal of the Right centre quite acceptable. "But," he said, "I must ask you a specific question. I have known you for a long time. What is your own opinion of the strength of the Right organization?" I replied that the Rights possessed enough forces to seize power and to hold it, adding that they had connections, sufficient connections, among military men. Dan replied that I was wrong there. Even if the Rights seized power, they could not retain it for any length of time without proper support, and above all the armed support of capitalist states. Furthermore, he said, you must work in such a way

98

as to undermine the economic and political might of the Soviet Union. I remember very clearly the expression he used: "You must not shrink from any means. Whoever fights for the overthrow of power and shrinks from using any particular means is a political Manilov. And the capitalist states must be helped even now in their struggle against the Soviet Union." Such were the results of my meeting with Dan. A few days later I was invited by Kibrik to Berlin. I went. This second meeting with Dan took place in Kibrik's apartment. Dan told me that he had managed to communicate with leaders of the Second International and asked me to convey to Rykov that the leaders of the Second International fully accepted the proposals which I had transmitted to them from the Right centre. Thereupon Dan reverted to the question that power could not be retained by the Rights without the assistance of the armed capitalist governments. He again stressed the point that I, in particular, as a member of a Right organization which was combating the Soviet power, should help the capitalist states in their struggle against the Soviet power, inasmuch as our aims coincided. I asked him what form this help could take. Dan did not give a direct and definite answer to this, but said that assistance could be of the most varied kind; if occasion to give assistance should lie in your path, you should give it. I also asked Dan how connections could be established between the Right centre and Dan in the future. Dan replied that I need not worry on this score; Rykov would find ways of establishing these connections. "But," he said, "I want you personally to maintain connections with me through Kibrik." That was the result of this meeting with Dan.

After my talk with Dan, which, as I said, took place in Kibrik's apartment, Dan left, and I remained for supper with Kibrik. I was to leave for the station after supper. During supper we drank rather heavily. On the plea of some engagement, Kibrik said that he could not accompany me to the station. He put me on a bus and I left him in order to return to Königstein.

VYSHINSKY: Did you get to the station?

CHERNOV: No, but I got to the Polizeipräsidium instead. In the bus several Germans tried to pick a quarrel with me. One of them pushed me, and I pushed him in return.

VYSHINSKY: Hard?

CHERNOV: Well, I am not so strong physically as to give a hard push; at any rate I pushed him as hard as I could.

VYSHINSKY: Well, and what happened?

CHERNOV: What happened was that three Germans seized hold of me, stopped the bus, put me into a taxi and drove me to the Polizeipräsidium.

At the Polizeipräsidium I protested and demanded to be released. I was told that I would have to await the arrival of the chief in the morning. I spent the night there. In the morning some kind of official who spoke Russian very well appeared, and I at once protested to him. He said he would have to report the matter to the chief. After some time a man appeared who introduced himself as Colonel Oberhaus. He pulled out a protocol and translated it to me. I was accused of maiming Germans, for which I was criminally liable. Moreover, I was told that a copy of the protocol would be sent to our Embassy. And thereupon he proposed that I should become an agent of the German intelligence service. I refused. Oberhaus then said that he knew something about my dealings in Germany. I asked him what he knew. He said that he knew about my meetings with Dan and showed me several photographs of my meetings with Dan, taken both in Königstein and in Berlin. At the same time he gave me a brief summary of the conversation with Dan.

VYSHINSKY: Whose?

CHERNOV: My conversation with Dan. His account contained a clear repetition of Dan's words. It then became absolutely obvious to me that the trap which had been set for me in Germany had been arranged by the German intelligence service with the full support of Dan himself and with Dan's participation, and that Dan himself was undoubtedly an agent of the German intelligence service, and so was Kibrik.

VYSHINSKY: And did what you were charged with in the Polizeipräsidium correspond to the truth?

CHERNOV: The protocol? It was drawn up tendentiously. I could not have maimed anyone.

VYSHINSKY: About the conversation with Dan?

CHERNOV: That did correspond with what Dan and I actually talked about.

VYSHINSKY: Did your conversation with Dan take place in anybody's presence?

CHERNOV: The conversation in Königstein took place privately. Kibrik conducted me to Dan's room, but then left.

VYSHINSKY: And so the police official could learn about the conversation only from you or from Dan?

CHERNOV: Yes.

VYSHINSKY: If you could not have transmitted the conversation, it means that the police learnt about it from Dan. And if Dan informed the police about it, it means that he is an agent of the police?

CHERNOV: Yes, otherwise he would not have transmitted it. After this I consented, and became a German spy.

VYSHINSKY: That is, you got caught yourself?

CHERNOV: Yes. This was followed by various formalities, questionnaires, and a signed pledge. Oberhaus instructed me about the work I was to perform in the Soviet Union on Germany's behalf. Seeing how upset I was, he said: "There is no need to get upset. You are fighting the Soviet power, and so are we, and even our methods of fighting will very likely coincide in the near future."

VYSHINSKY: Did this reassure you?

CHERNOV: It did not.

VYSHINSKY: But he tried to reassure you?

CHERNOV: The tasks set by Oberhaus amounted to this: I had to give systematic information to the German intelligence service on questions of interest to it which would be submitted to me through a representative of the German intelligence service in Moscow. I had also to organize diversive-wrecking activities in my field of work. As I was at that time working on grain collections, I had above all to do wrecking work in the sphere of grain collections.

VYSHINSKY: What form did your collaboration with the German intelligence service take?

CHERNOV: Oberhaus advised me, in order to avert exposure, not to extend my connections with the Rights too widely, but to maintain connections with a limited number of persons and to consolidate these connections. Oberhaus told me that I would not be disturbed in Moscow for some time, so as to enable me to arrange my spy work in the Soviet Union. And it is true that nobody came to see me at first. Several months passed and in 1930 I had a meeting with a representative of the German intelligence service.

VYSHINSKY: How did it take place?

CHERNOV: I was then either Assistant People's Commissar or a member of the Collegium of the People's Commissariat of Trade, I cannot recall which. The Information Bureau of the People's Commissariat of Foreign Affairs telephoned me and said that Paul Scheffer, correspondent of the German "Berliner Tageblatt," would come and see me to get some information. I was to give him information that was not of a confidential character. Shortly after Scheffer did come to see me and said that he had been sent by Colonel Oberhaus. He gave the password "Reinhold." That was my pseudonym as a German spy. I asked Scheffer what Colonel Oberhaus wanted. On that occasion he demanded information on the internal affairs of the Party, on the state of work among the Rights and Trotskyites, and on conditions in the rural districts. He moreover demanded special information about stocks of industrial goods. He was particularly interested in the stocks of industrial goods in the towns. He demanded information about the progress of the grain collections and about the grain mobilization stocks. Part of the information demanded—about the situation within the Party and about the work among the Rights—I gave him verbally on the spot; the figures I gave him a few days later.

After this I had a number of periodical meetings with Scheffer. I transmitted information to the German intelligence service, and through him received instructions from the latter about the organization of wrecking work. I had an especially long conversation with Scheffer on the organization of wrecking work in the sphere of grain collections and grain supplies. The chief task assigned to me by the German intelligence service at that time was to arrange to spoil grain within the country. This involved delaying the construction of storehouses and elevators, so as to create a discrepancy between the growing size of the grain collections and the available storage space. In this way, Scheffer said, two things would be achieved: firstly, the grain itself would be spoilt; and, secondly, the indignation of the peasants would be aroused, which was inevitable when they saw that grain was perishing. I was also asked to arrange for the wholesale contamination of storehouses by pests, and especially by corn beetle. Scheffer especially demanded that arrangements be made to contaminate the mobilization stocks with storehouse pests and corn beetle. These commissions that Scheffer gave me I carried out. Then Scheffer left the Soviet Union. Before his departure he told me that in view of the danger of exposure he would have to leave for Germany, but that the German intelligence service would not fail to establish connections with me.

My connections with representatives of the German intelligence service were resumed when I had already gone to work in the Committee of Agricultural Stocks. Espionage and wrecking activities became particularly intense after I was appointed People's Commissar of Agriculture. Several months after I had been appointed People's Commissar of Agriculture of the U.S.S.R., I was visited at the Commissariat by a certain Raivid, a former comrade of mine in the Menshevik organization in Ivanovo, who had been working in the People's Commissariat of Foreign Affairs for a long time. We met from time to time, and I was therefore not surprised when he came to see me at the People's Commissariat of Agriculture. But when we were alone in my office together, he said: "You and I have got to have a serious talk, Reinhold." That word was enough, everything was clear. It transpired that Raivid was a residential agent of the German intelligence service in the Soviet Union, and that he had received instructions from Oberhaus to establish connections with me. Raivid and I met several times. When I went to work at the People's Commissariat of Agriculture our meetings were devoted to working out a detailed program of wrecking and diversive work in the sphere of agriculture on fundamental and crucial questions. This program, which was drawn up in accordance with the demands of the German intelligence service, included wrecking activities in such fields as seed, crop rotation, machine and tractor stations and stock-breeding. The

German intelligence service made a special point of the organization of wrecking activities in the sphere of horse-breeding in order, as Raivid said, not to provide horses for the Red Army. As regards seed, we included in our program muddling up seed affairs, mixing up sorted seed and thus lowering the harvest yield in the country. As regards crop rotation, the idea was to plan the crop area incorrectly and thus place the collective farm peasants in such a position that they would be virtually unable to practise proper crop rotation and would be obliged to plough up meadows and pastures for crop growing. This would reduce the size of harvests in the country and at the same time rouse the indignation of the peasants, who would be unable to understand why they were being forced to plough up meadows and pastures when the collective farms wanted to develop stock-breeding and required fodder for the purpose.

As regards the machine and tractor stations, the aim was to put tractors, harvester combines and agricultural machines out of commission, to muddle the financial affairs of the machine and tractor stations, and for this purpose to place at the head of the machine and tractor stations useless people, people with bad records, and above all members of our Right organization.

As regards stock breeding, the aim was to kill off pedigree breed-stock and to strive for a high cattle mortality... to prevent the development of fodder resources and especially to infect cattle artificially with various kinds of bacteria in order to increase their mortality.

VYSHINSKY: Tell us in greater detail about the cattle mortality, where you got the bacteria from, what kind of bacteria, and so on.

CHERNOV: I must tell you what I told Rykov during my meetings with him in 1935. I told him that I had made preparations for certain acts of diversion, and Rykov gave his approval.

I performed the following acts of diversion. In order to cause heavy cattle mortality in Eastern Siberia, I instructed Ginsburg, Chief of the Veterinary Department, who belonged to the organization of the Rights, and through him the Chief of the Veterinary Supply Department, who also belonged to the organization of the Rights, not to supply anti-anthrax serum to Eastern Siberia, knowing that Eastern Siberia was particularly liable to anthrax. The serum was not supplied to Eastern Siberia. The preparations for this were made in 1935, and when there was an outbreak of anthrax there in 1936 it turned out that no serum was available, with the result that I cannot say how many exactly, but at any rate over 25,000 horses perished.

Secondly, I instructed Ginsburg and Boyarshinov, Chief of the Bacteriological Department, to artificially infect pigs with erysipelas in the Leningrad Region and with plague in the Voronezh Region and the Azov-Black Sea Territory. I chose these two bacteria because the pigs are inoculated not with dead microbes, but with live ones, only of reduced virulence. It was therefore quite simple from the technical standpoint to organize artificial infection. Secondly, in the case of these two diseases there is a rule that when plague breaks out in any particular district, all the pigs in that district have to be inoculated. This made it possible at once to spread the disease on a large scale.

For this purpose, three factories were selected at my suggestion: Kashintsevo, Orel and Stavropol. In these factories serums were made with virulent bacteria and given special serial numbers. Boyarshinov was informed of these serial numbers and he transmitted them to the chiefs of veterinary departments in the localities who could be relied upon in this matter, and they in turn transmitted them to veterinary surgeons who had anti-Soviet feelings and who in case of a heavy cattle mortality would not raise a big fuss.

... In this way these serums were distributed and artificial infection was carried out in these three regions.

It is difficult to estimate the results, but at any rate it may be taken for granted that several tens of thousands of pigs perished owing to this diversive act.

VYSHINSKY: Is that all?

CHERNOV: That is all with regard to diversive acts. As to my connections with the German intelligence service, I have nothing to add and would like to continue my testimony regarding my connections with the Right centre and with Rykov.

VYSHINSKY: One more question with regard to your connections with the German intelligence service. Did you receive any money from the intelligence service?

CHERNOV: Yes, I quite forgot about that.

VYSHINSKY: Why, of course, it is such a trifling matter that you forgot about it.

CHERNOV: It is not a trifling matter, of course, but I forgot about it. In Berlin I received 2,000 marks....

VYSHINSKY: How much did you receive in all?

CHERNOV: Roughly about 30,000 German marks and about 150,000 rubles in Soviet money. A considerable part of these sums was spent on my personal needs, but a certain part was spent in bribing members of the Right organization whom I thought it necessary to bribe.

VYSHINSKY: And so part of the money received was used for bribery, but the greater part for your personal needs.

CHERNOV: Absolutely right.

VYSHINSKY: Thus it may be said that you not only fell into

104

the net skilfully spread by the German intelligence service but that you deliberately sold yourself for money to the enemy?

CHERNOV: Absolutely right.

VYSHINSKY: Tell us about your subsequent connections with Rykov.

CHERNOV: I shall continue on the subject of my connections with the Right organization and with Rykov. In addition to those meetings with Rykov I have recounted, I had the following meeting with him in December 1930. He invited me himself and the meeting took place at his apartment. Rykov and Tomsky, who was also present at the meeting, were in a jubilant frame of mind.

The feeling was that a peasant uprising was inevitable in the near future, which, with proper leadership by the Right organization, might lead to the seizure of power in the country. Right there, Tomsky said among other things that the Right centre had taken measures to secure certain prominent posts for representatives of the Right organization. This, he claimed, was very necessary in order to accomplish a "palace coup" in the country. I there received instructions from Rykov also to organize wrecking activities. The task set me by Rykov was to arouse the anger of the peasants against the policy of the Party and against the Soviet government by extending to the middle peasants the repressive measures established for the kulaks, and to rouse discontent among the workers by disorganizing the supply of bread.

The next time I met Rykov, again on his invitation, was in October, it seems to me, but at any rate in the autumn of 1932. This meeting took place at the time when a profound change had taken place in the countryside. The collective farm movement had grown strong, the kulaks had been smashed and the rural districts were already beginning to feel tangible results from the industrialization of the country. Although Rykov attempted to maintain an air of serenity it was clear that he was nonplussed by the failure of the political predictions he had been making until then, and in his conversation with me he told me that we must go still more deeply underground and orientate ourselves for the seizure of power on the carrying out of a "palace coup." I said: "In 1930, too, you spoke to me about a 'palace coup.' What then is the difference between the line of 1930 and the line of 1932?" He answered that the difference was that in 1930 it was one of the possible variants, but that now it was the most decisive and most important variant for the seizure of power. As he put it, we must seize power in the country by means of a "palace coup," that is, the arrest and assassination of the leaders of the Party and the government.

VYSHINSKY: This was the second meeting since 1930?

CHERNOV: The first meeting was in 1930, but this was in 1932.

VYSHINSKY: When was the next meeting?

CHERNOV: The next meeting was in 1934, a few months after I was appointed People's Commissar of Agriculture of the U.S.S.R. Rykov invited me to his summer residence. This meeting took place in private and was mainly devoted to the organization of my work as a member of the Right organization in connection with my appointment to the post of People's Commissar of Agriculture of the U.S.S.R. The task Rykov set me was to organize my work in such a way as to undermine the collective farm system. For this purpose the guidance of the collective farms was to be conducted in such a way as to deprive the collective farmer of all interest in collective farm production, to which end collective farming was to be conducted in such a way that the collective farmer would receive next to nothing for his workdays. The plan of wrecking work in its entirety we did not draw up concretely, but agreed that I, together with a small group of members of the Right organization in the People's Commissariat of Agriculture, should draw up and proceed to carry out a concrete plan of wrecking measures in the sphere of agriculture.

My next and last meeting with Rykov took place either at the end of 1935 or in the beginning of 1936—I do not quite remember which. This was the time when the famous conferences were being held in the Kremlin between leaders of the Party and the government and the foremost people in agriculture. The instructions Rykov gave at this meeting were as follows. He said that we cannot but take note of the growth and consolidation of the collective farms in the country and the growth of new collective farm cadres revealed at these conferences. But this, he said, by no means implies that there are no forces in the countryside which we could organize. And as an example of these forces he pointed out the kulak elements who had returned from special exile settlements and the elements with anti-Soviet feelings from among the old rural intelligentsia—agronomists, doctors, stock-breeding experts, etc. These forces, he claimed, must be mobilized to the utmost and utilized for our purposes. And he particularly stressed the point that there were only two ways by which the Rights could seize power in the country, namely, the forcible removal of the leadership of the Party and the leadership of the government, that is, their arrest or assassination, or both. And he laid particular stress on the necessity for the defeat of the Soviet Union in a war with capitalist countries, should the latter attack us. And in this connection he particularly referred to the importance of organizing wrecking and diversive work, saying that since we needed the defeat of the Soviet Union for the conquest of power in the country, we should expedite this defeat, and should likewise expedite the outbreak of the war itself by diminishing the economic and defensive power of the Soviet Union. Such was the gist of our conversation in 1935. I repeat that at this meeting I informed Rykov about the diversive acts I have mentioned, particularly about the artificial infection of cattle, just as I informed him at every meeting about the wrecking work I had organized both in the sphere of grain collections in the Committee of Agricultural Stocks and in the sphere of agriculture in the People's Commissariat of Agriculture.

VYSHINSKY: Is that all? And so your last meeting with Rykov was in 1936?

CHERNOV: Either at the end of 1935 or at the beginning of 1936. I must add that Rykov told me that he could not see me any more because he feared exposure. He was being closely watched. He proposed that I establish connections with another, reserve centre through Lyubimov. [19]

VYSHINSKY: And so your first conspiratorial meeting with Rykov took place in 1928 and the last in 1936, or at the end of 1935?

CHERNOV: Correct.

VYSHINSKY: So that in 1928 you met Rykov and discussed with him your part in the struggle against the Soviet power?

CHERNOV: Correct.

VYSHINSKY: You carried out his commission to establish connections with Dan while you were abroad?

CHERNOV: Yes.

VYSHINSKY: Did you meet him in 1929?

CHERNOV: I met him in 1929 for a short while for information.

VYSHINSKY: In 1930 you again met him on the same basis of your common crimes?

CHERNOV: Yes.

VYSHINSKY: In 1932 you again met him on the basis of these same common crimes?

CHERNOV: Yes.

VYSHINSKY: In 1934 you again met him on the basis of this same common criminal activity, and, finally, at the end of 1935 or the beginning of 1936 you met him once more on this same common basis of criminal activity, and then, for reasons of secrecy, broke off connections with him?

CHERNOV: Yes.

VYSHINSKY: The character of your meetings with Rykov was that you received from Rykov orders and instructions with regard to your criminal activities? Is that so?

CHERNOV: It is.

VYSHINSKY: They had no connection with the official position of the accused Rykov?

CHERNOV: Absolutely none.

107

VYSHINSKY: You, while People's Commissar of Agriculture of the U.S.S.R., went to a man who held the post of People's Commissar of Post and Telegraph and received certain instructions from him? That is, the connections were exclusively criminal?

CHERNOV: Exclusively criminal.

VYSHINSKY: Exclusively criminal connections in the sphere of the organization of crimes against the Soviet power and against the Party.

Permit me to interrogate the accused Rykov.

Accused Rykov, do you agree with this estimate of your connections with Chernov?

RYKOV: After the meeting at which he reported on his meeting with Dan, I personally cannot recall all the rest of what Chernov said here, although much of what he says and relates coincided and coincides with the counter-revolutionary line and that counter-revolutionary work which I performed at the corresponding time. But as regards a "palace coup," I cannot admit that I could have informed Chernov of it, because we kept it the greatest secret, and I could have informed only those people who would be directly drawn into the matter. As to the other questions he touched on, I have no objections to make. When my turn comes I shall speak of the formulations of which Chernov spoke. I shall tell of my counter-revolutionary and treasonable activities.

VYSHINSKY: So what he says is essentially correct?

RYKOV. Yes, but as to the last meeting, I know nothing.

CHERNOV: How could Alexei Ivanovich have forgotten about these three meetings?

VYSHINSKY: Accused Rykov, during the period 1930-36, did you have meetings with other people in your criminal activities?

RYKOV: Of course.

VYSHINSKY: Numerous meetings?

RYKOV. Of course.

VYSHINSKY: And so you might have forgotten with whom you spoke and about what?

RYKOV: That I could completely have forgotten what Chernov says—five or six meetings—that cannot be.

VYSHINSKY: Did you have many accomplices like Chernov?

RYKOV: That was my mistake; but I do not consider him a very important accomplice. On the way from the restaurant to the station he managed to land in the Polizeipräsidium.

VYSHINSKY: Here, for example, are the prisoners in the dock; there are quite a number of your accomplices. Was Chernov one of them?

RYKOV: Yes.

VYSHINSKY: And did you, accused Chernov, have many leaders like Rykov?

CHERNOV: None except Rykov and the German intelligence service.

VYSHINSKY: I have no more questions.

CHERNOV: I have a question to ask Rykov.

How is it that you cannot explain? You are one of the chief leaders of the Right centre and I am the People's Commissar of Agriculture.

VYSHINSKY: You were.

CHERNOV: Yes, I was. That means, I am in charge of agriculture. You know that I am a member of your organization. How could you, having a member of your organization occupying the post of People's Commissar of Agriculture, not invite him to discuss the utilization of his position in the interests of the Right organization?

Please forgive me for my rudeness, but either you were a bad leader of the Right organization, which I do not think, or you do not want to confess. I cannot conceive that you could have forgotten, I do not want to say that I was a big personage and so on, but how you could have forgotten a meeting with the People's Commissar of Agriculture on the subject of wrecking work is hard to understand.

VYSHINSKY: Accused Chernov, you remember these meetings well?

CHERNOV: I remember them well, I remember some of the expressions well. I repeat that what I have told the Court was the whole truth.

THE PRESIDENT: Accused Rykov, do you want to reply to Chernov's question?

RYKOV: He has replied too well. Perhaps I should have done as he says. It was a mistake on my part.

THE PRESIDENT: The Court adjourns until 11 a.m. tomorrow.

[*Signed*] PRESIDENT: V. ULRICH

Army Military Jurist

President of the Military Collegium of the Supreme Court of the U.S.S.R.

SECRETARY: A. BATNER

Military Jurist First Rank

109

MORNING SESSION, MARCH 3, 1938

COMMANDANT OF THE COURT: The Court is coming, please rise.

THE PRESIDENT: Be seated. The session of the Military Collegium of the Supreme Court of the U.S.S.R. is resumed. We shall proceed to the examination of the accused Ivanov.

Accused Ivanov, do you confirm the testimony you gave during the preliminary investigation regarding your anti-Soviet activities?

IVANOV: Fully and entirely. I consider myself responsible and guilty of the gravest crimes. I was one of the active members of the group of the Rights, the "bloc of Rights and Trotskyites." For these gravest crimes I am prepared to bear any penalties that the Soviet Court may deem necessary to impose upon me, and to do everything within my power to expose all my treacherous activities and to divulge all the vileness, despicableness and treason to the whole Soviet Union, to the Party and to the people, and the treasonable and treacherous activities of the "bloc of Rights and Trotskyites" and of the group of the Rights.

THE PRESIDENT: Have you any questions, Comrade Procurator?

VYSHINSKY: Accused Ivanov, do you admit that you were a member of the underground Right-Trotskyite anti-Soviet organization?

IVANOV: I admit that I was an active member.

VYSHINSKY: Tell us, under what circumstances and when did you join this underground anti-Soviet organization?

IVANOV: Perhaps I may be permitted to mention certain criteria, what created the conditions and led me to adopt this path?

VYSHINSKY: That is what I am asking you.

IVANOV: My first fall dates back to 1911, when I was a student at the Tula gymnasium, in the eighth class. The tsarist Okhrana [1] managed to recruit me as one of its agents.

VYSHINSKY: How exactly were you recruited?

IVANOV: I was a very unruly element in the school. In the eighth class, the last class, I was several times threatened with expulsion.

110

VYSHINSKY: With what particular institution were you connected as an Okhrana agent; in what city?

IVANOV: In the city of Tula. I committed my first act of treachery in the following way. . . .

VYSHINSKY: I ask you: what institution were you connected with?

IVANOV: With the Okhrana Department of the Gendarmerie of the City of Tula.

VYSHINSKY: That is, with the Provincial Department of Gendarmerie in Tula?

IVANOV: Yes, in the city of Tula itself.

VYSHINSKY: What form did your work and activity as an Okhrana agent take?

IVANOV: In Tula I had taken part in a rowdy affair in the eighth class which led to the dismissal of the German language teacher, a woman, who was very much disliked by the students. I was one of the active instigators of this dismissal. I betrayed a group of students who had arranged this business—a certain Fromerd and Yudin.

VYSHINSKY: What next?

IVANOV: Later, before entering the Moscow University, and before leaving for Moscow, I severed connections with the Okhrana. For two or three months before my departure for Moscow I had no more connections with them. In 1912 I entered the Moscow University. In 1913 I took part in one of the strikes at the university. I was expelled from the university; a large number of students were expelled at that time. In Moscow the Okhrana department again laid hold of me.

VYSHINSKY: In Tula, with whom were you connected personally?

IVANOV: With Captain Mamatkazin.

VYSHINSKY: How long were you an agent of the Okhrana in Tula?

IVANOV: I was recruited at the end of 1911, and roughly in June or July 1912 connections were severed. . . .

VYSHINSKY: I want to elucidate the circumstances of this connection. So in Tula you were connected with Captain Mamatkazin as an agent of the Tula Department of the Gendarmerie. Did you have a secret pseudonym?

IVANOV: I did: "Samarin."

VYSHINSKY: Did you have a spy number?

IVANOV: I did: No. 163.

VYSHINSKY: Did you receive any remuneration for your services?

IVANOV: I received remuneration both in Moscow and in Tula.

VYSHINSKY: That means you were a paid . . . ?

IVANOV: A paid agent of the tsarist Okhrana.

VYSHINSKY: Was this the beginning of your political activities?

IVANOV: This was a shameful period in my life.

VYSHINSKY: Then you came to Moscow and entered the Moscow University in 1912.

IVANOV: Yes.

VYSHINSKY: You suffered no unpleasant consequences in connection with the strike? You averted them by your treachery?

IVANOV: Yes.

VYSHINSKY: You came to Moscow and entered the Moscow University in 1912?

IVANOV: Yes.

VYSHINSKY: What faculty?

IVANOV: The Medical Faculty.

VYSHINSKY: You came to Moscow. Did you bring no connections with the Okhrana along with you?

IVANOV: No, I had severed these connections.

VYSHINSKY: What form did the severance of your connections take?

IVANOV: For two months before I left for Moscow I went there no longer and was no longer disturbed by them. I did not pay the regular visit. . . .

VYSHINSKY: And they did not disturb you?

IVANOV: No, they did not.

VYSHINSKY: You did not sever connections by announcing that you did not wish to work any more?

IVANOV: No, I simply did not go there any more and they did not disturb me.

VYSHINSKY: And if they had disturbed you?

IVANOV: If they had disturbed me, as happened later, when I was all the time being threatened with exposure, I certainly would have gone.

VYSHINSKY: As happened . . .

IVANOV: As happened in 1913 in Moscow.

VYSHINSKY: And so we can put it that you did not sever connections, but that there was a temporary suspension of your provocateur activities for reasons that did not entirely depend upon you?

IVANOV: Correct.

VYSHINSKY: In 1913 you were active as an Okhrana agent?

IVANOV: Yes.

VYSHINSKY: In Moscow?

IVANOV: Yes.

VYSHINSKY: With whom were you connected?

IVANOV: With Captain Gryaznov and Lieutenant-Colonel Kolokolov.

VYSHINSKY: What form did your provocateur work take?

IVANOV: I gave information about the revolutionary movement in the student organizations, and information about individual comrades who were carrying on revolutionary work. For instance, I betrayed the revolutionaries Severny and Pomorov of the Tula Fellowship. In 1916 I betrayed Kaplun, one of the most active spirits in revolutionary work in the Medical Faculty.

VYSHINSKY: Who is this Kaplun?

IVANOV: I think he is at present a professor on questions of labour protection.

VYSHINSKY: Professor of Social Hygiene in the Moscow University?

IVANOV: I do not know. He mostly worked in Soviet institutions. He got an academic degree.

VYSHINSKY: He was a student at that time?

IVANOV: Yes, a student in the final course, and one of the most active spirits in revolutionary work. He was the head of our seniors.

VYSHINSKY: Under what circumstances did you betray him?

IVANOV: I do not remember exactly whether it was in 1915 or 1916. Lieutenant-Colonel Kolokolov summoned me and demanded information about Kaplun, who was known for his revolutionary activities in the Medical Faculty. It was then that I began giving information. In 1916, on Kaplun's initiative, a meeting of representatives of the student organizations was called in connection with the growing revolutionary movement. I betrayed this illegal meeting, and at the same time I betrayed Kaplun. I spent the night with him and tried to persuade him not to destroy the revolutionary literature he had, because I knew that he was to be arrested that night. Kaplun proved to be much cleverer than I, and more cautious with respect to the Okhrana: he had already destroyed this literature before the meeting. It is true that he was arrested, but the Okhrana could find nothing that directly incriminated him, such as revolutionary literature; and after a month of confinement, he was released.

I then gave information about the activities of the Bolshevik organization in the Commercial Institute. I had connections with Ter, the leader of the Bolsheviks in the Institute.

VYSHINSKY: And so you wormed your way in there too?

IVANOV: Yes, I was connected with the Bolshevik organization at the Institute, and I was told to gain access to the organization and to give information.

113

VYSHINSKY: Who told you to do this?

IVANOV: Lieutenant-Colonel Kolokolov.

VYSHINSKY: What information did you supply about this organization?

IVANOV: I gave information about the revolutionary sentiments and about the most energetic and active people in it. Then I gave warning that a meeting of students and workers was to be held. Ter was to have been seized at this meeting, but he managed to leap out of the window.

VYSHINSKY: Did you also betray any of the people belonging to this Bolshevik group to the Okhrana?

IVANOV: I betrayed only Ter, but he managed to get away.

VYSHINSKY: Did you commit other acts of treachery during this period?

IVANOV: I think that is all.

VYSHINSKY: How long were you an agent of the Moscow Okhrana?

IVANOV: From 1913 to the end of 1916.

VYSHINSKY: Did you receive remuneration?

IVANOV: Yes, I did.

VYSHINSKY: What remuneration did you receive?

IVANOV: From the Tula Okhrana I first received 15 rubles and then 20 rubles.

VYSHINSKY: And from the Moscow Okhrana?

IVANOV: I first received 30 rubles and 40 rubles and then rose to 60 and 75 rubles. As the quality of my work improved, my pay increased.

VYSHINSKY: You were connected with the Moscow Okhrana up to the end of 1916. And from the end of 1916?

IVANOV: At the end of 1916 I severed connections with the Okhrana.

VYSHINSKY: Just as you severed them in Tula?

IVANOV: No, I severed them for good. I made up my mind that, if necessary, I would even leave the university and clear out.

VYSHINSKY: What was the reason for this decision?

IVANOV: I was brought up in such conditions, I was so closely connected with the interests of the revolution and the working class. . . .

VYSHINSKY: How were you connected? You were connected just the other way round.

IVANOV: When I grew up . . .

VYSHINSKY: In the eighth class at school you became an agent-provocateur. At the time you were growing up you were an agent-provocateur.

IVANOV: Yes.

VYSHINSKY: At the age of 19 you were an agent-provocateur.

IVANOV: Yes.

VYSHINSKY: At the age of 20 you were an agent-provocateur.

IVANOV: Yes.

VYSHINSKY: Your whole growth was one of an agent-provocateur.

IVANOV: You did not understand me. . . .

VYSHINSKY: I ask you, why at the end of 1916 did you decide to sever connections with the Okhrana?

IVANOV: In the first place it weighed on my mind; and in the second place I was frightened by the growing revolutionary movement and the prospects of a victory for the working class; I feared that when the working class was victorious the documents of the Okhrana might fall into the hands of the revolutionary organizations and I would be exposed as an agent-provocateur.

VYSHINSKY: Well, that is a different story. You were just afraid of having to pay the reckoning.

IVANOV: That is so.

VYSHINSKY: Then what has your connection with the revolutionary movement got to do with it?

IVANOV: No, I did not say that it was my connection with the revolutionary movement.

VYSHINSKY: You talked about your revolutionary training. Your training was quite a definite one. You began your political training under the guidance of Captain Mamatkazin of the Tula Okhrana, and finished it under the guidance of Bukharin and Rykov. Do I understand you rightly?

IVANOV: That is so.

VYSHINSKY: Well, that was your political training.

When did you get into the Bolshevik Party?

IVANOV: In 1915.

VYSHINSKY: Under what circumstances? From personal conviction?

IVANOV: I was instructed by Lieutenant-Colonel Kolokolov to join the Bolshevik Party.

VYSHINSKY: So you joined the Party on the instructions of Lieutenant-Colonel Kolokolov of the Moscow Okhrana?

IVANOV: Yes.

VYSHINSKY: As part of your duties?

IVANOV: There can be no doubt about it.

VYSHINSKY: With what purpose?

IVANOV: With the purpose of obtaining more thorough information about the activities of the Bolshevik organization.

VYSHINSKY: With provocateur purposes?

IVANOV: Yes, with provocateur purposes.

VYSHINSKY: From what year did you reckon your membership in the Party?

IVANOV: I used to say when filling in questionnaires that I was a member of the Party since 1915.

VYSHINSKY: But as to your having joined the Party on the instructions of Lieutenant-Colonel Kolokolov you said nothing, of course?

IVANOV: That I did not tell anybody.

VYSHINSKY: Until when?

IVANOV: Until the moment of my arrest.

VYSHINSKY: Tell me, please, did you have any connections with the group of "Left Communists"?

IVANOV: Yes.

VYSHINSKY: And who brought you into this group?

IVANOV: As a matter of fact, nobody brought me into it, because my original sin and my fear that I might be exposed under the Soviet power drove me and spurred me into the camp of the enemies, and like a vulture drawn by the smell of carrion, I joined any hostile group that was fighting the Soviet power, because I reckoned that if the bourgeois regime were restored I would not be exposed.

VYSHINSKY: When did you join the "Left Communists"?

IVANOV: At the end of 1917 or the beginning of 1918.

VYSHINSKY: That means that you joined this group as an enemy who reckoned that through this group you would succeed in overthrowing the Soviet power?

IVANOV: Yes.

VYSHINSKY: And you explain this by the fact that you hoped to legalize your position in this way?

IVANOV: Yes.

VYSHINSKY: That means that you were acting as an enemy of Soviet power?

IVANOV: Yes.

VYSHINSKY: And the "Left Communists" were the most suitable group for you?

IVANOV: Yes, they were fighting the Soviet power and the Party.

VYSHINSKY: By provocateur methods. And that suited you very well?

IVANOV: I found in the "Left Communists" just what I needed as an enemy of the Soviet power and the working class.

VYSHINSKY: Specifically, what did you find in the group of the "Left Communists"?

IVANOV: An opportunity to combat the Soviet power and the Party.

VYSHINSKY: An opportunity to combat the revolution, to combat the working class? And so, if we examine this period,

116

we may say that beginning from 1911 and at least until 1918 you were waging a struggle against the working class?

IVANOV: I was both betraying and waging a struggle.

VYSHINSKY: Were you connected with Bukharin at that time?

IVANOV: We attended several conferences together. Then Bukharin one day suggested to me that, as a sign of protest against the Party and against Lenin's line, we must leave the Communist Party and form our own party. It was reckoned that this might lead to the collapse of the Communist Party and the victory of the "Left Communists." But at about this time the following transpired. I was working at that time as a Party organizer in the Basmanny district. I did not succeed in securing the support of the Party masses for the line of the "Left Communists." The masses solidly supported Lenin. It became clear to me that the whole work of the "Left Communists" was doomed to failure, to bankruptcy. I then left for the front.

VYSHINSKY: Why?

IVANOV: So as to break with the "Left Communists."

VYSHINSKY: Why did you leave for the front?

IVANOV: I left for the front. . . . (A pause.) I had certain vacillations, and then I thought—out of sight, out of mind, and that there would be less danger of my exposure as a former agent-provocateur.

VYSHINSKY: You were again running away from the danger of exposure—and not going in order to defend the Soviet system?

IVANOV: Oh, no.

VYSHINSKY: That is what interests me. What did you do then?

IVANOV: I then met Bukharin at the Tenth Party Congress, where we had the following conversation. He said that he differed with Lenin on fundamental questions; that he was engaged in mustering cadres, so that they might be ready at his, Bukharin's, first call to go into action against Lenin. This, in my opinion, was the prelude to the formation of the Bukharin "school."

VYSHINSKY: How did Bukharin expect to take action against Lenin? In what ways was he preparing to act?

IVANOV: He was in a fairly truculent mood. He was just waiting for a suitable moment. He wanted to have his own cadres.

VYSHINSKY: What for?

IVANOV: To remove Lenin.

VYSHINSKY: How to remove him?

IVANOV: Even by physical methods.

VYSHINSKY: And you talk about a school. A fine "school"!

IVANOV: It is known in the Party as the "school" of the "Left Communists."

VYSHINSKY: And in reality it is not a "school," but a gang, which Bukharin formed. Continue your account.

IVANOV: I referred to the Bukharin "school" by the term under which it is known.

VYSHINSKY: And in reality it is not a "school," but a gang.[2] And so your acquaintance with Bukharin is of old standing?

IVANOV: Our acquaintance was not interrupted until the moment of my arrest.

VYSHINSKY: I want to know, is your acquaintance with Bukharin of old standing, or not?

IVANOV: It is of old standing.

VYSHINSKY: It dates from the group of the "Left Communists," from the conspiratorial plans of 1918. Do I understand you rightly?

IVANOV: That is so.

VYSHINSKY: Go on with your account.

IVANOV: The conversation I had with Bukharin in 1926 is of interest. He bluntly said that we must prepare for an open fight against the Party. Bear this in mind, he said, that we are coming out in public, and by doing so we are furnishing a program for the consolidation of all the dissatisfied elements within the country. But that, he said, is not the chief and fundamental thing; the chief and fundamental thing is to work in secrecy for the recruitment of cadres, for drawing the most influential members of the Party into our net. By that time the feeling against the leadership of the Party was becoming very acute.

VYSHINSKY: What next?

IVANOV: In 1928 I was sent to the North Caucasus as the Second Secretary. Bukharin suggested to me that I should form a group of Rights in the North Caucasus. He added that the North Caucasus would play a very important part in our struggle against the Party and the Soviet power. He said that we must head a corresponding peasant movement, especially that of the Cossacks, a movement against the Soviet power. We must make it our task to transform the North Caucasus into a Russian Vendée. You know, he said, that capitalism has now entered a new phase of development, and at this new stage capitalism is displaying fairly high elements of organization and planning. Capitalism, he said, is revealing new and fresh strength, expressing itself in the progress of technique, which actually amounts to a technical revolution and the rejuvenation of capitalism, as it were. And that, correspondingly, we must revise our view of the contradictions, of the classes, of the class struggle, and so on. Fundamental amendments must be introduced to Marx. Marx's treatment of the question of

118

proletarian revolutions was no longer suitable. The doctrine of Lenin and Stalin that the epoch of imperialism is an epoch of proletarian revolutions was, he said, a most harmful utopia. This, in fact, was the position from which we proceeded, and which led us to fascism. Here I am obliged to anticipate a little. Bukharin and I returned to this question several times, because I just could not get it into my head, seeing that the contradictions of capitalist society were just forcing themselves to the surface. I mentioned facts to Bukharin which would now be clear to any schoolboy. I pointed to the growing acuteness of the relations between the capitalist states in their struggle for the redivision of markets (the seizure of Abyssinia by Italy, and the seizure of Manchuria by Japan). I pointed to the crisis of 1930. I pointed to the growth of unemployment. And in the end I pointed out that, as a matter of fact, fascism grew up on the acuteness of the class relations of capitalist society becoming extremely accentuated. Is it just such accentuation that the outrageous and bloodthirsty bourgeoisie needed so that capitalism could somehow extricate itself from the acute condition of capitalist society?

Bukharin said that I had not thought over this question deeply enough. Fascism, he said, corresponded to the latest trends in the development of capitalism. [3]

We arrived directly at fascism.

VYSHINSKY: Practically, what did Bukharin propose?

IVANOV: Practically, Bukharin proposed the formation of a group of Rights. I formed one. He proposed that I should form connections with hostile elements. This I also did. We formed connections with Cossack kulaks, with rabid elements among the émigrés, and did everything to prepare for a kulak uprising in the North Caucasus.

VYSHINSKY: That is, you adopted a number of practical measures in this direction?

IVANOV: Yes.

VYSHINSKY: On Bukharin's direct instructions?

IVANOV: Yes.

VYSHINSKY: Proceed.

IVANOV: Of most interest is my treacherous work in the Northern Territory.

VYSHINSKY: When were you sent to the Northern Territory?

IVANOV: In 1931. I went from the Caucasus as Secretary of the Northern Territory Committee. In 1931, April 1 or 2.

VYSHINSKY: Did you guide yourself by these instructions of Bukharin, about which you have just spoken, in subsequent years too?

IVANOV: Yes.

VYSHINSKY: As a general line?

119

IVANOV: Yes, my work in the Northern Territory may be divided into two periods. One period was 1931-32, and the other 1934.

VYSHINSKY: What is the difference?

IVANOV: In 1931-32 the Rights considered the seizure of power a foregone conclusion. So, at least, we thought.

VYSHINSKY: What do you mean by a foregone conclusion?

IVANOV: I shall tell you presently. We looked at it in this way. We took the difficulties of growth through which the country was passing to be a crisis of Socialist development; we took the rage of the kulaks to be a growth of dissatisfaction among the peasant masses, and on these grounds considered that the conditions were favourable for the seizure of power. Bukharin directly claimed that the power was just rushing into our hands.

VYSHINSKY: Just rushing into your hands?

IVANOV: Yes, just rushing into our hands.

VYSHINSKY: You had only to open the gates, so to speak?

IVANOV: Something like it.

VYSHINSKY: And how did Bukharin conceive the seizure of power, if the power was just rushing into your hands? You might just wait with arms folded.

IVANOV: When I left for the Northern Territory, I received instructions from Bukharin to organize . . .

VYSHINSKY: Answer my question, if you can. You said that Bukharin had the idea that the power was just rushing into your hands. I ask you, did Bukharin and his accomplices take any measures to ensure the success of the process, when the power was just rushing into your hands?

IVANOV: I said that in the Caucasus, in particular, we Rights were organizing the kulak elements for an uprising within the country. This was being done in other places too.

VYSHINSKY: But the North Caucasus is not decisive in this matter. I ask you, what instructions did Bukharin give in connection with his prognosis, which, as you see, was a profoundly mistaken one? What was his practical program?

IVANOV: His practical program was to prepare for an uprising.

VYSHINSKY: That is what I am asking you. Were there such instructions, or was it only talk?

IVANOV: No, there were instructions. When I was in the North Caucasus it was an orientation. When I was leaving for the Northern Territory instructions were given to prepare for an armed uprising.

VYSHINSKY: Did this follow from the aim of seizing power?

IVANOV: It followed from the aims of seizing power and of overthrowing the Soviet power.

VYSHINSKY: Did Bukharin and Rykov at that time raise the question of seizing power?

IVANOV: The question of seizing power was raised before 1931.

VYSHINSKY: And were definite instructions given you in this connection to organize insurrectionary bands in the North Caucasus?

IVANOV: Yes, to organize insurrectionary bands in the North Caucasus and later in the Northern Territory.

VYSHINSKY: This was in 1931?

IVANOV: Yes, it was in 1931. But I got the information from Bukharin in 1928 that a directing centre had been set up consisting of Bukharin, Tomsky and Rykov; and in 1929 he informed me that a bloc had been established between the Trotskyites, the Zinovievites and the Rights.

VYSHINSKY: In what year was that?

IVANOV: In 1929. I started very active work in the Northern Territory and formed a group of Rights. In 1934, when the victory of the Party and the growth of the Socialist economy had extraordinarily strengthened the influence of the Party among the masses, all this, of course, began to be felt by us very tangibly, and we then saw that the forces necessary for the seizure of power did not exist within the country itself. The question assumed a new aspect, which was given by Bukharin. I forgot to say that in 1932 Bukharin connected me with Lobov.[4]

VYSHINSKY: We are not interested just now with whom Bukharin connected you. I am interested in your connections with Bukharin, in your connections with the centre of the Rights.

IVANOV: In 1934 I received instructions from Bukharin.

VYSHINSKY: Where were you at that time?

IVANOV: I remained in the Northern Territory until October 1936.

VYSHINSKY: What instructions did you receive from Bukharin while you were in the Northern Territory?

IVANOV: The following, that we had no forces within the country.

VYSHINSKY: I am not asking you how he described the situation.

IVANOV: I cannot formulate what I want to say otherwise. I am going straight to the point.

VYSHINSKY: I am asking you what instructions Bukharin gave.

IVANOV: Bukharin set the task of proceeding to prepare the way through the forces of the Right organizations for the defeat of the Soviet power in case of intervention, in a war with the capitalist fascist states.

VYSHINSKY: There, now I am getting a straight answer. You will have plenty of time to say all you want. But just now

121

I am doing the questioning, and I put those questions which interest the Court. In 1934 Bukharin gave instructions to prepare the way for the defeat of the Soviet power under favourable conditions, in case of an attack by interventionists?

IVANOV: Yes, and he recommended the following series of measures: firstly, to proceed to organize insurrectionary groups in such a way, so that they might in time of war cut the lines of communication in the Northern Territory, because Archangel and the Northern Territory . . .

VYSHINSKY: "Because" does not interest us—we know why this was to be done. What interests us is his proposal that you should organize insurrectionary bands to fight the Soviet power.

IVANOV: Yes, to develop the insurrectionary bands, to develop diversive and wrecking activities and to form terrorist groups.

VYSHINSKY: Is that all?

IVANOV: I think so.

VYSHINSKY: What instructions did Bukharin give with regard to espionage?

IVANOV: He said that Lobov was specially engaged in organizing this, and that he was to inform me how this was to be carried on. He said: "You must, with the help of the Party organization, give every assistance to the residential agent who will be sent there, so as to fulfil the requirements of the British Intelligence Service."

VYSHINSKY: So Bukharin gave you instructions how to serve the British Intelligence Service?

IVANOV: Yes.

VYSHINSKY: And did you carry out these instructions?

IVANOV: I did, I performed services for, I sent material to and received instructions through this residential agent. And the directions received from the British Intelligence Service fully coincided with the directions I received from the Right centre.

VYSHINSKY: They fully coincided? So that sometimes you could not distinguish between the activities of the Right centre and those of the foreign intelligence service.

IVANOV: Yes, they fully coincided.

VYSHINSKY: That is not surprising. And what arguments did Bukharin give in support of his directions to you to get into connection with the British Intelligence Service?

IVANOV: He said that that country had very great interests in the Northern Territory.

VYSHINSKY: In which territory?

IVANOV: In the Northern Territory. He said that the Right centre had an agreement with that country about helping the

Rights to overthrow the Soviet power and about helping the Rights to maintain the power seized, and that this agreement provided for securing the interests of British timber firms with timber of the Northern Territory. Bukharin proposed that the sawmills should be handed over as a concession to the British, while the new sawmills that had been built under the Soviet power would have to be surrendered in payment of the tsarist debts. Then, in 1934, he suggested that we must already begin to make real payments in real values. He said that we must give advances to the British bourgeoisie so as, on the one hand, not to lose support, and, on the other, not to forfeit confidence. In accordance with these instructions, the following measures were carried out through Rosengoltz and Lobov.

The most valuable timber was sold at reduced prices. This involved a loss to the Soviet state of several million rubles in foreign currency. Bukharin explained this measure as being an advance to the British bourgeoisie in return for the support it had promised. Otherwise, he said, we would not be taken seriously, and we would forfeit confidence.

VYSHINSKY: Credit?

IVANOV: Yes.

VYSHINSKY: Now tell us about terrorist activities and terrorist plans.

IVANOV: Our organization in the Northern Territory was set the task of forming a terrorist group.

VYSHINSKY: Who set this task?

IVANOV: Bukharin. Bukharin reverted to this subject several times, particularly after the assassination of Kirov. He said that the shot fired at Kirov had shown that isolated terrorist acts could yield no results, that mass terrorist acts must be organized, and only then would we have results. His line was to do away with the leadership of the Party, and he argued as follows: if we succeed in doing so before a war, the position will be clear, and it is possible that immediate war on the Soviet Union will flare up. If, for any reason, we were to fail to put the leadership of the Party out of the way before a war, we were to do so during a war; and this would cause great dismay, undermine the fighting efficiency of the country and help radically to bring about the defeat of the Soviet power in a war with the imperialists. Bukharin asked us to name the persons whom we had enlisted as terrorists. We gave Bukharin the names of these people.

VYSHINSKY: Consequently, the organizing of terrorist acts also occupied a certain place in your criminal activities?

IVANOV: Yes.

VYSHINSKY: And this, you affirm, was done upon the direct instructions . . .

123

IVANOV: Of Bukharin.

VYSHINSKY: Only of Bukharin, or of others too?

IVANOV: Bukharin and Lobov.

VYSHINSKY: No, I mean among the accused in the present trial.

IVANOV: No, nobody else gave instructions.

VYSHINSKY: And so you acted under the direct instructions of Bukharin. In what year was that?

IVANOV: I first received instructions to organize a terrorist group in 1934. Pressure was brought to bear in 1935, when it was said that we were developing the work too slowly.

VYSHINSKY: What else have you to say about your wrecking activities?

IVANOV: We also carried on insurrectionary activities.

VYSHINSKY: You have already spoken about that.

IVANOV: We assembled insurrectionary groups, chiefly around Archangel, so as, at the moment of intervention, to cut off communication between Archangel and the central arteries of our country, and thus make it easier for the British to seize this timber region and most valuable port.

Then we carried on diversive activities, chiefly in the timber industry, because the Northern Territory is a timber region. These activities aimed at preventing the technical re-equipment of the timber industry, filling it with unreliable elements, wrecking the machinery centres and hampering timber-floating. In 1936, owing to the wrecking activities of our Right organization, the Northern Territory failed to supply considerable quantities of timber to the sawmills. This forced a number of the sawmills to stop work and increased the shortage of timber material in our country, thus severely affecting capital construction work in the country.

When I was in the People's Commissariat of the Timber Industry I continued these wrecking activities and the preparations for terrorist acts. Attention was chiefly devoted to hindering the technical re-equipment of lumbering, preventing the fulfilment of the plans of capital construction, especially in the cellulose and paper industry, in this way placing the country on a short paper ration and aiming a blow at the cultural revolution, interrupting the supply of exercise books and thus rousing discontent among the masses. We did everything we could to prevent the building of new plants and to hamper the work of the existing plants. We also deliberately refrained from carrying out a number of measures in the sphere of reconstruction which would have improved the work of the paper industry, and thus prevented the fulfilment of the program of paper output.

That, I think, is all. Perhaps you have some questions to ask me?

VYSHINSKY: And what circumstance terminated your criminal activities?

IVANOV: My arrest.

VYSHINSKY: Consequently, right up to your arrest . . .

IVANOV: Right up to my arrest I continued to belong to the bloc of Rights and Trotskyites and to carry on active undermining, espionage, terrorist, diversive and wrecking activities on the instructions of the centre of the Rights.

VYSHINSKY: I have no more questions at present.

THE PRESIDENT: Have the defence any questions to ask?

COUNSEL FOR DEFENCE: (Reply in the negative.)

BUKHARIN: I have a question to put. I want to put it to Citizen Ivanov. If I am not mistaken, the last time we met was in March 1936.

IVANOV: In my opinion, we met also after that. At one of the autumn plenums of the Central Committee of the Party you and I had a conversation. What we talked about was the depression that prevailed in the organization in connection with the victories of the Party, the great vacillations, that people were beginning to desert, and that we did not possess big forces. I want to recall the gist of the conversation, perhaps Bukharin will remember it. You and I, Citizen Bukharin, played the hypocrite to the Soviet government so often that you could get the whole calendar mixed up. I would remind you of the details of our conversation.

VYSHINSKY: The accused Bukharin asked you when you and he last met.

IVANOV: I met him in 1937. In 1937 he had already adopted a secretive attitude towards us.

VYSHINSKY: He had already adopted a secretive attitude towards you?

IVANOV: Yes, from fear that he might get "pinched." Citizen Bukharin has said that our connections were interrupted in March 1936. . . .

VYSHINSKY: He said nothing, he is only asking. You affirm that until your arrest—in what month was that? When were you arrested?

IVANOV: I was arrested after he was.

VYSHINSKY: That means that connections were not interrupted until his arrest?

IVANOV: They were not interrupted, but the meetings were casual ones; they took place in such conditions that nobody could have thought that we were arranging meetings with each other.

VYSHINSKY (to Bukharin): Do you deny that you had meetings with Ivanov until the moment of your arrest?

BUKHARIN: No, I do not deny it, but I simply asked Ivanov to remind me when we met the last time, where we met, and what we talked about.

IVANOV: We met several times during the course of 1936, and in particular in December or in November 1936. I put it to Bukharin that the organization was falling to pieces, that the victories of the Party and the successes of Socialist construction, and the enthusiasm of the masses for this construction, were having such an effect that vacillations were growing at an extraordinary pace, particularly in the peripheral part, that our assassination of Kirov had aroused the fury of the masses to an unprecedented degree, and that this was extremely hampering the treacherous and vile work of the Rights, and that here and there the masses themselves were exposing our followers. And I put it to him whether it did not follow from the situation that had developed in the country that we had suffered complete bankruptcy.

VYSHINSKY: This is what you said to Bukharin?

IVANOV: Yes. And never did I see Bukharin as angry and furious as he was then.

VYSHINSKY: When was that?

IVANOV: At the end of 1936. He attacked me violently, said that I was a coward, a panic-monger, that I was always bringing up the "masses," that we must not pander to the masses, that I should know that the Right organization will wage war on the masses, yet I wanted to pander to them.

VYSHINSKY: He wanted to wage war on the masses?

IVANOV: Yes. And he further put the question in this way: if there are deserters, we must adopt much more extensive measures to exterminate those who decide to repent publicly before the Soviet power, and thus expose our Right organization. The fact is that there were instructions in the Right organization to the effect that those who deserted the Rights and divulged their activities should be put out of the way. This was done to one of our people who was about to write to the People's Commissariat of Internal Affairs exposing the activities of the Rights in the North Caucasus. Lobov told me that one of these men had been put out of the way. And Bukharin plainly hinted that I must bear in mind that they would not stand on ceremony with anybody who funked or faltered, and that they had special people to carry out the necessary measures, meaning assassination.

In 1937 our conversation was also a very brief one.

VYSHINSKY: A brief one?

IVANOV: Brief because we were already very cautious. The whole organization was in a state of fear; I would say that the activities of the Rights were virtually on the eve of thorough

126

exposure. During this conversation in particular, I asked: where is the intervention, where is the attack on the Soviet Union? Bukharin told me that measures were being taken to induce the fascist countries—Japan and Germany—to take action without fail in 1937, and the chances of this were good.

VYSHINSKY: No more questions?

BUKHARIN: No.

VYSHINSKY: You have no more questions?

BUKHARIN: I have not received a reply to the question I put. I requested Ivanov to say, if he remembers everything so thoroughly, in what months we met in 1937. If he does not remember, let him say so.

THE PRESIDENT (to Ivanov): Reply briefly.

IVANOV: Why does Bukharin think that I must absolutely remember all the months in which I had conversations with him? I said that it was at the beginning of 1937. But it might have been in January or February.

VYSHINSKY: You do not remember?

IVANOV: I do not remember precisely whether it was in January or February, because we had so many conversations of all kinds that you can't remember everything.

THE PRESIDENT (to Vyshinsky): Have you any more questions?

VYSHINSKY: No.

THE PRESIDENT (to Bukharin): Have you any more questions?

BUKHARIN: No, I have no more questions.

THE PRESIDENT: The Court will adjourn for twenty minutes.

*   *   *

COMMANDANT OF THE COURT: The Court is coming, please rise.

THE PRESIDENT: Be seated. Comrade Procurator, have you anything to ask Ivanov?

VYSHINSKY: I would like to question Bukharin.

Accused Bukharin, the accused Ivanov said in this Court that in 1928, or even somewhat earlier, he already had conversations with you on the subject of the anti-Soviet work of the Right organization to which you belonged. Do you confirm this?

BUKHARIN: Yes. Permit me to say what I confirm....

VYSHINSKY: I am interested only in that question. Do you confirm it, or not?

BUKHARIN: Yes, I confirm it. Firstly, that I have been acquainted with Ivanov since the time of the Brest-Litovsk Peace, since 1918. During the Tenth Congress I really did advise Ivanov, believing that he held counter-revolutionary opinions, to continue anti-Party work.

VYSHINSKY: What I am interested in knowing just now is whether the accused Ivanov was right in saying that he had a conversation with you in 1928 about anti-Soviet work. Do you confirm that?

BUKHARIN: Yes.

VYSHINSKY: You consider that the accused Ivanov quite rightly stated that in 1927-28, when he was leaving for the North Caucasus, you gave him instructions?

BUKHARIN: It is perfectly true that when he was leaving for the North Caucasus, I, on behalf of the Right centre, gave him instructions regarding the recruitment of people and the formation of an organization there. Moreover, he had certain persons in mind, like Stepanov, Pivovarov, Tomachev and others.

And it is perfectly true that in 1931-32, to use his jargon, I passed him over to Lobov, who was to direct him.

Perfectly true is the assertion made by the accused Ivanov to the effect that I kept him informed of the stand of the Right centre, from the Ryutin platform[5] to the latest stands, of which the Court is fairly well informed.

It is quite true that I also met him later, in 1931-32, but I cannot recall the dates just now.

VYSHINSKY: That we shall ask later. I once more repeat that what interests me is 1928. Consequently, do you confirm this part of the testimony of the accused Ivanov?

BUKHARIN: I confirm that I had meetings with him at that time.

VYSHINSKY: And that you carried on those conversations with him, as he informed the Court, about anti-Party and anti-Soviet activities.

BUKHARIN: We did.

VYSHINSKY: The accused Ivanov testified that you proposed that he should form an organization of Rights in the North Caucasus with certain definite aims. Do you confirm that too?

BUKHARIN: He has got the dates mixed up.

VYSHINSKY: First of all, do you confirm the fact itself?

BUKHARIN: I confirm the fact itself that I instructed him to form an organization.

VYSHINSKY: A secret one?

BUKHARIN: A secret, illegal, counter-revolutionary one. But at that period the acute struggle against the Party and the Soviet government had not taken the forms . . .

VYSHINSKY: I am just now interested in the testimony of the accused Ivanov, which the Court has heard. He says that

Bukharin gave me, i.e., Ivanov, instructions to proceed to form a secret organization of Rights in the North Caucasus. Do you confirm this?

BUKHARIN: That part I do confirm.

VYSHINSKY: Consequently, in 1928 you had adopted the method of illegal, underground activities?

BUKHARIN: That was a moment of such transition . . .

VYSHINSKY: I am not asking you when it was. Is this a fact, or not a fact?

BUKHARIN: That I confirm.

VYSHINSKY: Did you also tell Ivanov at the time that a centre of the Right organization was already functioning?

BUKHARIN: I did.

VYSHINSKY: Consisting of whom?

BUKHARIN: Consisting of three persons: Tomsky, Rykov, and myself, Bukharin.

VYSHINSKY: Did you tell him that this centre was preparing for the overthrow of the Soviet power?

BUKHARIN: I did, but this refers to a later period.

VYSHINSKY: To which exactly?

BUKHARIN: I think it refers roughly to 1932-33.

VYSHINSKY: That is, somewhat later. But the fact that you had such a conversation with Ivanov you do confirm?

BUKHARIN: I do. I do not remember the date, nor the month, but that was the general orientation of the Right centre.

VYSHINSKY: And do you confirm that you said that you were preparing for open battles?

BUKHARIN: There could have been no open battles in 1926. When Ivanov says that we were preparing for open battles, he is mixing the dates.

VYSHINSKY: But during the preliminary investigation you said that it relates to 1926.

BUKHARIN: Yes, but not in the sense in which it is understood here, Citizen the State Prosecutor.

VYSHINSKY (to the Court): Please let me have Vol. V of Bukharin's testimony, p. 113. Allow me to read it.

BUKHARIN: Excuse me, what page?

VYSHINSKY: Page 113 of Bukharin's testimony, Vol. V. This is your testimony of December 25, 1937. Here, on p. 113, it says: "I again established connections with Ivanov during the Tenth Party Congress; I talked with him in the lobbies. . . . In 1926-27, when we were preparing for open battles against the Party, I advised Ivanov not to take part in the open attacks on the Party on the grounds that Ivanov was a practical man, and for the time being it was more expedient to keep him in reserve."

Do you confirm this?

BUKHARIN: Page 113 in my copy says something different.

VYSHINSKY: Is your signature there?

BUKHARIN: This is my signature, and the passage is perfectly correct. But I have a copy in which the page numbering is quite different.

THE PRESIDENT: Accused Bukharin, it is not a question of the page numbering.

VYSHINSKY: Accused Bukharin, did you tell Ivanov in 1926-27 that you, a group of Right conspirators, were preparing for open battles against the Party?

BUKHARIN: Excuse me, but as a matter of fact I was referring to open actions and not to open battles.

VYSHINSKY: Accused Bukharin, did the conversation which I have just quoted take place?

BUKHARIN: It did, but the words "open battles" did not mean violent open battles.

VYSHINSKY: You speak of open battles, and that is what you said in your conversation with Ivanov, too.

BUKHARIN: I was not referring to violent . . .

VYSHINSKY: Did you say that Ivanov should be kept in reserve?

BUKHARIN: Yes.

VYSHINSKY: Did you say that Ivanov should not get involved in the open fight?

BUKHARIN: Yes.

VYSHINSKY: You did refer to open battles?

BUKHARIN: Ivanov has got his dates muddled.

VYSHINSKY: Excuse me, he has got nothing muddled. We can see that it is you who are muddling it.

BUKHARIN: We did not refer to open battles in the sense of armed insurrection.

VYSHINSKY: I am referring to open battles.

BUKHARIN: I misunderstood you, Citizen State Prosecutor.

VYSHINSKY: I beg your pardon, you misunderstood me, Citizen Accused.

BUKHARIN: The incident is closed.

VYSHINSKY: Let us turn to your volume, p. 120. Just look for your testimony there.

BUKHARIN: I was arranging for this with Ivanov: "In 1926-27, when we were preparing for open battles against the Party, I advised Ivanov not to take part in the open battles, but to remain in reserve." I do not deny that.

VYSHINSKY: Then in 1927 Ivanov went to the North Caucasus, and you gave him instructions. Do you confirm that? I ask the question to check this. You gave him instructions to organize an illegal Right group. Is that true?

130

BUKHARIN: It is.

VYSHINSKY: An illegal group?

BUKHARIN: An illegal one.

VYSHINSKY: This you confirm. You also instructed him to carry out a number of tasks you gave him with regard to this organization in the period of 1928. It was not only a question of recruiting, but also of the organization of insurrectionary bands?

BUKHARIN: I did not go into the technical side of this business.

VYSHINSKY: I am not referring to the technical side of the organization of insurrectionary bands, but to the platform of the Rights, in which the line of insurrection was adopted. When you instructed Ivanov to form an illegal organization, did you say anything about insurrectionary bands?

BUKHARIN: I did not, and could not at that time.

VYSHINSKY: But what were the illegal organizations to do?

BUKHARIN: The illegal organizations were to muster forces for the fight against the Party, which was growing acute.

VYSHINSKY: Only preparations for a fight?

BUKHARIN: It was such a stage in the general development of the Right deviation.

VYSHINSKY: And when did you raise the question of insurrectionary bands?

BUKHARIN: The adoption of violence roughly relates to 1932.

VYSHINSKY: Where was Ivanov at that time?

BUKHARIN: This I do not remember.

VYSHINSKY: Accused Ivanov, where were you in 1932?

IVANOV: In 1932 I was in the Northern Territory.

VYSHINSKY: Was the question of organizing and forming insurrectionary bands discussed by you, and if so, in what form?

IVANOV: It was discussed. Bukharin bluntly put the question of establishing connections with the discontented kulak elements of the Cossacks.

VYSHINSKY: This was not in the Northern Territory, but in the North Caucasus?

IVANOV: Yes, in the North Caucasus.

VYSHINSKY: This refers not to 1932. Were you in the Northern Territory in 1932?

IVANOV: Yes, in 1932 I was in the Northern Territory.

VYSHINSKY: And was the question of preparing insurrectionary bands raised then?

IVANOV: The question of preparing insurrectionary bands was also put before me by Bukharin in 1932, when the question

131

was raised of creating Right organizations in the Northern Territory.

VYSHINSKY: In 1932 did not Bukharin speak about the necessity of strengthening insurrectionary bands?

IVANOV: He did.

VYSHINSKY: Hence you remember that you had two such talks—in 1928 and in 1932?

IVANOV: Yes.

VYSHINSKY: In connection with your work in the North Caucasus and in the Northern Territory?

IVANOV: Yes.

BUKHARIN (to the Court): I assert that in 1928 there was no talk at all about an insurrectionary orientation, as is evidenced by numerous documents and facts, including . . .

VYSHINSKY: But in 1929?

BUKHARIN: The fixation of the question about insurrectionary organizations that was approved by the Right centre was first indicated in what is called the Ryutin platform.

VYSHINSKY: The Ryutin platform, its first variant, in what period was that?

BUKHARIN: There was no variant at all. There was a preliminary conference, if I am not mistaken, in the spring of 1932 at which the theses were outlined. But in the platform which you mention—the platform of 1928-29—there was no reference to insurrection. . . .

VYSHINSKY: Hence, you assert that the question of insurrectionary bands was raised only in 1932?

BUKHARIN: The question of an insurrectionary orientation arose in 1932.

VYSHINSKY: The question of an "insurrectionary orientation." What is an "insurrectionary orientation"?

BUKHARIN: It means that every line has its strategy, tactics, organization, etc. An insurrectionary band is a category of organization, but not a category of strategy, and not even a category of tactics. In my terminology I usually distinguish between them because it seems to me that they can be distinguished. . . .

VYSHINSKY: Of course; they can. But I ask: in your activities there was a line of insurrectionary movement. Is this what you call an "insurrectionary orientation"?

BUKHARIN: Yes, tactics.

VYSHINSKY: And the organization of insurrectionary bands followed from these tactics?

BUKHARIN: Yes, it did.

VYSHINSKY: And what did you do in this matter? What instructions did you give?

132

BUKHARIN: I did not give Ivanov any instructions in this sense.

VYSHINSKY: But Ivanov says that instructions were given.

BUKHARIN: Quite naturally, Ivanov says . . .

VYSHINSKY: Yes, Ivanov says this, and you assert that you gave Ivanov no direct instructions, but that you had an "insurrectionary orientation."

BUKHARIN: It is quite natural that from this orientation the practical worker should draw corresponding conclusions. If I take such an orientation I am responsible for its conclusions which are implied. So that from the point of view of criminal law I request you to judge me for both the one and the other, and I will answer . . .

VYSHINSKY: You will be judged without your request.

BUKHARIN: Quite right, without my request. I do not think this is the time or place for witticisms. I too can be witty. . . .

VYSHINSKY: I do not intend to be witty or to compete with you in this. I only want to say that your request is of no material importance, because you will be judged whether you ask for it or not.

BUKHARIN: I am aware of this even without authoritative explanations, Citizen Procurator.

VYSHINSKY: If you are aware of this there was no need for you to mention it. I am asking you something else: Hence you admit that Ivanov's evidence as regards the line, the orientation towards an insurrectionary movement, is correct?

BUKHARIN: Yes, Citizen Procurator.

VYSHINSKY: In what manner did you inform Ivanov about your insurrectionary plans?

BUKHARIN: There were several conversations. . . .

VYSHINSKY: What conversations, and with whom?

BUKHARIN: With Ivanov.

VYSHINSKY: What did you talk about? In what form?

BUKHARIN: I informed Ivanov exclusively on the form of strategy and tactics.

VYSHINSKY: What is it if we say it without the words "strategy" and "tactics"?

BUKHARIN: I said that a period had set in when it was necessary to adopt mass tactics, to support insurrectionary kulak movements, etc.

VYSHINSKY: That is what I wanted to establish. You admit that you told Ivanov that it was necessary to support insurrectionary movements, every sort of kulak movement?

BUKHARIN: I admit it.

133

VYSHINSKY: Did you talk only about supporting, or also about organizing them?

BUKHARIN: In such detail, Citizen Procurator, I did not speak to him. . . .

VYSHINSKY: How did you picture it to yourself?

BUKHARIN: Naturally, when it is said that it is expedient to adopt these methods, then all the rest follows.

VYSHINSKY: That is?

BUKHARIN: That is, organization and leadership.

VYSHINSKY: Accused Bukharin, did you tell Ivanov that upon him devolved the task, set by the Right centre, of organizing an insurrectionary movement?

BUKHARIN: He might have understood it in that way.

VYSHINSKY: Accused Ivanov, did you understand it in that way?

IVANOV: The instructions were conveyed to me in sufficiently clear terms to enable me to understand their simple meaning. The point was raised that the kulaks were in an angry mood. These were the social forces on which we were to rely. Our task was to head the insurrection. And even in regard to the North Caucasus it was said, although in a somewhat different version, that the North Caucasus could provide considerable kulak cadres, that there the peasant and Cossack movement might start earlier than in any other place, and therefore we should take our place at the head of this movement.

VYSHINSKY: Bukharin, do you corroborate this?

BUKHARIN: This is correct, but not in relation to Ivanov. I said this to another person.

VYSHINSKY: The other person we shall discuss separately. What is important just now is whether the explanation given here coincides with the orientation towards insurrection, about which you have spoken.

BUKHARIN: I could not have said this to Ivanov because he was not in the North Caucasus in 1932.

VYSHINSKY: Ivanov, what year were you referring to?

IVANOV: I was speaking of the Northern Territory, but at the same time I said that in a somewhat different version this also applied to the North Caucasus.

VYSHINSKY: When did you leave the North Caucasus?

IVANOV: I left the North Caucasus on April 2 or 1, 1931.

VYSHINSKY: While you were in the North Caucasus when did you speak with Bukharin?

IVANOV: In 1928.

VYSHINSKY: And in 1929-30?

IVANOV: I was meeting him, but I do not think we talked about these things.

VYSHINSKY: But was there any talk about insurrection in 1932?

IVANOV: Yes, there was such talk.

VYSHINSKY: Permit me to sum up. Judging by the evidence of Ivanov and yours (to Bukharin), what can we regard as having been definitely established? Firstly, that you and Ivanov talked about an insurrectionary line. Is that right?

BUKHARIN: That is right.

VYSHINSKY: That you orientated Ivanov towards the necessity of utilizing kulak insurrections in the interests of the struggle against the Soviet power?

BUKHARIN: Yes.

VYSHINSKY: That you had in mind also the organization of these kulak insurrections?

BUKHARIN: Although I did not speak about them directly.

VYSHINSKY: Although you did not speak about them directly, nevertheless you orientated him towards them?

BUKHARIN: Quite right.

VYSHINSKY: And you assert that all this occurred in 1932?

BUKHARIN: Yes.

VYSHINSKY: And in 1928 you only talked about the illegal group of the Rights?

BUKHARIN: Quite right.

VYSHINSKY: The insurrectionary orientation was adopted nevertheless but without the details that Ivanov has spoken about?

BUKHARIN: In 1932, yes.

VYSHINSKY: You deny the conversation about an insurrectionary orientation in 1928?

BUKHARIN: Yes.

VYSHINSKY: But such a conversation took place in 1932?

BUKHARIN: Quite right. I corroborate this.

IVANOV: Permit me to put a question to Bukharin. Perhaps Bukharin will exert his memory and recall whether we had a conversation in 1928 about the growing discontent among the upper stratum of the rural population, and about a tendency towards a sharp expression of this discontent with the Soviet power. Let him answer this question.

BUKHARIN: Of course, in 1928 a conversation about the growing discontent did take place; I cannot deny it, because we were meeting in 1928. But I categorically deny that I spoke about insurrection in 1928.

IVANOV: Another question. Did Bukharin put it to me that in the carrying out of the line that was adopted by the Rights, the North Caucasus was of exceptionally great importance, and why it was of great importance?

135

BUKHARIN: It is quite true, Citizen Procurator and Citizens Judges, that when I spoke about the North Caucasus I said that the North Caucasus was one of the places where discontent among the peasantry was manifesting itself and will manifest itself most vividly, without, however, drawing any insurrectionary conclusions, because these arose at a much later period.

IVANOV: Bukharin said that an acute manifestation of discontent among the peasantry in the North Caucasus was possible. This comes very close to what I said about this conversation. In conformity with your conceptions did you not instruct me and the Right organization to clutch at this discontent and to do everything to work up the peasants against the Soviet power?

BUKHARIN: First you spoke about insurrection, but I spoke about the suitable social base for the Right organization, about recruiting members for this Right counter-revolutionary organization.

VYSHINSKY: With what object?

BUKHARIN: With the object of creating mass bases for the struggle against the Party line.

VYSHINSKY: Cossack, kulak circles for the struggle against the Party line?

BUKHARIN: Well, what of it?

VYSHINSKY: For the struggle against the Soviet power?

BUKHARIN: The struggle against the Party line is a struggle against the Soviet power.

VYSHINSKY: But the struggle against the Party line finds expression in other forms.

BUKHARIN: I think that the Citizen Procurator, the Citizens Judges and the whole country are interested in seeing how out of certain deviations monstrous conclusions are formed by the logic of the struggle. That is why I want to preserve a certain time-proportion in this respect. In 1928 the anti-Party platform was formulated. At the end of 1928 and the transition to 1929 the slogan was issued to form an illegal organization. In the course of the further intensification of the struggle all this led to what you know.

VYSHINSKY: The question is, did you not orientate Ivanov on the grounds that in your opinion there was favourable soil in the North Caucasus for insurrection against the Soviet power?

BUKHARIN: There was no talk about such an orientation at that time. The orientation was that there was soil there for growing discontent with the Soviet power.

VYSHINSKY: On whose part?

BUKHARIN: On the part of the kulak well-to-do strata of the peasantry, and partly also of the middle strata of the peasantry, as the middle peasantry there was very strong.

VYSHINSKY: Can we not draw from this the conclusion that

you orientated Ivanov towards underground counter-revolutionary work in which he would rely upon this kulak upper stratum in the struggle against the Soviet power?

BUKHARIN: At that time it was possible to formulate it in this way: every social base, in this case the kulak base, chemically produces within the Party not altogether sound elements, i.e., there it is easier to recruit for the illegal counter-revolutionary organization, even within the Party, people who would represent a certain potential force in the future. But this prospect was not fully developed at the time.

VYSHINSKY: But it was already outlined?

BUKHARIN: Potentially, in an embryonic form.

VYSHINSKY: Apart from this, you have no disagreements with Ivanov?

BUKHARIN: There are no important disagreements.

VYSHINSKY: Ivanov states that he learnt from you of the existence of a bloc between the Trotskyites, the Right groups and the nationalist groups. Do you corroborate this?

BUKHARIN: I do.

VYSHINSKY: And did you know about the negotiations which Ivanov and others carried on with capitalist countries?

BUKHARIN: Yes, this was at a much later period.

VYSHINSKY: Hence, Ivanov's statements about connections with the British Intelligence Service . . .

BUKHARIN: I was totally uninformed about the Intelligence Service and about plans.

VYSHINSKY: What were you informed about?

BUKHARIN: I informed Ivanov of the foreign-political orientation of the Right centre, I told him that in the fight against the Soviet power it was permissible to take advantage of a war situation, and a number of other things.

In short, as one of the leaders of the Right centre, it was my duty to communicate our line to one of the leaders of the periphery centre. What was this line? Briefly, this line was that in the fight against the Soviet power it is permissible to utilize a war situation and to make certain concessions to capitalist states for the purpose of neutralizing them, and sometimes for the purpose of obtaining their assistance.

VYSHINSKY: In other words, orientation towards assistance from certain foreign states.

BUKHARIN: Yes, it can be put that way.

VYSHINSKY: In other words, orientation towards the defeat of the U.S.S.R.

BUKHARIN: In general, summarized, I repeat, yes.

THE PRESIDENT: Are there any more questions?

VYSHINSKY: No.

BUKHARIN: Perhaps you will permit me, Citizen President, to say a few words regarding excursions into theory.

THE PRESIDENT: No. You may do so when you are examined. We will now proceed to examine the accused Zubarev.

Accused Zubarev, do you corroborate the testimony you gave during the investigation in the People's Commissariat of Internal Affairs and in the organs of the Procuratorship?

ZUBAREV: Yes, I do.

THE PRESIDENT: Fully?

ZUBAREV: I fully corroborate it.

THE PRESIDENT: Comrade Procurator, have you any questions?

VYSHINSKY: Accused Zubarev, when did you take the path of criminal activities in the counter-revolutionary organization of the Rights?

ZUBAREV: I was enlisted in the counter-revolutionary organization of the Rights in 1929.

VYSHINSKY: And since then?

ZUBAREV: And since then I carried on active work up to the day of my arrest.

VYSHINSKY: What was the active criminal work which you continued up to the day of your arrest?

ZUBAREV: In 1929, I was enlisted in the organization of the Rights by Alexander Petrovich Smirnov,[6] with whom I had been acquainted since 1919. On meeting him in the beginning of 1928 I expressed my dissatisfaction and disagreement with the Party line in respect to the policy in the rural districts. He entirely supported my opinion and strengthened me in it. Knowing my counter-revolutionary views, he in 1929, in May or June, in Moscow, gave me a detailed description of the political state of the country, of the growing discontent in the rural districts owing to the grain collections and to the employment of extraordinary measures against the kulak upper stratum of the rural population, owing to the restriction of the private initiative of the rural population and the decline and diminution in sown area, particularly in the extensive farming districts, the Urals in particular. He developed the point of view that it would be impossible for the Rights to change this state of things by internal Party methods, and that the only path left was that of struggle against the Soviet power. He then informed me of the existence of the Right organization, and I learnt for the first time in 1929 that he was a member of this organization. It was then also that I first learnt of the existence of a Union centre of this organization.

Then he went on to say that the Rights attached great importance to the Urals, that the Urals were important for two reasons (I am speaking not of the present Urals Region, but of the former Urals

138

Region, which included the present Chelyabinsk Region, so that this region, which is not only a very important industrial district, but also a very important agricultural district, comprised the whole of the eastern part of the Urals); that as regards industry and agriculture, the Urals were extremely important in this respect, and that they (and he in particular) counted on my participation in counter-revolutionary work.

When I consented he at once told me that I would not be the only one working in the Urals, that there was already an active member of the counter-revolutionary organization there, very influential, that he was already directly connected with the Union centre through Rykov. He mentioned Kabakov.

VYSHINSKY: When did the connections with Rykov begin?

ZUBAREV: Connections with Rykov began in 1930, when he came to the Party conference in Sverdlovsk.

VYSHINSKY: Under what circumstances did the connection arise between you and Rykov as the leader of the Right conspiratorial centre?

ZUBAREV: I was then on Party work. During the conference I had quite a long talk with Rykov.

VYSHINSKY: What about?

ZUBAREV: Rykov referred to A. P. Smirnov and stated that he had heard from him that I was an active member of the Right organization. I described to him the general situation in the Urals, the state of our organization and told him that already at the end of 1929, in December, Kabakov and I had organized a regional leading group which co-ordinated the whole work. I told him who belonged to this group: Kabakov, myself, Sovetnikov and others. I told him of the work I had done on Smirnov's instructions and on his, Rykov's, instructions, conveyed by Kabakov.

The work at that time in the main consisted of preparing cadres, of uniting the scattered forces we then had in the organization. Rykov approved of this work, and he in turn gave me a detailed description of the state of the country at the time, that is, in the spring of 1930, when the situation was extremely tense in the rural districts, in the period of the class struggle that followed in connection with mass collectivization and the policy of expropriating the kulaks.

He characterized the situation as extremely strained and said that, owing to mass collectivization, the expropriation of the kulaks and the employment of administrative measures, spontaneous armed risings were breaking out in a number of districts; that the policy of expropriating the kulaks had affected not only the kulak upper stratum but sometimes also certain well-to-do middle strata of the rural population, and that this great drama in the rural districts had also created a hostile attitude towards the Party's policy. He said there and then that the Party was responsible for this mess and would have to clean it up itself, and as far as we were concerned, the worse, the better. Rykov said that it would be ridiculous on our part if we did not wage our struggle to bring about this kulak insurrection, if we ourselves took absolutely no measures to organize such a kulak movement and did not take the lead of it. Rykov said that first of all we should take advantage of these factors to fan discontent in the rural districts. The tasks which Rykov then put before me during this conversation can be reduced to three main points.

The first was wrecking work in the rural districts: disruption of the sowing campaign by delaying the issue and supply of seeds, reducing their quality, which would naturally rouse anger among the population. On the other hand, measures that hindered the strengthening of the collective farms were adopted in order to rouse discontent among the peasant population.

As regards industry, no definite tasks were put as regards wrecking; at least, no direct and definite instructions were given.

In addition, we were to create and consolidate cadres in large-scale industry and to entrench ourselves in its most important branches in the Urals, and not to scatter our forces in this work; industry was too varied, and so we were to concentrate our work on the most important branches of industry, and in the most important plants.

The second point. This was to excite the population by various provocative measures, by disorganizing the supply of staple food products, and particularly disorganizing public catering. This was done in a number of places in 1932, particularly in Perm, Lisva, and, as far as I know, in Berezniki in the Kizel district.

The third point. The consolidation of all the elements hostile to the Soviet power and the formation of a bloc with the other organizations in the Urals. In particular, in respect to the Trotskyites, Zinovievites, Socialist-Revolutionaries, it was impressed upon us that we were to get in touch with them and organize connections and contact without losing our independence.

This, in substance, is the line which I received. I learnt from Kabakov that he had had separately conversations, rather lengthy ones, with Rykov in his railway car at the same time, and the contents, the substance of their conversations I learnt from Kabakov himself, who told me about them. The substance of their conversations amounted to the same as what I have just stated.

VYSHINSKY (to the Court): Permit me to question the accused Rykov.

Accused Rykov, what have you to say about this part of the accused Zubarev's evidence? Do you corroborate the statement about the meeting?

RYKOV: Yes.

VYSHINSKY: And the conversations, instructions?

RYKOV: I corroborate the talks about my opinions concerning the temper prevailing in the rural districts at that time. I also had to give and gave instructions. But the main thing here are the conclusions. In respect to the conclusions the main position on wrecking . . .

VYSHINSKY: First about the facts, and then about conclusions. Did you give Zubarev any instructions?

RYKOV: Yes.

VYSHINSKY: When?

RYKOV: In May 1930.

VYSHINSKY: Hence, you gave instructions secretly to recruit members for the organization of the Rights?

RYKOV: Yes.

VYSHINSKY: You corroborate this?

RYKOV: Yes.

VYSHINSKY: Do you want to clear up any points on subsequent instructions that you gave Zubarev in respect to his criminal activities?

RYKOV: Yes.

VYSHINSKY: In the main, what he said is right?

RYKOV: In the main it can be said he is right. In respect to the rural districts, I spoke about—expressing myself in our language—sabotaging the policy of the Party in the rural districts in respect to collectivization and supporting individual farming in the rural districts.

VYSHINSKY: You gave the line to sabotage the government's measures in respect to collectivization, to disrupt collectivization. . . .

RYKOV: And to support individual peasant farming.

VYSHINSKY: For the purpose of disrupting collectivization?

RYKOV: The one excluded the other.

VYSHINSKY: Did you give any line on sabotaging the Party's policy?

RYKOV: Well, of course, and the Party's policy in the rural districts in general.

VYSHINSKY: You corroborate this?

RYKOV: Yes.

VYSHINSKY: Be seated. (To the Court.) Permit me to question the accused Zubarev.

Accused Zubarev, tell us what you did concretely to commit crimes against the Soviet government.

ZUBAREV: In the sphere of agriculture we had at the head members of our . . .

VYSHINSKY: It is not important for me what members

141

of your organization you will name. What is important for me is what you, Zubarev, did in committing crimes against the Soviet government.

ZUBAREV: I gave instructions in the sphere of agriculture to disrupt grain collections, to encourage hostile moods in connection with grain deliveries, to resist collectivization, to resist the measures the Party and the government were carrying out to strengthen the collective farms.

VYSHINSKY: This was in what year?

ZUBAREV: I gave these instructions when I was in the Urals in 1931.

VYSHINSKY: And did you give any instructions to organize kulak insurrections?

ZUBAREV: I did. They were direct corollaries of these measures.

VYSHINSKY: Tell us what you remember of this part.

ZUBAREV: What we did in respect to kulak insurrections and in the sphere of organizational measures? We set up organizational groups in the periphery. Of course, at that time there was nothing else of a definite nature that we could do.

VYSHINSKY: With what object?

ZUBAREV: With the object of being ready at the proper moment to lead such insurrections and insurrectionary movements.

VYSHINSKY: Did you do this on your own initiative or not?

ZUBAREV: I carried out the instructions I had received from Smirnov and Rykov. Kabakov, who all the time maintained direct connections with Rykov and Tomsky, also had this line.

VYSHINSKY: And then in 1932 and 1933?

ZUBAREV: I must say that in 1931, towards the end of the year, I went to Moscow, but I learnt of a number of measures that were being carried out in the Urals from members of the Urals organization whom I met in Moscow. I did not directly give instructions myself. I left at the end of September and did not return to the Urals, and my connections were maintained only by meeting individual members of the organization. But I knew about the wrecking work that was going on in industry and about the connections the Urals organization had with the Trotskyites and Socialist-Revolutionaries.

VYSHINSKY: When was that?

ZUBAREV: In 1932, 1933 and 1934. I knew this from a number of members, and directly from Kabakov.

VYSHINSKY: What wrecking acts were committed as a result of your activities?

ZUBAREV: I gave wrecking instructions which caused damage to the Soviet state in the sphere of agriculture in the Urals. As for my work in Moscow, my counter-revolutionary activities here started in the middle of 1933.

142

VYSHINSKY: Tell us the nature of your wrecking activities..

ZUBAREV: When I was working in the seed cultivation department of the People's Commissariat of Agriculture of the U.S.S.R., they were of the nature that the accused Chernov spoke about yesterday: causing confusion in seed cultivation, lowering the quality of the seeds, employing bad quality materials, bad sifting, careless storing, and the result of all this was not only a reduction in yield, but also a hostile mood of the peasantry, dissatisfaction with these so-called selected seeds.

VYSHINSKY: During what period did you commit these crimes?

ZUBAREV: They were committed at the end of 1933 and the beginning of 1934.

VYSHINSKY: And then?

ZUBAREV: And then in March 1934 I left the People's Commissariat of Agriculture of the U.S.S.R. and went to the People's Commissariat of Agriculture of the R.S.F.S.R. There was our organization in the People's Commissariat of Agriculture of the R.S.F.S.R. and I was able to establish connections with this organization through Muralov, as Muralov, while being a member of this organization, had for a long time been People's Commissar of Agriculture of the R.S.F.S.R., and his Assistant Commissar was Lisitsin. I knew from Muralov that Lisitsin too was a member of our organization.

VYSHINSKY: What was the nature of your criminal activities in the People's Commissariat of Agriculture of the R.S.F.S.R.?

ZUBAREV: Here my criminal activities consisted first of all in wrongly planning the sowing of vegetables; in particular, little attention was paid to the development of vegetable growing in our eastern districts, where the development of vegetable growing was of enormous importance, especially in view of the development of industry, in particular in the Far Eastern Territory and in the West Siberian Territory. The shipping of vegetables from the principal vegetable-growing districts in Central Russia was economically extremely difficult and loaded the railways with a very unprofitable freight—this was the first point. Secondly, exactly the same kind of work was carried on in respect to retarding the development of fruit-tree nurseries. Fruit growing had recently begun to develop very rapidly and the collective farm population was beginning to present a growing demand owing to their increased prosperity, but we were unable to meet this demand. The development of nurseries was also retarded as one of the wrecking measures.

In respect to state farms, the main wrecking activities were that up to the last moment no proper rotation of crops was established, and in a number of state farms there was no rotation of crops at all. All this naturally reduced the yields. A large number of state farms which possessed large herds of cattle were left without fodder owing to the wrong crop rotation, and as a result we had the dying off of cattle and slow development of the livestock farming. Why do I speak only of this compass of measures? Because in the People's Commissariat of Agriculture of the R.S.F.S.R. the compass of our measures was extremely limited, as the principal activities were concentrated in the People's Commissariat of Agriculture of the U.S.S.R.

VYSHINSKY: Did you know that the program of this centre and of the whole group of the bloc of Rights and Trotskyites included terrorist acts?

ZUBAREV: Yes, I did know.

VYSHINSKY: So you knew. Were you personally engaged in organizing terrorist acts?

ZUBAREV: Yes.

VYSHINSKY: When and against whom?

ZUBAREV: At the end of 1936, approximately in December, we—Lisitsin and I—received instructions to organize a terrorist group in the People's Commissariat of Agriculture of the R.S.F.S.R. This group consisted of . . .

VYSHINSKY: Who belonged to it is not important just now. Did you belong to this group?

ZUBAREV: Yes, I belonged to it.

VYSHINSKY: Did you organize this group?

ZUBAREV: I was one of its members and one of its organizers.

VYSHINSKY: Against whom did you intend to commit your dastardly terrorist acts?

ZUBAREV: At first we had no definite persons in mind, but generally we intended to commit terrorist acts against the leading members of the Central Committee of the C.P.S.U. (Bolsheviks), in particular, against the members of the Political Bureau. In view of our position, in view of our connections and great possibilities for organizing terrorist acts, our choice fell on Molotov.

VYSHINSKY: On Molotov—the Chairman of the Council of People's Commissars of the U.S.S.R.?

ZUBAREV: Yes, on Molotov.

VYSHINSKY: And did you have any other criminal designs of the same kind?

ZUBAREV: We confined ourselves to that. We saw no other possibilities. At first the question was raised about Stalin, Kaganovich, Voroshilov and Molotov, but we limited ourselves to Molotov for the reasons I have just stated.

VYSHINSKY: That is, for technical reasons?

ZUBAREV: For technical reasons, and according to our possibilities.

VYSHINSKY: Tell us under what circumstances you became an agent of the tsarist Okhrana.

144

ZUBAREV: Not the Okhrana, but the tsarist police.

VYSHINSKY: Is there any difference?

ZUBAREV: There is a slight difference, but in substance they are the same.

VYSHINSKY: I think so too.

ZUBAREV: In 1908, in the village where my father lived, and where I was staying at the time, a large force of police arrived to make a search. During the search a considerable quantity of literature was found.

VYSHINSKY: Of what sort?

ZUBAREV: Illegal literature. Inspector Vasilyev, who was in charge of the search, put it to me like this: "If you, Zubarev, want to escape punishment, the only way you can do so is to accept my proposal that you become an agent of the police." I did not immediately give him a definite reply but said that if I decided to accept I would call upon him.

Some time later I called on him in his apartment in the town of Kotelnich and received from him instructions to provide him with information on the membership of the Kotelnich organization, on the character of some of its most active leaders—Chibisov, Petukhov and Popov—and with information about the match factory and the military garrison. This was in December-November 1908. In March I called upon him a second time and then I left the Vyatka Province and went to the Ufa Province, where I obtained a situation as a bookkeeper in a co-operative society in the district town. At first I had no occasion to meet the police, but in the middle of 1910 I established connections with the police inspector of Sterlitamak.

VYSHINSKY: What sort of connections?

ZUBAREV: As an agent.

VYSHINSKY: That is to say, you became an agent of the police in Sterlitamak?

ZUBAREV: Yes. Inspector Vasilyev told me that he had sent notification to my new place of residence. That is when my work started, and I was given the pseudonym of "Paren."

VYSHINSKY: This was your second pseudonym?

ZUBAREV: Yes. My first was "Vasily."

VYSHINSKY: Did you have another pseudonym?

ZUBAREV: In Ufa my pseudonym was "Prokhor."

VYSHINSKY: When was this?

ZUBAREV: In the beginning of 1916.

VYSHINSKY: What other occupation did you then have, apart from your work as an agent-provocateur? What was your official position?

ZUBAREV: I was working in the town of Sterlitamak as the district co-operative instructor.

VYSHINSKY: Whom did you betray?

ZUBAREV: The members of the staff of the Co-operative Society and of the Zemstvo.[7] In Sterlitamak I was instructed to give information about the political exiles, of whom there was a large number in Sterlitamak.

VYSHINSKY: You gave information about the political exiles?

ZUBAREV: Yes.

VYSHINSKY: Did you give information about the Bolshevik exiles?

ZUBAREV: There was one Social-Democrat there, the agronomist Silin, and one other Social-Democrat whose name I cannot now recall.

VYSHINSKY: So you find it hard to remember all those you betrayed?

ZUBAREV: At all events, since I do not deny the fact itself...

VYSHINSKY: Well, I say that you cannot remember them all. And so at the end of 1915 or beginning of 1916 you moved to Ufa?

ZUBAREV: Yes.

VYSHINSKY: Under what circumstances? What drew you to Ufa?

ZUBAREV: The Provincial Zemstvo offered me the post of provincial co-operative instructor. I went to Ufa, and six weeks later I was mobilized. . . .

VYSHINSKY: When you arrived in Ufa you resumed your connections with the police?

ZUBAREV: Yes, at the beginning of February 1916.

VYSHINSKY: And it was then that you were given the pseudonym of "Prokhor"?

ZUBAREV: Yes.

VYSHINSKY: And then you were called up for the army?

ZUBAREV: Yes.

VYSHINSKY: And while you were in the army did you continue to inform the police on political matters?

ZUBAREV: After my departure from Ufa, no.

VYSHINSKY: I ask when you were in the army. . . .

ZUBAREV: At all events, this business depressed me very much, for my becoming an agent of the tsarist Okhrana was not called forth by any natural organic vice.

VYSHINSKY: By inorganic vice?

ZUBAREV: I want to say that I . . .

VYSHINSKY: Whether it was called forth by organic vice or inorganic vice we shall ascertain later.

And so you established connections with the police in 1908?

ZUBAREV: Yes.

VYSHINSKY: These connections continued for a number of years. Then you found yourself in Sterlitamak, and here you also established connections with the police because Inspector Vasilyev had informed the district where you lived about you. In 1910 you lived in Sterlitamak, and you also lived there in 1911.

ZUBAREV: I lived there until 1914.

VYSHINSKY: During all this time you maintained connections with the police?

ZUBAREV: Yes.

VYSHINSKY: Thus in 1910, 1911, 1912, 1913, 1914 and part of 1915 you were connected with the police, while living in Sterlitamak.

ZUBAREV: Yes.

VYSHINSKY: Then you moved to Ufa and again established connections with the police. After that you were called up to the army. While you were in the army, did you give the police information about revolutionary sentiments in the army?

ZUBAREV: I received instructions to report the political sentiments of the military unit to which I belonged.

VYSHINSKY: Did you do that?

ZUBAREV: Yes, I did it once, and then I left Ufa.

VYSHINSKY: You had no further occasion to do so?

ZUBAREV: No.

VYSHINSKY: Thus, you were connected with the police for a long period of time, right up to the revolution?

ZUBAREV: Yes.

VYSHINSKY: Did you receive any remuneration for this work?

ZUBAREV: On two occasions Inspector Vasilyev gave me thirty rubles.

VYSHINSKY: Thirty pieces of silver on each occasion?

ZUBAREV: Yes.

VYSHINSKY: Twice as much as Judas received?

ZUBAREV: Yes.

THE PRESIDENT: Have you engaged in espionage activities?

ZUBAREV: I forgot to mention this.

THE PRESIDENT: Have you engaged in espionage activities?

ZUBAREV: Yes.

THE PRESIDENT: Tell us about your espionage activities.

ZUBAREV: My espionage activities began at the end of 1935. I was drawn into this organization for supplying secret information by Sulimov's secretary, Ivanov. I supplied secret information about agriculture on two occasions—in January and December 1936. I gave details about the state of the rural districts, grain

147

reserves, seed and food stocks, particularly fodder, and reported on the condition of the cattle. I learnt from Ivanov that this information was given for the benefit of fascist Germany. Who definitely maintained the connections, I, for quite understandable reasons, was not informed, and I do not know.

VYSHINSKY: I request that Inspector Vasilyev, who enlisted Zubarev, be called as a witness in order to verify this circumstance.

THE PRESIDENT (to Zubarev): Sit down for the time being.

The Court has decided to grant the Procurator's request and to call Vasilyev into Court in the capacity of witness.

VYSHINSKY: I ask permission to interrogate him immediately. I have arranged for him to be called, but he is outside the Court room.

THE PRESIDENT: Comrade Commandant, lead in the witness Vasilyev.

(The Commandant leads in Vasilyev.)

Is your name Vasilyev?

VASILYEV: It is.

THE PRESIDENT: What is your name and patronymic?

VASILYEV: Dmitry Nikolayevich.

THE PRESIDENT: When were you born?

VASILYEV: In 1870.

THE PRESIDENT: In which towns did you live in 1907, 1908, 1909 and 1910?

VASILYEV: In the town of Kotelnich.

THE PRESIDENT: What position did you occupy?

VASILYEV: I was District Inspector of District No. 4.

THE PRESIDENT: From what year and until what year were you inspector?

VASILYEV: From 1906 to 1917.

THE PRESIDENT: During the period you were inspector did you enlist anyone as an agent-provocateur?

VASILYEV: Yes.

THE PRESIDENT: In particular, did you enlist Zubarev?

VASILYEV: Zubarev, yes sir.

THE PRESIDENT: Tell us in a few words how you did this.

VASILYEV: The police inspector in the Smerdinsk District—in the village where Prokopy Timofeyevich Zubarev lived—reported to me that young people gathered in his father's house, sang revolutionary songs and read revolutionary literature. Well, I, of course, in the performance of my duties, went to the village with rural inspector Konev, searched the place, and indeed found a large number of revolutionary publications. I took the latter away and, of course, I had to arrest Zubarev. In my office Zubarev told me that there were some more revolutionary-minded people in the village and named two persons, although he did not tell me their surnames, and said that he would point them out. I reported this to the Chief Inspector. The inspector instructed me to enlist him and to get a signed pledge from him.

THE PRESIDENT: What was the nature of this pledge?

VASILYEV: To the effect that he undertook to supply the police with information. In making the pledge he said that his pseudonym would be "Vasily."

THE PRESIDENT: Did he say it?

VASILYEV: Yes, he said it. I remember it very well.

THE PRESIDENT: And did he speak about money?

VASILYEV: After that he spoke about money.

THE PRESIDENT: What pay was fixed?

VASILYEV: The inspector sent him thirty rubles.

THE PRESIDENT: Did you ever give him any more money?

VASILYEV: I distinctly remember one occasion, but I may have given him more, I do not deny it.

VYSHINSKY: How long were you connected with Zubarev?

VASILYEV: From 1908 to 1909.

VYSHINSKY: About how long?

VASILYEV: About a year.

VYSHINSKY: Over a year?

VASILYEV: Yes. I established connections at the beginning of 1908, and at the beginning of 1909 he left the Kotelnich District.

VYSHINSKY: And did you know his family?

VASILYEV: No, I did not. I was in charge of six volosts and had to look after a lot of people.

VYSHINSKY: How is it that you remember him so well? Much time has elapsed since then, and yet you remember this Zubarev so well.

VASILYEV: I just remember.

VYSHINSKY: You remember him through your work at that time?

VASILYEV: That is so.

VYSHINSKY: Did he meet you again?

VASILYEV: I have not set eyes on him since 1909. He was a young man then, and now he is no doubt a middle-aged man.

VYSHINSKY: I should think so! You were younger then too. (To the President.) May I question Zubarev?

THE PRESIDENT: Accused Zubarev.

VYSHINSKY: Do you remember, is this the Vasilyev who was the inspector at that time?

ZUBAREV: Thirty years have elapsed since then and it is

149

hard for me to remember, but I think that is the man. . . . I do not deny it.

VYSHINSKY: Does he resemble him?

ZUBAREV: Yes.

VYSHINSKY: He was younger then?

ZUBAREV: Of course.

VYSHINSKY: Did you receive the money from Vasilyev, or from some other person? And to whom did you give the information?

ZUBAREV: Yes, I received the money from Vasilyev and gave the information to Vasilyev.

VYSHINSKY: How many times, do you remember?

ZUBAREV: I went to see him twice.

VYSHIN KY: Where did he live then?

ZUBAREV: In Kotelnich.

VYSHINSKY: And you reported to him in Kotelnich?

ZUBAREV: Yes.

VYSHINSKY: And where were you arrested?

ZUBAREV: I was not arrested then.

VYSHINSKY: But he took you in custody with the literature?

ZUBAREV: Yes, but he put such terms to me . . .

VYSHINSKY: Was a search made in your house?

ZUBAREV: Yes.

VYSHINSKY: Was illegal literature found in your house?

ZUBAREV: Yes.

VYSHINSKY: And you were taken in custody because of this?

ZUBAREV: Yes, I was taken in custody, but the following terms were proposed, that if I gave information . . .

VYSHINSKY: Then he made you sign a pledge?

ZUBAREV: I do not remember now, but I think it was so.

VYSHINSKY: But you clearly remember this fact?

ZUBAREV: Yes. Later on I left Kotelnich and sent information to Sterlitamak.

VYSHINSKY: Did you yourself choose the pseudonym of "Vasily"?

ZUBAREV: I do not remember whether I adopted it myself, or whether he proposed it; I do not remember, and I would not deny that he gave it to me, or that I chose it myself, but the fact occurred.

VYSHINSKY: Do you affirm that the witness Dmitry Nikolayevich Vasilyev recalls to your mind Inspector Vasilyev, who enlisted you in the service of the police?

ZUBAREV: Yes, I do.

VYSHINSKY: I have no more questions.

150

THE PRESIDENT: Accused Zubarev, have you any questions to put to the witness?

ZUBAREV: I said in the evidence I gave the Court that I was enlisted by Inspector Vasilyev for service in the police.

THE PRESIDENT: In that case the witness may be allowed to go?

VYSHINSKY: Yes.

THE PRESIDENT: You may go.

(To Vyshinsky.) Have you any more questions to put to Zubarev?

VYSHINSKY: No.

THE PRESIDENT: Adjournment until 6 p.m.

[*Signed*] PRESIDENT: **V. ULRICH**

Army Military Jurist

President of the Military Collegum of the Supreme Court of the U.S.S.R.

SECRETARY: **A. BATNER**

Military Jurist First Rank

EVENING SESSION, MARCH 3, 1938

COMMANDANT OF THE COURT: The Court is coming, please rise.

THE PRESIDENT: Be seated. The session is resumed. We shall proceed to examine the accused Krestinsky.

VYSHINSKY: Before interrogating Krestinsky, may I put a few questions to the accused Rakovsky?

THE PRESIDENT: You may.

VYSHINSKY: Accused Rakovsky, have you pleaded guilty to the crimes with which you are charged?

RAKOVSKY: I have.

VYSHINSKY: You also heard Krestinsky's reply, when, in answer to the question of the Court, he declared that he was not a Trotskyite and had not committed the crimes to which he had confessed in the preliminary investigation.

I would like to ask you, as one of the most prominent representatives and leaders of the Trotskyite underground organization in the U.S.S.R., what you know about the Trotskyite activities of Krestinsky in this recent period.

RAKOVSKY: First of all I must deal with the testimony, or rather the statements, which Krestinsky made in this Court yesterday.

VYSHINSKY: Yes, that is just what I am speaking of.

RAKOVSKY: In order to prove that he had parted with Trotskyism, Krestinsky declared that at the end of 1927 he had sent a letter to Trotsky in which he dissociated himself from the Trotskyite positions. If I am not mistaken, that was the meaning of the statement that Krestinsky made in this Court yesterday?

VYSHINSKY: That is how we all understood it.

RAKOVSKY: I am acquainted with this letter of Krestinsky's.

VYSHINSKY: You are acquainted with it?

RAKOVSKY: Trotsky gave it to me to read. And not to me alone. But in order to bring out the meaning of this letter, I must first mention one fact.

In 1927, several weeks before Krestinsky sent this letter, on the eve of the Plenum of the Central Committee just before the Fifteenth Congress, I stopped on my way back to Moscow in Berlin, as always in the Embassy, where Krestinsky was then working. Kamenev was with me. He had come from Rome and was also on his way to the Plenum of the Central Committee. An exchange of opinions took place in Berlin then between Kamenev, Krestinsky and myself, as people who held the same views.

VYSHINSKY: As people who held the same views?

RAKOVSKY: Yes, quite naturally, as people who held the same views. Krestinsky had before then shown no signs of withdrawing from the opposition. At our meeting in Berlin we jointly discussed what stand the opposition should take at the forthcoming Plenum. Krestinsky remained in Berlin. He was of the opinion that we should continue further to manoeuvre.

VYSHINSKY: To manoeuvre?

RAKOVSKY: To manoeuvre.

VYSHINSKY: That is, to double-deal?

RAKOVSKY: That word was not used in those days.

VYSHINSKY: But the meaning?

RAKOVSKY: The meaning was the same.

I shall not mention the other disputes that arose among us. Some time later, when I was already in Moscow, Trotsky showed me Krestinsky's letter.

VYSHINSKY: When was that?

RAKOVSKY: I think it was in the early part of December 1927.

VYSHINSKY: Do you recall what was in that letter?

RAKOVSKY: I cannot recall the exact contents, but the general impression was that it was a manoeuvre. When I read this letter of Krestinsky's, I said to Trotsky: "Krestinsky is preparing what in legal language is called an 'alibi.'" Trotsky confirmed this. And so it subsequently turned out to be; for when the Central Committee of the C.P.S.U. (Bolsheviks) inquired of the Ambassadors who shared Trotskyite views what their attitude was to the expulsion of the leaders of the opposition from the Party, Krestinsky wrote a letter to the Central Committee in which he referred to this "alibi."

VYSHINSKY: He cited this letter to Trotsky as proof of his rupture with Trotskyism?

RAKOVSKY: Yes, he cited this letter as proof that he had withdrawn. Krestinsky's letter to the Central Committee was published in the newspapers in 1928. I do not remember what passages from Krestinsky's letter were published. He kept a copy. I cannot say what passages from his letter were quoted, but there was a reference to his letter.

I, too, stand here as an accused man. I have no right to burden any of my accomplices with new charges. I think it will be enough if I describe the impression which was produced then, and which has remained now. I do not think that this document testifies to Krestinsky's withdrawal from the Trotskyite opposition. This was not a temporary infatuation. It was a struggle that had lasted seven or eight years, a struggle between the Trotskyites and the Party. And how can it be expected that it was enough to compel oneself to sit down for a half-hour or an hour and write a document, for the whole past, the whole ideology, all the habits and connections to disappear?

VYSHINSKY: Consequently, the letter to which the accused Krestinsky referred here as a proof of his rupture with Trotsky and the Trotskyites, you consider to be nothing but a manoeuvre, a document which was to serve as his "alibi," if necessary?

RAKOVSKY: That is true.

VYSHINSKY: Consequently, if I were to ask whether Krestinsky was a Trotskyite in November 1927 and later, what would be your answer?

RAKOVSKY: Yes, Krestinsky was a Trotskyite and never broke with Trotskyism.

VYSHINSKY: Consequently, how do you evaluate the statement made here yesterday by the accused Krestinsky to the effect that he was not a Trotskyite, or, at least, that he has not been a Trotskyite since November 1927?

RAKOVSKY: That it does not correspond with the facts.

VYSHINSKY: Do you know that the accused Krestinsky was a Trotskyite later too?

RAKOVSKY: I do.

VYSHINSKY: Can you cite any facts to prove it?

RAKOVSKY: I can. With the permission of the Court, I will ask Krestinsky himself.

THE PRESIDENT: You may.

RAKOVSKY (to Krestinsky): Nikolai Nikolayevich, did you write to me when I was in exile?

KRESTINSKY: Yes, I sent you a letter through your daughter when she went to Saratov.

VYSHINSKY: Allow me to ask the accused Krestinsky. What year was that?

KRESTINSKY: It was in 1928.

RAKOVSKY: It was in 1929, in August or in July. In 1928 I was in Astrakhan.

VYSHINSKY: Accused Krestinsky, and where did you send the letter?

RAKOVSKY: He wrote to Saratov.

KRESTINSKY: I do not remember the exact year. But I then asked Kaganovich to transfer Khristian Georgievich from Astrakhan to Saratov, alluding to our friendly relations. The request was granted. Well, when he arrived in Saratov, his daughter went to see him, and through her I sent a letter to him. Permit me . . .

VYSHINSKY: Pardon me. We do everything in order here. . . .

KRESTINSKY: Perhaps I can shorten your labours.

VYSHINSKY: I have no need to have them shortened, all the more since the statements you made yesterday do not testify to a desire on your part to shorten the trial.

KRESTINSKY: But perhaps I . . .

THE PRESIDENT: Your turn will come, accused Krestinsky.

VYSHINSKY: I would ask you, accused Rakovsky, to tell us what the accused Krestinsky wrote to you in 1929 while you were living in exile in Saratov.

RAKOVSKY: Krestinsky wrote in that letter that I should return to the Party, naturally with the object of continuing Trotskyite activities.

VYSHINSKY: What for?

RAKOVSKY: He wrote nothing in the letter that was obviously unlawful.

VYSHINSKY: And so you are now establishing the fact that he maintained connections with you, although you were an exiled Trotskyite?

RAKOVSKY: Yes, as well as his desire, as that of other Trotskyites, to preserve the Trotskyite cadres, as far as possible, by penetrating into the Party.

VYSHINSKY: That is, he tried to persuade you, from tactical motives, and in the Trotskyite interests, to return to the Party?

RAKOVSKY: That is how I understood it.

VYSHINSKY: Allow me to put a question to the accused Krestinsky.

Accused Krestinsky, did the accused Rakovsky understand the contents of your letter properly?

KRESTINSKY: He did.

VYSHINSKY: I have to make the following request of the Court. The documents taken from Krestinsky during the search have at my request now been examined. Among them was a copy of his letter to Trotsky dated November 27, 1927, the very letter to which Krestinsky referred yesterday, and of which Rakovsky is speaking.

I request to be allowed to hand this copy of the letter to Rakovsky and Krestinsky and to ask them whether it is to this letter to Trotsky they are both referring; after which I request to be allowed to put a few more questions.

(The copy of the letter of November 27, 1927, is handed to Krestinsky and then to Rakovsky.)

KRESTINSKY: That is the letter.

VYSHINSKY: Please hand the copy of this letter to the accused Rakovsky.

155

RAKOVSKY: The author of the letter remembers it better than I do.

VYSHINSKY: It will only take a couple of minutes, but the fact will be established.

RAKOVSKY (reads the letter): Yes, as far as I remember, this is the letter.

VYSHINSKY: I ask that Rakovsky be handed an excerpt from the newspaper "Ekonomicheskaya Zhizn" of April 8, 1928, which carries the heading: "Excerpt from Krestinsky's Letter of March 22, 1928." Is this what he was referring to when he spoke of the letter Krestinsky sent to the Central Committee after he had sent his letter to Trotsky?

RAKOVSKY: Yes, this is what I was referring to.

VYSHINSKY: And so, all the facts have been established.

RAKOVSKY: I read this in the "Pravda" or the "Izvestia," but it might have been published in all the newspapers.

KRESTINSKY: This was on April 8.

VYSHINSKY: But the letter is dated March 22?

KRESTINSKY: I do not remember the date of the letter.

RAKOVSKY: I remember that there were two letters sent by Trotskyite Ambassadors: Antonov-Ovseyenko[1] and Krestinsky.

VYSHINSKY: And so all the facts have been established. Do you not remember, accused Rakovsky, that the letter to which you just referred began just like the copy of this letter—"Dear Lev Davidovich"?

RAKOVSKY: That was the usual form.

VYSHINSKY: Accused Rakovsky, do you remember the following passage from Krestinsky's personal letter to Trotsky, as it is expressed in the copy? Krestinsky writes: "It is my profound conviction that the tactics of the opposition during the past half-year have been profoundly erroneous and detrimental to the aims of the opposition itself, and one might say tragically wrong."

May one draw the conclusion from this paragraph that there is any condemnation of Trotskyism here?

RAKOVSKY: No. Krestinsky is arguing like a man who belongs to the Trotskyite organization. He proceeds from Trotskyite premises. He speaks in the interests of the Trotskyite organization and the Trotskyite aims. This is just what he declared in Berlin, as I have already said.

VYSHINSKY: Consequently, all that we have here is a simple estimate of the tactical line of the Trotskyites given by a man, in this case Krestinsky, who adheres to the ground of the Trotskyite struggle against the Soviet power?

RAKOVSKY: Yes, that is so.

VYSHINSKY: Allow me to question Krestinsky. Would it be correct so to interpret this passage from the letter to Trotsky?

KRESTINSKY: Yes.

VYSHINSKY: The copy of this letter further says:

"It is absurd to talk of preserving cadres when they have already been virtually destroyed by the incorrect policy of the opposition itself. After all, you cannot regard a couple of hundred comrades who have been expelled and outlawed as cadres. These are cadres for prison and exile, and not for the continuation of the struggle within the Party. It is even more absurd to talk of the preservation of influence over the masses. Where has it happened in history that a group which has been utterly defeated in the struggle owing to its mistakes has been able to preserve influence over the masses? And yet it should be clear to any but the blind that the premature action, which was doomed to failure, and the subsequent complete defeat were the result of mistakes and bad and incorrect leadership.

"Whether by capitulation or by irreconcilable tactics, loss of influence is inevitable. But in the former case it may be possible, slowly, gradually and by persistent work within the Party and the Soviet apparatus, to restore, to again earn the confidence of the masses and influence over the masses."

What do we find here? It seems to me to be an evaluation of the tactical line of the Trotskyites from the standpoint of the interests of the Trotskyite struggle against the Party, and not a break with Trotskyism.

RAKOVSKY: Yes, that is so; I fully confirm that.

VYSHINSKY (to Krestinsky): You have heard the detailed explanation Rakovsky has given of your so-called departure from Trotskyism. Do you consider Rakovsky's explanation correct?

KRESTINSKY: What he says is right.

THE PRESIDENT: You confirm what Rakovsky said?

KRESTINSKY: Yes, I do.

VYSHINSKY: If what Rakovsky said is true, will you continue to deceive the Court and to deny that the testimony you gave in the preliminary investigation was true?

KRESTINSKY: I fully confirm the testimony I gave in the preliminary investigation.

VYSHINSKY: I have no questions to ask Rakovsky.

I have one question to ask Krestinsky: What, then, is the meaning of the statement you made yesterday, which cannot be regarded otherwise than as a piece of Trotskyite provocation in court?

KRESTINSKY: Yesterday, under the influence of a momentary keen feeling of false shame, evoked by the atmosphere of the dock and the painful impression created by the public reading of the indictment, which was aggravated by my poor health, I could not bring myself to tell the truth, I could not bring myself to say

157

that I was guilty. And instead of saying, "Yes, I am guilty," I almost mechanically answered, "No, I am not guilty."

VYSHINSKY: Mechanically?

KRESTINSKY: In the face of world public opinion, I had not the strength to admit the truth that I had been conducting a Trotskyite struggle all along. I request the Court to register my statement that I fully and completely admit that I am guilty of all the gravest charges brought against me personally, and that I admit my complete responsibility for the treason and treachery I have committed.

VYSHINSKY: I have nothing more to ask the accused Krestinsky for the present.

THE PRESIDENT: Accused Krestinsky, be seated.

We shall now proceed to examine the accused Rykov.

Accused Rykov, do you confirm the testimony you gave in the preliminary investigation?

RYKOV: I do.

THE PRESIDENT: Comrade Procurator, have you any questions to put to the accused Rykov?

VYSHINSKY: I have a number of questions.

Accused Rykov, tell us, when did your underground, conspiratorial activities against the Soviet government begin?

RYKOV: Essentially, they began in 1928.

VYSHINSKY: Did they assume shape in 1928?

RYKOV: Perhaps; it is difficult to remember.

VYSHINSKY: Approximately at that period.

Tell us, in what were your anti-Soviet activities expressed at that time; what immediate organizational tasks and what aims did you set yourselves?

RYKOV: At that time, from 1928 to 1930 . . .

VYSHINSKY: And subsequently?

RYKOV: I speak of this period because it was all of one type. I actively fought the policy of the Party and the Soviet government, and chiefly the policy of the Party towards the peasantry. This activity was expressed in my, so to speak, legal utterances. In this period the illegal organization utilized the legal opportunities.

VYSHINSKY: Tell us about the illegal activities. It is the illegal activities that interest me.

RYKOV: In this period the one could not be separated from the other, because the illegal organization in this period existed in order to utilize legal opportunities. Legal opportunities had the following result: they afforded the possibility of intercourse with people and sections of the population, of which the illegal organization was deprived in the following period. Therefore the directing centre, to which I belonged, acted legally and utilized all opportunities. Therefore, as to me, I made legal public utterances at that period; I was Chairman of the Council of People's Commissars, and therefore my legal utterances possessed a special significance, which the Party at that time still allowed me.

VYSHINSKY: What were your relations in 1928-29 with Yagoda?

RYKOV: Everything in my relations with Yagoda was illegal. Already at that period, side by side with the legal part, i.e., the group of members of the counter-revolutionary Right organization who acted legally, we had cadres who were specially kept secret with the object of organizing the further struggle against the Party. One of these people was Yagoda, with whom at that period, and prior to that period, I was connected personally, and from whom I received special information, which I used for my attacks upon the policy of the Party in the rural districts. When later, at a meeting of the Political Bureau, Yagoda's sympathy with us on the question of the extraordinary measures against the kulaks in the matter of the grain collections came to light, he after a while performed a double-dealing manoeuvre and proclaimed himself to be a supporter of the Party, while actually remaining a member of our counter-revolutionary organization. Moreover, this was done not only with my knowledge, but, as far as I can remember, on my advice.

VYSHINSKY: Did you have an understanding with Yagoda that no repressive measures were to be adopted against the members of your underground organization?

RYKOV: Of course.

VYSHINSKY: Was there an understanding with Yagoda that he was to use his official position to protect the underground organization of the Rights?

RYKOV: Yes.

VYSHINSKY: And what official position did he hold at that time?

RYKOV: He was Vice-Chairman, under Chairman of the O.G.P.U., Menzhinsky.

VYSHINSKY: Vice-Chairman of the O.G.P.U?

RYKOV: Yes. That is chiefly why we endeavoured to keep him on a secret footing.

VYSHINSKY (to the Court): Permit me to question Yagoda. Accused Yagoda, do you confirm this part of Rykov's testimony?

YAGODA: I confirm the fact, but not its formulation.

VYSHINSKY: You do not like the formulation?

YAGODA: The fact is true, but not as Rykov puts it.

VYSHINSKY: Was this in 1929?

YAGODA: It was.

VYSHINSKY (to Rykov): Accused Rykov, you say that this was in 1929?

RYKOV: Yes, it was in 1929.

VYSHINSKY: At any rate, it was when you, accused Yagoda, were Vice-Chairman of the O.G.P.U. and when it was your duty to combat underground groups?

YAGODA: Yes.

VYSHINSKY: Consequently, you committed direct high treason?

YAGODA: Yes.

VYSHINSKY: Be seated. Accused Rykov, continue.

RYKOV: I shall pursue the subject of Yagoda. From the very beginning of our open struggle against the Party, a number of the members of our counter-revolutionary Right organization did not openly proclaim that they supported the Rights. To this group, in addition to Yagoda, belonged such people as Antipov, Razumov and Rumyantsev.

VYSHINSKY: And of the people who are in the dock?

RYKOV: Here?

VYSHINSKY: Sitting to the right of you.

RYKOV: As regards Ivanov, he performed a manoeuvre in this respect. He was known to belong to the Right deviation. He was also one of the first to manoeuvre. I know of nobody else here. Bukharin and I acted openly; as to the others, I cannot say whether there were open acts in defence of the program of the Rights. Regarding Ivanov, I can say that there were. There even existed separate groups, like the whole of the Leningrad group, consisting of Komarov and a number of others.

Thus at this period of the so-called open struggle, in addition to the legal and open struggle, there at once began to form an illegal centre of the Rights, consisting of Bukharin, Tomsky and myself. It arose of itself, because the three of us belonged to the Political Bureau at one and the same time. The direction of the struggle was in our hands. This centre held on and continued its counter-revolutionary work until quite recently.

The illegal work consisted in the fact that in that period, 1928-30, similar groups began to be created elsewhere on the territory of the Soviet Union. I cannot give a precise enumeration of what groups were formed, where and in what number. There were a number of members of our organization in various places, as has been enumerated, including people like Kabakov, secretary . . .

VYSHINSKY: That is unnecessary.

RYKOV: The chief components of the counter-revolutionary organization in Moscow were Tomsky and his trade unionists, Bukharin and his connections, in particular his disciples and his "school," I myself with a number of my followers, and Uglanov with a group of his Moscow followers.[2] This at once created the organization of the Rights. Until 1930 there proceeded a process of enlargement of this organization and of utilizing public utterances to recruit followers and to create a definite popularity for the organization.

We utilized the Trade Union Congress for this purpose, for the purpose of fighting the Party. Practically every one of the 93 people who voted for Tomsky and against the Party at the Trade Union Congress joined our counter-revolutionary organization.[3]

And so there were elements of double-dealing, of illegal work concealed from the Party from the very beginning.

There were various shades of opinion regarding a legal or illegal counter-revolutionary organization. One of the members, like Antipov, let us say, and a number of others, at once insisted on the early adoption of illegal methods, not attributing the slightest importance to the legal struggle and considering that a legal footing only led to the exposure of cadres, that it promised no chance of success; but certain members of the organization, a large number of them, had a high opinion of legal action. When at plenums, conferences and congresses of the Party the position of the Rights was systematically exposed, it became perfectly clear that it would be impossible to maintain a legal position. Thereupon began a series of declarations of abandonment of Right views. The purpose of all these declarations was to deceive the Party. The centre, to which I also belonged, gave direct instructions that such declarations should be submitted.

Somewhat later, among the last, Bukharin, Tomsky and I submitted a statement renouncing the advocacy of the Right platform.[4] It was designed to deceive the Party. After the Party Congress had passed a resolution declaring that the views of the Rights were incompatible with membership of the Party, we decided to adopt an illegal footing completely. There were some absolutely secret methods of utilizing the legal press; but they rarely succeeded, and could not succeed; and we had therefore to assume an illegal footing.

Thus from 1930 onwards the counter-revolutionary organization was 100 per cent illegal; its work was based on deceiving the Party.

Apart from the declaration I had submitted, we, and I in particular, published in the newspaper several articles criticizing our own statements and views. This was designed for the same purpose—deception.

VYSHINSKY: So deceit of the Party was a system you practised very widely?

RYKOV: Yes, of course, it was a system that was practised very widely. I have cited as an example the report I made to the

Urals Regional Conference. This was in 1930. It is characteristic of this report that, at a time when the chief link of the whole work of the Party, the working class and the peasantry, was the struggle for collectivization and for the liquidation of the kulaks as a class, I made a report in which this thesis was entirely omitted. Here I employed silence, a silence which in many cases speaks far louder than publicity. I employed this method at a conference in Sverdlovsk, about which Zubarev has told you, and at which I met him. Such was the situation in 1930. Today I can mention several people.

VYSHINSKY: That does not interest me. I am interested in another question. Did your directing centre function in the period 1928-29?

RYKOV: Yes, the trio functioned from the outset.

VYSHINSKY: Of whom did it consist?

RYKOV: Bukharin, Tomsky and myself.

VYSHINSKY: Consequently, it may be directly affirmed that as far back as 1928 the illegal group of Rights already had their directing centre in the persons of this trio?

RYKOV: Of course.

VYSHINSKY: Let us pass to the next period.

RYKOV: The next period was 1930-33. This was the period when there evolved the most criminal methods of work and aims that the counter-revolutionary organization set itself. I must say that it would be wrong to assert that in the period 1928-30 none of the Rights spoke in favour of adopting such methods as terrorism.

VYSHINSKY: Were there such?

RYKOV: Of course. At that period certain persons were already demanding the adoption of such methods; but these were only the heralds of what was subsequently adopted in the shape of the tactics of the counter-revolutionary Right organization. As regards lines of principle, the so-called Ryutin program was characteristic of the period 1930-33. This Ryutin program was discussed twice in 1932 at Tomsky's summer residence with my participation. In addition to myself, there were present at the first meeting Bukharin and Tomsky and a number of other persons, among them Vasily Schmidt[5] and Uglanov.

VYSHINSKY: Was Bukharin there?

RYKOV: Bukharin was at the first meeting, when the original theses were drawn up.

VYSHINSKY: Was he at the second meeting?

RYKOV: Bukharin was not present at the second meeting. He was on vacation; but later, having acquainted himself with the platform, he fully approved and identified himself with it.

VYSHINSKY: You and Tomsky were present at the second meeting?

RYKOV: At the first meeting I, Tomsky, Bukharin, Uglanov and Schmidt were present.

VYSHINSKY: Vasily?

RYKOV: Yes.

VYSHINSKY: Vasily Schmidt?

RYKOV: Yes.

VYSHINSKY: And who was present at the second meeting?

RYKOV: The same people were present at the second meeting, except for Bukharin, and with the addition of two other persons, whom I have mentioned, and certain persons whose names I do not know—they were invited by Uglanov and took part. Here both the content and form are interesting. The platform was called after Ryutin, because it was published by supporters of the Rights, the Ryutin group, from Uglanov's Moscow organization.

During the investigation instituted in connection with this platform, this group took the whole responsibility upon itself. This had been decided on beforehand, so that we ourselves should not be called to account for the platform. We managed to do this thanks to the fact that Yagoda was at the head of the O.G.P.U.

VYSHINSKY: So Yagoda shielded you?

RYKOV: And to make it easier to do this, the program itself contained a phrase which expressed a certain sense of aloofness from Bukharin, Tomsky and myself; it said something to the effect that these three were waste steam. This was done from motives of double-dealing.

VYSHINSKY: So that even then there were elements of terrorism in your activities?

RYKOV: The formulation was essentially one of tactics. The platform recognized (as far as I remember, and I do remember, for I had a share in editing it) methods of violence in changing the leadership of the Party and of the country—terrorism and uprisings. It was formulated so broadly as to constitute an instruction that measures of violence should be applied in whatever forms might prove to be at our disposal. The second formulation was the uniting of those forces, those organizations, which were combating the Party and the government of the U.S.S.R. These two theses were fundamental and decisive in the Ryutin platform and at the same time for the whole subsequent period.

How was this program put into effect? This period was marked by an acute class struggle in the countryside and the strong resistance of the kulaks, the peasant bourgeoisie, to the government and the Party. This laid a special imprint on the period. During this period our counter-revolutionary work aimed at relying on, and it to a certain degree did rely on, the forces of counter-revolution which had at that time become activized. I am referring to the kulak actions, the kulak risings, the kulak sabotage which at that time was fairly widespread. We adopted all the forms of utilizing the anti-Soviet, bourgeois forces in the countryside for combating the Party and the government—from utilizing actions that had already matured to the deliberate organization of kulak uprisings. As an example, I can quote two cases in which the centre took a direct part. Of course, the centre could not direct each particular action in every locality, but in two instances, which are of significance in connection with the present case, this did take place. I am referring to the North Caucasus and Siberia.

VYSHINSKY: The North Caucasus—what year are you referring to?

RYKOV: In this case it is difficult to distinguish. . . . I think it was 1931, 1932 and 1933.

VYSHINSKY: 1930 is not included?

RYKOV (after a silence): I fear to make a mistake.

VYSHINSKY: What about the dispute which occurred this morning between the accused Bukharin and the accused Ivanov regarding the line for an insurrectionary movement in the North Caucasus? According to your recollection, was there such a line?

RYKOV: My own personal participation in the counter-revolutionary work of the centre dates from a later period and is connected with the dispatch of Eismont to the Caucasus in 1932.

VYSHINSKY: But you said that in 1928 you were connected with Ivanov?

RYKOV: Who, I?

VYSHINSKY: No, the Right group.

RYKOV: I heard Ivanov say today that he belonged to the Right group, but I had no personal connections with him.

VYSHINSKY: So this was a separate line of Bukharin and Ivanov?

RYKOV: I do not know. After all, every member of the centre could not have dealings with all the members of the organization.

VYSHINSKY: That is clear, but Bukharin and Ivanov were connected by underground work. Did you know that Ivanov had a share in it?

RYKOV: I did not. It may be that I have forgotten the fact, but the name Ivanov has no place in my memory.

VYSHINSKY: But is it possible that individual members of your centre had their own people and did not inform each other about all the people?

RYKOV: This, in my opinion, is not only possible but absolutely inevitable, because it was not a question of a hundred or so people, but of far more numerous cadres. It is quite possible that not everybody knew all the members of the organization.

VYSHINSKY: Even in the case of such an important underground worker as Ivanov?

RYKOV: Even in that case.

VYSHINSKY: Continue.

RYKOV: The Right centre devoted special attention to the North Caucasus owing to its high proportion of Cossacks and wealthy peasants, and the specific character of its traditions, and also in view of its political and economic importance as a region bordering on the Ukraine, possessing a large number of national republics and supplying a large quantity of grain.

Eismont[6] went there specially in 1932 with the purpose of organizing our participation in the kulak movement, inasmuch as it was developing fairly strongly. Eismont went there with my knowledge and after a preliminary talk with me, with the object, as I have already said, of sharpening the kulak movement in the North Caucasus in every way and of helping it to spread. Later on he told me that he had got in touch with Pivovarov, and in addition to Eismont. Slepkov[7] one of the prominent members of the Bukharin organization, was sent there. He was sent with Bukharin's knowledge and on his initiative.

VYSHINSKY: With Bukharin's knowledge?

RYKOV: On his initiative. I don't think Bukharin will deny that. I sent Eismont and Smirnov, while he sent Slepkov.

VYSHINSKY: With what concrete instructions did Slepkov go there?

RYKOV: The detailed instructions were given by Bukharin, but the principal instructions, as I have already said, were to sharpen the dissatisfaction of the kulaks in every way, including every kind of open action.

VYSHINSKY: In other words, to organize kulak actions, kulak insurrections?

RYKOV: Of course. That is what I said. Only, in those cases where there were no prospects for armed action, to organize unarmed actions.

VYSHINSKY: That was Slepkov's task?

RYKOV: That was the task which in my opinion must have been given him.

VYSHINSKY: Bukharin gave it?

RYKOV: Bukharin gave it with our knowledge, so that I regard myself as being fully responsible for it.

VYSHINSKY: What do you say, accused Bukharin?

BUKHARIN: I corroborate all that Rykov has said here up to now. Slepkov was sent to the North Caucasus precisely for this purpose. It must be said for the sake of historical exactitude. . . .

VYSHINSKY: Don't trouble to speak for history, accused Bukharin. History will itself record what will be interesting for history. Now Rykov said here that with the knowledge of the centre, on the direct instructions of the centre, and in particular, with his

165

own, Rykov's, and your, Bukharin's, instructions, in the North Caucasus, in 1931 or 1932 . . .

BUKHARIN: I think it was in the spring of 1932.

RYKOV: Yes, it was in 1932.

VYSHINSKY: So that, in the spring of 1932, on the direct instructions of the centre, and in particular of Rykov and Bukharin, Slepkov, one of your closest colleagues in the underground organization, is sent to the North Caucasus for the purpose of doing everything, as Rykov said, to organize kulak risings. Is that right?

BUKHARIN: But I have said that I corroborate everything that Rykov has said here from the first word to the last.

VYSHINSKY: Hence, you sent Slepkov to organize kulak insurrections in the North Caucasus?

BUKHARIN: Hence, I sent him for the purpose of raising insurrections.

VYSHINSKY: Did you personally instruct Slepkov?

BUKHARIN: Slepkov needed no instruction whatever, because he was a sufficiently qualified person.

VYSHINSKY: Qualified in what respect?

BUKHARIN: Qualified for the purpose of drawing the necessary organizational and practical conclusions.

VYSHINSKY: That is to say, qualified also for the purpose of raising insurrections?

BUKHARIN: And for the purpose of raising insurrections. The task then was to sharpen kulak discontent with the Soviet power in every way, to fan this discontent, to organize cadres. and to organize actions, including armed kulak insurrections.

VYSHINSKY: That is exactly what I wanted to know.

BUKHARIN: And that is exactly what I say.

VYSHINSKY: Now we can pass to Siberia.

RYKOV: As for Siberia, I know from what Bukharin said. . . .

VYSHINSKY: What about?

RYKOV: About the fact that Yakovenko was doing the same kind of work in Siberia as was being done in the North Caucasus, that is to say, he was striving to rouse the kulaks to insurrection. He frequently met Bukharin and talked with him. Of course, Bukharin gave him the line, gave him instructions and urged him.

VYSHINSKY (to the Court): Permit me to question Bukharin on this matter.

BUKHARIN: All I need do here is to say more or less emphatically, because I suggested to Yakovenko a plan. . . .

VYSHINSKY: What plan?

BUKHARIN: A plan of insurrection with the aid of partisans in some region of Siberia.

VYSHINSKY: So this fact did take place?

166

BUKHARIN: This fact did take place. I reported this at a meeting of the centre, I think the whole trio were present.

VYSHINSKY: But Rykov appears to be denying it.

BUKHARIN: I am speaking as I remember it.

VYSHINSKY: Did the accused Rykov correctly relate the fact about your sending Yakovenko to Siberia for the purpose of organizing kulak insurrections?

BUKHARIN: He did. Yakovenko accidentally met me in Serebryanny Bor. He said that sufficient forces were available for the purpose of raising an insurrection. At first I did not consent, but said I would consult my colleagues. I formally submitted the question to the centre for discussion.

VYSHINSKY: In 1932?

BUKHARIN: Yes. They expressed displeasure at my failing to give Yakovenko an affirmative answer at once.

VYSHINSKY: Had you given an affirmative answer?

BUKHARIN: No, they expressed displeasure because I had not given an affirmative answer.

VYSHINSKY: Please, will you repeat this? I did not hear.

BUKHARIN: Excuse me, perhaps I am not speaking loud enough. After this decision was arrived at I informed Yakovenko of it.

VYSHINSKY: What did you tell Yakovenko?

BUKHARIN: I told him, without going into the details of the technical side, that the centre was in favour of exciting the movement and of raising insurrection.

VYSHINSKY: And did he go?

BUKHARIN: Yes, he went.

VYSHINSKY: Well, and were there kulak risings in Siberia?

BUKHARIN: Yes, there were.

VYSHINSKY: Do you remember, was that in the Biisk District?

BUKHARIN: I do not remember, perhaps it was in the Biisk District.

VYSHINSKY: That is not so essential.

BUKHARIN: No, it is not so essential.

VYSHINSKY: Tell us, what official work did you do apart from organizing kulak insurrections?

BUKHARIN: I was a member of the Central Committee, a member of the Central Executive Committee.

VYSHINSKY: And later?

BUKHARIN: Later I worked at the People's Commissariat of Heavy Industry.

VYSHINSKY: In what capacity?

BUKHARIN: In the capacity of director of one of the departments.

VYSHINSKY: Which?

BUKHARIN: The scientific and technical.

VYSHINSKY: And simultaneously, as a joint occupation, you directed the organization of kulak insurrections?

BUKHARIN: Ironically it can be called a joint occupation, but, as I have already said, I don't intend to be witty here.

VYSHINSKY: In 1932 you took the path of open treason. Is that right or not?

BUKHARIN: Quite right. I have said that I date this with the Ryutin platform.

VYSHINSKY: That means 1930?

BUKHARIN: The Ryutin platform was adopted at the notorious conference held in the autumn of 1932, or in the summer, and it was approved at the meeting of which Alexei Ivanovich Rykov spoke.

VYSHINSKY: That means 1932?

BUKHARIN: The autumn of 1932.

VYSHINSKY: That date marks the beginning of your high treason?

BUKHARIN: Yes, that date.

VYSHINSKY: But before that date there were other dates, about which we shall speak later on.

BUKHARIN: Yes, there undoubtedly were other dates.

VYSHINSKY: 1918, for example?

BUKHARIN: This stands somewhat separately. . . .

VYSHINSKY: We will speak about it separately, but I am now speaking about your activities.

BUKHARIN: I am speaking, Citizen Procurator, from the point of view of the evolution of the Right deviation which grew into a counter-revolutionary, terrorist, treasonable group.

VYSHINSKY: This process of evolution was consummated in 1932?

BUKHARIN: Yes, it was consummated and assumed definite ideological shape.

VYSHINSKY: I am interested now not in ideology, but in criminology.

BUKHARIN: But ideology may also be criminal; actions are performed by thinking people.

VYSHINSKY: That may be so, but what interests us is action, practice.

BUKHARIN: I have been questioned so many times about the Ryutin platform, perhaps this is a mistake on the part of the investigation, but I must say . . .

VYSHINSKY: And so, you yourself date your activities as a conspirator and traitor from 1932 in connection with the evolution of the Right deviation into a counter-revolutionary organization. Is that right?

168

BUKHARIN: That is right.

VYSHINSKY: And so, you have to your account preparation for and organization of kulak insurrections in the North Caucasus, and preparation for and organization of kulak insurrections in Western Siberia. Is that so?

BUKHARIN: That is so.

VYSHINSKY (to Rykov): Accused Rykov, was this known to you too? Was this done with your knowledge?

RYKOV: Of course. As for the dates, in my opinion this is a formal question. And before the infant, the Ryutin platform, could be born, there had to be pregnancy, pregnancy with a document like the Ryutin program, and this was quite definitely loss of virginity.

VYSHINSKY: Well, that's clear.

RYKOV: Connected with the North Caucasus there is still another criminal factor, and that is the connection with the Socialist-Revolutionaries, which we had discussed previously to this especially in connection with kulak insurrections, and also in connection with the fact that some of the members of the centre, and of the illegal organization generally, considered that it was necessary to establish contact with, to utilize, the kulak movement for the work of the Right organization and the organization of the Socialist-Revolutionaries. Connection with the Socialist-Revolutionaries on the basis of joint anti-Soviet kulak risings was, as Eismont informed me, actually established in the North Caucasus. But these movements, of course, created an extremely tense situation in the country, and increased the aspirations, expectations and hopes of the Rights of coming into power. Although these movements were in fact kulak, that is to say anti-Soviet movements, on the other hand, we nevertheless regarded them as a mass movement in the country, which served as a support for the Right deviation.

I remember a discussion we had on this subject in the trio and also among the followers of the Right deviation. Here many argued and quoted the example of the Kronstadt uprising and urged that with the aid of kulak risings it would be possible to create not one, but several Kronstadts, and achieve corresponding political success. [8]

This is the first thing that is characteristic of the crimes we committed in the period of 1930-33.

In this period also the views of the Rights on the question of terrorism took shape.

VYSHINSKY: On terrorism?

RYKOV: On the question of terrorism it is also difficult to establish an absolutely exact dividing line, say, the fifth of such-and-such a month and such-and-such a year. Terrorist moods began to develop as far back as 1930, as far as I know. They found expression in Radin, who stood close to me. Approximately in 1932 our positive attitude toward the application of terrorism took shape as a method of struggle for power and found practical expression. I cannot conceive of theoretical terrorism. When people talk about terrorism it is a purely practical thing. One can't indulge in the theory of terrorism without practice. As soon as the line was adopted, corresponding organizational and practical conclusions were drawn from it at once; that is to say, a number of terrorist groups were formed. I myself gave a number of terrorist instructions to a number of persons, apart from those who stood close to me, like Nesterov and Radin. I conveyed these instructions also to the nationalist organizations; I discussed the question of terrorism with the members of the Pan-Tyurkic and Byelorussian nationalist organizations, and soon the terrorist line and the corresponding conclusions drawn from it were widely adopted. In addition to these discussions on this question I had others. Nesterov later reported that on my instructions an organization had been formed in Sverdlovsk, in the Urals.

Later on, in 1935, I had a talk about terrorism with Kotov,[9] a leading member of the Moscow Right organization. Approximately in 1934, I instructed my former secretary Artemenko to watch for passing government automobiles.

Other members of our counter-revolutionary organization adopted similar measures. But we never passed any definite decision that such-and-such a member of the government is to be killed. The centre of the Right organization never adopted such a decision; but its work consisted of preparing such an attitude towards terrorism and such a state of terrorist cadres as would enable such a decision to be carried out whenever the centre adopted one.

In this period also terrorist connections were established with the Socialist-Revolutionary Semyonov through Bukharin. I did not know Semyonov personally. Bukharin told me that through Semyonov he was preparing for an attempt on the life of Stalin. Later on, as far as I remember, we discussed the question of establishing contact with the Socialist-Revolutionaries on this matter, and this contact was established through Bukharin, who had the firmest connections. I also had a conversation about terrorism with Beloborodov while travelling to a health resort in the North Caucasus. This was approximately in 1934.[10]

VYSHINSKY (to the Court): Permit me to dwell on the role of Semyonov.

THE PRESIDENT: You may.

VYSHINSKY: Accused Rykov, how do you know about Bukharin's connection with this Socialist-Revolutionary terrorist Semyonov?

RYKOV: I heard about it from Bukharin, who told me that he had had connections with Semyonov ever since the trial of the Socialist-Revolutionaries in connection with the attempt on the life of Lenin; as is well known, at this trial Bukharin defended Semyonov.[11]

VYSHINSKY: Bukharin defended Semyonov?

RYKOV: Yes.

VYSHINSKY: Did you ever meet Semyonov at Bukharin's?

RYKOV: One day I visited Bukharin at his apartment and I found a stranger sitting there who left after my arrival.

VYSHINSKY: When you spoke about this you had Semyonov in mind?

RYKOV: Yes.

VYSHINSKY: Bukharin told you that this was the Semyonov who was organizing the attempt on the life of Stalin?

RYKOV: Whether it was he who was organizing it I cannot say.

VYSHINSKY: Were you posted on the organization of this attempt?

RYKOV: I was not posted on this matter, but evidently I knew about it.

VYSHINSKY: During the preliminary investigation you said— that is why I am asking you about it—"In 1932 or in the beginning of 1933, on visiting Bukharin, I found there a stranger in his apartment who left soon after. After his departure Bukharin told me that this was the Semyonov whom he had known since the trial of the Socialist-Revolutionaries, at which he defended him" (this is what you have just now testified), "and he went on to say that the Socialist-Revolutionaries were preparing an attempt on the lives of Stalin and Kaganovich. Bukharin and I accepted this communication with satisfaction, as its execution would have facilitated the counter-revolutionary activities of the Rights." Do you corroborate this episode?

RYKOV: Yes.

VYSHINSKY (to the Court): Permit me to question the accused Bukharin.

Accused Bukharin, do you corroborate this?

BUKHARIN: In the main I corroborate it, but there are a number . . .

VYSHINSKY: Let us take things in their order.

BUKHARIN: But I wanted to clear up . . .

VYSHINSKY: Accused Bukharin, I want to explain to you that you will have time to clear things up and explain when you are examined. At present I am interrogating you on a question that is connected with another of the accused. Is the accused Rykov telling the truth when he says that in 1932-33 he found a man in your apartment whom you called Semyonov?

171

BUKHARIN: It is possible, I do not remember definitely whether he saw Semyonov and whether that scene took place. . . .

VYSHINSKY: But you were connected with Semyonov?

BUKHARIN: Yes, I was connected with him. Rykov knew about this connection because I myself told him about it. Whether this was the form . . .

VYSHINSKY: That is not important. The important thing for me now is to establish whether you were connected with the Socialist-Revolutionary terrorist Semyonov.

BUKHARIN: That is true, but Semyonov was a member of the Party.

VYSHINSKY: You, too, were a member of the Party.

BUKHARIN: As for Semyonov, I . . .

VYSHINSKY: You defended him?

BUKHARIN: Yes.

VYSHINSKY: You, while being a member not only of the Communist Party but of its Central Committee, organized terrorist acts against the leaders of the Party?

BUKHARIN. Quite true.

VYSHINSKY: Therefore, the fact that Semyonov was formally a member of the Communist Party makes no difference. Were you connected with him as with a Communist or a Socialist-Revolutionary?

BUKHARIN: I do not think I was connected with him as with a Socialist-Revolutionary but as with a terrorist who sympathized with the Rights.

VYSHINSKY: That is why it is no use harping on the fact that he was a member of the Communist Party.

BUKHARIN: I did not want to minimize my guilt, I wanted to aggravate it.

VYSHINSKY: I do not want to aggravate your guilt, I am talking about facts. Were you connected with Semyonov, the Socialist-Revolutionary terrorist; were they terrorist connections?

BUKHARIN: They did not start as terrorist connections.

VYSHINSKY: I am not asking how they started, I am asking what they were at that time.

BUKHARIN: At that time they were terrorist connections.

VYSHINSKY: You had then learnt from Semyonov that preparations were being made for an attempt on the lives of Comrades Stalin and Kaganovich?

BUKHARIN: No, Rykov is not putting it quite correctly. The position was as follows. Semyonov reported that he had connections with various Socialist-Revolutionary terrorist groups, and as he knew the moods among the Right counter-revolutionary organizations concerning terrorism, he proposed that these connections be utilized.

172

VYSHINSKY: For what purpose?

BUKHARIN: For terrorist activities.

VYSHINSKY: Of what kind?

BUKHARIN: For terrorist activities against the leadership of the Party.

VYSHINSKY: That is?

BUKHARIN: A number of members of the Political Bureau were mentioned.

VYSHINSKY: Including whom?

BUKHARIN: Including Stalin and Kaganovich.

VYSHINSKY: And so, in 1932 you and Semyonov talked about this, that an attempt should be organized on the lives of Comrade Stalin and of Comrade Kaganovich.

BUKHARIN: I did not say that it should; I am saying what happened.

VYSHINSKY: I say that in 1932 you had a talk on this, that an attempt was being prepared on the lives of Comrades Stalin and Kaganovich.

BUKHARIN: If you formulate it like that, it gives it an absolutely concrete character.

VYSHINSKY: Very concrete.

BUKHARIN: At that time we talked about terrorist acts against the leading men of the Party.

VYSHINSKY: Was it a theoretical talk?

BUKHARIN: No. Organizing groups is not a theoretical talk.

VYSHINSKY: What did you talk about?

BUKHARIN: We talked about terrorist plans on the organization of preparations to carry out this plan against members of the Political Bureau.

VYSHINSKY: Including whom?

BUKHARIN: Including Stalin and Kaganovich.

VYSHINSKY: That, then, is concrete.

BUKHARIN. Quite concrete. I wanted to decipher and say exactly what actually happened.

VYSHINSKY: I ask the Court to permit me to read the testimony given by the accused Bukharin during the preliminary investigation.

THE PRESIDENT: You may.

VYSHINSKY: Pages 105-06; when the Procurator of the Union interrogated you on December 1, you, accused Bukharin, testified as follows: "I want to state the truth and I declare that I reported this proposal" (this is preceded by the reference to Semyonov's proposal) "to a conference of the centre and we decided to instruct Semyonov to organize terrorist groups."

BUKHARIN: Yes.

173

VYSHINSKY: This is right?

BUKHARIN: Right.

VYSHINSKY: This precisely refers to 1932?

BUKHARIN: Quite true.

VYSHINSKY: Thus, in 1932, you on the decision of the centre of the Right organization instructed Semyonov to organize a terrorist group. Is that so, or not?

BUKHARIN: It is so.

VYSHINSKY: Why did you instruct him to organize a terrorist group?

BUKHARIN: In order to commit terrorist acts.

VYSHINSKY: Against whom?

BUKHARIN: Against members of the Political Bureau.

VYSHINSKY: Including whom?

BUKHARIN: Including Stalin.

VYSHINSKY: Hence, we may say that the Right centre decided in 1932 to commit terrorist acts against members of the Political Bureau, including Comrade Stalin and Comrade Kaganovich. and instructed Semyonov to carry them out. Is this so?

BUKHARIN: In the sense of a line, it is so.

VYSHINSKY: Yes or no?

BUKHARIN: But this does not mean that the whole machine had been set and the signal had been given.

VYSHINSKY: We know how machines are set and how they operate.

BUKHARIN: I say this for the sake of exactitude.

VYSHINSKY: Well, we have achieved exactitude. Please be seated. Continue, accused Rykov.

RYKOV: I repeat, I cannot guarantee that my memory is absolutely exact. But I remember the episode literally in such a way that . . .

VYSHINSKY: That you accepted with satisfaction Bukharin's communication to Semyonov, or Semyonov's communication to Bukharin, or Semyonov's and Bukharin's communication?

RYKOV: This means that considered from a political point of view the most odious thing about the whole matter is that we wanted to use others to . . .

VYSHINSKY: To do what?

RYKOV: Commit terrorist acts.

VYSHINSKY: Was that put concretely, or only theoretically?

RYKOV: I have already said that theoretical terrorism does not exist for me.

VYSHINSKY: I understand it that way too.

RYKOV: But the centre did not adopt a decision in such-and-such a year to kill such-and-such a member of the Political Bureau or of the government. The centre took measures that would enable such a decision to be put into effect if one were adopted. . . .

VYSHINSKY: In either case it was a matter of utilizing the Socialist-Revolutionary terrorists for an attempt on the lives of Comrade Stalin and Comrade Kaganovich.

RYKOV: Yes, that is how I understood it. And here it appears a disagreement arises between me and Bukharin. I thought that Semyonov was organizing this as a member of another organization. The version that Bukharin outlined to the effect that I instructed Semyonov to create some kind of special terrorist organization I hear for the first time.

BUKHARIN: It is very simple. . . .

VYSHINSKY: Very simple.

BUKHARIN: It is quite understandable. The understandability lies in what I said: I do not refute Rykov when he says that he met Semyonov in my apartment. He might have met him. But this is not the point. Semyonov might have told him, I might have told him, Semyonov might have told him first and I might have told him afterwards, both of us might have told him. The fact is that Semyonov made a proposal; this proposal became known not only to me, but also to my accomplices in crime at that time, and they agreed. I quite agree with Rykov that there is an even more odious element in this; using the Socialist-Revolutionaries as cat's-paws—this is quite understandable. But I say that there was, of course, an undoubted attempt to utilize Socialist-Revolutionary terrorist forces for the purpose of waging a criminally treacherous fight against the leadership of the Party. Since I was connected with Semyonov, then undoubtedly, in this case, the initiative belonged to me.

I cannot under any circumstances minimize, whitewash in one form or another or belittle my initiative in this case.

VYSHINSKY: And so the initiative was yours?

BUKHARIN: I think Semyonov made the proposal to me, but as far as my accomplices, the Rights, were concerned . . .

VYSHINSKY: Tomsky and Rykov?

BUKHARIN: Yes, here I took the initiative.

VYSHINSKY: And in the case of Semyonov whose initiative was it?

BUKHARIN: I do not remember, perhaps it was mine. At all events, I do not deny it.

VYSHINSKY: So, accused Bukharin, maybe in this it was your initiative in organizing the terrorist act against Comrade Stalin?

BUKHARIN: This I have admitted. But the whole point is, and I want to emphasize this, that my initiative does not exclude the fact that in this case Semyonov received the consent of my

175

two colleagues. I again emphasize that this does not exclude my initiative in this matter, on the contrary. . . .

VYSHINSKY: Permit me to establish that you, Bukharin, as a member of the centre of the Right underground organization, had underground conspiratorial connections with a Socialist-Revolutionary terrorist who, together with you, was preparing the organization of an attempt on the lives of Comrade Stalin and other members of the Political Bureau, and that these preparations of terrorist acts were being made with the knowledge and approval of the Right centre, including Tomsky and Rykov.

BUKHARIN: No, I think, not including, because they were the only ones who knew about it.

VYSHINSKY: Well, you, Tomsky and Rykov?

BUKHARIN: Yes.

VYSHINSKY (to Rykov): Does Rykov agree with this?

RYKOV: Yes.

VYSHINSKY: So there are no disagreements on this point?

BUKHARIN: I want to emphasize that the initiative in this matter lies on my shoulders.

VYSHINSKY: Your initiative in relation to Rykov and Tomsky?

BUKHARIN: Quite true.

VYSHINSKY: So that here the Socialist-Revolutionary line and the Bukharin line converged?

BUKHARIN: This, too, is possible.

VYSHINSKY: I have no more questions for the time being.

THE PRESIDENT: Adjournment for 20 minutes.

* * *

COMMANDANT OF THE COURT: The Court is coming, please rise.

THE PRESIDENT: Be seated.

We shall continue the examination of the accused Rykov. Comrade Procurator, have you any more questions?

VYSHINSKY: Yes, of course. (To Rykov.) We have analysed part of your crimes. We stopped approximately at 1933.

RYKOV: The end of this period coincided with the liquidation of the kulaks. In connection with this the Rights lost their last social base—the kulaks. The next period is characterized by the creation of an exclusively conspiratorial type of organization and the employment of the sharpest methods of struggle against the Party and the government. This particularly includes one of the attempts that was made to prepare for a "palace coup."

VYSHINSKY: To when does this refer?

RYKOV: This plan aimed to arrest the members of the govern-ment in connection with a violent coup carried out by the conspiratorial organization with the aid of a special organization created for the purpose of bringing about this coup. As far as I remember, this idea arose among the Rights in 1933-34, when it began to assume a more or less definite shape. But, as in the case of terrorism, when utterances in favour of terrorism were heard before terrorism had been adopted by the centre of the Right organization, so on the question of the "palace coup," individual members of the Right organization expressed themselves in favour of this method of conspiratorial activity before the Right centre definitely shaped this idea and tried to carry it out. This applies in particular to me, when in 1930 one of the members of the Right organization came to me with a fully worked out plan for a "palace coup," with a plan to arrest the government with the aid of a small specially prepared armed force. At that time I had not yet discussed this either with Tomsky or with Bukharin. This question arose in 1933. The mainstay of this counter-revolutionary plan was Yenukidze, who had become an active member of the Right organization in 1933. An important role was played by Yagoda, who was at the head of the G.P.U. These were the starting points that enabled us to proceed with the organization of the coup. To be more precise, subsequently the Right centre together with Yenukidze and Tomsky from time to time informed me about the progress of the preparations and execution of this plan. What month this was is not important; I remember that the first piece of information I received was about the group of Kremlin officials, and the principal figures here were Yagoda, Peterson, Gorbachov and Yegorov; I have in mind not the Chief of the General Staff—I don't know what he *is doing now—but Yegorov, the chief of the Kremlin military school. These three names played a great role in the life of the Kremlin and were in command of the school and of the entire administrative routine in the Kremlin. Several times Tomsky informed me about the enlistment through these persons— Yenukidze and Yegorov—of a group of military officials, headed by Tukhachevsky, who also prepared to accept this plan and were working in this direction. He mentioned the names of Uborevich and Kork. This is the basis of the relationships which afforded the possibility of carrying out, or at all events of attempting to carry out, the plan from the point of view of inflicting real damage, internal damage, apart from connections with abroad. We did not succeed in making a real attempt, but it might have inflicted a very serious wound upon Socialist liberty.

I cannot speak of the details of this work because it was kept very secret. A group was formed including very influential people—a military group. This group, from the underground viewpoint, worked independently of the other underground groups and it was the only one.

177

The question arose of how to co-ordinate the forces of the counter-revolution for the purpose of carrying out the "palace coup." For this purpose a centre was formed including the Trotskyites and Zinovievites: Kamenev, Pyatakov, Yenukidze, and also myself, Bukharin and Tomsky. Our task was to weld all the forces around this centre. With this centre were connected Tukhachevsky's military group and Yagoda's group.

In 1934 we already discussed the possibility of a tactical utilization of this organization in connection with the Seventeenth Party Congress that was about to be held. I do not remember exactly whether it was on the advice of Tomsky or perhaps of Yenukidze, but the question was raised of bringing about the coup during the Seventeenth Party Congress when all responsible workers would gather, and it would be possible to arrest simultaneously with most prominent members of the government, also those workers from the republics and regions who could offer resistance to the coup. But this plan was rejected. I think that apart from Tomsky hardly anyone supported it. What prompted its rejection? Clearly, the principal reason was that the conditions in the country precluded all likelihood of success. The compact unity of the Party, the popularity of the government and the absence of any discontent in the country, of course, made such an attempt a sheer adventure, absolutely futile, and this was the reason why it was rejected. The organization remained in existence. This proposal was discussed at a certain time, although, I repeat, it was rejected by everybody, including myself. Tomsky was the only one in favour of it. This corroborates the indictment, particularly those points which refer to this as one of the biggest counter-revolutionary undertakings. In this connection I must deal with the first paragraph of the indictment—our stake on defeat and on the assistance of the international bourgeoisie. All this refers, at all events the main part of it refers, to the period after 1933 in conformity with the ideological, political and practical line, which could be explained only by the loss of the last basis in the country. Those who persist in their counter-revolutionary struggle resort to the measures, methods and allies that we resorted to in the period after 1933. This refers to the "centre's" connections with the German fascists. Naturally, we, and I personally, tried to tone down our testimony on this question because this is a very bad thing. We depicted the situation so as to make it appear that we had not discussed these connections in the centre beforehand. Actually the situation was that Tomsky had taken the initiative. Bukharin and I heard about it afterwards. But all these are formal points, because all of us, I and Bukharin, never hesitated for a moment in deciding that Tomsky was right, and had he asked us, we would have said it was the proper thing to do. At all events, without reproaching him in the least, we proceeded to discuss the results of the soundings, as we called them, but in reality treasonable negotiations that had been going on. What is characteristic of these negotiations? The characteristic thing is that Karakhan reported that the German fascists were, of course, very well disposed towards the prospect of the Rights coming into power and would welcome it very much.[12] ... And in respect to their military operations against the Soviet Union, they would agree to co-operation, peaceful cohabitation, on the condition that definite economic privileges were given, made in the form of concessions, privileges in foreign trade, and so forth—that is to say, what Bukharin had proposed at one time, namely, that we could come to an arrangement with the Germans by means of concessions of this kind without territorial concessions. He said that the Germans insisted on the national republics receiving the right freely to secede from the Union.

VYSHINSKY: What did it mean in essence?

RYKOV: It meant that the largest national republics were to be wrested from the U.S.S.R., that they would attempt to turn them into territories adjacent to their own states, convert them into their vassals and thus obtain an opportunity for an attack on the rest of the Union. They would thus come close to the heart of the U.S.S.R. The possibility of waging a successful war against the U.S.S.R. would thus be facilitated for them.

VYSHINSKY: They would use this as a cover?

RYKOV: They would conceal their designs behind this.

VYSHINSKY: Consequently, this meant dismemberment of the U.S.S.R., wresting a number of republics from it?

RYKOV: Yes.

VYSHINSKY: Preparing a base for the fascists, for their attack and victory?

RYKOV: Yes, that is unquestionably so.

VYSHINSKY: Not only tools, but also conscious accomplices?

RYKOV: I do not know whether it is better to be a conscious or unconscious tool. One is as bad as the other.

VYSHINSKY: You picture it as if you just became the victims of the fascist designs.

RYKOV: No. But in all our aspirations we were not people going to the very end with regard to fascism; after all, we did confine our understanding to definite concessions. But we were tools in the sense that this understanding, all that led up to this understanding, facilitated for fascism the possibility of annulling it.

VYSHINSKY: You pursued your criminal objects at the cost of treason?

RYKOV: Of course.

VYSHINSKY: And you did it consciously?

179

RYKOV: Of course.

VYSHINSKY: And in this sense you were no tools?

RYKOV: Of course, there were negotiations . . .

VYSHINSKY: That the fascists wanted to use you—that is a separate matter. You wanted to use them too, for your aims.

RYKOV: No, I think that objectively it is clear that the movement of the Rights and the nationalist movement in our country are a reflection of the fascist and bourgeois encirclement which exists, because if there were no bourgeois encirclement and if there were no fascism, the Right deviation in the U.S.S.R. could not give rise to them; but they created quite a number of bourgeois groups. Objectively, that is so.

VYSHINSKY: That is clear, of course. But your plans reduced themselves to seizing power at the cost of treason?

RYKOV: Well, you know, there is treason and treason.

VYSHINSKY: Proceed.

RYKOV: Thus, our struggle with the Party began to develop, the methods of the struggle and the aims of the struggle were becoming clearer all the time. Then came the contact centre.

VYSHINSKY: This contact centre was a result of the organization of the "bloc of Rights and Trotskyites"?

RYKOV: It is hard to tell. The expression . . .

VYSHINSKY: What I want to say is that, besides the contact centre, there was a preliminary agreement between you, which you called a bloc.

RYKOV: Not a bloc, but formally we understood it to be a bloc with the Trotskyites since 1935. I say formally. But, in addition to formal organizational relations, there were, of course, elements of a bloc which found their expression in meetings between members of one organization and the other. Tomsky frequently met Zinoviev and Kamenev. Bukharin also met them. These were not the relationships of a formal bloc. But such meetings and conversations on political subjects established relations which, politically and in fact, without their being given the form of a bloc, meant a co-ordination of the activities of those organizations, or a bloc between them.

VYSHINSKY: Will it be right or wrong to say that in the period of the years 1932-33 a group was organized which we may call the Anti-Soviet Bloc of Rights and Trotskyites?

RYKOV: It was so in fact. Its organizational expression, since 1933-34, was the so-called contact centre.

VYSHINSKY: That's it, now; the contact centre represented a further step in putting the organizational relations on a formal basis?

RYKOV: Yes. In fact and politically that is a correct way of putting it.

VYSHINSKY: That is correct. And that bloc set itself the aim of—how do you formulate it?

RYKOV: It set itself the aim of overthrowing the Soviet system by forcible means, by means of treason and by means of an agreement with the fascist forces abroad.

VYSHINSKY: On what conditions?

RYKOV: On the conditions of dismembering the U.S.S.R., of severing the national republics. At the same time I must say that, after Karakhan's soundings, that was not our answer to the Germans. I shall tell about this later. As a matter of fact, our answer to their proposals went much further and was much worse than our formal acceptance of their conditions.

VYSHINSKY: This bloc, you said, included the Rights. Who else was included in this bloc?

RYKOV: The Rights, the Trotskyites and the Zinovievites.

VYSHINSKY: The Zinovievites, and then certain national-ist groups in the Union republics, say in Byelorussia?

RYKOV: Yes. I reserve the national republics for the con-cluding section of my testimony. I shall speak of that.

VYSHINSKY: Were the Socialist-Revolutionaries included?

RYKOV: In some of the republics.

VYSHINSKY: The Mensheviks were included. Through them you were connected with Nikolayevsky and Dan abroad. And, finally, there were separate bourgeois-nationalist groups in the national republics. For instance, in Byelorussia. Who was there of the accused?

RYKOV: Of the accused—Sharangovich.

VYSHINSKY: Is it known to you that he was a member of the bloc?

RYKOV: I learnt of it from Goloded and Chervyakov.

VYSHINSKY: And what about Sharangovich? Were you not personally connected with him?

RYKOV: No.

VYSHINSKY: But you knew from others that he was con-nected with the bloc?

RYKOV: I cannot say that.

VYSHINSKY: Accused Sharangovich, were you a member of the "bloc of Rights and Trotskyites"?

SHARANGOVICH: I was directly connected with Antipov and I knew of Goloded's connections with Rykov.

VYSHINSKY (to Rykov): And in Central Asia?

RYKOV: With the Pan-Tyurkic organizations.

VYSHINSKY: With whom?

RYKOV: With Ryskulov and Faizulla Khodjayev.

VYSHINSKY: Accused Faizulla Khodjayev, do you corro-borate this?

KHODJAYEV: I do.

VYSHINSKY: That you were a member of this bloc?

KHODJAYEV: I maintained direct relations with Rykov, later I was connected with Bukharin.

VYSHINSKY: Directly in matters concerning the conspiracy?

KHODJAYEV: In matters concerning the conspiracy.

VYSHINSKY: Accused Bukharin, is Faizulla Khodjayev's evidence correct?

BUKHARIN: It is.

VYSHINSKY (to Rykov): And were you not connected with Ikramov?

RYKOV: Personally I was not connected with Ikramov.

VYSHINSKY: Accused Ikramov, were you a member of the "bloc of Rights and Trotskyites"?

IKRAMOV: I was connected with the group of Rights through Bukharin. I may say that I was enlisted by Bukharin. After he began to slander the Party and Lenin in connection with the national question with regard to the thesis that the backward countries can attain Socialism with the assistance of the proletariat without passing through the stage of capitalism; he said that this was a lie, that it was wrong. When he began to speak openly on the national question, I told him of my bourgeois-nationalist organization and I formed a bloc with Bukharin in 1933. I spoke to him after that.

VYSHINSKY: Accused Bukharin, do you corroborate Ikramov's evidence?

BUKHARIN: I do.

VYSHINSKY: Hence the bloc included Trotskyites, Zinovievites, Rights, bourgeois nationalists, Central Asiatic groups, Byelorussian groups, and, through Grinko, Ukrainian groups.

RYKOV: We just began to make connections with Grinko.

VYSHINSKY: Accused Grinko, were you a member of the "bloc of Rights and Trotskyites"?

GRINKO: Yes, but I became a member somewhat later, in 1935. I joined as a representative of the Ukrainian national-fascist organization.

VYSHINSKY: Whom were you connected with?

GRINKO: With Rykov and Bukharin.

VYSHINSKY: As you have stated in your evidence?

GRINKO: Yes.

RYKOV: I must say that with regard to Grinko I knew that he was a Right, I had talks with him, I knew that he represented the Ukraine, but I did not know that he was an official representative.

VYSHINSKY: He showed you no credentials?

RYKOV: It is not a question of credentials. . . .

VYSHINSKY: But you knew Grinko as an old Borotbist, or didn't you?

RYKOV: Of course I knew, and I knew many others, but not every one of them was a representative of an organization.

VYSHINSKY: Why, did you regard him just as an individual, as Grinko?

RYKOV: I knew that he must be a member of this organization. . . .

VYSHINSKY: That he was not only a member, but a leader of the organization?

RYKOV: I could suspect what his role was, but I did not know.

VYSHINSKY (to the Court): Permit me to interrogate the accused Grinko. Accused Grinko, was it a case where he could only suspect your role as leader of the nationalist organization in the Ukraine, or was the case different?

GRINKO: Rykov is not telling the truth, because my connection with the centre of Rights and Trotskyites through Rykov began with my telling him, in one of our conversations, about the national-fascist organization in the Ukraine, about its desire to co-operate with the central conspiratorial organizations, and about the connections of the nationalist fascist organization with the German and Polish fascists.

VYSHINSKY: Accused Rykov, did Grinko speak to you about the things which he has just now told us?

RYKOV: No, I do not remember.

VYSHINSKY: You do not remember? And you, accused Grinko, do you affirm this?

GRINKO: I do.

VYSHINSKY: And besides Rykov, with whom else were you connected?

GRINKO: With Bukharin. Also with Antipov. But my connections with Bukharin did not refer to the work in the Ukraine, but to the undermining activities which I, as a member of the centre of the bloc, representing the Ukrainian organization, carried on on an all-Union scale.

VYSHINSKY: Accused Bukharin, do you corroborate Grinko's evidence?

BUKHARIN: I knew that he was a member of the bloc, I had conversations with him, and I also knew that he was in a general way connected with the nationalist Ukrainian circles. I must say, since there is some confusion and misunderstanding here concerning this question: the point is that the "bloc of Rights and Trotskyites" was an organization that had not taken final shape. It took final shape only in this contact centre. It is therefore quite natural that there were no credentials nor representatives in the common organization; one could speak of representatives only with regard to an organized body, but with regard to the bloc this question did not arise.

VYSHINSKY: I only want to ascertain whether you regarded Grinko's part in this common conspiratorial group as that of one of the leaders of the nationalist Ukrainian organization.

BUKHARIN: When you speak of a "group," do you mean the entire totality of the organization?

VYSHINSKY: Of course.

BUKHARIN: We did not regard him as a representative, but we did regard him as a man who, in fact, expressed the corresponding tendencies.

VYSHINSKY: That is, you had in mind that through Grinko you were dealing with the entire nationalist Ukrainian group?

BUKHARIN: A definite connection was established, he was a representative, but not in the formal sense, but in the sense of conveying the tendencies.

VYSHINSKY: It is not a question of representation, but a question of participation. . . .

BUKHARIN: It was a question of applying in the "bloc of Rights and Trotskyites" that complex of ideas, the complex of those measures which Grinko dragged in his wake.

VYSHINSKY: Is the Prosecution justified in formulating this point in the following way: the "bloc of Rights and Trotskyites" in the broad sense of the word, as we have just spoken of it, which is accused of having committed a whole series of crimes, as stated in the indictment, included Trotskyites, Zinovievites, Rights, bourgeois nationalists in the persons of Ikramov, Khodjayev, Grinko, Sharangovich and the nationalist groups standing behind them?

BUKHARIN: If you are referring to the "bloc of Rights and Trotskyites" in its entirety, and not to the group on top, I think it is quite right to pose the question the way you do it.

VYSHINSKY: Permit me to interrogate Krestinsky.

Accused Krestinsky, do you know that the Trotskyites belonged to the "bloc of Rights and Trotskyites" of which we are speaking here?

KRESTINSKY: I learnt from Pyatakov, when he spoke to me about this in February 1935, that an organization had been formed, which united the Rights, Trotskyites and military men, and which set itself the aim of preparing for a military coup. I also knew that the leading centre included Rykov, Bukharin, Rudzutak and Yagoda from the Rights, Tukhachevsky and Gamarnik from the military, and Pyatakov from the Trotskyites. He never told me that representatives of national-democratic organizations were included in this centre, and when I was in this centre with Rosengoltz in 1937, there were no representatives of these organizations in the centre then either.

As for the joining of forces, there is no doubt that this

184

same centre which united the Rights, the Trotskyites and the military group relied for support on the national-democratic organizations as well, but I did not know what the organizational form of this combination was.

VYSHINSKY: Hence, you confirm that the "bloc of Rights and Trotskyites," as an organization of anti-Soviet forces, included those groups of which the accused Bukharin spoke here, such as the Rights, Zinovievites, Trotskyites, bourgeois-nationalist groups, etc.

KRESTINSKY: With regard to the bourgeois-nationalist groups I am not certain that I could say that they were included on a basis of equality.

VYSHINSKY: Nor do I say that they were included on a basis of equality. What has the basis of equality got to do with it? It was not the League of Nations!

KRESTINSKY: When we speak of the organizational structure . . .

VYSHINSKY: I am not speaking of the organizational structure, but of the political connections. You say that you learnt it from Pyatakov, and that you personally . . .

KRESTINSKY: In 1937, when I joined the centre together with Rosengoltz, after Pyatakov was out, and we were there for three or four months, we had no personal connections with them. . . .

VYSHINSKY: Were you personally a member of this contact centre?

KRESTINSKY: I did not know it by this name.

VYSHINSKY: Each of you called it his own name. But in essence?

KRESTINSKY: In 1937, after a number of arrests, this centre comprised Rosengoltz and myself from the Trotskyites, Rudzutak and Yagoda from the Rights, and Tukhachevsky and Gamarnik from the military group.

VYSHINSKY: And where was Rykov?

KRESTINSKY: Rykov had either been arrested or he was not around. This was not earlier than February 1937.

VYSHINSKY: Accused Rykov, when were you arrested?

RYKOV: February 27, 1937.

KRESTINSKY: Personally I was in contact only with Rudzutak, for the contact with Yagoda was maintained by Rudzutak; we did not meet all together.

VYSHINSKY: Consequently, you knew about the existence of this union of anti-Soviet forces not only because Pyatakov told you; you convinced yourself of it personally?

KRESTINSKY: That is right.

185

VYSHINSKY: Accused Rykov, proceed.

RYKOV: If we consider that all the other questions have to a certain extent been exhausted, the main subject now is the question of the national republics.

VYSHINSKY: We will specially interrogate Sharangovich, Khodjayev and the others later on; then we shall speak about it in greater detail.

RYKOV: Of the main subjects, just the subject of the national republics remains.

VYSHINSKY: I want to put some questions with regard to the bloc and methods of its criminal activity. Did both you and Bukharin accept a defeatist line, or did Bukharin have a different point of view on this subject?

RYKOV: We gave no explicit formulations, but, in any case, I know of no existing ·differences of opinion on this subject. I remember that once, in my presence, Bukharin formulated the idea of opening the front.

VYSHINSKY: Perhaps you will tell us about it in greater detail?

RYKOV: I should prefer to give a general exposition of the question. The indictment speaks of active and passive methods. It will be sufficient to enumerate here a number of facts: the existence of a military group, headed by Tukhachevsky, which was connected with our centre and which aimed at taking advantage of a war to overthrow the government. This meant preparing for intervention pure and simple. Our dealings with the Germans, which we intensified in every way, were meant to stimulate in every way an armed attack, inasmuch as in this sphere the conspiratorial organization had entered into treasonable relations with them. Is that an active or a passive method? Among the important measures this is the sharpest thing that could be thought of in this form. Take the work in Byelorussia. . . . We had only Karakhan to maintain connections, while there connections were maintained through Ulyanov and a number of other persons. There the relations were much closer and more businesslike than was the case with Karakhan.

VYSHINSKY: Was there a connection with the Polish intelligence service?

RYKOV: This connection was maintained through the Byelorussian Polish organization and through Ulyanov. The relations were very close. Contact existed on the question of the so-called independence of Byelorussia. There was also a number of other matters, including work carried on by the Byelorussian organization among the Byelorussians in Poland, and the assistance in this respect was of a mutual kind: the Byelorussian organization gave assistance to the Pilsudskyites,[13] the Polish fascists, in their work within the Communist Party of Western Byelorussia, and they in their turn gave their assistance in the work here. Whether this kind of relations be considered active or passive, they represented very real preparation.

VYSHINSKY: A plan of treasonable activities?

RYKOV: Yes.

VYSHINSKY: At the preliminary investigation you said that in the negotiations with the Poles you agreed to the severing of Byelorussia from the U.S.S.R. On the basis of what facts did you say that?

RYKOV: On the basis of the relations with the Byelorussian organization. I was connected with such of their leaders as Goloded and Chervyakov.

VYSHINSKY: What was your personal line in this question?

RYKOV: This question was duly discussed in the centre, and all of us, myself, Bukharin and Tomsky, were unanimous that in case such a national movement did arise we would permit this secession.

VYSHINSKY: That is, severance?

RYKOV: That is clear, secession or severance. We used milder expressions.

VYSHINSKY: You bluntly agreed to such a treasonable act as the severance of Byelorussia from the U.S.S.R. for Poland?

RYKOV: To its independence. Byelorussia was supposed to come under the protectorate of Poland.

VYSHINSKY: As a vassal. (To Bukharin.) Accused Bukharin, do you agree with Rykov on this question?

BUKHARIN: I must say that Rykov's memory is failing him here.

VYSHINSKY: Did you, like Rykov, maintain a defeatist position?

BUKHARIN: No, but I am responsible for this affair.

VYSHINSKY: That you are responsible—that is a different matter. I must establish the fact: did you discuss with Rykov and Tomsky the question of opening the front?

BUKHARIN: I did, not with Rykov, but with Tomsky.

VYSHINSKY: What about?

BUKHARIN: This refers . . .

VYSHINSKY: It is of no consequence, when and why; that is a different question.

BUKHARIN: I had a conversation with Tomsky; he spoke about the idea of opening the front.

VYSHINSKY: There was a conversation with Tomsky about opening the front. Opening the front to whom?

BUKHARIN: Against the U.S.S.R.

187

VYSHINSKY: Opening the front to whom?

BUKHARIN: To Germany.

VYSHINSKY: Hence, there was talk of opening the front to Germany.

BUKHARIN: It was a question of our attitude. I want to say that no instructions were worked out during this conversation.

VYSHINSKY: About instructions later.

I am speaking of facts, such as took place. You confirm that you discussed it with Tomsky, that in case of necessity the front was to be opened.

BUKHARIN: I do not recall that.

VYSHINSKY: And do you, accused Rykov, recall it?

RYKOV: Of course, to open the front in case of war.

VYSHINSKY (to Bukharin): So you did not object.

BUKHARIN: It is self-understood that horses eat oats.

You say: what does it mean, opening the front to the enemy? Tomsky said that that was his opinion, but I objected.

VYSHINSKY: Wait a while, it still remains to be seen how you objected. We want to establish what actually happened. So Tomsky told you that it would be necessary or expedient to open the front?

BUKHARIN: Yes, he inclined to this opinion.

VYSHINSKY: That it would be expedient to open the front to the Germans in case of war?

BUKHARIN: Yes, in case of war.

VYSHINSKY: And what does this mean?

BUKHARIN: It means high treason.

VYSHINSKY: And as to how to open the front, who spoke to you about that?

BUKHARIN: Tomsky spoke about it, that there was such an opinion among the military men.

VYSHINSKY: Which military men?

BUKHARIN: The Right conspirators.

VYSHINSKY: Concretely, who?

BUKHARIN: He named Tukhachevsky, and Kork, if I am not mistaken; then the Trotskyites.

VYSHINSKY: That means that Kork, Tukhachevsky and the Trotskyites generally intended to open the front in case of war with Germany, and it was of this that Tomsky spoke to you?

BUKHARIN: Yes, that there was such an opinion among them.

VYSHINSKY: An opinion or a plan?

BUKHARIN: I would not say a plan. Perhaps it was a plan, but in a very cursory conversation. . . .

188

VYSHINSKY: And was Tukhachevsky a member of this group?

BUKHARIN: I have already explained. . . .

VYSHINSKY: I am asking: Were Tukhachevsky and the military group of conspirators members of your bloc?

BUKHARIN: They were.

VYSHINSKY: And they discussed with the members of the bloc?

BUKHARIN: Quite right.

VYSHINSKY: When members of a bloc discuss such things, it may be said that it is a plan.

BUKHARIN: It becomes a plan when all the i's are dotted.

VYSHINSKY: Can it be said that Tomsky dotted the i's?

BUKHARIN: It can.

VYSHINSKY: So that is established. And you were opposed to this?

BUKHARIN: Yes, I was opposed.

VYSHINSKY: And your opinion, accused Rykov? Can it be said that Bukharin accepted the standpoint of defeat of the U.S.S.R.?

RYKOV: I only want to tell of what actually occurred in my presence. (To Bukharin.) It is from you I first heard the term "opening the front."

VYSHINSKY: And what exactly was it that you heard?

RYKOV: That is what I want to tell. Perhaps it was a continuation of a previous discussion or conversation with Tomsky, I do not at all exclude this possibility; but we were there, the three of us—you, Tomsky and myself—and then you expressed the idea that in case the front is opened it will be necessary, in order to forestall seizure of power by the military group, to adopt definite measures against a military dictatorship.

VYSHINSKY (to Bukharin): Is that true?

BUKHARIN: That is true.

RYKOV: That is to say, that at that time Bukharin, in my presence, discussed the question of how to avoid in case of the front being opened . . .

VYSHINSKY: With whom did he discuss it?

RYKOV: I say there were Tomsky, Bukharin and myself. There was nobody else. He discussed the question of how to avoid the danger of Napoleonism, of a military dictatorship, in case of the front being opened.

VYSHINSKY: And whom did you suspect of this Napoleonism?

RYKOV: I do not remember. The question was discussed in general terms. The leader of the military group was Tukhachevsky. I cannot say whether his name was mentioned or not.

VYSHINSKY: In a word, you were apprehensive lest Tukhachevsky imagine himself a Napoleon?

RYKOV: I set forth what Bukharin said. That was the first time I heard the term "opening the front." I say I heard it when Bukharin expounded this and therefore I said in my deposition that before that I had not heard, I had not come across this idea, and I had not spoken of it to Tomsky. I said that in this respect Bukharin adopted an extreme position, because I first heard the words "opening the front" from Bukharin, and exactly in the sense which I have here explained. When he spoke, he said not a word to the effect that there were scoundrels who wanted to open the front, or similar things; there was not a word said to this effect.

VYSHINSKY: And what about Bukharin? Was he in favour of it?

RYKOV: He spoke about this calmly: in case of the front being opened, that is, in order to avoid such danger, something or other has to be done. But if one raises the question that it will be necessary to adopt some measures in order to avoid a definite danger, one speaks of it only if one considers the consummation of the thing itself admissible.

VYSHINSKY: Correct.

RYKOV: Therefore my impression was that at any rate Bukharin considers it permissible.

VYSHINSKY: Correct.

RYKOV: According to my opinion, this cannot be understood or interpreted in any other way.

VYSHINSKY: May I ask you this: did Bukharin pursue a defeatist line in this question?

RYKOV: This is too elementary.

VYSHINSKY: There are elementary things which it will do no harm to repeat. Yes or no?

RYKOV: Of course, yes.

VYSHINSKY: May we say that Bukharin's standpoint was that of defeat for the U.S.S.R.?

RYKOV: Knowing Bukharin as I do, I should say that perhaps he did not consider it the only thing, but he considered it as something that could be discussed, something that could be realized under definite conditions.

VYSHINSKY: I do not say the only thing possible, but one of the means—to open the gates to the enemy. Is that correct?

RYKOV: Yes, but as something possible, not indispensable.

VYSHINSKY: Of course, as something possible, not indispensable; that is to say, this was not the only road along which he was pursuing his aim. Isn't that treason?

RYKOV: Yes.

VYSHINSKY: Do you consider Bukharin a traitor?

RYKOV: A traitor, like myself.

VYSHINSKY: Do you corroborate the evidence you gave before the Procurator of the U.S.S.R.? (Reads.) ". . . as for our defeatist position, Bukharin shared it fully."

RYKOV: I must introduce a correction: he was the first to discuss it in my presence.

VYSHINSKY: Of course not in your absence.

RYKOV: But in general he discussed it with somebody before he spoke to me.

VYSHINSKY: If we consider you, Bukharin and Tomsky the centre of the Right section of the "bloc of Rights and Trotsky-ites," from whom in this centre did you first hear about the necessity of a preliminary agreement between your organization and foreign states?

RYKOV: I was just as much a member of the centre as he, and if such things were spoken of in my presence and I did not hand that person over to you, then I must answer for it.

VYSHINSKY: You are trying here to pose as a person of noble mind; but how was it in actual fact: did he speak to you or did you speak to him?

RYKOV: I wrote of this, I did not think it would be this way.

VYSHINSKY: But you said that he was the first to discuss it in your presence. Consequently, it was not you who spoke to him but he who spoke to you. Is that correct?

RYKOV: Yes.

VYSHINSKY: But both of you are responsible for this in an equal degree. He spoke to you. Was the initiative yours, or Bukharin's?

RYKOV: The initiative of introducing the subject?

VYSHINSKY: Yes.

RYKOV: That is so.

VYSHINSKY: Further: "He assumed an extremely favourable attitude towards the information concerning the negotiations with the German fascist circles." Do you corroborate this?

RYKOV: Yes, yes.

VYSHINSKY: Do you corroborate this?

RYKOV: Yes. Permit me to introduce more exactitude. The favourable attitude consisted in the fact that when we discussed the question of a rapprochement with the Germans, of avoiding war with them, Bukharin proposed that we make a number of concessions.

VYSHINSKY: Further: "As for our defeatist position, Bukharin shared it fully." Do you corroborate this?

RYKOV: Yes.

VYSHINSKY: "And he spoke in favour of this position even in sharper terms than we." Who is "we"?

RYKOV: I had Tomsky and myself in mind. I am referring to the question of opening the front. We did not discuss in detail how to avoid one thing, another, or a third.

VYSHINSKY: Further: ". . . and as a defeatist he spoke even in sharper terms than we."

RYKOV: It might perhaps be better here to change the formulation. I do not want to appear better in this respect than he. We are the same.

VYSHINSKY: These are your motives. But what about the facts?

RYKOV: They were the same as the motives, because I absolutely . . .

VYSHINSKY: Facts cannot be the same as motives. Facts are facts. You want to make Bukharin's position easier in connection with this question.

RYKOV: It is not that I want to make it easier for him, but I do not want to make it easier for myself at Bukharin's expense.

VYSHINSKY: During the preliminary investigation, did you state the truth or not?

RYKOV: Of course I stated the truth. I think that everybody understands that I am a sufficiently grown-up and experienced man and know how to make such differentiations. Suppose I did say one thing or another. I am older than he and my responsibility is not lessened or mitigated.

VYSHINSKY: May I put the question differently? Did Bukharin speak in favour of this position, of the defeatist position, as you say, in sufficiently sharp terms, in just as sharp terms as you?

RYKOV: Yes.

VYSHINSKY: And further: "He made the proposal and formulated the idea of opening the front to the Germans in case of war."

RYKOV: It is here that I must add that he thus formulated in my presence the question of the danger of seizure of power.

VYSHINSKY: Do you corroborate this?

RYKOV: Yes.

VYSHINSKY: Thus, when Bukharin says that he was opposed to the defeatist position, is he right or not?

RYKOV: Here I did not understand Bukharin, and do not understand him. The main thing is that a man of politics answers for his actions and for the results of his political actions. This is the one thing that must be demanded both of me and of him, and not at all the way he thinks. Then it will be of interest.

VYSHINSKY: I have no more questions to the accused Rykov.

THE PRESIDENT: Accused Rykov, in your depositions dealing with the work of the organization of the Rights in Byelorussia you noted that in fact your organization of the Rights in Byelorussia turned into an espionage agency of the Polish General Staff. Is that right?

RYKOV: Yes.

THE PRESIDENT: And further you stated in the same deposition that your organization of the Rights in Byelorussia received the same kind of instructions from the Polish General Staff, on the one hand, and on the other hand, from the centre of the Rights. How are we to understand this?

RYKOV: In what sense the same kind?

THE PRESIDENT: As regards wrecking work, that it was necessary to bring about a decrease in the number of livestock.

RYKOV: Even more than that. These instructions, as Goloded said, were duly received from the Poles. I do not recall that he spoke of having received these instructions from the centre.

THE PRESIDENT: But the instructions which your organization in Byelorussia was receiving from the Poles coincided with the instructions given by your centre?

RYKOV: I do not remember what instructions were given; in any event, I gave no instructions.

THE PRESIDENT: Did your centre give instructions with regard to wrecking in the sphere of agriculture, in the sphere of livestock raising?

RYKOV: No. No instructions were given in this sphere.

THE PRESIDENT: But if organizations which are subordinate to you receive instructions from the Polish intelligence service to engage in wrecking activities in the sphere of livestock raising, and, particularly, with regard to bringing about a decrease in the number of horses, and to perpetrate other acts of diversion, and if you know about it, how is it to be understood?

RYKOV: How is it to be understood? It is one of the elements of treason. I used to receive information after the damage had been done. I am guilty of covering up these acts. In any case the organizations of this type were large organizations, and they decided things on their own.

THE PRESIDENT: In the same deposition you say that "in Byelorussia the organizations of the Rights had set the task to turn Byelorussia into a base for an offensive by the Poles for the purpose of severing Byelorussia from the U.S.S.R. in the interests of Poland. These instructions of ours coincided with identical instructions which the Byelorussian organizations received from the Polish General Staff."

RYKOV: This is an unfortunate expression.

THE PRESIDENT: Why unfortunate? It is exactly what it

193

says in the record of your deposition: "our instructions coincided with the instructions of the Polish General Staff." This follows from your depositions and such is the conclusion. During your deposition you said in reply to a question: "as a result the organization of the Rights in Byelorussia actually turned into an espionage agency of the Polish General Staff."

RYKOV: This is correct. But there is a certain aspect here which consists in the fact that, besides the Right centre, besides fascist Poland, there were the Byelorussian nationalist organizations.

THE PRESIDENT: You were referring to the organization of the Rights.

RYKOV: These nationalist organizations had their own opinion, their line, their theses and their decisions.

THE PRESIDENT: You stated in your deposition: "Our instructions coincided with the instructions of the Polish General Staff." Here we must understand it to refer to the instructions of the centre—of Bukharin, Rykov, Tomsky.

RYKOV: When I wrote this, my object was to give a characterization of the ultimate political result.

THE PRESIDENT: The result was that your organizations in Byelorussia turned into an espionage agency of the Polish General Staff.

RYKOV: This is the formulation of the political results and not of very definite organizational relations.

THE PRESIDENT: Did your organizations of the Rights in Byelorussia engage in wrecking work in agriculture and in road-building on the instructions of the Polish General Staff?

RYKOV: I learnt of two cases from Goloded: one referred to the horses, the other referred to cows.

THE PRESIDENT: Why was it necessary for the Polish intelligence service to give instructions to carry out wrecking activities in road-building?

RYKOV: Apparently, this was done in order to impede the movement of our troops to defend the borders of the Soviet state.

THE PRESIDENT: How did you conceive of the role of your organization of the Rights in Byelorussia in respect of bringing about disintegration in the revolutionary movement of Western Byelorussia?

RYKOV: I have already explained this. I said that there was an exchange of services between our Byelorussian organization and the fascists. At the request of the Poles the counter-revolutionary Byelorussians sent people to Poland to work in the Polish Communist organizations in the spirit of the Byelorussian organization.

THE PRESIDENT: For what purpose were people sent? For work as agents-provocateurs, or for some other work?

RYKOV: The Poles, of course, used them for provocatory purposes, but this was hardly their immediate task.

They wanted at the same time to bring about the disintegration of the revolutionary movement among the Byelorussians, the disintegration of the Communist Party there, in order to set up in its place a Byelorussian organization which would set itself not only and not so much the aim of espionage as definite political aims.

THE PRESIDENT: Is it or is it not a fact that the organization of the Rights planted agents-provocateurs in the Communist organizations abroad, in Western Byelorussia?

RYKOV. That is true.

THE PRESIDENT: If you have stated that the organization of the Rights on the territory of Byelorussia was, as you say, an espionage agency of the Polish General Staff, what then can be said of the organization of the Rights on the territory of the Ukraine? Whose espionage agency or the organ of which General Staff was that organization?

RYKOV: I do not know exactly what the relations were there. I had no detailed conversations on this subject. But, in my opinion, the situation must have been analogous to what it was in Byelorussia, that is to say, that it was an espionage agency of German-Polish fascism.

THE PRESIDENT: Thus, your organization on the territory of the Ukraine was in actual fact an organization of German-Polish fascism?

RYKOV: Yes.

THE PRESIDENT: Your organization in the Northern Territory was also an agency of the intelligence service of a foreign state?

RYKOV: (No reply.)

THE PRESIDENT: You heard the evidence given by Ivanov?

RYKOV: As regards his espionage work?

THE PRESIDENT: Yes, and as regards possible concessions of timber and sawmills to British capitalists.

RYKOV: I heard that.

THE PRESIDENT: Do you agree with it? Was it so? At least, did Ivanov get such plans from your centre?

RYKOV: I did not know of that and gave no such instructions. At least . . .

THE PRESIDENT: Tell us, what kind of conversation did you have with Yenukidze as to the necessity of murdering Maxim Gorky?

RYKOV: I . . .

195

VYSHINSKY: Permit me to request that this be postponed until the time when we clear up this entire episode, since one question will hardly bring out anything, inasmuch as this question is linked up with quite a number of other questions. I would ask that this be postponed until we clear up the whole matter.

RYKOV: That is why I did not touch . . .

THE PRESIDENT: Tell us, accused Rykov, when you gave your evidence about the work of the organization of the Rights in the North Caucasus, did you mention that you had dealings with a whiteguard Cossack organization?

RYKOV: Alongside with things of secondary importance I failed to mention here one essential matter, the question of the Cossacks, of the Cossack organization of the Rights, which was formed there. It began to be formed in the period of 1930-31. Subsequently, Pivovarov informed me about the organization of the work in the Cossack organization.

It took final shape approximately in 1934, when Larin was at the head of it. . . .

THE PRESIDENT: I am interested in the nature of the connections which this organization had.

RYKOV: Of all the organizations this was probably the most extreme Right organization. In addition to Cossacks it included returned émigrés who, as Pivovarov told us, maintained their connections with the remnants of the Cossack armies which remained abroad, and in their work they received aid from those Cossack White armies. Through them and with them conversations were carried on to the effect that if an insurrection should take place in Central Asia, these same remnants of Cossack organizations abroad even promised the assistance of a landing party. This is what I learnt from Pivovarov about the Cossack organizations.

THE PRESIDENT: And who was to make up the intended landing party, White émigrés?

RYKOV: I said—the remnants of the Cossack White armies abroad.

VYSHINSKY (to the Court): If you will permit, I have two questions to ask Krestinsky in connection with the evidence given by the accused Rykov.

Accused Krestinsky, tell us, please, what do you know of the participation of the Tukhachevsky group in the "bloc of Rights and Trotskyites"?

KRESTINSKY: I know the following about Tukhachevsky's participation. When I met Trotsky in Meran in October 1933, he pointed out to me that in orientating ourselves on a coup d'état, we should under no circumstances rely for support solely on our Trotskyite forces, because their numbers were not sufficient for this purpose, but that we must come to an agreement both with the Rights and with the military group. He paid particular attention to Tukhachevsky, a man with an adventurous bent who lays claim to the first place in the army and would probably be ready to take many chances. He asked me to convey this opinion of his to Pyatakov and to talk with Tukhachevsky personally.

VYSHINSKY: Did you talk to Tukhachevsky?

KRESTINSKY: I had a talk with him in the beginning of 1934, after Pyatakov had spoken to him, and I told him of my talk with Trotsky. Tukhachevsky said that in principle he was favourably disposed not only to the joining of forces but also to the fact that such a task was being posed. But the question, he said, requires deliberation, the possibilities have to be established, and after that he would come to an understanding with Pyatakov on this subject. I found out from Pyatakov in February 1935 that an understanding had been reached, but I did not ask Pyatakov when the understanding was reached and when exactly this centre came into being. Subsequently I spoke to Tukhachevsky several times on this subject. This was in the second half of 1935, in 1936 and in 1937. I carried on such conversations on more than one occasion. During one of the conversations in 1935 he mentioned several people, on whose support he relied. He mentioned, among others, Yakir, Uborevich, Kork and Eidemann. During another conversation later on, a very important conversation which took place at the Extraordinary Eighth Congress of Soviets, Tukhachevsky urged the necessity of hastening the coup. The point was that we had linked up the coup with our defeatist orientation and timed it for the beginning of war, when Germany would attack the Soviet Union. But as this attack was being delayed, so was the practical consummation of the coup being delayed. At that period the gradual smashing up of the counter-revolutionary forces had begun. Pyatakov and Radek had been arrested, arrests of Trotskyites had begun, and Tukhachevsky began to fear that if this business were further delayed it would spell ruin for the entire undertaking. Therefore he raised the question of hastening the counter-revolutionary action. We discussed the matter with Gamarnik and Rudzutak, and came to the conclusion that Tukhachevsky was right. After that I asked in writing through Bessonov for Trotsky's opinion and received from him an answer in the affirmative. All these questions which are connected with Tukhachevsky, Trotsky, and so on—is it worth bringing them out here?

VYSHINSKY: I am satisfied with your answer.

Accused Rosengoltz, do you corroborate this part of Krestinsky's evidence?

ROSENGOLTZ: Yes, I do.

VYSHINSKY: Did you have occasion to speak to Tukhachevsky and Krestinsky?

ROSENGOLTZ: In the end of March 1937 I discussed with Krestinsky the question of hastening the organization of the coup.

VYSHINSKY: You will speak of this in detail during your examination. At present I have no more questions to you.

I have one question to ask the accused Chernov. Accused Chernov, I should like to dwell on your connection with the correspondent of the "Berliner Tageblatt," Paul Scheffer. You spoke of it yesterday. Under what circumstances did you establish contact with him? Did he visit you, or did you find him?

CHERNOV: I spoke of this yesterday. I repeat: they called me up from the Information Bureau of the People's Commissariat of Foreign Affairs and told me that I was to receive the correspondent of the "Berliner Tageblatt," Paul Scheffer, and give him information of a non-confidential character for use in the press. This was in the spring of 1929.

VYSHINSKY: Not 1930?

CHERNOV: No, 1929.

VYSHINSKY: Yesterday, I think, you said 1930.

CHERNOV: That must be a misunderstanding. If I said that it was in 1930, it was a slip of the tongue.

VYSHINSKY: Did you meet him once or several times?

CHERNOV: Several times in the course of 1929, until the connection with him broke.

VYSHINSKY: And what caused the connection to break?

CHERNOV: He said he was afraid of being exposed and was leaving the Soviet Union. I cannot say exactly when it was— either towards the end of 1929 or in 1930; rather, I would say, it was in 1929.

VYSHINSKY: Perhaps Krestinsky remembers?

KRESTINSKY: I think that Scheffer left the Soviet Union before my return from Berlin.

CHERNOV: That is what I say.

VYSHINSKY: You say either towards the end of 1929 or the beginning of 1930.

CHERNOV: During the preliminary investigation I stated both the period I was meeting Scheffer and the period when the connection broke.

VYSHINSKY: During the preliminary investigation you stated over your signature, on p. 45 of Volume VIII: at the end of 1929, or perhaps in 1930, Scheffer left the U.S.S.R. and the connection broke.

CHERNOV: Apparently, it was a slip of the tongue, or I was nervous.

198

VYSHINSKY: In any event, you remember that he left soon after this. Did you have a talk with him about his leaving?

CHERNOV: I did.

VYSHINSKY: I have no more questions.

THE PRESIDENT: The Court is adjourned until 11 a.m.

[Signed] PRESIDENT: V. ULRICH

Army Military Jurist
*President of the Military Collegium of
the Supreme Court of the U.S.S.R.*

SECRETARY: A. BATNER

Military Jurist First Rank

Summary of Morning Session

MARCH 4, 1938

Examination of the Accused SHARANGOVICH:

Sharangovich confirms the testimony he gave at the preliminary investigation and confesses to his "treasonable and treacherous crimes." According to his testimony, he became a traitor in 1921 when on his release from a Polish prisoner-of-war camp he was recruited by the Polish intelligence service. He was put in contact with an agent in the Byelorussian Republic and while attached to the Procurator's office gave information concerning cases of espionage then being processed. These activities were terminated in 1924-1925 but were resumed in 1932-1933. By this time he was a member of "the national-fascist anti-Soviet organization in Byelorussia." Sharangovich testifies that this organization received instructions from "the Moscow centre of the Rights . . . from Rykov and Bukharin personally." Two Byelorussian leaders, Goloded and Chervyakov, met with Rykov and Bukharin in 1932 and regularly thereafter.

The aim of the organization, the defendant states, was the overthrow of Soviet power in Byelorussia and the restoration of capitalism, and the "severance of Byelorussia from the Soviet Union" in the event of war with facist states. The means utilized include wrecking, diversion, and terrorism. Contact was established with the Polish General Staff. Sharangovich testifies that while Second Secretary of the Central Committee of the Communist Party of Byelorussia (1932) he carried on wrecking in the sphere of agriculture and slowed down collectivization. He "muddled up the sowing areas," "spread plague among pigs," provoked discontent among the peasants, and "caused a wide outbreak of anemia" that resulted in the death of approximately 30,000 horses. In addition, he conducted wrecking activities in industry and on the cultural front. Terrorist groups were formed and a terrorist act against Voroshilov and other Party leaders was planned in 1936. This was done on Rvkov's instructions. Sharangovich concludes by confessing to all of the charges.

Examination of the Accused KHODJAYEV:

Khodjayev testifies that his crimes began in 1920 in Bokhara when he joined a bourgeois-nationalist organization. During the nineteen twenties, while posing as a pro-Soviet leader, he marshalled bourgeois-nationalist forces against Soviet power. By 1928 he and the accused Ikramov headed anti-Soviet activities in Uzbekistan.

Khodjayev states that he met Rykov in Moscow in 1930 and at that time they formed an alliance of Uzbek nationalists and Rights designed to overthrow the Soviet government and the Party leadership.

At this point Vyshinsky questions Ikramov, who testifies that the two groups (his and that of Khodjayev) joined together not on their own initiative in 1928 but under pressure from Bukharin in 1933. Khodjayev continues to insist that the correct date is 1928. Resuming his testimony, he states that his group prepared a Five-Year Plan designed to give Uzbekistan a "self-contained economy" independent of the Soviet Union; however, Moscow revised their target figures. It was therefore necessary to stir discontent among the people. They destroyed the crop rotation system, caused deficiencies in cattle breeding and silk cultivation, and carried on general wrecking activities. Ikramov, as head of the Uzbek Party, and Khodjayev, as head of the government, directed these operations. Ikramov confirms this account, adding that they received directions from the Trotskyites in the person of the defendant Zelensky. Zelensky corroborates this testimony.

Khodjayev testifies that in 1930 Rykov spoke of the necessity of removing the present Stalinist leadership because the Party line was disastrous and the Rights must come to power. It was at this time that the alliance between the Rights and the Uzbek nationalists was concluded. Bukharin came to Uzbekistan in 1930 and discussed the alliance with Ikramov. In 1934, Antipov, a representative of the Rights centre, also journeyed to Uzbekistan. He criticized the Uzbek organization and demanded that wrecking activity be stepped up and that contact be made with England. According to Khodjayev's testimony, Bukharin repeated these demands at a meeting with him in Tashkent in 1936. Bukharin reported that an agreement had been reached with fascist Germany and that one with Japan was near. It was necessary, however, to accommodate England in regard to the Central Asian Republics. When Uzbekistan broke away from the Soviet Union it would have to become a "British protectorate."

Khodjayev concludes with a recitation of his wrecking activities; spreading discontent among the peasant population through "harsh administration and by overdoing things"; bringing about a decrease in livestock and silk cultivation; sabotage in construction, power stations, and cement works. In addition, terrorist and insurrectionary groups were formed on his instructions. Khodjayev states that he has betrayed the people of Bokhara, of Uzbekistan, of the U.S.S.R., and the confidence of Stalin.

EVENING SESSION, MARCH 4, 1938

COMMANDANT OF THE COURT: The Court is coming, please rise.

THE PRESIDENT: Please be seated. The session is resumed. We shall proceed to the examination of the accused Rosengoltz.

Do you confirm the testimony you gave at the preliminary investigation?

ROSENGOLTZ: Yes.

THE PRESIDENT: Comrade Procurator, have you any questions?

VYSHINSKY: Yes.

THE PRESIDENT: Please put them.

VYSHINSKY: Accused Rosengoltz, tell us briefly about your criminal activities, beginning from the moment that opened the road for you to the "bloc of Rights and Trotskyites."

ROSENGOLTZ: I shall say a few words about an earlier period.

As you know, I was a member of the Trotskyite trade union opposition during the trade union discussion in 1920-21.[1] Then, in 1923, I signed what was known as the "Platform of the Forty-Six," although with considerable reservations.[2]

At the beginning of 1925 I began to entertain certain differences with Trotsky in connection with the demand I made of him that he should admit the erroneousness of the theory of so-called "permanent revolution." He categorically refused to do this and the result was a certain cooling off of relations and certain divergences.[3]

My relations with Trotsky were restored, although not directly. In 1929 Krestinsky brought me Trotsky's instructions that I and Krestinsky should conceal our real attitude and as far as possible occupy responsible posts, maintaining a waiting attitude until the necessary forces in the country should, as Trotsky thought, gain the upper hand and we could take part in the organization of a new power.

This was the situation roughly until 1933. In 1933, in connection with the new directions and with our own decisions, we entered upon the path of greater or, to speak frankly, of intensive criminal activities.

Firstly, what meetings did I have during this time?

Krestinsky's letter was received at the beginning of 1933.

202

VYSHINSKY: But before 1933, say in 1929, were you in correspondence with Trotsky when Trotsky was already abroad?[4]

ROSENGOLTZ: You are referring to 1929?

VYSHINSKY: Yes, I ask you, were you in correspondence with Trotsky in 1929? Or perhaps you received through a third person, or in written form, instructions from Trotsky?

ROSENGOLTZ: The chief thing was the arrival of Krestinsky, who transmitted verbal instructions.

VYSHINSKY: And so in 1929 Krestinsky brought you instructions from Trotsky?

ROSENGOLTZ: Yes.

VYSHINSKY: What have you to say on this score, accused Krestinsky?

KRESTINSKY: There is a certain inaccuracy here. I met Trotsky's son at the end of 1929. I was at that time working abroad and could transmit these instructions to Rosengoltz only at the beginning of 1930.

VYSHINSKY: The difference between the end of 1929 and the beginning of 1930 is not a big one. What I want to establish is whether you actually did transmit certain instructions to Rosengoltz from Trotsky. And so this was at the end of 1929, or at the beginning of 1930?

ROSENGOLTZ: I have already said so.

VYSHINSKY: And so, at the end of 1929, or rather at the beginning of 1930, you received certain instructions through Krestinsky?

ROSENGOLTZ: I have already said so.

Further, in 1933 Krestinsky received a letter from abroad. Then, when Krestinsky was abroad himself, he had a meeting. I was abroad in 1933 and had a meeting with Sedov in Felden in Austria. I had several long conversations with him near the house where I lived. I next saw Sedov in 1934 in Karlsbad.

VYSHINSKY: What was the substance of your conversations?

ROSENGOLTZ: Sedov transmitted the following basic instructions from Trotsky. I shall here set forth the instructions which I received during my conversations with Sedov and which were transmitted through Krestinsky; in the main they coincided. This is with regard to connections with the Rights. It was recommended to form connections with the Rights and to carry on the work in contact with them.

VYSHINSKY: With whom specifically?

ROSENGOLTZ: That I was not told. Krestinsky told me about it, but mentioned no names, except Tukhachevsky's.

VYSHINSKY: But it was understood?

ROSENGOLTZ: Krestinsky said that he had instructions with regard to Rykov and Rudzutak. Sedov spoke a lot about the necessity of the maximum, the closest possible connections with Tukhachevsky, inasmuch as, in Trotsky's opinion, Tukhachevsky and the military group were to be the decisive force of the counter-revolutionary action. During the conversation it was also revealed that Trotsky entertained fears regarding Tukhachevsky's Bonapartist tendencies. In the course of one conversation Sedov said that Trotsky in this respect even expressed the fear that if Tukhachevsky successfully accomplished a military coup, it was possible that he would not allow Trotsky into Moscow, and in this connection he referred to the necessity for the greatest vigilance on our part. In fulfilment of these directions regarding connections . . .

VYSHINSKY: In what was this vigilance to consist?

ROSENGOLTZ: Trotsky therefore proposed that during the coup d'état we should everywhere place our own people, people who would be faithful to Trotskyism and who could be relied upon as regards vigilance. I will not mention a number of technical trifles which are of no significance here.

In fulfilment of these instructions, Krestinsky formed connections with Tukhachevsky. During the whole of this period, from 1933 to 1937, I had connections with Rykov and Rudzutak. The most important subject of these conversations with Sedov was the proposed composition of the government.

VYSHINSKY: Well, we can speak about that a little later on. For the present tell us about the substance of your criminal activities.

ROSENGOLTZ: I shall enumerate the main points. Sedov also conveyed directions from Trotsky about the organization of terrorism, stating that at that period these instructions about terrorism should have no direct practical bearing on Krestinsky and myself from motives of secrecy, since special instructions were being given on this score to the terrorist organization of Ivan Nikitich Smirnov.[5] In 1933 directions and instructions were received with regard to wrecking in the sphere of foreign trade. As Sedov had told me that Trotsky had an agreement with certain German circles, from this standpoint wrecking was of very essential importance to Trotsky for the maintenance of his prestige and the preservation of the agreement. The principal line in wrecking was to further the interests of Germany and Japan in the sphere of foreign trade. The question was then raised—and it was put several times and very persistently on the part of Trotsky and Sedov—of financing the Trotskyite movement through the channels of foreign trade. In 1935-36 there was also a certain exchange of letters between Moscow and abroad on these questions. I shall dwell on the letter of 1937, which Krestinsky received already after the Pyatakov trial.

VYSHINSKY: This was already in 1937?

ROSENGOLTZ: Yes, yes.

VYSHINSKY: And somewhat earlier? I would like to dwell, let us say, on 1935 or even 1934, that second meeting of yours in Karlsbad.

ROSENGOLTZ: I have spoken about that.

VYSHINSKY: I know that you have spoken about it. How was the question of war put on that occasion?

ROSENGOLTZ: In regard to war, Trotsky's line was for defeat.

VYSHINSKY: Was it expected that there would be a war? When?

ROSENGOLTZ: In 1935 or 1936.

VYSHINSKY: So Trotsky expected that a war would break out in 1935-36, and in this connection . . .

ROSENGOLTZ: The question of a coup was raised. Furthermore, a change in the line took place here, because at first it was a question of the desirability and necessity for effecting a military coup to coincide with the period of the possible outbreak of war. Only a difference of a few weeks could have been involved. And then, in view of the obvious delay of the war, the desirability of expediting the coup was urged—this was already in 1937—without awaiting military events.

VYSHINSKY: Very good. And so in 1934, during your conversations with Sedov, reference was made to a war in 1935-36 and it was said that the stake should be on defeat.

ROSENGOLTZ: Yes, yes.

VYSHINSKY: Did you not have occasion in 1934 to speak to any of the leaders of the bloc on this subject?

ROSENGOLTZ: I cannot remember so precisely with regard to 1934; it is difficult to recall individual dates.

VYSHINSKY: But did you meet Rykov in 1934?

ROSENGOLTZ: I certainly did. At any rate, such an exchange and contact did exist after the receipt of these instructions.

VYSHINSKY: They did exist?

ROSENGOLTZ: Yes.

VYSHINSKY: Continue.

ROSENGOLTZ: In 1937 . . .

VYSHINSKY: Before going on to 1937, just one other question. Did you have occasion to speak to Rykov on this subject in 1936?

ROSENGOLTZ: There was talk about this throughout this period: in 1934, in 1935 and in 1936.

VYSHINSKY: Preparations were being made?

ROSENGOLTZ: Yes, yes. Rykov chiefly staked on and hoped for an uprising in the countryside.

VYSHINSKY: This was before 1936, but what was the chief stake in 1936?

ROSENGOLTZ: On a military coup, on Tukhachevsky's group.

VYSHINSKY: Do you not recall what Rykov's attitude was

205

generally towards the delay of the counter-revolutionary action?

ROSENGOLTZ: He regarded the delay of action very unfavourably.

VYSHINSKY: He was nervous?

ROSENGOLTZ: He was very nervous, of course. Rykov and others feared that the delay might result in a number of exposures.

VYSHINSKY: Did Rykov tell you that Tukhachevsky was promising to act, but did not act?

ROSENGOLTZ: Yes.

VYSHINSKY: And who else said this?

ROSENGOLTZ: This was also said by Krestinsky, and Sedov transmitted Trotsky's opinion. So that this was a constant and basic subject in the conversations.

VYSHINSKY: Allow me to question the accused Krestinsky and Rykov.

Accused Krestinsky, do you confirm the testimony of the accused Rosengoltz?

KRESTINSKY: Yes, but there is some, relatively insignificant, inaccuracy.

VYSHINSKY: But in the main?

KRESTINSKY: In the main, yes. But the inaccuracy is that I did not receive a letter from Trotsky in 1933, at the beginning of the year. It was Radek, apparently, who received a letter from him.

VYSHINSKY: And did you know about the letter to Radek?

KRESTINSKY: I knew about it from Radek.

VYSHINSKY: Did he show it to you?

KRESTINSKY: No, he told me about it.

VYSHINSKY: And so you knew?

KRESTINSKY: Yes, I did. But I began to receive letters after the meeting in Meran, and I spoke to Tukhachevsky not in 1933, but in 1934.

VYSHINSKY: Accused Krestinsky, tell us, did you tell Rosengoltz in 1936 that Tukhachevsky was procrastinating with the counter-revolutionary action?

KRESTINSKY: I did, but in my opinion it was in a different way.

VYSHINSKY: Did you speak on this subject, or not?

KRESTINSKY: Yes. The fact of the matter is that in 1933 Trotsky spoke to me in Meran and developed the defeatist theory in detail.

VYSHINSKY: You will tell us about that later. Just now, in connection with the testimony which the Court has heard from the accused Rosengoltz, who stated that in 1936 Rykov was

206

nervous and said that Tukhachevsky kept on appointing dates for the execution of his criminal plan—an uprising—and postponing them. Rosengoltz said that Krestinsky also spoke of this. I ask, is it true?

KRESTINSKY: That is not so, because on Trotsky's instructions, it was agreed with Tukhachevsky from the very beginning that the action should be timed with war. At the end of 1936 the question was raised simultaneously both by Trotsky abroad, in the letter to Radek, and by Tukhachevsky himself, that the coup should be expedited and not be timed to the outbreak of war.

VYSHINSKY: That is, to act without waiting for war?

KRESTINSKY: Yes.

VYSHINSKY: That is, to expedite war, to hurry?

KRESTINSKY: Yes.

VYSHINSKY: And so Tukhachevsky was in a hurry?

KRESTINSKY: At the end of 1936 Tukhachevsky began to be in a hurry.

VYSHINSKY: And did you hurry him at that time?

KRESTINSKY: I agreed with him.

VYSHINSKY: Did you hurry him, or not?

KRESTINSKY: I did not hurry him, but I agreed with him.

VYSHINSKY: And so you thought that the counter-revolutionary action should be expedited, that is, you should hurry. If you held that view, it means that you hurried him?

KRESTINSKY: Yes, but it was at a later period.

VYSHINSKY: At the end of 1936? What I must know is whether you were possessed with impatience, whether you were in a hurry to expedite Tukhachevsky's uprising, and whether you told Rosengoltz about this.

KRESTINSKY: Yes, in 1936.

VYSHINSKY: And so he is telling the truth?

KRESTINSKY: This was in November 1936.

VYSHINSKY: But November 1936 is 1936?

KRESTINSKY: Yes.

VYSHINSKY: Permit me to question the accused Rykov. Accused Rykov, is the accused Rosengoltz stating the matter correctly?

RYKOV: With regard to Tukhachevsky?

VYSHINSKY: Did you speak to Tukhachevsky?

RYKOV: To Tukhachevsky? No.

VYSHINSKY: Did you speak to Rosengoltz?

RYKOV: I spoke to Rosengoltz once or twice.

VYSHINSKY: About the fact that you were in a hurry? And did you say that Tukhachevsky must be hurried?

RYKOV: No, there was no such talk.

VYSHINSKY: Accused Rosengoltz, where did the meeting take place?

ROSENGOLTZ: The meeting with Alexei Ivanovich Rykov took place in the lobby of the Council of People's Commissars, and I quite definitely remember that there was such a conversation.

VYSHINSKY: There was?

RYKOV: I just as definitely remember that there was no such conversation.

VYSHINSKY: But were you aware of the actions which Tukhachevsky was planning?

RYKOV: I stated yesterday that there was a military group, connected with a coup and a conspiracy.

VYSHINSKY: And do you confirm it today?

RYKOV: Yes.

VYSHINSKY: You do not recall such a conversation with Rosengoltz, but the fact itself remains?

RYKOV: Yes.

VYSHINSKY: But were you connected with the conspiratorial group?

RYKOV: I was connected with it through Tomsky and Yenukidze.

VYSHINSKY: Through Tomsky and Yenukidze?

RYKOV: Just so.

VYSHINSKY (to Rosengoltz): Do you recall what Krestinsky and Rykov said on the subject?

ROSENGOLTZ: Yes.

VYSHINSKY: How did you react to the arrest of Pyatakov in this connection?

ROSENGOLTZ: Already after the trial of Pyatakov a letter was received from Trotsky in which he put it that Tukhachevsky's military coup must be expedited to the maximum. There was a meeting in my apartment in this connection.

VYSHINSKY: What sort of a letter was this, can't you give more details?

ROSENGOLTZ: Trotsky raised several questions in it. First of all, he pointed out that if we procrastinated, the result would be that all the counter-revolutionary forces would be smashed piecemeal. Therefore, inasmuch as the cadres had already been considerably demolished, a number of possible actions should be expedited to the maximum.

VYSHINSKY: For example?

ROSENGOLTZ: Two questions chiefly were raised: the first was to retaliate to the Court sentence on Pyatakov by terrorist acts,

VYSHINSKY: That is, to the sentence of the Court?

ROSENGOLTZ: As a retaliation to the sentence of the Court condemning Pyatakov to be shot, it was proposed to organize terrorist acts.

VYSHINSKY: Against whom?

ROSENGOLTZ: Against leaders of the Party and the government, and to expedite a military coup to the maximum.

VYSHINSKY: Was there nothing else in this letter?

ROSENGOLTZ: It was demanded that Krestinsky and I should be more active.

VYSHINSKY: And did not this letter contain Trotsky's opinion about Pyatakov's conduct in Court? Do you not recall that Trotsky gave his appraisal of Pyatakov's conduct in Court in admitting his crimes?

ROSENGOLTZ: I do not exactly remember this point. I have a clearer recollection of the two points I have mentioned: regarding the demand for action in Trotsky's proposal to retaliate by terrorist acts, and the point about expediting a military coup.

VYSHINSKY: These two questions relate to criminal activities as such, while the third question relates to tactics. (To the Court.) Permit me to question the accused Krestinsky.

Accused Krestinsky, do you recall what Trotsky wrote in this letter?

KRESTINSKY: In one of the letters, received in the first quarter of 1937 along Arkady Pavlovich's lines . . .

VYSHINSKY: What does "along Arkady Pavlovich's lines" mean?

KRESTINSKY: Through his foreign connections.

VYSHINSKY: Through Rosengoltz?

KRESTINSKY: Yes. After Bessonov's departure and his arrest, my connections were broken. In this letter Trotsky expressed his disgust with Pyatakov's conduct. He demanded that in future, in a similar case, we should not behave in this way.

VYSHINSKY: How then to behave?

KRESTINSKY: Not to admit one's guilt.

VYSHINSKY: These were Trotsky's instructions even at that time?

KRESTINSKY: Yes. It was a sort of detail, an unimportant part of the letter; it was not regarded as anything of vital importance; a few sentences were devoted to it.

VYSHINSKY: In the preliminary investigation you testified (p. 72): "The second letter . . . In this letter Trotsky sharply criticized Pyatakov's conduct at the trial and proposed that in the event of further arrests we should not admit our guilt and refuse to give testimony." Is that correct?

KRESTINSKY: Yes.

VYSHINSKY: It was so?

KRESTINSKY: Yes.

VYSHINSKY: Perhaps your conduct in Court two days ago was also dictated by these directions?

KRESTINSKY: No.

VYSHINSKY: But you remembered these instructions of Trotsky?

KRESTINSKY: I did, but it was not this that dictated my conduct. It was connected with the facts I mentioned yesterday.

VYSHINSKY: When were you arrested?

KRESTINSKY: At the end of May.

VYSHINSKY: And when did you confess your guilt at the preliminary investigation?

KRESTINSKY: As to the principal crime, the one that was hardest of all for me to admit, namely, about my connections with the German intelligence service and General Seeckt, I confessed after the lapse of a week, at the first interrogation.

VYSHINSKY: But for a week you denied it?

KRESTINSKY: I confessed it at the end of the first interrogation.

VYSHINSKY: Was it because you wanted to carry out Trotsky's instructions that you denied your guilt?

KRESTINSKY: No. I just hoped that I would be believed and that . . .

VYSHINSKY: You would succeed in the deception?

KRESTINSKY: That I would succeed in the deception and thus save myself.

VYSHINSKY: But you did not succeed!

KRESTINSKY: No.

VYSHINSKY: Accused Rosengoltz, continue.

ROSENGOLTZ: The point I stopped at was the conference we had with Tukhachevsky. It took place at the end of March. At the confrontation, Krestinsky introduced a correction and said that it was at the beginning of April; but the difference is of no importance. There was a conference with Tukhachevsky.

VYSHINSKY: Where was this conference held?

ROSENGOLTZ: In my apartment.

VYSHINSKY: There was a conference in your apartment. With whom?

ROSENGOLTZ: With Tukhachevsky and Krestinsky.

VYSHINSKY: When was this conference held? Let me have the exact date.

ROSENGOLTZ: It was at the end of March 1937.

VYSHINSKY: Continue.

ROSENGOLTZ: At this conference Tukhachevsky stated that he counted definitely on the possibility of a coup and mentioned the date. He believed that by May 15, in the first half of May, he would succeed in carrying out this military coup.

VYSHINSKY: What was the plan for this counter-revolutionary action?

ROSENGOLTZ: Tukhachevsky had a number of variants. One of them, the one on which he counted most, was the possibility for a group of military men, his adherents, gathering in his apartment on some pretext or other, making their way into the Kremlin, seizing the Kremlin telephone exchange, and killing the leaders of the Party and the government.

VYSHINSKY: Was this his plan, or was it your joint plan?

ROSENGOLTZ: We did not discuss this plan of his. He merely told us of it as one of the variants on which he placed great hopes.

VYSHINSKY: And you left it to him to act?

ROSENGOLTZ: Well, of course. We could not go into these questions.

VYSHINSKY: And why did he inform you of this plan?

ROSENGOLTZ: Inasmuch as we in general advanced the proposition of a military coup.

VYSHINSKY: As the leaders of this action?

ROSENGOLTZ: Yes, yes.

VYSHINSKY: Of this plot?

ROSENGOLTZ: Yes, yes.

VYSHINSKY: Allow me to ask Krestinsky now. (To Krestinsky.) Do you confirm this?

KRESTINSKY: Yes, I do. This conference took place in Rosengoltz's apartment. It was at the beginning of April. At this conference we referred to Yagoda's arrest as a fact. I learnt about Yagoda's arrest on April 2 or 3. So it was in April.

VYSHINSKY: Were you also informed of Yagoda's part in the plot?

KRESTINSKY: Yes, I spoke about that yesterday.

VYSHINSKY: Be seated.

Accused Rosengoltz, continue.

ROSENGOLTZ: The question of a terrorist act was raised. Krestinsky and I discussed the possibility there and then of a terrorist act against Molotov, Chairman of the Council of People's Commissars.

VYSHINSKY: Accused Krestinsky, did you discuss the commission of a terrorist act against Vyacheslav Mikhailovich Molotov?

KRESTINSKY: We discussed the question in a different way—in its wider aspects. . . .

VYSHINSKY: Did you discuss this question?

KRESTINSKY: He and I spoke generally about the necessity of renewing the terrorist activities of the Trotskyites, which had

211

been suspended after the death of Pyatakov, and I discussed this point with Rosengoltz and Gamarnik. We discussed the necessity of terrorist acts against the leaders of the Party and the government.

VYSHINSKY: Against whom exactly?

KRESTINSKY: We had in mind Stalin, Molotov and Kaganovich, but we did not discuss specifically a terrorist act against Molotov in detail.

VYSHINSKY: I am not interested in details. Did you talk about preparations for a terrorist act against Comrade Molotov?

KRESTINSKY: Not about preparations, but about the necessity for preparations.

VYSHINSKY: And so you discussed the necessity of preparations for a terrorist act in order to commit it?

KRESTINSKY: Yes, of course.

VYSHINSKY: Be seated.

Accused Rosengoltz, continue.

ROSENGOLTZ: Now about certain of the more important lines of these crimes and criminal activities. . . .

VYSHINSKY: Allow me first of all to put one question. After Yagoda's arrest, did Krestinsky express his demands that the armed uprising should be expedited?

ROSENGOLTZ: He had expressed this all along, both during 1936 and during 1937.

VYSHINSKY: But after Yagoda's arrest?

ROSENGOLTZ: I cannot recall with such precision the date of the arrest, when it took place; but at any rate this should coincide, because he raised this question in March, and it was raised again in April.

VYSHINSKY: I am interested in knowing, was Krestinsky's part in your plot fairly active, or not?

ROSENGOLTZ: Krestinsky put the question quite clearly that the coup should be expedited.

VYSHINSKY: It is one thing to put the question clearly, it is another to direct the affair—to hurry, to organize, to insist upon the execution of the plan of the plot.

ROSENGOLTZ: All the negotiations with Tukhachevsky were conducted by Krestinsky, with the exception of one conference which was held in my apartment.

VYSHINSKY: As far as I understand, it was part of your conception that your principal hope in this criminal design rested with the Tukhachevsky group. Is that so?

ROSENGOLTZ: Yes.

VYSHINSKY: Who held direct and immediate contact with this group?

ROSENGOLTZ: Krestinsky.

VYSHINSKY: Consequently, in a certain measure, as a member of the bloc, he organized the activities of this group. Do I under-nd rightly?

ROSENGOLTZ: Of course.

VYSHINSKY: Consequently, he played one of the leading parts in this affair?

ROSENGOLTZ: He hurried Tukhachevsky all the time. . . .

VYSHINSKY: And when you stated at the preliminary investigation that after Yagoda's arrest, or even earlier, after Pyatakov's arrest, Krestinsky put the question to Tukhachevsky particularly sharply, that is how it was in reality? It is indicative of the energy displayed by Krestinsky in this affair?

ROSENGOLTZ: I have no wish to, and have no grounds for singling out Krestinsky especially. . . .

VYSHINSKY: You have no grounds, but I have. I am asking you, as a man who organized this sinister plot together with Krestinsky.

ROSENGOLTZ: Krestinsky, like myself, considered it necessary to expedite this coup and systematically hurried Tukhachevsky.

VYSHINSKY: Accused Krestinsky, is it true that you systematically hurried Tukhachevsky to effect the coup?

KRESTINSKY: Ever since November 1936 I was decidedly in favour of expediting this coup to the maximum. I had no need to hurry Tukhachevsky, because he was of the same mind himself, and he himself put this question to us—to the Rights, to me, to Rosengoltz and Rudzutak—and asked our consent to carry out this action without waiting for the armed attack. And so there was no need to hurry him. Our minds were one on the question of the coup.

VYSHINSKY (to Rosengoltz): Rosengoltz, why do you assert that Krestinsky systematically hurried Tukhachevsky to effect the coup?

ROSENGOLTZ: Because he told me about it himself: he said that he had been conducting negotiations for a considerable time and that Tukhachevsky was giving him promises and fixing dates which he did not adhere to.

VYSHINSKY: Accused Krestinsky, did you express the idea that this act had to be expedited?

KRESTINSKY: I could not do this before November 1936, because it was obvious to all of us at that time that this action could not take place before the Soviet Union was attacked by foreign states. But after this we had talks together and discussed how the action could be expedited. This was in March 1937, when from the time of Tukhachevsky's return from his vacation to the end of March I spoke to him several times on this subject, and then told Rosengoltz, but not to the effect that Tukhachevsky had appointed a definite date and was not adhering to it, because no date whatever was fixed. The talk in Rosengoltz's apartment was more explicit. Tukhachevsky was preparing to go to London for the coronation of the King of England so as not to arouse suspicion. But when it was learnt that his trip had been cancelled, he said that he would start a revolt in the early part of May.

VYSHINSKY: So Tukhachevsky declared that he would start a revolt in the early part of May?

KRESTINSKY: Yes, he did.

VYSHINSKY: Accused Rosengoltz, continue.

ROSENGOLTZ: I now want to deal with the criminal utilization of the channels of the People's Commissariat of Foreign Trade in my Trotskyite activities.

VYSHINSKY (to Rosengoltz): What have you to say about your meetings with Gamarnik?

ROSENGOLTZ: I confirm the testimony I gave at the preliminary investigation.

VYSHINSKY: Which exactly?

ROSENGOLTZ: As regards Gamarnik, the chief point is that Gamarnik told us of his proposal, which apparently had the consent of Tukhachevsky, that it was possible to seize the building of the People's Commissariat of Internal Affairs during the military coup. Gamarnik assumed that this attack would be carried out by some military unit under his direct command, believing that he enjoyed sufficient Party, political prestige in the army. He calculated that in this affair he would have the support of some of the commanders, especially the dare-devils. I remember that he mentioned the name of Gorbachov.

VYSHINSKY: And so in addition to your having been informed by Tukhachevsky of his plans for a criminal plot, you were also informed of these plans by Gamarnik?

ROSENGOLTZ: Yes.

VYSHINSKY: Did Krestinsky take part in these conversations with Gamarnik and in the discussion of this plan?

ROSENGOLTZ: He was not present at this conversation.

VYSHINSKY: But he was on some other occasion?

ROSENGOLTZ: My conversations with Gamarnik were held without Krestinsky.

VYSHINSKY: Krestinsky did not take part in them?

ROSENGOLTZ: No.

VYSHINSKY: And do you know whether Krestinsky had similar conversations with Gamarnik?

ROSENGOLTZ: I do not know of these conversations which Krestinsky had with Gamarnik.

VYSHINSKY: You do not know? (To Krestinsky.) Krestinsky, what have you to say about this?

KRESTINSKY: I had one conversation with Gamarnik together with Arkady Pavlovich Rosengoltz, where the question of terrorism was discussed. When we saw that this business, with which we had not been associated in Pyatakov's time, was left unattended in our Trotskyite ranks after he was shot, and at the same time it was clear and Trotsky had written that terrorist acts were necessary, the three of us met to discuss what was to be done. And at this meeting we unanimously came to the conclusion that of the three of us Rosengoltz and I were not suited to take up this job, because by the nature of our work and our contacts we were not connected with those groups of Party members and citizens who could undertake the task of preparing and committing terrorist acts.

VYSHINSKY: In short, Gamarnik took it over?

KRESTINSKY: Yes. And after this neither of us, Rosengoltz or myself, discussed with him concretely what he was doing, but he used to tell us that he was making progress, that he was selecting cadres, selecting groups.

ROSENGOLTZ: Concerning the utilization of our foreign trade connections for criminal Trotskyite purposes, I might say that Ivan Nikitich Smirnov utilized the channels of foreign trade in his time. I knew that Golzman was active in the foreign trade, then there was a man named Gerzberg who worked in Berlin and had connections with Trotsky, then Birkenhof maintained connections with Trotsky and with Gaven. More recently it was Krayevsky and Shostak. But the main connections were maintained through the People's Commissariat of Foreign Affairs, since Krestinsky had the mail service in his own hands.

VYSHINSKY: So diplomatic mail was used?

ROSENGOLTZ: Yes, we used the diplomatic mail and persons who had diplomatic passports so that they could carry everything they liked.

VYSHINSKY: Proceed.

ROSENGOLTZ: Foreign trade was criminally utilized by way of using and stealing funds to finance the Trotskyite movement. Without dwelling on quite a number of perhaps insignificant dealings, I shall mention two of the most important examples. The first was an operation carried out by Krayevsky to the amount of $300,000, which were transmitted to the Trotskyite organization or directly to Trotsky.

VYSHINSKY: Put at Trotsky's disposal?

ROSENGOLTZ: Yes.

VYSHINSKY: By Krayevsky?

ROSENGOLTZ: Yes.

VYSHINSKY: On your instructions?

ROSENGOLTZ: Yes. This was done through the corresponding

firms by using Sedov as a broker; later this financing was organized also by me personally, when I came to terms with a certain official person in Moscow when we were concluding an agreement.

VYSHINSKY: With what official person?

ROSENGOLTZ: With the representative of a certain state.

VYSHINSKY: A foreign state?

ROSENGOLTZ: Yes. Terms according to which Trotsky was to receive approximately $110,000 annually in the course of three years.

VYSHINSKY: So you arranged that Trotsky was regularly and properly supplied with funds?

ROSENGOLTZ: Yes.

VYSHINSKY: These were the bigger operations; what about the smaller ones? For example, did you transmit £2,000 to Trotsky in 1933?

ROSENGOLTZ: That was done without me, but I knew of it, of course; I am saying it not in order to absolve myself but for the sake of exactitude.

VYSHINSKY: This was done through the channels of foreign trade, and you were then . . .

ROSENGOLTZ: I was People's Commissar of Foreign Trade, and with my sanction and knowledge . . .

VYSHINSKY: That is to say, by you. So £2,000 were transmitted. This is also a large sum, but it is a trifle compared with $110,000. And was there another £15,000 transmitted to Trotsky in 1934?

ROSENGOLTZ: Yes, yes.

VYSHINSKY: £15,000—that is not a mere trifle, it is £15,000.

ROSENGOLTZ: Yes, £15,000; then another time again £10,000.

VYSHINSKY: £15,000, then £10,000, then £2,000, that already makes £27,000.

ROSENGOLTZ: And another 20,000 marks.

VYSHINSKY: That is to say, a rather considerable amount of money?

ROSENGOLTZ: Oh yes, I mentioned in the beginning only two sums, the largest.

VYSHINSKY: I understand. Add to this another $300,000. During what period?

ROSENGOLTZ: That was since 1933.

VYSHINSKY: And since 1931?

ROSENGOLTZ: Oh yes, $300,000 through Exportles.

VYSHINSKY: Through Exportles—that is a separate item. What have you got to state further?

ROSENGOLTZ: Now I want to mention also that at an earlier period—in 1923, in connection with a business contact I had . . .

VYSHINSKY: With whom?

ROSENGOLTZ: With German military circles. Trotsky told me to supply Seeckt with information about the Soviet air force.

VYSHINSKY: And did you supply it?

ROSENGOLTZ: Yes, I supplied this information.

VYSHINSKY: Besides transmitting money to Trotsky, you also gave espionage information to Seeckt?

ROSENGOLTZ: Yes, yes. This was in 1923.

VYSHINSKY: And later, and afterwards?

ROSENGOLTZ: Beginning with 1931, information was transmitted concerning orders to be placed abroad in the line of foreign trade.

VYSHINSKY: Confidential, state information?

ROSENGOLTZ: Yes.

VYSHINSKY: You have thus served a foreign intelligence service during a long period of time?

ROSENGOLTZ: Information of this kind was given beginning with 1931 up to 1935 and in 1936.

VYSHINSKY: And in 1937?

ROSENGOLTZ: None.

VYSHINSKY: Why?

ROSENGOLTZ: I am merely stating what the picture was.

VYSHINSKY: But why such a picture? Why did you not transmit anything in 1937?

ROSENGOLTZ: We had no meetings.

VYSHINSKY: Because there was no suitable occasion?

ROSENGOLTZ: No, there was no occasion.

VYSHINSKY: And in 1923 you supplied General Seeckt with espionage information on Trotsky's instructions?

ROSENGOLTZ: Yes, yes.

VYSHINSKY: Do you know whether there was anybody else who transmitted to Seeckt similar information at that time?

ROSENGOLTZ: I knew that Krestinsky had some kind of an illegal connection with the Reichswehr.

VYSHINSKY: When did you know about it?

ROSENGOLTZ: Approximately during that same period and somewhat later. I cannot say exactly; but I did not know what was the nature of this connection.

VYSHINSKY: Perhaps the accused Krestinsky will tell us about the nature of this connection?

Accused Krestinsky, what was the connection with the Reichswehr to which Rosengoltz is referring?

KRESTINSKY: In 1921 Trotsky told me to take advantage of a meeting with Seeckt during official negotiations [6] to propose to him, to Seeckt, that he grant Trotsky a regular subsidy for the development of illegal Trotskyite activities; at the same time he told me that, if Seeckt will put up a counter-demand that we render him services in the sphere of espionage, we should and may accept it. I shall speak later about the conversation I had with Trotsky when he gave me these instructions. I put the question before Seeckt and named the sum of 250,000 gold marks, that is $60,000, a year. General Seeckt, after consulting his assistant, the chief of staff, agreed in principle and put up the counter-demand that certain confidential and important information of a military nature should be transmitted to him, even if not regularly, by Trotsky in Moscow or through me. In addition he was to receive assistance in obtaining visas for some persons whom they needed and whom they would send to the Soviet Union as spies. This counter-demand of General Seeckt was accepted and in 1923 this agreement had been put in effect.

VYSHINSKY: Did you transmit espionage information?

KRESTINSKY: I would say, not I, but we, the Russian Trotskyites. But there were cases when I personally gave this information to General Seeckt.

VYSHINSKY: You gave it personally?

KRESTINSKY: Yes. I also received money on several occasions.

VYSHINSKY: From whom did you receive money?

KRESTINSKY: From General Seeckt.

VYSHINSKY: Where?

KRESTINSKY: In his office. I handed over the money to Trotsky personally during my visits to Moscow.

VYSHINSKY: Personally?

KRESTINSKY: Yes, without resorting to anybody's services.

VYSHINSKY: In what year did the negotiations with Seeckt begin?

KRESTINSKY: It was in the spring and summer of 1922. In the indictment it says 1921. This is of no great consequence, but this first meeting of an official nature, which Trotsky suggested that I take advantage of, occurred in the winter of 1921-22.

VYSHINSKY: So this meeting was taken advantage of?

KRESTINSKY: On learning of these meetings, Trotsky suggested that I take advantage of the last one, which took place at the end of the spring or in the summer of 1922. This is of no consequence from the point of view of the charges against me.

VYSHINSKY: So you established connections with the Reichswehr in the person of General Seeckt in the winter of 1921-22, that is to say, since 1921?

KRESTINSKY: The connection of a criminal nature was established in 1922.

VYSHINSKY: You first arranged the connection, and then?

KRESTINSKY: And then it developed into a criminal connection.

VYSHINSKY: So it developed into a criminal connection?

KRESTINSKY: Yes, since 1922, into a criminal connection.

VYSHINSKY: Be seated.

So you, Rosengoltz, established connections with the German intelligence service already in 1923?

ROSENGOLTZ: With Seeckt directly.

VYSHINSKY: Do you draw a line between the two?

ROSENGOLTZ: I am saying it merely for the sake of exactitude.

VYSHINSKY: So since 1923 you, accused Rosengoltz, began to supply espionage information to foreign states?

ROSENGOLTZ: That is right.

VYSHINSKY: Proceed.

ROSENGOLTZ: I must also state, although I said it in my testimony during the preliminary investigation, that in 1926 I gave information to Farbman,[7] an English journalist, who at the same time was a Trotskyite. This was information concerning the foreign policy of the U.S.S.R. After that, during 1932-35, I gave information about orders placed abroad to the editor of the "British-Russian Gazette," Talbot, who came to me on his behalf.

Now as regards wrecking activities. I want to state that in these wrecking activities our aim was to help mainly Germany, and partly Japan.

Of the most important acts of this wrecking, which clearly constituted also treacherous activity, I shall mention the conclusion of the oil agreement with Germany, I shall mention the fact that gold tailings were exported to Germany when it would have been more rational to treat them in the Soviet Union. Further, the export of zinc concentrates, the advance exports, then the export of pig iron to Japan at reduced prices and in large quantities at a time when there·was an acute shortage of pig iron on the market, the delay in placing orders for tonnage, which entailed extra expenditures, the inclusion of a number of disadvantageous terms in contracts, for example, the formulation of the clause concerning force-majeure, also the delays in exports to Mongolia and to Western China.

It is necessary to note especially the wrecking activities which followed from our aim of working for defeat—the delay in the import of materials needed for defence.

VYSHINSKY: You will tell of this in greater detail at the in camera session. I think that there is no need to dwell on this question at present.

219

ROSENGOLTZ: Well, this in fact covers all that is of importance.

THE PRESIDENT: Have you any more questions to the accused, Comrade Procurator?

VYSHINSKY: No.

THE PRESIDENT: Be seated, please.

VYSHINSKY: Permit me to interrogate Krestinsky.

THE PRESIDENT: Accused Krestinsky, tell the Court briefly of your counter-revolutionary activities without dwelling on those points which have already been cleared up.

KRESTINSKY: I began my illegal Trotskyite activities at the end of 1921, when on Trotsky's suggestion I consented to the formation of an illegal Trotskyite organization and to my joining its centre, which was to be made up of Trotsky, Pyatakov, Serebryakov, Preobrazhensky [8] and myself, Krestinsky. Trotsky made this proposal to me immediately after the Tenth Congress. At that time I rejected this proposal, because it seemed to me that my differences with the Party were of a casual nature and that, after my return from my summer vacation for cure, I would be able to go on with my Party work without feeling restricted in my rights, and that I had no grounds or motives for any kind of joint activities with Trotsky. But when it turned out during my cure abroad that I was appointed to the Berlin post, and when my request, which I made after my return, that this appointment be rescinded was rejected, Trotsky began to impress upon me that this appointment was not dictated by business motives, that I was not fit for work abroad, that I did not know the language, that I did not know foreign countries, and that this step was taken in order to remove me from Party work forever. As a result of this kind of systematic influence exerted on me, which went on for several weeks, I consented to join this organization, which was clearly a violation both of the Party rules and of the special decision of the Tenth Congress prohibiting the formation of groups. As yet, this was an offence of an inner Party nature, which would not have entailed any serious consequences for me if I had reported it to the Party leadership. A year later I committed a crime—I refer to the one I spoke about during the examination of the accused Rosengoltz—the agreement I concluded on Trotsky's instructions with General Seeckt, with the Reichswehr in his person, about financing the Trotskyite organization in exchange for services of an espionage nature which we undertook in this connection to render the Reichswehr. When Trotsky gave me these instructions my attitude towards them was mainly of great apprehension, but apprehension not out of fear, but, so to speak, out of some inner shuddering, and I pointed out that this means espionage and treason to the fatherland. But

220

Trotsky argued that our line in foreign policy coincided with that of Germany at that period, that Germany was in a state of ruin after the war, and that in any event, in view of the existence of revenge sentiments in Germany with regard to France, England and Poland, a clash between Germany and the Soviet Union, or Soviet Russia at that time, in the near future was out of the question, and that therefore we could agree to this deal without actually committing a grave crime. Blinded by my factional bitterness, I permitted myself to be convinced by these unsound, childish arguments. The agreement was concluded.

VYSHINSKY: These arguments, were treasonable rather than childish.

KRESTINSKY: Childish on account of their not being convincing, on account of their emptiness and on account of the ease with which even a child could parry them.

VYSHINSKY: But you are not a child.

KRESTINSKY: That is why I say that, although these were arguments which would not be convincing even for a youngster, for a child, still I permitted myself to be convinced by these arguments.

VYSHINSKY: Why did you permit yourself to be convinced?

KRESTINSKY: I have said already: blinded by my factional bitterness, by my desire to fight the leadership.

VYSHINSKY: Perhaps it was not particularly necessary to try to convince you.

KRESTINSKY: I have said already that my first objections I raised from tradition, from an inner impulse independent of reason. It was a feeling of repulsion, unconscious, but I subjected it to reason. . . .

VYSHINSKY: To Trotskyite reason?

KRESTINSKY: Yes, to Trotskyite reason, which permitted me to be persuaded by these Trotskyite treasonable arguments. Since 1923 the agreement with Seeckt was carried out mainly in Moscow, and sometimes in Berlin. But, of course, inasmuch as I was the person who concluded this agreement, inasmuch as I carried it out at times, and inasmuch as I was a member of the organization on behalf of which this agreement was concluded, I naturally bear full political responsibility also for those acts which were committed in Moscow. This agreement did not remain unchanged: in 1926 the Reichswehr raised the question of repudiating this agreement. I think that this was a tactical step with the object of putting greater demands to us. . . .

VYSHINSKY: Who do you mean, "us"?

KRESTINSKY: The Trotskyites. At that time we had already become accustomed to receiving sums regularly, in sound currency. . . .

VYSHINSKY: You had become accustomed to receiving money from foreign intelligence services?

KRESTINSKY: Yes. This money went for the Trotskyite work which was developing abroad in various countries, for publishing literature and so forth. . . .

VYSHINSKY: What is the "and so forth"?

KRESTINSKY: For travelling expenses, for agitators, for maintaining certain professional workers in various countries. . . .

VYSHINSKY: For the purpose of organizing espionage?

KRESTINSKY: I think that at that period, it is possible, we did not need money for the organization of espionage.

VYSHINSKY: Rosengoltz supplied espionage information in 1923. Why then was there no need of money?

KRESTINSKY: There was no need for him to spend money in this connection.

VYSHINSKY: Not for him, but perhaps there was need for somebody else. Is it not a fact that your Trotskyite organization already engaged in espionage at that time?

KRESTINSKY: Yes, but the money which was received went not for "production expenses," but for . . .

VYSHINSKY: You cannot vouch that the money was used for that purpose, nor that it was not used.

KRESTINSKY: I cannot. Probably Trotsky obtained this information free of charge from Trotskyites who occupied positions in various institutions.

VYSHINSKY: If Rosengoltz and Krestinsky occupied positions in one place, why could there not have been Rosengoltzes and Krestinskys occupying positions in other places who also needed 250,000 marks? In a word, may we say that the money went for all kinds of Trotskyite criminal purposes?

KRESTINSKY: In 1926, when the struggle of the Trotskyite groups abroad against the Party leadership was at its height, both in Moscow and among the fraternal parties a refusal to accept this money might have undermined the struggle of the Trotskyites. Therefore when Seeckt gave warning that he intended to stop these subsidies, I naturally raised the question as to the conditions on which he would consent to extend the agreement. Then he advanced the proposal that the espionage information which was being transmitted to him not regularly but from time to time should now assume a more regular character, and, in addition, that the Trotskyite organization should pledge that in case it assumed power during a possible new world war, this Trotskyite government would take into consideration the just demands of the German bourgeoisie, that is to say, mainly demands for concessions and for the conclusion of treaties of a different kind.

After I consulted Trotsky—I do not remember whether

it was in the beginning of the summer, when Trotsky was taking medical treatment in Berlin, or later—and having received his consent, I answered General Seeckt in the affirmative and our information began to assume a more systematic character, no longer sporadic, as it had been before. Verbally, promises were made with regard to a future post-war agreement.

VYSHINSKY: Thus, you kept on receiving money?

KRESTINSKY: Yes, we kept on receiving money.

VYSHINSKY: Will you tell us how much money you received altogether?

KRESTINSKY: Beginning with 1923 until 1930 we received annually 250,000 German marks in gold.

VYSHINSKY: This makes approximately two million gold marks during these years?

KRESTINSKY: Yes, approximately two million gold marks.

VYSHINSKY: This is the sum of which you know?

KRESTINSKY: Yes, this is the sum of which I know.

VYSHINSKY: This agreement which was concluded in 1923 was in effect until 1930?

KRESTINSKY: Through me until 1930. Up to the end of 1927 the stipulations of this agreement were carried out mainly in Moscow. After that, from the end of 1927 almost to the end of 1928, in the course of about 10 months there was an interruption in the receipt of money because after Trotskyism had been smashed I was isolated, I did not know of Trotsky's plans, I received no information or instructions from him, and therefore I would not know what to do with the money if I received it. On the other hand, the German side was not inclined to spur me on because they realized what my position was at that time, they read in the papers of my renunciation, they took it for granted that I was probably being watched and that in all probability I had no information which could be of interest to them. This went on until October 1928, when I received a letter from Trotsky, who at that time was in exile in Alma-Ata, which was brought to me by Reich.

VYSHINSKY: Reich-Johannson?

KRESTINSKY: No, that was an entirely different person. Reich-Johannson was Bessonov's man, with whom he maintained connections.

This letter contained Trotsky's instructions that I was to receive from the Germans the money, which he proposed to hand over either to Maslow[9] or to Trotsky's French friends, that is Rosmer, Madeleine Paz, and others. [10]

I got in touch with General Seeckt. At that time he had resigned and occupied no post whatever. But I had no contact with his successors, and did not address myself to them. I addressed myself to Seeckt, told him that the connections in Moscow were cut off, that

I had definite instructions and asked him to assist me in this business. He volunteered to talk it over with Hammerstein and to obtain the money. He obtained the money.

VYSHINSKY: And who is this Hammerstein?

KRESTINSKY: Hammerstein was at that time the chief of staff of the Reichswehr, and in 1930 he became Commander in Chief of the Reichswehr. Seeckt received this money and I visited him—I do not remember whether it was at that time or later, but I visited him. During our meeting he, without referring to our obligation to supply espionage information, engaged me in a political conversation on international questions with the idea of obtaining some information from me. I do not remember what exactly the conversation was about at that time, but during previous meetings with him I had given him information concerning Dovgalevsky's negotiations with the French for an agreement which was then being negotiated; I informed him of this before it was made public. Then I informed him of Lyubimov's negotiations with Mussolini or with Mussolini's assistants concerning a trade agreement, a credit deal; again I informed him of this before and more fully than it was later publicly announced. I do not remember what we spoke about during this first visit. I did give him some information of a confidential nature.

VYSHINSKY: Did he pay the money?

KRESTINSKY: Yes, he gave money.

VYSHINSKY: Did he know what he was giving it for?

KRESTINSKY: He knew, but I carried on the conversation in such a way as not to talk especially on this subject.

VYSHINSKY: But did you talk of it previously, before that? Did you settle the question of money with him beforehand?

KRESTINSKY: Of course.

Before I received the money, Maslow telephoned me and asked me in cryptic language whether anybody had visited me and whether I had anything to transmit to him. My attitude to Maslow was a negative one, I considered him an unprincipled person. I disliked him not because of any of his Trotskyite or treacherous tendencies, but I considered him a person with no principles in these matters.

VYSHINSKY: Which matters?

KRESTINSKY: Trotskyite matters.

VYSHINSKY: And do you consider yourself a man of principles?

KRESTINSKY: Well, I was a Trotskyite, but he could be a Trotskyite today, renounce Trotskyism tomorrow and then become a Trotskyite again. . . .

VYSHINSKY: Have you been a Trotskyite all the time?

KRESTINSKY: I did adhere more or less constantly to one point of view. I had certain differences of opinion, there were vacillations. . . .

224

VYSHINSKY: But you have been a Trotskyite all the time?

KRESTINSKY: Yes. But while in the Trotskyite ranks I had certain differences with Trotsky, certain vacillations, but I adhered to this Trotskyite line all the time.

VYSHINSKY: Have you been a Trotskyite all the time?

KRESTINSKY: Yes. I told Maslow that I had no money for him, but that I had some for Rosmer and Madeleine Paz. Ten days later he telephoned and said that Madeleine Paz had arrived and that she was stopping at the Hotel "Excelsior." I met her there and I gave her the money. It continued this way until the autumn of 1930. When I was leaving Germany I considered two possibilities: the first possibility—to arrange the connection with Seeckt through Sedov, whom I had met before my departure and established contact, or else to arrange the connection through Putna, who had been appointed military attaché in Berlin just before my departure, and concerning whom I learnt from Smirnov that he was a Trotskyite, and I thought that he was still a Trotskyite, but I had no opportunity to talk to him about the money from Seeckt being handed over to him. I sent word to Sedov that he should try to come to Berlin before I left and I told Seeckt that somebody would come to see him on my behalf or on Trotsky's behalf. If Sedov or Putna should come, he would not have to ask them for any written recommendation or identification and he could deal with them safely.[1] If, however, it should be somebody else, then he must have a letter from Trotsky or a note from me. On that we agreed. Sedov had not arrived prior to my departure, and I left without putting anybody in touch with Seeckt; I let it take place after my departure, when Sedov would turn up. I left instructions with Yakubovich, the second counsellor of the Embassy, who was my assistant in the Trotskyite affairs, to the effect that he was to direct Sedov to Seeckt. Sedov did not get to Seeckt. In 1931, when Pyatakov went to Berlin to complete the credit agreement and to place orders, I. N. Smirnov also went with him. I told Pyatakov then of the understanding that I had reached with Seeckt and suggested that he should find out whether Putna was a member of our organization, and, if so, that he should make him take part in this business. Pyatakov said that he would do this, and when he returned he said that things had been arranged and that Putna had accepted and was maintaining this connection. Thus I had no longer any connection with the money affairs. Putna took care of these, and later Trotsky and Sedov directly, and later on this developed into a more comprehensive agreement. Now I shall tell about my meetings. . . .

VYSHINSKY: Inasmuch as you are winding up the story of this period of your criminal activities, I want to get more precise information on one question. You said that in the winter of

1921-22 you evolved your calculations on the German Reichswehr.

KRESTINSKY: The plans to utilize the German Reichswehr for criminal Trotskyite purposes appeared in the spring of 1922.

VYSHINSKY: Did your Trotskyite organization maintain contact with Seeckt even before 1921?

KRESTINSKY: There was a contact with him of which I do not want to speak at an open session. It was a contact established by a member of our organization who at that time was not yet a member of our organization, and it was not a contact of a Trotskyite nature.

VYSHINSKY: If you please, we shall not speak of everything in open session. But something may be said right now. In the first place, who was Kopp?

KRESTINSKY: Generally speaking, Kopp was an old Menshevik.

VYSHINSKY: What were his relations with Trotsky?

KRESTINSKY: He maintained good relations, both business and personal, with Trotsky, even before the war and before the revolution.

VYSHINSKY: And in Party relations?

KRESTINSKY: When I speak of business relations, I refer to his Party affairs, which at that time were Menshevik.

VYSHINSKY: Hence he was connected with Trotsky in Menshevism and in Trotskyism.

KRESTINSKY: If we consider . . .

VYSHINSKY: We all know what we may consider.

KRESTINSKY: I simply do not know whether he was a Trotskyite of the pre-war formation.

VYSHINSKY: I am not asking you about the formation, I am asking you, who was Kopp? Was he at that time extremely close to Trotsky?

KRESTINSKY: He was a man close to Trotsky.

VYSHINSKY: As a Menshevik?

KRESTINSKY: As a Menshevik.

VYSHINSKY: As one who shared Trotskyite views?

KRESTINSKY: I think he was more of a Menshevik than a Trotskyite.

VYSHINSKY: And I think that Trotsky was more of a Menshevik than a Trotskyite. Well, so there is no contradiction between what we say.

KRESTINSKY: There is no contradiction.

VYSHINSKY: Did you have a talk with Trotsky and Kopp about obtaining funds for secret Trotskyite work?

KRESTINSKY: This talk took place in the spring of 1922.

VYSHINSKY: So Kopp did engage in Trotskyite secret work?

KRESTINSKY: Oh, yes.

VYSHINSKY: So we may say that Kopp was a Trotskyite?

KRESTINSKY: But not during the period to which you referred.

VYSHINSKY: But up to that period he was a Menshevik who was connected with Trotsky. I see no difference here. This is a matter for the Institute of Party History.

KRESTINSKY: No, but . . .

VYSHINSKY: You say that in July 1920 this same Kopp established contact with Seeckt in connection with a matter of which you apparently do not intend to speak here but of which you will tell us at the in camera session.

KRESTINSKY: It was Seeckt who got in touch with Kopp.

VYSHINSKY: Kopp was at that time the representative of the Red Cross for the repatriation of the prisoners of war; what business did he have with Seeckt?

KRESTINSKY: At that time he was actually our unofficial representative in Berlin.

VYSHINSKY: Whether yours or not yours, that we shall clear up later. But while he was the representative of the Red Cross in 1920, Kopp had contact with General Seeckt. Is that true?

KRESTINSKY: Yes.

VYSHINSKY: From this I draw the conclusion that, not only in 1921 and 1922, but as early as 1920, Trotsky sent out feelers through Kopp and found his way to Seeckt.

KRESTINSKY: I do not know the details of this, there were official meetings at that time.

VYSHINSKY: Is such a conclusion natural?

KRESTINSKY: I know of the other aspect of this matter, the purely official aspect.

VYSHINSKY: You know of the purely official aspect, but is the question of money an official aspect?

KRESTINSKY: Official.

VYSHINSKY: The question of money for Trotskyite purposes from the German Reichswehr—is that an official aspect or not?

KRESTINSKY: This was the secret Trotskyite aspect, a criminal thing.

VYSHINSKY: Which refers to 1921-22?

KRESTINSKY: To 1922.

VYSHINSKY: Did you say that in the winter of 1921 you already had meetings and conversations with General Seeckt about this?

KRESTINSKY: Not about this.

VYSHINSKY: Permit me to read the following passage in Vol. III, p. 13 reverse: "During these conversations the question

227

of funds for secret Trotskyite work was raised. . . . . This question of financial means was raised by Trotsky. . . ."

KRESTINSKY: That is right.

VYSHINSKY: ". . . who had met certain difficulties in utilizing office funds for secret Trotskyite purposes. Kopp then suggested that an attempt be made to obtain the necessary funds from the German Reichswehr. The following circumstance favoured this. As early as June 1920 . . . " etc.

"Thus contact between Kopp and General Seeckt had already been established. . . ."

This is what the accused Krestinsky testified on June 9, 1937. Accused Krestinsky, do you confirm this?

KRESTINSKY: Oh, yes, fully, but a few lines before that it says that this conversation between me, Trotsky and Kopp took place at the time when I was here for the Eleventh Congress.

VYSHINSKY: But this was preceded by a conversation which Kopp had with Seeckt in 1920, and which you are here trying to represent as an official contact, but I think that that already was the first step in your Trotskyite treasonable connections with General Seeckt, for which you took advantage of your official position. Do you confirm this?

KRESTINSKY: Oh, yes.

THE PRESIDENT: Comrade Procurator, have you any questions concerning this part of the testimony?

VYSHINSKY: No. Accused Krestinsky, proceed.

KRESTINSKY: In 1929, in the autumn, I think it was in September, when I was on my vacation in Kissingen, in the South of Germany, Yakubovich telephoned me from Berlin and informed me—it was done in cryptic language—that Trotsky's son wanted to see me on his father's instructions. I suggested that he come to Kissingen. On the following day, or the day after, Sedov and Yakubovich arrived. They stopped in different hotels. Sedov stopped in the hotel "Englische Hof," which was not frequented by Soviet citizens. We had our meeting in this hotel.

Since Rosengoltz spoke of this in general outline, I shall tell in greater detail about the information and the instructions which I received. Sedov's information was to the effect that Trotsky advised the exiled and expelled Trotskyites to hand in statements declaring that they renounced the opposition struggle and asking to be reinstated in the Party. He mentioned particularly that I could speak frankly to Pyatakov and Radek, although Pyatakov had handed in a statement on his renunciation of Trotskyism in 1928 and Radek, I think, in 1929. And he pointed out that they were still followers of Trotskyism.

He said further that it was necessary to give up work among

228

the masses. Up to that time, the work of the Trotskyites was orientated towards winning over the masses and coming, as it were, to power in the Party and then in the Soviet Union by means of wide mass work, of winning followers. Now Trotsky thought that it was utopian in the first place, and, finally, that it was impossible inasmuch as he proposed that we get back into the Party by deception and that we continue our activities in secret. It was impossible simultaneously to carry on in secret and pose as honest people faithful to the Party, and at the same time to carry on work among the masses in order to draw them into the ranks of the Trotskyites. It was necessary to try to preserve the skeleton organization; to see to it that these people got into the Party and Soviet organizations and tried to occupy there more or less independent responsible posts, so as to proceed in strict secrecy with the work of drawing into the organization new individual followers from among trustworthy people in order to increase and strengthen the backbone of the cadre organization.

The question as to when and how these cadres would be used for the purpose of assuming power in the Party and in the Soviet state had not been raised at that time. When Rosengoltz spoke, when he told about the meeting, he said that the substance of the meeting was that he and I should occupy responsible posts and work in strict secrecy. But it was not quite so. The instructions were to the effect that we should worm our way into the Party, to occupy responsible posts there, and it referred to all and not only to us.

VYSHINSKY: I did not quite get you. You say that these instructions referred not only to you?

KRESTINSKY: Not only to the two of us, but to all the others.

VYSHINSKY: But to you also?

KRESTINSKY: I am speaking in wider terms. We were not supposed to limit ourselves to going under cover and biding our time. I was to keep up the connection with the Reichswehr, getting money from them and transmitting information to them, I was to organize the connections between Trotsky and his agents in Europe and the Trotskyites in the Soviet Union. It is true that, as far as Rosengoltz was concerned, he was not given any concrete tasks in connection with any particular work of his, except that he was to occupy some post. I was commissioned to inform Pyatakov and Rosengoltz of this conversation. I informed Pyatakov of it that same year, towards the end of my vacation. Rosengoltz I informed of it in the beginning of 1930; then, a year later, early in October 1930, I went to Moscow for permanent work in the capacity of Assistant People's Commissar of Foreign

Affairs. I have already told you what I did with regard to this connection with the Reichswehr. In short, with Pyatakov's and Smirnov's help it was handed over to Putna.

The connection with Trotsky was established in the following way. Yakubovich stayed on in Berlin for approximately a year after my departure, and we agreed with him that, if necessary, he would receive letters from me in the diplomatic mail to forward to Trotsky, and that during his meetings with Sedov he would arrange with him as to the addresses in Paris to which these letters were to be forwarded.

In addition, since I had by that time established a connection with another worker of the Embassy, Stern, who entertained Trotskyite sympathies, I agreed with him that if Yakubovich were to leave Berlin sooner than he, Stern, then my request to Stern was that he should take over these my commissions and instructions from Yakubovich, which was done because when Yakubovich left in 1931, while Stern remained until 1932, Yakubovich handed over to Stern the Paris addresses and the information as to the connection with Trotsky through Paris; he informed him of this in complete detail. Up to 1933 I was really not supposed to do any other work in Moscow. I did not agree to that, but when in the course of our work a need was felt to convey information concerning events in the Soviet Union, information which did not appear in the Soviet press and which did not get abroad through foreign correspondents in the regular way, in any case when there was need for it, for our Trotskyite reasons and, besides, Radek asked me for it, I arranged through certain members of my staff in the Press Department of the People's Commissariat of Foreign Affairs that certain foreign correspondents should be supplied with confidential information.

VYSHINSKY: Who exactly of the foreign correspondents?

KRESTINSKY: I do not mention their names because Mironov, who was in charge of this business, did not give me their exact names. I should not like to make guesses.

VYSHINSKY: In the indictment the name of Scheffer is mentioned.

KRESTINSKY: Scheffer—that is a different affair. Scheffer left Germany after I had left and we did not have him in mind in this case.

VYSHINSKY: And was he not being supplied through others?

KRESTINSKY: I cannot tell definitely. He left for America.

VYSHINSKY: But this is of no consequence.

KRESTINSKY: I cannot say definitely.

VYSHINSKY: Mention some of the foreign correspondents. It would be interesting to know whom you supplied.

KRESTINSKY: We had in mind German correspondents.

VYSHINSKY: And their names?

KRESTINSKY: I do not want to mention their names. Some of them were mentioned to me, but they were not mentioned openly.

VYSHINSKY: The President warned us, both sides, that we may not mention any surnames and names of official representatives of foreign states. Foreign correspondents do not belong to this category.

KRESTINSKY: Of course. Inasmuch as Mironov did not mention the names to me, but only spoke of them, I was just guessing.

VYSHINSKY: Do you know their names?

KRESTINSKY: I guess, I presume.

VYSHINSKY: What do you presume?

KRESTINSKY: I presume that it was Baum, I presume that it was Just, that it was Guenther Stein, and William Stein, because Mironov was closely connected with them through his work and personally.

VYSHINSKY: And were you connected with them?

KRESTINSKY: I was connected with them officially.

VYSHINSKY: But you arranged for this connection?

KRESTINSKY: I organized the matter of Mironov's supplying information to foreign correspondents.

VYSHINSKY: Information which you were interested in publishing for Trotskyite purposes?

KRESTINSKY: Yes.

VYSHINSKY: You organized this business?

KRESTINSKY: Yes. I have already said that, of course, I bear full responsibility for this business. I am only mentioning that I personally was not directly connected with them.

VYSHINSKY: I am not speaking of direct connections. There is a certain division of labour here: you were the organizer, he was the executor, and they, were they your accomplices?

KRESTINSKY: Of course.

VYSHINSKY: Hence, you enlisted the services of some foreign correspondents in order to establish espionage connections? Is that right?

KRESTINSKY: Yes. Through Pyatakov and partly through Radek I was kept somewhat informed of the general work and I showed interest in the problems of the work. Up to 1929 the position was as follows: money was received, let us say, from the Reichswehr; this money was spent for mass work. . . .

VYSHINSKY: What kind of mass work?

KRESTINSKY: Trotskyite work. Theoretically it might have been presumed that through this mass work the Trotskyites would come to power in the Party and in the state. . . .

VYSHINSKY: How do you mean "come to power"?

KRESTINSKY: During the period up to 1929 there were prospects that the Trotskyites would come to power not through a conspiracy, not through insurrections, but through obtaining influence among the masses, by making use of money obtained abroad. This was the conception up to 1929. But after 1929, when we had given up mass work, this conception was no more valid, and no new conception had been reasoned out to the end, no new conception had been advanced. There was money, there were cadres, these cadres were being preserved and enlarged little by little, but how these cadres and their leader Trotsky would come to power—that question remained unsolved. Early in 1933 instructions were received through Ivan Nikitich Smirnov and through Radek about terrorism, about wrecking activities. But terrorism and wrecking activities are auxiliary methods, but not methods of seizing power; terrorism is . . .

VYSHINSKY: We know what terrorism is. . . .

KRESTINSKY: I want to say what its political importance is. . . .

VYSHINSKY: We know that.

KRESTINSKY: By means of terrorism one person or another may be killed, it may be possible to disorganize the government to a certain extent, but you cannot seize power by this means.

VYSHINSKY: And how can it be seized?

KRESTINSKY: This was the question which confronted us, and in our brief conversations with Pyatakov we were thinking, we were saying that without help from the outside, that is to say, without intervention, without armed assistance from outside, we could not manage, and when I went abroad . . .

VYSHINSKY: Without armed assistance? Whose?

KRESTINSKY: Of the foreign bourgeoisie, of the bourgeois states. And so, when I went abroad in 1933 I had in mind that I would clear up the prospects in my conversation with Trotsky and that we would map out a course, because, as it was, our work was futile and offered no prospects. When I met Trotsky in Meran . . .

VYSHINSKY: Tell us how your meeting with Trotsky in Meran was arranged.

KRESTINSKY: I stopped in Berlin for a few days on my way. In Berlin the counsellor of our Embassy was Bessonov, our man, a Trotskyite who was supposed to have connections with Trotsky because when he left for Berlin in May 1933 I told him to establish such connections.

VYSHINSKY: You instructed him?

KRESTINSKY: Yes, I instructed him to establish this connection. It happened that Yakubovich and Stern had left Germany

232

and my connection was cut off. Pyatakov had a connection through his people, who were going to Germany to place orders, but this was not a regular connection and therefore it was necessary to establish a connection through the Embassy in Berlin so that we might take advantage of the diplomatic mail. And this was entrusted to Bessonov. I told him that it was necessary to inform Trotsky that I wanted to see him.

VYSHINSKY: So Bessonov told us here the real truth?

KRESTINSKY: Yes.

VYSHINSKY: And at first you tried to deny it?

KRESTINSKY: But this was at first, and I told you what considerations prompted me to deny it.

VYSHINSKY: I am not accusing you, I only want to establish the fact.

KRESTINSKY: On the first day, when I denied my guilt, since I could not bring myself to admit it publicly, I naturally, as a logical conclusion from this, denied also what Rosengoltz and Bessonov said.

VYSHINSKY: But you must agree that by this you put Bessonov in the position of a liar.

KRESTINSKY: Well, what of it? I lied myself. Since I put myself in the position of a liar, it was so much easier to put others in the same position.

VYSHINSKY: That is your logic.

KRESTINSKY: When I told him that I wanted to meet Trotsky he said that there was a possibility of arranging it. At the same time I said that I would stay in Kissingen to the end of September and that I would spend the rest of the time up to the 10th of October in Meran, and I gave him the address of the Kissingen sanatorium in which I always stopped, and also my address in Meran. I had stopped there twice in the same hotel and I thought that this hotel still existed. I told him that it would be easy to find me at this address (I was going under my own name).

I was still in Kissingen when Bessonov telephoned and told me that the meeting would take place in Meran; in the meantime I had received confirmation that the hotel, in which I had stopped eight years before that, still existed; that was the hotel "Bavaria." Trotsky arrived in Meran around the 10th of October together with Sedov. Reich, as Bessonov said, had not come with him, at least I did not hear about it, I saw only the father and the son.

VYSHINSKY: And the holy ghost?

KRESTINSKY: No, the holy ghost . . .

VYSHINSKY: Was hovering over you?

KRESTINSKY: Or else he remained in Paris, if we might consider this Reich the holy ghost.

Trotsky, as he told me, arrived with somebody else's French passport and he travelled by the route of which Bessonov spoke, that is to say, over the Franco-Italian border, and not through Switzerland and Germany. For Trotsky, the questions which bothered us in Moscow were irrevocably settled and he himself proceeded to expound his instructions with regard to this. He said that as since 1929 we had developed into an organization of a conspiratorial type, it was natural that the seizure of power could be consummated only by force. But our conspiratorial organization was unable to carry out any coup by itself. It was necessary to come to an explicit agreement on this score with some bourgeois state. He remarked that the embryo of such an agreement was our agreement with the Reichswehr, but this agreement in no way satisfied either the Trotskyites or the German side for two reasons: first, the other party to this agreement was only the Reichswehr, and not the German government as a whole. If under the previous governments, the Reichswehr had played a decisive role and we could reckon with it as with the government as a whole, now, with Hitler's coming to power and with Hitler's striving to subordinate the Reichswehr to himself, and with a certain wariness in the attitude of some of the leaders of the Reichswehr towards Hitler's attempts to penetrate into the Reichswehr, the German government could no longer be identified with the Reichswehr, and it was necessary to see to it that not only the Reichswehr, but the German government as a whole, became the other party to our agreement. This is first.

Second. What was the substance of our agreement with the Reichswehr? We were receiving a small sum of money and they were receiving espionage information which they would need during an armed attack. But the German government, Hitler particularly, wanted colonies, territory, and not only espionage information. And he was prepared to be satisfied with Soviet territory instead of the colonies for which he would have to fight England, America and France. As for us, we do not need the 250,000 gold marks, we need the German armed forces in order to come to power with their assistance. And it is towards this end that the work should be carried on. This work means a treasonable agreement with a foreign government about using foreign armed forces in order to achieve victory over the Red Army and in order to open the road to power for the Trotskyites. But even if the Soviet Union is attacked, let us say, by Germany, that does not as yet make it possible to seize the machinery of power unless certain internal forces have been prepared along these lines. But the Trotskyites as such are not sufficiently numerous and strong to create such an organization by themselves. It is necessary to have strongholds both in the towns and in the countryside among the petty bourgeoisie and the kulaks, and there it is mainly the Rights who have the connections. Finally, it is necessary to have a stronghold, an organization in the Red Army, among the commanders, in order, with our united effort, to seize the most vital places at the necessary moment and to come to power, to replace the present government, which must be arrested, by a government of our own which has been prepared beforehand.

From this it followed: the first line to take was for an agreement with foreign governments, the second for combining the forces of the Trotskyites, the Rights and the military conspirators within the Soviet Union.

In speaking about the Rights, about the necessity of establishing organizational connections with them, Trotsky said that we should not confine ourselves to Rykov, Bukharin and Tomsky, because although they were the recognized leaders of the Rights, they had already been compromised to a great extent and were under surveillance, and that it was necessary to make the connection through Rudzutak, who for many years had occupied a post in the Soviet government with Rykov in the capacity of his assistant and nobody had ever known of any differences between him and the Party; therefore it was necessary to take him into consideration and establish connections with him.

As for the military men, Trotsky, in speaking of them, mentioned only one name, that of Tukhachevsky, as a man of a Bonapartist type, an adventurer, an ambitious man who strove not only for a military but also for a military-political role and who would unquestionably make common cause with us.

Further Trotsky developed the idea of the necessity of terrorism, wrecking activities and diversions. In speaking of them, Trotsky considered diversionist acts and acts of terrorism from the point of view both of applying them in time of war for the purpose of disorganizing the defensive capacity of the Red Army, for disorganizing the government by the moment of the coup d'état, and at the same time, these diversionist and terrorist acts would make his, Trotsky's, position stronger and would give him more confidence in his negotiations with foreign governments, because he would be able to refer to the fact that his followers in the Soviet Union were both sufficiently strong and sufficiently active.

He undertook to carry on the negotiations with the Germans. As for the Japanese, of whom he spoke as a force with which it was also necessary to come to terms, he said that, for the time being, it was difficult for him to establish direct connections with them, that it would be necessary to carry on conversations with them in Moscow, that it was necessary in this connection to use Sokolnikov,[12] who was working in the People's Commissariat of Foreign Affairs and, as it happened, was in charge of eastern affairs. And inasmuch as this conversation would be held only with an official person, and the preliminary conversation would only be in the nature of soundings, it would be sufficient to confine ourselves at first to general statements to the effect that if a government of a bloc of the opposition groups assumed power in the Soviet Union, it would display a favourable attitude towards the Japanese and take into consideration the wishes of the Japanese during the discussion and settlement of the controversies existing between the Soviet government and the Japanese government. He asked me to get in touch with Pyatakov with regard to all these policies and particularly with regard to the necessity of getting in touch with the Japanese. In addition he said that I should not be content with the talks which Pyatakov would have with Tukhachevsky and Rudzutak, but that I should also see them, because I would be in a position to tell them of my personal talk with Trotsky, of my personal impressions, and that would exert a somewhat greater influence in that direction.

VYSHINSKY: I beg your pardon, are you with this winding up your explanations concerning your meeting with Trotsky in Meran?

KRESTINSKY: With this I am winding up the story of my meeting with Trotsky in Meran. During the meeting in Meran he drew my attention to the necessity of using several people. He spoke to me of Rosengoltz.

VYSHINSKY: I am only interested in Rosengoltz, who is one of the accused in the present case. What did he tell you about Rosengoltz?

KRESTINSKY: The first to speak to me about Rosengoltz was Sedov, as early as 1925; he asked me to convey the gist of our conversation to Rosengoltz. And in 1933 Trotsky spoke to me, saying that Rosengoltz had so far remained inactive; but Rosengoltz, he said, is, generally speaking, a very active man, persistent, tenacious, a man with wide connections both through his military work and through his Party work, through his work at the front, with varied circles of former Trotskyites and generally with wide circles; that in this respect, in the sense of his knowing people, he is second only to Serebryakov. But Serebryakov was now removed from affairs and had no connections, while Rosengoltz was a man who had connections with people, an influential man, and it was necessary to spur on his activity in connection with this question and to draw him into the work. He also spoke of the necessity for Rosengoltz to develop wrecking activities in his department.

VYSHINSKY: Did you convey this to Rosengoltz?

KRESTINSKY: I conveyed it to Rosengoltz.

THE PRESIDENT: Adjournment for 30 minutes.

* * *

COMMANDANT OF THE COURT: The Court is coming, please rise.

THE PRESIDENT: Please be seated. The session is resumed.

Accused Krestinsky, please continue, only make it shorter, do not dwell on the circumstances with regard to which you have already made replies.

KRESTINSKY: But I must explain the consequences of my actions after my return from abroad. When I returned I immediately informed Pyatakov and Rosengoltz of my talk. Pyatakov talked it over with Tukhachevsky and Rudzutak. Perhaps he spoke to other Rights, perhaps also to Gamarnik, but I don't know. He informed me that he had spoken to Tukhachevsky and Rudzutak.

In February 1934, I met both Tukhachevsky and Rudzutak, told them the substance of my conversation, and got from both of them a confirmation in principle, their acceptance of the line for an understanding with foreign states for their military assistance, for a defeatist policy, for setting up a united organization within the country; they even told me that for them it was not a question of principle but a question of the necessity of ascertaining what their forces were, and that they would then give a final reply to Pyatakov as the chief representative of the Trotskyite organization in the U.S.S.R.

Even before I received information from Pyatakov to the effect that things had been set in motion and that an understanding had been concluded, I had also begun to select forces in my organization, in the Commissariat of Foreign Affairs, and to select those on whom I could rely in case of a counter-revolutionary coup, although it was clear to me that a coup was not a matter of the near future, nor even of the nearest one or two years, since this matter was being linked up with the beginning of a war with Germany and, presumably, at the same time with Japan, because Germany would not attack without Japan, they would attack together.

In the beginning of 1935 Pyatakov informed me that an understanding had been reached, named the composition of the centre of which I spoke yesterday, and told me that myself and Rosengoltz, while not joining the centre, would work under its direction, mainly in connection with the planning and preparing of the future government machinery. Here was a division of labour. We

237

were told that we would be connected in this work with Rudzutak from the Rights, and with Tukhachevsky. My impression was that only Rudzutak was mentioned. But Rosengoltz took an active part in this and he subsequently spoke to me of his meetings with Rykov. In general, it was Rykov and Rudzutak from the Rights, and Tukhachevsky from the military group. There was no such thing as my knowing of the connections with Tukhachevsky and Rosengoltz's not knowing of them; but, as part of the division of labour, he took upon himself mainly the connections with the Rights, although I was the one who used to see Rudzutak, and, as far as Tukhachevsky was concerned, it was mainly I, but he also. He spoke of a meeting in 1937; I also had the impression, and I spoke of it at the investigation, that during one of the first meetings at Rudzutak's country house, he was not there; I am saying what I heard from Rosengoltz.

But, inasmuch as later, during the confrontation and here, Rosengoltz said that he met Tukhachevsky and spoke to him for the first time in 1937, and I told what I heard from Rosengoltz, so evidently that is the way it happened.

And now with regard to setting the date for taking action. From the very moment of my meeting in Meran it was considered definitely established that our action was to be timed with the outbreak of war, and that therefore we, here, in the Union, could not independently set the date for Tukhachevsky's action, and we did not do it. This question was outside Rosengoltz's and my competence; we were connected with Tukhachevsky, Rudzutak and Rykov, but conversations with regard to questions of high politics or the date when action was to be taken were carried on by Pyatakov.

Therefore, up to the autumn of 1936, up to Pyatakov's arrest, I had no occasion to speak on these subjects either to Tukhachevsky or to Rosengoltz, inasmuch as this question was outside the sphere of our discussions. We were waiting for the war to begin, we were waiting for the attack.

After Pyatakov and Radek had been arrested, when Bessonov was going to Berlin, I took advantage of this and sent verbal information to Trotsky to the effect that after I had taken up this question with Rosengoltz and Rudzutak I could formulate the situation as follows: we think that quite a large number of Trotskyites have been arrested, but nevertheless the main forces of this anti-Soviet bloc—the Trotskyites, the Rights and the military conspirators—are as yet not affected, have not been smashed, that action could be taken, and that for this purpose it is essential for the centre that foreign action should be hastened. This was in October 1936. But late in November 1936 Tukhachevsky spoke to me excitedly and in grave terms at the Extraordinary Eighth

Congress of Soviets. He said arrests had begun and there was no reason to think that things would stop with the arrests which had already been made. Apparently the smashing up of the Trotskyites and the Rights would go on. The fact that Yagoda was removed from the People's Commissariat of Internal Affairs indicated that it was not only a question of dissatisfaction with his insufficiently active work in the People's Commissariat of Internal Affairs. Apparently, this indicated political mistrust of him, Yagoda, not just as Yagoda, the former People's Commissar of Internal Affairs, but as an active Rightist, as a member of the united centre, and it was possible that they would unearth these things. And if they unearthed this they would also unearth the facts about the military group, and then we would have to give up all hopes for a coup. He drew the conclusion: there was no use waiting for intervention. It was necessary to act on our own. To begin on our own—that was difficult, that was dangerous; but on the other hand there were chances that it might succeed. The military organization, he said, is a big one and well-prepared and he said he thought it necessary to take action. And it was with regard to this that we were to request an answer.

And so he asked me to give him an answer on behalf of our organization, and, if it was possible for me, to convey it to the Rights, so that it would not be necessary for him to get in touch with the Rights in this connection. I then spoke on this subject to Rosengoltz. I think I did not speak at that time to Gamarnik. Tukhachevsky spoke not only for himself, but also on behalf of the counter-revolutionary organization of the military men, and Gamarnik was a member of the military organization and a member of the common centre, in which he represented the military group. I talked it over with Rosengoltz, then I talked it over with Rudzutak, and we came to the conclusion that Tukhachevsky was right, that time was pressing. We decided to ask for Trotsky's opinion. As a rule I did not write to him about such questions, I preferred to convey the information verbally. I sent a letter to Trotsky with the diplomatic mail through Bessonov.

The letter dealt with the necessity of changing the line according to which our internal coup was necessarily to be connected with a war. I said that the coup must be hastened. Without consulting Tukhachevsky and the rest, I put to Trotsky in this letter certain other questions in case he replied in the affirmative. It was clear to me that in the case of a coup of this kind we would have to conceal the true purposes of the coup, we would have to make a statement to the population, to the army and to the foreign states; and so I put the question this way: firstly, it would be the proper thing in our statements to the population not to mention that our coup was

239

designed for the overthrow of the existing, Socialist, order. We were prepared to restore capitalist relations in the U.S.S.R. and to make territorial concessions to the bourgeois states with which we had already come to an agreement.

We dared not declare this openly to the Soviet people. I put before Trotsky the question that we should issue suitable statements to the population and the army, in which we would evade all questions connected with the true purposes of our coup, that is, we would deceive the people and pose in the guise of Soviet rebels: we would overthrow a bad Soviet government and re-establish a good Soviet government, which is the same as . . .

VYSHINSKY: That was your line of reasoning?

KRESTINSKY: That is how we were going to speak to the population, that is what we were going to say; but privately we reasoned otherwise. Then it was decided that also in the statements to the foreign states we would not say that we were changing the whole foundation of the state and that we agreed to certain territorial concessions; in our statement to the population and the army and in our statements to the foreign states we would say that, while we pursued a policy of peace, were reducing armaments, etc., we would nevertheless take action in defence of the frontiers of the Soviet Union and would not allow forcible severance of any parts from the Soviet Union.

In my letter I asked Trotsky's opinion on the question of the dissolution of the state farms and collective farms. It seemed to me that economically, from the point of view of the productivity of labour, the collective form had justified itself in the eyes of the collective farm peasants; I thought it would be better for the time being to preserve this form while somewhat changing the relations inside the collective farms so as to provide an opportunity for an upper stratum to evolve. That is why I considered that in any case we should not be too outspoken on this question.

Bessonov conveyed this letter to Trotsky, who at that time was still in Norway. My impression then was that Bessonov did it by sending for Sedov, but as it turns out he sent the letter through Reich-Johannson, and a reply was received to this letter. Trotsky replied that he agreed.

VYSHINSKY: When did you get the reply?

KRESTINSKY: This reply in all probability came at the end of December or the beginning of January. It is difficult for me to tell you the exact date now. Our conversations were held at the congress in November, I sent the letter in the beginning of December, the reply apparently came at the end of December, or perhaps in the beginning of January. . . .

VYSHINSKY: Or perhaps in the middle of December?

KRESTINSKY: No, it could not have been in the middle of December because of the time that had to elapse while the letter went to Norway and a reply was received. . . . It transpired that Trotsky on his own initiative raised the question of hastening the coup and sent these instructions in a different, roundabout way in a letter addressed to Rosengoltz. Rosengoltz received this letter approximately at the same time or somewhat later (I think through Shostak). And so, after this reply was received, we began to make more direct preparations for the coup; Tukhachevsky was given a free hand, he was given carte blanche to get on with the job directly. It was about the beginning of February that Rosengoltz and myself were officially made members of the centre. In November Rosengoltz, Gamarnik and myself had to take over the leadership of the Trotskyite organization. Pyatakov was out of it, Radek also. We had to conduct conversations with Tukhachevsky and Rudzutak without reporting to anyone on the Trotskyite side, because there were no people over us to give us instructions and lead us; we had to correspond directly with Trotsky, and not through Pyatakov, as had been the case previously, when Pyatakov was alive. This being so, we told Rudzutak that from now on he should reckon with us as the main representatives of the Trotskyites and count us in this centre, which existed although it did not meet in full force. At the time, in February, Tukhachevsky was absent—on vacation in Sochi. When leaving on vacation, he gave his confederates and assistants among the military instructions to get ready. Then we had a conference in Rosengoltz's apartment, about which Rosengoltz has told you. I shall not repeat the gist of the conference because Rosengoltz has given it you in fair detail. At this conference the date of the coup was fixed—the second half of May. But at the very beginning of May it transpired that Tukhachevsky was not going to London. By this time Rudzutak had returned from Central Asia. After Rudzutak's return and when it became known that Tukhachevsky was not going to London, he declared that he could accomplish this coup in the first half of May. Ever since 1935 I had been in contact with three responsible officials of the Moscow Party organization who were covert Trotskyites—Postolovsky, Furer and Korytny, who were busy getting covert Trotskyites into responsible jobs in the Moscow region and city organizations, were maintaining contact with the Party for Moscow—and they knew from me that the time might come when a certain number of promotions would be needed for the central apparatus also.

I got in touch with them and told them that the time for action was drawing nearer, and therefore they must draw up lists of people in Moscow to be arrested and removed from their posts at the outbreak of the coup, and lists of people who could be appointed to these vacancies. As at the time a whole series of local district conferences was taking place in Moscow and various changes in personnel were being made, it was settled that I would have the lists approximately by May 12. But early in May the debacle of the counter-revolutionary organization began, changes on the active list of the military department were published, Gamarnik was removed from his post of First Assistant People's Commissar and Tukhachevsky from his post of Second Assistant People's Commissar, Tukhachevsky was transferred to Samara, Yakir from Kiev, Uborevich from Byelorussia, while Kork and Eidemann were arrested. It became clear that a coup was now impossible, so that the question whether the coup should take place in the middle of May became obviously irrelevant.

I began to get ready for my arrest. I talked matters over with Rosengoltz. Rosengoltz did not expect to come to grief, and undertook to continue connections with Trotsky. I also warned the Moscow men that in case I was arrested they must get in touch with Rosengoltz. A few days later I was arrested.

I want to supplement my testimony somewhat. I have not spoken of my connections with Trotsky after I returned from abroad. These connections were maintained through Berlin and Bessonov, and only after Trotsky removed to Oslo, through our Minister in Oslo, Yakubovich, whose name I mentioned as the go-between in my meeting with Sedov in 1929.

In the autumn of 1935 Trotsky, through Yakubovich, reproached us all for insufficient activity. He did not mean activity in the sense of accelerating the coup, because this was bound up with external circumstances and outbreak of war, but in the sense of developing terrorist and diversive activities. This I conveyed to all the leading comrades.

Then Pyatakov went abroad, and a large number of letters passed through Bessonov. There were quite a few letters from Pyatakov, which for the most part were conveyed through Bessonov, sometimes through Yakubovich, and when Yakubovich left in the winter of 1935 our situation was reported through him. Through Bessonov in 1934 I communicated the results of my conversations with Rosengoltz, Rudzutak and Tukhachevsky. Through Bessonov I communicated that a committee had been formed in 1935, although in all probability Pyatakov had spoken of this before me, but I also considered it my duty to make it known.

The question of terrorist activity. Rosengoltz was telling the truth when he said here that this business was centralized, that Smirnov was attending to it. Soon he was arrested and Mrachkovsky took over the job. Then these questions were taken over by Pyatakov, but when Pyatakov was dead and this business was left without anybody in charge, Gamarnik undertook it.

During a meeting with Tukhachevsky the latter insisted that certain terrorist acts were to be committed before the counter-revolutionary coup. Rosengoltz and I were doubtful about this, not from the point of view of principle, but from the point of view of political expediency.

We were of the opinion that these terrorist acts preceding the coup might create a less favourable situation for the coup, they would put the government, the masses of the workers, and the Red Army on their guard; furthermore, as a result of this or that terrorist act, radical reprisals might follow against many of the arrested, and we were calculating on them as our cadres. If during the coup the premises of the People's Commissariat of Internal Affairs and the prisons should be seized, we anticipated getting back a number of important people, notably Pyatakov, who would be assigned responsible work. Since Tukhachevsky insisted on terrorist acts, primarily against Molotov and Voroshilov, we gave our consent, and told him that terrorists for these acts would be provided. Gamarnik, who on this question was acting in a dual position—on behalf of the military organization and of our organization—told us that he also had some picked men for terrorist acts.

That, I think, is all I can say about my activity and the activity of the people associated with me in terrorist, underground, conspiratorial and treasonable work.

VYSHINSKY: After all your vacillations and contradictory statements here in Court, do you now plead guilty to the charges brought against you?

KRESTINSKY: I do.

VYSHINSKY: You admit that throughout our revolution you have been one of the most active and direct participants of the Trotskyite organization?

KRESTINSKY: Not throughout the revolution, but from 1921.

VYSHINSKY: You admit that ever since 1921 you have been supplying regular spy information to the German intelligence service?

KRESTINSKY: Actually ever since 1923, although an understanding was reached in 1922.

VYSHINSKY: That is the argument we had about dates.

KRESTINSKY: It is not an argument about dates; at the session in camera I will go into greater detail about it.

VYSHINSKY: Well, all right. In any case, you admit today that you are a German spy of long standing, which you reckon at least from 1923, while we reckon from 1921.

KRESTINSKY: Actually from 1923, although an understanding was reached in 1922. I consider that the crime had already been perpetrated when I came to an agreement with the Trotskyite organization to that effect.

VYSHINSKY: Do you plead guilty to being an active member of the "bloc of Rights and Trotskyites"?

KRESTINSKY: Yes, I was an active member of the conspiratorial "bloc of Rights and Trotskyites."

VYSHINSKY: From the moment when the bloc was formed?

KRESTINSKY: It was formed somewhat earlier; I joined it somewhat later, but I was ready to join this bloc ever since my meeting with Trotsky.

VYSHINSKY: But before you joined this bloc your activities could hardly be distinguished from the activities of the bloc. Your organization more and more approached the main tasks which were afterwards embodied in the program of the bloc?

KRESTINSKY: Yes, yes. I have been a member of this organization from the beginning of 1935.

VYSHINSKY: Further, you are not only a member, but one of the organizers of the conspiracy against the Soviet power?

KRESTINSKY: Yes.

VYSHINSKY: You admit it?

KRESTINSKY: Yes. Up to 1937 I was not a member of the central group, but one of the participants.

VYSHINSKY: But you were a member of the group attached to the centre?

KRESTINSKY: Yes, I was a member of the group attached to the centre.

VYSHINSKY: Further you made direct preparations and took part in drawing up a plan for an anti-Soviet coup d'état in the U.S.S.R.?

KRESTINSKY: Yes.

VYSHINSKY: By means of an armed insurrection reinforced with terrorist acts ...

KRESTINSKY: Yes.

VYSHINSKY: Calculating on the U.S.S.R. being involved in a war and defeated?

KRESTINSKY: Yes.

VYSHINSKY: With all the political consequences which might ensue from this fact?

KRESTINSKY: Yes.

VYSHINSKY: To this too you plead wholly and entirely guilty?

KRESTINSKY: Yes.

VYSHINSKY: And, finally, you took a hand in discussing and preparing terrorist acts against Comrade Stalin, Comrade Molotov, and Comrade Kaganovich?

KRESTINSKY: I admit it.

VYSHINSKY: Do you know whether besides Gamarnik your accomplice Rosengoltz also undertook a special task to commit a terrorist act? . . .

KRESTINSKY: No.

VYSHINSKY: Besides Gamarnik, who undertook the task of organizing this act?

KRESTINSKY: I had not heard about it from him.

VYSHINSKY: Didn't he inform you about this?

KRESTINSKY: No.

VYSHINSKY (to the President): May I ask the accused Rosengoltz?

THE PRESIDENT: You may.

VYSHINSKY: Accused Rosengoltz, did you personally have the criminal intent to commit a terrorist act against any of the leaders of the Soviet government?

ROSENGOLTZ: Yes, I testified to this and I confirm it.

VYSHINSKY: You personally intended to commit a terrorist act?

ROSENGOLTZ: Yes.

VYSHINSKY: Perhaps you will say against whom?

ROSENGOLTZ: As I testified at the preliminary investigation, against Joseph Vissarionovich Stalin.

VYSHINSKY: I have no more questions to Krestinsky.

THE PRESIDENT: Accused Rakovsky, do you confirm the testimony you gave at the preliminary investigation?

RAKOVSKY: I confirm it entirely.

THE PRESIDENT (to Vyshinsky): Have you any questions?

VYSHINSKY: Yes. Accused Rakovsky, tell us briefly to what you plead guilty in the present case.

RAKOVSKY: Allow me to make a preliminary remark.

VYSHINSKY: If it is not very long.

RAKOVSKY: It is very short.

VYSHINSKY: By all means.

RAKOVSKY: From the trials which have taken place and the trial which is being heard here the third day, the conclusion might be drawn, I think, that I was somewhat on the fringe of things, because no one would suppose, of course, that my name would be hushed up. But I say this not to absolve myself of any responsibility whatsoever. Not at all. I just want to say that along with these organizations, there is standing before you a man guilty of high treason, who was connected with them by certain threads—some horizontal, and some vertical, and they all led to

245

Trotsky. This, so to speak, is the guiding force in all these conspiracies, in all these treacheries and treasons against the Soviet Union, against the leaders of the government and the Party. Such is my preliminary remark.

My treasonable activities are divided into two periods. Between these two periods lies my exile. Only this factor prevented me from deeper complicity in all these centres which were formed here. In so far as my treasonable activities bear a more systematic character after my exile, I intend to begin with the second period and then return to the first period.

Having received permission to go for treatment to Lake Shirlo in 1932, I met Nikolai Ivanovich Muralov in the summer in Novosibirsk, where I was stopping over on my way.[14] And it was there, in July, or the beginning of August, that I held a conversation with him. He told me that he had highly important news, and then he told me that instructions had been received from Trotsky to change over to new, terrorist methods of struggle. When I asked him to explain what they consisted of, he said: terrorist methods of struggle. Trotsky pointed out that after the defeat of the opposition, after the rebuff which it had received from the Party and the working class, what with the dissension and demoralization which ensued in its own ranks, the old methods of struggle would not lead to seizure of power. I must tell you, not with the intention of creating for myself any circumstances mitigating my offence, but because it corresponds to the truth, that Muralov's information dumbfounded me and at the same time evoked a strong reaction. I was in exile, isolated, occupying myself with all kinds of theoretical calculations, and what was taking place in Moscow, where the leaders of the Trotskyite underground opposition were living in a dense atmosphere of sectarianism, nursing their usual rancour there—between this atmosphere and mine, of course, there certainly was a difference. In Moscow this evolution of Trotskyism, which is natural, progressed at a rapid tempo. I was not prepared for this; I told Muralov: I strongly object to tactics which cut across all the past, all the traditions of the labour movement, not only in Russia, but throughout the world. I asked him to write to Trotsky, because although he gave me Trotsky's address, I could not write from Barnaul, where I was, inasmuch as my correspondence was under certain control.

This took place in July or August 1932. One and a half years later, in February 1934, I sent a telegram to the Central Committee of the C.P.S.U., saying that I had completely disarmed myself both ideologically and organizationally and asked to be reinstated in the Party. This telegram was insincere, I was lying.[15] It was my deliberate intention to hide from the Party and the government my association with the Intelligence Service ever since 1924, and

Trotsky's association with the Intelligence Service ever since 1926. I was going to conceal my conversation with Muralov in 1932 and the conversation which took place in 1934 in Novosibirsk, where I stopped over on my way after I had received permission to return to Moscow. I met Muralov on the street, and he said to me, "You are going back at a moment when all your comrades in the struggle have returned to active underground work." Muralov considered that I should have stayed in exile so that my stay there would preserve those remnants of Trotskyite cadres who were in exile at that time.

When I arrived in Moscow in May, I met Sosnovsky. Sosnovsky told me that the former leaders of the old Trotskyite opposition were returning again to active underground work; this was a period which would soon come to an end, a period of certain hesitations. I wrote to Trotsky and again pointed out that the tactics he recommended were reckless and pointed out that his position was groundless, because judging by my impressions in Moscow and in exile, the actual aspect of the country completely contradicted the gloomy predictions which the Trotskyite opposition gave.

In the second half of July 1934 I received a letter from Trotsky. I had written to Trotsky in Copenhagen and I received a reply by the method which I suggested in my letter.

In his reply Trotsky first of all tried to dispel my favourable impression of Socialist construction. He wrote that I was yielding to the mystic influence of statistical data, without considering the process under the surface, and so on and so forth. As regards the tactics he recommended, he wrote that he, of course, understood that after such a long period in exile, in view of my age, fatigue, etc., I was not in a condition to take part in the active work of the opposition in its full scope. In the letter he asked me to utilize my extensive connections with political circles abroad, primarily "Left" circles. I understood the import of these instructions as follows: capitalist aggression against the Soviet Union must be strengthened and intensified.

This was a compromise, this was, so to speak, meeting my wishes in the sense that they recommended me somewhat more congenial methods, in the sense of making use of my acquaintances, of my former connections. I agreed to this proposal. I will not enter here into psychological explanations, why and wherefore. From this moment I already stood with both feet on the positions of Trotskyism, or rather on the positions of neo-Trotskyism, if I might use the term.

In September 1934 I was sent to Tokyo at the head of the Soviet Red Cross Delegation to an international conference of Red Cross Societies, which was to take place there in October. The day after I arrived in Tokyo, I was stopped in the corridor of the Japanese Red Cross building by a certain prominent public man of Japan. I can mention his name.

THE PRESIDENT: No, there is no need.

RAKOVSKY: Very well, I will name him at the session in camera. He invited me to tea. I made his acquaintance. He held a position which had some relation to my mission—I want to say, not my mission as one who belonged to the opposition, but my governmental mission. I accepted his amiable invitation. During the conversation this person (here I omit various compliments, commonplaces, flattering remarks) said that the interests of the political trend to which I belonged in the U.S.S.R. and the interests of a certain government fully coincided, and that he personally welcomed my arrival in Tokyo because it would give him the opportunity to discuss certain questions concerning both sides; and in particular, he declared that for a certain government and for himself my estimate of the political situation in the Soviet Union would be of extraordinary value.

I must say that I did not anticipate a conversation like this, it took me unawares. I said that, firstly, I was not, nor did I belong to or take any part in the leading circles of my country. I now occupied a very modest position, a modest post in the People's Commissariat of Public Health, and unfortunately, in this connection I could not be of any service to them. I evaded further conversation and left.

I am giving you the gist of it, of course, without vouching for every word. I wanted to ascertain the motives which prompted such a proposal. The same evening I had a talk with the Ambassador, Yurenev, whom I had known as a Trotskyite ever since 1926, when I spent a summer with him in the south of France at Saint-Jean-de-Luz. I told him of the rather strange words of the person I have mentioned. I am representing it in a somewhat more pointed form, because usually such things are wrapped up in a lot of verbiage without any pretext for protest being given. I told Yurenev that the idea here was to enlist me as a spy, as an informer for a certain government.

Then Yurenev drew a letter from his pocket and told me: "The question is decided, there is no need to hesitate." He even said: "The die is cast." He showed me Pyatakov's letter, which I myself had brought him from Moscow. It was sent to me under such circumstances that I could not know its contents.

I must tell you that when I arrived in Moscow after sending my statement to the Party, I immediately went for a cure. Then I came back, started work, and in two months left for Tokyo. During this time I had the opportunity to see only Sosnovsky, and went twice on business to the People's Commissariat of Foreign Affairs, where I met Krestinsky, with whom I exchanged

248

a few words. I will speak of this later. But on the whole this was the period when I was trying to get back into the Party and in general avoided any meetings with known oppositionists.

Just before my departure I received by messenger of the People's Commissariat of Heavy Industry an envelope addressed to me in the People's Commissariat of Health. In this envelope there was a second envelope, addressed to Yurenev, and a note for me. The note was from Pyatakov. In this note he congratulated me on my return and asked me to take the letter to Yurenev and insist on Yurenev's compliance with his request. The letter was not coded. The contents of this letter related to the methods used in Japan for making alloys of non-ferrous metals; Pyatakov asked Yurenev to let him know what methods were used there and at the same time to send him literature on the subject available in Japan in English and German. But when after my conversation with the well-known public man I have mentioned Yurenev drew this letter from his pocket, besides the uncoded text there was another text which had been written in invisible ink. Then Yurenev read to me first of all what concerned me. Pyatakov had written to him: Rakovsky, apart from his ill health, has another reason for being cautious; this is his desire to get back into the Party; so that in this sense we must spare him, but as far as possible utilize his stay in Tokyo. Then came literally the following phrase: "It is likely that a certain government will itself take steps in this direction" (that is, in the direction of utilizing Rakovsky). Further Pyatakov wrote to Yurenev about Bogomolov, the Ambassador in China, pointing out that a certain government was dissatisfied with his political line, that he was helping Great Britain more than he was the said government.

Further it was pointed out that Yurenev must try to make all possible use of Sabanin, the director of the legal department of the People's Commissariat of Foreign Affairs, while he was in Tokyo. Finally, Yurenev said, reading the letter: "But this is what I find difficult to do." The letter contained instructions that he must take advantage of the well-known negotiations concerning the sale of the Chinese Eastern Railway so that something might accrue to the benefit of the Trotskyites.

I have told you approximately the contents of Pyatakov's letter to Yurenev. Yurenev was connected with the Trotskyite underground in Moscow, with Pyatakov.

On the second or third day after my conversation with Yurenev, after a certain banquet to which all the delegates to the Red Cross Conference had been invited, at the end of the dinner somebody approached me and said that a certain personage of high standing, present at this dinner, wished to make my acquaintance.

249

The official personage stated that he was very pleased to make my acquaintance, etc. Then he went on to say that our interests coincided with the interests of a certain state, that an agreement had been reached between the Trotskyites in the U.S.S.R. and the representatives of a certain state, but that we did not know the exact terms of this agreement yet.

The prominent public man who had spoken to me did so, as I learnt, on the instructions of this high personage. After this I had two more meetings with the public man....

THE PRESIDENT: Excuse me, accused Rakovsky. Seeing that it is now ten o'clock and your evidence will last another hour at least, you will conclude tomorrow.

The Court is adjourned until 11 a.m.

[Signed] PRESIDENT: V. ULRICH

Army Military Jurist

President of the Military Collegium of the Supreme Court of the U.S.S.R.

SECRETARY: A. BATNER

Military Jurist First Rank

MORNING SESSION, MARCH 5, 1938

COMMANDANT OF THE COURT: The Court is coming, please rise.

THE PRESIDENT: Please be seated. The session is resumed. Accused Rakovsky, you may conclude your evidence.

RAKOVSKY: Yesterday I concluded with the statement that, after my conversation with the high personage who was close to the Japanese government, I had three talks with the public man of whom I have spoken, the man at the head of a big public organization in Japan.

During the second and third meeting with the public man who headed a big public organization in Japan we established the nature of the information which I promised to supply to the agents of the Japanese intelligence service in Moscow and also the technique of transmitting this information. While still in Tokyo, I drew into this work Dr. Naida, secretary of the Red Cross Delegation, of whom I already knew that he was a member of the underground counter-revolutionary terrorist organization. I sent Dr. Naida with my card to the public man and he arranged with him as to how and with whom Dr. Naida was to meet in Moscow; it was he who acted as liaison agent between me and the Japanese intelligence service. In Tokyo I had yet another meeting, with a third person. All such international conferences, as you probably know, are accompanied by all kinds of receptions, dinners, shows, meetings, which usually serve as a background for very serious conversations, quite legitimate, but sometimes not legitimate. I have in mind recruiting for various purposes. I was introduced to this third person by the second high personage. He asked me to take coffee with him—this was after dinner; we sat down at a table and began to talk.

I shall not reproduce the whole conversation, and it is not necessary either; I shall give it to you in substance.' He started the conversation by saying: "We are aware that you are a very close friend and adherent of Mr. Trotsky. I must ask you to write to him that a certain government is dissatisfied with his articles on the Chinese question and also with the behaviour of the Chinese Trotskyites. We have a right to expect a different line of conduct on the part of Mr. Trotsky. Mr. Trotsky ought to under-

251

stand what is necessary for the certain government. There is no need to go into details, but it is clear that an incident provoked in China would be a desirable pretext for intervening in China." I wrote to Trotsky about all this—about my negotiations in Tokyo, about my conversations with Yurenev, about my meetings, and, of course, about this last proposition.

I also kept Yurenev informed of all my talks. During the last week I fell ill owing to an inflammation of the veins of my right leg, and I stayed in the Embassy. I am mentioning this because it gave me and Yurenev an opportunity to see more of each other. He would come to me—the other members of the delegation were, of course, away at such times—he would come to me and we would talk about our common Trotskyite affairs. Yurenev was very much worried by one circumstance. "We have gotten," he said, "into such a mess that sometimes one does not know how to behave. One is afraid that by satisfying one of our partners we may offend another. For instance, here at present, antagonism is arising between Great Britain and Japan in connection with the Chinese question, while we have to maintain connections both with the British and Japanese intelligence services."...

VYSHINSKY: Who do you mean, "we"?

RAKOVSKY: The Trotskyites. "The Moscow centre, in this case Pyatakov, is complaining that Bogomolov is taking the side of the British. And here I have to find my bearings in all this."... I told him: you are exaggerating the difficulty of your position. What do we have to proceed from? We Trotskyites have to play three cards at the present moment: the German, Japanese and British. It was not quite clear to me, at that time at least, what the German card promised. Personally I thought that the possibility was not excluded that Hitler would seek a rapprochement with the government of the U.S.S.R. I cited the policy of Richelieu: in his own country he exterminated the Protestants, while in his foreign policy he concluded alliances with the Protestant German princes. The relations between Germany and Poland were still in the stage of their inception at the time Japan, on the other hand, was a potent aggressor against the U.S.S.R. For us Trotskyites the Japanese card was extremely important, but, on the other hand, we should not overrate the importance of Japan as our ally against the Soviet government. Even if Japanese aggression could force its way into the territory of the U.S.S.R., it would be lost in the vast spaces, and in the taiga. As for Great Britain, the situation was rather more serious. At that moment Great Britain was antagonistic to Japan. I am telling you about our private conversations which ought to show why we pursued one line or another. At the moment there was antagonism between ourselves and Japan, but it should not be forgotten that England once headed a coalition against the French Revolution and fought on for twenty-five years.

THE PRESIDENT: You should dwell less on the past and speak more about the Trotskyite organization.

RAKOVSKY: Thus, the conclusion was that it was necessary to maintain the connection with the British Intelligence Service, but to pay attention to the Japanese intelligence service at the present time.

VYSHINSKY: I did not quite get you. You say: it was necessary to maintain the connection with the British Intelligence Service and to pay attention to the Japanese intelligence service.

RAKOVSKY: To pay the main attention.

VYSHINSKY: Hence, to serve both the Japanese and British intelligence services, and in addition also the German.

RAKOVSKY: According to my personal opinion at the time, this latter was a mere prospect.

VYSHINSKY: From Krestinsky's evidence you saw that it was not a mere prospect.

What intelligence services were you personally connected with?

RAKOVSKY: The British and the Japanese.

VYSHINSKY: And Krestinsky? Accused Krestinsky, what intelligence service were you connected with?

KRESTINSKY: The German.

VYSHINSKY: Prospectively or actually?

KRESTINSKY: Actually.

VYSHINSKY: Actually? Proceed, please.

RAKOVSKY: I returned from Tokyo with the credentials of a Japanese spy in my pocket. In my present state of mind I do not find it difficult to say so openly, to admit openly before the people's Court what formerly I would not bring myself to admit to my own conscience. It took me a short time, only a few months one might say, to consummate that evolution of Trotskyism which it took other Trotskyites several years to consummate. I say a few months, because up to that time I was at a loose end, I was not actively engaged. Trotskyism passed through a period of passive defeatism when it was maliciously gleeful over every mistake, every failure in the sphere of Party development and every failure of the Soviet government in the sphere of Socialist construction. Even during that period there had already been certain links, and in my person too, with one intelligence service or another. I shall speak of this when I deal with my connections with the British Intelligence Service. As I said yesterday, this was a sporadic connection. The second period was the period of active defeatism, a period when one does not wait for mistakes

253

or failures, for mistakes in internal work, but begins to cause them by wrecking activities carried on according to a definite system and program; when one no longer waits for offers to come from the outside, by chance, but begins to look for connections; espionage then becomes a system. This very evolution of Trotskyism—from passive defeatism to active defeatism—I passed through during the period of 1934. Formerly Trotskyism posed as a definite ideological current; now it has completely exposed itself in my person. In 1934 I already saw that all the theoretical and ideological premises—all that was a thing of the past, all that was of no consequence whatever, including the notorious scholastic theory of the impossibility of building Socialism in a single country. Now we became a school of espionage, wrecking, treason, terrorism. We were the vanguard of foreign aggression, of international fascism, and not only in the U.S.S.R., but also in Spain, China, throughout the world. Clearly, there was some kind of inner connection here with our past. Nobody, I think, will put an equation mark between us and the fascists. This would be a distortion of the whole picture and harmful to the truth, harmful to the struggle against the Trotskyites. There were other, far-reaching calculations here. The whole policy was a policy of adventurism, but we told ourselves (nor did I conceal it in my conversation with Yurenev) that I would write to Trotsky that what we were doing was a policy of putting everything at stake, of everything for everything, but if a risky venture succeeds, the adventurers are called great statesmen. What were our calculations? I must return to my conversations with Yurenev, because I think that they are characteristic.

Now, let us take the question of Japanese aggression. It might cause enormous dissatisfaction in the country and then we would appear as friends, already bound by the ties of co-operation, in the role of the saviours of the fatherland. And then we would already apply the program concerning the Maritime Region, the Amur Region, and so forth.

When I returned to Moscow I continued to be sick until January 15, 1935. Professor Pletnev, by the way, who is present here, and other physicians attended me. Kazakov gave me lysate injections.

During this period Sosnovsky[1] came to see me. Yes, I forgot to mention one important detail, namely, that Yurenev sent a reply to Pyatakov in a letter, written in the same way, of course, about the connection with the intelligence service and about espionage work. It was written in invisible ink. I informed Sosnovsky of all my conversations in Japan and handed over to him Yurenev's letter to Pyatakov, written in invisible ink. During 1935 and the first half of 1936, that is to say, before the trial

254

of Kamenev and Zinoviev, I transmitted five reports to the Japanese intelligence service through Naida. I shall not dwell on the problems which I analysed. These problems are not the essential thing. I informed them—mainly about the effect which the abolition of the ration card system had on the level of wages, about the condition of the collective farms, about the way the industrial and financial plan was being carried out. I consciously presented the situation and my conclusions in a very pessimistic light, painting things in extremely dark colours. I did this in order to whet the appetites of the aggressors.

In the beginning of 1935 I received a second letter from Trotsky. He again dwelt on the subject which he dealt with in his first letter and gave instructions on the necessity of isolating Stalin, of internationally isolating the Soviet Union. This time he dwelt already more concretely on the arguments which I was to use for the international isolation of the Soviet Union.

Of course, he referred first of all to the Left elements abroad. With regard to them it was necessary to play on their pacifist sentiments. It was necessary to represent things in such a light that the U.S.S.R. might become a cause of war. If I should have occasion to talk to the British Labourites, I was to approach them from the point of view that these elements in Great Britain were afraid of the reintroduction of compulsory military service, which would be inevitable in case of war. As far as the Right elements abroad were concerned, matters were simpler; their sentiments against the Soviet Union were quite clear and definite. With them we could speak frankly. As for the democratic elements, we must deal with them not by a frontal attack but through a flanking movement. Soon an occasion arose on which I could apply these instructions of Trotsky. This was during the visit of the French Prime Minister Laval.[2] Among the journalists who came from France with Laval was Emile Buré, an old close friend of mine in France, who had gone over to the camp of the Right Republicans and become director of one of the largest and most influential French newspapers, "L' Ordre." I went to see him in the hotel "Metropole" with the object of convincing him that a rapprochement between France and the Soviet Union was fraught with danger, that it might lead to a new preventive war on the part of Germany. I told him that this was not the opinion only of myself, because I knew the sentiments of the entire opposition, their defeatist sentiments.

VYSHINSKY: What opposition? When was that?

RAKOVSKY: This was in the middle of 1935, when Laval was on a visit to Moscow.

VYSHINSKY: In this case, what opposition are you talking about?

255

RAKOVSKY: I am talking both of the Rights and the Trotskyites.

VYSHINSKY: But what kind of an opposition are they? They are a bandit gang of counter-revolutionaries.

RAKOVSKY: Citizen Procurator, you must excuse me, for a long time this term . . .

VYSHINSKY: In your explanations today you are generally permitting yourself to use quite a number of such expressions, as if you were forgetting that you are being tried here as a member of a counter-revolutionary bandit, espionage, diversionist organization of traitors. I consider it my duty to remind you of this in my interrogation of you and to ask you to keep closer to the substance of the treasonable crimes which you have committed, to speak without philosophy and other such things which are entirely out of place here.

RAKOVSKY: Buré replied to me: France cannot remain isolated in face of the growing militarization of Germany. The aggressor must be put in a strait-jacket; this is the only means to crush war. I wrote to Trotsky about this reply. I repeat, this was in the summer of 1935, when Laval was on a visit in Moscow.

In the beginning of January 1936 Pyatakov telephoned me from his office in the People's Commissariat of Heavy Industry and uttered a short phrase in French: "Our friend is dissatisfied with you, you are not active." I hung up the receiver, because I considered it absolutely out of place to carry on a conversation of this kind over the telephone.

Some time later I met Radek, and he told me of Pyatakov's trip to Oslo. This meeting took place in the beginning of July, during a reception given to the International Commission on Hygiene, which is under the auspices of the League of Nations. Radek informed me of the negotiations between the Germans and Trotsky, and asked for my co-operation. In his opinion it was necessary to support Trotsky in Moscow, that is to say, with the representatives of the German intelligence service in Moscow. I made some critical remarks in this connection, but that is of no consequence. What is important is that when I was leaving for the South with this delegation I agreed with Radek that upon my return from the South I would visit him at his country house; at that time Radek gave me the address of his country house in Khimki.

Very shortly after my return from the South (I returned at the end of July), the Kamenev and Zinoviev trial began and I saw no more of Radek.

I return now to my treasonable activities prior to my exile, and I shall begin with evidence dealing with the way I became an agent of the Intelligence Service.

It happened in the end of 1924. After the fall of the MacDonald government two Englishmen, Armstrong and Leckart, whom I knew personally, came to visit me at the Embassy in London.

VYSHINSKY: Who were they?

RAKOVSKY: Armstrong was a former naval officer: Leckart and Armstrong belonged to the circle of the well-known British capitalist Lord Inverforth, a former minister in the Lloyd George cabinet. I had met Armstrong in Lausanne shortly after my arrival there in the beginning of 1923 during the Lausanne negotiations.[3] He came there and arranged for a meeting between our People's Commissar and Lord Curzon, but he did that in a different connection.

VYSHINSKY: That is to say, in what different connection?

RAKOVSKY: In connection with the Foreign Office.

VYSHINSKY: And when you met him in 1924, in what connection was that?

RAKOVSKY: I first met him, as I said, in Lausanne, and then I met Armstrong, who was a close acquaintance of Berns, the naval attaché of our Embassy, and together with Armstrong and Berns I had a meeting with Lord Inverforth with reference to arranging for credits; so that I met him that time. . . .

VYSHINSKY: I am not interested in the meetings you had with various lords; I am interested in your criminal activities on behalf of the British Intelligence Service.

RAKOVSKY: But since you asked me when I met Armstrong . . .

VYSHINSKY: I asked you, and you said that Armstrong came to see you in 1924.

RAKOVSKY: At the end of 1924.

VYSHINSKY: You said that when you met him this time it was in a different connection, so I am asking you, in what different connection?

RAKOVSKY: In connection with negotiations for opening credits in England.

VYSHINSKY: That is to say, also in an official capacity?

RAKOVSKY: It was in an official capacity, while I was carrying out instructions.

VYSHINSKY: How did it come about that you were recruited by the British Intelligence Service? This is what interests us. This is what we accuse you of.

RAKOVSKY: Citizen Procurator, I took it that you were asking when I became acquainted with Armstrong.

VYSHINSKY: In 1923. You answered that.

RAKOVSKY: And then I met him in London, prior to this.

VYSHINSKY: If I understood you correctly at the preliminary investigation, and if I understood correctly what is contained in

257

the records of the preliminary investigation, you were already enlisted as an agent of the Intelligence Service in 1924. Is that so?

RAKOVSKY: It is.

VYSHINSKY: Tell us under what circumstances you were enlisted, under what circumstances you became an agent of the Intelligence Service in 1924.

RAKOVSKY: I shall take the liberty of repeating this part: after the fall of the MacDonald government in November 1924 Armstrong and Leckart, whom I had known before and in a different connection, called on me.

VYSHINSKY: Well, if you please, how did your enlistment take place? I understand that it may not be very pleasant for you to speak of it now, but it is essential.

RAKOVSKY: I have explained everything in my testimony and here.

VYSHINSKY: In this case, will you be so kind as to tell us about just this question, about this fact, how you were enlisted?

RAKOVSKY: Armstrong said: "We have great sympathy for you, we want to warn you of a danger which is threatening you." He took out from his pocket a slip of paper which he showed me.

VYSHINSKY: What kind of a slip of paper?

RAKOVSKY: It was a letter, typewritten and bearing my forged signature.

VYSHINSKY: Was it really forged?

RAKOVSKY: It was.

VYSHINSKY: And to whom was this letter addressed?

RAKOVSKY: There was no address.

VYSHINSKY: For whom was it intended?

RAKOVSKY: I shall tell you the contents of the letter.

VYSHINSKY: You do not want me to ask you any questions?

RAKOVSKY: No, not that, I have no right.

VYSHINSKY: You have a right.

RAKOVSKY: Ask questions if you please, it may so happen that your questions will refer to what I want to tell and I shall answer willingly.

VYSHINSKY: For whom was this letter intended?

RAKOVSKY: This letter was written to Germany, but there was no address.

VYSHINSKY: The letter was intended for Germany?

RAKOVSKY: It followed from the contents that it was intended for the German government.

VYSHINSKY: For the German intelligence service?

RAKOVSKY: Possibly.

VYSHINSKY: What did the letter say?

RAKOVSKY: The letter said approximately the following:

"I am enclosing a list of Rumanian commercial firms and newspaper offices which should be won over to the side of Germany in order to draw Rumania itself into the war on the side of Germany."

VYSHINSKY: What is the meaning of these contents of the letter?

RAKOVSKY: The contents of the letter meant that there existed a connection between me and the German intelligence service, the German government, or some German organization.

VYSHINSKY: And you helped Germany in enlisting Rumanian citizens on Rumanian territory to aid Germany?

RAKOVSKY: Yes.

VYSHINSKY: Was that what it was about?

RAKOVSKY: Yes.

VYSHINSKY: And tell us, were you in Rumania at the time to which this letter refers?

RAKOVSKY: At the time to which this letter refers?

VYSHINSKY: Yes.

RAKOVSKY: The letter was dated Berne, October 1915, but at that time I was not at Berne.

VYSHINSKY: But were you in Rumania?

RAKOVSKY: Yes, of course, I was connected with the labour movement.

VYSHINSKY: You leave the labour movement out of this; I am not speaking of the labour movement, which, according to your own evidence, you betrayed in 1924. Did you say that you became an agent of the British Intelligence Service in 1924?

RAKOVSKY: I did.

VYSHINSKY: Is that betrayal of the working class? We may as well clarify this point once we have touched on this question.

RAKOVSKY: I did betray.

VYSHINSKY: Therefore speak less of the labour movement and dwell on the questions which are more closely related to this trial. In what year were you in Rumania?

RAKOVSKY: I was in Rumania from 1904 to 1907 and from 1912 to 1917.

VYSHINSKY: Were you in Rumania during the war?

RAKOVSKY: I was.

VYSHINSKY: What was your official occupation in Rumania? What were your means of existence?

RAKOVSKY: My means of existence?

VYSHINSKY: Yes.

RAKOVSKY: I was the son of a wealthy man.

VYSHINSKY: Who was he? What did his wealth consist of? Was he a manufacturer or a landowner?

RAKOVSKY: My father was a landlord.

259

VYSHINSKY: A landlord?

RAKOVSKY: Yes.

VYSHINSKY: Did he own any industrial enterprise?

RAKOVSKY: He owned no industrial enterprise.

VYSHINSKY: Any commercial enterprise?

RAKOVSKY: He did not engage in commerce.

VYSHINSKY: What did he engage in?

RAKOVSKY: My father died in 1903.

VYSHINSKY: I am not reproaching you on account of your father. You yourself mentioned him. I am asking, what were your means of existence?

RAKOVSKY: My means of existence were the income I received from my father's property.

VYSHINSKY: So you lived on income which you received as a rentier?

RAKOVSKY: As a rural proprietor.

VYSHINSKY: That is to say, as a landlord?

RAKOVSKY: Yes.

VYSHINSKY: Hence, it was not only your father who was a landlord, but you also were a landlord, an exploiter?

RAKOVSKY: Well, of course I was an exploiter. The fact is I lived on an income; and income, as is well known, accrues from surplus value.

VYSHINSKY: And the surplus value was in your hands?

RAKOVSKY: Yes, the surplus value was in my hands.

VYSHINSKY: Hence I am not mistaken when I say that you were a landlord?

RAKOVSKY: You are not mistaken.

VYSHINSKY: Well, now. It was important for me to establish whence you received your income.

RAKOVSKY: But it is important for me to say what this income was spent for.

VYSHINSKY: This is a different matter. Did you at that time maintain relations with various landlord and capitalist circles to any extent?

RAKOVSKY: To a very small extent. If I had to make a loan in a bank, then I had business relations with that bank. As a matter of fact, I lived in Rumania for a very short period of time.

VYSHINSKY: But you lived in Rumania all through the war?

RAKOVSKY: Yes.

VYSHINSKY: I want to put the question bluntly: I have a grave suspicion that your signature on the letter which Armstrong presented to you, a letter addressed to the German intelligence service, was not forged but was actually signed by you, because you were then already an agent of the German intelligence service. Is this right or wrong?

RAKOVSKY: Absolutely wrong.

VYSHINSKY: Let us then pass on to the further business, to your co-operation with the British Intelligence Service. Proceed.

RAKOVSKY: When Armstrong and Leckart showed me this document I said: "Why, this is a gross forgery." The document was dated October 15 at Berne, and at that time I was in Rumania, not in Berne. And then, what was the sense of my writing to the German government about Rumanian commercial firms and Rumanian newspapers, when Rumania, which had been a military ally of Germany for dozens of years, was a German agency—there were German firms, German daily newspapers, German banks there—what could I tell them? Why, the Germans knew a thousand times better what Rumania was and what Rumanian commercial houses were. This was an absurdity. It was not only a forgery, but a stupid forgery. Then they remarked: "You maintain that the Zinoviev letter is a forgery too, but here is the result: the fall of the MacDonald government and the forthcoming annulment of the treaty which you signed with the British government." I must tell you that I retorted with extreme indignation: "You are just blackmailers." This they denied, stating that in calling on me they were actuated by the best of intentions. "Do you know," they asked me, "why you received your agrément in England?" I said that I did. They were hinting at the fact that the agrément given me in England when I was first appointed Ambassador had been held back by the British government in connection with a certain campaign which had begun in the British press. Later the British government granted it, when it became convinced that this campaign was based on sheer calumny—I was alleged to have made a speech in Kharkov that I was going to England to organize the social revolution. Then they told me: "No, you do not know everything, we have been making inquiries about you from Mr. Eastman (Eastman, the American Trotskyite) and learnt that you belong to Mr. Trotsky's faction, and that you are on intimate terms with him.[4] And only in consideration of this circumstance did the Intelligence Service consent to your being accredited Ambassador to this country." This statement changed the whole situation. They said: "No, we are not here as your enemies." I told them: "First of all, I must have confirmation that you really represent the Intelligence Service in this case" Shortly after, I was invited to dinner in a restaurant in Oxford Street, where there was a person whom they introduced as the chief of the Russian department of the Intelligence Service. I do not remember his name exactly, this was in 1924; if my memory does not fail me, it was either Richardson or Robertson. He confirmed that Armstrong and Leckart were acting on behalf of the Intelligence Service, that the question at issue concerned the formation of close, friendly relations between certain political trends, that here there was no need to speak of vulgar espionage, etc. But inasmuch as Richardson or Robertson was a stranger to me, I said: "I must have extra confirmation from an official person, someone I know."

VYSHINSKY: And the man you were talking to, what was his name, do you remember?

RAKOVSKY: I said that I do not remember exactly.

VYSHINSKY: You said either Robertson or Richardson?

RAKOVSKY: Perhaps it was Nicholson, something like that. They promised that I would be given this confirmation. After this I went to Moscow. For me it was important to gain time. I arrived in Moscow and told Trotsky. Trotsky said that the forged letter was a pretext for conversation, that this was something to think about. "In general, it must be borne in mind that our situation," said Trotsky, "is such that we will soon amount to nothing. You have been shifted from the Ukraine; prior to this, while Lenin was still alive, Krestinsky, Serebryakov, Preobrazhensky and Smirnov were removed from the Central Committee."

THE PRESIDENT: You are dealing with your connection with the British Intelligence Service, but instead are enumerating who was removed from the Central Committee in what year. This is all known.

RAKOVSKY: Trotsky agreed that connections with the British Intelligence Service should be established, and, so to speak, gave me his blessing in this enterprise. He pressed me to be extremely careful and to ascertain in what way they could be of service to Trotskyism. Soon after returning to London I was invited to see a certain official person, who confirmed that the proposal made by the Intelligence Service had indeed been sanctioned. On their part Armstrong and Leckart said that the liaison agent between me and them would be the journalist Farbman. For this purpose I enlisted two more employees of the Embassy as liaison agents. This happened in the beginning of 1925. Before leaving London I managed to hand over a document, a review of Soviet policy in the Central Asia national republics from the point of view of a man who wanted to encourage a hostile attitude toward the U.S.S.R. In October of the same year, 1925, I was transferred to Paris as Ambassador. In this position it was difficult for me to maintain direct connections with the Intelligence Service.

When Farbman came to see me next, we consulted together and decided to enlist Mdivani for direct work for the Intelligence Service.

VYSHINSKY: You are going into the question of whom to

enlist, while we are interested to know what you did, what espionage services you performed.

RAKOVSKY: Recruiting.

VYSHINSKY: You have spoken about this. Further, apart from recruiting?

RAKOVSKY: Then my connections with the Intelligence Service were broken off, from the time I left London—rather not my connections but my reports.

VYSHINSKY: The supplying of information?

RAKOVSKY: Yes.

VYSHINSKY: And then it was resumed?

RAKOVSKY: Yes.

VYSHINSKY: In what year?

RAKOVSKY: Ten years later.

VYSHINSKY: That is to say?

RAKOVSKY: I resumed furnishing information at the beginning of 1936. My connections were resumed after a lapse of ten years.

VYSHINSKY: And then you began supplying information.

RAKOVSKY: Yes.

VYSHINSKY: Under what circumstances were your connections resumed?

RAKOVSKY: In the summer of 1934, after I returned from exile, my connections were resumed. An acquaintance of mine came to Moscow, an Englishwoman who reminded me that contact with the Intelligence Service ought to be resumed.

VYSHINSKY: Why did this question interest the Englishwoman?

RAKOVSKY: I had known her in London. It can be affirmed that she herself was connected with the Intelligence Service.

VYSHINSKY: In other words, a British woman spy?

RAKOVSKY: Yes.

VYSHINSKY: What is her name?

RAKOVSKY: Lady Paget.

VYSHINSKY: Lady Paget. What is her position in society?

RAKOVSKY: She is a well-known philanthropist; during the war she had a hospital in Kiev.

VYSHINSKY: That is how you regarded her—a philanthropist?

RAKOVSKY: As a sideline.

VYSHINSKY: Just as you are a philanthropist as a sideline?

RAKOVSKY: (No reply.)

VYSHINSKY: You resumed this contact through Paget also with Trotsky's knowledge?

RAKOVSKY: No.

VYSHINSKY: Have you been in contact with Trotsky since 1934?

RAKOVSKY: Yes. I wrote to him in 1934, rather in 1935.

VYSHINSKY: You informed Trotsky of this connection of yours with the Intelligence Service through Lady Paget?

RAKOVSKY: No.

VYSHINSKY: You did not specially inform him?

RAKOVSKY: No.

VYSHINSKY: Tell us what you know of Trotsky's connections with the Intelligence Service.

RAKOVSKY: It was just before Trotsky's exile to Alma-Ata. At first he was to have been sent to Astrakhan, but he managed to get this rescinded and changed to Alma-Ata instead. Calling on him at his apartment in Granovsky Street, I found him very pleased that Astrakhan was changed for Alma-Ata. I was surprised. After all, it was several days' journey from Frunze to Alma-Ata (at that time there was no railway there). He replied: "But it is nearer to the Chinese border," and he pointed to a roll of maps. He gave me to understand that he intended to make his escape. I asked him how his escape could be organized across Western China, through deserts, over mountains, without resources. "The Intelligence Service will help me," said Trotsky. And here he told me in strict confidence that he had made criminal contact with the Intelligence Service in 1926.

VYSHINSKY: Through whom?

RAKOVSKY: Through one of the representatives of the Lena Goldfields concession.[5]

VYSHINSKY: Did he have anything to do with this concession firm?

RAKOVSKY: At that time he was chairman of the Chief Concessions Board.

VYSHINSKY: So when he was chairman of the Chief Concessions Board he made contact with the Intelligence Service through a representative of the Lena Goldfields?

RAKOVSKY: Absolutely correct. He told me another fact. He had already managed to render a certain service to the British Intelligence Service. This was at the beginning of 1927. According to him, in return for certain services rendered him by this organization, he helped the Conservatives to bring about the rupture of relations with the U.S.S.R. He had advised the Intelligence Service that a convenient incident could be brought about by organizing a raid on Arcos.[6] He mentioned certain London Trotskyites who were employed there, including one Müller or Miller, through whom specially fabricated documents were planted on the Arcos premises to be found during the raid, and that he had in this way given Joynson

264

Hicks (then Home Secretary) something by which to convince his colleagues of the necessity of breaking off diplomatic relations between the U.S.S.R. and England. The opposition at that time expected that it would be able to take advantage of the difficulties. I myself had been connected with the Intelligence Service since the end of 1924, that is why I easily understood all that Trotsky told me of his connection with the Intelligence Service. I must mention another fact of my treasonable work, dating back to 1927: my negotiations with Right capitalist circles in France. This began during the July Plenum of 1927. After Stalin's speech, where he came out sharply against the so-called Clemenceau thesis of Trotsky, I had dinner with Trotsky and asked him: "I can't understand why Stalin puts the question so sharply. I see no particular point in this comparison with Clemenceau." Trotsky rejoined: "Stalin understands perfectly well what he is doing. Stalin considers that if the gulf between the opposition and the Party gets wider, then by the very logic of things the opposition must adopt consistent defeatist positions." The next day I had another talk with Trotsky. He said: "I have come to the conclusion that we must give instructions to our confederates abroad, Ambassadors and trade representatives, to sound out the conservative circles in the capitalist countries to which they have been accredited to what extent the Trotsky-ites can count on their support." I told him that in France it is principally up to Pyatakov. He asked me to inform him about this.

THE PRESIDENT: Accused Rakovsky, has what you are saying now any bearing on your connections with the British Intelligence Service?

RAKOVSKY: It has.

THE PRESIDENT: You are giving evidence on your connection with the British Intelligence Service. You went on to 1934, and now you are going back to 1927.

RAKOVSKY: I have nothing more to say on the British Intelligence Service. If you have any questions . . .

THE PRESIDENT: I understood that in 1934 you resumed your connection with the British Intelligence Service and your work in it, and now you have reverted again to 1927. Tell us, after the attempts to enlist you in the British Intelligence Service in 1934, did you take any part in the work of the British Intelligence Service?

RAKOVSKY: Yes. I have already said that in the beginning of 1936 I again began to supply them with information. I gave them an analysis of the new Constitution from the standpoint of the relations between the peripheral republics and the centre, furthermore, my analysis of the new Constitution was absolutely unfavourable.

THE PRESIDENT: To whom did you give this analysis?

RAKOVSKY: Donskoy came to me.

THE PRESIDENT: Who is Donskoy?

RAKOVSKY: An employee of the People's Commissariat of Health. I passed on this analysis through him. This was at the beginning of 1936.

THE PRESIDENT: This was the last information you gave?

RAKOVSKY: It was.

THE PRESIDENT (to Vyshinsky): Have you any questions?

VYSHINSKY: No.

RAKOVSKY: Now I can return . . .

THE PRESIDENT: Then that will do.

VYSHINSKY: No. I have no more questions to ask on this part of the testimony of the accused, but he has to continue his testimony.

THE PRESIDENT (to Rakovsky): What else do you want to talk about?

RAKOVSKY: I want to speak on the negotiations which Trotsky instructed me to conduct in France in the summer of 1927.

THE PRESIDENT: If you please.

RAKOVSKY: I met the deputy Nicole in Roye. Nicole is a very big flax spinner in the north, a factory owner. I knew him because he bought flax from us. I made his acquaintance the first time I arrived in Paris, and knew that he belonged to Right Republican circles. When I met him, he himself opened the conversation, because the incidents at the Plenum were being discussed by the whole French press. In short, a conversation began in connection with the Plenum. I asked him then what opportunities or prospects there were for the opposition—whether support could be sought among French capitalist circles aggressively inclined to the U.S.S.R. He replied: "Of course, and to a larger extent than you perhaps expect." But this, as he said, would mainly depend on two circumstances. The first circumstance was that the opposition should become indeed a real force, and the second circumstance was to what extent the opposition would agree to concessions for French capital.

The second conversation I had in Paris also took place in 1927, in September, and was with the deputy Louis Dreyfus, a big grain merchant. I must say that both the conversation and the conclusion were analogous to those which I had with Nicole.

Now about my counter-revolutionary connections. I have nothing more to say about my treasonable activities in the period

266

preceding my exile. Now about my counter-revolutionary connections. When I returned from exile in 1934, I met Sosnovsky and kept in touch with him. In March 1935 Sosnovsky informed me that a bloc had been formed between the Rights and the Trotskyites quite a long time ago, but when, in what period, he did not say. He told me that complete agreement had been reached as to aims and methods—espionage, diversion, wrecking. He mentioned a detail like this: the Rights spoke of the advantages of the tactics they followed in regard to the Party, because, unlike the Trotskyites, who gave open battle and thereby exposed all their cadres, the Rights had given instructions to all their cadres to exercise the greatest secrecy, so as to be invulnerable. That is how they were preserving their cadres. I am giving you in general outline what Sosnovsky said to me then.

Another underground worker whom I met in 1934 was Krestinsky. I visited him twice at the People's Commissariat in connection with my trip to Tokyo. At that time Litvinov [8] was away and Krestinsky was temporarily taking his place. Our first conversation for the most part concerned my forthcoming speech at the Tokyo conference. Towards the end he congratulated me on my statement . . .

VYSHINSKY: On what?

RAKOVSKY: On my statement.

VYSHINSKY: To whom?

RAKOVSKY: To the Central Committee. I told him I was back at work again. During the first conversation Krestinsky looked at me and said nothing. We were sort of feeling out each other. The second time I saw him he said he was engaged in underground work.

VYSHINSKY: As a Trotskyite?

RAKOVSKY: As a Trotskyite. As to the nature of his work, we had a talk when I returned from Tokyo. But I must say I did not meet Krestinsky after that and had no conversations of any kind with him. I met Bukharin on the street in 1934, when he was on his way to make a report at the International Writers'Congress.[9] This was the only time we met. I saw Rykov once in the Council of People's Commissars. My last meeting with Sosnovsky took place in December 1935.

VYSHINSKY: Tell me, how would you briefly formulate your admission of guilt before the Soviet Union?

RAKOVSKY: I admit that beginning with 1924 I became a traitor to the Soviet Socialist fatherland.

VYSHINSKY: And your activity—at first factional, then counter-revolutionary underground Trotskyite criminal activity—began in what year?

RAKOVSKY: I have been personally acquainted with Trotsky

since 1903. This acquaintance grew closer and I was his intimate friend.

VYSHINSKY: His political friend?

RAKOVSKY: Political when political questions were concerned.

VYSHINSKY: And his personal friend?

RAKOVSKY: And personal.

VYSHINSKY: And such you have remained until recently?

RAKOVSKY: And such I have remained until recently.

VYSHINSKY: Consequently, for nearly thirty-five years you have been bound to Trotsky by political and personal friendship.

RAKOVSKY: Yes.

VYSHINSKY: You waged a struggle against the Party and the Soviet government?

RAKOVSKY: In 1921 the trade union discussion was, one might say, a "trial of strength." And from the end of 1924 clandestine connections were formed which came within the provisions of the Criminal Code.

VYSHINSKY: From 1924 clandestine, criminal connections punishable by Soviet law, and criminal activity began?

RAKOVSKY: Which I have recounted.

VYSHINSKY: Which you have admitted. For the sake of what did you Trotskyites wage this struggle against the Soviet state?

RAKOVSKY: For the sake of the seizure of power.

VYSHINSKY: And further, seizure of power for what object?

RAKOVSKY: The main object was to destroy the achievements which exist at the present moment.

VYSHINSKY: That is to say, in other words, to destroy the Socialist order?

RAKOVSKY: The return, I do not say openly, of the capitalist system. . . .

VYSHINSKY: You won't say this openly?

RAKOVSKY: I want to say that it did not figure in my mind as an open, obvious aim, but in my subconscious mind I cannot help realizing that this is what I was after.

VYSHINSKY: What premise and what historical prognosis did you act upon?

RAKOVSKY: A very indefinite prognosis. This was an adventure—if power can be seized, all right, if not . . .

VYSHINSKY: But first of all you proceeded from the main Trotskyite thesis that in the U.S.S.R., taken alone, its economic and cultural level being what it is, it is impossible to build Socialist society.

RAKOVSKY: This ideological premise went by the board.

268

VYSHINSKY: It subsequently went by the board because it was replaced by some other premise?

RAKOVSKY: There was no ideological premise whatsoever.

VYSHINSKY: There was no ideological premise whatsoever?

RAKOVSKY: No.

VYSHINSKY: And the object was a rabid struggle against the Socialist state for the purpose of seizing power in the interests—when all's said and done, whose interests?

RAKOVSKY: Citizen Prosecutor, if I tell you that we wanted to seize power in order to hand it over to the fascists, we would not only be the criminals we are, but we would be fools. But . . .

VYSHINSKY: But?

RAKOVSKY: But when we thought it possible to seize power and to hold it without handing it over to the fascists, it was insanity, it was a utopia.

VYSHINSKY: Consequently, if you had managed to seize power it would inevitably have fallen into the hands of the fascists?

RAKOVSKY: I share this estimate entirely.

VYSHINSKY: So you wanted to seize power with the help of the fascists?

RAKOVSKY: With the help of the fascists.

VYSHINSKY: If the fascists secured the seizure of power for you, in whose hands would the power be?

RAKOVSKY: History knows. . . .

VYSHINSKY: No, you leave history alone.

RAKOVSKY: No standard answer can be given to this question. But, if you like, the result would have been something like the Petliura regime in the Ukraine.

VYSHINSKY: "Something like" depends on many circumstances which you do not control. I ask you, did the Trotskyites and the "bloc of Rights and Trotskyites," whose representatives are sitting here in the dock, figure on seizing power and destroying Soviet government by their own efforts?

RAKOVSKY: No.

VYSHINSKY: No? On whose help was the "bloc of Rights and Trotskyites" relying for the seizure of power? Whose help?

RAKOVSKY: The help of an aggressor, a fascist aggressor.

VYSHINSKY: As a result of the defeat, the dismemberment of the U.S.S.R., and so forth, which we have already elucidated here. I ask you now: if your bloc figured on seizing power, with the help of fascist aggressors, and this was your only hope, in whose hands would this power be—in the hands of the bloc or in the hands of the fascist aggressors?

RAKOVSKY: In the long run it would have fallen into the hands of the fascist aggressors.

VYSHINSKY: In the long run, and from the very outset. Consequently your "bloc of Rights and Trotskyites" was one of the detachments of the fascist aggressors, and you, as one of the most active and most prominent Trotskyites and leaders of the Trotskyite underground in the U.S.S.R., admit yourself guilty of this?

RAKOVSKY: I admit it.

VYSHINSKY: And you personally furthered the aims and interests of this fascism?

RAKOVSKY: I admit it.

VYSHINSKY: You acted by methods of espionage? . . .

RAKOVSKY: I admit it.

VYSHINSKY: Preparing the defeat of the U.S.S.R. in a coming war in case of attack on the Soviet Union?

RAKOVSKY: I admit it.

VYSHINSKY: Preparing to weaken the might and defence capacity of the U.S.S.R. by methods of wrecking, diversion and terrorism?

RAKOVSKY: I admit it.

VYSHINSKY: Is this reality or fantasy? Or, as you call it, an adventure?

RAKOVSKY: You have misunderstood me. I say adventure in the sense of achieving ends. Seizing power.

VYSHINSKY: Of course, all this is an adventure, because it is unattainable.

RAKOVSKY: Because it could not have succeeded.

VYSHINSKY: And never will succeed.

RAKOVSKY: I don't doubt it.

VYSHINSKY: But this was a real program?

RAKOVSKY: Yes.

VYSHINSKY: That is how it was in reality?

RAKOVSKY: That is how it was, yes.

VYSHINSKY: With your participation?

RAKOVSKY: With my participation.

VYSHINSKY: What you have done is high treason?

RAKOVSKY: I have said so already.

VYSHINSKY: This is not only treason to the Soviet state, but treason to the whole international labour movement? You plead guilty to this?

RAKOVSKY: I do.

VYSHINSKY: I have no more questions.

RAKOVSKY: I must say that I have pleaded guilty to this from the moment when I decided to give complete, exhaustive and frank testimony. For eight months I denied everything and refused to testify.

VYSHINSKY: Following the instructions and tactics of the Trotskyites?

RAKOVSKY: It is the application of the old revolutionary practices and the application of the counter-revolutionary practices.

VYSHINSKY: What have you got to do with revolutionary practices? You have still some phraseology left, but that is another matter.

RAKOVSKY: But it cannot be denied that I once belonged to . . .

VYSHINSKY: But you were arrested not once upon a time, but now, by the Soviet authorities, and you imagined that you could use against the investigation authorities of the Soviet state the old methods which you used once when you were among revolutionaries?

RAKOVSKY: It means that for eight months I continued to live with the same old Trotskyite counter-revolutionary ideology.

VYSHINSKY: That is what I am saying. And not only the ideology, but the tactics as well.

RAKOVSKY: And the tactics. And then—if you will allow me, I will say.

VYSHINSKY: And then, as they say, you laid down your arms.

RAKOVSKY: I will tell you what prompted me . . .

VYSHINSKY: I have no objection if you will deal briefly with this, without long historical digressions. No objections, on my part.

RAKOVSKY: Very briefly. As I said, it was only in the eighth month that I began to make a clean breast of my main activities.

VYSHINSKY: Criminal activities.

RAKOVSKY: My criminal activities, of course. But before this the thought frequently arose in my mind: was I doing right in denying? Nobody will deny that imprisonment, solitude in general, makes people undertake a revaluation of values. But I remember, and will never forget as long as I live, the circumstances which finally impelled me to give evidence. During one of the examinations, this was in the summer, I learnt, in the first place, that Japanese aggression had begun against China, against the Chinese people, I learnt of Germany's and Italy's undisguised aggression against the Spanish people. . . .

I learnt of the feverish preparations which all the fascist states were making to unleash a world war. What a reader usually absorbs every day in small doses in telegrams, I received at once in a big dose. This had a stunning effect on me. All my past rose before me. Of course this past may be reduced to naught and will be obliterated by my disgraceful actions, but as an inner motive, nothing and nobody can do anything against it. All my past rose before me, my responsibilities, and it became clear to me that I myself was a party to this, that I was responsible, that I myself had helped the aggressors with my treasonable

271

activities. I knew that I was not alone, that I was harbouring illusions about them. Former heads of the government, former People's Commissars, former Assistant People's Commissars, former Ambassadors had become entangled in this web. And then I became a judge over myself, I sat in judgment over myself. This is a court which no one will reproach with being biased. I sat in judgment over myself. I had given myself to the labour movement from my youth, and where had I got to? I had reached a stage when I facilitated the vilest work with my actions, I had facilitated the fascist aggressors' preparations to destroy culture, civilization, all the achievements of democracy, all the achievements of the working class.

That is what induced me to speak, that is what overcame my obstinacy, my false shame born of vanity, fear for my own fate, which was not worthy of a man who had once taken part in the revolutionary movement. My rancour, which all of us harboured, some to a greater and some to a lesser extent, rancour against the leadership, rancour against particular individuals, had played a great part. Rancour and ambition fell from me. I considered that from now on my duty was to help in this struggle against the aggressor, that I would go and expose myself fully and entirely, and I told the investigator that on the following day I would begin to give complete, exhaustive testimony. I must say that the testimony which I gave here is absolutely complete, sincere and exhaustive.

THE PRESIDENT: Adjournment for twenty minutes.

* * *

COMMANDANT OF THE COURT: The Court is coming, please rise.

THE PRESIDENT: Please be seated. The session is resumed. We will proceed to the examination of the accused Zelensky. Accused Zelensky, do you confirm the testimony you gave at the preliminary investigation?

ZELENSKY: Yes, I do. And I request the Court to permit me to recount the incriminating episodes of my treacherous and criminal activity as a member of the counter-revolutionary traitorous "bloc of Rights and Trotskyites," whose aim it was to restore capitalism in the Land of Soviets.

THE PRESIDENT: Briefly and more to the point.

ZELENSKY: First of all I must dwell on my gravest crime— my work in the tsarist Okhrana. I was an agent of the Samara branch of the Okhrana from 1911 until 1913. The circumstances under which I was recruited were as follows: in the summer of 1911 my home was searched, and a number of documents were found there incriminating me as a member of the Social-Democratic organization. I was taken to the gendarmerie headquarters, and examined by Colonel Betipazh, who told me that either they would stage a trial and send me to penal servitude or I would have to become an informer of the Okhrana. I knew several cases where the Samara Okhrana had engineered trials of this kind. My courage failed me, and instead of refusing I agreed to become an informer, yielded to persuasion, and committed treason and treachery to the cause of the revolution.

I have no mitigating circumstances to plead. I cannot plead youth, since I was twenty-one years of age, I cannot plead inexperience, since I had been taking part in the revolutionary movement since 1906. Twice before the incident in Samara I had been arrested, exiled, and so had had my "baptism of fire." This makes my crime all the more grave.

When I was recruited I was given the pseudonym "Ochkasty." I was instructed to give reports on the work of the local Social-Democratic Bolshevik group and its struggle against the Liquidators. Subsequently, I regularly received money for this treacherous work, 25, 40, 50 and even 100 rubles. This went on until February 1912.

In this period my treacherous criminal work consisted of the following. I gave information about the work of the Bolsheviks in the mutual aid society of the printers' club and the work of the Bolsheviks in the consumers' co-operative society. I gave a general description of the work of the Bolshevik Social-Democratic group in Samara. It goes without saying that I used to meet at a secret rendezvous an officer of the gendarmerie. I did not know his name; he was called Vasily Konstantinovich. I used to tell him the names of the leading workers of the Samara organization. The promise which the gendarmes made when they first began to persuade me, namely, that I would not be forced to give any names, of course proved false. At first general information was demanded, and then the names of active participants in the revolutionary movement. I betrayed a number of people, and they were arrested. Apart from acting as an informer, the gendarmes commissioned me to act as an agent-provocateur: I was instructed to get in touch with the newspaper men on the local newspapers. This I did not succeed in doing because I had very strained personal relations with the Social-Democrats working on one newspaper, and in the case of the other newspaper, where the editor was the late Svidersky, the fact of the matter was that Svidersky at that time held views that actually were Cadet views.[10] I was instructed to organize a printshop. I was instructed to organize the collection of membership dues and issue receipt books with seals, that is to say, I was instructed to prepare material evidence, so that in the event of the organization being arrested this would provide grounds for a trial under Article 102 and for a sentence of penal servitude. In February 1912 I was arrested along with the people I had given away: Buyanov, Blagodarova, Levin, Vulfson, Kuchmenko. In 1912 Serebryakov came to Samara in connection with the preparations for the January Conference, and again after the January Conference. I reported Serebryakov's arrival and he was arrested together with us. I also reported the address which Serebryakov had brought for contacts with abroad. When I was arrested and put in the Samara prison, I wrote to Betipazh, requesting to be summoned for examination, because I wanted to know the reasons for my arrest. Betipazh summoned me and said that the reason for my arrest was to safeguard me. "The better for you that we arrested you." I remained in prison for six months, after which I was exiled to Narym Territory. Before starting out, I was visited in prison by the same officer of the gendarmerie with whom I had had meetings at the secret rendezvous, and he demanded that I report from my place of exile about the moods among the exiles.

I must say that apart from being in direct contact with the gendarme officer, the Okhrana put me in touch with another agent—the provocateur Polonko, who delivered part of the information which I supplied, that is to say, he was the liaison man.

Having put me under obligation to send information from exile, the gendarme headquarters gave me a secret address for correspondence, namely, Averbuch's print shop. I was told by the investigator that later, on the basis of this testimony, Averbuch, when examined, fully confirmed what I had said. Thus when I arrived in Narym as an exile I was already a traitor to the labour movement.

Of course it would be ludicrous to say just now, and this is not the time nor the place, how I was tormented by my own treachery. From Narym I sent two letters, after which my contact with the Okhrana was broken off. I must explain the circumstances under which this rupture took place. As it seemed to me then, I had two possibilities of breaking off connections. The first possibility of making an honest confession, if one might speak of an honest intent in a case like this, was to report my treachery to the Party organization, hand myself over for judgment by the Party organization and abide by the decision of the Party organization. This was the only proper honest course in the present crime.

I did not adopt this course. I broke off connections in the following way. At the beginning of 1913 I fell seriously ill. After this, when the thaw set in, I was sent to a small place in the Narym Territory called Barabel, where there were only a few exiles, and by spring I managed to reach Narym. Inasmuch as I hid

274

my crimes from the Party organizations and the Party members, I enjoyed their trust as a Party member. I accepted at that time the proposal of Alexander Smirnov . . .

VYSHINSKY: You are going over to the next part of your testimony.

ZELENSKY: At first I should like to say everything that concerns . . .

VYSHINSKY: I think we had better finish first with this period of your work in the Okhrana.

ZELENSKY: Just as you like.

VYSHINSKY: About your work as an informer, as an Okhrana agent, as agent of the Samara Gendarmerie Headquarters, have you said everything already, or do you wish to add anything?

ZELENSKY: I think that is all.

VYSHINSKY (to the Court): Then allow me to put a few questions.

THE PRESIDENT: You may.

VYSHINSKY: In what month were you recruited?

ZELENSKY: It was in the summer—I think in June or July.

VYSHINSKY: June or July of what year?

ZELENSKY: 1911.

VYSHINSKY: Do you know whether the gendarmerie headquarters took any interest in you when you were under arrest in 1912?

ZELENSKY: I do not understand. . . .

VYSHINSKY: You were arrested in 1912?

ZELENSKY: Yes, I was. I have already mentioned this.

VYSHINSKY: Do you not know whether the gendarmerie headquarters took an interest in you personally when you were under arrest in 1912? Didn't they inquire from other Okhrana branches about the reasons for your arrest, what had happened to you, and so forth?

ZELENSKY: I do not know. They probably did make inquiries, but I know nothing about it.

VYSHINSKY: You do not know?

ZELENSKY: I think that since I was arraigned in other places they would probably make inquiries.

VYSHINSKY: In August 1911 or in the spring of 1911— I have no exact information—you were searched?

ZELENSKY: That was the very search after which I was taken to the gendarmerie headquarters where I was recruited.

VYSHINSKY: And you were recruited?

ZELENSKY: Yes.

VYSHINSKY: Before this occasion you had no connections at all with the Okhrana?

275

ZELENSKY: No.

VYSHINSKY: Then how do you explain that on August 11, 1911, the chief of the Saratov Provincial Gendarmerie Headquarters sent a letter of inquiry through the district under his supervision, in which he wrote that "from letters received through our agents it seems that the Zelensky you have arrested was apparently searched by you in the spring or summer of this year. Seeing that no reports have been forthcoming from you concerning this matter, please notify us whether this is the case, and, if so, what was the reason for his being searched, and also the results of the search." So it appears that the chief of the Saratov Gendarmerie specially inquired about your case on August 11, 1911. How do you explain this?

ZELENSKY: I myself am a native of Saratov, in Saratov I was brought up for charges, then again I was connected with certain Saratov Party men, was in correspondence with them, and it is very possible that to the extent that my correspondence with these people was under surveillance this might have interested the gendarmes.

VYSHINSKY: Irrespective of the fact that you were an agent of the Okhrana?

ZELENSKY: Irrespective.

VYSHINSKY: And perhaps in this connection too?

ZELENSKY: I do not know.

VYSHINSKY: Were you aware that on September 4, 1911, the chief of the Orenburg Provincial Gendarmerie Headquarters inquired: "Please notify me what could have happened to Zelensky recently." The chief of the Samara Provincial Gendarmerie Headquarters did the same thing. So it seems that three gendarmerie headquarters were taking an interest in you: the Samara gendarmerie, where you were recruited in July 1911, then the Saratov gendarmerie—on August 11, 1911, and lastly the Orenburg Gendarmerie Headquarters in the month of September.

ZELENSKY: Yes.

VYSHINSKY: It seems to be a rather wide periphery.

ZELENSKY: That was the periphery where I worked.

VYSHINSKY: "What could have happened to Zelensky recently"—what does this mean?

ZELENSKY: I cannot give any explanations on the matter.

VYSHINSKY: You cannot? You yourself cannot give an explanation for it? I have an explanation, but I would like to hear you explain it.

ZELENSKY: I explain it in the following way. I worked in Orenburg, I was arrested in Orenburg. In Orenburg I also had connections and people with whom I was in contact. I think that

276

in so far as at the time of my arrest and prior to my arrest my work in Saratov and in Orenburg was known to the authorities, the gendarmerie headquarters in these places, having received notification of my arrest, would naturally be interested to know if there was evidence in the possession of the Saratov Gendarmerie Headquarters which could incriminate or expose anyone in Orenburg or Saratov corresponding or otherwise connected with me.

VYSHINSKY: But look at the formulation. "Please notify me what could have happened to Zelensky recently." This formulation is very definite: it seems to say—Zelensky is our man, and you arrest him. What is the matter? What has happened to him? That is the only way to understand it. Or perhaps it could be understood differently?

ZELENSKY: I can say the following. . . .

VYSHINSKY: Can it be understood in this way?

ZELENSKY: Yes, it can, but it can also be understood in another way.

VYSHINSKY: In 1912 where were you imprisoned?

ZELENSKY: In Samara.

VYSHINSKY: You did not make any application to his honour the chief? . . .

ZELENSKY: I made an application asking to be summoned for examination.

VYSHINSKY: For examination?

ZELENSKY: Yes.

VYSHINSKY: Not to elucidate certain questions?

ZELENSKY: I have already said that I asked to be summoned . . .

VYSHINSKY: For examination?

ZELENSKY: Yes. That was written in my petition. I intended to find out the reasons for my arrest.

VYSHINSKY: For a revolutionary the reason for his arrest is quite naturally his revolutionary activity. And you thought they would tell you who had given you away?

ZELENSKY: No, not who had given me away.

VYSHINSKY: What did you want?

ZELENSKY: I made an application requesting to be summoned for examination.

VYSHINSKY: But I think that was not what you wrote. Allow me to read out your statement, you can dispute it afterwards.

ZELENSKY: Pardon me, allow me to say, perhaps it is not worth your wasting time.

VYSHINSKY: Allow me to waste time and read it out.

"To His Honour Chief of the Samara Gendarmerie Headquarters. Petition. I have the honour to request you humbly to summon me to headquarters, or to come to the Samara Province prison, to

277

clear up the questions connected with my arrest, and also to allow me to see my brother, Yakov Abramovich Zelensky." Was not your brother an agent of the Gendarmerie Headquarters?

ZELENSKY: No, not this one, but another brother.

VYSHINSKY: What was his name?

ZELENSKY: Alexander.

VYSHINSKY: He was also an agent of the Gendarmerie Headquarters?

ZELENSKY: Yes.

VYSHINSKY: Which one?

ZELENSKY: Also of Samara.

VYSHINSKY: Also of Samara?

ZELENSKY: Also of Samara.

VYSHINSKY: So you started a family business?

ZELENSKY: (No reply.)

VYSHINSKY: Do you know that in 1913 the Chief of Police became interested in you, and why? His inquiry to the Samara Provincial Gendarmerie Headquarters reads: "In view of need, I ask you kindly to inform me where Isaac Abramovich Zelensky has been exiled and for what term." That was you?

ZELENSKY: Yes.

VYSHINSKY: In July 1911 you are recruited as an agent of the Samara Gendarmerie Headquarters; the Saratov Gendarmerie Headquarters in August and the Orenburg Gendarmerie Headquarters in September inquire what could have happened to you. Finally, in January 1913 a Chief of Police inquires where you have been exiled and for what term. So they all seek contact with you and are anxious to know what has happened to you. Is that so, or not?

ZELENSKY (after a silence): I think . . .

VYSHINSKY: I ask you, is this a fact?

ZELENSKY: Such are the facts.

VYSHINSKY: Were you acquainted with Polonko?

ZELENSKY: I was not acquainted; he was an agent, a provocateur.

VYSHINSKY: What had you to do with him?

ZELENSKY: He was an agent of the Okhrana and I was instructed to get in touch with the Okhrana through Polonko.

VYSHINSKY: I have no questions now. But I ask the Court to verify this, to take Vol. LI of the present case, there you will find a record made by the Acting Chief of the Gendarmerie Headquarters, Istomin. This record of the Gendarmerie Headquarters says: "Polonko, Alexander Alexandrovich, druggist's apprentice, railway employee . . ."

ZELENSKY: I don't know his family tree.

278

VYSHINSKY: Not his family tree, but it is a fact that "Alexander Alexandrovich Polonko was a secret agent of the Samara Province Gendarmerie Headquarters under the pseudonym 'Novikov.' " You knew his pseudonym—"Novikov"?

ZELENSKY: No.

VYSHINSKY: And what was your pseudonym?

ZELENSKY: "Ochkasty."

VYSHINSKY: Why?

ZELENSKY: Evidently because I wore spectacles.

VYSHINSKY: No, I do not think that was the reason. And what other pseudonym?

ZELENSKY: "Salaf."

VYSHINSKY: Why?

ZELENSKY: I don't know.

VYSHINSKY: According to a record of the same Gendarmerie Headquarters, Polonko, in 1910, was receiving 40 rubles a month. Payment was made on payroll No. 25 for the year 1910: "September-October—60 rubles, November-December—40 rubles. . . . February—60 rubles, March—60 rubles, April—100 rubles." What about you?

ZELENSKY: Also—25, 40, 50 and also 100.

VYSHINSKY: So you were being promoted parallel with Polonko?

ZELENSKY: Yes.

VYSHINSKY: So we have documentary proof of Polonko. Do you know Averbuch?

ZELENSKY: I don't know him personally, but that is the name to which I was to address letters for the Okhrana from my place of exile.

VYSHINSKY: From exile you sent letters care of Averbuch? Who was Averbuch?

ZELENSKY: The proprietor of a printshop.

VYSHINSKY: And an Okhrana agent simultaneously?

ZELENSKY: Probably, yes.

VYSHINSKY: If you sent your letters from exile to his address, and he was to pass them on to the Okhrana, he was probably an agent of the Okhrana?

ZELENSKY: Yes.

VYSHINSKY: I ask the Court to ascertain that in the same volume, Vol. LI, on p. 24, there is a record of the examination of Leib Moiseyevich Averbuch, who was arrested in December 1937. Is that the man?

ZELENSKY: I said that I do not know his name.

VYSHINSKY: "I do not know his name." But Averbuch is Averbuch?

ZELENSKY: I think it is the same man.

VYSHINSKY: And here is what Averbuch says in his testimony: "Furthermore, my address was used by the Samara Gendarmerie Headquarters and by agents of the Gendarmerie Headquarters, even those who were in exile. I remember that the reports of a certain Isaac Abramovich, who was in exile, passed through me." That was you?

ZELENSKY: I think so.

VYSHINSKY: "I passed his letters on to the Gendarmerie Headquarters." Question: "To whom personally did you give Isaac Abramovich's letters?" Answer: "I do not remember the person's name." Question: "How many letters did you pass on?" Answer: "Altogether between 1913 and 1916 I passed on four or five letters to the Gendarmerie Headquarters."

ZELENSKY: I was not in Narym between 1913 and 1916.

VYSHINSKY: You are not the only one concerned, there might have been letters from others. And, in so far as you are concerned, is it a fact?

ZELENSKY: It is.

VYSHINSKY: Further on he says: "I do not know Isaac Abramovich by the surname of Zelensky. From the letters which I passed on to the Gendarmerie Headquarters I knew an Isaac Abramovich, whose surname I do not know, whose letters I received and passed on to the Gendarmerie Headquarters." He himself received 50 rubles a month, you received more. Do you confirm all this, accused Zelensky?

ZELENSKY: I do.

VYSHINSKY: Please tell us whether there was an occasion when the accused Yagoda called on you in 1924 and showed you these photographs and fingerprints from the Gendarmerie Headquarters.

ZELENSKY: Yes.

VYSHINSKY (to the President): May I ask the accused Yagoda?

THE PRESIDENT: Yes.

VYSHINSKY: Accused Yagoda, do you confirm this fact?

YAGODA: Yes. This was his brother's dossier.

VYSHINSKY: This was his brother's dossier?

YAGODA: Yes, his brother had been arrested, Zelensky was very perturbed. His brother was an agent-provocateur and was shot in 1924.

VYSHINSKY: And you handed over this material to Zelensky? Why?

YAGODA: I did not hand it over. Dzerzhinsky told me to show the dossier to Zelensky. I told Zelensky to come over. At that time he was Secretary of the Moscow Committee of the Party. He did not come, but telephoned, asking me to come.

VYSHINSKY: Did you go?

YAGODA: I did. I showed him the whole dossier. Zelensky was very perturbed and asked me to leave the dossier with him.

VYSHINSKY: And you left it?

YAGODA: No, I took it back.

VYSHINSKY: How is it that these dossiers were found in his possession?

YAGODA: I do not remember.

ZELENSKY: He brought me my brother's dossier and my own personal Samara records.

VYSHINSKY: These records?

ZELENSKY: Yes. I asked him to give me these two photographs.

VYSHINSKY: Two?

ZELENSKY: Two or as many as there were.

VYSHINSKY: One, two, three, four, five, six, seven, eight, nine photographs altogether.

ZELENSKY: But they are all on one card.

VYSHINSKY: One card, but nine photographs.

ZELENSKY: Yes.

VYSHINSKY: Now you may proceed with your epic.

ZELENSKY: But these photographs do not prove . . . They prove that I was detained for interrogation by the gendarmerie on the charge of belonging to a Social-Democratic organization.

VYSHINSKY: Here it is important for me to establish the accused Yagoda's evidence that you were perturbed, that you showed concern, and as a result of this concern and uneasiness, nine photographs of this brother of yours, the agent-provocateur, got into your possession.

ZELENSKY: Not my brother's, but my photographs. And another print remained in the dossier.

VYSHINSKY: And this was left with you?

ZELENSKY: Yes.

VYSHINSKY: Who were you then?

ZELENSKY: Secretary of the Moscow Committee.

VYSHINSKY: Did you inform the Central Committee of the Party about this fact then?

ZELENSKY: About my brother? Yes?

VYSHINSKY: No, about yourself.

ZELENSKY: No, I did not.

VYSHINSKY: So you concealed it all? Now continue.

ZELENSKY: So I escaped from exile; I took advantage of the confidence placed in me by Party people, and went to Tsaritsyn with a commission to restore the Party organization there and run the campaign in connection with the new elections to the sick benefit societies. I worked in Tsaritsyn for from two to two and a half months, was arrested and sent back to Narym. In Narym I continued to conceal the crimes I had committed against the Party;

I finished my term of exile, after which I continued to do Party work and kept in touch with the Party organization. I worked near Moscow—in Bogorodsk—in the power transmission plant, worked in Sormovo, and in September 1915 was arrested again and exiled to Verkholensk, Irkutsk Province, after more than eight months' detention in jail. In Irkutsk I likewise continued to conceal my complicity, my previous provocateur work, from my fellow exiles. I escaped from exile in Irkutsk in December 1916. It was in the city of Irkutsk, where I met my brother on my way from exile, that I learnt that he had also been recruited by the Okhrana, and, instead of exposing him, I suggested that he break off all connections with the Party organization. I don't know whether he did so or not, because in February 1917 he was exposed, declared an agent-provocateur, arrested and put on trial. This is, so to speak, the first shameful epic of my criminal life. I became connected with the Rights at the end of 1928 or in 1929.

Before telling you the nature of my connection with the Rights, I want to dwell on another anti-Party and criminal action of mine, which the Party knew about, but which had not been sufficiently elucidated.

I want to speak of the letter which I wrote to Kamenev from Tashkent in the summer of 1924. I want to speak of this not for the purpose of throwing light just on my own crimes, but because it is of certain public interest and deals with certain matters that throw light on the status of the Moscow organizations at that time and on Kamenev's preparation for an attack on the Party as far back as the summer of 1924. My letter was regarded as the letter of a man resentful at being removed from a post. Actually, this was not the case. The letter undoubtedly was of a factional nature. The letter contained an anti-Party, anti-Leninist attempt to contrast Lenin's line with Stalin's line. The letter is evidence that even then there was the intention to organize an anti-Party struggle against Stalin. The gist of the matter was as follows. Kamenev was doing everything to cultivate sentiments of "local interests first," he was out to make the Moscow organization in actual fact a patrimony.

VYSHINSKY: Perhaps you could be more brief with this, Kamenev does not interest us now.

ZELENSKY: It is a question of the situation and the tendencies which might arise.

VYSHINSKY: We are not interested in the tendencies which might arise; we are concerned with the facts establishing your criminal activities. You can say all the rest in your last plea; at present the Court examination is in progress. So please give us the facts concerning your criminal activity as a member of the Right and Trotskyite and anti-Soviet plot and bloc. You are going a long way around.

ZELENSKY: That is what I am talking about.

THE PRESIDENT: Regarding this letter there is your testimony, which is of no particular interest to the open Court session, and has no direct bearing on the case.

ZELENSKY: It has a bearing on the case in the sense that it shows that in the summer of 1924 Kamenev was preparing to start a struggle against the Central Committee of the Party.

VYSHINSKY: That is also known.

ZELENSKY: And I was an accomplice in this.

VYSHINSKY: Well, say so; you were Kamenev's accomplice in his anti-Soviet struggle as far back as 1924.

ZELENSKY: At that time there was no anti-Soviet struggle yet, it was in preparation.

VYSHINSKY: But to all intents and purposes this was a struggle against the Party and against the Soviet state?

ZELENSKY: Now the question concerning my wrecking work. I joined the Right organization at the end of 1928 or at the beginning of 1929 for the reasons stated in the indictment, out of fear that my criminal activity would be exposed.

VYSHINSKY: What criminal activity?

ZELENSKY: Provocateur activity.

VYSHINSKY: Well, say so.

ZELENSKY: I joined the Right organization not only for this reason but because the line adopted by the Party at that time, the offensive against the kulaks, the final liquidation of the kulaks, the last exploiter class, had an especially violent effect on me and precipitated me into the camp of counter-revolution. I got in touch with Smirnov. I did so because I had been acquainted with him previously and was intimate with him, and because contact with him seemed the most convenient, since he held a high Party post. I was recruited by A. P. Smirnov. When I arrived from Tashkent I participated in a number of meetings of the Rights which took place at Smirnov's home in the course of 1929-30. A number of people took part in these meetings, whose names I mentioned in my testimony and which I will make public here with your permission.

VYSHINSKY: It is not important who took part in meetings ten years ago. Were any of the accused there?

ZELENSKY: No.

VYSHINSKY: Did you take part in them?

ZELENSKY: Yes.

VYSHINSKY: Well, speak of yourself first of all.

ZELENSKY: At the meetings the line of the Party was sharply criticized, and a line of struggle against the Central Committee

283

of the Party was worked out. During one of the visits Smirnov told me that the Rights had their centre, consisting of Bukharin, Rykov, Tomsky, Uglanov and himself, Smirnov.

Speaking of the centre's tactics in the period of 1929-30, I must point out that Smirnov expressed strong dissatisfaction even then. He considered that the line of the Rights—Bukharin's and Tomsky's—was not sufficiently vigorous and resolute. He demanded more vigorous moves, more vigorous actions in the struggle to change the leadership. Even then he expressed the opinion that a bloc with Kamenev and Zinoviev was essential.

In 1929-30 Smirnov gave me a number of instructions concerning the disruption of collectivization in Central Asia.

These instructions were as follows: everything must be done, as Smirnov expressed himself, to preserve the big farms, meaning kulak farms; everything must be done to check the development of the collective movement, check and disrupt the organization of collective farms. He said it was necessary to support the bourgeois-nationalist organization in its struggle against the Party. I transmitted these directions. As regards Central Asia, they consisted concretely in the fact that I submitted a plan of collectivization to the Central Committee of the Party considerably minimizing the actual possibilities and constituting a slowed-down pace of development. The plan of collectivization which I submitted for the first five-year period provided for the possibility of collectivizing 52 per cent of the peasant holdings. The Central Committee rejected this plan and fixed the percentage of collectivization at 68 per cent.

Instead of organizing a struggle to carry out this plan by doing everything to intensify organizational and economic work in the collective farms and training cadres, on arriving in Tashkent I issued the slogan "Overtake and surpass the foremost collectivized districts of the Soviet Union!" In line with this direction, the local organizations worked out a plan of rapid collectivization and proceeded to organize collective farms by methods of compulsion.

This method of disrupting the organization of collective farms was seized upon by the national-chauvinist organizations, which engineered a number of excesses. When discontent assumed considerable proportions and these gross mistakes in collectivization could not be concealed from the Central Committee, I gave instructions that, instead of rectifying the mistakes, matters should be so arranged that people would leave the collective farms and nothing should be done to prevent it. Under this seemingly legal formula a way was opened for kulak agitation and kulak activity aimed at breaking up the collective farms. As a result of the exodus from the collective farms, the number of households associated in collective farms, which had reached 55 per cent by the end of 1930, was reduced to 28 per cent, that is to say, 15 to 18 per cent dropped out of the collective farms. Besides this wrecking activity which I carried on in the sphere of collective farm development, I supported the Rights in the national republics, including Faizulla Khodjayev in Uzbekistan, Atabayev in Turkmenia, Khadjibayev in Tadjikistan, etc.

After I was removed from Tashkent and arrived in Moscow, I continued to keep in touch with Smirnov, as a representative of the centre of the Rights. At the end of 1931 or the beginning of 1932, Smirnov, in speaking of the failure of the tactics of the Rights to disrupt collective farm development, initiated me into the Ryutin platform. The Ryutin platform, as you know, was a platform for the restoration of capitalism. Speaking of this platform, Smirnov told me of the new tactics which had been outlined by the centre of the Rights, and which consisted in the following: the use of double-dealing, a conspirative form of organization, the adoption of tactics of wrecking, diversion, destruction, training insurrectionary cadres, the adoption of terrorism. . .

Speaking of the necessity for concentrating our forces in the struggle to remove the leadership of the Party and the country, Smirnov, expressing the opinion of the centre, in which I also concurred, considered that any means were permissible, meaning thereby struggle by means of insurrection and by means of terrorism.

After Smirnov was exposed as a Right, I began to maintain contact with Antipov, whom I knew as an active participant in the counter-revolutionary organization of the Rights. From him I received instructions to proceed more actively with wrecking work in the co-operatives and in the Centrosoyuz. The object which the organization of the Rights set itself in the wrecking work in the sphere of trade consisted in the following: Antipov and all the Rights attached special importance to the disorganization of those branches of economy which most immediately affected the population: housing, co-operatives, trade, commodity circulation, etc.

THE PRESIDENT: You are speaking of the history of the organization of the Rights. You had better tell us about your wrecking activities; as it is, you are speaking like a witness, and saying nothing about yourself.

ZELENSKY: Every accused is at the same time a witness.

THE PRESIDENT: All right, but don't forget to speak of your own wrecking activities.

ZELENSKY: I am giving evidence as to the content of the wrecking activities and the aims which the wrecking activities pursued. I think it is important.

So, the purpose of the wrecking activities was to arouse discontent among the population with regard to the supply service, discontent with the work of the organs of supply and trade, in the given case the work of the co-operative bodies, and thereby provoke discontent against the government, that is to say, it was done with a manifest provocative intent.

How did I put these wrecking activities into practice? I recruited, both in the Centrosoyuz and in its branches . . .

THE PRESIDENT: You need not mention names.

ZELENSKY: All right. I recruited several officials. The content of the wrecking activities consisted in the following. The Rights engineered interruptions in the supply of commodities of everyday use to the trading organizations. Thus, for instance, interruptions of this kind were engineered in the Kursk Region in the first quarter of 1936, in the sugar supply. Many shops were out of sugar for two or three weeks. Similar interruptions were engineered in the Leningrad Region in the makhorka supply; there were similar interruptions in the summer of 1936 in the bread trade in a number of rural districts of the Byelorussian S.S.R. situated near the frontier.

To give you some idea of the character of these interruptions, I will point out the following: out of 30,000 shops inspected by the co-operative trade sections of the Soviets and by trade inspectors, there was no salt in 3,700 shops in the first quarter of 1936. Out of 42,000 shops, 2,000 shops had no sugar on sale. In the third quarter of 1936, 1,600 shops out of 36,000 had no makhorka, so that these were not isolated cases, but rather widespread.

The Rights did nothing to combat short measure, short weight and overcharging the public. What is more, they furthered this criminal business. . . .

THE PRESIDENT: Speak about yourself, not about them.

ZELENSKY: All right. This was done in the following way.

VYSHINSKY: You are referring to overcharging?

ZELENSKY: Yes.

VYSHINSKY: And how did matters stand with regard to butter, thanks to your criminal activity?

ZELENSKY: I am coming to that. I intend to speak of it.

VYSHINSKY: How matters stood with butter, this is of interest to me at this stage of the investigation. You have spoken of salt, of sugar, how you held back these commodities from sale

286

to the population by sabotage, etc. But how did matters stand with butter?

ZELENSKY: We don't sell butter in the rural districts.

VYSHINSKY: I am not asking you what you sell. You were above all selling the main thing—your country. I am speaking about what measures were taken by your organization to disrupt trade and deprive the population of prime necessities. Apart from sugar and salt, do you know anything concerning butter?

ZELENSKY: I told you that the co-operatives do not sell butter in the rural districts.

VYSHINSKY: You are not a co-operator, you are a member of a conspiratorial organization. Do you know anything about butter?

ZELENSKY: No.

VYSHINSKY: For instance, that you did not supply cheap grades of butter?

ZELENSKY: That is another matter altogether.

VYSHINSKY: What do you mean, another matter?

ZELENSKY: I can explain this to you now. I want to tell you what bore relation . . .

VYSHINSKY: No, you are dividing your activities into two parts: your activity as a co-operator and your activity as a conspirator. But I want you to speak here not as a co-operator, but as a conspirator.

ZELENSKY: Quite true, but might I be allowed some continuity in my account?

VYSHINSKY: You are not delivering a report here.

ZELENSKY: But in respect of the account of my criminal activity there must be some continuity?

VYSHINSKY: Continuity in my opinion consists in answers being given to the questions that are put to you by the Court investigation, and I am asking you: have you any knowledge of criminal operations with regard to supplying the population with butter, particularly cheap grades of butter, or not? Operations which were effected on the orders of your "bloc of Rights and Trotskyites"; are they known to you or not?

ZELENSKY: Yes, they are.

VYSHINSKY: In what did they consist?

ZELENSKY: They consisted in the following: in making butter, all the produce-purchasing organizations used the international standards fixing quality of butter.

VYSHINSKY: That is not the point.

ZELENSKY: That is the point.

VYSHINSKY: No.

ZELENSKY: What do you mean? This was done . . .

287

THE PRESIDENT: Accused Zelensky, no cross-talk and keep to the point.

VYSHINSKY: You want to explain the technicalities of this business and I want to get to the bottom of this business. You said at the preliminary investigation that the destructive character of your work consisted in the following: the adopted scale of grades of butter had the result that there was only butter of the highest grade, no cheap butter reached the market.

ZELENSKY: That is what I just wanted to explain.

VYSHINSKY: Is it a fact, or not?

ZELENSKY: It is.

VYSHINSKY: Further. This affected the budget of the consumer. Is that so, or not?

ZELENSKY: Yes.

VYSHINSKY: Did this rouse satisfaction or dissatisfaction on the part of the public?

ZELENSKY: Dissatisfaction.

VYSHINSKY: Is this what you were striving for?

ZELENSKY: It was.

VYSHINSKY: Did your organization strive for it?

ZELENSKY: It did.

VYSHINSKY: And was the butter which was issued for sale always of good quality, or did you try to spoil its quality too?

ZELENSKY: Yes.

VYSHINSKY: Were there cases when members of your organization connected with the butter business threw glass into the butter?

ZELENSKY: There were cases when glass was found in butter.

VYSHINSKY: Glass was not "found," but thrown into the butter. You understand the difference: thrown into the butter. Were there such cases, or not?

ZELENSKY: There were cases when glass was thrown into the butter.

VYSHINSKY: Were there cases when your accomplices, fellow participators in the criminal plot against the Soviet power and the Soviet people, threw nails into the butter?

ZELENSKY: There were.

VYSHINSKY: For what purpose? To make it "tastier"?

ZELENSKY: That is clear.

VYSHINSKY: Well, that is organizing wrecking and diversive activities. Do you admit that you are guilty of this?

ZELENSKY: I do.

VYSHINSKY: Yet you say: "We did not engage in this, it is not a co-operative matter."

Are you a member of the conspiratorial "bloc of Rights and Trotskyites"?

288

ZELENSKY: I am.

VYSHINSKY: Did you take part in the wrecking, diversive, terrorist and espionage work of this bloc?

ZELENSKY: I did take part in wrecking and diversive work.

VYSHINSKY: About espionage work you so far say nothing?

ZELENSKY: (No reply.)

VYSHINSKY: Do you answer for all the criminal activities of the bloc?

ZELENSKY: I do.

VYSHINSKY: Including diversive activities?

ZELENSKY: Yes.

VYSHINSKY: For the nails, for the glass in the butter, which hacked the throats and stomachs of our people?

ZELENSKY: I answer for it. May I continue?

THE PRESIDENT: You may.

ZELENSKY: I was telling about the wrecking activities with regard to short measure, short weight and overcharging, which were made possible owing to the fact that the local wholesale organizations had no price lists.

VYSHINSKY: You are again talking about overcharging. But what about eggs?

ZELENSKY: In that case, please establish the order of interrogation.

THE PRESIDENT: Accused Zelensky, when you make your speech in defence or your last plea, nobody will interrupt you. But now, when questions are put to the accused, be good enough to answer.

ZELENSKY: I am answering all the questions.

THE PRESIDENT: Accused Zelensky, the Procurator of the U.S.S.R. is questioning you. You may answer or not; you may say nothing at all and take your seat. But if you are put questions, be good enough to answer.

VYSHINSKY: You are talking about overcharging, but I am interested in questions which are closer to butter. I want first to speak about eggs, and then about overcharging. Did you take the same sort of measures as in the case of butter with regard to the supply of eggs to the public? That is another question that interests the public. For example, was there a case, or cases, when periodical attempts were made to leave Moscow without eggs. Were there such cases?

ZELENSKY: Yes, there were.

VYSHINSKY: Was there a case in 1936 when Moscow was left without eggs through your fault, through the fault not of you personally, but of one of the active participators in this conspiratorial bloc?

ZELENSKY: There was.

VYSHINSKY: Do you remember when this made itself most acutely felt?

ZELENSKY: I cannot recall the month just now, but I can mention the following fact. In 1936 fifty carloads of eggs were allowed to spoil, from wrecking motives.

VYSHINSKY: Fifty carloads of eggs? Where was this, in Moscow?

ZELENSKY: Yes.

VYSHINSKY: Deliberately?

ZELENSKY: I presume so.

VYSHINSKY: You only presume so? But who did this? I am not asking for the name, but who in relation to your organization?

ZELENSKY: It was done by a man whom I had placed in charge of this organization, Kulinovsky, manager of the egg and poultry department, and by the manager of the Moscow office, whom I had not recruited, but who I presume was a member of the organization.

VYSHINSKY: But they performed this operation with your knowledge?

ZELENSKY: No, I learnt about it later.

VYSHINSKY: So it was on their own initiative?

ZELENSKY: Apparently.

VYSHINSKY: Were there not instructions to wreck wherever possible?

ZELENSKY: There were.

VYSHINSKY: And they, being placed in charge of the egg business, did wrecking work on this job? Was this with your knowledge?

ZELENSKY: Yes, this was with my knowledge.

VYSHINSKY: Can this be called on their own initiative?

ZELENSKY: No, it was on my responsibility.

VYSHINSKY: As a member . . .

ZELENSKY: Of a counter-revolutionary organization.

VYSHINSKY: And who were you at that time?

ZELENSKY: The chairman of the Centrosoyuz.

VYSHINSKY: That means that it was your duty to supply the population with foodstuffs?

ZELENSKY: Yes.

VYSHINSKY: And that is the way you supplied the population with foodstuffs. And did you not mix nails with the eggs?

ZELENSKY: No.

VYSHINSKY: Why? It did not work? The shells interfered? Now you may continue.

ZELENSKY: I consider overcharging, short measure and short weight to be wrecking in no less a degree.

VYSHINSKY: Yes, that is a serious matter.

290

ZELENSKY: And I want to divulge the mechanism of this matter.

VYSHINSKY: Tell us first what it consisted in and then you can go on to the mechanism.

ZELENSKY: It seems to me that the question of overcharging, short measure and short weight should be clear to everybody; it is very obvious. It consists in the following: when a man comes into a shop to make a purchase, he is overcharged, given short measure and short weight, that is, he is named a price higher than the one at which the goods should be sold, or is given shorter weight than he is entitled to, or is sold goods not of the proper quality.

VYSHINSKY: Why is this done?

ZELENSKY: To arouse discontent among the population.

VYSHINSKY: That is, with provocative purposes?

ZELENSKY: Of course. The mechanism of this business consists in the fact that the wholesale organizations have no price lists.

And so the auditing organizations and the consumers themselves are unable to verify the prices charged. Prices are fixed by the trading organizations or by the salesmen in the shops very often at their own discretion, that is, without control. And so it is almost impossible to detect a man who overcharges the consumer. This matter assumed a serious and widespread character. To give some idea of the extent of this wrecking work, I may mention that of 135,000 shops that were inspected by the Co-operative Trade Inspectorate, cases of overcharging and defrauding purchasers were established in 13,000 shops. The actual number was considerably larger.

Another important form of wrecking, also designed to arouse the discontent of the population, was the freezing of trade by despatching goods to the wrong districts or at the wrong times. For example, there were cases when summer goods were sent in winter, and, vice versa, when winter goods arrived in the shops in summer.

VYSHINSKY: That is, the public was offered felt boots in summer and summer shoes in winter?

ZELENSKY: Yes.

VYSHINSKY: Was this your plan?

ZELENSKY: Yes.

VYSHINSKY: Was this accidental, or was it a plan and a system?

ZELENSKY: Seeing that it was wrecking work, there can be no question of its having been accidental.

VYSHINSKY: Hence it was done deliberately, on your instructions?

ZELENSKY: Yes.

VYSHINSKY: With the same provocative purposes?

ZELENSKY: Yes.

VYSHINSKY: What dimensions did this wrecking work assume?

ZELENSKY: The to*al dimensions assumed by this economic wrecking were as follows: as a rule, any particular stocks of goods in the trading system were 1 or 1.5 per cent in excess, which totalled 100,000,000-150,000,000 rubles. . . .

Actually, the amount of frozen trade was much larger, because in certain regions—in West Siberia, for example, the Kursk Region and Saratov—the actual stocks of goods exceeded the plan by an 8 to 10 days' supply, and so on. I must mention one other method of wrecking, in the shipping and the freezing of goods. In the last quarter of 1936, the goods required for grain purchasing were determined. Goods were sent to all the regions in which grain was to be purchased, but it was found that in the Tatar and Bashkir Republics and other places grain purchasing was not proceeding satisfactorily. However, the goods reserved for the grain-purchasing fund were kept there for five or six months, and only after the lapse of this period was the question raised of taking them off the reserve. The public saw the goods in the shops and was unable to purchase them, which in its turn aroused acute dissatisfaction among the population.

I must deal with one other important question, namely the encouragement of embezzlement and theft.

THE PRESIDENT: More briefly, please.

ZELENSKY: The assistance I gave to embezzlement and theft took two forms. I gave directions to draw up wrecking instructions governing accountancy. The wrecking feature here was that I sanctioned group entries of trade operations on what was called the group system, which diminished the opportunities for control. Furthermore, I drastically curtailed bookkeeping and preserved a fairly high degree of diary accounting, which considerably diminished the opportunities for controlling outstanding advances.

I deliberately hampered the work of the auditing commissions of the rural consumers' societies. It is impossible to combat embezzlement and theft without the work of the auditing commissions and without the organization of public control. I deliberately refrained from taking measures to organize this work. I should also mention that we took measures to disrupt the records of the shareholders and the records of share capital contributed, which hampered the enlistment of shareholders in the management of co-operative affairs. These are the chief forms and branches of work that were embraced by the wrecking activities which I organized and for which I bear full responsibility.

I want to say the following. We wreckers could carry on our work on such a broad scale only because we had confederates. Our confederates in trade were the wrecking organizations in the People's Commissariat of Internal Trade and the State Planning Commission. Our confederates were those who should have audited and controlled, that is, Antipov, yet he was the man from whom I directly received instructions on wrecking activities.

But I would like to mention two other confederates. They are the following: in our wrecking activities we took advantage of inter-departmental friction and bureaucratic red-tape of all kinds in the Soviet organizations. This enabled us to mask our wrecking work; and wrecking work was made possible by the existence of such a confederate as the opportunist, tolerant and philistine attitude of many Communists and non-Party people, who were tolerant towards all manifestations of petty wrecking, as though they were trifling defects of an objective character. Measures were taken along the lines of the People's Commissariat of Internal Affairs to eradicate wrecking activities. But while wreckers like myself can be eradicated by arrest, such confederates cannot be eliminated by the organs of the People's Commissariat of Internal Affairs, but matters must be so organized . . .

THE PRESIDENT: We shall manage without your help.

ZELENSKY: I must deal with one other question. The Rights attributed great importance to the utilization of the co-operative apparatus for anti-Soviet purposes. I had instructions, and I pursued the aim of contaminating the apparatus with alien, hostile, anti-Soviet and insurrectionary elements. How contaminated the apparatus of the Centrosoyuz was may be judged from the fact that when I was in charge of it about 15 per cent of the staff of the Centrosoyuz consisted of former Mensheviks, Socialist-Revolutionaries, anarchists, Trotskyites, etc. In certain regions the number of alien elements, former members of other parties, Kolchak officers,[11] and so on as, for example, in the Krasnoyarsk Territory, Irkutsk and West Siberia—was considerably higher.

I gave instructions that these people should not be expelled from the apparatus, having in mind that, in view of the wide ramification of the apparatus of the co-operative societies in the rural districts, these people might always act as a centre of attraction for all kinds of anti-Soviet elements and act as the organizers of all kinds of insurrectionary groups and bands.

The Rights also intended to utilize the co-operatives at the forthcoming elections to the Supreme Soviet. But we managed to do nothing here, because arrest intervened. The Rights intended to utilize the rural apparatus for the nomination of their candidates first and foremost to the local co-operative bodies.

VYSHINSKY: Did you conduct secret counter-revolutionary work while you were in Central Asia?

ZELENSKY: While I was in Central Asia I carried on the work of which I have spoken. I worked to frustrate collectivization.

VYSHINSKY: Did you carry on undermining, counter-revolutionary work there?

ZELENSKY: I worked to frustrate collectivization, which was counter-revolutionary, undermining work.

VYSHINSKY: And so you did conduct undermining, counter-revolutionary work. Do I understand you rightly?

ZELENSKY: Yes.

VYSHINSKY: Then you came to Moscow? In what year was that?

ZELENSKY: In 1931.

VYSHINSKY: After this, did you break off connections with your accomplices in Central Asia?

ZELENSKY: I did not form any organization in Central Asia.

VYSHINSKY: I am not talking about an organization, I am talking about your connections. Did you break off connections?

ZELENSKY: I did.

VYSHINSKY: And while in Moscow, did you take part in illegal meetings together with Ikramov?

ZELENSKY: I attended an illegal meeting with Ikramov at Smirnov's place somewhere in 1929 or 1930.

VYSHINSKY: And who invited Ikramov there? Do you remember?

ZELENSKY: It may have been I.

VYSHINSKY: Permit me to question the accused Ikramov.

Accused Ikramov, do you recall how it was you attended illegal meetings in 1929 or 1930?

IKRAMOV: Whether legal or illegal, I cannot say now, but there was a meeting at Smirnov's place to which Zelensky invited me. All the Rights were present at this meeting.

VYSHINSKY: Who invited you?

IKRAMOV: I was there twice; once I was invited by Zelensky, and the other time by Antipov.

VYSHINSKY (to Ikramov): Were you invited by Zelensky?

IKRAMOV: Yes.

VYSHINSKY: Did he take you there?

IKRAMOV: Yes.

VYSHINSKY: Did he put you in contact?

IKRAMOV: No.

294

VYSHINSKY: But what?

IKRAMOV: I do not know why it was, but there was no open anti-Soviet talk; the talk was in hints.

VYSHINSKY: And did not some of those present at this meeting express sharp opposition to the policy of the Soviet power?

IKRAMOV: I wanted to speak about that in my testimony.

VYSHINSKY: Were there such utterances?

IKRAMOV: There were.

VYSHINSKY: There were. Why, then, do you say that there were not?

IKRAMOV: There were hints.

VYSHINSKY: But fairly broad hints. For instance, were not direct calumnies uttered at this meeting against Kirov?

IKRAMOV: There were.

VYSHINSKY: Were they hints or calumnies?

IKRAMOV: Open calumnies.

VYSHINSKY: Anti-Soviet calumnies?

IKRAMOV: Yes.

VYSHINSKY: And was Zelensky there?

IKRAMOV: Yes.

VYSHINSKY: Accused Zelensky, is that true?

ZELENSKY: Yes.

VYSHINSKY: I have no more questions.

THE PRESIDENT: You did not say anything about your anti-Soviet connections abroad. Tell us in a few words how you attempted to utilize certain personal connections abroad for anti-Soviet purposes.

ZELENSKY: I utilized the foreign bureau of the Centrosoyuz for the purpose of circulating tendentious and false information about the state of the co-operative movement and its relations with the Soviet government. Stressing the independent character of the co-operative movement, and exaggerating its economic and political significance, I endeavoured to say . . .

VYSHINSKY: You tell us plainly: did you, while chairman of the Centrosoyuz, utilize your position in the apparatus, in which there was a foreign bureau, for anti-Soviet, counter-revolutionary activities abroad?

ZELENSKY: I think that the circulation of tendentious . . .

VYSHINSKY: Tendentious, provocative information with an anti-Soviet bias. Is that anti-Soviet activity?

ZELENSKY: All the bulletins were carefully censored.

THE PRESIDENT: We are not speaking of official communications.

ZELENSKY: There were no others.

VYSHINSKY: There was tendentiousness?

ZELENSKY: Yes.

VYSHINSKY: It passed the censorship, yet remained?

ZELENSKY: Yes.

VYSHINSKY: You managed to utilize legal opportunities for illegal ends?

ZELENSKY: (No reply.)

THE PRESIDENT: Did you attempt to come to an arrangement with British circles about possible assistance in the event of an uprising against the Soviet power?

ZELENSKY: I gave testimony on this point to the Procurator.

THE PRESIDENT: Your testimony contains the phrase: "To come to an understanding with these leaders for possible assistance in the event of an uprising against the Soviet power." Do you confirm this, or not?

ZELENSKY: I do.

THE PRESIDENT: How did you endeavour to utilize this?

ZELENSKY: At a meeting with a certain Alexander . . .

THE PRESIDENT: Who is this Alexander?

ZELENSKY: The leader of the British Co-operative Party, which is affiliated to the Labour Party. When he was passing through here, I asked him what the attitude of the British co-operators would be if the Rights were to come to power in the Soviet Union; what assistance they could give to a government of Rights.

THE PRESIDENT: Did Alexander promise assistance, or did he refrain from replying?

ZELENSKY: Alexander said that he would welcome a Right government. As to help, he said that the British co-operators could at any rate guarantee such credits and such assistance as was granted to the Soviet government during the time of the embargo.

THE PRESIDENT: Have you any other questions, Comrade Procurator?

VYSHINSKY: No.

THE PRESIDENT: Adjournment until six o'clock.

[*Signed*] PRESIDENT: V. ULRICH

Army Military Jurist

President of the Military Collegium of the Supreme Court of the U.S.S.R.

SECRETARY: A. BATNER

Military Jurist First Rank

EVENING SESSION, MARCH 5, 1938

COMMANDANT OF THE COURT: The Court is coming, please rise.

THE PRESIDENT: Please be seated. The session is resumed.

Accused Ikramov, do you corroborate the testimony which you gave at the preliminary investigation?

IKRAMOV: I corroborate it in full.

THE PRESIDENT: Tell us briefly about your anti-Soviet activities.

IKRAMOV: I began my anti-Soviet activities in 1928. True, as early as September 1918 I joined a legal youth organization of a nationalist type. I joined the Trotskyite opposition in 1923.

In 1928 I was in fact one of the leaders of the counter-revolutionary nationalist organization, which was, in essence, a national-fascist organization. This organization was called "Milli-Istiklal," which means "national independence." This name speaks for itself. What other independence could these people expect when there was Soviet power, what other kind of independence except bourgeois restorationist independence? I was a member of this organization. We fought for bourgeois independence. Yesterday I spoke about direct guidance. Direct guidance consists in the following: at that time we could not undertake any important concrete action, we had to gather forces, train cadres; for this purpose it was necessary to accept into the higher educational institutions people who would later on become our loyal cadres, that is to say, we recruited young people from an environment which was socially alien to Soviet power. In training these people, we figured that through them we would be able to get hold of the Soviet and Party apparatus, so that at the necessary moment we might effect a coup with the help of these forces. At that time these two tasks were the immediate tasks which we set ourselves, and there were no others. It can probably be seen from the material which I furnished during the preliminary investigation, both in the People's Commissariat of Internal Affairs and in the Procurator's Office, that at the time this organization was formed, and for two or three years after, it was not the kind of organization which it is today; because as, on the one hand, the Soviet power was growing stronger, and, on the other hand, the cadres of this nationalist counter-revolutionary organization were growing in numbers, new elements of struggle against the Soviet power appeared in the activities of this organization.

In 1930, in connection with the murder of Abid Saidov by a group of young people belonging to this organization, a number of people were arrested, about seven or eight. I learnt about this in Kislovodsk. When I came to Moscow I went to the O.G.P.U. and found out the reasons for their arrest. Kaul or Kaval—I do not remember which—and Sobolev told me about the murder and the arrest. Then I told myself that the arrest was a thing which could not be undone and that now it was necessary to protect the people who still remained.

How could we protect them? Simply to say that those arrested were not guilty would be ridiculous, that would be no way of protecting them. Therefore we took the line of double-dealing, that is to say, Karimov, Rakhimi and myself came out in the Party organization with speeches denouncing these people. In this way we succeeded in preserving the remaining cadres.

However, I did not confine myself to this, and in 1932 (perhaps I am not sure about the year, is it of any importance?) I began to intercede on behalf of some of the arrested people of this group—Ramzi, Kachimbek, Nazirov and others, asking for their release.

VYSHINSKY: And what about Batu?

IKRAMOV: I did not intercede in behalf of this immediate perpetrator of the murder; I was somewhat angry with him because he took the road of terrorism at a time when it was not necessary to do so, and this was a blow to our organization. It was my opinion that by his acts he was cutting the branch on which we were sitting. That is what I thought of his conduct. I succeeded in bringing about the release of Ramzi.

VYSHINSKY: Did Ramzi commit this murder together with Batu?

IKRAMOV: No, he did not take part in the murder, because he was not in Uzbekistan.

VYSHINSKY: And did Batu take part in it?

IKRAMOV: I spoke about this yesterday. I can only speak on the basis of the official record.

VYSHINSKY: But at that time Ramzi was exposed as a member of your organization, was he not?

IKRAMOV: I do not remember. Kachimbek and Nazirov were exposed.

VYSHINSKY: And did Nazirov take part in the murder?

IKRAMOV: No.

VYSHINSKY: And who of them did take part in the murder?

IKRAMOV: I can only say what is in the official records.

Of those who participated in this murder I remember Batu, Saidov . . .

VYSHINSKY: Is that Nasyr Saidov?

IKRAMOV: Yes, Nasyr Saidov. I think Sadyr Kadyrov also took part in the murder. I do not remember the others.

VYSHINSKY: Were they all members of this organization?

IKRAMOV: Yes.

VYSHINSKY: Of which you were also a member?

IKRAMOV: Yes.

VYSHINSKY: And did you intercede in their behalf with the consent of the other members of the organization?

IKRAMOV: I must say that I no longer asked the opinion of the others on questions referring to wrecking activities in the interests of our organization. You know, Citizen Procurator, and you yourself realize that my crime is so much the graver because, as former Secretary of the Central Committee of Uzbek-istan, I enjoyed the great confidence of the leadership of the Party and the Soviet government. I took advantage of this and acted independently.

VYSHINSKY: Did you discuss with other members of your organization, with Karimov, Shir-Mukhamedov and others, the questions of terrorism, of tactics, and so forth?

IKRAMOV: When I saw that the organization was falling to pieces, I summoned Karimov and Shir-Mukhamedov and told them that we must gather our forces and take resolute action, that it was necessary to do real work.

VYSHINSKY: And about terrorism?

IKRAMOV: In this connection we discussed the question of terrorism and agreed that for the time being terrorism would do us no good whatever.

VYSHINSKY: For the time being?

IKRAMOV: It would do us no good whatever. For the time being it was necessary for us to have a program of gathering forces, the more so since Abid Saidov had not exposed a single member of our organization and, on the contrary, had praised Ikramov at the Court trial. And it was he whom the "Milli-Ittikhadists" had to kill. I was terribly disgusted with this conduct in regard to Abid Saidov. We decided then not to engage in terrorism, but to gather forces and not to go beyond the program which I have explained.

VYSHINSKY: Does it mean that you decided not to engage in terrorism for tactical reasons or as a matter of principle?

IKRAMOV: Both as a matter of principle and for tactical reasons. The principle was that we would never achieve our goal by means of individual terrorist acts.

VYSHINSKY: And how did you intend to act?

IKRAMOV: There I spoke plainly. Here I deliberately did not want to speak. I said that it was necessary to employ the Bolshevik tactics of winning the masses.

VYSHINSKY: The masses? You wanted to win the masses? But it was exactly the masses that you did not succeed in winning.

IKRAMOV: I would ask you to please take pity on my Russian language. I shall explain first, so that you should put your questions later, as you did in the case of Sharangovich.

VYSHINSKY: I shall try not to interfere with your explanations, but, on the contrary, only to be helpful. What interests me is the following: this general question of terrorism is one thing, but what about the things that Abid Saidov did, about the question of whether methods of terrorism should or should not be applied to local people who opposed your organization? How was this question settled?

IKRAMOV: With regard to terrorism—that it was in no case permissible.

VYSHINSKY: You said, "for the time being." At that time you thought it would do you no good. Hence it was for tactical considerations?

IKRAMOV: No, it was also for considerations of principle.

VYSHINSKY: That it was doing no good?

IKRAMOV: Yes, that it was doing no good and was only preventing us from achieving our aim.

VYSHINSKY: Which aim?

IKRAMOV: We may kill one, but the Soviet power is strong and would find us all out.

VYSHINSKY: Well, that is what I say, these are tactical considerations.

IKRAMOV: And considerations of principle. We wanted to win the people.

VYSHINSKY: You had one principle—not to be smashed.

IKRAMOV: No, in addition we also wanted to win the masses.

VYSHINSKY: Did you succeed in that?

IKRAMOV: I also want to tell . . .

VYSHINSKY: No, you had better answer the question first: did you succeed in winning the masses?

IKRAMOV: No, we did not succeed.

VYSHINSKY: And you will never succeed.

IKRAMOV: And praised be god if we never succeed.

VYSHINSKY: And what measures did you mean to adopt in order to protect yourself from those honest citizens who were exposing you? Why was Abid Saidov murdered?

IKRAMOV: Abid Saidov was a dishonest person, and I am

300

convinced that he would have landed in jail or made his getaway. He had once been an organizer of the Basmachi movement.

VYSHINSKY: He might have been in prison—that is your opinion. But you are there already. So do not tell us that he was dishonest. Why was he murdered?

IKRAMOV: I can state only what the official record says.

VYSHINSKY: What do you know from the official record, why was Abid Saidov killed?

IKRAMOV: Because he denounced the "Milli-Istiklal."

VYSHINSKY: That is to say, your counter-revolutionary organization?

IKRAMOV: Yes.

VYSHINSKY: Hence he acted as an honest citizen?

IKRAMOV: Possibly.

VYSHINSKY: What do you mean—"possibly"? I think that he acted as an honest man in denouncing a counter-revolutionary organization. He died for that, did he not?

IKRAMOV: Yes.

VYSHINSKY: He died for the Soviet power?

IKRAMOV: Yes.

VYSHINSKY: So how dare you say that he was a dishonest person?

IKRAMOV: He had been one of the organizers of the Basmachi movement.

VYSHINSKY: It is one thing who he had been. But the question is what he became. He became a man who exposed you.

IKRAMOV: No, not us.

VYSHINSKY: Did he expose the counter-revolutionary organization?

IKRAMOV: Yes.

VYSHINSKY: But you were also a member of the counter-revolutionary organization?

IKRAMOV: Yes.

VYSHINSKY: Consequently, he exposed you.

Now I am asking you, did you discuss the measures to take to prevent your organization from being exposed? What did you decide with regard to this?

IKRAMOV: We discussed this question and adopted the following decision: to persecute such people as bad people, and to fire them from the places where they worked so that they would not be in our way.

VYSHINSKY: To declare that these people were anti-Soviet, perhaps nationalists, persecute them—in short, to resort to every kind of provocative means. Is that so?

IKRAMOV: It is.

VYSHINSKY: Is that honest?

IKRAMOV: No.

VYSHINSKY: So now I am reminding you what you said with regard to Abid Saidov—that he was a dishonest person. By this manoeuvre you were really trying to hide your real face. Were those your tactics?

IKRAMOV: Yes, that is right.

VYSHINSKY: And in this way you wanted to gather your cadres?

IKRAMOV: Yes.

VYSHINSKY: Proceed.

IKRAMOV: As the Soviet power was becoming stronger and the class struggle more intense, new problems arose before us.

VYSHINSKY: Permit me to put one more question. Perhaps I am interfering with you a little, but I shall put one more question to you and try not to interfere any more. I have the following question to ask you: when did you adopt these provocative tactics?

IKRAMOV: In 1931.

VYSHINSKY: Did you discuss this question with your people? Did you meet with them, did you give them instructions to this effect?

IKRAMOV: Yes, this is what happened and I gave instructions to this effect.

As the class struggle was becoming intensified, new questions arose in Uzbekistan. One of them was the question of collectivization. Zelensky spoke here about his slogan "To overtake and surpass." This is correct. Such a slogan was given. I paraphrased Zelensky's slogan and gave the following slogan: Uzbekistan is a cotton district, an agricultural district, therefore we must not lag behind the foremost districts of the Soviet Union with regard to collectivization. As a result there were mass actions against the collective farms in a number of districts.

VYSHINSKY: That is to say, this slogan was a provocative slogan?

IKRAMOV: Yes, it was a provocative slogan.

VYSHINSKY: What was the practical result of this provocative slogan of yours?

IKRAMOV: Mass actions against collectivization.

VYSHINSKY: And first of all it was a blow at the dekhkans.

IKRAMOV: This is true, it was a blow at the dekhkans. It was also a blow at collectivization and meant the ruin of peasant farms.

VYSHINSKY: But later the situation of the peasant farms improved?

IKRAMOV: Yes, it improved.

VYSHINSKY: So this manoeuvre of yours was exposed?

IKRAMOV: It was foiled.

VYSHINSKY: It was foiled—that means your manoeuvre was exposed. Proceed.

IKRAMOV: With the object of upsetting the order of crop rotation, we gave instructions that all the irrigated cultivated lands should be sown to cotton. Thus we brought it about that there was no fodder for the cattle and the dekhkans were not allowed to raise food crops and vegetables for themselves. I am referring to melons, watermelons, onions, carrots and other important crops. All this aroused discontent among the dekhkans.

VYSHINSKY: And how did you utilize this discontent?

IKRAMOV: There was no chance for this discontent to grow stronger. One year we carried out our line, but the next year the Party and the Soviet government came down upon us and corrected the line.

Now I want to speak about the bloc between our nationalist organization and the centre of the Rights. They wanted to enlist me, to make me a participator in the organization of the Rights, as early as 1931. That is why they invited me twice to come to A. P. Smirnov's country house. This was before and during the Sixteenth Congress of the Party.

VYSHINSKY: Who invited you the first time?

IKRAMOV: The first time, I think, it was Smirnov who invited me, I cannot say exactly. I went to Zelensky, and he took me to Smirnov. The second time it was Antipov who invited me.

VYSHINSKY: This morning you said that Zelensky invited you.

IKRAMOV: I cannot say with certainty.

VYSHINSKY: Did you know where Smirnov's country house was located?

IKRAMOV: I knew that his country house was in Serebryanny Bor.

VYSHINSKY: I am not asking about now, but did you know then?

IKRAMOV: Yes.

VYSHINSKY: Did Zelensky know?

IKRAMOV: Perhaps he knew.

VYSHINSKY: Then who of you took whom?

IKRAMOV: He took me. At that stage I was not enlisted and did not establish a bloc. Therefore I think that I should pass on to the direct counter-revolutionary bloc connections with the Rights which did exist. I established direct counter-revolutionary connections with the Rights in 1933 in Tashkent. Bukharin came to Central Asia for a rest. Up to that time I had not been on any terms of friendship with him. He sent a telegram saying that he was coming for a rest. He came to me and stayed seven or eight days in my apartment. We went hunting together, we went to

303

the country house together, we spent all the time in each other's company. During this time we established connections—organizational and political connections—with the Right counter-revolutionary organization and with the Right centre. Bukharin first broached the subject of collectivization, of the collective farms, saying that this was a wrong line. He repeated the old, well-known Bukharin thesis of military-feudal exploitation of the peasantry.[1]

VYSHINSKY: In 1933?

IKRAMOV: Yes.

He compared the collective farms with the corvée system.[2]

Then he went on to discuss the question of industrialization, he pressed this matter all the time.

VYSHINSKY: In what sense did he press this matter?

IKRAMOV: I did not want to speak of this, because Bukharin's conception is well-known. Bukharin further said that the Party and the Soviet government were pursuing a wrong line, that industrialization was unnecessary, that industrialization was leading to ruin.

VYSHINSKY: Industrialization leading to ruin?

IKRAMOV: Yes.

At the same time he said that he did not believe in Lenin's thesis that the backward colonial countries could attain Socialism with the assistance of the advanced proletariat, without going through the stage of capitalism. Bukharin held the opinion that neither was this possible in the republics such as those of Central Asia, and that they would inevitably have to pass through the stage of normal capitalist development.

VYSHINSKY: That is to say, he proposed to restore capitalism in Uzbekistan?

IKRAMOV: Yes, exactly that. I agreed with him, that is how he enrolled me. Bukharin asked me, "You agree?" "I agree." "Will you work with us?" "I will," I said. And right then and there I told him that I was a counter-revolutionary not from today, that I was no novice, but a leader of a similar counter-revolutionary organization. I told him of my organization, and we came to an understanding that we would act jointly, that the political line was one, and that we must also establish one organizational line. Then he formulated our understanding in the following way: we have one aim—to overthrow the leadership of the Party and the Soviet government and assume power ourselves in order to achieve this goal.

VYSHINSKY: That is to say?

IKRAMOV: The restoration of capitalism.

VYSHINSKY: In its entirety?

IKRAMOV: Yes, not only in Uzbekistan but in the whole Union as well. Then he said: "What are your tactics?" I said:

"To gather forces and effect a counter-revolutionary coup."
The ultimate object was to wrest Uzbekistan away from the Soviet
Union. He said that our methods were petty, that we were willing
to wait until the Soviet government would experience hard times
and then we would act. And he cited Turgenev's words to the
effect that a Russian waits for a miracle to happen, for the unexpected, that he places his hopes in god, that a Russian leaves matters
to chance. No, he said, it is better to act. We approve of your
work with regard to the severance of Uzbekistan. With regard to this question there was an understanding between the
Rights and the Ukrainian nationalists, the Byelorussian nationalists and the nationalists of other republics. He said, "other,"
but I did not ask which other. Thus politically we were fully in
accord. Then Bukharin set us a number of tasks. The first—wrecking
activities, the second—kulak insurrection. He linked these two
questions up, saying that unless we organized armed struggle we
could not achieve our goal. He said that it was necessary to organize
the kulaks, to take advantage of religious fanaticism, to enlist the
priests and thus create an insurrectionary organization. As for
wrecking activities, at first I did not quite get what he was
driving at. I was afraid that if we, the leaders, engaged in
wrecking activities ourselves, then tomorrow the people would say:
"Go to prison yourselves." He replied: "You are queer fellows if
you think that people will speak about what you are doing. In each
such case it is necessary to say that this is the line of the Soviet
government, and thus the Soviet government is to blame. This
will help to turn the people against the Soviet government. There
are few kulaks now, the priests are also few, but it is necessary
to organize the broad masses to follow their lead. But how are the
broad masses to be organized if everything goes well, if everything
is developing? It is necessary to arouse discontent with the object
of organizing insurrectionary groups among them.

I agreed. Further he said that the program of the Rights included the point about terrorism. He went on to cite the theses
which two months later became known as the Ryutin platform for
the removal of the leadership of the Party.

VYSHINSKY: He told you about them as early as that?

IKRAMOV: Oh, yes. A month later I learnt about this platform officially.

VYSHINSKY: And you immediately recognized it?

IKRAMOV: It was the same program which Bukharin had explained to me verbally, and now I got it in written form. With
regard to terrorism he set us no immediate tasks. Then he pointed
out that it would be absolutely necessary to engage in diversionist
destructive activities. These were the tasks which he set us at that
time. I agreed, and said that we would get down to work. I shall

first enumerate all the points of the program, and then I will tell how we acted.

VYSHINSKY: You are calling this the points of a program?

IKRAMOV: It was the program which served as a basis for our actions.

VYSHINSKY: This is what he explained to you in 1933?

IKRAMOV: Yes. In August or September.

VYSHINSKY: During the few days that he spent with you as your guest?

IKRAMOV: Yes.

VYSHINSKY: Is that all that Bukharin said and conveyed to you?

IKRAMOV: This is all. Then there were other meetings and other questions.

VYSHINSKY: Did that happen in other years?

IKRAMOV: Yes.

VYSHINSKY: I want to question Bukharin. Did you meet Ikramov in 1933?

BUKHARIN: Yes, I stayed with him for several days in 1933.

VYSHINSKY: So he is telling the truth?

BUKHARIN: Absolutely the truth.

VYSHINSKY: Did you discuss political subjects?

BUKHARIN: We did.

VYSHINSKY: Is Ikramov presenting them correctly?

BUKHARIN: In substance I spoke to him along the lines of the Ryutin platform.

VYSHINSKY: So in substance he is presenting it correctly?

BUKHARIN: That depends on what you consider the substance.

VYSHINSKY: Did you propose to him to join you in the struggle against the Soviet government?

BUKHARIN: Yes.

VYSHINSKY: Further, did you speak to him about the methods which should be applied in this struggle?

BUKHARIN: About the methods which were included in the Ryutin platform. It also contained a vague allusion to terrorism.

VYSHINSKY: Did you talk to him about wrecking activities as well?

BUKHARIN: No, I did not.

VYSHINSKY: So he is not telling the truth?

BUKHARIN: He has, apparently, confused things.

VYSHINSKY: Perhaps you spoke to him about this somewhat later?

BUKHARIN: The fact of the matter is that during the confrontation Ikramov denied that he carried on any conversations of a political nature. I made him confess.

VYSHINSKY: It happens that one refuses to talk and later overreaches himself.

BUKHARIN: And later wants to overreach himself.

VYSHINSKY: That happens. That is why we are trying to verify it.

BUKHARIN: I want to say that I do not deny that I gave him all the directions, that I recruited him and that I was the first to enroll him in the Right organization.

VYSHINSKY: You admit that? I am putting the question to you: he is not overreaching, he is telling the truth, is he not?

BUKHARIN: Yes.

VYSHINSKY: You were the first to enroll him in the counter-revolutionary organization of the Rights, were you not?

BUKHARIN: I was.

VYSHINSKY: For struggle against the Soviet government?

BUKHARIN: Yes.

VYSHINSKY: You explained to him the points in the Ryutin platform?

BUKHARIN: Yes.

VYSHINSKY: Do you deny that you spoke about wrecking activities and acts of diversion on that occasion?

BUKHARIN: That was the first conversation . . . .

VYSHINSKY: Why do you not answer my question?

BUKHARIN: I am giving the reasons for my negative answer.

VYSHINSKY: It is not your reasons that I want.

BUKHARIN: My answer is in the negative.

VYSHINSKY: Did you talk to Ikramov about wrecking activities and acts of diversion in subsequent years?

BUKHARIN: No, I did not.

VYSHINSKY: Accused Ikramov, here Bukharin is accusing you of trying to overreach yourself.

IKRAMOV: Before I was arrested I denied. Now I have no intention of hiding behind Bukharin or "our leaders," but I must say that we learnt from them. . . .

VYSHINSKY: What?

IKRAMOV: You are witness to the fact and you know for how many days we denied, how many times my "leaders" denied this at the Plenum of the Central Committee. Our arsenal is the same, our methods of denial are the same.

VYSHINSKY (to Ikramov): Do you now affirm that Bukharin spoke to you about wrecking activities?

IKRAMOV: We had another conversation with him. This was in 1935, I do not remember the date. He was finding fault here with somebody, because the dates and the month had been confused. I can point out the circumstances that attended this conversation. It was on Zubovsky Boulevard, in a new apartment block, on the

307

fourth or fifth floor. That was where we met. Besides ourselves, there was my wife, his wife and some woman whom they called Aunt Sonya. We had supper in the kitchen, and then Bukharin led me into another room and there we had our conversation.

VYSHINSKY (to Bukharin): Was there an Aunt Sonya?

BUKHARIN: If you are interested in the matrimonial aspect, then that is a different matter.

VYSHINSKY: I am asking you: did you talk to him about wrecking activities?

BUKHARIN: Your formulations are not quite clear, Citizen Procurator, it is not quite clear what you want to ask.

VYSHINSKY: Accused Bukharin, I am asking you whether you recall these circumstances.

BUKHARIN: Yes.

VYSHINSKY: Did this meeting with Ikramov in 1935 take place?

BUKHARIN: It did.

VYSHINSKY: What was its purport?

BUKHARIN: I did not say a word to him about politics.

VYSHINSKY (to Ikramov): Is he telling the truth?

IKRAMOV: No, he is not.

VYSHINSKY (to Bukharin): And what bound you and Ikramov? Was he a member of your organization?

BUKHARIN: Yes, I recruited him in 1933.

VYSHINSKY: And was he still a member of your organization in 1935?

BUKHARIN: I think so.

VYSHINSKY: And why do you think so if you did not discuss this subject with him?

BUKHARIN: I know that Ikramov is a sufficiently serious man, and if he undertook a definite obligation, if he agreed to a whole series of directions, he would not retreat. The most essential thing which Ikramov did not mention in his evidence today was a certain conversation. Here it appears that I came from Moscow and said that Lenin's thesis on non-capitalist evolution was wrong, and so let us establish capitalism in Uzbekistan. I am not that stupid, I could not argue the way Ikramov has testified here. The conversation began . . .

VYSHINSKY: I am not interested in what the conversation began with, I am asking you, was there a meeting on the fourth floor in 1935?

BUKHARIN: I answered, Citizen Procurator, that during that meeting there was not a word spoken about politics.

VYSHINSKY: What did you talk about?

BUKHARIN: About tea, about the weather, about what the

308

weather was in Turkestan; but we did not discuss politics. Why did we not discuss them? Because . . .

VYSHINSKY: Because you assume that, in 1935, when you talked about the weather in Turkestan and Uzbekistan, Ikramov was still a member of your counter-revolutionary organization.

BUKHARIN: During the first conversation Ikramov was in a highly emotional state. He was bitter against the leadership of the Party in connection with events which had taken place in Kazakhstan.

VYSHINSKY: Was that in 1933?

BUKHARIN: Yes.

VYSHINSKY: And in 1935?

BUKHARIN: I say that in 1935 I had no such conversation with him, but I did load him with a charge of this kind in 1933. I formed the conviction that he was so strongly attached to the anti-Party and counter-revolutionary organization that he would necessarily continue in this state.

VYSHINSKY: And you, the leader of an underground organization, met a member of your organization, one whom you enlisted, met him two years later, and did not try to verify whether he still adhered to the positions of your counter-revolutionary organization, you showed no interest in this, but began to discuss the weather in Uzbekistan. Is this how it was, or not?

BUKHARIN: No, this is not how it was. You are putting a question which contains in itself an ironical reply. As it happened, I figured that I would meet Ikramov again, but by chance this meeting did not take place because he did not find me in.

VYSHINSKY: You have an extraordinarily good memory for exactly those meetings which did not take place.

BUKHARIN: I do not remember the meetings which did not take place, because they are a phantom, but I do remember those which did materialize.

VYSHINSKY: You are trying to convince us that when you met your accomplice you did not discuss counter-revolutionary subjects with him?

BUKHARIN: I did not discuss them with him not out of virtue, but because the circumstances did not favour such a discussion.

VYSHINSKY: Ikramov, what have you got to say?

IKRAMOV: He is absolutely right in what he says about Kazakhstan. We did talk about Kazakhstan. He said that in coming he was looking through the window of the railway car and what he saw was something terrible. I agreed with him. I have already explained what kind of a person I had been before that. I gave him my consent immediately.

VYSHINSKY: That was in 1933?

IKRAMOV: Yes.

309

VYSHINSKY: But what about 1935? Bukharin denies that in that year you had a conversation with him on the fourth floor of a certain house on Zubovsky Boulevard and that you discussed your counter-revolutionary work.

IKRAMOV: The circumstances were indeed such. . . . There were three outsiders present.

VYSHINSKY: Was there only one room in the apartment?

IKRAMOV: We had supper in the kitchen, then we went to another room, a well-furnished room. . . .

VYSHINSKY: Hence there was another room, a separate room in which two people could have a chat undisturbed.

IKRAMOV: Yes.

VYSHINSKY: Why is it then that Bukharin says that circumstances were not favourable?

IKRAMOV: Let the Court judge for itself. There were three rooms in the apartment. I remember well that we had supper in the kitchen. Then it was so arranged that we, the two men, had to go out. You understand?

VYSHINSKY: I understand.

Accused Bukharin, did you, after 1933, in general maintain anti-Soviet contact with Ikramov?

BUKHARIN: I met him in the years 1933-34 or in 1932-33, I do not remember exactly.

VYSHINSKY: Did you meet him after that time when you enrolled him?

BUKHARIN: I did.

VYSHINSKY: Did you talk to him on subjects connected with your anti-Soviet activity?

BUKHARIN: I did.

VYSHINSKY: This is the main thing. Be seated.

Accused Ikramov, proceed.

IKRAMOV: The main conversation was to the following effect. Bukharin said, why have we got two groups—Faizulla Khodjayev's and Ikramov's? We ought to work together, but why could I not be in one organization with Faizulla, why aren't our activities combined? That would in no way aggravate my crimes. . . .

VYSHINSKY: But in the long run you came to an understanding with Khodjayev?

IKRAMOV: In the years 1925-27 there was an acute struggle going on between me and Faizulla Khodjayev. I do not want to say that I was a Communist, but perhaps there was a subconscious feeling that I was an ally, a temporary fellow-traveller. When the land and irrigation reform was introduced (of those present here Ivanov and Zelensky remember it), I was one of those who showed active initiative in carrying out the land reform. I was entrusted with the chairmanship and I saw the thing through. Perhaps, since

310

I was a bourgeois national-democrat, the actual consummation of this work, the liquidation of feudal economy, was to my liking.

VYSHINSKY: But it was not to Khodjayev's liking?

IKRAMOV: He himself testified yesterday with regard to the "Group of the Eighteen." At the Second Party Conference of Uzbekistan the question was discussed, and it was pointed out that in essence this group came out in favour of rejecting the land and irrigation reform.[3]

VYSHINSKÝ: We heard this yesterday.

IKRAMOV: In connection with this question a struggle for cadres developed. . . .

VYSHINSKY: How did your struggle with Khodjayev end?

IKRAMOV: It ended with the victory of the Party line, which I defended.

VYSHINSKY: Did you form an alliance with Khodjayev?

IKRAMOV: Yes.

VYSHINSKY: Against whom?

IKRAMOV: Against the Soviet government.

VYSHINSKY: So at first you fought and then you became reconciled?

IKRAMOV: Yes.

VYSHINSKY: And you began to fight the Soviet government together?

IKRAMOV: Yes.

VYSHINSKY: Khodjayev, is this correct?

KHODJAYEV: With your permission, I should like to give my explanations with regard to this question.

THE PRESIDENT: You may.

KHODJAYEV: I want to say that Ikramov is not quite correct in what he says—that up to 1933, before his conversation with Bukharin, there was no co-ordination of action between me and him.

VYSHINSKY: There was?

KHODJAYEV: There was. In 1925 I indeed did not agree with the form of the land and irrigation reform. It was too much to the detriment of the bai[4] and kulak upper stratum of the countryside.

VYSHINSKY: This was not to your liking?

KHODJAYEV: It was not to my liking and I opposed it. It is true that at that time this group of three, that is to say, Zelensky, Ikramov and Ivanov, taking cover behind the Party line, the correct Party line, defeated me.

VYSHINSKY: But they took cover?

KHODJAYEV: Of course.

VYSHINSKY: Why do you think that they were taking cover?

KHODJAYEV: Because Zelensky has told you who he was, Ivanov has told you who he was, Ikramov tried to deny, but that didn't work either. Consequently, they were taking cover.

311

VYSHINSKY: Correct.

KHODJAYEV: I want to say that my sins were more or less known. This made it easier for them to flay me. In 1926-27 I carried on no joint activity with Ikramov, but since 1928 we have worked together.

VYSHINSKY: In what sense have you worked?

KHODJAYEV: In the sense of carrying on wrecking activities. I do not put any other sense into these words. Ikramov is wrong in trying to say that only after Bukharin brought pressure to bear on him in 1933 did he accept the position of wrecking and work together with me. In this way he is trying to exonerate himself of part of the guilt, just as he was trying to lay at the door of Karimov the leadership of the nationalist organization. I think that this is unworthy of Ikramov.

IKRAMOV: Permit me to continue.

VYSHINSKY: No, just a moment. I want to put some more questions to the accused Khodjayev. But, after all, did Bukharin play any role in uniting your counter-revolutionary forces?

KHODJAYEV: Yes.

VYSHINSKY: What role?

KHODJAYEV: In the sense that although, beginning with 1928, we worked together with Ikramov, we did wrecking work together, the struggle for influence in Uzbekistan at times interfered, if I may say so, with the fruitfulness of this anti-Soviet activity. Therefore, first Bukharin in the conversation to which Ikramov is referring (I did not speak to Bukharin directly at that time), and then Antipov, said that I ought to join hands with Ikramov. They said that we should work together, that we should carry on the struggle together. . . .

VYSHINSKY: Against?

KHODJAYEV: Against the Soviet government, against the Party, against the leadership of the Party.

VYSHINSKY: Is this true, accused Ikramov?

IKRAMOV: It is. If I had been permitted, I would have said the same.

VYSHINSKY: Do you confirm what Khodjayev is saying here—that Bukharin played a tremendous role in the amalgamation of your counter-revolutionary forces?

IKRAMOV: Well, of course.

VYSHINSKY: And does Bukharin confirm this?

BUKHARIN: I should like to say . . .

VYSHINSKY: Not just now.

IKRAMOV: I want to say that beginning with 1925, inasmuch as there was such an acute struggle going on up to 1929, up to the Fourth Kurultai,[5] there was no unity between me and Faizulla.

312

After the Fourth Kurultai there was such joint action. Here it is only a matter of detail.

VYSHINSKY: But for appearances' sake, you still kept on fighting between yourselves?

IKRAMOV: No, we did not fight for appearances' sake.

VYSHINSKY: Why, you are fighting now. So how can you deny that you were fighting?

IKRAMOV: That was not a sincere fight, it was just a sham.

VYSHINSKY: Cock-fights?

IKRAMOV: Not even cock-fights. Cocks sometimes fight until blood is drawn.

VYSHINSKY: There were no fights even of this nature?

IKRAMOV: No.

VYSHINSKY: Not even cock-fights?

IKRAMOV: No.

VYSHINSKY: At first it was a tacit fight, and then Bukharin came and reconciled you in essence as well. Do I understand you right?

IKRAMOV: Yes. I will tell you about it.

VYSHINSKY: Please.

IKRAMOV: In our underground nationalist organization, we had come to an understanding to try not to admit any of the nationalists into this organization. Not because we had no need of them, but because there was a pile of material about each of them.

VYSHINSKY: Where?

IKRAMOV: In the organs of the Soviet government which have access to all documents. Very many of them who worked in various spheres were exposed by the Party and by the people; the press wrote about it. Therefore, in order to succeed in preserving complete secrecy, we decided not to admit these people. Yesterday Faizulla found proof somewhere that I was trying to keep something back. I am not holding anything back. Whatever facts there were I am telling about. What did we do? We did not admit these people. Khodjayev says that during 1925-28 there was a lull in his activities, he had no people. Most of our People's Commissars were Pan-Tyurkists and nationalists: Khidyr Aliyev, Khadjibayev, Kurbanov and others. They were all people who were connected with Faizulla. The acute struggle left a certain imprint on us with regard to each other. They might have been in Uzbekistan today. In 1933 we might perhaps have come to terms with them. At present there is no difference between me and them. Since 1931 there has been no difference.

VYSHINSKY: And with Bukharin?

IKRAMOV: With Bukharin, since 1933.

VYSHINSKY: What, then, was Bukharin's role?

313

IKRAMOV: Bukharin said, "Why have you got two groups? You ought to unite." I gave him no definite answer at the time. At the end of 1934 Antipov came to visit us. He told me that, on instructions of the centre of the Rights, it was absolutely necessary to unite our two organizations, so that there should be an understanding with regard to all questions and joint action. He did not demand formal unity, but unity in essence. After that the actual union of our two organizations was effected, just as it was in the case between the Trotskyites and the Rights, but at the same time each of our organizations preserved its own loathsome face. That is why, when I spoke of this yesterday, I said that since 1929 there has been tacit co-ordination of work between Faizulla and me. I spoke about this. Why then does he say here that I am trying to place the blame on somebody? This is not true. I am not laying my guilt at anybody's door. Such an understanding between the two organizations was established in 1934. The three of us—Antipov, Khodjayev and Ikramov—met together. We came to an understanding with regard to the joint activities of our organizations.

Now further, why did we not want to admit the old nationalist intellectuals? When Burnashev put the question before me in 1928 that it was necessary for me to effect a rapprochement with Khodjayev, at that time I really thought: here is a clever man, a capable man, we may effect a rapprochement. But at that time I received a note from a certain Mukhitdinov saying that he had sent a statement to the Central Asia Bureau or to the G.P.U. in which he repented of his counter-revolutionary crimes and in which he told the most terrible things about Faizulla. I thought: now the question will shortly come up for discussion, and I, together with Faizulla, might be exposed too soon. He testified that he had received Enver Pasha—that was a well-known Turkish adventurer.[6] So everything was not quite on the level there. We were both sullied, birds of a feather, only I had a tactical consideration.

VYSHINSKY: There was material against him, but there was none against you?

IKRAMOV: There was none against me.

VYSHINSKY: So you figured that you ought not to have anything to do with him, that it was dangerous, that you might be exposed yourself?

IKRAMOV: Yes, that is correct. I have spoken about it and I have not hidden behind anything. I do not want to minimize my crimes.

VYSHINSKY: Accused Khodjayev, what have you got to say about the Basmachi Maxum?

KHODJAYEV: Maxum was the chief of a militia detachment attached to the Chairman of the Revolutionary Committee. In

1921 we disarmed him in Bokhara, but he escaped. Soon after he was caught and put on trial. This was after the orientation towards the Basmachis was accepted.

VYSHINSKY: Accepted by whom?

KHODJAYEV: By us.

VYSHINSKY: That is to say, you helped him to avoid being called to account?

KHODJAYEV: He was amnestied.

VYSHINSKY: Did you have a Basmachi orientation?

In the first place, Mukhitdinov was an important Basmachi.

KHODJAYEV: Not a Basmachi, he was a national-democrat.

VYSHINSKY: Did you maintain contact with him?

KHODJAYEV: Maxum was connected with him. He might have compromised me.

VYSHINSKY: And to what extent might he have compromised you?

KHODJAYEV: I do not understand what Ikramov has been saying here. The note to which Ikramov has been referring is in the records of my case.

VYSHINSKY: Was Maxum there?

KHODJAYEV: Yes, he was.

VYSHINSKY: Did you have a meeting with Enver Pasha?

KHODJAYEV: We had three meetings.

VYSHINSKY: When?

KHODJAYEV: Two meetings in Bokhara were official, one meeting in my apartment was unofficial.

VYSHINSKY: What were the purposes of this meeting?

KHODJAYEV: The purpose of the last meeting was to discuss Enver Pasha's proposal as to what line the Bokhara government was to take with regard to the Soviet Union and what tactics were necessary.

VYSHINSKY: You concealed these meetings from the Soviet government, did you not?

KHODJAYEV: Absolutely.

VYSHINSKY: Was that what Maxum's note referred to?

KHODJAYEV: No, he merely stated that he was not reporting anything that would implicate him in counter-revolution and that he was trying to make me responsible for the Bokhara counter-revolutionary nationalist organization. This was done with a purpose, and I sent him a note in answer to this then.

VYSHINSKY: And did he refer to your connection with some people?

KHODJAYEV: Yes.

Permit me to add to this. Zelensky here spoke apparently very truthfully about his activities in Central Asia. He said that he supported the Rights, Faizulla Khodjayev and Atabayev. It was not myself whom Zelensky supported, but Mukhitdinov, who had an English orientation, but he said not a word of this.

VYSHINSKY: We shall ask him now.

Accused Zelensky, tell us, did this episode with Mukhitdinov take place?

ZELENSKY: I had to come out against Khodjayev from time to time, otherwise I would have exposed myself. Now as for Mukhitdinov. It is the first time I hear he was awarded the Order of the Banner of Labour.

VYSHINSKY: Who awarded it to him?

ZELENSKY: I do not know.

KHODJAYEV: He was awarded the Order in 1936 or 1937 by decision of the Central Executive Commitee of Uzbekistan on a proposal made by Zelensky and Ikramov. I can produce the corresponding documents dealing with this question.

ZELENSKY: I have no idea.

IKRAMOV: I once travelled with Mukhitdinov from Moscow in the same railway car. I saw the man once. He was an extremely hateful man. I entertained such hatred for him. All the time he was flaunting the Tadjik question, setting up the Tadjiks in opposition to the Uzbeks. I never saw a more hateful man than he.

VYSHINSKY: But you tell us, did he get an Order?

IKRAMOV: I simply do not remember it. Perhaps Faizulla has just made a mistake. I might award one to anybody, but not to this Mukhitdinov.

VYSHINSKY: And was Zelensky Secretary at that time?

IKRAMOV: Yes.

VYSHINSKY: In any event, if he was awarded, it could not have been decided without Zelensky.

IKRAMOV: It could have been decided.

VYSHINSKY: How so, without the Secretary of the Central Asia Bureau?

IKRAMOV: It sometimes happened that the Central Committee of Uzbekistan considered such questions by itself.

VYSHINSKY: This is an isolated episode. I have gone into it at the request of Faizulla Khodjayev. While Zelensky has not resumed his seat, may I question him with regard to one circumstance?

(To Zelensky.) In what year were you in Central Asia?

ZELENSKY: In 1924.

VYSHINSKY: And how long did you stay there?

ZELENSKY: Until January 1931.

VYSHINSKY: So you spent seven years there?

ZELENSKY: Yes.

VYSHINSKY: During these seven years, while you were engaged in counter-revolutionary wrecking activities, did you have any connections with Ikramov and Khodjayev?

ZELENSKY: I had no connections with Ikramov, but I did cover up Khodjayev's new line.

VYSHINSKY: So you pursued your line independently?

ZELENSKY: Independently.

VYSHINSKY: And how can you explain the fact that you did not get in touch with the one or the other?

ZELENSKY: There was no need. Perhaps I was a little afraid of them.

VYSHINSKY: What were you afraid of?

ZELENSKY: Exposure.

VYSHINSKY: Exposure? So it was from considerations of secrecy? And did you see what they were engaged in?

ZELENSKY: Well, you see, I must say that with regard to Ikramov I had no doubts up to 1928 that he maintained the positions of the Party, only giving in from time to time to his nationalist tendencies.

VYSHINSKY: And since 1928?

ZELENSKY: Since 1928 I had begun to realize more clearly that Ikramov was connected with a nationalist organization, and when the "Milli-Istiklal" organization was exposed, then, for reasons of self-preservation, I came out very strongly against Ikramov—this is known from the records of the Fourth Kurultai—I raised the question of his being removed from his post and even of having him arrested.

VYSHINSKY: By way of insuring yourself?

ZELENSKY: Yes.

VYSHINSKY: Hence, by way of insuring yourself.

ZELENSKY: Yes.

VYSHINSKY: Consequently, you knew of his counter-revolutionary activity, and what you did you did in essence for the purpose of insuring yourself?

ZELENSKY: I did not know of it, but I presumed.

VYSHINSKY: Did you raise the question of arrest only on the basis of a presumption? You say that for the purpose of insuring yourself you raised the question of having Ikramov arrested.

ZELENSKY: I did.

VYSHINSKY: On what grounds? Why should he be arrested?

ZELENSKY: When the "Milli-Istiklal" was exposed, a number of the members of this organization said in their depositions in the organs of the O.G.P.U. that Ikramov was the actual leader of this organization.

VYSHINSKY: Consequently, you knew from the depositions of a number of members that Ikramov was the leader?

317

ZELENSKY: Yes.

VYSHINSKY: And, in order to insure yourself, you raised the question of having Ikramov arrested?

ZELENSKY: Yes.

VYSHINSKY: But did you actually fight against his counter-revolutionary activities?

ZELENSKY: I was very soon recalled from there.

VYSHINSKY: No, but you say that it became clear to you in 1928 that Ikramov was carrying on nationalist counter-revolutionary work.

ZELENSKY: Yes, it became clear. Formally, I waged a fight against him.

VYSHINSKY: But actually you did not wage a fight against him?

ZELENSKY: Actually, I did not, and could not.

VYSHINSKY: Why could you not?

ZELENSKY: Faizulla has already described me here as . . .

VYSHINSKY: Do you agree with the description Faizulla gave of you?

ZELENSKY: I myself gave such a description of myself—actually, I did not fight; I could not fight, because I myself was a traitor.

IKRAMOV: Well, to continue. Under the direct leadership of Antipov, and on the instructions of the Right centre, a bloc of both nationalist organizations was formed. Antipov informed me about the German-Japanese orientation and about the connections with the Germans and Japanese. He also told me that there was a military group, and that in the event of war they would act by opening the front to the attacking forces of the interventionists. He then said that we too must act. We did not at that time speak about wrecking yet; there was no wrecking at that time. On the question of insurrection no practical instructions had been given to the organizations, and he therefore said that we must act.

At the second meeting with Bukharin he said nothing about politics, but told me why he had connected us with Antipov. He said that it would not do for him and me to meet, but Antipov visited Central Asia nearly every year on cotton business and the position he occupied was such that I could always go and see him on business. We agreed that permanent contact should be maintained with Antipov. He asked me about actions. I told him that we were carrying on some wrecking work. He said that it was entirely inadequate, that it must be extended, that we must act, that no time must be lost.

The third meeting dealt with connections with England. Faizulla spoke about that yesterday. It is true that Faizulla Khodjayev informed me in October 1936 that Bukharin had spoken to him, that Bukharin was very optimistic about the capitalist stabilization of European countries, especially of the fascist states. He said that we must orientate ourselves on England. As the question was a serious and important one, at the end of November or the beginning of December 1936 I asked Bukharin about it. He replied in the affirmative.

VYSHINSKY: Bukharin replied in the affirmative?

IKRAMOV: Yes.

VYSHINSKY: Where did he say that?

IKRAMOV: It was during the Congress of Soviets in November or the beginning of December 1936. During the Congress of Soviets I met Bukharin on the staircase; nobody was about, and I asked him about this. He answered in the affirmative, and formulated it as follows: if there will not be a war just now, if there will not be intervention soon, it is all over with our business. They will bag us all, yet we cannot expedite war because of England, which in certain respects is an international arbiter. As long as she does not decide one way or another, as long as she does not arrive at some decision, there will be no war. But at present, in the war that is brewing, the British will not raise the question until it is clear to them what they can get, and where. It is well known, Bukharin said, that the British have long had their eyes on Turkestan as a choice morsel. If such proposals are made, the British perhaps would more quickly come over to the side of an aggressor against the Soviet Union.

That is why I believed Faizulla Khodjayev when he told me about the orientation on England. In Uzbekistan, the people hate the imperialists, especially the British. Before they used to come and trade with us, then there were their representatives, they went back through this way. They know that in India . . .

THE PRESIDENT: Accused Ikramov, you must not deal with the internal affairs of other states. Let us have your testimony.

IKRAMOV: The people of Uzbekistan would rise up against such a proposal, no matter who made it. We would be flung out neck and crop. I was not the sort of man to be easily frightened, but the sentiments of the nation alarmed me. I decided to verify what Faizulla Khodjayev had told me in October 1936.

It was Antipov who told me about terrorism. I said to him, "How is this, you instructed us to form a terrorist group in Uzbekistan?" He replied that it was to test our readiness, but actually it would be done here. If anybody wanted to come to us—they would hardly get there. He boasted that whoever the Rights had decided to kill would never reach Central Asia.

VYSHINSKY: Who said that?

IKRAMOV: Antipov.

I was connected in Tadjikistan—through Rakhimbayev—

319

with a nationalist counter-revolutionary organization of the same type as the one in Uzbekistan. True, there was only one occasion when we talked about it, but I was connected with the Tadjik counter-revolutionary organization through Rakhimbayev. If necessary, I can tell you in detail. . . .

VYSHINSKY: The investigation on that case is not yet completed, so that it would be better if you did not give any details.

IKRAMOV: Faizulla told me that he had formed, or was forming, contacts with the organization in Turkmenistan. I did not question him about details.

Permit me now to relate what our nationalist counter-revolutionary organization did in execution of its plan, of its program. After Bukharin had rebuked me for inadequate activity, I myself committed a direct wrecking act. In 1935, we—Lyubimov, Faizulla Khodjayev and I—jointly issued directions, signed by Lyubimov and Ikramov (they were not signed by Faizulla, I think) that cotton with a moisture content exceeding the standard fixed by the government of the Union should be accepted, as a result of which 14,000 tons of cotton perished, of which 2,600 tons were sent to the cotton-wool factory, and the rest graded at lower qualities. The loss amounted to several million rubles.

VYSHINSKY: Was this done by you deliberately?

IKRAMOV: Of course. If it had been accidental, I would not have spoken about it here. Wrecking work was done in the caracul business. We did not do it ourselves directly, but through members of our organization. The grades were lowered. In 1936, owing to wrong methods of treatment, there was a 27 per cent lowering of grades. In 1937 caracul skins were damaged wholesale during steam treatment—a huge number of skins were scalded. This was also done by members of our organization (Sata Khodjayev was working there).

Wrecking activities were also carried on in the municipal enterprises of Tashkent and Bokhara. A member of our organization named Tadjiyev was active in Tashkent—he did wrecking work in the planning of the drainage system and in building construction.

Here is an example of wrecking work in the sphere of building construction. Tashkent is divided into two parts: the old town and the new town. There is no drainage system in the old town, there are extensive stretches of territory where houses cannot be built. In addition, there are many cesspools. Building operations were begun on the new premises of the People's Commissariat of Post and Telegraph, but in view of the fact that there were nineteen cesspools, the laying of the foundation had to be begun at a depth of 30 or 40 metres.

There was also wrecking work in the municipal enterprises of

Bokhara. The city was allowed to fall to pieces. Houses were sold off. The inhabitants were called upon to pay intolerable rates, they abandoned their houses, which were then sold off.

The funds granted by the government of the U.S.S.R. for district development were deliberately dissipated on numerous projects so as to secure the minimum effect. In 1937 uncompleted construction work amounted to a total of 34,000,000 rubles.

VYSHINSKY: All because of the wasteful distribution of funds?

IKRAMOV: Yes. That was the work of Karimov and Faizulla Khodjayev.

VYSHINSKY: Not yours?

IKRAMOV: I had no direct connection with it, but it goes without saying that I must be held no less responsible.

VYSHINSKY: Was it done with your knowledge?

IKRAMOV: Of course. And if I had wanted to, I could have exposed it. Wrecking on an equally large scale, to which we closed our eyes, took place in the building operations of the People's Commissariat of Light Industry, at the cotton plants and the silk mills. I cannot remember the figures just now, but enormous sums were invested in building operations that were carried over from year to year. I think that the building operations of the People's Commissariat of Light Industry in the silk branch were planned at 300,000,000 rubles. Of this, 80,000,000 rubles have been invested in construction work, and the remainder is carried over from year to year in the form of uncompleted construction. In Namangan the construction of a silk-winding mill was begun. About one and a half or two million rubles were spent, but in the middle of the year it was said that the building job would have to be put into conservation. I was very much astonished, because I did not know the technique of this business. It was said that half a million rubles would be required for conservation purposes, and the People's Commissariat of Light Industry did in fact assign half a million rubles for conservation purposes.

Five million rubles were spent on the construction of a cotton ginning plant in Bokhara. The plant was ready, but could not function, even though the machinery had been delivered. Why? Because there were no presses.

VYSHINSKY: How much does a press cost?

IKRAMOV: Probably about 100,000 or 200,000 rubles. Even the houses for the workers and office staffs have been built, but the plant is at a standstill and is now being used as a storehouse.

VYSHINSKY: Who is responsible for that?

IKRAMOV: The People's Commissariat of Light Industry is responsible for it, in particular. But I also am responsible, of course, as a man who closed his eyes to it.

321

VYSHINSKY: You shielded it?

IKRAMOV: Of course. I pretended that I saw nothing. The same applies to the cotton warehouses. That is what I have to say in reference to wrecking work. Now as to insurrections. Faizulla spoke about this in his testimony.

VYSHINSKY: What did you do to organize insurrectionary bands?

IKRAMOV: We gave them instructions to this effect. What was actually done, I do not know. But Baltabayev said that Almazov had told him that he had already started on this work in the Margalan district and that he already had some cadres.

VYSHINSKY: That is, you mustered cadres?

IKRAMOV: Then Faizulla, I think it was, told me that preparations in this direction were being made in Bokhara. That is what I have to say about my crimes against the Soviet power. If I may sum up, I would formulate my crimes as follows: treason to the Socialist fatherland and treason to the Soviet people, in the first place to the Uzbek people, who had nurtured me and reared me.

THE PRESIDENT (to Vyshinsky): Have you any questions to put to the accused Ikramov?

VYSHINSKY: No.

THE PRESIDENT: Adjournment for half an hour.

*   *   *

COMMANDANT OF THE COURT: The Court is coming, please rise.

THE PRESIDENT: Please be seated. The session is resumed.

(To Vyshinsky.) Have you any questions to put to the accused Ikramov?

VYSHINSKY: I have a question to put to the accused Bessonov.

THE PRESIDENT: Very well.

VYSHINSKY: Accused Bessonov, I would like you to give us more precise information about your meeting with the Socialist-Revolutionary Maslov. You told us on the first day of the trial that you had received instructions from Pyatakov to establish connections with the Socialist-Revolutionaries?

BESSONOV: Yes, I did say that.

VYSHINSKY: Through whom did you do this?

BESSONOV: I am referring to connections with the "Trudovaya Krestyanskaya Partia."

VYSHINSKY: A Socialist-Revolutionary Party?

BESSONOV: The base of which consisted of remnants of the old Socialist-Revolutionary Party.

VYSHINSKY: And so you were referring to connections with the "Trudovaya Krestyanskaya Partia," which was made up of remnants of the old Socialist-Revolutionary Party?

BESSONOV: Yes, that is so.

VYSHINSKY: Continue.

BESSONOV: In the autumn of 1934, during one of my usual meetings with Pyatakov, he referred for the first time to my Socialist-Revolutionary past, and, in particular, questioned me very closely about the Vologda period of my activities. I gave him a detailed description of the active figures in the Northern group of the Socialist-Revolutionary Party, in particular of Sergei Semyonovich Maslov, who was in the past, and is at present, a leader of the "Trudovaya Krestyanskaya Partia," which he had founded while in exile abroad. I asked Pyatakov why he was interested in my Socialist-Revolutionary past. Pyatakov said that he had reasons, which had been partly suggested by conversations with the Rights and had partly arisen in his own mind independently. And, indeed, before I left for Berlin, about a month after this conversation, Pyatakov asked me to go and see Maslov, justifying the necessity for this meeting by the following arguments. Firstly, he had information, coming from the "bloc of Rights and Trotskyites," that the "Trudovaya Krestyanskaya Partia" possessed fairly considerable cadres among the rural intelligentsia, chiefly among co-operative officials and agronomists. Its program and tactics were such as to make it an organization with which contact could easily and should be established. As I knew Maslov very well from past work, when I was still in the Socialist-Revolutionary Party, and as I was permanently residing abroad, it seemed to him that I was a suitable person to sound out the ground for an agreement with the "Trudovaya Krestyanskaya Partia."

VYSHINSKY: An agreement of the "Trudovaya Krestyanskaya Partia" with whom?

BESSONOV: Pyatakov spoke in his own name, that is, in the name of the Trotskyites and of the bloc. As I have said, the idea of the agreement arose in his mind partly independently, partly under the influence of conversations with the Rights.

VYSHINSKY: Do you remember with whom he conducted these conversations?

BESSONOV: He did not mention any names.

VYSHINSKY: But whom did he have in mind?

BESSONOV: I think it was somebody working in the People's Commissariat of Agriculture, because in the course of subsequent negotiations with Maslov I learnt that people working in the Commissariat of Agriculture were involved.

Somewhat later, after my meeting with Maslov, I received instructions to connect Maslov with people working in Czechoslovakia.

VYSHINSKY: Did your meeting with Maslov take place?

BESSONOV: It did; not in 1934, however, but in 1935, in the summer.

VYSHINSKY: Where did it take place?

BESSONOV: In Prague.

VYSHINSKY: Why in Prague?

BESSONOV: Maslov is permanently resident in Prague.

VYSHINSKY: How long has he been living there?

BESSONOV: As far as I know, he has been living in Prague since 1922 or the end of 1921.

VYSHINSKY: Did he settle in Prague shortly after the October Revolution?

BESSONOV: I cannot say exactly, but I think that Maslov emigrated from the Soviet Union in 1921.

VYSHINSKY: In a word, as far as you know he had been living in Prague for a long time?

BESSONOV: Yes.

VYSHINSKY: What was he doing there?

BESSONOV: He was publishing magazines and newspapers.

VYSHINSKY: On what funds?

BESSONOV: That was elucidated during my talk with him. . . .

VYSHINSKY: On what funds was he publishing newspapers and magazines?

BESSONOV: At the beginning of the conversation—that question interested me too—I elucidated what he possessed.

VYSHINSKY: Or on what funds he was living?

BESSONOV: He was living quite well. He depends upon his old friends. When I asked him about this aspect of the matter, Maslov said that he received funds from the "Trudovaya Krestyanskaya Partia." This party was formed in 1921.

VYSHINSKY: I am not interested how it was formed, or what its ideas are, but on what funds it existed.

BESSONOV: You want me to say on what funds?

VYSHINSKY:·Yes, if you know.

BESSONOV: He said: the same as you. I spoke to him in the name of Pyatakov.

VYSHINSKY: Who was this "you"?

BESSONOV: "You" means the Trotskyites. He said that if you are not squeamish about receiving funds for your activities, still less can you expect Maslov to be. He frankly said that he had sources of financial aid among Polish, Rumanian and Yugoslavian circles.

VYSHINSKY: That is, to put it bluntly, how should this be interpreted in the language of actual relations?

BESSONOV: In each of these countries there is a fairly large section of the ruling class which is interested both in the activities

324

of the "Trudovaya Krestyanskaya Partia" and in the activities of the "bloc of Rights and Trotskyites."

VYSHINSKY: That is, in other words, they were maintained by them?

BESSONOV: By these circles.

VYSHINSKY: By these reactionary, bourgeois circles?

BESSONOV: Yes.

VYSHINSKY: And were not the Socialist-Revolutionaries connected with intelligence services?

BESSONOV: I learnt at the beginning of the conversation with Maslov that he was connected with the Henlein organization.

VYSHINSKY: What sort of an organization is that?

BESSONOV: The Henlein organization is so well known ...

VYSHINSKY: Tell us about it all the same.

BESSONOV: It is an organization which is pursuing the aim of uniting Bohemia to Germany. It is an organization which is a fascist organization in both form and content.

VYSHINSKY: Maslov published his newspapers and magazines, and at the same time he and his organization were maintained by reactionary bourgeois circles—Polish, Rumanian and Bulgarian?

BESSONOV: Yes.

VYSHINSKY: He was in addition connected with other organizations?

BESSONOV: He was connected with the Henlein organization.

VYSHINSKY: What sort of an organization is that? What is it?

BESSONOV: An agency of German fascism in Czechoslovakia.

VYSHINSKY: Consequently, he is connected with the German intelligence service?

BESSONOV: I am accustomed to precision in such matters. . . .

THE PRESIDENT: Will you speak a little louder, please?

BESSONOV: It is an organization of fascist agents directed by the Foreign Department of the National-Socialist Party, which has its headquarters in Munich and which is one of the organizations of German fascism for the development of aggression, but which, strictly speaking, cannot be called an intelligence service.

VYSHINSKY: It pursues its specific tasks, and works in accordance with a common plan with the intelligence service?

BESSONOV: Quite right.

VYSHINSKY: What did you talk to Maslov about?

BESSONOV: I explained to him the substance of the instructions I had received from Pyatakov. After explaining in fairly great detail what the "Trudovaya Krestyanskaya Partia," in his opinion, or as he described it, had at its disposal in the Soviet Union, about which I have given detailed information during the preliminary investigation—I do not know if it is necessary to speak about

325

it here—Maslov mentioned three conditions on which he was prepared to place his organization under the general control of the "bloc of Rights and Trotskyites." These conditions, which were very heterogeneous, contained an agreement on certain questions of program. He referred in particular to the rural question and the national question, but stressed the fact that this was of no essential importance. His main condition was that he should be immediately given a certain sum of money by the "bloc of Rights and Trotskyites," both in foreign currency and in Soviet currency. Then the work of the "Trudovaya Krestyanskaya Partia" was to be afforded the legal opportunities which the bloc possessed. In return for these conditions, he thought it possible to give directions to his organization in the Soviet Union and to subordinate the work of the "Trudovaya Krestyanskaya Partia" to the "bloc of Rights and Trotskyites" along all lines. Of course, I could not reply to all these questions. But in 1936 I put Maslov in touch with Trotsky's representative, who came to an arrangement with him on this point.

VYSHINSKY: Tell us, when talking to you, did Maslov express the wish to be put in contact with Trotsky?

BESSONOV: He said that he had tried to establish contact with Trotsky through a Czech Trotskyite.

VYSHINSKY: But did he not say on whose initiative, who it was that first expressed the desire to arrange a meeting with Trotsky? Did he not refer to the Henlein?

BESSONOV: He did. I mentioned this in the preliminary investigation. That is how it was. He did refer to the Henlein. He said that preparations had recently been made for amalgamation with the Henlein organization, and that in the near future an amalgamation would take place of all the opposition groups which were active in the Soviet Union and co-ordinating their activities with the appropriate organs of fascist Germany.

VYSHINSKY: That is, all the fascist groups?

BESSONOV: Yes.

VYSHINSKY: How did he regard this prospect of connections with Trotsky?

BESSONOV: This connection was established by me.

VYSHINSKY: That is, the commission you had to establish contact between Maslov and Trotsky was fulfilled by you, and an agreement was arrived at as a result? That agreement was based on those few conditions you have mentioned?

BESSONOV: These conditions form an integral part of it. As to the organizational side, there were two conditions: firstly, that the "Trudovaya Krestyanskaya Partia" was to be given a certain sum of money by the "bloc of Rights and Trotskyites" in foreign currency and Soviet currency, and that the "bloc of Rights and Trots-

326

kyites" was to place at the disposal of Maslov, and hence of the "Trudovaya Krestyanskaya Partia," the legal opportunities which the "bloc of Rights and Trotskyites" possessed in view of the official positions held by its members. Whether this agreement included an arrangement on questions of program, which Maslov himself did not consider very essential, I cannot say; but I do in fact consider that this question did not have any serious significance in the negotiations, a point which Maslov himself stressed.

VYSHINSKY: Did you in your talk with Maslov refer in one degree or an other to Bukharin and Rykov?

BESSONOV: Maslov said that he was very well informed on the development of the anti-Soviet groups within the Soviet Union, and that he was informed both by reports received from his foreign friends, as he put it, and by reports he received directly from his nuclei in the Soviet Union.

In addition, he said that he had taken steps to establish contact with some of the Rights. In this connection he mentioned the name of A. I. Muralov of the People's Commissariat of Agriculture, with whom he had established connections through some co-operator, whose name I cannot now recall.

VYSHINSKY: Consequently, he was aware of the anti-Soviet activities of Bukharin and Rykov?

BESSONOV: Undoubtedly.

VYSHINSKY: And had connections with the Rights himself?

BESSONOV: He described this contact as a step towards the establishment of stable organizational connections with the Rights.

VYSHINSKY: There was an organizational contact, which subsequently, thanks to his measures, was transformed into stable organizational connections?

BESSONOV: Yes, in 1935.

VYSHINSKY: What else can you say in addition to what you have said?

BESSONOV: Only perhaps about what the "Trudovaya Krestyanskaya Partia" had at its disposal.

VYSHINSKY: This concerns the investigation of the case of the "Trudovaya Krestyanskaya Partia" rather than the present case. I have no more questions.

THE PRESIDENT: We shall now proceed to the interrogation of the accused Bukharin.

BUKHARIN: I have a request to make to the Court on the following two points: firstly, to give me the opportunity of freely presenting my case to the Court, and, secondly, to permit me at the beginning of my statement to dwell more or less, as far as time will permit, on an analysis of the ideological and political stand of the criminal "bloc of Rights and Trotskyites," for the following reasons: firstly, because comparatively little has been said about it, secondly, because it has a certain public interest, and thirdly, because Citizen the Public Prosecutor put this question at the previous session, if I am not mistaken.

VYSHINSKY: If the accused Bukharin intends in any way to restrict the right of the State Prosecutor to put him questions in the course of his explanations, I think that Comrade the President should explain to Bukharin that the right of the Prosecutor to put questions is based on law. I therefore ask that this request should be denied, as provided in the Code of Criminal Procedure.

BUKHARIN: That is not what I meant by my request.

THE PRESIDENT: The first question to the accused Bukharin: Do you confirm the testimony you gave at the preliminary investigation about your anti-Soviet activities?

BUKHARIN: I confirm my testimony fully and entirely.

THE PRESIDENT: What do you wish to say about your anti-Soviet activities? And Comrade the Procurator is entitled to put questions.

VYSHINSKY: Allow me to begin the interrogation of the accused Bukharin. Formulate briefly what exactly it is you plead guilty to.

BUKHARIN: Firstly, to belonging to the counter-revolutionary "bloc of Rights and Trotskyites."

VYSHINSKY: Since what year?

BUKHARIN: From the moment the bloc was formed. Even before that, I plead guilty to belonging to the counter-revolutionary organization of the Rights.

VYSHINSKY: Since what year?

BUKHARIN: Roughly since 1928. I plead guilty to being one of the outstanding leaders of this "bloc of Rights and Trotskyites." Consequently, I plead guilty to what directly follows from this, the sum total of crimes committed by this counter-revolutionary organization, irrespective of whether or not I knew of, whether or not I took a direct part, in any particular act. Because I am responsible as one of the leaders and not as a cog of this counter-revolutionary organization.

VYSHINSKY: What aims were pursued by this counter-revolutionary organization?

BUKHARIN: This counter-revolutionary organization, to formulate it briefly . . .

VYSHINSKY: Yes, briefly for the present.

BUKHARIN: The principal aim it pursued although, so to speak, it did not fully realize it, and did not dot all the "i's"—was essentially the aim of restoring capitalist relations in the U.S.S.R.

VYSHINSKY: The overthrow of the Soviet power?

328

BUKHARIN: The overthrow of the Soviet power was a means to this end.

VYSHINSKY: By means of?

BUKHARIN: As is known . . .

VYSHINSKY: By means of a forcible overthrow?

BUKHARIN: Yes, by means of the forcible overthrow of this power.

VYSHINSKY: With the help of?

BUKHARIN: With the help of all the difficulties encountered by the Soviet power; in particular, with the help of a war which prognostically was in prospect.

VYSHINSKY: Which was prognostically in prospect, with whose help?

BUKHARIN: With the help of foreign states.

VYSHINSKY: On condition?

BUKHARIN: On condition, to put it concretely, of a number of concessions.

VYSHINSKY: To the extent of . . .

BUKHARIN: To the extent of the cession of territory.

VYSHINSKY: That is?

BUKHARIN: If all the "i's" are dotted—on condition of the dismemberment of the U.S.S.R.

VYSHINSKY: The severance of whole regions and republics from the U.S.S.R.?

BUKHARIN: Yes.

VYSHINSKY: For example?

BUKHARIN: The Ukraine, the Maritime Region, Byelorussia.

VYSHINSKY: In whose favour?

BUKHARIN: In favour of the corresponding states, whose geographical and political . . .

VYSHINSKY: Which exactly?

BUKHARIN: In favour of Germany, in favour of Japan, and partly in favour of England.

VYSHINSKY: So, that was the agreement with the circles concerned? I know of one agreement which the bloc had.

BUKHARIN: Yes, the bloc had an agreement.

VYSHINSKY: And also by means of weakening the defensive power?

BUKHARIN: You see, this question was not discussed, at least not in my presence.

VYSHINSKY: And what was the position with regard to wrecking?

BUKHARIN: The position with regard to wrecking was that in the end, especially under pressure of the Trotskyite part of the so-called contact centre, which arose roughly in 1933, despite

329

a number of internal differences and manipulatory political mechanics, which are of no interest to the investigation, after
various vicissitudes, disputes and so on, the orientation on wrecking
was adopted.

VYSHINSKY: Did it tend to weaken the defensive power of
our country?

BUKHARIN: Naturally.

VYSHINSKY: Consequently, there was an orientation on the
weakening, the undermining of defensive power?

BUKHARIN: Not formally, but essentially it was so.

VYSHINSKY: But the actions and activity in this direction
were clear?

BUKHARIN: Yes.

VYSHINSKY: Can you say the same about diversive acts?

BUKHARIN: With regard to diversive acts—by virtue of
the division of labour and my definite functions, of which you
know—I mainly occupied myself with the problematics of general
leadership and with the ideological side; this, of course, did not
exclude either my being aware of the practical side of the matter,
or the adoption of a number of practical steps on my part.

VYSHINSKY: As I understand you, there was a division of
labour among you.

BUKHARIN: But I, Citizen Procurator, say that I bear responsibility for the bloc.

VYSHINSKY: But the bloc which you headed set itself the
aim of organizing diversive acts?

BUKHARIN: As far as I can judge by various things that
rise in my memory, this was made dependent on concrete circumstances and concrete conditions.

VYSHINSKY: As you see from the trial, the circumstances
were concrete enough. Did you and Khodjayev discuss the fact that
too little wrecking was being done, and being done badly?

BUKHARIN: About accelerating wrecking there was no talk.

VYSHINSKY: Permit me to question the accused Khodjayev.

THE PRESIDENT: You may.

VYSHINSKY: Accused Khodjayev, did you discuss with
Bukharin the question of accelerating wrecking activities?

KHODJAYEV: In August 1936, when I spoke to Bukharin
in my country house, he said that wrecking work was feeble in
our nationalist organization.

VYSHINSKY: And what ought to be done about it?

KHODJAYEV: To intensify it, and not only intensify the
wrecking work, but to proceed to the organization of uprisings,
terrorism, and so on.

VYSHINSKY: Accused Bukharin, is what Khodjayev say
correct?

BUKHARIN: No.

VYSHINSKY: Was the organization of an insurrectionary movement one of your aims?

BUKHARIN: There was an insurrectionary orientation.

VYSHINSKY: There was an orientation? Did you send Slepkov to the North Caucasus to organize this business? Did you send Yakovenko to Biisk for the same purpose?

BUKHARIN: Yes.

VYSHINSKY: And is this not what Khodjayev says in relation to Central Asia?

BUKHARIN: I thought that when you asked about Central Asia my answer should deal only with Central Asia.

VYSHINSKY: And so, you deny this fact with regard to Central Asia, but not the line of the bloc, whereas I asked you about the line of the bloc.

BUKHARIN: And I said that the question was decided from case to case, depending upon geographical, political and other conditions.

VYSHINSKY: You deny Khodjayev's testimony? I invited Khodjayev just now to testify against you because I consider it important to illustrate the fact that your "bloc of Rights and Trotskyites" gave instructions from case to case, as you put it, depending upon circumstances, for the organization of an insurrectionary, diversionist and wrecking movement. Do you agree with that?

BUKHARIN: I agree with that. Only I must clarify it, so as to avoid confusion. The uprisings you are referring to took place in 1930, whereas the "bloc of Rights and Trotskyites" was organized, as you are aware, Citizen Procurator, in 1933.

VYSHINSKY: But its tactics did not differ in any way from the tactics of your Right centre. Do you agree with that?

BUKHARIN: Yes.

VYSHINSKY: That is, the organization of an insurrectionary movement was part of the activities of the "bloc of Rights and Trotskyites" as well?

BUKHARIN: It was.

VYSHINSKY: And you bear responsibility for it?

BUKHARIN: I have already said that I bear responsibility for the sum total of the actions.

VYSHINSKY: Did the bloc stand for the organization of terrorist acts, the assassination of leaders of the Party and the Soviet government?

BUKHARIN: It did, and I think that the organization of this must be dated back roughly to 1932, the autumn.

VYSHINSKY: And what was your relation to the assassination of Sergei Mironovich Kirov? Was this assassination also committed with the knowledge and on the instructions of the "bloc of Rights and Trotskyites"?

BUKHARIN: That I did not know.

VYSHINSKY: I ask you, was this assassination committed with the knowledge and on the instructions of the "bloc of Rights and Trotskyites"?

BUKHARIN: And I repeat that I do not know, Citizen Procurator.

VYSHINSKY: You did not know about this specifically in relation to the assassination of S. M. Kirov?

BUKHARIN: Not specifically, but . . .

VYSHINSKY: Permit me to question the accused Rykov.

THE PRESIDENT: You may.

VYSHINSKY: Accused Rykov, what do you know about the assassination of Sergei Mironovich Kirov?

RYKOV: I know nothing about the participation of the Rights or the Right part of the bloc in the assassination of Kirov.

VYSHINSKY: In general, were you aware of preparations for terrorist acts, for the assassination of members of the Party and the government?

RYKOV: As one of the leaders of the Right part of this bloc, I took part in the organization of a number of terrorist groups and in preparations for terrorist acts. As I have said in my testimony, I do not know of a single decision of the Right centre, through which I was related with the "bloc of Rights and Trotskyites," about the actual commission of assassinations. . . .

VYSHINSKY: About the actual commission. So. Do you know that one of the aims of the "bloc of Rights and Trotskyites" was to organize and commit terrorist acts against leaders of the Party and the government?

RYKOV: I said more than that, I said that I personally organized terrorist groups. But you are asking me whether I knew of such aims through some third person.

VYSHINSKY: I am asking whether the "bloc of Rights and Trotskyites" had any relation to the assassination of Comrade Kirov.

RYKOV: I have no information regarding the relation of the Right part to this assassination, and therefore I am convinced to this day that the assassination of Kirov was carried out by the Trotskyites without the knowledge of the Rights. Of course, I might not have known about it.

VYSHINSKY: Were you connected with Yenukidze?

RYKOV: With Yenukidze? Very little.

VYSHINSKY: Was he a member of the "bloc of Rights and Trotskyites"?

RYKOV: He was, since 1933.

VYSHINSKY: Which part did he represent in this bloc, the Trotskyites or the Rights? To which did he gravitate?

RYKOV: He must have represented the Right part.

VYSHINSKY: Very well; please be seated. Permit me to question the accused Yagoda. Accused Yagoda, do you know that Yenukidze, of whom the accused Rykov just spoke, represented the Right part of the bloc and that he had direct relation to the organization of the assassination of Sergei Mironovich Kirov?

YAGODA: Both Rykov and Bukharin are telling lies. Rykov and Yenukidze were present at the meeting of the centre where the question of assassinating S. M. Kirov was discussed.

VYSHINSKY: Did the Rights have any relation to this?

YAGODA: Direct relation, because it was a bloc of Rights and Trotskyites.

VYSHINSKY: Did the accused Rykov and Bukharin in particular have any relation to the assassination?

YAGODA: Direct relation.

VYSHINSKY: Did you, as a member of the "bloc of Rights and Trotskyites," have any relation to this assassination?

YAGODA: I did.

VYSHINSKY: Are Bukharin and Rykov telling the truth when they say that they knew nothing about it?

YAGODA: That cannot be so, because when Yenukidze told me that they, that is, the "bloc of Rights and Trotskyites," had decided at a joint meeting to commit a terrorist act against Kirov, I categorically objected. . . .

VYSHINSKY: Why?

YAGODA: I declared that I would never permit any terrorist acts. I regarded it as absolutely unnecessary.

VYSHINSKY: And dangerous for the organization?

YAGODA: Of course.

VYSHINSKY: Nevertheless?

YAGODA: Nevertheless Yenukidze confirmed . . .

VYSHINSKY: What?

YAGODA: That at this meeting they . . .

VYSHINSKY: Who were they?

YAGODA: Rykov and Yenukidze at first categorically objected. . . .

VYSHINSKY: To what?

YAGODA: To the commission of a terrorist act. But under the pressure of the remaining part of the "bloc of Rights and Trotskyites" . . .

VYSHINSKY: Principally the Trotskyites?

YAGODA: Yes, under the pressure of the remaining part of

333

the "bloc of Rights and Trotskyites," they gave their consent. So Yenukidze told me.

VYSHINSKY: After this, did you personally take any measures to effect the assassination of Sergei Mironovich Kirov?

YAGODA: I personally?

VYSHINSKY: Yes, as a member of the bloc.

YAGODA: I gave instructions . . .

VYSHINSKY: To whom?

YAGODA: To Zaporozhetz in Leningrad. That is not quite how it was.

VYSHINSKY: We shall speak about that later. What I want now is to elucidate the part played by Rykov and Bukharin in this villainous act.

YAGODA: I gave instructions to Zaporozhetz. When Nikolayev was detained . . .

VYSHINSKY: The first time?

YAGODA: Yes. Zaporozhetz came to Moscow and reported to me that a man had been detained . . .

VYSHINSKY: In whose briefcase . . .

YAGODA: There was a revolver and a diary. And he released him.

VYSHINSKY: And you approved of this?

YAGODA: I just took note of the fact.

VYSHINSKY: And then you gave instructions not to place obstacles in the way of the murder of Sergei Mironovich Kirov?

YAGODA: Yes, I did. . . . It was not like that.

VYSHINSKY: In a somewhat different form?

YAGODA: It was not like that, but it is not important.

VYSHINSKY: Did you give instructions?

YAGODA: I have confirmed that.

VYSHINSKY: You have. Be seated.

THE PRESIDENT (to Vyshinsky): Have you any more questions?

VYSHINSKY: I have another question to put to Bukharin. Was your attitude to terrorism positive or negative, to terrorism against Soviet statesmen?

BUKHARIN: I understand. The question of terrorism arose for the first time for me in a conversation with Pyatakov, and I must say that I knew that Trotsky was insisting on terrorist tactics. At that time I objected.

VYSHINSKY: When was that?

BUKHARIN: In the end Pyatakov and I found a common language under the formula that it would all work out in the end and that all differences would be ironed out in one way or another. And then I have reported to you, Citizen State Prosecutor . . .

VYSHINSKY: You reported to the Court in my presence . . .

334

BUKHARIN: I reported to the Court in your presence that actually the orientation on terrorism, strictly speaking, was already contained in the Ryutin platform.

VYSHINSKY: I understand. I want to know whether your attitude towards terrorism was a positive one?

BUKHARIN: What do you mean by that?

VYSHINSKY: That you were in favour of the assassination of leaders of our Party and the government.

BUKHARIN: You ask whether I, as a member of the centre of Rights and Trotskyites, was in favour of . . .

VYSHINSKY: Terrorist acts.

BUKHARIN: I was.

VYSHINSKY: Against whom?

BUKHARIN: Against the leaders of the Party and the government.

VYSHINSKY: You will tell us the details later. You came to favour this roughly in 1929-30?

BUKHARIN: No, I think it was roughly in 1932.

VYSHINSKY: But were you not in favour of the assassination of leaders of our Party and government in 1918?

BUKHARIN: No, I was not.

VYSHINSKY: Were you in favour of the arrest of Lenin?

BUKHARIN: His arrest? There were two such cases—about the first of which I told Lenin himself; as to the second, I kept silent about it for reasons of secrecy—regarding which, if you like, I can speak in greater detail. It did take place.

VYSHINSKY: Did it take place?

BUKHARIN: Yes.

VYSHINSKY: And about the assassination of Vladimir Ilyich?

BUKHARIN: The first time it was proposed to keep him under restraint for twenty-four hours. There was such a formula. But in the second case . . .

VYSHINSKY: But if Vladimir Ilyich were to resist arrest?

BUKHARIN: But Vladimir Ilyich, as you know, never entered into armed conflicts. He was not a brawler.

VYSHINSKY: And so you expected that when you came to arrest him, Vladimir Ilyich would not resist?

BUKHARIN: You see, I can mention the case of another man. When the "Left" Socialist-Revolutionaries arrested Dzerzhinsky,[7] he did not offer armed resistance either.

VYSHINSKY: That always depends upon the particular circumstances of the case. And so, in this case you counted that there would be no resistance?

BUKHARIN: Yes.

VYSHINSKY: And did you not count upon the arrest of Comrade Stalin in 1918?

BUKHARIN: At that time there were several talks about . . .

VYSHINSKY: I am not asking about talks, but about a plan for the arrest of Comrade Stalin.

BUKHARIN: And I say that if I do not agree with your description of it as a plan, then permit me to prove to the Court how it was in actual fact. Then, it may be said, it was not a plan, but a talk.

VYSHINSKY: What about?

BUKHARIN: There was the same talk about the formation of a new government of "Left Communists."

VYSHINSKY: And I ask you, did you have a plan for the arrest of Comrade Stalin in 1918?

BUKHARIN: Not of Stalin, but there was a plan for the arrest of Lenin, Stalin and Sverdlov.

VYSHINSKY: All three: Lenin, Stalin and Sverdlov?

BUKHARIN: Quite so.

VYSHINSKY: And so, not Comrade Stalin, but Comrades Stalin, Lenin and Sverdlov?

BUKHARIN: Exactly.

VYSHINSKY: There was a plan of arrest?

BUKHARIN: I say that there was not a plan, but talks on the subject.

VYSHINSKY: And what about the assassination of Comrades Stalin, Lenin and Sverdlov?

BUKHARIN: Under no circumstances.

VYSHINSKY: I shall request the Court at the end of today's session, or at the next session of the Court, to call as witnesses on this question Yakovleva, a former active member of the group of "Left Communists," Ossinsky and Mantsev, former active members of the so-called group of "Left Communists," and then the "Left" Socialist-Revolutionaries, Karelin and Kamkov, members of the Central Committee of the "Left" Socialist-Revolutionaries, in order to question them whether Bukharin and the "Left Communists," whom he headed at the time, together with the "Left" Socialist-Revolutionaries, had a plan, and what kind of plan, for the arrest and assassination of Comrades Lenin, Stalin and Sverdlov. I have no more questions for the present.

BUKHARIN: May I begin?

THE PRESIDENT (after conferring with the Members of the Court): The Court has decided to grant the request of the State Prosecutor to summon as witnesses Yakovleva, Ossinsky, Mantsev, Karelin and Kamkov.

VYSHINSKY: That fully satisfies me.

THE PRESIDENT: You have no more questions to put to Bukharin for the present?

VYSHINSKY: Not for the present.

THE PRESIDENT: I must explain to the accused Bukharin that it is not a speech for the defence he must make, nor a last plea.

BUKHARIN: I understand that.

THE PRESIDENT: And so, if you want to say anything about your criminal anti-Soviet activities, you may do so.

BUKHARIN: I want to deal with the subject of the restoration of capitalism. May I?

VYSHINSKY: Of course, that is your chief speciality.

BUKHARIN: I want first to deal with ideological positions, not in the sense of declining responsibility for practical, criminal counter-revolutionary activities. I have not the slightest desire that the proletarian Court should conceive such an opinion. I want to reply to the question which Citizen the State Prosecutor put to Rakovsky, namely, for the sake of what did the "bloc of Rights and Trotskyites" carry on such a criminal struggle against the Soviet power? I realize that I am not a lecturer and must not preach a sermon here, but that I am an accused person who must bear responsibility as a criminal, facing the Court of the proletarian country. But just because it seems to me that this trial is of public importance, and because this question has been dealt with extremely little, I thought that it would be useful to dwell on the program which has never been written down anywhere, on the practical program of the "bloc of Rights and Trotskyites," and to decipher one formula, namely, what is meant by the restoration of capitalism, in the way it was visualized and conceived in the circles of the "bloc of Rights and Trotskyites." I repeat that in desiring to dwell upon this aspect of the matter I have no wish to disclaim responsibility for various practical things, for my counter-revolutionary crimes. But I want to say that I was not one of the cogs of counter-revolution, but one of the leaders of counter-revolution; and as one of the leaders I play and answer in a far greater degree, bear far greater responsibility than any of the cogs. And so I cannot be suspected of wanting to wriggle out of or repudiate responsibility, even if I were not a member of the Right and Trotskyite organization. The Court and the public opinion of our country, like the public opinion of other countries, as far as progressive mankind is concerned, can judge how people sank to such depths, how we all became rabid counter-revolutionaries, traitors to the Socialist fatherland, and how we turned into spies, terrorists and restorers of capitalism, and what, in the end, were the ideas and political standpoint of the "bloc of Rights and Trotskyites." We embarked on treachery, crime and treason. But for the sake of what did we embark on this? We turned into an insurrectionary band, we organized terrorist groups, engaged in wrecking activities, wanted to overthrow the valiant leadership of Stalin, the Soviet government of the proletariat.

337

One of the very widespread replies is that through the logic of the struggle we were forced to become counter-revolutionaries, plotters and traitors, that we were led to the shame, to the crime, that has brought us into the criminal dock. I need not say that such things do not happen in public life; here there is a logic, the logic of the struggle is combined with the methods of the struggle, with the platform.

I want to dwell on these facts, although I am convinced that actually such a terminology may sound rather strange in relation to such criminal activities, but nevertheless it seems important to me to dwell on this.

It has been proved many times, and repeated tens of thousands of times, that the Right deviation, from the moment of its inception, when it was still in an embryo, from the moment of its inception set itself the aim of restoring capitalism. I do not intend to speak about this. I want to speak of another aspect of the matter, from a far more important standpoint, from the objective side of this matter, because here there arises the problem of accountability and judgment from the standpoint of the crimes revealed in Court, all the more so because I am one of the leaders in the dock. We must here start from the beginning.

The Right counter-revolutionaries seemed at first to be a "deviation"; they seemed, at a first glance, to be people who began with discontent in connection with collectivization, in connection with industrialization, with the fact, as they claimed, that industrialization was destroying production. This, at a first glance, seemed to be the chief thing. Then the Ryutin platform appeared. When all the state machines, when all the means, when all the best forces were flung into the industrialization of the country, into collectivization, we found ourselves, literally in twenty-four hours, on the other shore, we found ourselves with the kulaks, with the counter-revolutionaries, we found ourselves with the capitalist remnants which still existed at the time in the sphere of trade. Hence it follows that the basic meaning, the judgment, from the subjective standpoint, is clear. Here we went through a very interesting process, an over-estimation of individual enterprise, a crawling over to its idealization, the idealization of the property-owner. Such was the evolution. Our program was—the prosperous peasant farm of the individual, but in fact the kulak became an end in itself. We were ironical about the collective farms. We, the counter-revolutionary plotters, came at that time more and more to display the psychology that collective farms were music of the future.[8] What was necessary was to develop rich property-owners. This was the tremendous change that took place in our standpoint and psychology. In 1917 it would never have occurred to any of the members of the Party, myself included, to pity Whiteguards who had been killed; yet in the period of the liquidation of the kulaks, in 1929-30, we pitied the expropriated kulaks, from so-called humanitarian motives. To whom would it have occurred in 1919 to blame the dislocation of our economic life on the Bolsheviks, and not on sabotage? To nobody. It would have sounded as frank and open treason. Yet I myself in 1928 invented the formula about the military-feudal exploitation of the peasantry, that is, I put the blame for the costs of the class struggle not on the class which was hostile to the proletariat, but on the leaders of the proletariat itself. This was already a swing of 180 degrees. This meant that ideological and political platforms grew into counter-revolutionary platforms. Kulak farming and kulak interests actually became a point of program. The logic of the struggle led to the logic of ideas and to a change of our psychology, to the counter-revolutionizing of our aims.

Take industry. At first we raised an outcry about over-industrialization, about over-straining the budget, and so on. But as a matter of fact this was a program demand, it was the ideal of a kulak agrarian country with an industrial appendage. And psychologically? Psychologically, we, who at one time had advocated Socialist industrialism, began to regard with a shrug of the shoulders, with irony, and then with anger at bottom, our huge, gigantically growing factories as monstrous gluttons which consumed everything, deprived the broad masses of articles of consumption, and represented a certain danger. The heroic efforts of the foremost workers . . .

THE PRESIDENT: Accused Bukharin, you have again not understood me. You are not making your last plea now. You were asked to testify to your anti-Soviet, counter-revolutionary activities, but you are giving us a lecture. In your last plea you may say whatever you like. I am explaining this to you for the third time.

BUKHARIN: Then permit me very briefly . . .

VYSHINSKY: Tell me, accused Bukharin, how all this took shape in practice in your anti-Soviet activities.

BUKHARIN: Then permit me to enumerate certain points of program. And then I will immediately pass on to relate my practical counter-revolutionary activities. May I, Citizen the President?

THE PRESIDENT: Only more briefly, if you please. You will have an opportunity to make a speech as your own Counsel for Defence.

BUKHARIN: This is not my defence, it is my self-accusation. I have not said a single word in my defence. If my program stand were to be formulated practically, it would be, in the economic sphere, state capitalism,[9] the prosperous muzhik[10] individual, the curtailment of the collective farms, foreign concessions, surrender of the monopoly of foreign trade, and, as a result—the restoration of capitalism in the country.

339

VYSHINSKY: What did your aims amount to? What general prognosis did you make?

BUKHARIN: The prognosis was that there would be a heavy list towards capitalism.

VYSHINSKY: And what transpired?

BUKHARIN: What transpired was quite different.

VYSHINSKY: What transpired was the complete victory of Socialism.

BUKHARIN: The complete victory of Socialism.

VYSHINSKY: And the complete collapse of your prognosis.

BUKHARIN: And the complete collapse of our prognosis. Inside the country our actual program—this I think must be said with all emphasis—was a lapse into bourgeois-democratic freedom, coalition, because from the bloc with the Mensheviks, Socialist-Revolutionaries, and the like, it follows that there would be freedom of parties, freedom of coalition, and follows quite logically from the combination of forces for struggle, because if allies are chosen for overthrowing the government, on the day after the possible victory they would be partners in power. A lapse not only into the ways of bourgeois-democratic freedom, but in the political sense into ways where there are undoubtedly elements of Caesarism.

VYSHINSKY: Say fascism simply.

BUKHARIN: Since in the circles of the "bloc of Rights and Trotskyites" there was an ideological orientation towards the kulaks and at the same time an orientation towards a "palace revolution" and a coup d'état, towards a military conspiracy and a praetorian guard of counter-revolutionaries, this is nothing other than elements of fascism.

Since the features of state capitalism about which I spoke operate in the sphere of economics . . .

VYSHINSKY: In short, you lapsed into outright rabid fascism.

BUKHARIN: Yes, that is correct, although we did not dot all the "i's." That is the formulation characterizing us as conspirators, restorers of capitalism, true from all points of view. And quite naturally, this was accompanied by a disintegration and degeneration of the whole ideology, our entire practice and methods of struggle.

Now permit me to go straight on with an account of my criminal activity.

VYSHINSKY: Perhaps as a preliminary I might ask you two or three questions of a biographical nature.

BUKHARIN: By all means.

VYSHINSKY: Have you lived in Austria?

BUKHARIN: I have.

VYSHINSKY: For long?

BUKHARIN: 1912 to 1913.

340

VYSHINSKY: You had no connections with the Austrian police?

BUKHARIN: None.

VYSHINSKY: Have you lived in America?

BUKHARIN: Yes.

VYSHINSKY: For long?

BUKHARIN: Yes.

VYSHINSKY: How many months?

BUKHARIN: About seven months.

VYSHINSKY: In America you were not connected with the police?

BUKHARIN: Absolutely not.

VYSHINSKY: On your way from America to Russia you passed through . . .

BUKHARIN: Through Japan.

VYSHINSKY: Did you stop there for long?

BUKHARIN: A week.

VYSHINSKY: You were not recruited during this week?

BUKHARIN: If it pleases you to put such questions . . .

VYSHINSKY: The Code of Criminal Procedure gives me the right to put such questions.

THE PRESIDENT: The Prosecutor has all the more right to put such a question because Bukharin is charged with attempting to assassinate the leaders of the Party as far back as 1918, with raising a hand against the life of Vladimir Ilyich Lenin in 1918.

VYSHINSKY: I am not overstepping the Code of Criminal Procedure. If you like, you can say "no," but I may ask.

BUKHARIN: Quite right.

THE PRESIDENT: The consent of the accused is not required.

VYSHINSKY: You made no connections with the police?

BUKHARIN: Absolutely.

VYSHINSKY: Like Chernov in the bus. I am asking you about connections with some police authority.

BUKHARIN: I had no connections with any police authorities whatsoever.

VYSHINSKY: Then why was it so easy for you to join a bloc which was engaged in espionage work?

BUKHARIN: Concerning espionage work I know absolutely nothing.

VYSHINSKY: What do you mean, you don't know?

BUKHARIN: Just that.

VYSHINSKY: And what was the bloc engaged in?

BUKHARIN: Two people testified here about espionage, Sharangovich and Ivanov, that is to say, two agents-provocateurs.

341

VYSHINSKY: Accused Bukharin, do you consider Rykov an agent-provocateur?

BUKHARIN: No, I do not.

VYSHINSKY (to Rykov): Accused Rykov, do you know that the "bloc of Rights and Trotskyites" conducted espionage work?

RYKOV: I know there were organizations that conducted espionage work.

VYSHINSKY: Tell me, did the Byelorussian national-fascist organization, which was part of your "bloc of Rights and Trotskyites" and which was led by the accused Sharangovich, conduct espionage work?

RYKOV: I have already spoken about that.

VYSHINSKY: It conducted espionage work?

RYKOV: Yes.

VYSHINSKY: It was connected with the Polish intelligence service?

RYKOV: Yes.

VYSHINSKY: You knew about this?

RYKOV: I did.

VYSHINSKY: And Bukharin did not know?

RYKOV: In my opinion, Bukharin also knew.

VYSHINSKY: So, accused Bukharin, it is not Sharangovich who says so, but your pal Rykov.

BUKHARIN: Nevertheless I did not know.

THE PRESIDENT: Comrade Prosecutor, have you any more questions?

VYSHINSKY: I want to make myself clear to the accused Bukharin. Do you understand now why I asked you about Austria?

BUKHARIN: My connection with the Austrian police consisted in my imprisonment in an Austrian fortress.

VYSHINSKY: Accused Sharangovich, you were a Polish spy, although you have been in prison?

SHARANGOVICH: Yes, although I have been in prison.

BUKHARIN: I have been in a Swedish prison, twice in a Russian prison, and in a German prison.

VYSHINSKY: The fact that you have been in jail is no proof that you could not have been a spy.

Accused Rykov, you confirm that after all his terms of confinement in the prisons of various countries, Bukharin, with you, knew of Sharangovich's spy connection with the Polish intelligence service? Knew about it and approved of it?

RYKOV: I knew of organizations which conducted espionage work.

VYSHINSKY: The fact that Bukharin had been in various prisons did not prevent him from approving his accomplices' connections with the Polish intelligence service. You understand this?

RYKOV: No, I do not.

VYSHINSKY: Bukharin understands it.

BUKHARIN: I understand, but I deny it.

THE PRESIDENT: Continue.

BUKHARIN: I must speak briefly about the various stages. Practically speaking, the foundations for my counter-revolutionary activity as far as the Right deviation is concerned, its evolution down to the "bloc of Rights and Trotskyites," with corresponding methods of struggle, with corresponding criminal actions, were laid deliberately as far back as 1919-20, when from my pupils at the Sverdlov University I mustered a distinct group, which began to develop very quickly into a faction. The membership of this group is known. It is in the material of the investigation, and as far as I can judge by the remarks of Citizen the Procurator he has information on the subject.[11]

VYSHINSKY: Among your pupils was Slepkov, the man you sent to the North Caucasus to organize insurrections?

BUKHARIN: Quite true. I can cite several more facts.

VYSHINSKY: Of the same kind?

BUKHARIN: No, not of the same kind.

VYSHINSKY: But of the same type?

BUKHARIN: No.

VYSHINSKY: Well, something similar to it?

BUKHARIN: Excuse me, I cannot explain everything in one word.

VYSHINSKY: Continue.

BUKHARIN: A certain nucleus of cadres was formed which subsequently became one of the component parts in the aggregate counter-revolutionary organization of the Rights, and then, consequently, of the "bloc of Rights and Trotskyites."

About 1923 I wrote a so-called memorandum, which was to be handed to the Central Committee; however, I did not submit it and it passed into circulation among the circles of this school among whom certain views became current which subsequently grew, blossomed and bore correspondingly poisonous fruit. In this memorandum I said that in the leadership of the Party one crisis would give place .[12] .

VYSHINSKY: What you wrote in it is not of the slightest interest to us now.

BUKHARIN: In 1928, when elements of a crisis appeared in the country in the relations between the proletariat and the peasantry, and the Party leadership, headed by Stalin, mapped out a course of overcoming the difficulties and of an offensive against the kulaks, the opposition began to take shape—at first only as an opposition.[13] One of the episodes was that in that year I went to G. G. Yagoda, then head of the O.G.P.U., to get tendentiously picked data; he gave me suitably picked data, which I then used to form my counter-revolutionary ideology and corresponding actions based on this ideology.

VYSHINSKY: When did your counter-revolutionary Right organization take shape?

BUKHARIN: My rapprochement with Tomsky and Rykov dates approximately to 1928-29—then contacts and sounding out the then members of the Central Committee, illegal conferences which were illegal in respect of the Central Committee; consequently, the organization overstepped the bounds of Soviet state legality, and it was on this basis that there quickly arose a peculiar organization of the leadership of the Right organization, which may be depicted as a hierarchy, approximately like this: the trio—Rykov, Tomsky and myself, who were members of the Political Bureau at that time, opposition members of the Central Committee who by virtue of their views had already developed into a counter-revolutionary grouping; then various groupings, the chief component parts of which should be listed as follows: Bukharin and his notorious school in the first place, Tomsky and his trade union cadres in the second place, Rykov and his secretaries and people of the Soviet apparatus in the third place, Uglanov with Moscow district officials and a group in the Industrial Academy in the fourth place. In this manner the upper clique of this counter-revolutionary organization was formed.

VYSHINSKY: And where did Yagoda come in?

BUKHARIN: Yagoda stood aside.

VYSHINSKY: Was he connected with you?

BUKHARIN: Yes, he was.

VYSHINSKY: He helped you to pick tendentious data?

BUKHARIN: Quite right.

VYSHINSKY: So, he was a participant . . .

BUKHARIN: I am speaking now about the hierarchy of the leadership, and therefore as far as Yagoda . . .

VYSHINSKY: I simply did not want the accused Yagoda to be slighted.

BUKHARIN: Here began the quest for blocs. Firstly, my meeting with Kamenev at his apartment. Secondly, a meeting with Pyatakov in the hospital, at which Kamenev was present. Thirdly, a meeting with Kamenev at Schmidt's country house.

I forgot to say that in 1928 on the basis of and in connection with a statement made by representatives of a whole group in the Central Committee, at that time an opposition group, but who were already swinging to counter-revolutionary views, and on the basis of a corresponding plan, I drew up the so-called platform of 1928.[1]

I am mentioning it not because it was widely circulated and not because its ideas, as you know, formed the basis of all practical

344

steps at that time and it became the principle underlying the ideology, but because at the second sounding out of the Trotskyite-Zinovievite circles, namely at the meeting with Kamenev and Pyatakov, I showed the economic section of this platform to the persons referred to.

I do not know whether you are interested in a detailed . . .

THE PRESIDENT: I think these episodes could be related more briefly.

BUKHARIN: Very well. The meeting with Kamenev at his apartment. Here there were extremely slanderous conversations about the leadership of the Party, the Party regime, the organization of hunger, civil war in the country, scurrilous attacks on the Party leadership, and so on and so forth.

The meeting in the hospital. I repeat that inasmuch as the economic platform met with some disparagement, no agreement was reached on this occasion, but we sounded and tested each other, and an attempt at an agreement was made.

Thirdly, and lastly, the meeting at the country house of Vasily Schmidt, who was not there himself and at which myself, my secretary Tseitlin, Kamenev and Tomsky were present. On this occasion the conversation was comparatively short and consisted in a discussion of the tactics which we opposition members of the Central Committee should pursue at the forthcoming Plenum of the Central Committee. Kamenev's position was that of urging us on to taking action, but we were also waiting for an opportunity. So that I regard all these three attempts as quests for criminal connections and a criminal bloc against the Party leadership and the Party with those circles which were grouped around Kamenev and Zinoviev on the one hand, and the Trotskyite Pyatakov on the other.

The next stage in the development of the counter-revolutionary organization of the Rights began in 1930-31. At that time there was a great sharpening of the class struggle, of kulak sabotage, kulak resistance to the policy of the Party, etc.

I consider this stage the transition to "double entry book-keeping" all along the line. The trio became an illegal centre and therefore, whereas this trio had previously been at the head of the opposition circles, now it became the centre of an illegal counter-revolutionary organization. And inasmuch as they, I repeat, were illegal in relation to the Party, they became thereby illegal in relation to the Soviet authorities.

Close to this illegal centre was Yenukidze, who had contact with this centre through Tomsky. Uglanov, whose influence in the Party organization was quite considerable because only a short time back he had been leading the Moscow Party organization, was also close to the centre at that time.

345

Around this time, approximately towards the end of 1931, the members of the so-called school were transferred to work outside of Moscow—to Voronezh, Samara, Leningrad, Novosibirsk—and this transfer was utilized for counter-revolutionary purposes even then.

VYSHINSKY: How was it utilized?

BUKHARIN: It was utilized in the sense that we members of this illegal trio, members of the Right centre, myself among them, gave these demoralized people a direct charge, a direct commission, primarily about recruiting people. As regards Yagoda, if my memory does not fail me, according to A. I. Rykov he at that time demanded a special status for himself, insisting on it particularly just then.

VYSHINSKY: A special status in what sense?

BUKHARIN: A special status within the Right organization in the sense of specially secretive forms of concealment, which is quite understandable in view of the position he held in the official Soviet hierarchy.

VYSHINSKY: He got this status?

BUKHARIN: He got this status. About the autumn of 1932 the next stage in the development of the Right organization began, namely the transition to tactics of a forcible overthrow of Soviet power.

VYSHINSKY: What year do you date it from?

BUKHARIN: I date it approximately from the summer of 1932. But, in general, Citizen State Prosecutor, I must say that it should be borne in mind that all this division into periods is of an arbitrary character, because, for example, if I take the fact of Yakovenko's having been sent with my permission and the permission of the Right centre, I have referred to facts concerning which you have questioned me and concerning which I gave you an affirmative reply. They relate to an earlier period. From this I only draw the conclusion that if dates do not coincide, this can in no wise serve to disprove the criminal nature of one or another act, because there was no clear line of demarcation here. Furthermore, in some cases, as in the case of Yakovenko, there was such a hectic situation that it gave rise to a corresponding criminal reaction on our part.

Proceeding to the tactics of forcible overthrow in general, I make note of the time when the so-called Ryutin platform was formulated. Much has been said here about the Ryutin platform, and perhaps there is no need to dwell upon it. It was called the Ryutin platform for reasons of secrecy, as an insurance against exposure; it was called the Ryutin platform in order to conceal the Right centre and its top leadership.

346

Furthermore, I must say in addition: I think that the Ryutin platform—that is why I permit myself to hold your attention for a few minutes longer—the Ryutin platform, as far as I can remember during the trial, the platform of the Right counter-revolutionary organization, was perhaps already actually a common platform of the other groupings, including the Kamenev-Zinoviev and Trotskyite groupings.

It was just at this very moment that the situation became such that Trotsky had to throw off his Leftist uniform. When it came to exact formulations of what had to be done after all, his Right platform came into evidence at once, that is, he had to speak of decollectivization, etc.

VYSHINSKY: That is, you equipped Trotskyism ideologically too?

BUKHARIN: Quite true. Here the correlation of forces was such that Trotsky insisted on more drastic methods of struggle, and we to a certain extent armed him ideologically. (To Vyshinsky.) Is that all I need say about the Ryutin platform?

VYSHINSKY: That is your affair.

BUKHARIN: No, I am asking if it interests you or not.

VYSHINSKY: I am interested in your crimes.

BUKHARIN: Very well, but these crimes are so numerous, Citizen Procurator, that it is necessary to pick out the most important.

VYSHINSKY: I am interested in all of them—not in a selection, but from beginning to end.

THE PRESIDENT: So far you are still beating about the bush, you are saying nothing about your crimes.

BUKHARIN: So you do not consider an illegal organization a crime, nor do you consider the Ryutin platform a crime?

VYSHINSKY: That is not the question, but you are told you are beating about the bush.

THE PRESIDENT: Accused Bukharin, I request you not to engage in cross-talk, but to speak if you want to speak.

BUKHARIN: I will speak.

THE PRESIDENT: According to procedure, the session should close in fifteen minutes. I ask you to wind up your thoughts or to finish.

VYSHINSKY: You mentioned Yagoda. I would like to question Yagoda. Accused Yagoda, please tell us if you demanded of the bloc that you should be put in a specially secret position.

YAGODA: Yes, there was such a demand on my part.

VYSHINSKY: Do you remember under what circumstances this took place and with whom you spoke about it?

YAGODA: I spoke with Rykov.

347

VYSHINSKY: Accused Rykov, do you confirm this?

RYKOV: I confirm it, I have already spoken about this in my preliminary testimony.

VYSHINSKY: Continue.

BUKHARIN: The Ryutin platform registered the transition to the tactics of overthrowing the Soviet power by force.

In this connection, I think I should dwell on the conference of 1932. Those people who had been sent to various places outside Moscow, consisting for the most part of "young people," returned from their localities and on the initiative of Slepkov and with my sanction called a conference at the end of the summer of 1932, at which reports from the localities were made.

VYSHINSKY: Illegal?

BUKHARIN: Illegal. The conference was illegal, the work was illegal, the reports were illegal and the reports were about illegal work.

VYSHINSKY: The conference was counter-revolutionary, the reports were counter-revolutionary, and the reports were about counter-revolutionary work.

BUKHARIN: Yes, the whole thing was counter-revolutionary.

Incidentally, one of the points on the agenda of this conference was the question of the Ryutin platform, and the conference approved this Ryutin platform. After this there was a conference of the "trio," plus Uglanov. I was not present at this conference because I was on my vacation, but when I returned from my vacation I fully agreed with this platform and I bear full responsibility for it. The Ryutin platform was approved on behalf of the Right centre. The essential points of the Ryutin platform were: a "palace coup," terrorism, steering a course for a direct alliance with the Trotskyites. Around this time the idea of a "palace coup" was maturing in the Right circles, and not only in the upper circles, but also, as far as I remember, among a section of those working outside of Moscow. At first this idea came from Tomsky, who was in contact with Yenukidze. This thought occurred to Tomsky in connection with the possibilities of using the official position of Yenukidze, who had charge of the Kremlin guard at that time. Here we have the logic of the struggle and the disappearance of avenues for legal work, the development of this idea, the consolidation of the ties between Tomsky and Yenukidze, and between Rykov and Yagoda. Tomsky said that Yenukidze agreed to take an active part in this coup. Tomsky also said that Yenukidze had enlisted Peterson. And here, speaking ironically, from an academic formulation of the question, the question matured into a practical formulation, because elements of the organization of this coup were present.

348

Consequently, it was already then that the plan was being made and the organizational forces picked to carry it out, that is to say, the recruiting of people for a "palace coup " This was when the political bloc with Kamenev and Zinoviev originated. In this period we had meetings also with Syrtsov and Lominadze.

I must say, only I ask the Court not to understand it as a desire to mitigate the charges against me, that the political tendencies in this group were not entirely undifferentiated, that the Rights were not united with the Trotskyites: the Trotskyites counted on terrorism while the Rights put their hopes in an insurrectionary movement. The Rights urged the organization on to mass action.

I think this is no mitigation, but in this case I am telling you what took place and what was known from the reports which were given then. We counted on enlisting the masses.

I had talks with Pyatakov, Tomsky and Rykov. Rykov had talks with Kamenev, and Zinoviev with Pyatakov.

In the summer of 1932 I had a second conversation with Pyatakov in the People's Commissariat of Heavy Industry. At that time this was a very simple matter for me, since I was working under Pyatakov. At that time he was my boss. I had to go into his private office on business, and I could do so without arousing suspicion. Neither did the fact that I would sit in his private office for so long arouse any suspicion. There was no telling what business had to be transacted.

VYSHINSKY: You made use of all the legal opportunities for illegal conversations.

BUKHARIN: I utilized legal opportunities for anti-Soviet, illegal purposes. In this talk, which took place in the summer of 1932, Pyatakov told me of his meeting with Sedov concerning Trotsky's policy of terrorism. At that time Pyatakov and I considered that these were not our ideas, but we decided that we would find a common language very soon and that our differences in the struggle against Soviet power would be overcome. Tomsky and Rykov, I may be mistaken, spoke with Kamenev and Sokolnikov. I remember that at that time Tomsky particularly insisted on a coup d'état and a concentration of all forces, while the members of the Right centre orientated themselves on an insurrectionary movement.

By the end of 1932—the Ryutin platform dates to the autumn or the end of the summer of 1932, the conference dates . . .

THE PRESIDENT: The session is drawing to a close, conclude.

BUKHARIN: Then I will merely conclude the thought that the counter-revolutionary bloc of Rights, Trotskyites and Kamenev-Zinovievites was formed at the end of 1932.

THE PRESIDENT: The Court is adjourned until March 7, 11 a.m.

[Signed] PRESIDENT: V. ULRICH
Army Military Jurist
*President of the Military Collegium of
the Supreme Court of the U.S.S.R.*

SECRETARY: A. BATNER
Military Jurist First Rank

350

MORNING SESSION, MARCH 7, 1938

COMMANDANT OF THE COURT: The Court is coming, please rise.

THE PRESIDENT: Please be seated. The session is resumed. Accused Bukharin, continue your testimony about your anti-Soviet activities.

BUKHARIN: Very well. The day before yesterday I finished by saying that at the end of 1932 the bloc of Rights, Trotskyites and Zinovievites was formed on the basis of the Ryutin platform. By that time terrorist sentiments had already begun to develop among the participants of the counter-revolutionary organization of the Rights. They were to be marked among my so-called disciples, in the Matveyev group surrounding Uglanov, among Rykov's supporters and among certain trade union functionaries, as was at one time disclosed in the press. The formation of the group of conspirators in the Red Army relates to that period. I heard of it from Tomsky, who was directly informed of it by Yenukidze, with whom he had personal connections, and with whom in addition it was more convenient for him to be in contact because they lived along the same corridor in the Kremlin.

Both of them, Tomsky and Yenukidze, as I heard—though "heard" is not a particularly suitable word; rather I was informed by Tomsky and Yenukidze, who told me that in the upper ranks of the Red Army the Rights, Zinovievites and Trotskyites had then united their forces; names were mentioned to me—I don't vouch that I remember them all exactly—but those I have remembered are Tukhachevsky, Kork, Primakov[1] and Putna.

Thus the connections with the centre of the Rights followed the line of: the military group, Yenukidze, Tomsky and the rest. Approximately at this time, i.e., towards the end of 1932 or the beginning of 1933, the so-called contact centre was formed, which included representatives of various anti-Party counter-revolutionary trends, including the Rights.

In returning to the story or to the evidence regarding the criminal activity of the counter-revolutionary Right bloc, I wish firstly to deal with the idea of the coup d'état as one of the central criminal ideas, and the practical preparations that corresponded to it, because this very idea and the corresponding practical prep-

351

arations developed in conformity with various periods and the general political situation in the various stages of its development.

The inception of the idea of the coup d'état among us Right conspirators relates approximately to the years 1929-30, and at that time this coup d'état in its embryo form was conceived, or rather was spoken of, as a coup d'état on relatively a very narrow basis. I would say that it was an idea of a circumscribed coup d'état, or rather of a "palace coup" (I again fear to say so, lest the impression be got that I wish to shirk responsibility here), and was for the first time expressed by Tomsky in connection with the circumstance that at that time Yenukidze, who was personally connected with Tomsky and was frequently in his company, had charge of the Kremlin guard; at the same time there was a possibility for Rykov, who was Chairman of the Council of People's Commissars, to make use of his official position. In this connection there were a number of legal opportunities and loopholes facilitating all kinds of secret criminal activities, and therefore this could serve as a definite condition under which this "palace coup" could be effected. It dates approximately to the years 1929-30, but at that time they did not proceed to carry the "palace coup" into effect, and did not do so, strictly speaking, for two reasons: the one reason was a wider one . . .

VYSHINSKY: Why they did not proceed to put it into effect is not so interesting as why they did; why they did not, why it did not take place, is of no interest to us.

BUKHARIN: Very good, I shall not dwell on this if it is not of interest.

VYSHINSKY: You have already reached the year 1933.

BUKHARIN: The reason I wanted to refer to this question is that it is connected with the practical preparations. . . .

VYSHINSKY: So speak of the practical preparations, instead of telling us why this or that did not take place. The Court is interested in knowing what took place, and why.

BUKHARIN: Yes, but every negation contains an affirmation, Citizen Procurator. Spinoza once said that in the sphere of determination . . .

VYSHINSKY. Speak concretely: how were you preparing the seizure of power, with whose aid, by what means, with what aims and objects in view?

BUKHARIN: Since we did not undertake a "palace coup" for reasons which you are not interested in listening to here, we proceeded to orientate ourselves on kulak revolts. . . .

VYSHINSKY. What is the meaning of the expression "palace

coup"? Am I to understand that this means the direct seizure of power, the seizure of power by the forces of your bloc?

BUKHARIN: Absolutely correct; politically—by the forces of the bloc. But why do I say "palace coup"? This means by forces organizationally concentrated in the Kremlin.

VYSHINSKY: By such forces as would prove to be at your disposal, but not necessarily by forces that were in the Kremlin?

BUKHARIN: Absolutely correct.

VYSHINSKY: Then would it not be better to speak not of a "palace coup," but of an attempt to seize power by means of an armed uprising?

BUKHARIN: No, it is not quite correct to speak of an armed uprising.

VYSHINSKY: Why not? You wished to seize power with arms in hand?

BUKHARIN: An armed uprising is a mass affair, while here it was a matter of a narrower . . .

VYSHINSKY: What masses? You had no masses with you.

BUKHARIN: Consequently it is not an uprising.

VYSHINSKY: An uprising with the aid of a group.

BUKHARIN: If you choose to define an uprising by a group as an uprising, then it is correct.

VYSHINSKY: In any case, it is more correct than to speak of a "palace coup," which is supposed to take place in some palace.

BUKHARIN: When speaking of a "palace coup," I had in view . . .

VYSHINSKY: A group of plotters?

BUKHARIN: Absolutely correct.

VYSHINSKY: I believe it will be better to call it so. Tell me, how did you prepare the group of plotters for the seizure of power?

BUKHARIN: That refers to the following period. Perhaps you will allow me to relate the facts in chronological order, as I have my material arranged, at first about the "palace coup," then the transition to an uprising, from an uprising to, strictly speaking, a coup d'état.

VYSHINSKY: Tell me, what was the main object of the group of plotters in this sphere?

BUKHARIN: Even at that period the main object was the overthrow of the Soviet government by force.

VYSHINSKY: Well, tell us then how you were preparing for the overthrow of the Soviet government by force.

BUKHARIN: At that period we were already discussing the

353

question of the overthrow of the Soviet government by force, with the aid of a group of military participants in the plot.

VYSHINSKY: A group?

BUKHARIN: Yes.

VYSHINSKY: A group of participants in your plot?

BUKHARIN: Absolutely correct.

VYSHINSKY: In the persons of Tukhachevsky, Primakov and some others?

BUKHARIN: There was the Yenukidze group as well.

VYSHINSKY: We have already spoken of the Yenukidze group.

BUKHARIN: Absolutely correct. In 1931-32, in connection with the changed political situation, the main stress was laid on the development of the insurrectionary movement, and the counter-revolutionary Right organization, headed by the centre of the Rights, provoked several kulak revolts which, Citizen Procurator, were already dealt with in part when you questioned me in connection with Yakovenko, Slepkov, etc.

VYSHINSKY: On your direct instructions and under your leadership?

BUKHARIN: Absolutely correct. I can mention here yet another fact which has not been referred to. At that time I spoke about myself. I sent Slepkov to prepare a kulak revolt in the Kuban. Rykov sent Eismont to the Caucasus, and he entered into connections with the Right-winger Pivovarov and the Trotskyite Beloborodov; this has been referred to during the Court investigation. In addition I can tell the Court that I was informed by P. Petrovsky and Zaitsev of kulak sabotage as a sort of preliminary stage preceding sharper forms of struggle.

VYSHINSKY: In so far as you have mentioned Eismont, I ask you to testify regarding your connections with Whiteguard circles and German fascists.

BUKHARIN: I don't understand what you have in view.

VYSHINSKY: I repeat, tell the Court of your connections, of connections between your conspiratorial group and Whiteguard circles abroad and the German fascists. Is the question clear?

BUKHARIN: I do not know of this. In any case, I don't remember.

VYSHINSKY (to the Court): Allow me to ask Rykov. Did you hear my question? What can you say in this regard?

RYKOV: I knew from Pivovarov that the Cossack League, organized on the instructions, on the advice of Slepkov . . .

VYSHINSKY: The Whiteguard Cossack League?

RYKOV: Yes. . . . That through the re-emigrants who made up the forces of this counter-revolutionary organization, it was connected with the remnants of the Cossack émigrés abroad, and this connection was facilitated by the aid received from the German fascists.

VYSHINSKY: So that the group of conspirators in the North Caucasus, of which you knew from Pivovarov's words, was in contact with the Whiteguard Cossack League abroad, and with the German fascists.

RYKOV: Yes, that's so.

VYSHINSKY: Accused Bukharin, did you know of this, did you know Pivovarov?

BUKHARIN: I did not know Pivovarov.

VYSHINSKY: What was Pivovarov's position in the North Caucasus?

BUKHARIN: He was at the head of Soviet state power in the North Caucasus.

VYSHINSKY: So you knew that Pivovarov was Chairman of the Territorial Executive Committee in the North Caucasus?

BUKHARIN: I knew that he was Chairman of the Territorial Executive Committee, but I did not know him personally.

VYSHINSKY: Rykov knew that Pivovarov was the head of a local group of traitors and counter-revolutionaries in the North Caucasus, and that he was connected with Whiteguard Cossack circles abroad, but you, Bukharin, did not know this?

BUKHARIN: I don't dispute the possibility of such a fact, but I did not know it.

VYSHINSKY: Was it a fact, or was it not, that Pivovarov was connected with Whiteguard Cossack circles abroad?

BUKHARIN: I cannot deny it. I can only conjecture that it could be so, since our line was to make use of all forces.

VYSHINSKY: Including Whiteguard forces as well?

BUKHARIN: That was not excluded.

VYSHINSKY: Was that clear to you?

BUKHARIN: I don't deny that this was possible, but I cannot recall it with a sufficient degree of exactitude, there is not the material in my mind to enable me to remember about connections with the Whiteguard Cossack League abroad.

VYSHINSKY: I ask you, was there such a fact as the one mentioned by Rykov, who knew of it as one of the leaders of your organization?

BUKHARIN: There is no such fact in my mind. But I cannot deny the possibility of such a fact. What is more, it is very likely that such connections existed.

VYSHINSKY: You wish to present matters as if you were not practically concerned with these crimes.

BUKHARIN: How so, when I sent Yakovenko to Siberia to

organize armed kulak insurrections, and sent Slepkov to the North Caucasus for the same purpose?

VYSHINSKY: Accused Rykov, did Bukharin know of this fact, or did he not?

RYKOV: The initiative of the organization of this League, according to Pivovarov, belonged to Slepkov, who was sent to the North Caucasus by Bukharin, and who, I presume, was given definite instructions and directives by Bukharin.

VYSHINSKY: So then, Slepkov was sent to the North Caucasus on Bukharin's initiative. Accused Bukharin, do you confirm this?

BUKHARIN: I sent Slepkov there as an individual skilled in the organization of the insurrectionary movement. But once he got there, found his bearings and learnt what organizations there were, Slepkov could undertake certain steps without me.

VYSHINSKY: Do you bear responsibility for these criminal acts as one of the leaders of the organization?

BUKHARIN: Undoubtedly I do bear responsibility.

VYSHINSKY: For the connections of your organization with Whiteguard Cossack circles and German fascists?

BUKHARIN: Of course I do.

VYSHINSKY: Was there such a fact?

BUKHARIN: If others say that there was such a fact, then there was.

RYKOV: I categorically assert that such a commission was given, that Slepkov was sent to the North Caucasus because he played an important role and was able to gather a counter-revolutionary organization together. I do not know whether he spoke to Bukharin on this point, but the initiative there, according to Pivovarov, belonged to Slepkov.

VYSHINSKY: Consequently, these connections followed Bukharin's line?

RYKOV: The idea followed Bukharin's line.

VYSHINSKY: The idea and the practical application of it.

RYKOV: Slepkov did it.

BUKHARIN: I don't deny having sent Slepkov there. I sent him to establish contact with Whiteguard Cossack circles.

VYSHINSKY: Was this included in the plan of your leadership?

BUKHARIN: I did not specifically say so.

VYSHINSKY: Do you assert that you were unaware of the contacts with German fascists and Whiteguard Cossack circles?

BUKHARIN: I did not know.

VYSHINSKY: Rykov knew, Slepkov knew, but you did not?

BUKHARIN: They were there on the spot.

VYSHINSKY: Did you send Slepkov there?

BUKHARIN: Yes, I did.

VYSHINSKY: Were you connected with Slepkov when he was there?

BUKHARIN: No.

VYSHINSKY: Did you talk to him about what he did there?

BUKHARIN: Later on?

VYSHINSKY: Yes, later on.

BUKHARIN: We had no detailed conversation.

VYSHINSKY: But did you meet him?

BUKHARIN: I met him once.

VYSHINSKY: You met once, and this was enough to enable you to discover whether he had fulfilled your commission or not.

BUKHARIN: No, we did not speak about it.

VYSHINSKY: Tell me, what was the subject of your conversation?

BUKHARIN: We talked very little.

VYSHINSKY: You sent Slepkov to organize a kulak insurrection. Slepkov engaged in the organization of this insurrection and worked in this direction.

BUKHARIN: He did not give me a detailed reply.

VYSHINSKY: I ask you, was this so or not?

BUKHARIN: I sent him.

VYSHINSKY: Did he fulfil your instructions?

BUKHARIN: Apparently he did.

VYSHINSKY: Apparently?

BUKHARIN: Yes.

VYSHINSKY: But did he speak to you about it?

BUKHARIN: I say that I met him once.

VYSHINSKY: Did Slepkov tell you how he had fulfilled your commission?

BUKHARIN: I don't remember his having said much.

VYSHINSKY: But why do you say that he did not speak in detail?

BUKHARIN: He spoke in general.

VYSHINSKY: He spoke in general?

BUKHARIN: Yes, in general.

VYSHINSKY: If he spoke in general, then he spoke?

BUKHARIN: If he spoke in general, then he spoke.

VYSHINSKY: But you have only just said that he did not speak.

BUKHARIN: He did not speak in detail.

VYSHINSKY: I ask you, accused Bukharin, did you send Slepkov to organize Whiteguard kulak insurrections?

BUKHARIN: Yes.

VYSHINSKY: Did he inform you how he had fulfilled your commission?

BUKHARIN: He did not say how he had fulfilled it.

VYSHINSKY: But how did he fulfil it?

BUKHARIN: He said that there were disorders there.

VYSHINSKY: Not insurrections, but disorders?

BUKHARIN: The conversation rapidly passed to another topic, about the preparations for the conference in 1932.

VYSHINSKY: Your conversations of course passed very rapidly from one topic to another.

It is important for me to establish that at that time in the North Caucasus there was a part of your Right-wing plotting organization.

BUKHARIN: Yes.

VYSHINSKY: So it is a fact?

BUKHARIN: It is.

VYSHINSKY: That you knew about it?

BUKHARIN: Yes.

VYSHINSKY: That you sent Slepkov there to establish contact with this organization. That Slepkov did something there in this direction of which he spoke to you. . . . Is that a fact?

BUKHARIN: It is.

VYSHINSKY: That there were kulak disorders there. Is that a fact?

BUKHARIN: It is.

VYSHINSKY: That this was connected with his activity. Is that a fact?

BUKHARIN: It is.

VYSHINSKY: And was connected with your activity. Is that a fact?

BUKHARIN: It is.

VYSHINSKY: Further, it is known that this North Caucasus group was in contact with Whiteguard Cossack émigré circles. . . . Is that a fact or not?

BUKHARIN: I have told you that I cannot deny this fact, Citizen Procurator.

VYSHINSKY: Accused Bukharin, is it a fact or not that a group of your confederates in the North Caucasus was connected with Whiteguard émigré Cossack circles abroad? Is that a fact or not? Rykov says it is, Slepkov says it is.

BUKHARIN: If Rykov says it is, I have no grounds for not believing him.

VYSHINSKY: Can you answer me without philosophy?

BUKHARIN: This is not philosophy.

VYSHINSKY: Without philosophical twists and turns.

BUKHARIN: I have testified that I had explanations on this question.

VYSHINSKY: Answer me "No."

BUKHARIN: I cannot say "No," and I cannot deny that it did take place.

VYSHINSKY: So the answer is neither "Yes" nor "No"?

BUKHARIN: Nothing of the kind, because facts exist regardless of whether they are in anybody's mind. This is a problem of the reality of the outer world. I am no solipsist.

VYSHINSKY: So that regardless of whether this fact entered your mind or not, you as a plotter and leader were aware of it?

BUKHARIN: I was not aware of it.

VYSHINSKY: You were not?

BUKHARIN: But I can say the following in reply to your question: since this thing was included in the general plan, I consider it likely, and since Rykov speaks of it in a positive fashion, I have no grounds for denying it.

VYSHINSKY: Consequently, it is a fact?

BUKHARIN: From the point of view of mathematical probability it can be said, with very great probability, that it is a fact.

VYSHINSKY: So that you are unable to give a plain answer?

BUKHARIN: Not "unable," but there are some questions that cannot be answered outright "Yes" or "No," as you are perfectly well aware from elementary logic.

VYSHINSKY: Allow me to ask Rykov again: was Bukharin aware of this fact?

RYKOV: I did not speak to him about it.

VYSHINSKY: Now, did Bukharin know about it or not?

RYKOV: I personally think with mathematical probability that he should have known of it.

VYSHINSKY: That's clear. Accused Bukharin, were you aware that Karakhan was a participant in the conspiratorial group of Rights and Trotskyites?

BUKHARIN: I was.

VYSHINSKY: Were you aware that Karakhan was a German spy?

BUKHARIN: No, I was not aware of that.

VYSHINSKY (to Rykov): Were you aware, accused Rykov, that Karakhan was a German spy?

RYKOV: No, I was not.

VYSHINSKY: Were you not aware that Karakhan was engaged in negotiations with certain German circles?

RYKOV: Negotiations regarding the centre of the Rights?

VYSHINSKY: Yes, of course, regarding the centre of the Rights.

RYKOV: Yes, yes.

VYSHINSKY: Treasonable negotiations?

RYKOV: Treasonable.

VYSHINSKY: With whom did he conduct these negotiations, with what institution?

RYKOV: (No reply.)

VYSHINSKY: Well?

RYKOV: I don't know that.

VYSHINSKY: In that case, tell the Court: what was the line of the negotiations?

RYKOV: The line was. . . At that time negotiations were conducted with German government circles.

VYSHINSKY: With which circles?

RYKOV: On the question of their attitude to the Rights, to a possible coup d'état by the Rights.

VYSHINSKY: Were there negotiations regarding the organization of the defeat of the U.S.S.R., or not?

RYKOV: I don't know that.

VYSHINSKY: Then I wish to remind Rykov of the following testimony given by him at the preliminary investigation—Vol. I, p. 112: "Consequently not only the Tukhachevsky group, which was a component part of our organization, worked to prepare the defeat of the U.S.S.R. This defeat was prepared for by our entire international orientation and Karakhan's negotiations." Is that correct?

RYKOV: It is.

VYSHINSKY: Then what follows from this?

RYKOV: I had in view defeat not in the direct sense of the word. I had in view that if a group of plotters in any country engages in negotiations with the enemy, then, firstly, the very fact of these negotiations in itself must assist in hastening war—the enemy will the sooner undertake his offensive the more support he has within the country—and, secondly, the ability of the country to defend itself, and of the other to attack, correspondingly changes, that is, the defence weakens while the offensive becomes stronger.

VYSHINSKY: So then this fact took place?

RYKOV: Yes.

VYSHINSKY: And further: "In our very international orientation, our starting point was that we needed to receive support from the international bourgeoisie, and we linked up our activity and the success of our counter-revolutionary work in the U.S.S.R. with direct aid from fascism." In brackets it states: "Karakhan's negotiations." Can the conclusion be drawn from this that Karakhan, with your knowledge, engaged in negotiations with fascist circles regarding support for your treasonable activity on definite conditions? Was that the case?

RYKOV: Yes.

VYSHINSKY: And what were the conditions?

RYKOV: Firstly, a number of economic concessions, and secondly the so-called dismemberment of the U.S.S.R.

VYSHINSKY: What does that mean?

RYKOV: That means the separation of the national republics and placing them under a protectorate, or making them dependent, formally not dependent, but actually dependent on . . .

VYSHINSKY: That is to say, territorial concessions?

RYKOV: Of course.

VYSHINSKY: Did Karakhan propose in the name of your bloc to cede to the Germans some part of the territory of the Soviet Union?

RYKOV: The matter was somewhat different.

VYSHINSKY: I speak of the meaning of these concessions.

RYKOV: I myself did not meet Karakhan. I know this from Tomsky, who explained it in my presence and in that of Bukharin.

VYSHINSKY: So that means Bukharin also knew? Allow me to ask Bukharin. Did you know?

BUKHARIN: I did.

RYKOV: He explained it in this way: the German fascists accept these conditions, i.e., privileges as regards concessions, trade agreements, etc., but on their part they demand that the national republics be given the right to free separation.

VYSHINSKY: Well, and what does that mean?

RYKOV: It was not what we proposed. This was a new demand on the part of the Germans. In plain language, this means, of course, the dismemberment of the U.S.S.R.

VYSHINSKY: That is to say, handing over part of the U.S.S.R. to the Germans?

RYKOV: Of course.

VYSHINSKY: That is to say, you were aware that Karakhan, with your knowledge, engaged in negotiations with German circles to hand over part of the U.S.S.R. Precisely what part?

RYKOV: There was no talk about that.

VYSHINSKY: Did your plan include a point about severing the Ukraine for the Germans, or did it not?

RYKOV: I personally cannot say about the Ukraine, I repeat, not because we were against the Ukraine being severed.

VYSHINSKY: But were you against or for its being severed?

RYKOV: There was simply no talk among us about the Ukraine being severed, and the question was not decided then.

VYSHINSKY: Did you have in view severing the Ukraine in favour of German fascism?

RYKOV: Such was the formula.

VYSHINSKY: Not a formula—but in practice?

RYKOV: In practice the question at issue could be that of Byelorussia.

VYSHINSKY: And of the Ukraine?

RYKOV: No. We could not decide this question without the consent of the Ukrainian counter-revolutionary organizations.

VYSHINSKY: Then I address myself to the accused Bukharin. Did you in 1934 engage in negotiations with Radek on this subject?

BUKHARIN: Not negotiations, but conversations.

VYSHINSKY: All right, conversations. Did they take place or not?

BUKHARIN: They did, only not about that.

VYSHINSKY: Then about what?

BUKHARIN: Radek told me of his negotiations with Trotsky, that Trotsky had engaged in negotiations with the German fascists regarding territorial concessions in return for help to the counter-revolutionary organizations.

VYSHINSKY: That's it, that's it.

BUKHARIN: I then objected to Radek.

VYSHINSKY: Did Radek tell you that on Trotsky's instructions the Ukraine was to be ceded, yielded to the Germans?

BUKHARIN: I definitely remember about the Ukraine.

VYSHINSKY: Were there such conversations or not?

BUKHARIN: Yes.

VYSHINSKY: And about the Far East?

BUKHARIN: About the Ukraine I definitely remember; there was talk of other regions, but I do not remember which.

VYSHINSKY: You testified as follows: "Trotsky, while urging the intensification of terrorism, yet considers the main chance for the advent of the bloc to power to be the defeat of the U.S.S.R. in a war against Germany and Japan at the cost of territorial concessions (the Ukraine to the Germans, and the Far East to the Japanese)." Was that so?

BUKHARIN: Yes, it was

VYSHINSKY: That is to say, these are the concessions?

BUKHARIN: I was not in agreement.

VYSHINSKY: Further it states: "I did not object to the idea of an understanding with Germany and Japan, but did not agree with Trotsky on the extent."

BUKHARIN: Read the next phrase as well, where the extent and character are explained.

VYSHINSKY: I have read and want to speak about this.

BUKHARIN: I said I was against territorial concessions.

VYSHINSKY: No. I want to speak about this. And so Radek told you that Trotsky gave instructions to cede the Ukraine to the Germans. Did he say this?

BUKHARIN: He did, but I did not consider Trotsky's instructions as binding on me.

362

VYSHINSKY: Was Rykov aware of this conversation with Radek, or not?

RYKOV: Whom are you asking?

VYSHINSKY: Bukharin.

BUKHARIN: I don't remember whether I told Rykov.

VYSHINSKY: And Rykov?

RYKOV: He did not tell me.

VYSHINSKY: Consequently you were unaware of Bukharin's conversation with Radek?

RYKOV: (No reply.)

VYSHINSKY: But did he talk privately to Bukharin?

RYKOV: Who?

VYSHINSKY: Radek. Accused Bukharin, how did Radek talk to you? What post did you occupy at that time?

BUKHARIN: It is not a matter of the post.

VYSHINSKY: What post did you occupy?

BUKHARIN: I was the editor of the "Izvestia."

VYSHINSKY: Did you talk to Radek as the editor of the "Izvestia," or as a member of the plotting organization?

BUKHARIN: You understand perfectly well that I spoke to him as a member of the plotting organization.

VYSHINSKY: Rykov and Tomsky then constituted the centre, and under these conditions you said nothing of this conversation with Radek?

BUKHARIN: Excuse me, I wish to answer this question. I cannot answer every question in one word. I do not possess sufficient ability for that.

The conditions under which we met were of a conspiratorial character, since we hardly met together at all, but spoke from time to time, making use of meetings in corridors, in the streets, etc. It may have happened that I did not tell him of this conversation. I say this not in order to whitewash Rykov; it is to be explained by the conspiratorial methods that existed in the organization of the Rights.

VYSHINSKY: Do you deny that you passed on to Rykov such a serious conversation as the one you had with Radek? Did you not tell Rykov about your serious conversations with Radek?

BUKHARIN: Citizen Procurator, I did not consider Trotsky's directions as obligatory for us all.

VYSHINSKY: I am not speaking of directions, but of conversations.

BUKHARIN: I do not remember and therefore cannot say whether I spoke of this. I don't remember this.

VYSHINSKY: You do not deny, but you don't remember. I will ask Rykov. Accused Rykov, when you spoke of dismemberment, which parts of the U.S.S.R. did you have in mind?

RYKOV: When Tomsky reported on the additional demands of the German fascists to the Rights, we accepted this proposal in the main in its general form.

VYSHINSKY: What was in question here, or what parts of the U.S.S.R.?

RYKOV: There was no specific talk regarding which republics, which parts of the U.S.S.R.

VYSHINSKY: At the preliminary investigation, and here in Court, you testified that Karakhan engaged in negotiations with the German fascists regarding help for your plot. Was that a fact or was it not?

RYKOV: Regarding help for the plot? If political aid is meant, then it was to secure a favourable attitude towards it.

VYSHINSKY: In return for what?

RYKOV: I have already enumerated.

VYSHINSKY: Territorial concessions. What part of the U.S.S.R. did this concern?

RYKOV: We did not specify this.

VYSHINSKY: You did not define this?

RYKOV: No, we did not.

VYSHINSKY: But did you have a definite part of the U.S.S.R. in mind or not? Or did you speak in the general abstract?

RYKOV: What happened was what I have already stated.

VYSHINSKY: That is to say?

RYKOV: We accepted conditions favourable to the practical activity of the centre of the Rights. This was put into effect in our work, in our guidance regarding Byelorussia.

VYSHINSKY: So then the Germans were concerned about Byelorussia? For whose benefit?

RYKOV: I cannot say what the Germans were concerned about.

VYSHINSKY: They were concerned that you might hand over Byelorussia to whom? Not to the Germans?

RYKOV: To the Poles.

VYSHINSKY: But what about the Germans? It would appear that the Germans were fussing around for the benefit of others. For whom? The Poles? The Germans render you a service, and in return for this you hand over Byelorussia to the Poles. They turn out to be in a ridiculous position.

RYKOV: (No reply.)

VYSHINSKY: I revert to the first question. Consequently, Karakhan engaged in negotiations with the Germans. Apparently this took place with the knowledge of your bloc. Did Bukharin know of this?

RYKOV: Tomsky told me and Bukharin of this.

VYSHINSKY: So, then, was Bukharin aware of this?

Accused Bukharin, were you aware of this?

BUKHARIN: Citizen Procurator, I have already said twice that I was.

VYSHINSKY: Did you endorse this?

BUKHARIN: What exactly does "this" mean?

VYSHINSKY: What you have already said twice.

BUKHARIN: I did not endorse it. At the preliminary investigation I gave detailed testimony to the effect that Karakhan . . .

VYSHINSKY: Did you endorse it?

BUKHARIN: I was faced with the fact itself, because Karakhan . . .

VYSHINSKY: Did you endorse these negotiations conducted by Karakhan with the German fascists?

BUKHARIN: Citizen Procurator, I say that this was a political fact.

VYSHINSKY: Did you endorse Karakhan's negotiations with the German fascists on behalf of the bloc?

BUKHARIN: In general, as regards the negotiations . . . I endorsed, that is to say, considered it expedient . . .

VYSHINSKY: Not in general, but the negotiations conducted by Karakhan?

BUKHARIN: I have already explained to you, Citizen Procurator, that the situation was such that Karakhan went without a preliminary decision of the joint centre and returned . . .

VYSHINSKY: Were you aware that Karakhan was engaged in negotiations with the German fascists?

BUKHARIN: I was. I knew of this from Tomsky, from Karakhan himself . . .

VYSHINSKY: Did you endorse these negotiations?

BUKHARIN: Or disavow? I did not disavow them; consequently I endorsed them.

VYSHINSKY: I ask you, did you endorse them, or not?

BUKHARIN: I repeat, Citizen Procurator: since I did not disavow them, I consequently endorsed them.

VYSHINSKY: Consequently, you endorsed them?

BUKHARIN: If I did not disavow them, consequently I endorsed them.

VYSHINSKY: That's what I am asking you: that is to say you endorsed them?

BUKHARIN: So then "consequently" is the same as "that is to say."

VYSHINSKY: What do you mean, "that is to say"?

BUKHARIN: That is to say, I endorsed them.

VYSHINSKY: But you say that you learnt of this post factum.

BUKHARIN: Yes, the one does not contradict the other in the slightest.

365

VYSHINSKY: Allow me to question the accused Rykov.

THE PRESIDENT: You may.

VYSHINSKY: Accused Rykov, did Karakhan undertake these negotiations on his own initiative?

RYKOV: He undertook them on the instructions, on the initiative of Tomsky. But Bukharin and I endorsed this initiative when these negotiations were reported to us.

VYSHINSKY: Did you endorse not only the fact of the negotiations but also the initiative, that is, the affair as a whole?

RYKOV: We are neither of us little children. If you don't endorse such things, then you must fight against them. One cannot play with neutrality in such things.

VYSHINSKY: And so it can be established that Karakhan conducted negotiations with the German fascists with Bukharin's knowledge. Accused Rykov, do you confirm this?

RYKOV: Yes.

BUKHARIN: What is the meaning of "with Bukharin's knowledge"? It was not the case that I knew that he was going there.

VYSHINSKY: I am not speaking about his going there. Do you know what initiative means? . . .

BUKHARIN: I can guess vaguely.

VYSHINSKY: Vaguely? I see that your position compels you to guess vaguely about very clear things.

BUKHARIN: Possibly.

VYSHINSKY: The accused Rykov has just testified to the Court in your presence that Karakhan began negotiations with the Germans not on his own initiative, but on that of Tomsky. . . .

BUKHARIN: But then neither Rykov nor I knew of this.

VYSHINSKY: But when you learnt later, did you endorse it?

BUKHARIN: Rykov has already stated that in such cases there can be no such thing as neutrality: if I did not put an end to them, then I endorsed them. But this is a paraphrase of what I said: if I did not disavow them, I endorsed them.

VYSHINSKY: And so, accused Bukharin, you bear responsibility for these negotiations of Karakhan with the Germans?

BUKHARIN: Undoubtedly.

VYSHINSKY: For the negotiations regarding the preparations for defeat?

BUKHARIN: The question was not put that way.

VYSHINSKY: Regarding help to you?

BUKHARIN: In general I spoke of help . . . of neutralization . . .

VYSHINSKY: Rykov has already explained to you.

BUKHARIN: It seems to me that he is explaining to the Court, and not to me.

VYSHINSKY: He explained that the very fact of the negotiations with the enemy means assisting him.

BUKHARIN: Well, yes, in that sense, but I draw a difference—that was not how the question was dealt with from the legal aspect, because . . .

VYSHINSKY: How was help to have been rendered? In assisting the success of the conspiracy?

BUKHARIN: During the conspiracy there might be German intervention against us in general. . . .

That has to be neutralized, and that means help.

VYSHINSKY: That is to say, that they should help you to maintain power.

BUKHARIN: To neutralize them and thereby to help us in maintaining power.

VYSHINSKY: At the price of certain concessions?

BUKHARIN: Yes.

VYSHINSKY: The accused Rykov stated that at that period the question of severing Byelorussia was discussed. Is that how I am to understand it?

BUKHARIN: My impression of it is quite a different one.

RYKOV: Tomsky informed us that the Germans had told Karakhan that, in addition to economic concessions, the German fascists insisted on the national republics being given the right of secession. We immediately understood and interpreted it as meaning the dismemberment of the U.S.S.R.

VYSHINSKY: That is to say, as meaning the surrender of Byelorussia?

RYKOV: And thereupon, as far as I remember (and one must not and cannot forget such things), we accepted it in this general form.

VYSHINSKY: Who is meant by "we"?

RYKOV: I, Bukharin and Tomsky.

VYSHINSKY: Is that correct, accused Bukharin?

BUKHARIN: Not altogether, not about Byelorussia, but about the Ukraine.

VYSHINSKY: So, now it's about the Ukraine. But till now we were dealing with Byelorussia?

BUKHARIN: You have not questioned me on this point, so that logically there is nothing contradictory in what I say.

VYSHINSKY: Allow me to show the accused Rykov his testimony, Vol. I, p. 119, where it says: "I must, however, say that the question of the orientation on Poland with a view to securing her support in case of our advent to power arose considerably earlier, namely, in 1930-31." Do you confirm this?

RYKOV: Yes.

VYSHINSKY: Bukharin, do you confirm this?

BUKHARIN: I don't know and don't remember this.

VYSHINSKY: Accused Rykov, whom did you have in mind when you referred to this question?

RYKOV: I referred to my relations with the representatives of the Byelorussian organization.

VYSHINSKY: But did you not discuss this question with Bukharin?

RYKOV: I cannot assert that.

VYSHINSKY: Then allow me to read out your further testimony: "At that period this question was on several occasions the subject of discussion between myself, Bukharin and Tomsky, on the one hand," etc. Thus I ask you: so you did discuss this question with Bukharin?

RYKOV: "This question" meant the agreement with the counter-revolutionary Byelorussian organization. Perhaps I did not express myself quite correctly, but that was what I had in view.

VYSHINSKY: Apparently you had in view what was in view. Here it is clearly stated that the question of an orientation on Poland was discussed in 1930-31. And further it states: "In this period," that is, precisely at that time, this question, that is, the question of the orientation on Poland.

RYKOV (after a silence): There is no such thing in my testimony, perhaps there is some other word. . . .

VYSHINSKY: Here every word plays a big part.

RYKOV: That is absolutely correct.

VYSHINSKY: It says outright: at that period this question, that is, the question which was spoken of before, the question of the orientation on Poland. Please read it.

(Rykov is handed his testimony given at the preliminary investigation.)

RYKOV: Here it states: "At that period this question . . ." this refers to the whole of the previous paragraph, and not to the last phrase of the paragraph at all.

VYSHINSKY: I read further: "The general formula we then agreed on amounted to this, that in the negotiations with the Poles, with whom contacts had already been restored by that time through Chervyakov, we would agree to the Byelorussian Soviet Republic being severed from the U.S.S.R."

Is that so? With whom did you discuss this question?

RYKOV: I discussed this with Goloded and Chervyakov, they were aware of the matter.

VYSHINSKY: They were aware of the matter? And was Bukharin aware of it?

BUKHARIN: I did not meet Chervyakov.

VYSHINSKY: That you didn't meet Chervyakov is not the

point. I am speaking of Rykov. I submit to him these three paragraphs from his testimony. The first reads: "I must, however, say that the question of the orientation on Poland was repeatedly discussed in 1930-31." The second paragraph: "In this period, i.e., in the period 1930-31, this question, i.e., the question spoken of previously, the question of the orientation on Poland, was on several occasions a subject of discussion between myself, Bukharin, Tomsky and Chervyakov, former Chairman of the Central Executive Committee of Byelorussia. Chervyakov has been a covert, but exceptionally active participant of the Right organization since 1928." The third paragraph: "The general formula we then agreed on amounted to this, that in the negotiations with the Poles, with whom contacts had already been restored by that time through Chervyakov, we would agree to the Byelorussian Soviet Republic being severed from the U.S.S.R."

Do you confirm this?

RYKOV: Yes.

VYSHINSKY: Accused Bukharin, did you know of all this?

BUKHARIN: In 1930 such a question could not arise. Hitler was not yet in power at that time.

VYSHINSKY: But this question was raised. The history of your treachery did not begin with Hitler

BUKHARIN: That is true.

VYSHINSKY: Did you have conversations with Rykov and Tomsky in 1930-31?

BUKHARIN: I don't remember.

VYSHINSKY: Now Rykov testifies to the fact that there were such conversations. I ask you, were there such conversations or not? Yes or no?

BUKHARIN: And I say I don't remember. I have the right to tell the Court not what you want, but what really happened.

VYSHINSKY: I don't demand this of you.

BUKHARIN: I have the right to say to the Court, and do say, I don't remember.

VYSHINSKY: You don't remember? Accused Rykov, what do you say?

RYKOV: The first report of this was made by Tomsky; he referred to Chervyakov, who had been at his country house. And then the three of us discussed this question on the strength of Tomsky's report and adopted this proposal regarding contact with the counter-revolutionary Byelorussian organization. At any rate it was in Bukharin's presence.

VYSHINSKY: Since this was in Bukharin's presence, Bukharin knew of it.

369

Allow me to address myself to Sharangovich, one of the leaders of the Byelorussian underground organization of plotters. Accused Sharangovich, what have you to say in this regard?

SHARANGOVICH: Both Goloded and Chervyakov informed our organization of this line, as of an accomplished fact. Besides, I must say that Tomsky never figured in conversations regarding this line; Rykov and Bukharin were mentioned. In addition, Chervyakov had several conversations with Bukharin, after which he not only informed me, but informed our organization, at a meeting of the centre, making reference to Bukharin and Rykov.

VYSHINSKY: The following paragraph from Rykov's reply: "There were several variations which consisted exactly in this. The idea was to give this compensation to Poland in the event of our coming to power in war time. The factors giving rise to the war, the attack by the imperialist powers (Poland and Germany), the war we were engineering in order to come to power, we did everything possible to sharpen and stimulate this factor in all our practical activities."

Do you confirm this testimony of yours?

RYKOV: I do.

VYSHINSKY: Whom did you have in view?

RYKOV: I had in view the centre of the Rights.

VYSHINSKY: Whom personally?

RYKOV: I have already said quite a lot about this.

VYSHINSKY: I want you not to be ashamed and to say it here.

RYKOV: I had Bukharin in mind. The centre consisted of three persons: myself, Bukharin and Tomsky. Consequently this refers to Bukharin as well.

VYSHINSKY: Consequently this refers to Bukharin as well?

RYKOV: Of course.

VYSHINSKY: Accused Bukharin, do you confirm this?

BUKHARIN: In general the centre possessed such a line.

VYSHINSKY: The next paragraph of Rykov's reply, page 120, reads as follows: "Chervyakov developed exceptionally intensive work in Byelorussia in his relations with the Poles. He was connected with them in his illegal activities. He drew all the practical conclusions from these instructions of ours." Do you confirm this, Rykov?

RYKOV: Of course.

VYSHINSKY: Consequently, Chervyakov and the people connected with you maintained systematic connections with the Poles?

RYKOV: Yes.

VYSHINSKY: They were executing your instructions?

370

about your conversation with Bukharin concerning the espionage connections of the Byelorussian organization with the Poles?

RYKOV: In this conversation there was no special emphasis put on its being an espionage connection.

VYSHINSKY: I am speaking of the nature of the connection, of its essence.

RYKOV: It was inevitable. Under these conditions, any kind of connection with the Poles automatically and inevitably—and everybody understands that—very rapidly develops into espionage connections.

VYSHINSKY: Not only was it inevitable that they should develop, but they did develop?

RYKOV: Yes.

VYSHINSKY: Under your leadership?

RYKOV: I mean to say that we did not personally direct this development; however, it is not a question of direct leadership but of general leadership. We absolutely and definitely bear responsibility for this.

VYSHINSKY: There is no point in making a pious face, accused Bukharin. Better admit what exists. And what exists is the following: you had a group of your accomplices, fellow-conspirators in Byelorussia, headed by Goloded, Chervyakov and Sharangovich. Is that right, Sharangovich?

SHARANGOVICH: It is.

VYSHINSKY: And on Bukharin's and Rykov's instructions, and under their leadership, you established connections with the Polish intelligence service and with the Polish General Staff? Is that right, Sharangovich?

SHARANGOVICH: Absolutely right.

VYSHINSKY: Under your leadership also with regard to the espionage connections. Is that right, Sharangovich?

SHARANGOVICH: Absolutely right.

VYSHINSKY: Consequently, who was the organizer of the espionage in which you engaged?

SHARANGOVICH: Rykov, Bukharin.

VYSHINSKY: Hence, they were spies.

SHARANGOVICH: Quite right.

VYSHINSKY: Just as . . .

SHARANGOVICH: As I myself.

VYSHINSKY: Be seated. (To Rykov.) Accused Rykov, did Goloded tell you in 1932 that all more or less important appointments of people to responsible posts in Byelorussia were first co-ordinated with the Polish intelligence service?

RYKOV: Yes.

VYSHINSKY: Did Bukharin know of this?

RYKOV: I cannot say.

371

about your conversation with Bukharin concerning the espionage connections of the Byelorussian organization with the Poles?

RYKOV: In this conversation there was no special emphasis put on its being an espionage connection.

VYSHINSKY: I am speaking of the nature of the connection, of its essence.

RYKOV: It was inevitable. Under these conditions, any kind of connection with the Poles automatically and inevitably—and everybody understands that—very rapidly develops into espionage connections.

VYSHINSKY: Not only was it inevitable that they should develop, but they did develop?

RYKOV: Yes.

VYSHINSKY: Under your leadership?

RYKOV: I mean to say that we did not personally direct this development; however, it is not a question of direct leadership but of general leadership. We absolutely and definitely bear responsibility for this.

VYSHINSKY: There is no point in making a pious face, accused Bukharin. Better admit what exists. And what exists is the following: you had a group of your accomplices, fellow-conspirators in Byelorussia, headed by Goloded, Chervyakov and Sharangovich. Is that right, Sharangovich?

SHARANGOVICH: It is.

VYSHINSKY: And on Bukharin's and Rykov's instructions, and under their leadership, you established connections with the Polish intelligence service and with the Polish General Staff? Is that right, Sharangovich?

SHARANGOVICH: Absolutely right.

VYSHINSKY: Under your leadership also with regard to the espionage connections. Is that right, Sharangovich?

SHARANGOVICH: Absolutely right.

VYSHINSKY: Consequently, who was the organizer of the espionage in which you engaged?

SHARANGOVICH: Rykov, Bukharin.

VYSHINSKY: Hence, they were spies.

SHARANGOVICH: Quite right.

VYSHINSKY: Just as . . .

SHARANGOVICH: As I myself.

VYSHINSKY: Be seated. (To Rykov.) Accused Rykov, did Goloded tell you in 1932 that all more or less important appointments of people to responsible posts in Byelorussia were first co-ordinated with the Polish intelligence service?

RYKOV: Yes.

VYSHINSKY: Did Bukharin know of this?

RYKOV: I cannot say.

VYSHINSKY: You do not know? You do not want to betray your pal?

RYKOV: What I mean to say is that in those cases when I know that he is not telling the truth, I am exposing him, but in those cases when I do not know, I cannot and shall not do it.

VYSHINSKY: I am asking you with regard to the fact that the Poles were giving their consent to the various appointments to official posts in Byelorussia. Was this known to your leading centre?

RYKOV: I knew of it. As for Bukharin, I never spoke to him about it. I also knew that Chervyakov and Goloded maintained connections, not only with me, but with Bukharin and Tomsky as well. Whether or not they spoke of this to Bukharin I cannot say, because I was not present at those conversations.

VYSHINSKY: Do you think that it would have been natural for Goloded to speak to Bukharin about this question? Or did they have to keep it a secret from Bukharin?

RYKOV: I think that, naturally, he spoke to Bukharin, but what they talked about I do not know.

VYSHINSKY: I shall ask you now by way of making a supposition: do you suppose that Bukharin knew of this?

RYKOV: This circumstance ... I prefer to speak only of what I know; and as to what I do not know—my position in this Court room is not such as to allow me to advance suppositions.

VYSHINSKY: And did you have any conversations with Bukharin about the affairs of the conspiracy in Byelorussia?

RYKOV: The only conversation which took place and which I remember—perhaps there were others but I have no recollection of them—that was during the early stage of our relations, which sprang up as a result of Tomsky's information.

VYSHINSKY: Why, you yourself said that even during the period of 1931 there were several occasions when you and Bukharin spoke about these questions. I have just reminded you of pages 119-20 of the case.

RYKOV: But the conversations related not only to what you are asking about ...

VYSHINSKY: Did you speak to Bukharin on several occasions?

RYKOV: About the fact that there was an organization in Byelorussia, that work was already being carried on....

VYSHINSKY: What kind of work?

RYKOV: Counter-revolutionary work in support of our ...

VYSHINSKY: Which included also espionage work?

RYKOV: I do not recall any conversations dealing especially with this espionage work. I do not exclude the possibility that there were such conversations, but I do not remember.

VYSHINSKY: Tell us, please, were there any instructions received from the Poles with regard to undermining the defence capacity?

RYKOV: I know of two cases. You asked me the same question two sessions before this. I mentioned two cases which are known to me—these refer to horses and road-building. You asked, why road-building? I answered: apparently in order to impede the movement of our troops.

VYSHINSKY: Did Bukharin know of this? Of this instruction of the Polish intelligence service to disrupt and destroy our defence capacity?

RYKOV: This question, like the previous ones, I cannot answer.

VYSHINSKY: Were you aware of the treasonable activities of the Polish spy Ulyanov?

RYKOV: I was.

VYSHINSKY: Did Bukharin know about it?

RYKOV: I do not know.

VYSHINSKY: Were you aware of the treasonable activities of the Polish spy Benek?

RYKOV: I was.

VYSHINSKY: Was Bukharin aware of it?

RYKOV: I do not know.

VYSHINSKY: Permit me then, Comrade President, to read page 127 of the record which contains the following question to Rykov and his reply: "Question: With regard to being informed of and directing the activities of your organization in Byelorussia, you are talking all the time almost exclusively about yourself; but what was the role of the other members of the centre? Answer: What I have deposed here . . ." And what you deposed there was about Benek, about Ulyanov, about the instructions of the Poles concerning undermining the defence capacity, about the appointment of official persons with the knowledge of the Polish intelligence service—did you depose that?

RYKOV: And something else besides.

VYSHINSKY: Did you depose that?

RYKOV: Yes.

VYSHINSKY: "What I have deposed here was, of course, known to the other members of the centre, to Bukharin and Tomsky." Do you confirm this?

RYKOV: This refers to all our relations with Byelorussia.

VYSHINSKY: No, you will not wriggle out of this, I shall read further. . . . "What I have deposed here," and what you deposed here refers to the Polish instructions to damage the strategical means of communication—this is on page 123 of the record, it refers to the treasonable espionage work of Benek—page 124 of the record, it refers to the treasonable espionage work of Ulyanov—pages 125 and 126 of the record. Finally, this is page 127, where it says: "From Chervyakov's information I retained in memory the most important thing, namely, that the leadership of our organization in Byelorussia received active assistance from the Polish intelligence service in corrupting the revolutionary movement in Western Byelorussia," etc. And the question: "You are talking about yourself, but tell us about your accomplices who knew about this." The answer: "The other members of the centre—Bukharin and Tomsky—knew of it too."

RYKOV: You have there the word "obviously." It implies that this is a supposition on my part, that my certainty is not based on direct facts.

VYSHINSKY: I asked you and you answered that you preferred to talk about the things which you knew.

RYKOV: But I made the reservation there—"obviously."

VYSHINSKY: In this case, I shall read on: "Bukharin and Tomsky knew . . ." Here you do not say "obviously," but you say, Bukharin and Tomsky knew, Schmidt was partly initiated into these affairs—you are referring to Vasily Schmidt—"But I dwelt more on my own role for the reason that, by a decision of the centre, the main connections with the Byelorussian anti-Soviet organization of the Rights were concentrated in my hands." Is this clear?

RYKOV: It is clear to me.

BUKHARIN: I was not asked a single word about this during the preliminary investigation, and you, Citizen Procurator, did not question me for three months, not a single word.

VYSHINSKY: I am questioning you now. This is my right.

BUKHARIN: But at the preliminary investigation . . .

VYSHINSKY: Be so kind as not to instruct me how to conduct a preliminary investigation, the more so since you do not understand a thing about it. You understand more about the affairs for which you find yourself in the dock.

BUKHARIN: Possibly.

VYSHINSKY: Was the accused Rykov, by your decision, put in charge of the connections with the counter-revolutionary organizations?

BUKHARIN: In a general way, he was put in charge.

VYSHINSKY: And your status was that of a secret member?

BUKHARIN: Inside there was no status of secrecy.

VYSHINSKY: With regard to connections with the Byelorussian group?

BUKHARIN: Generally everything was done with secrecy.

VYSHINSKY: But your status was that of particular secrecy?

BUKHARIN: This term cannot be applied here, it does not fit.

VYSHINSKY: Do you want to argue about the term?

BUKHARIN: No, I do not want to argue, on the contrary, I keep silent.

VYSHINSKY: I ask the Court to authenticate this. What I have cited here is fully identical with what was written in the original record signed by Rykov. And I request that this be presented to Rykov so that he may identify his signature.

RYKOV: I do not deny it.

VYSHINSKY: The word "obviously" refers to the previous sentence, but with regard to Bukharin there is no "obviously." "Bukharin and Tomsky knew, Schmidt was partly initiated."

THE PRESIDENT: I corroborate that these quotations correspond to the original record which has Rykov's signature on each page.

RYKOV: I affirm that the word "obviously" refers to what has been read.

VYSHINSKY: The word "obviously" is not there.

RYKOV: My deposition—"Bukharin and Tomsky knew, Schmidt was partly initiated"—should be understood with the word "obviously." I am not a very good stylist. If I said the word "obviously" in the first sentence, and the second sentence represents a paraphrase of the first sentence, the word "obviously" is implied.

VYSHINSKY: According to your supposition, did Bukharin know of these espionage connections, or did he not?

RYKOV: He should have known, but in less detail and in fewer particulars than I knew. But which details, which particulars, which facts out of those I related and knew in greater detail than he, that I cannot tell.

VYSHINSKY: If by the decision of the centre you were entrusted with maintaining the connections with the Byelorussian group, that means that you knew all the details of the connections.

RYKOV: No.

VYSHINSKY: Through the connections which you maintained you should have known everything.

RYKOV: No.

VYSHINSKY: Through the connections which you maintained you should have known everything you were doing.

RYKOV: I should have known what I was doing? I don't understand what you are driving at.

VYSHINSKY: I am asking you, were you supposed to know what you were doing?

RYKOV: What I was doing?

VYSHINSKY: Of course.

RYKOV: That is to say, you are asking me whether I was in a state of consciousness or unconsciousness? Always in a state of consciousness.

376

VYSHINSKY: And did Bukharin know everything?

RYKOV: I did not speak to Bukharin about details.

VYSHINSKY: I am not asking you about details but about the substance. Did Bukharin know the substance?

RYKOV: Bukharin was informed about the substance of the connection and knew about it.

VYSHINSKY: That is what I wanted to establish. Permit me to consider it established that Rykov and Bukharin knew the substance of the treasonable connection which included espionage. Is that correct, Rykov?

RYKOV: That is, espionage followed.

BUKHARIN: So it appears that I knew something from which something followed.

VYSHINSKY: You will argue it out at leisure.

RYKOV: I am afraid that there will be no leisure.

VYSHINSKY: That is for the Court to decide. I have no more questions.

THE PRESIDENT: Accused Bukharin, proceed.

BUKHARIN: In 1933-34 the kulaks were already smashed, an insurrectionary movement ceased to be a real possibility, and therefore in the centre of the Right organization a period again set in when the orientation toward a counter-revolutionary conspiratorial coup became the central idea. Thus, from a "palace coup," from a combination of a coup with a mass insurrection, and from an orientation toward a mass insurrection with the corresponding practical conclusions, we passed on to counter-revolutionary plotting pure and simple. And the central idea became that of a coup d'état which was to be accomplished by means of an armed conspiracy.

The forces of the conspiracy were: the forces of Yenukidze plus Yagoda, their organizations in the Kremlin and in the People's Commissariat of Internal Affairs; Yenukidze also succeeded around that time in enlisting, as far as I can remember, the former commandant of the Kremlin, Peterson, who, apropos, was in his time the commandant of Trotsky's train.[2]

Then there was the military organization of the conspirators: Tukhachevsky, Kork and others.

VYSHINSKY: What year was that?

BUKHARIN: I think it was in 1933-34.

VYSHINSKY: And at the same time you carried on negotiations of a defeatist and treasonable nature with Khodjayev?

BUKHARIN: I had one single talk with Khodjayev in 1936.

VYSHINSKY: In 1936. And what was this talk about?

BUKHARIN: Which—this?

VYSHINSKY: The one you had with Khodjayev.

BUKHARIN: In 1936?

VYSHINSKY: Yes.

BUKHARIN: Properly speaking, I heard Khodjayev's evidence, I heard what he said in Court, and I have quite a number of corrections to proffer to what was said.

VYSHINSKY: First we shall deal with those matters which require no corrections, and you will proffer your corrections later.

BUKHARIN: As you say.

VYSHINSKY: Did you tell Khodjayev that there already existed an agreement with fascist Germany?

BUKHARIN: No, I did not.

VYSHINSKY (to the Court): Permit me to question the accused Khodjayev.

Accused Khodjayev, did Bukharin talk with you?

KHODJAYEV: Yes, he did.

VYSHINSKY: How, when, where, and about what specifically?

KHODJAYEV: It was in the month of August, when Bukharin came to Tashkent. . . .

VYSHINSKY: Recount briefly what you have stated in Court.

KHODJAYEV: I gave my testimony during the preliminary investigation, I also gave it in Court. The conversation between me and Bukharin took place at my country house in Chimgan.

BUKHARIN: I stated the same.

KHODJAYEV: After reviewing the international situation of the U.S.S.R., after reviewing the situation in various European countries—I spoke about this in detail in my preliminary testimony—and then after reviewing the internal situation of the Soviet Union, Bukharin said that it was necessary so to direct our activities that these activities should help to bring about the defeat of the Union.

VYSHINSKY: That is to say, he considered this a natural process?

KHODJAYEV: According to what he said, the internal and international situation were leading up to this. He said that we, the Rights, had an agreement with fascist Germany, and that we were planning an agreement with Japan.

VYSHINSKY: Accused Bukharin, were you with Khodjayev at his country place?

BUKHARIN: I was.

VYSHINSKY: Did you carry on a conversation?

BUKHARIN: I carried on a conversation and kept my head on my shoulders all the time, but it does not follow from this that I dealt with the things of which Khodjayev just spoke; this was the first conversation. . . .

VYSHINSKY: It is of no consequence whether it was the first

378

or not the first. Do you confirm that there was such a conversation?

BUKHARIN: Not such a conversation, but a different one, and also secret.

VYSHINSKY: I am not asking you about conversations in general, but about this conversation.

BUKHARIN: In Hegel's "Logic" the word "this" is considered to be the most difficult word. ...

VYSHINSKY: I ask the Court to explain to the accused Bukharin that he is here not in the capacity of a philosopher, but a criminal, and he would do better to refrain from talking here about Hegel's philosophy, it would be better first of all for Hegel's philosophy....

BUKHARIN: A philosopher may be a criminal.

VYSHINSKY: Yes, that is to say, those who imagine themselves to be philosophers turn out to be spies. Philosophy is out of place here. I am asking you about that conversation of which Khodjayev just spoke; do you confirm it or do you deny it?

BUKHARIN: I do not understand the word "that." We had a conversation at the country house.

VYSHINSKY: What is there that you can't understand? The conversation, the contents of which were here related by Khodjayev. Is this clear?

BUKHARIN: If you are referring to the contents of the conversation, then the contents were somewhat different; but this conversation at the country house did take place.

VYSHINSKY: What different contents?

BUKHARIN: It was the first time in my life that I spoke to Khodjayev about politics. This explains the nature of the conversation. I told him that it was necessary for us to be prepared to overthrow the Soviet government by forcible means, and that for this purpose it was necessary to take advantage of possible mass movements which might occur there. Secondly ...

VYSHINSKY: What has that got to do with the agreement with fascist Germany?

BUKHARIN: I said nothing about an agreement.

VYSHINSKY: Accused Khodjayev, did Bukharin speak about an agreement?

KHODJAYEV: I confirm that he said the things of which he spoke here, but immediately after that he spoke about an agreement with Germany.

VYSHINSKY: Was there any talk about England?

KHODJAYEV: Yes, there was. He said that an agreement with England was being considered and that the Right centre would, on its part, take measures to effect this agreement, and that we, the centre of the nationalist organization of Uzbekistan, must, on our part, also take the necessary steps in this direction.

VYSHINSKY: Namely?

KHODJAYEV: In the sense of establishing connections with the British resident agents.

VYSHINSKY: Through whom?

KHODJAYEV: With regard to the question of "through whom," we, myself and Bukharin, established this not in the sense of an instruction but merely in the course of the conversation.

VYSHINSKY: It was a consultation?

KHODJAYEV: Yes.

VYSHINSKY: Accused Bukharin, do you confirm this part of Khodjayev's evidence?

BUKHARIN: I told Khodjayev that in our foreign political orientation we must make use of all keys, including the British.

VYSHINSKY: So you spoke not about a British orientation, but about British keys?

BUKHARIN: If it pleases you, about British keys.

VYSHINSKY: And could you say it in plainer words?

BUKHARIN: In foreign policy we orientated ourselves exclusively on the neutralization of Japan and Germany and on their assistance, which, however, did not preclude the necessity of taking advantage of the international contradictions. . . .

VYSHINSKY: Toward whom did you consider it necessary to orientate yourselves?

BUKHARIN: I beg your pardon, it is I who am speaking and not you.

THE PRESIDENT: Accused Bukharin, do not forget that it is not you who regulates the questions and answers here.

VYSHINSKY: I am asking you: what was your opinion? Towards whom were you to orientate yourselves?

BUKHARIN: I told him that it was necessary to take advantage of the international contradictions. . . .

VYSHINSKY: Accused Bukharin, do you confirm Khodjayev's evidence?

BUKHARIN: I said that we would have to deal with various foreign states, and that it was impossible to deal with only one group, but that it would be necessary to deal with the others as well.

VYSHINSKY: Hence, you did tell Khodjayev that it would be necessary to orientate yourselves towards certain foreign states?

BUKHARIN: You see, I gave up using the expression "orientation" because of its ambiguity, and therefore I am making it more precise. . . .

VYSHINSKY: Well, now make it more precise.

BUKHARIN: I told him . . .

VYSHINSKY: Was there any talk of England?

BUKHARIN: There was.

VYSHINSKY: Was there any talk of Japan?

BUKHARIN: There was.

VYSHINSKY: Was there any talk of Germany?

BUKHARIN: There was.

VYSHINSKY: Was there any talk to the effect that it was necessary to utilize both the ones and the others in the interests of your struggle against the Soviet government?

BUKHARIN: The question was not put that way. After all, it was the first time I spoke to Khodjayev.

VYSHINSKY: And you spoke of overthrowing the Soviet government this first time!

BUKHARIN: Yes, for a very simple reason. There is nothing for you to gesticulate about.

THE PRESIDENT: Accused Bukharin, do not forget where you are now.

BUKHARIN: This conversation was carried on in terms which spelt absolute secrecy, and not a single word was said. . . .

VYSHINSKY: I am not asking you about terms, I am asking you about the contents of the conversation.

BUKHARIN: I am using the same words which I used in my testimony during the preliminary investigation. . . .

VYSHINSKY: But I am not speaking about words. I will be compelled to cut the interrogation short because you apparently are following definite tactics and do not want to tell the truth, hiding behind a flood of words, pettifogging, making digressions into the sphere of politics, of philosophy, theory and so forth—which you might as well forget about once and for all, because you are charged with espionage and, according to all the material of the investigation, you are obviously a spy of an intelligence service. Therefore stop pettifogging. If this is the way you want to defend yourself I shall cut the interrogation short.

BUKHARIN: I am answering your questions.

VYSHINSKY: Did you talk with Khodjayev about overthrowing the Soviet government, which your conspiratorial group was preparing for?

BUKHARIN: I spoke in vague nebulous formulas.

VYSHINSKY: But such formulas as he could understand?

BUKHARIN: Perfectly right.

VYSHINSKY (to Khodjayev): Did you understand?

KHODJAYEV: Absolutely.

VYSHINSKY: Hence, it is not a question of words but of the contents. Did you say that it was necessary to orientate yourselves in your foreign relations towards various foreign states, and to make use of the internal contradictions and international contradictions in the interests of the struggle of your group of conspirators against the Soviet government?

BUKHARIN: Right.

VYSHINSKY: Did you say it?

BUKHARIN: I did.

VYSHINSKY: Hence, Khodjayev is right when he says that you spoke to him about connections with British spies.

BUKHARIN: But there was nothing of this.

VYSHINSKY (to Khodjayev): Was it so, Khodjayev?

KHODJAYEV: It was.

BUKHARIN: But this is nonsense, because assistance is not determined by spies. . . .

KHODJAYEV: I do not say spies, but resident agents.

VYSHINSKY: As you see, not just spies but resident agents.

KHODJAYEV: We established with him that it was best to act either through some Tadjik people or to send a person to Afghanistan.

VYSHINSKY (to Bukharin): Do you deny this?

BUKHARIN: I do. Nobody asked me about this.

VYSHINSKY: Well, I am asking you.

BUKHARIN: During the year I spent in prison I was not once asked about it.

VYSHINSKY: We are asking you here in an open proletarian Court, we are asking you here in this Court before the whole world.

BUKHARIN: But you did not ask me about this before.

VYSHINSKY: I am asking you again, on the basis of the testimony which was here given against you: do you choose to admit before the Soviet Court by what intelligence service you were enlisted—the British, German or Japanese?

BUKHARIN: None.

VYSHINSKY: I have no more questions to put to Bukharin.

THE PRESIDENT: Adjournment for 30 minutes.

*　　*　　*

COMMANDANT OF THE COURT: The Court is coming, please rise.

THE PRESIDENT: Please be seated. The session is resumed.

Accused Bukharin, proceed with your evidence; only speak more to the point.

BUKHARIN: All right, I shall.

I said last that an organization of a criminal counter-revolutionary conspiracy was created, which included the forces of Yenukidze, of Yagoda, the organization in the Kremlin, in the People's Commissariat of Internal Affairs, the military organization and forces of the Moscow garrison under the leadership of the conspirators of the military group, which, as is self-understood, did not exclude the utilization of other forces and cadres which were made up of the Trotskyites and Zinovievites. The more so that in the military group itself, which was the immediate organizer of the forces on which devolved the actual organization of the military coup, there had existed for a comparatively long period a bloc between the Rights, Trotskyites and Zinovievites, who, if my memory does not fail me, had joined this military group before the contact centre was organized.

During the period preceding the Seventeenth Party Congress, Tomsky broached the idea that the coup d'état with the help of the armed counter-revolutionary forces should be timed exactly for the opening of the Seventeenth Party Congress. According to Tomsky's idea, an integral part of this coup was to be a monstrous crime—the arrest of the Seventeenth Party Congress.[3]

This idea of Tomsky's was subjected to a discussion, though a very cursory one; but objections to this idea were raised on all hands. I am afraid of making an error, but it seems to me that it happened this way: that first this was discussed in the Right centre, but, since it was turned down there, the question was discussed in the so-called contact centre.

Pyatakov objected to this idea not for considerations of principle, but for considerations of tactics, because that would have aroused extreme indignation among the masses. In a word, objections were voiced not for considerations of principle, but for purely tactical considerations. This idea was rejected. But the fact alone that this idea was conceived and that it was subjected to a discussion speaks sufficiently clearly of the whole monstrosity and criminality of an organization of this sort.

I must say that at a much earlier period I personally had already given instructions to Semyonov to organize terrorist groups and reported this to our Right centre. It was accepted. Thus, I, more than any other member of the centre, am responsible for the organization of Semyonov's terrorist groups.

I must also stop to continue a thought which I have already touched on in part, or the facts which I have mentioned—our allying with various counter-revolutionary forces, especially and particularly with the Socialist-Revolutionaries and the Mensheviks. As regards my direct practical activities at that time, and not only my theoretical formulations, I must testify that I tried to establish a connection of this kind through a number of intermediaries and also personally. I also charged the Socialist-Revolutionary Semyonov—who was mentioned during the interrogation the day before yesterday—to get in touch with the underground members of the Socialist-Revolutionary Central Committee, who, if I am not mistaken, were then in exile (which does not alter the case), and consequently I am directly responsible for it not only as a member of the Right centre, but directly responsible in the immediate sense of the word.

Secondly, I tried to establish contact with organizations and groups of Socialist-Revolutionaries abroad through a certain Chlenov. This was one of the men in our diplomatic service, whom I had known years ago, since our school days, when he was a member of a Social-Democratic organization of that time. I say this not by way of a digression into history, but to explain and show why I felt such confidence in him despite the conspiratorial nature of the work of that time. And he tried to establish connections with the Central Committee of the Socialist-Revolutionaries; when he returned, he had no time to discuss the matter with me in detail, but from this conversation I ascertained approximately the following. The Socialist-Revolutionaries agreed in principle to support the bloc and maintain contact with the Rights, Trotskyites, Zinovievites, and the like. But they demanded formal guarantees, almost in written form, their conditions being that the peasant policy should be changed in the spirit of a kulak orientation, that the Socialist-Revolutionary and Menshevik Parties should be legalized—which obviously implied that the government which would be set up if the conspiracy were successful would be a coalition government.

Furthermore, during my last trip abroad in 1936, after the conversation with Rykov, I established contact with the Menshevik Nikolayevsky, who is very close to the leading circles of the Menshevik Party. From the conversation with Nikolayevsky I ascertained that he knew about the agreements between the Rights, Zinoviev's and Kamenev's people, and the Trotskyites, and that in general he was in the know of all that was going on, including the Ryutin platform.[4] The concrete and new element of our conversation was that in the event of the exposure of the centre of the Rights, or the contact centre, or the upper organization of the conspiracy generally, there would be, through Nikolayevsky, an understanding with the leaders of the Second International that they would launch a suitable campaign in the press.

Besides myself, some other prominent leaders of the organization of Rights and Trotskyites (in this case I can speak about the Rights, I have no information about the others) also had contact, were establishing criminal connections with representatives of counter-revolutionary organizations which had been set up long ago. Rykov had connections with the Mensheviks through Nikolayevsky. I forgot to say that my meeting with

Nikolayevsky was facilitated for me, and not only facilitated, but camouflaged, by the fact that I had to meet with this Nikolayevsky by virtue of my official business.[5] Thus I had a quite legitimate cover behind which I could carry on counter-revolutionary conversations and make agreements of one kind or another. Smirnov, or Foma, as he was called, had important connections of long standing. These connections had been made when he was still in the People's Commissariat of Agriculture, where, as you know, there were a number of prominent figures of the Socialist-Revolutionary and kindred movements. Everybody knows that some of them have been tried for wrecking. And Smirnov on his part was likewise arranging connections with the Socialist-Revolutionaries.

Thus, there is not a shadow of doubt—and I admit it fully and entirely—that apart from the bloc with the Trotskyites, Zinovievites, Kamenevites and bourgeois-nationalist organizations, there was also absolutely direct and real contact with Socialist-Revolutionaries and Mensheviks, for which I myself was to a large extent directly to blame of course, as a leader of the centre of the Rights. This meant in the first place the underground Socialist-Revolutionaries who had remained here, that is to say, the former Central Committee of the official Party of Socialist-Revolutionaries, and, in the second place, the organization abroad, which was principally rallied around such a person as Mark Vishnyak, the former secretary of the Constituent Assembly.[6]

After the great debacle of the Trotskyites and Zinovievites in connection with the assassination of Sergei Mironovich Kirov, after this . . .

VYSHINSKY: You want to go on to another period already, but I would like to ask some questions in connection with the Socialist-Revolutionaries. Bessonov testified here concerning his journey to Prague and his meeting with Sergei Maslov. In Bessonov's conversation with Maslov reference was made to Bukharin and Rykov. Bessonov said so here. You remember?

BUKHARIN: I thought he said he had been informed about the underground activities of Bukharin and Rykov.

VYSHINSKY: That is what I want to ask Bessonov before you continue. Accused Bessonov, did Maslov tell you that he knew about Bukharin's underground activity?

BESSONOV: He said that he was aware of the counter-revolutionary views of the Right opposition and their underground activities.

VYSHINSKY: Accused Bukharin, did you have direct connections with Maslov?

BUKHARIN: No.

VYSHINSKY: You knew what Maslov was doing in Prague,

385

that he was the organizer of a counter-revolutionary kulak party, that he was living on an income derived from a foreign intelligence service and from his newspapers and journals? Is that so, accused Bessonov?

BESSONOV: Quite true.

VYSHINSKY: Through whom did he obtain his information?

BUKHARIN: I do not know, but I think it was through the surviving members of the Socialist-Revolutionary Central Committee abroad.

VYSHINSKY: You were connected with the Central Committee of the Socialist-Revolutionaries?

BUKHARIN: Through Chlenov I was connected with Rapoport.

VYSHINSKY: A Socialist-Revolutionary?

BUKHARIN: This Rapoport was connected with Mark Vishnyak.

VYSHINSKY: And they were connected?

BUKHARIN: I do not know, but I can guess. You know that old acquaintances usually keep in touch in emigration.

VYSHINSKY: So you suppose that Sergei Maslov was informed about your underground activities through members of the Central Committee of the Socialist-Revolutionary organization abroad or . . .

BUKHARIN: Or through Rapoport or Vishnyak.

VYSHINSKY: And in regard to Rykov through Nikolayevsky?

BUKHARIN: No, I do not think so.

VYSHINSKY: Accused Rykov, have you any conjectures as to where Sergei Maslov could have obtained his information?

RYKOV: I have no information and no conjectures on this point.

VYSHINSKY: Did you inform your Menshevik connections about your underground activity?

RYKOV: No.

VYSHINSKY: Then how was it?

RYKOV: They knew that I was conducting work against the Central Committee.

VYSHINSKY: How did they know?

RYKOV: They knew it from me.

VYSHINSKY: But you said . . .

RYKOV: I understood you to mean that a certain organization was conducting work, but what kind of work . . .

VYSHINSKY: Underground, anti-Soviet. Did they know?

RYKOV: They knew it to this extent, but they did not know more concrete things.

VYSHINSKY: And there was no need for them to know more concrete things. So we may suppose that the émigré circle with which Nikolayevsky was associated was informed about your underground activities by him?

RYKOV: I can say nothing about this.

VYSHINSKY: This is not experts' evidence but an elucidation of your connections.

RYKOV: I have spoken about my connections. You are asking if this contact passed to Maslov?

VYSHINSKY: Of course.

RYKOV: Yes.

VYSHINSKY: You informed Nikolayevsky about your underground work?

RYKOV: Yes.

VYSHINSKY: Accused Bukharin, from Bessonov's testimony it can be taken that Maslov maintained contact with the Rights and was posted on their counter-revolutionary activities. You, as the leader of this counter-revolutionary organization, were consequently also in the sphere of this contact. Do you confirm this?

BUKHARIN: I was not in the sphere of this contact. I was in the sphere of contact with the Socialist-Revolutionaries. I have no information as to what they were doing, but in reply to your question I make a conjecture as to the possible channel.

VYSHINSKY: Through what channels this could pass?

BUKHARIN: Yes, the channels through which this could pass.

VYSHINSKY: Accused Bukharin, proceed.

BUKHARIN: So, I left off at the question of the composition of the "bloc of Rights and Trotskyites," which, as it appears from the entire material, is called the centre of Rights and Trotskyites but actually has a much broader content not only from the point of view of its hangers-on or its environment, but from the point of view of its very composition.

VYSHINSKY: In speaking about these connections of your centre and your bloc, you have said nothing about connections with the foreign intelligence service and fascist circles.

BUKHARIN: I have nothing to testify on this subject.

VYSHINSKY. Apart from what you have testified already?

BUKHARIN: Yes. Apart from what I have testified.

VYSHINSKY: Proceed.

BUKHARIN: When the fascists came to power in Germany, exchanges of opinion commenced among the leaders of the counter-revolutionary organizations concerning the possibility of utilizing foreign states in connection with a war situation. Here I must say frankly, and I tell the Court what I precisely remember, that in this major question, which is a very important subject for the Court's consideration and for the determination of the legal sanction, the Trotskyites were outright for territorial concessions, while on the whole the leading circles of the Right counter-revolutionary organization were primarily concerned with concessions, trade agreements, duties, prices, supplies of raw material, fuel, etc.—in short, various concessions of an economic nature. When I began my testimony I told the Court that I, as one of the leaders of the counter-revolutionary bloc, am not just as a cog in the wheel, bear responsibility for absolutely everything done by this organization. But in so far as concrete things are concerned, I think that it can be said of this case that the guiding principle in the bloc, the most active political principle in the sense of the acuteness of the struggle, in the sense of far-reaching criminal connections, etc., was after all the Trotskyite section. I repeat, I say this not in order to disclaim the responsibility of the Right section, since in this case from the point of view of criminology it is not important who first said "a," who repeated this "a," who exposed and reported it; but from the point of view of the internal mechanics of this case and from the point of view of elucidating the personal role of Trotsky, who, unfortunately, is beyond the reach of the Court,[7] I think this question has a certain importance, and that is why I make bold to emphasize it here.

In the summer of 1934 Radek told me that directions had been received from Trotsky, that Trotsky was conducting negotiations with the Germans, that Trotsky had already promised the Germans a number of territorial concessions, including the Ukraine. If my memory does not fail me, territorial concessions to Japan were also mentioned. In general, in these negotiations Trotsky already behaved not only as a conspirator who hopes to get power by means of an armed coup at some future date, but already felt himself the master of Soviet land, which he wants to convert from Soviet to non-Soviet.

I must say that then, at that time, I remonstrated with Radek. Radek confirms this in his testimony, just as he confirmed at a confrontation with me that I objected to this, that I considered it essential that he, Radek, should write and tell Trotsky that he was going too far in these negotiations, that he might compromise not only himself, but all his allies, us Right conspirators in particular, and that this meant certain disaster for us. It seemed to me that with the growth of mass patriotism, which is beyond all doubt, this point of view of Trotsky's was politically and tactically inexpedient from the standpoint of the plan of the conspiracy itself, and that much greater caution was needed.

VYSHINSKY: Who said that?

BUKHARIN: I said it. I even considered that preliminary negotiations were not needed.

VYSHINSKY: To avoid exposure?

BUKHARIN: No, there were also other considerations. . . .

VYSHINSKY: As you have just said, you pointed out then that this might lead too far. . . . You were afraid of exposure?

BUKHARIN: I do not speak of exposure in the sense of arrest, but in the sense that the whole business might have come to grief.

VYSHINSKY: I am also speaking of this. You expressed this point of view out of caution, to save your plot from ruin?

BUKHARIN: This will have to be turned round a bit. . . .

VYSHINSKY: You can turn it round as much as you like. . . . What year was this?

BUKHARIN: The conversation with Radek took place in the summer of 1934.

VYSHINSKY: And the conversation with Karakhan was later?

BUKHARIN: It took place after his arrival in Moscow in 1935.

VYSHINSKY: And was this conversation with Karakhan preceaed by a conversation with Yenukidze, or was the conversation with Yenukidze on this topic later?

BUKHARIN: The first conversation was with Tomsky.

VYSHINSKY: So, the conversation with Tomsky was the basis?

BUKHARIN: There were three conversations on this subject.

VYSHINSKY: We will proceed to that later. Continue.

BUKHARIN: Must I dwell on the internal aspect of the affair, on the conversations that took place, or is this of no interest?

VYSHINSKY: That depends on what the conversations were about.

BUKHARIN: Of course they were not about the weather.

VYSHINSKY: Tell the Court about your crimes.

BUKHARIN: Tomsky considered it permissible to take advantage of war and preliminary agreements with Germany. This I opposed by the following arguments. I said that in the first place if Germany were to intervene in one way or another during the war to help the counter-revolutionary coup, then, as it always happens, Germany, being rather a strong military and technical factor, would inevitably put her feet on the table and tear up any preliminary agreement which had been concluded. Secondly, I advanced the argument that since this was to be a military coup, then by virtue of the very logic of things the military group of the conspirators would have extraordinary influence, and, as always happens in these cases, it would be just that section of the joint upper group of the counter-revolutionary circles that would command great material forces, and consequently political forces, and that hence a peculiar Bonapartist danger might arise. And Bonapartists—I was thinking particularly of Tukhachevsky—would start out by making short shrift of their allies and so-called inspirers in Napoleon style. In my conversations I always called Tukhachevsky a "poten-

389

tial little Napoleon," and you know how Napoleon dealt with the so-called ideologists.

VYSHINSKY: And you considered yourself an ideologist?

BUKHARIN: Both an ideologist of a counter-revolutionary coup and a practical man. You, of course, would prefer to hear that I consider myself a spy, but I never considered myself a spy, nor do I now.

VYSHINSKY: It would be more correct if you did.

BUKHARIN: That is your opinion, but my opinion is different.

VYSHINSKY: We shall see what the opinion of the Court is. Tell us how you conducted this "ideological" conversation with Tomsky then or at any other time; did Tomsky propose two variants for the seizure of power?

BUKHARIN: I am coming to that in the next few words.

VYSHINSKY: I'll wait.

BUKHARIN: Very well. I wanted to say that after these preliminary conversations in 1935—I do not know what other factors played a part before the adoption of any decision on the part of the Right centre and on the part of the contact centre: whether Tomsky was being pressed by Yenukidze or the military circles, or jointly by Yenukidze, the Trotskyites and the Zinovievites—but the fact is that Karakhan left without a preliminary conversation with the members of the leading centre, with the exception of Tomsky.

Now I want to tell the Court what I remember concerning the three conversations that took place after Karakhan's arrival. The first conversation was with Tomsky, the second with Yenukidze and the third with Karakhan, who introduced certain details and an added coefficient into the conversation.

As I remember, Tomsky told me that Karakhan had arrived at an agreement with Germany on more advantageous terms than Trotsky.

VYSHINSKY: First of all, tell us about Tomsky. I am interested in your talk with Tomsky concerning your plan of a coup d'état, as you call it, the seizure of power. When did you have a conversation about opening the front to the Germans?

BUKHARIN: I am coming to that now.

VYSHINSKY: Can you touch on the question of how you and Tomsky were going to open the front to the Germans in case of war?

BUKHARIN: I will speak about this a bit later.

VYSHINSKY: You do not care to speak on the subject that interests the investigation now?

BUKHARIN: I shall speak about this front.

VYSHINSKY: I put the question for the third time. When did you have a conversation about opening the front to the Germans?

BUKHARIN: When I asked Tomsky how he conceived the mechanics of the coup he said this was the business of the military organization, which was to open the front.

VYSHINSKY: So Tomsky was preparing to open the front?

BUKHARIN: He did not say that.

VYSHINSKY: Yes or no?

BUKHARIN: I asked how he visualized the mechanism of this intervention.

VYSHINSKY: Whose intervention?

BUKHARIN: Of certain foreign states.

VYSHINSKY: Did he say how it was conceived ?

BUKHARIN: Tomsky did say.

VYSHINSKY: Tomsky said, "Open the front"?

BUKHARIN: I will put it exactly.

VYSHINSKY: What did he say?

BUKHARIN: Tomsky said that this was a matter for the military organization, which was to open the front.

VYSHINSKY: Why was it to open the front?

BUKHARIN: He did not say.

VYSHINSKY: Why was it to open the front?

BUKHARIN: From my point of view, it ought not to open the front.

VYSHINSKY: From the point of view of your organization?

BUKHARIN: From the point of view of our organization.

VYSHINSKY: Were they to open the front from the point of view of Tomsky, or not?

BUKHARIN: From the point of view of Tomsky? At any rate, he did not object to this point of view.

VYSHINSKY: He agreed?

BUKHARIN: Since he did not object, it means that most likely he three-quarters agreed.

VYSHINSKY: He nevertheless kept one-quarter in reserve?

BUKHARIN: I only wanted to stress the point.

VYSHINSKY: I am asking you. Answer the question.

BUKHARIN: Citizen Procurator, you said that every word was very important to the Court.

VYSHINSKY: Permit me to read Bukharin's testimony, Vol. V, pp. 95-96: "Tomsky told me that two variants were discussed: the case where the new government would be formed in time of peace," and this meant that the conspirators would organize a new government in time of peace, and "the case where it would be organized in time of war; in the latter case the Germans were demanding big economic concessions," concessions of which I have already spoken, "and were insisting upon cessions of territory." Tell us, is this true or not?

BUKHARIN: Yes, that is all true.

391

VYSHINSKY (continues to read): "I asked Tomsky how the mechanism of the coup was visualized in this connection. He said that this was the business of the military organization, which was to open the front to the Germans."

BUKHARIN: Yes, correct.

VYSHINSKY: Did Tomsky agree with this, or not?

BUKHARIN: He said "was to" ("dolzhna"); but the meaning of these words is "müssen" and not "sollen."

VYSHINSKY: Leave your philology aside. In Russian "was to" means "was to."

BUKHARIN: It means that the military circles had the idea that in that case these military circles . . .

VYSHINSKY: No, not the idea, but they were to. That means . . .

BUKHARIN: No, it does not mean.

VYSHINSKY: So they were not to open the front?

BUKHARIN: From whose point of view? Tomsky told me what the military said, what Yenukidze said.

VYSHINSKY: And what did you testify?

BUKHARIN: I know very well what I testified.

VYSHINSKY: "Tomsky said that the coup was the business of the military organization, which was to open the front to the Germans." Is the question clear?

BUKHARIN: I said that I asked Tomsky: "How is the mechanism of this intervention visualized?" He answered: "This is the business of the military organization, which is to open the front to the Germans." Whereupon I said . . .

VYSHINSKY: No more for the present. They were to open the front. That is, they intended to open the front to the Germans?

BUKHARIN: Yes.

VYSHINSKY: In which circles?

BUKHARIN: In the circles of the military organization.

VYSHINSKY: Did Tomsky agree to this?

BUKHARIN: He did not say so directly.

VYSHINSKY: He three-quarters agreed?

BUKHARIN: I am telling you that from what he said it followed that he probably agreed to this.

VYSHINSKY: And when he told you this, did you object?

BUKHARIN: I did.

VYSHINSKY: And why did you not write "I objected"?

BUKHARIN: That is written here later on.

VYSHINSKY: What is written later on is something entirely different.

BUKHARIN: That means that I objected.

VYSHINSKY: What is written later is: "Whereupon I said that in that case . . ." In which case?

392

BUKHARIN: In case the front were opened.

VYSHINSKY: Right. "In that case it would be expedient to try those guilty of the defeat at the front. This will enable us to win over the masses by playing on patriotic slogans."

BUKHARIN: But permit me, I will explain that to you, if you will allow me.

VYSHINSKY: One moment. Let us examine it in order, in order. Was this your objection?

BUKHARIN: Yes.

VYSHINSKY: Is that what you told him: "The front must not be opened"?

BUKHARIN: Yes.

VYSHINSKY: But where is this written?

BUKHARIN: It is not written, but it is self-understood.

VYSHINSKY: And what does playing on patriotic slogans mean?

BUKHARIN: The word "play" here was not meant in an odious sense. . . .

VYSHINSKY: "Was to" is not meant in its right sense, and "play" is not meant in its right sense.

BUKHARIN: "Was to" in Russian has two meanings.

VYSHINSKY: And we want to have one meaning here.

BUKHARIN: That is what you would like, but I am entitled not to agree with you. It is well known that in German "sollen" and "müssen" have two meanings . . .

VYSHINSKY: You are accustomed to speak in German, but we are speaking in the Soviet language.

BUKHARIN: The German language in itself is not odious.

VYSHINSKY: You are continuing to speak in German, you are already accustomed to negotiate with the Germans in their language. But here we speak in Russian. When Tomsky told you that it was necessary to open the front to the Germans, then, if you objected, you should have said as follows: "I objected, I said that I would not consent to such a betrayal, to such treason." Did you say that?

BUKHARIN: No, I did not. But if I said that it was necessary . . .

VYSHINSKY: To play on patriotic slogans, that is, to speculate on them, to pretend that somebody committed treason, but that you were patriots. . . .

BUKHARIN: That is not quite so, because in other parts of my testimony, including the confrontation with Radek, and during all the conversations with Radek, I objected to what Radek said and declared that Tomsky did not understand. . . .

VYSHINSKY: Accused Bukharin, that you have here employed a jesuitical method, a perfidious method, is borne out by the fol-

393

lowing. Permit me to read further: "I had in mind that by this, that is, by the conviction of those guilty of the defeat, we would be able at the same time to rid ourselves of the Bonapartist danger that alarmed me."

BUKHARIN: Yes, quite true.

VYSHINSKY: So that is how you "objected" to the opening of the front.

BUKHARIN: One task by no means interferes with the other.

VYSHINSKY: One task is the opening of the front. . . .

BUKHARIN: No, not the opening of the front.

VYSHINSKY: To try those guilty of defeat at the front, to play on patriotic slogans, and thus get off scot free.

BUKHARIN: An entirely different orientation.

VYSHINSKY: That is the conversation you had with Tomsky. Is it correctly recorded here?

BUKHARIN: Correctly, of course, but you did not read everything.

VYSHINSKY: I have read three paragraphs; are they correctly recorded?

BUKHARIN: The three paragraphs are quite correctly recorded.

VYSHINSKY: Did you speak to Yenukidze on this subject?

BUKHARIN: I did speak to Yenukidze.

VYSHINSKY: Did you speak to Karakhan?

BUKHARIN: I did.

VYSHINSKY: What did Yenukidze and Karakhan say on this subject?

BUKHARIN: Yenukidze . . .

VYSHINSKY: In general confirmed this?

BUKHARIN: In general he confirmed it. Tomsky learnt this from Karakhan and Yenukidze.

VYSHINSKY: That is?

BUKHARIN: They confirmed, firstly, that Karakhan had concluded an agreement with the Germans on conditions of economic concessions of territories, to which Karakhan did not reply, saying that this matter must be discussed. It included a formula regarding the severance of the Union Republics. Thirdly, about pacts.

VYSHINSKY: Thirdly, about opening the front?

BUKHARIN: Thirdly, about the pacts of mutual assistance of the U.S.S.R. with Czechoslovakia and France.

VYSHINSKY: Did you have a pact with them?

BUKHARIN: I am conveying what Tomsky said about what he was told by Karakhan. That is what he said. The Germans demanded the annulment of these pacts.

VYSHINSKY: Of whom with whom?

BUKHARIN: Of the new government.

394

VYSHINSKY: You thought that you were already the government?

BUKHARIN: We did not think so, but Karakhan said that in case . . .

VYSHINSKY: Was it sanctioned?

BUKHARIN: We did not afterwards object, which means that we sanctioned it.

VYSHINSKY: That is, you thought that you were acting as a government?

BUKHARIN: The meaning of the pact . . .

VYSHINSKY: Then you would break the alliance with Czechoslovakia? [8]

BUKHARIN: You did not let me finish. Karakhan replied to this in the affirmative. We reckoned on deceiving the Germans and on not fulfilling this demand.

VYSHINSKY: And so you built everything on deception. And they reckoned on deceiving you?

BUKHARIN: That always happens.

VYSHINSKY: On using you and then throwing you on to the muck heap.

BUKHARIN: That is so.

VYSHINSKY: In general, both of you lost.

BUKHARIN: Happily, that is so.

VYSHINSKY: Happily for us, that is so. And did you talk to Karakhan about opening the front?

BUKHARIN: Karakhan said that the Germans were demanding a military alliance with Germany.

VYSHINSKY: And are the gates closed to an ally?

BUKHARIN: Karakhan gave me an answer to this question.

VYSHINSKY: That the gates are closed to an ally?

BUKHARIN: No.

VYSHINSKY: That means to open the gates?

BUKHARIN: Pardon me, there was no alliance yet.

VYSHINSKY: But there were expectations, plans?

BUKHARIN: Well, just now the Soviet Union has an alliance with France, but that does not mean that it opens the Soviet frontiers.

VYSHINSKY: What did you have?

BUKHARIN: We had nothing; there were verbal plans.

VYSHINSKY: You do not want to admit that you were the initiator of the proposal to open the front in case of an attack by the Germans.

BUKHARIN: No. But Rykov affirms this because it is now perfectly clear. . . .

VYSHINSKY: But Rykov confirms that Bukharin was the initiator of this idea. Accused Rykov, is that correct?

395

RYKOV: I first heard about opening the front from Bukharin.

BUKHARIN: And that is true. But that does not mean that I was the initiator. It was after the conversation with Tomsky.

VYSHINSKY (to Rykov): Did Bukharin object to it?

RYKOV: He did not object in my presence.

VYSHINSKY: Be seated. (To Bukharin.) Continue your account. I consider that the question of opening the front is clear. I have no more questions.

BUKHARIN. I forgot to say and mention that when Trotsky was negotiating with the Germans, the Rights were already a component part of the "bloc of Rights and Trotskyites" and that consequently they were partners to these negotiations, even in spite of the fact that Trotsky did this on his own initiative, independently of any preliminary arrangement.

That in the main is all I have to say, I think.

THE PRESIDENT: Comrade Procurator, the accused Bukharin has finished his testimony.

VYSHINSKY: I have no questions to put.

THE PRESIDENT. Comrade Procurator, we have now to settle the question of summoning the witnesses. Or shall we proceed to interrogate Bukharin on the events of 1918?

VYSHINSKY: I have already done so.

THE PRESIDENT: We must decide at what time to summon the witnesses: now, or after the adjournment?

VYSHINSKY: If the witnesses are present I would request to have them called in now.

THE PRESIDENT: The first witness to be called is Yakovleva?

VYSHINSKY: Yes.

THE PRESIDENT: Call in the witness.

VYSHINSKY: While the witness is being called in, permit me to put to Bukharin a question in connection with his testimony at the preliminary investigation—p. 94, Vol. V. May I read it?

THE PRESIDENT: You may.

VYSHINSKY: "We clearly perceived the gigantic growth of Soviet patriotism, which growth was connected with the tangible growth of the might, strength and prosperity of the broad masses, the extraordinary popularity of Stalin's slogan that we would not surrender a single inch of Soviet land, which in our eyes was a perfectly obvious indication of this growing patriotism." Do you confirm this?

BUKHARIN: I do.

VYSHINSKY: "To set ourselves up against this slogan, however cunning our political calculations might be, would most certainly have meant isolating ourselves from the masses once

396

and for all, rendering our position meaningless in advance, and our plans utterly hopeless." Do you confirm this?

BUKHARIN: I confirm it fully.

VYSHINSKY: I have no more questions.

THE PRESIDENT: Be seated.

(Witness Yakovleva enters the Court.)

THE PRESIDENT: Is your name Yakovleva, Varvara Nikolayevna?

YAKOVLEVA: Yes, Yakovleva, Varvara Nikolayevna.

THE PRESIDENT: You are summoned in the case of Bukharin, Nikolai Ivanovich. You are called upon to tell the Court the truth. As you have been summoned at the request of the Procurator of the U.S.S.R., he has the right to interrogate you.

VYSHINSKY (to Yakovleva): Do you recall your participation in the group of "Left Communists" in 1918?

YAKOVLEVA: Very clearly.

VYSHINSKY: Tell us, briefly, who was the principal organizer and leader of this group?

YAKOVLEVA: Its ideological leader was Bukharin.

VYSHINSKY: Who was the organizer of the activities of this group?

YAKOVLEVA: The factional centre of the anti-Soviet group of "Left Communists" was the Moscow Regional Bureau. It was elected at a regional Party conference, had a fairly large number of members, including peripheral functionaries. Then it set up what was called the narrow bureau for its permanent organizational and directing work. At the end of 1917 and the beginning of 1918 this narrow bureau consisted entirely of "Left Communists," and it represented the factional centre of the group of "Left Communists."

VYSHINSKY: Who was the leader of this centre?

YAKOVLEVA: The ideological leader was Bukharin. Then there were a number of public persons who formulated the ideology of the "Left Communists." They included Preobrazhensky, Radek and Ossinsky.

VYSHINSKY: I am interested in the particulars about Bukharin, inasmuch as he is charged in this case. We need this for a characterization of him.

Tell us, what was Bukharin's attitude to the peace negotiations in Brest-Litovsk, to the conclusion of the Brest-Litovsk Peace?

YAKOVLEVA: Bukharin, like the whole group of the "Left Communists," was opposed to the conclusion of peace with the Germans.

VYSHINSKY: What measures did he take to frustrate the conclusion of peace?

YAKOVLEVA: There were a number of utterances in the press and in Party circles, and then there were the illegal activities of the group of "Left Communists," which were directed towards the same ends.

VYSHINSKY: In what did the underground anti-Soviet activities of the group of "Left Communists" consist? Perhaps you recall the most outstanding facts characteristic of its activities?

YAKOVLEVA: What I know about the illegal activities of the anti-Soviet group of so-called "Left Communists" is the following: I mentioned the narrow bureau, which was the factional centre of the group. I was the secretary of the Regional Bureau, but when I left for Leningrad—this was at the beginning of December 1917—the secretary of the bureau was Mantsev. At the end of February 1918, a meeting of the Moscow Regional Bureau was held at which the question of concluding peace with the Germans was discussed. At this meeting, Stukov, a member of the Bureau, moved a resolution on this question and spoke in favour of this motion, expressing the idea that in the political struggle against the conclusion of peace with the Germans, in the political struggle on the question of war and peace, we must not only not shrink from replacing the leadership of the Party and the government, but we must not even shrink from the arrest of the leading, most resolute part of the government, as represented by Lenin, Stalin and Sverdlov. And if the struggle were to become more acute, we must not shrink even from their physical extermination.

VYSHINSKY: From the physical extermination of whom?

YAKOVLEVA: Of the leaders of the Party: Lenin, Stalin and Sverdlov.

VYSHINSKY: This was proclaimed at a secret meeting of the bureau?

YAKOVLEVA: It was not a secret meeting, it was an open meeting of the narrow bureau of the Moscow Regional Bureau.

VYSHINSKY: And so it might be said that this was a meeting of "Left Communists." There were no others present?

YAKOVLEVA: No.

VYSHINSKY: This was said by Stukov?

YAKOVLEVA: Yes. Stukov also said that in a political struggle we must not only not shrink from replacing the government and even from arresting its leading and politically irreconcilable section, but even from the loss of the Soviet power, which in the event of the conclusion of peace with the Germans would become a mere formality. Stukov's draft resolution and his speech at this meeting were recorded in the minutes book of the Moscow Regional Bureau.

In May 1918, in connection with the Moscow Regional Conference, Mantsev and I were preparing to hand over the materials of the Regional Bureau, and Mantsev told me that Bukharin insisted on the removal of this draft resolution and the record of Stukov's speech from the minutes book of the Regional Bureau, for the reason that it was necessary to avoid politically compromising the position of the Moscow Regional Bureau and the exposure of its illegal activities. Guided by this argument, Mantsev and I removed (tore out or cut out) from the minutes book and destroyed the pages that contained the record of Stukov's speech and his draft resolution.

It should be mentioned that this was that very meeting of the Moscow Regional Bureau about which Lenin wrote in his article "Strange and Monstrous." In this article Lenin referred to the explanatory text accompanying the resolution.

The page from the minutes book of the Regional Bureau we destroyed was this explanatory text accompanying the resolution.

I must also say something about the origin of this document. I was not present at the meeting of the Regional Bureau in question. I was at that time in Leningrad. I returned to Moscow very soon after this meeting, two or three days later. Having acquainted myself with the minutes of the Regional Bureau, I spoke to Stukov and told him that the resolution he had moved was politically unjustified and also criticized his speech rather sharply. Stukov told me that he did not bear responsibility for the political justification of this motion, and that on this subject I must address myself to Bukharin, for he had received this draft resolution from Bukharin in Leningrad just before the meeting of the Regional Bureau, together with a letter in which Bukharin instructed him, Stukov, as to the character of his speech in support of the motion.

Shortly after this, I had a talk with Bukharin on the subject. This was before the Seventh Party Congress. I asked Bukharin whether what Stukov had said was true. Bukharin confirmed that the draft resolution was sent to Stukov by him, Bukharin, and that he had instructed Stukov how to speak in support of the motion. He had advised him to elucidate to the members of the Regional Bureau the possible prospects of the political struggle on the question of war and peace, and he thereupon said roughly the same as what was contained in Stukov's speech and what I have just related. I told Bukharin that I had until then believed that Stukov's idea about the arrest and deposal of the government was Stukov's personal standpoint. Bukharin rejoined that among the "Left Communists" there were people who were able with logical consistency and thoroughness to envisage all the possible prospects of the struggle. He considered Stukov one of these people. He considered that Stukov would not fear to put the question bluntly and sharply, and that is why he had instructed Stukov to draft the resolution and to expound to the members of the Regional Bureau the ideas I have mentioned.

At the same time Bukharin told me that he was not the only one who thought in this way, that he, Bukharin, had had a frank talk on the subject with Trotsky, and that Trotsky also thought that the political struggle on the question of war and peace had only just begun; that the "Left Communists" must envisage the possibility of this struggle going beyond the confines of the Party, and that allies must be sought who could be relied upon in this struggle. Trotsky had told Bukharin that the "Left" Socialist-Revolutionaries, whose position on the question of the war was already fairly clear, might prove to be such allies.

Bukharin also said that Trotsky too believed that the struggle might assume most aggressive forms, involving not only the replacement of the government, but also the overthrow of the government and the physical extermination of leading people in the government and the Party. He thereupon mentioned Lenin, Stalin and Sverdlov.

At the same time Bukharin informed me that in the course of this conversation Trotsky had frankly told him that his, Trotsky's, halfway position on the question of the conclusion of peace was nothing but a tactical manoeuvre, that he simply did not dare to come out actively in favour of the position of the "Left Communists," that is, against the conclusion of peace, that he was a new man in the Party and if he openly adopted the position of the "Left Communists" it would be said that Trotsky had joined the Party in order to fight Lenin. [9]

During this conversation, when telling me of Trotsky's line and of the possible allies of the "Left Communists," Bukharin also referred to Zinoviev and Kamenev. He said that Zinoviev and Kamenev occupied an extremely vacillating position on the question of war and peace, and that during the fight over this question they had in private conversations repeatedly expressed themselves to Bukharin directly in favour of the position of the "Left Communists." Bukharin said that Zinoviev and Kamenev dared not come out openly against Lenin, that they had been compromised by their position during the October days on the question of the October uprising, of the Socialist revolution, and that therefore they did not dare to come out against Lenin openly.[10] He said that Zinoviev and Kamenev, like Bukharin and Trotsky, also thought that the political struggle on the question of war and peace might go beyond the confines of the Party, and that in that case the "Left Communists" must think of allies on whom they could rely. But, Bukharin said, on the question of allies Zinoviev and Kamenev went farther than Trotsky and considered that the Mensheviks and Right Socialist-Revolutionaries might also become such allies. Bukharin said that Zinoviev and Kamenev, even though

400

they had come out in favour of the conclusion of peace, were opposed to Lenin, did not believe in the victory of the revolution, and did not believe that the Bolsheviks could retain power. They considered the victory of counter-revolution inevitable and that this counter-revolution would be an unprecedentedly bloody one.

I soon had occasion to hear from Zinoviev himself his opinion on this question. This was somewhat later, during the Seventh Party Congress. One day Bukharin took me to see Zinoviev in the Hotel Astoria. When we arrived, Zinoviev at once began to talk about counter-revolution. He said that it was mustering its forces, that it would go badly with us, and that the bloodshed would be extraordinary. Bukharin turned the conversation to the question of the conclusion of peace. Zinoviev took up the subject and said roughly as follows: "Well, the conclusion of peace will help to accomplish the historically inevitable and inexorably approaching counter-revolution by more peaceful means and with less bloodshed. After the conclusion of peace the Soviet power will be obliged, under the joint pressure of the Germans and the internal counter-revolution, to make concessions and, in particular, to include other parties in the government." He said that in general the conclusion of peace with the Germans would be one more proof that Zinoviev and Kamenev were right, of the correctness of their view that the time was not ripe for a Socialist revolution. "After the conclusion of peace, the Germans, supported by the forces of internal counter-revolution, will switch the revolution over to bourgeois-democratic lines and liquidate the October Revolution." And when I, in great astonishment, asked Zinoviev whether this was the reason why he favoured the conclusion of peace with the Germans, he was greatly embarrassed and said: "Of course not. I only consider that if the forces of the revolution prove inadequate and the counter-revolution inevitable, the Germans, and the conclusion of peace with the Germans, may play a positive part." Thus the position of Zinoviev on the question of peace really proved to have had nothing in common with the position of Lenin. Zinoviev's position was thoroughly capitulationist; and as a matter of fact I then got the impression that he dreamed of peace as one of the means of liquidating the Socialist revolution. Somewhat later...

VYSHINSKY: What was Bukharin's attitude to this question?

YAKOVLEVA: Bukharin was present.

VYSHINSKY: Did he express himself?

YAKOVLEVA: When we left, Bukharin said to me: "Zinoviev was embarrassed, you put him such awkward, tactless questions. Nevertheless, he has said enough to make his position clear."

I answered that Zinoviev had said more than enough, but I could not understand why Bukharin referred to Zinoviev and Kamenev as allies of the "Left Communists," as people whom he hoped to win over to his side; in my opinion, we did not need capitulators. To this Bukharin rejoined that I, Yakovleva, was unable to take a long view.

VYSHINSKY: A long view?

YAKOVLEVA: Yes.

VYSHINSKY: What does that mean?

YAKOVLEVA: At that time I did not attach any significance to it, but later on I thought over what it meant, namely, that if you go beyond the confines of the Party, then even Trotsky, even Zinoviev and Kamenev, would be of use, and that this was exactly the reason for the talk about the allies which the "Left Communists" were to have in mind should they suffer defeat within the Party.

VYSHINSKY: Irrespective of what these allies represented?

YAKOVLEVA: Yes.

VYSHINSKY: Continue.

YAKOVLEVA: What I have still to say about the illegal activities of the group of "Left Communists" relates to a somewhat later period, roughly to the end of April or to May. At that time it was already perfectly clear that the "Left Communists" had suffered severe defeat in the Party. This was shown by the Seventh Party Congress, it was shown by the position of the majority of the organizations in the localities after the Seventh Party Congress, and, finally, it was shown by the very attitude of the population and the Party circles towards the conclusion of peace, which took place at that time. Roughly at the end of April, perhaps it may have been at the beginning of May—I cannot say exactly—there was an illegal meeting, a private illegal conference of the group of "Left Communists."

As far as I can recall there were present: Pyatakov, Preobrazhensky, Bukharin, Stukov, Lobov, Maximovsky, Mantsev, Kizelshtein and I. At this meeting Bukharin made a report. He said that the "Left Communists" had suffered defeat in the Party, but that this did not remove the question of the "ruinous" consequences of the Brest-Litovsk Peace, that the "Left Communists" must not lay down their arms, and that allies must be sought outside the Party. Such allies were the "Left" Socialist-Revolutionaries; their position on the question of war and peace at that time had become perfectly definite. In connection with the conclusion of peace they had resigned from the government. Their Second Congress had taken place, and it had endorsed the resignation of the "Left" Socialist-Revolutionaries from the government and their opposition to the conclusion of peace. Bukharin informed this conference that already in February the "Left" Socialist-

402

Revolutionaries had started negotiations with the "Left Communists" for the joint formation of a government, and that he therefore considered it expedient once more to start negotiations with the "Left" Socialist-Revolutionaries for the formation of a joint government. It should be mentioned that in the course of his report Bukharin again enlarged on the same ideas about the prospects of the struggle over the question of peace which had been expounded before by Stukov and of which he had spoken about to me in the conversation which I have just related. He spoke about the possibility of extremely aggressive forms of struggle, that the question of the government itself and of the formation of a government from "Left Communists" and "Left" Socialist-Revolutionaries was already perfectly clear, that in the course of the struggle for this the question might arise of the arrest of the leading group of the government as represented by Lenin, Stalin and Sverdlov, and that if the struggle became more acute even the physical extermination of the most resolute group of the leaders of the Soviet government was probable. Some time later, very soon after this, another conference was called, consisting roughly of the same people. The conference adopted Bukharin's proposal to start negotiations with the "Left" Socialist-Revolutionaries about the joint formation of the government, and to ascertain their views. It was also agreed that these negotiations should be conducted by Bukharin and Pyatakov. Somewhat later, very soon afterwards, a conference was again summoned consisting roughly of the same people. At this second conference Bukharin reported that the negotiations had taken place, that they had negotiated with Kamkov, Karelin and Proshyan, that the "Left" Socialist-Revolutionaries agreed to the joint formation of the government with the "Left Communists," had hinted that they already had a concrete plan for the seizure of power and the arrest of the government and that they made it a definite condition that the "Left Communists" should take part in the organizational preparations for the seizure of power and the replacement of the government.

Bukharin proposed that consent should be given in principle to the "Left" Socialist-Revolutionaries about taking such a part in the organizational preparations, and that negotiations with them should be continued on this basis. The conference endorsed Bukharin's view and resolved that the negotiations should be continued on the basis mentioned. A few days after this conference, the Moscow Regional Conference took place, at which the "Left Communists" were again completely smashed, and the Regional Bureau dissolved. The "Left Communists" lost their organizational force and their organizational base and generally speaking ceased to be an organizational force of any kind. Thus the "Left" Socialist-Revolutionaries received no organizational assistance from the

"Left Communists" and did their job with their own forces. I am referring to the July revolt.

That is all I know about the illegal activities of the "Left Communists."

VYSHINSKY: Consequently, judging by your evidence, you affirm that in 1918, immediately after the October Revolution, during the period when the Brest-Litovsk Peace was being concluded, there existed an anti-Soviet conspiracy in which Bukharin and his group of so-called "Left Communists," Trotsky and his group and the "Left" Socialist-Revolutionaries took part?

YAKOVLEVA: There undoubtedly was a conspiracy with the "Left" Socialist-Revolutionaries inasmuch as quite definite negotiations were conducted with them.

VYSHINSKY: What was the role of Bukharin in this affair?

YAKOVLEVA: I have stated that Bukharin himself proposed that these negotiations should be conducted, and that he conducted them in conjunction with Pyatakov.

VYSHINSKY: That is, his role was a perfectly practical one, as a leader of this conspiracy?

YAKOVLEVA: Yes.

VYSHINSKY: You confirm this?

YAKOVLEVA: I do.

VYSHINSKY: Further, you confirm that Bukharin spoke of the necessity of not shrinking in the course of a struggle from the arrest of the leaders of the Party and the·government?

YAKOVLEVA: He said that in the course of the struggle it might so happen that we must not shrink from this.

VYSHINSKY: He had in mind?

YAKOVLEVA: He had in mind determination and political irreconcilability, that is, readiness to fight to the end for the overthrow of the leaders of the Party I have mentioned.

VYSHINSKY: You said that it was Lenin, Stalin and Sverdlov that he had in mind?

YAKOVLEVA: Yes, these names were mentioned by Stukov.

VYSHINSKY: And did Bukharin mention them?

YAKOVLEVA: I also heard them from Bukharin.

VYSHINSKY: You heard them?

YAKOVLEVA: I heard the same from Bukharin.

VYSHINSKY: You confirm to the Court that Bukharin also told you that the assassination of Lenin, as the head of the Soviet state, and Stalin and Sverdlov, as leaders of the Party and the government, was politically expedient and necessary.

YAKOVLEVA: Bukharin spoke about that. Of course, he spoke of it cursorily, veiling it in a number of vague and unnecessary theoretical arguments, as Bukharin likes to do generálly. He wrapped up this idea like a cocoon in a host of lengthy explanations, but he said it.

VYSHINSKY: Accused Bukharin, do you want to say anything?

BUKHARIN: I can speak on the sum total of what Varvara Nikolayevna said.

VYSHINSKY: Accused Bukharin, were you the organizer and leader of the so-called group of "Left Communists" in 1918?

BUKHARIN: I was one of the organizers.

VYSHINSKY: You were one of the organizers of this group?

BUKHARIN: Yes.

VYSHINSKY: Did you at this period conduct illegal work, fighting the Soviet power?

BUKHARIN: Here one must deal with various periods. If it is a question of the period prior to the Brest-Litovsk Peace, there was nothing illegal in the strict meaning of the term, for the simple reason that everybody knew about the struggle, there was an open organ of this struggle, conversations took place openly. . . .

VYSHINSKY: Did you speak openly of the arrest of Lenin, Stalin and Sverdlov?

BUKHARIN: There was talk of arrest, but not of physical extermination. This was not in the period prior to the Brest-Litovsk Peace, but after. Before the Brest-Litovsk Peace the principal orientation of the "Left Communists" was to gain a majority in the Party by legal means. . . .

VYSHINSKY: What legal means?

BUKHARIN: Discussions, voting at meetings, and so on.

VYSHINSKY: And when did the hope of this disappear?

BUKHARIN: That was after the Brest-Litovsk Peace. I want to clarify this question in order to refute V. N. Yakovleva's evidence. She speaks of a period prior to the Brest-Litovsk Peace, which is patent nonsense, because at that time we and the Trotsky-ites had the majority in the Central Committee and we hoped to win the majority in the Party, so that to speak of conspiratorial activities at that time is nonsense. At that time I had one conversation with Pyatakov, when Karelin and Kamkov came and said that they proposed to set up a new government. . . .

VYSHINSKY: When was that?

BUKHARIN: It was before the Brest-Litovsk Peace. They proposed to form a government by arresting Lenin for 24 hours.

VYSHINSKY: And so we may say that prior to the conclusion of the Peace of Brest-Litovsk you had a conversation with the "Left" Socialist-Revolutionaries, Karelin and Kamkov, about the formation of a new government, that is, by first overthrowing the government headed by Lenin? Was there such a conversation?

BUKHARIN: There was.

VYSHINSKY: About the arrest of Lenin?

405

BUKHARIN: The Socialist-Revolutionaries spoke of that.

VYSHINSKY: As you put it, the Socialist-Revolutionaries spoke about the arrest of Lenin; but the witness Yakovleva affirms that Bukharin too spoke about the arrest of Lenin.

BUKHARIN: She is mixing it up with another question. She asserts that the conversation took place before the conclusion of the Brest-Litovsk Peace.

VYSHINSKY: I ask you, were there before the conclusion of the Brest-Litovsk Peace negotiations with the Socialist-Revolutionaries about the arrest of Lenin?

BUKHARIN: Yes.

VYSHINSKY: And were there also negotiations after the conclusion of the Brest-Litovsk Peace?

BUKHARIN: After the conclusion of the Brest-Litovsk Peace such a conversation really took place.

VYSHINSKY: And there had also been the other conversation?

BUKHARIN: The difference is that in the first conversation a negative answer was given.

VYSHINSKY: I am not asking you about the answer, but about the facts which took place. Was there a conversation with Karelin and Kamkov about the arrest of Lenin?

BUKHARIN: I confirm that there was.

VYSHINSKY: Before the Brest-Litovsk Peace?

BUKHARIN: Yes.

VYSHINSKY: And were there also negotiations after the conclusion of the Brest-Litovsk Peace?

BUKHARIN: There were.

VYSHINSKY: What about?

BUKHARIN: About political contact.

VYSHINSKY: And about arrest?

BUKHARIN: And about the arrest of the trio Yakovleva has mentioned.

VYSHINSKY: Of whom exactly?

BUKHARIN: Of Lenin, Stalin and Sverdlov.

VYSHINSKY: Also for 24 hours?

BUKHARIN: This formula was not employed then.

VYSHINSKY: And how were they to be arrested? And what for?

BUKHARIN: In order to form a new government.

VYSHINSKY: And what was to be done with the arrested?

BUKHARIN: There was no talk of physical extermination.

VYSHINSKY: But it was not precluded?

BUKHARIN: On the contrary, we all thought that the safety of these persons must be guarded at all costs.

406

VYSHINSKY: When a government is overthrown and arrested, are not forcible methods resorted to?

BUKHARIN: Yes.

VYSHINSKY: Did you envisage adopting forcible methods when making the arrest? Is this true or not?

BUKHARIN: It is.

VYSHINSKY: But what do forcible methods involve? Did you determine that precisely?

BUKHARIN: No, we did not.

VYSHINSKY: And so you decided to act as circumstances permitted and dictated?

BUKHARIN: Just so.

VYSHINSKY: But circumstances might dictate very decisive action?

BUKHARIN: Yes, but the fact is that neither did the "Left Communists" hold a fatalistic standpoint, but reckoned with the circumstances. This did not mean that circumstances dictated anything and everything.

VYSHINSKY: Let us for the present establish what is undisputed. Before the Brest-Litovsk Peace there was talk about the arrest of Vladimir Ilyich Lenin; after the Brest-Litovsk Peace there were negotiations about the arrest of Lenin, Stalin and Sverdlov and the forcible overthrow of the government. Is that correct?

BUKHARIN: It is correct on the whole.

VYSHINSKY: Moreover, when the forcible overthrow of the Soviet power and the arrest of Comrades Lenin, Stalin and Sverdlov were spoken of, forcible methods were actually spoken of, but which exactly were not mentioned?

BUKHARIN: That is so. All that was said was that their safety must be guaranteed at all costs.

VYSHINSKY: Witness Yakovleva, what do you say to this? Is Bukharin speaking the truth?

YAKOVLEVA: I was not present during his negotiations with the "Left" Socialist-Revolutionaries.

VYSHINSKY: What did he tell you?

YAKOVLEVA: He told me that such a possibility was not precluded.

VYSHINSKY: What possibility?

YAKOVLEVA: That the possibility of physical extermination, that is, assassination, was not precluded.

VYSHINSKY: Did he speak to you about this?

YAKOVLEVA: He did.

VYSHINSKY: And he did not say that this was absolutely precluded, because the safety and inviolability of these persons was assured?

YAKOVLEVA: I did not hear him say that.

407

VYSHINSKY: And about assassination?

YAKOVLEVA: That I did hear, but I repeat that this conversation was of such a character that he did not stress the matter....

VYSHINSKY: But he spoke about it?

YAKOVLEVA: He did.

VYSHINSKY: I have no more questions to put to Bukharin and Yakovleva.

BUKHARIN: Have I the right to question the witness?

THE PRESIDENT: You have.

BUKHARIN: I have many questions to ask.

VYSHINSKY: Perhaps we could leave it to the evening session.

THE PRESIDENT: Since according to the procedure there is to be an adjournment at three o'clock, I now declare the adjournment.

VYSHINSKY: Excuse me, if we are going to suspend the examination of the witness Yakovleva until the evening session, I request the opportunity to make a few remarks.

THE PRESIDENT: You may.

VYSHINSKY: Firstly, about a statement connected with the charge brought against the accused Pletnev and Levin. I want to submit this statement to the Counsel of the accused mentioned, and then request permission to read it.

(The statement is submitted to the Counsel for Defence).

THE PRESIDENT: Have the Counsel for Defence acquainted themselves with the statement?

COUNSEL FOR DEFENCE KOMMODOV: The Counsel for Defence has no objection to the statement being attached to the records.

THE PRESIDENT: The Court attaches the statement to the records.

VYSHINSKY: Permit me to read the statement. (Reads.)

"To the Procurator of the U.S.S.R., Comrade Vyshinsky,

"Having acquainted myself with the indictment published on March 3, 1938, in the case of the conspiratorial bloc of Rights and Trotskyites, I consider it my duty to inform you of the following:

"In my capacity as physician of the Medical Administration of the Kremlin, I was assigned to Alexei Maximovich Gorky at his summer house during his last illness for the performance of intravenous infusions.

"I perfectly recall that in the early days of A. M. Gorky's illness he was given many heart stimulants which were administered both internally and by means of intravenous infusions, and injections.

"Thus, I personally, on the instructions of the physicians in attendance, and chiefly of L. G. Levin, performed the following

408

injections and intravenous infusions: digalen, cardiosol, glucose, and glucose together with strophanthus and strophanthin (I think it was German).

"I draw your attention to the fact that from the very early days of A. M. Gorky's illness these heart stimulants were administered in large quantities.

"During one of the infusions of strophanthin I expressed to Dr. L. G. Levin my doubts about the use of strophanthin, which caused me alarm and which I feared to administer. It is significant that Levin at once discontinued further infusions of strophanthin. This is all the more remarkable because I am not a therapeutical specialist and from this standpoint my opinion, under normal conditions, could not have been of any particular importance to Dr. L. G. Levin.

"It must also be mentioned that the infusion of strophanthin (intravenous) was performed in conjunction with digalen (during this period).

"About ten days before A. M. Gorky's death, Prof. Pletnev, who had come to Gorky's summer residence for consultation purposes, seeing that I was preparing to make the usual infusion (I do not remember of what exactly), cynically said to me: 'Why do you do that? A patient in such a condition should be allowed to die in peace.'

"I at once reported Pletnev's statement to Dr. Levin, who said that the infusions should be continued.

"If necessary, I can confirm the above in Court and I answer for what I have written.

"Dr. M. Y. Belostotsky."

VYSHINSKY: I request the Court to have Dr. Belostotsky summoned to give evidence as a witness.

At the same time, in order to elucidate the circumstances connected with the slaying of A. M. Gorky, Comrades Menzhinsky and Kuibyshev and M. A. Peshkov, Gorky's son, and with the attempt on the life of Comrade N. I. Yezhov, I request that a commission of medical experts be appointed, consisting of the following:

1. Prof. Nikolai Adolfovich Shereshevsky, Scientist of Merit,

2. Prof. Dmitry Alexandrovich Burmin, Scientist of Merit,

3. Prof. Vladimir Nikitich Vinogradov,

4. Prof. Dmitry Mikhailovich Rossisky,

5. Vladimir Dmitrievich Zipalov, Doctor of Medicine.

If my request to appoint a commission of medical experts consisting of the persons mentioned is granted, permit me to submit the questions to them at the evening session.

THE PRESIDENT: Has the Counsel for Defence any objection to summoning the witness and appointing the commission of experts?

COUNSEL FOR DEFENCE KOMMODOV: The Counsel for Defence have no objection to summoning the witness and the experts.

THE PRESIDENT: The Court grants the request of Comrade Vyshinsky, Procurator of the U.S.S.R., to summon Dr. Belostotsky, Maximilian Yulianovich, as a witness, and also to the summoning of an expert commission consisting of the five persons mentioned by the Procurator, Comrade Vyshinsky.

Adjournment till 6 p.m.

[*Signed*] PRESIDENT: V. ULRICH
Army Military Jurist
President of the Military Collegium of
the Supreme Court of the U.S.S.R.

SECRETARY: A. BATNER
Military Jurist First Rank

COMMANDANT OF THE COURT: The Court is coming, please rise.

THE PRESIDENT: Please be seated. The session is resumed.

Comrade Commandant, call witness Yakovleva. (Witness Yakovleva enters the Court.) Accused Bukharin, have you any questions to put to witness Yakovleva?

BUKHARIN: Yes, I have several, if you will allow me.

THE PRESIDENT: Please.

BUKHARIN: Firstly, I wish to ask witness Yakovleva whether she is aware that I was the first during the struggle agianst Trotsky to give publicity to the conversation with Kamkov and Karelin?[1]

YAKOVLEVA: I am aware of that, but I am also aware of the point that when Bukharin, in the heat of the Party's.struggle against Trotsky, reported on this fact, he did not tell the whole story, far from it.

BUKHARIN: That's another question....

THE PRESIDENT: Accused Bukharin, let her finish.

YAKOVLEVA: He did not have the courage to pull the whole curtain aside, and only raised a tiny corner of it. I am aware of that too.

THE PRESIDENT: What other questions are there?

BUKHARIN: I have another question....

VYSHINSKY: Excuse me. I have a question to put to witness Yakovleva. What in your opinion did Bukharin conceal, what did he suppress?

YAKOVLEVA: He suppressed all that I have told the Court today.

VYSHINSKY: That is to say?

YAKOVLEVA: That is to say, the fact that there was a plot between the "Left Communists" and the "Left" Socialist-Revolutionaries.

VYSHINSKY: It was organized with the direct, active, leading...

YAKOVLEVA: ... part being played by Bukharin himself.

VYSHINSKY (to Bukharin): Is that true?

BUKHARIN: What I testified is true.

VYSHINSKY: Is that true?

BUKHARIN: What Yakovleva says regarding the period prior to the Brest-Litovsk Peace is untrue.

VYSHINSKY (to Bukharin): I am not talking of that. Is it true that you were one of the organizers of the plot against the Soviet power, that is to say, of the plot of the "Left Communists" and the "Left" Socialist-Revolutionaries?

BUKHARIN: I testified to that effect. Now I wish to ask whether witness Yakovleva was aware that Kuibyshev, Menzhinsky and Yaroslavsky[2] belonged to the "Left Communists"?

VYSHINSKY: I ask this question to be ruled out as having no bearing on the case.

THE PRESIDENT: You need not answer this question, as it has no bearing on the case.

BUKHARIN: Then I ask Citizen the President to explain to me whether I have the right to put such questions as I wish, or whether my questions are determined by Citizen the Procurator.

THE PRESIDENT: Accused Bukharin, Yakovleva was called here to give testimony as to your anti-Soviet activity, the activity of Nikolai Ivanovich Bukharin. In connection with her testimony you wished to put several questions to her in relation to matters concerning you, and not any other persons.

BUKHARIN: Quite so, but I ask for an explanation from Citizen the President as to whether I have the right to put such questions as I consider necessary to put, or whether their character is determined by someone else, particularly, by Citizen the Procurator. In that case, of course, I cannot put questions.

THE PRESIDENT: You put one question and received a reply to it. Do you still wish to put questions?

BUKHARIN: Yes, very much so.

VYSHINSKY: Allow me to make the following remark: I consider it necessary to explain Article 257 of the Code of Criminal Procedure, which defines, firstly, that the President guides the Court investigation, and, secondly, that at the Court investigation the President rules out of the Court investigation and the speeches for the prosecution and the defence all points that have no bearing on the case under trial.

BUKHARIN: Then, Citizen Procurator, I ask for an explanation. . . .

THE PRESIDENT: Citizen the Procurator will give you no explanation.

BUKHARIN: Then I ask Citizen the President of the Court to explain to me whether the question of the composition of the central group of the "Left Communists" has any bearing on the case or not?

THE PRESIDENT: I completely rule out your question. Have you any questions to witness Yakovleva as far as you are concerned, or not?

BUKHARIN: I still have a number of questions.

VYSHINSKY: I ask permission to explain the contents of Article 257 of the Code of Criminal Procedure to Bukharin, in order to avoid further misunderstanding, and to ensure that the accused Bukharin does not put such questions in the future.

THE PRESIDENT: I quote Article 257 of the Code of Criminal Procedure of the R.S.F.S.R.:

"The president at a Court trial shall direct the course of the trial, endeavour to keep the Court investigation and the speeches for the prosecution and the defence free of everything extraneous to the case under examination, and direct the Court investigation in the way best calculated to elicit the truth."

BUKHARIN: Am I to understand this as meaning that you bar this question as having no relation to the point at issue?

THE PRESIDENT: Accused Bukharin, if you have questions to witness Yakovleva, put specific questions to her.

BUKHARIN: Yes, I have questions. I ask witness Yakovleva to say whether she denies that in the Central Committee prior to the Brest-Litovsk Peace the majority of the votes was held by the "Left Communists" plus the Trotskyites.

THE PRESIDENT: What bearing has this question on your criminal role?

BUKHARIN: It has this much bearing, that I wish thereby to motivate and explain the point that it was absolutely senseless to strive for a plot . . .

THE PRESIDENT: The Court is interested in your role in the plot against the leaders of the Soviet government, and this is now the subject of the testimony.

BUKHARIN: Good, then allow me to put the following question. Does witness Yakovleva deny that the "Left Communists" prior to the Party Congress strove to receive a majority in the Party by legal means?

THE PRESIDENT: The question has nothing whatever to do with the charge preferred against you of organizing a plot against the Soviet power, and therefore I rule it irrelevant.

BUKHARIN: Does Yakovleva deny that I was one of the members of the Presidium of the Congress in Moscow, one of the members of the Presidium which at the time of the murder of Mirbach arrested the faction of "Left" Socialist-Revolutionaries?

THE PRESIDENT: This question has no bearing whatsoever on your criminal activity. I rule it irrelevant.

BUKHARIN: Does witness Yakovleva deny that in 1919 I was

413

wounded at a meeting of the Moscow Committee by a "Left" Socialist-Revolutionary bomb?

THE PRESIDENT: This question has nothing whatever to do with the charge against you of being concerned in a plot. I rule this question irrelevant also.

BUKHARIN: I have no more questions.

THE PRESIDENT: Comrade Procurator, have you any questions to witness Yakovleva?

VYSHINSKY: I have a question to Bukharin. For all that, I am interested in whether you were one of the organizers of the plot against the Soviet power in 1918.

BUKHARIN: I, Citizen Procurator, gave testimony on this point and had a confrontation in your presence. I stated that I admitted myself...

VYSHINSKY: I ask you. If you choose to answer, speak; if you do not, don't reply. I ask you, in 1918 were you one of the organizers of the plot of "Left Communists" and "Left" Socialist-Revolutionaries against the Soviet power?

BUKHARIN: Of the preparation of such a plot, yes.

VYSHINSKY: Despite all the questions you have put to witness Yakovleva, this question can be solved thus: that you were one of the organizers of a plot against the Soviet power.

BUKHARIN: But I am speaking of exact dates and exact facts, and say: Yes, there was a moment when I was a participant in negotiations of a conspiratorial character, undertaken through Pyatakov.

VYSHINSKY: How long did this "moment" continue?

BUKHARIN: It continued for a comparatively short time, for the simple reason...

VYSHINSKY: Approximately how long, though?

BUKHARIN: I think about several months.

VYSHINSKY: A moment of your conspiratorial activity in 1918 that continued for several months.

BUKHARIN: This activity was expressed in negotiations.

VYSHINSKY: In negotiations, calculated on success, in preparing all kinds of measures, etc.

With whom specifically did you conduct negotiations about the plot?

BUKHARIN: I admit two criminal conversations.

The first conversation was with Karelin, Pyatakov and Kamkov prior to the Brest-Litovsk Peace.

VYSHINSKY: You consider this conversation a criminal one?

BUKHARIN: I consider the conversation a criminal one because...

VYSHINSKY: I did not ask why. I only asked, do you consider this conversation a criminal one?

414

BUKHARIN: Yes, I think it was. Another criminal conversation took place with Pyatakov, who was commissioned to conduct negotiations of a similar character with the group of "Left" Socialist-Revolutionaries, with Kamkov, Karelin and somebody else.

VYSHINSKY: Did you personally have any dealings with any of the "Left" Socialist-Revolutionaries on the question of the plot?

BUKHARIN: I had no dealings on these questions.

VYSHINSKY: Did you have any conversation with Karelin?

BUKHARIN: I had a general conversation with Karelin, but had no conversations regarding a plot. And then a catastrophic change in the situation took place, I was sent to Germany.

VYSHINSKY: Excuse me, did you have no conversation with Karelin?

BUKHARIN: I did not.

VYSHINSKY: And with Kamkov?

BUKHARIN: Nor with Kamkov.

VYSHINSKY: I ask you: did you, in 1918, in connection with your conspiratorial plans, have a conversation with Kamkov, member of the Central Committee of the Party of "Left" Socialist-Revolutionaries? Did you or did you not?

BUKHARIN: I say I did not. I had one conversation . . .

VYSHINSKY: Excuse me. Did you or did you not? You can't answer that way. Did you or did you not have a conversation?

BUKHARIN: I did not after the Brest-Litovsk Peace, but prior to the Brest-Litovsk Peace I had one conversation.

VYSHINSKY: I ask you: did you have a conversation with Kamkov regarding a plot, on a subject of a conspiratorial character?

BUKHARIN: I have said that prior to the Brest-Litovsk Peace I had one conversation, but it cannot be interpreted as you are doing.

VYSHINSKY: Allow me to cite Vol. IV, p. 92, where Kamkov testifies as follows: "Bukharin told me: the struggle within our Party against Lenin's position on the Brest-Litovsk Peace is assuming acute forms. Within our ranks the question is being discussed of creating a new government consisting of 'Left' Socialist-Revolutionaries and 'Left Communists.' Bukharin mentioned Pyatakov as a possible candidate for leader of the new government, and stated that the idea was to bring about the change of government by arresting its members, headed by Lenin."

Did such a conversation take place?

BUKHARIN: Not quite such, but something like it.

VYSHINSKY: Something like it. I have no more questions.

THE PRESIDENT: Witness Yakovleva, you are not needed any longer.

VYSHINSKY: I would ask that she be left in the Court room during the examination of other witnesses for confrontations that may be necessary.

THE PRESIDENT: Comrade Commandant, ask witness Ossinsky in. (Witness Ossinsky enters the Court.)

THE PRESIDENT (to Ossinsky): Is your name Valerian Valerianovich Ossinsky?

OSSINSKY: Quite so.

THE PRESIDENT: You are called here as a witness in the Bukharin case. You are asked to testify the truth.

OSSINSKY: At your service.

THE PRESIDENT: Comrade Procurator, have you any questions to put to Ossinsky?

VYSHINSKY: Yes, of course.

THE PRESIDENT: Very well.

VYSHINSKY: Witness Ossinsky, what do you know of the activity of the accused Bukharin connected with his participation in the group of so-called "Left Communists"? I speak of his criminal activities. Do you know of any facts in this sphere or not; if you do, then what facts?

OSSINSKY: Only relating to the year 1918, or to 1917 as well?

VYSHINSKY: If you have facts relating to 1917, then by all means, I do not object.

OSSINSKY: Bukharin was the leader of the so-called "Left Communist" faction, which took shape in the second half of November 1917 in connection with differences that arose on the question of the conclusion of the Brest-Litovsk Peace with the Central Powers. Nikolai Ivanovich Bukharin was the leader of this faction, in which I also took part as a member of the centre. In the beginning, the activity of the faction followed legal lines, although from the very outset the struggle against Lenin's Party leadership was exceptionally acute, and gradually grew more so; by February 1918 the struggle found expression in the resolution of the Moscow Regional Bureau of the Party, regarding which Lenin wrote his article "Strange and Monstrous." As is well known, in this resolution the Moscow Regional Bureau declared in advance that should the Brest-Litovsk Peace be concluded, the Soviet power would become a mere formality, and that it, the bureau, would not subordinate itself to instructions coming from the Central Committee led by V. I. Lenin. This was the legal expression of the great sharpening of the anti-Party struggle waged by the "Left Communist" faction. Simultaneously with this, illegal criminal activity was also begun.

The first information I received regarding this side of the activity of the "Left Communist" faction led by Bukharin was at the beginning of March 1918 from V. N. Yakovleva (one of

416

the active members of the group of "Left Communists"). My official position at that time was that of chairman of the Supreme Council of National Economy. I had been away, had been in Kharkov and returned in the first week or so of March to Leningrad, where I had my permanent abode at that time. On my return I met with Varvara Nikolayevna Yakovleva as my immediate assistant in the Supreme Council of National Economy (where she was business manager). Yakovleva told me what had taken place in my absence and informed me that an illegal meeting of the Moscow Regional Bureau and of other "Left Communists" had taken place, in which Bukharin, Yakovleva, Lomov, Mantsev, Stukov and others had participated. At this meeting the question had been raised that a very sharp and vigorous line must be taken against Lenin's leadership of the Party and the Soviets, the line of seizing power, of overthrowing Lenin's government and placing it under arrest; Yakovleva stated that Bukharin was inclined to the idea that with the arrest of Lenin, Stalin and Sverdlov, the necessity would arise of physically removing, or, to speak more clearly, of exterminating them as the three most outstanding Party and Soviet leaders, as the people carrying on a most consistent struggle for the conclusion of the Brest-Litovsk Peace, the most dangerous opponents of the "Left Communists."

At the preliminary investigation I answered from memory that Bukharin had also taken part in this meeting. I cannot make this assertion for certain, but what I can assert with absolute certainty is that these proposals were introduced and adopted by the inner circle of members of the Moscow Regional Bureau on the initiative, on the instructions and with the complete agreement of Bukharin.

VYSHINSKY: But what grounds have you for asserting that these proposals were adopted on the initiative, on the instructions and with the complete agreement of Bukharin?

OSSINSKY: That was what Yakovleva told me. Simultaneously with this, a proposal was introduced about the formation of a bloc with the "Left" Socialist-Revolutionaries and the conduct of negotiations in this direction with the "Left" Socialist-Revolutionaries. These negotiations were to be conducted, on the one hand, by Stukov and Bukharin, and, on the other hand, by the "Left" Socialist-Revolutionaries Kamkov, Karelin and Proshyan. It was then decided to prepare the Moscow Regional Party organization for the appropriate action to seize power and arrest the government. It was intended to time the action for the arrival of the government in Moscow, since here was the main citadel of the "Left Communists"—the Moscow Regional Bureau, which was in our hands—and it was therefore natural to concentrate such action at that point and to fix it for that moment. I came

417

to the conclusion that I must ask Bukharin himself about this. Our conversation took place a couple of days later. I put the question to Bukharin as to whether Yakovleva had exactly passed on the decisions adopted by the inner circle of members of the Regional Bureau according to his, Bukharin's, line. Bukharin confirmed the point that Yakovleva had given me an exact outline of the decision, and that he agreed with this decision. I then asked him whether, if a line was taken for an undertaking fraught with such vast consequences, Bukharin could state that this undertaking had a sufficiently solid political basis and whether one could consider the combined efforts of the "Left Communists" and Socialist-Revolutionaries to be such a basis. In reply to this question Bukharin stated that my question and the element of doubt that it contained were justified, that he was already taking steps to provide the plan outlined with a wider basis. He gave me a review and characterization of the political groupings—both inside and outside the Party—that could be drawn into this bloc. First of all, he spoke in this connection of Zinoviev and Kamenev and of those who surrounded them, and put the question in this way: at first sight it might appear that Zinoviev and Kamenev were not suitable partners to be drawn into such a bloc, because Zinoviev was then (and that was the case) making speeches at meetings, making reports, etc., in favour of the Brest-Litovsk Peace; but this behaviour of Zinoviev and Kamenev was only a very artful double game, calculated primarily on restoring confidence in themselves both among the Party leadership and the masses of Party members, a confidence seriously undermined by the blackleg behaviour in the pre-October and October days of these people, whose reputation had been very seriously damaged. By coming forward as a unit solid with the Party leadership they strove above all to restore this confidence. But this by no means implied that they had abandoned their intention of waging a struggle against the Party leadership.

Zinoviev and Kamenev regarded the situation thus: the Socialist revolution in Russia could not be successful, Russia was destined to become transformed into a bourgeois-democratic state, and hence they considered the Brest-Litovsk Peace to be a defeat for Lenin's policy. In order to conduct a struggle against the Party they were ready, by reason of their lack of principle, to form a bloc with anybody at all, including the "Left Communists." Therefore they wanted negotiations, and negotiations had begun.

Bukharin stated that despite the damage undoubtedly done to the political reputations of these people, which they were striving to recover, they possessed quite a following, and therefore could prove to be quite a weighty factor in the bloc.

After this Bukharin proceeded to give an estimate of Trotsky's

418

position, and stated that the situation with Trotsky was approximately the same as that with Zinoviev and Kamenev. Outwardly Trotsky was not coming forward either as a supporter of the "Left Communists" or as an opponent of the Brest-Litovsk Peace. To outward appearance he occupied the intermediary position of "Neither peace nor war.[3]"He had selected this position as a cover, so as not to demonstrate openly that he was conductiong a struggle against Lenin. He was agreed to enter the bloc, where he would prove to be quite a weighty factor. Bukharin spoke of a third force that must be drawn into the bloc, being gathered together by the "Left Communists." This was the Socialist-Revolutionaries. The disagreements between the "Left" Socialist-Revolutionaries and the Right Socialist-Revolutionaries on the question of withdrawing Russia from the imperialist war were exceptionally acute. The viewpoint of the Right Socialist-Revolutionaries was that this war must be continued to a victorious conclusion, while the "Left" Socialist-Revolutionaries supported the position of the Bolsheviks on this question. But at that moment, when the "Left" Socialist-Revolutionaries were opposing the Brest-Litovsk Peace, it was absolutely clear that the disagreements on this question had been smoothed over, and that thus a certain identity of viewpoint was being established between the "Left" and Right Socialist-Revolutionaries, and that therefore the "Left" Socialist-Revolutionaries on the one hand could be used as a framework that could be extended to the Right Socialist-Revolutionaries, thus enabling the basis of the bloc to be extended, and also the Right Socialist-Revolutionaries could be included, who, it goes without saying, would support any measure directed against the Party leadership and against the measures of the Soviet power. Therefore in the struggle against Lenin they would undoubtedly prove to be allies. The Right Socialist-Revolutionaries still constituted quite a considerable political force, they had a considerable number of active supporters, considerable contacts in the rural districts, and therefore their incorporation would strengthen and extend this bloc.

When Bukharin finished the review of these propositions of his, which at that time already had begun to be carried into effect, I put the question to him as to why it was that such important changes in the policy of the "Left Communist" faction were being adopted independently, while I in particular had only just learnt of the still further extension of the bloc. In reply to this Bukharin told me that there was no need for me to feel offended, for I had been away, while on the other hand such agreements and negotiations on such agreements demanded exceptionally strict secrecy, a point on which, by the way, certain partners-to-be in this agreement, particularly Zinoviev and Kamenev, insisted; because, should there be any exposure of such a secret prior to the plan outlined being carried through, or should this plan meet with failure, any publication of this secret would lead to all the participants in this affair being absolutely irreparably compromised. Therefore, since I had put this question to him, he, as a member of the centre of these "Left Communists," gave me this information, but I was not to inform anybody of this, apart from those who knew of it, and was to keep the information I had received a strict secret.

That was my conversation with Bukharin, which, so to speak, cleared up the point at that moment as to the direction being taken by the activity of the "Left Communist" faction.

A few days later I had a conversation with V. N. Yakovleva. She informed me that together with Bukharin she had had a conversation with Zinoviev, who had declared for a struggle against Lenin's government, and that Zinoviev was ready for an agreement with us "Left Communists."

Subsequently I met Karelin, member of the Central Committee of the "Left" Socialist-Revolutionaries, the only leader of the "Left" Socialist-Revolutionaries whom I had known from pre-revolutionary times. And so, aware that negotiations were to be conducted with him, and that therefore I was not violating secrecy in this respect, I raised the question: "How about the agreement regarding the proposal made by Bukharin to you concerning the seizure of power, the arrest of the government connected with this, and all the consequences following therefrom?" That approximately was how I expressed myself. In reply to this Karelin stated that all these proposals were acceptable, that the "Left" Socialist-Revolutionaries were accepting them, and that they were making the corresponding preparations in their organization for the fulfilment of these decisions.

Here I must remark that on meeting Yakovleva and Lomov, who were members of the Moscow Regional Bureau, I received the information from them that the Moscow Regional organization was also preparing to undertake the necessary action at the right moment. Subsequently, at a much later time, I again inquired of Bukharin as to whether the bloc had taken complete shape and whether the negotiations were concluded. This was at the end of April or the beginning of May. Bukharin told me in reply that the bloc was established, that all the political groupings indicated had declared their agreement to join the bloc, and had joined forces on this basis. Later, however, as is well known, this plan fell through and was not put into operation. This took place, as is well known, as a result of the following circumstances. At the May conference...

VYSHINSKY: The plan fell through. That's all to the good. We are interested in the facts which actually did take place.

OSSINSKY: This in fact is the point to which I shall pass, with the aid of a certain intervening link.

VYSHINSKY: By all means. Only you have been called here as a witness at my request, and what interests me is not what did not take place, but what did.

OSSINSKY: Well, this plan was not fulfilled because at the conference of the Moscow Regional Party organization held in May, the "Left Communists" met with defeat, were thoroughly routed by Lenin, and the basis for the execution of this plan was, as far as the "Left Communists" were concerned, knocked out of their hands. This led to considerable confusion in the ranks of the "Left Communists." The revolt of the "Left" Socialist-Revolutionaries was carried through in fulfilment of the plan outlined by us "Left Communists," but it was crushed. This revolt was precisely one of the results of the fulfilment of the line adopted by the "Left Communists" as far back as the end of February 1918. A further result of the line of the bloc . . .

VYSHINSKY: So then you assert that the revolt of the "Left" Socialist-Revolutionaries in July 1918 was carried through by the "Left" Socialist-Revolutionaries in accordance with the line drawn up by the "Left Communists." Whose line was this?

OSSINSKY: The line of the bloc.

VYSHINSKY: Which bloc?

OSSINSKY: The bloc made up of "Left" Socialist-Revolutionaries, "Left Communists," Zinovievites and Trotskyites.

VYSHINSKY: Consequently the plans of this bloc included . . .?

OSSINSKY: The plans of this bloc included, first of all, the seizure of power.

VYSHINSKY: And for this?

OSSINSKY: For this armed action was needed.

VYSHINSKY: Now was it the "Left" Socialist-Revolutionaries who carried through this armed action in July 1918?

OSSINSKY: Without any doubt whatsoever.

VYSHINSKY: But Bukharin interested himself here in asking of witness Yakovleva, who was examined before you, how it could be, since he was engaged in crushing the "Left" Socialist-Revolutionary revolt. So it appears that he did not crush, but prepared the "Left" Socialist-Revolutionary revolt. Is that how I am to understand you?

OSSINSKY: Yes.

VYSHINSKY: Now can you, as a living witness, explain whether Bukharin suppressed the revolt of the "Left" Socialist-Revolutionaries?

OSSINSKY: I know nothing of this.

VYSHINSKY: But did he prepare the revolt of the "Left-" Socialist-Revolutionaries?

421

OSSINSKY: Without a doubt, he prepared it ideologically and prepared its organizational side by negotiating with the "Left" Socialist-Revolutionaries.

VYSHINSKY: Were the "Left Communists," including yourself, aware of the preparations for the revolt of the "Left" Socialist-Revolutionaries at that time?

OSSINSKY: I, in particular, was not aware of the specific action. This was not my speciality. My political speciality was of a literary and ideological kind.

VYSHINSKY: What were you aware of?

OSSINSKY: I was aware that the "Left" Socialist-Revolutionaries were conducting preparations for armed action.

VYSHINSKY: Were you as a "Left Communist," as a member of the group of "Left Communists" and one of the leaders of this group, aware of the fact that the "Left" Socialist-Revolutionaries were preparing a revolt?

OSSINSKY: Yes, I was, and in the sense that in reply to the question I put to Karelin as to whether this agreement had been accepted and on what scale, I received the reply that it had been fully accepted, and that the "Left" Socialist-Revolutionaries were preparing to put it into operation.

VYSHINSKY: And was Bukharin informed of this?

OSSINSKY: Undoubtedly.

VYSHINSKY: Because he himself carried on the negotiations.

OSSINSKY: Of course.

VYSHINSKY: And how do you know that he carried on negotiations?

OSSINSKY: I heard it from Yakovleva and from Bukharin himself.

VYSHINSKY: You heard it from Bukharin. And about the intended arrest of the government, from whom did you hear that?

OSSINSKY: I heard this first from Yakovleva, and then Bukharin corroborated it.

VYSHINSKY: And was it a plan not only to arrest the leaders of the Party and government, but to assassinate them too?

OSSINSKY: It is beyond doubt that a plan of this kind existed as a guiding line and a main perspective in settling the question of what was to be done with the arrested members of the government.

VYSHINSKY: Whom concretely?

OSSINSKY: Lenin, Stalin, Sverdlov.

VYSHINSKY: From whom did you find out that it was the intention of the bloc of conspirators to assassinate Comrades Lenin, Stalin and Sverdlov in 1918?

OSSINSKY: From Yakovleva in the first place, and then from Bukharin.

VYSHINSKY: Did Bukharin personally corroborate this intention?

OSSINSKY: Yes.

VYSHINSKY: And what was your attitude to this?

OSSINSKY: What was my attitude? Do you want to know my political attitude or my subjective attitude? However, I'll put my subjective attitude aside. Since I did not oppose this and did not object, consequently I agreed with this.

VYSHINSKY: And you did not inform anybody about this?

OSSINSKY: I did not inform anybody, consequently I agreed with this.

VYSHINSKY: I have no more questions.

THE PRESIDENT: Accused Bukharin, have you any questions to put to witness Ossinsky?

BUKHARIN: I have. In the first place, I should like to ask Ossinsky whether he could tell us something about the central group of the "Left Communists" in Petersburg. Whom did it consist of?

THE PRESIDENT: This question has no bearing on the conspiracy.

BUKHARIN: It has, because inasmuch as negotiations were carried on . . .

THE PRESIDENT: We are now concerned with the accused Bukharin.

BUKHARIN: Why, I am appearing here as a representative of the group of "Left Communists" and its centre. When we are asked about the Right and Leftist centre, that concerns us, but if it relates to the centre of the group of "Left Communists," we cannot talk. . . .

THE PRESIDENT: In any event the case concerns Nikolai Ivanovich Bukharin.

BUKHARIN: Citizen the Procurator stated that this was not the case because, owing to the lapse of the time limit prescribed by law, there is no case.

THE PRESIDENT: Accused Bukharin, do you want to put questions to witness Ossinsky?

BUKHARIN: Yes, I do. I want to ask witness Ossinsky whether Ossinsky was a member of the central group of "Left Communists."

OSSINSKY: Of course I was.

BUKHARIN: I want to find out from witness Ossinsky whether he wrote the general theses which served as the main platform of the "Left Communists" in that period.

OSSINSKY: Quite right.

VYSHINSKY: Together with whom did you write those theses?

OSSINSKY: Together with Bukharin, Radek and Preobrazhensky.

BUKHARIN: And who was the author of the basic text of those theses?

OSSINSKY: The author of the basic text was Ossinsky.

VYSHINSKY: And who edited it?

OSSINSKY: It was edited by all those participating, including Nikolai Ivanovich Bukharin.

BUKHARIN: Then I should like to ask witness Ossinsky whether he was in Moscow on the eve of the October uprising.

OSSINSKY: Yes, on the eve of the October uprising I was in Moscow.

BUKHARIN: I should also like to know whether witness Ossinsky was in Moscow during the October uprising.

THE PRESIDENT: What need is there for these questions?

BUKHARIN: I need them for my defence, because later on I will have no opportunity to get answers to these questions.

VYSHINSKY: If the accused Bukharin states that he needs these questions for his defence and since, according to our laws, each accused has the right to defence in its full scope, I plead that this question be not ruled out.

BUKHARIN: In this case I plead for putting again all the questions which the Court ruled out before.

THE PRESIDENT: Accused Bukharin, do not engage in obstructing the work of the Court.

VYSHINSKY: If the accused Bukharin has need of putting all these questions for his defence, I, as Prosecutor, do not object to these questions being put here.

THE PRESIDENT: But the Court objects to these questions being put here, because they have no bearing on the case.

VYSHINSKY: I submit to the decision of the Court.

BUKHARIN: I submit, too.

THE PRESIDENT: Comrade Commandant, call witness Mantsev.

(Witness Mantsev enters the Court.)

THE PRESIDENT (to Mantsev): Are you Vasily Nikolayevich Mantsev?

MANTSEV: Yes.

THE PRESIDENT: You have been called as a witness in the case of Nikolai Ivanovich Bukharin. You are requested to tell the truth.

Comrade Procurator, have you any questions to put to witness Mantsev?

VYSHINSKY: I have. Witness Mantsev, did you belong to the group of "Left Communists" in 1918?

MANTSEV: Yes, I did.

VYSHINSKY: What was your role in this group, that of a rank-and-file member, or a leading role?

MANTSEV: A leading role.

VYSHINSKY: Who were the other most active members of this group?

MANTSEV: The centre for all the practical work of the "Left Communists" was the Moscow Regional Bureau, the leading nucleus of which was made up entirely of "Left Communists." Bukharin was the leader of the faction of the "Left Communists."

VYSHINSKY: What were the relations between the group of the "Left Communists" and the group of the "Left" Socialist-Revolutionaries at that time? Do you remember?

MANTSEV: I do.

VYSHINSKY: Can you tell us briefly about it?

MANTSEV: I can. As early as the month of April, after the Seventh Congress of the Party and the Fourth Congress of Soviets, I learnt that the leadership of the faction of "Left Communists" was carrying on negotiations about a bloc, about an alliance with the "Left" Socialist-Revolutionaries with the conspiratorial object of overthrowing the Soviet government, for the purpose of effecting a counter-revolutionary coup. At one of the meetings of the Regional Bureau, at which almost all the members of the faction of "Left Communists" were present in full force—Yakovleva, myself, Lomov, Maksimovsky, Stukov, Kizelshtein and a number of others who took an immediate part in directing the activities of the faction—Bukharin delivered a report in which he declared that, after the Brest-Litovsk Peace had been endorsed by the Congress of the Party and the Congress of Soviets, there was only one road left—the road of insurrection against the Soviet government, of overthrowing the Soviet government. In the course of the same report he stated that he considered it an indispensable condition for the success of the coup to arrest and, in case of necessity, to physically exterminate, in plain words to murder, the leaders of the Party and the government—Lenin, Stalin and Sverdlov.

VYSHINSKY: Did you hear it yourself?

MANTSEV: Yes, I heard it myself, just as all those who were present at that meeting heard it. Then he stated that he was carrying on, or rather that he had brought to a successful issue, negotiations with "Left" Socialist-Revolutionaries concerning an alliance with them; he also informed those who at that time were in the leadership of the faction that the "Left" Socialist-Revolutionaries, like the "Left Communists," were then preparing for an insurrection against the Soviet government. Bukharin confirmed the existence of an alliance between the "Left Communists" and the "Left" Socialist-Revolutionaries for the purpose of overthrowing the Soviet government. He said that he personally conducted the

425

negotiations. I also heard that, of the "Left Communists," the following people took part in these negotiations: Stukov and Ossinsky.

At this meeting Bukharin was instructed to continue the negotiations with the "Left" Socialist-Revolutionaries.

VYSHINSKY: Is this all?

MANTSEV: No, not all.

VYSHINSKY: Proceed.

MANTSEV: The fact of the matter is that earlier, in February, it was not Bukharin who delivered a report, but . . .

VYSHINSKY: What year was that?

MANTSEV: 1918. Stukov delivered a report, and he declared at the time that he was speaking on Bukharin's direct instructions. Stukov was a member of the Regional Bureau of the Party and one of the leaders of the faction of the "Left Communists."

I forgot to mention that Bukharin characterized the existing Soviet government, which was headed by Lenin, as a government betraying the interests of the proletarian revolution, as a bourgeois-kulak government. It was as early as February or towards the end of February that Stukov, on Bukharin's direct instructions, already then raised the question of overthrowing this government and of making preparations for organizing an insurrection against this government.

VYSHINSKY: When was that?

MANTSEV: That was towards the end of February 1918.

VYSHINSKY: Tell us, was this circumstance recorded in the minutes?

MANTSEV: That is what I want to speak about. It was recorded in the minutes.

VYSHINSKY: And what happened to those minutes?

MANTSEV: As a rule, the minutes of the meetings of the Regional Bureau were recorded in the minutes book. This was an ordinary office ledger in which the secretary entered the minutes. At that time I was secretary, and before me it was Yakovleva. The minutes were usually recorded either by me or by Yakovleva. These minutes were recorded by me.

VYSHINSKY: And what happened to these minutes?

MANTSEV: Permit me to digress somewhat. At the Moscow Regional Conference in 1918 the "Left Communists" suffered defeat. The majority of the conference declared in favour of the line of the Central Committee of the Party, and towards the end of the conference, during the elections, the list of the Central Committee obtained a majority. Out of the seven members included in the list of the Central Committee, five adhered to the line of the Central Committee, to Lenin's line, and two of the elected were members of the "Left Communists"—myself and Lomov.

At a meeting of the faction of the "Left Communists," which took place at the end of the conference, it was decided to disband the faction, and to discontinue factional activities. I must say that this was insincere, because at the same meeting of the faction it was decided that Lomov and myself should refuse to participate in the work of the Regional Committee of the Party, the majority of which consisted of adherents of the Central Committee. After the meeting of the faction a flying meeting was held of the former members of the Regional Bureau of the "Left Communists," at which all those of whom I have spoken were present. On a motion of Bukharin, and for the purpose of concealing from the Party the real stand taken by the "Left Communists" with regard to the Central Committee of the Party and the government (and it consisted in the fact that we were preparing for the overthrow of the government), this meeting commissioned Yakovleva and myself to destroy that entry in the minutes of which I have spoken. And this I did.

VYSHINSKY: Destroy it?

MANTSEV: Yakovleva and I destroyed these minutes that same evening or at night.

VYSHINSKY: And you left nothing for history?

MANTSEV: We destroyed it then so that nothing was left at that time and, consequently, for history.

VYSHINSKY: I have no questions to Mantsev, for the time being.

BUKHARIN (to the Court): I have one question which consists in the following: Does Citizen Mantsev remember that he, with a detachment of the Cheka, conducted the operation against the Anarchists—the allies of the "Left" Socialist-Revolutionaries—who threw a bomb in Leontievsky Street, which bomb exploded while it was hurtling through the air. Does Citizen Mantsev confirm that he conducted this operation?

MANTSEV: Yes, I cônfirm it.

BUKHARIN: I have no more questions.

VYSHINSKY: What year was that?

MANTSEV: The end of 1919.

VYSHINSKY: Were you then a member of the group of "Left Communists"?

MANTSEV: There was no such group then.

VYSHINSKY: And when this group of "Left Communists" existed, did you take action against the Socialist-Revolutionaries?

MANTSEV: Yes.

VYSHINSKY: I have no more questions.

THE PRESIDENT: Adjournment for 15 minutes.

* * *

427

COMMANDANT OF THE COURT: The Court is coming, please rise.

THE PRESIDENT: Please be seated. The session is resumed. Comrade Procurator, have you any more questions to put to witness Mantsev?

VYSHINSKY: I have questions to put to Bukharin.

THE PRESIDENT: You may.

VYSHINSKY: Accused Bukharin, what have you got to say with regard to the testimony of witness Mantsev?

BUKHARIN: I must say the following with regard to the testimony of witness Mantsev: I delivered a report at the bureau of the Moscow organization; I do not remember it, but I do not deny it either. However, I absolutely exclude the possibility that I should have spoken in my report in the spirit which Mantsev described here. As for the line for a forcible overthrow of the Soviet government, I have already replied that there was such a moment, and when it was, and that I admit. As for the statement that I allegedly gave instructions with regard to the removal of some passage from the minutes, I consider, in the first place, that . . .

VYSHINSKY: Did you give such instructions?

BUKHARIN: I beg your pardon, I consider, in the first place . . .

VYSHINSKY: Did you give such instructions?

BUKHARIN: No, I gave no such instructions.

VYSHINSKY: But the minutes disappeared.

BUKHARIN: The minutes disappeared, that is an accomplished fact, but I have . . .

VYSHINSKY: Did they disappear by themselves?

BUKHARIN: No, not by themselves, but everything that happens in the world, including the disappearance of minutes, you cannot . . .

VYSHINSKY: But did you have anything to do with it?

BUKHARIN: No, I had nothing to do with it.

VYSHINSKY: Consequently, you assert that Mantsev's testimony in this part and the testimony of witness Yakovleva are false?

BUKHARIN: Yes, I do.

VYSHINSKY: How do you explain the fact that they are not telling the truth?

BUKHARIN: You had better ask them about it.

VYSHINSKY: We shall ask them directly. Witnesses Yakovleva and Mantsev, the accused Bukharin here says that in this case you are not telling the truth about him. What can you say about this?

YAKOVLEVA: I can say the following. I heard Mantsev's testimony. I was not present at this meeting where this decision was adopted—it was a sort of flying faction meeting; and it was apparently by chance that I was not present. Mantsev

428

simply conveyed to me the decision. When we were preparing the material of the Regional Bureau, I heard that Bukharin insisted that not the whole minutes but a certain part of the minutes be removed, namely the part in which was recorded Stukov's speech and the draft resolution which he proposed at the meeting of the faction of the Regional Bureau. The reasons given were that if this passage were left it might expose the illegal activities of the "Left Communists" and serve to condemn the political position of the Moscow Bureau. As I have already testified, Mantsev and myself removed this passage.

VYSHINSKY: Witness Mantsev, what have you to say?

MANTSEV: I confirm the testimony which I have given. The fact of the matter is that it was not at a faction meeting, but there was a special meeting called for this purpose, at which Bukharin, who knew that there was such an entry in the minutes of the former members of the Regional Bureau, of the members of the faction of "Left Communists," made this proposal. The meeting was called specially for this purpose, because it was a very small meeting and did not last very long.

VYSHINSKY: A flying meeting?

MANTSEV: He proposed that these minutes be removed from the minutes book in order to conceal the conspiratorial activities of the "Left Communists."

VYSHINSKY: Were these the reasons he advanced?

MANTSEV: I do not remember whether Yakovleva was there, but this passage was removed.

VYSHINSKY: You did it together with Yakovleva?

MANTSEV: Together with Yakovleva.

VYSHINSKY (to Bukharin): And do you maintain your position?

BUKHARIN: Of course.

VYSHINSKY: Now the following question: Accused Bukharin, do you confirm that you had the intention of placing Comrades Lenin, Stalin and Sverdlov under arrest?

BUKHARIN: Yes, I confirm it, there was such a moment.

VYSHINSKY: Such a plan?

BUKHARIN: I do not say a plan.

VYSHINSKY: Such an intention?

BUKHARIN: Such an intention.

VYSHINSKY: Initiative?

BUKHARIN: Yes.

VYSHINSKY: And who was the initiator of this intention? Was it you?

BUKHARIN: The initiator of this intention was Trotsky.

VYSHINSKY: Did Trotsky commission you with it?

BUKHARIN: No, our relations were not of the kind that he could commission me with anything.

VYSHINSKY: Why then did you accept Trotsky's initiative and begin to put it into effect?

BUKHARIN: Because there was a certain inclination among the leading group of the "Left Communists" to accept this plan.

VYSHINSKY: So you agreed with Trotsky's initiative, and supported his initiative in the question of placing Lenin, Stalin and Sverdlov under arrest, because you yourself had a similar plan?

BUKHARIN: In the question of negotiations with regard to this with the leading group of the "Left" Socialist-Revolutionaries.

VYSHINSKY: Was Trotsky the initiator of the idea of placing Lenin, Stalin and Sverdlov under arrest?

BUKHARIN: Yes, quite right.

VYSHINSKY: Did you agree to this?

BUKHARIN: Yes, quite right.

VYSHINSKY: Did you support this?

BUKHARIN: As a matter of fact I did.

VYSHINSKY: And you started negotiations with the "Left" Socialist-Revolutionaries about putting this plan into effect, is that right?

BUKHARIN: Yes, that's right.

VYSHINSKY: With the object of forcible overthrow...

BUKHARIN: With the object, as Trotsky formulated it at the time, of forming a new Cabinet.

VYSHINSKY: A Cabinet?

BUKHARIN: Yes.

VYSHINSKY: At the same time, it was not excluded, of course, that forcible means would be adopted with regard to Lenin, Stalin and Sverdlov?

BUKHARIN: Yes, if we consider that placing under arrest is a forcible means...

VYSHINSKY: And besides arrest?

BUKHARIN: No, nothing besides arrest; if you are referring to physical extermination, I repeat that there was no mention of it.

VYSHINSKY: But what did Stukov report?

BUKHARIN: I do not know what Stukov said.

VYSHINSKY: Did Yakovleva speak to you about Stukov's information?

BUKHARIN: Stukov gave no information whatever to Yakovleva in my presence.

VYSHINSKY: I am asking you, did Yakovleva speak to you about the report delivered by Stukov?

BUKHARIN: In my opinion, she did not.

VYSHINSKY: Witness Yakovleva, did you speak to Bukharin about Stukov's report?

YAKOVLEVA: Stukov told me that it was on Bukharin's instructions that he delivered his report in which he argued in favour of this affair. In this report Stukov spoke. as a prospect of the development of the political struggle, also of the arrest of the government in the persons of Lenin, Stalin and Sverdlov, and even, in case of an intensification of the struggle, the possibility of the physical extermination of these three leaders of the Party. I informed Bukharin about this and he corroborated it.

VYSHINSKY: Accused Bukharin, do you confirm this?

BUKHARIN: This is impossible, because Yakovleva is referring to this as relating to the period prior to the Brest-Litovsk Peace, which, as I have already proved, I think, sufficiently convincingly, would be absurd from every point of view.

VYSHINSKY: You are speaking about the conclusions, while I am speaking about the facts.

BUKHARIN: I deny the fact. When there are two people concerned, I have the right of proof by contrary proposition.

VYSHINSKY: Do you deny this fact?

BUKHARIN: Of course.

VYSHINSKY: Of course? But they confirm it. (To Mantsev.) You also confirm that there was talk about the physical extermination of Lenin, Stalin and Sverdlov?

MANTSEV: Yes.

BUKHARIN: I object to what Yakovleva is saying because she is referring to the period before Brest-Litovsk, while Ossinsky is speaking about the period after Brest-Litovsk. They must first agree between themselves. . . .

VYSHINSKY: And what period are you referring to?

BUKHARIN: I am referring to the second period, the second period, when there was a plan of arrest, there was the intention, and initiative, the author of which was Trotsky; it was actually accepted and approved of.

VYSHINSKY: The initiative was not yours?

BUKHARIN: Since Trotsky . . .

VYSHINSKY: Answer the question: yours, or not yours?

BUKHARIN: This was Trotsky's initiative, and I am not Trotsky; consequently, it was not mine.

VYSHINSKY: Do you repudiate the initiative?

BUKHARIN: I repudiate the initiative but I do not repudiate the approbation.

VYSHINSKY: The reason I am putting the question this way is that I have the testimony of the witnesses, who say that you, together with Trotsky, were the initiator, that you were also the initiator; that is why I am asking you, but you are denying it.

BUKHARIN: Yes, I deny it.

VYSHINSKY: But you have said that you approved of it?

BUKHARIN: Yes.

VYSHINSKY: And I am asking: When, after the Brest-Litovsk Peace, you intended to arrest Comrades Lenin, Stalin and Sverdlov, was it for the purpose of overthrowing the government, was it to be a part of the violent struggle? Do I understand you right?

BUKHARIN: Well, that's what I am saying: that it was intended, and that this particular act could have been accomplished in such a way as to be violent but not sanguinary, and therefore there can be no . . .

VYSHINSKY: Violent but not sanguinary?

BUKHARIN: You arrested me, that is an act of violence; however, I am still alive, but perhaps I will not be alive and I am almost certain of it, yet I am still alive, which is testified to by the fact that I am speaking from this dock.

VYSHINSKY: This is an unnecessary digression from the interrogation.

BUKHARIN: I am telling you what was.

VYSHINSKY: I only want to establish where you drew the line between violent arrest in the course of the struggle and murder. Where did you draw the line?

BUKHARIN: There was talk at the time that it was necessary to ensure and guarantee the full safety of the mentioned persons.

VYSHINSKY: That is what you are asserting, but Yakovleva says that it was exactly the other way around; so she is not telling the truth?

BUKHARIN: I do not agree with this and I say that she is not telling the truth.

VYSHINSKY: Hence Mantsev is not telling the truth either?

BUKHARIN: Yes, he also is not telling the truth. I am telling what I knew, and as for what they knew, it is a matter of their conscience to tell about it.

VYSHINSKY: You must somehow explain the fact that three of your former accomplices are speaking against you.

BUKHARIN: You see, I have neither sufficient material nor the psychological requisites to clear up this question.

VYSHINSKY: You cannot explain.

BUKHARIN: Not that I cannot, I simply refuse to explain.

VYSHINSKY: Witness Ossinsky, do you categorically affirm that you were aware from Bukharin of the proposed arrest and murder of Comrades Lenin, Stalin and Sverdlov?

OSSINSKY: I confirm this. I have already said that I learnt of this from Yakovleva in the formulation which I reported to Bukharin, who confirmed it.

VYSHINSKY: Consequently?

432

OSSINSKY: Bukharin is not speaking the truth now.

VYSHINSKY: Do you, witness Yakovleva, also think that Bukharin is not speaking the truth?

YAKOVLEVA: Yes, I have said that I heard from Bukharin about the physical extermination of the three leaders of the Party.

VYSHINSKY: Consequently, in denying this now, Bukharin is not speaking the truth?

YAKOVLEVA: Yes, Bukharin does not wish to speak the truth.

VYSHINSKY: But were there cases when Bukharin, while pretending to speak the truth, was not speaking the truth?

YAKOVLEVA: It seems to me that, while pretending to speak the truth about the conspiracy of "Left Communists" and "Left" Socialist-Revolutionaries, he is not speaking the truth. This is already a historical fact. And now he himself admits, in reply to your question he was compelled to state, that he has not told the whole truth.

VYSHINSKY: Is this correct?

BUKHARIN: When I said . . .

VYSHINSKY: Is it correct that at the time you did not tell the whole truth?

BUKHARIN: At that time Yakovleva denied even this half truth, but from this one cannot draw the conclusion that she is speaking the truth.

VYSHINSKY: When we come to discuss her conduct we shall speak of her. But it is not only Yakovleva who speaks of this fact now; Yakovleva and Ossinsky speak of it. . . .

BUKHARIN: But they all denied this half truth.

VYSHINSKY (to Yakovleva): Why did you deny this at one time?

YAKOVLEVA: We denied this at the time, I personally at any rate, because we had then not yet disarmed ourselves in the struggle against the Party and acted as people who wished to hide the truth from the Party. But when we had disarmed ourselves we considered it necessary to speak of everything that took place.

VYSHINSKY: Apparently Bukharin has not yet disarmed?

YAKOVLEVA: Apparently.

THE PRESIDENT: I intend to allow all the witnesses to remain in the Court room for the time being.

VYSHINSKY: I ask leave to put one more question to Mantsev.

Witness Mantsev, tell the Court, please, about this operation against the Anarchists' House, against this nest of anarchists, about which Bukharin spoke.

MANTSEV: This was the anarchist organization which organized the explosion on the premises of the Moscow Committee of the Communist Party.

VYSHINSKY: What relations had these anarchists to the "Left Communists"?

MANTSEV: The "Left Communists" were not functioning then.

VYSHINSKY: But when the "Left Communists" were functioning, did they have any relation to these anarchists?

MANTSEV: At that time this group, these anarchists, were not in Moscow.

VYSHINSKY: In what capacity did you act in the liquidation of this anarchist nest at that time?

MANTSEV: I acted against them in the capacity of Assistant Chairman of the Moscow Extraordinary Commission.

VYSHINSKY: That means you acted not on your own personal desire but in accordance with your official position?

MANTSEV: Yes, in accordance with the position I occupied.

VYSHINSKY: Well, was this attempt organized and directed specially against Bukharin?

MANTSEV: This attempt had no relation to Bukharin whatsoever.

VYSHINSKY: But whom did it have relation to?

MANTSEV: The attempt was directed against the Moscow Committee of the Communist Party.

VYSHINSKY: And was Bukharin the secretary of the Moscow Committee at that time?

MANTSEV: He was not the secretary.

VYSHINSKY: Was he present at this meeting of the Moscow Committee?

MANTSEV: In my opinion, he was not.

BUKHARIN: What do you mean, I was not present? I was contused during the explosion.

MANTSEV: It is possible he was there, I do not remember it.

BUKHARIN: I was present and delivered a report on the conspiracy of the National Centre, the investigation of which I was conducting in the Cheka.

MANTSEV: I must say that this is of no essential importance for the matter under discussion.

VYSHINSKY: But Bukharin thinks that this attempt was directed against him.

MANTSEV: This is not correct. I personally conducted the arrests of these anarchists, I personally interrogated them, and not one of the arrested even mentioned a word about an attempt against Bukharin.

VYSHINSKY: That means Bukharin got into this business accidentally?

MANTSEV: He got into it accidentally. These anarchists were fighting against the Bolshevik Party and made their attempt against the Moscow Committee of the Party. Bukharin had nothing to do with it.

VYSHINSKY: That means this cannot be put down to Bukharin's credit?

MANTSEV: No, it cannot.

Allow me to deal some more with the question as to who issued the instructions on the physical extermination of the leaders of the Party. I knew that besides the alliance with the "Left" Socialist-Revolutionaries, the "Left Communists" made common cause with Trotsky. I learnt of this in the very last days preceding the dissolution of the "Left Communist" group. But regarding the conspiracy, regarding the proposed assassination, I knew that this was the proposal of Bukharin, the leader of our faction.

VYSHINSKY: Did you have occasion to visit Trotsky and speak to him on this subject?

MANTSEV: Yes, I visited Trotsky and spoke to him of this.

VYSHINSKY: Did Trotsky speak to you of the necessity of murdering Lenin, Stalin and Sverdlov?

MANTSEV: Yes, Trotsky spoke of this.

VYSHINSKY: Consequently, when Bukharin declares that the initiative came also from Trotsky, he is speaking the truth?

MANTSEV: Yes, in this case he is speaking the truth.

VYSHINSKY: That means, it can be said that Trotsky together with Bukharin were planning to kill Lenin, Stalin and Sverdlov?

MANTSEV: Yes, this is true.

VYSHINSKY: How did you come to know of this plan?

MANTSEV: I learnt of it from Yakovleva, from Trotsky and others personally.

VYSHINSKY: Trotsky spoke of the necessity of murdering Lenin and Stalin?

MANTSEV: Yes, he did.

VYSHINSKY: Did Bukharin tell you that he was himself inciting the murder of Lenin and Stalin?

MANTSEV: This was a decision.

VYSHINSKY: Whose decision?

MANTSEV: A decision of the leading body of the "Left Communists."

VYSHINSKY: Taken on whose initiative?

MANTSEV: On the initiative of Bukharin.

VYSHINSKY: Now tell the Court about 1919.

MANTSEV: After the dissolution of the faction at the Regional Party Conference in May, the faction made a decision that Lomov and myself, who had been elected to the Regional Bureau on the Central Committee slate, should refuse to participate in the work of the Regional Bureau. This was proof of hypocrisy. The very decision regarding the dissolution of the "Left Communist" faction was insincere; the members of this faction continued to hold the same convictions as they had held before.

435

Personally, I had no contact nor meetings with the members of the former "Left Communist" faction up to the autumn of 1919. At that time I was engaged in work in the Moscow Extraordinary Commission. In the autumn of 1919 I met such people as Kizelshtein, Maximovsky, Bukharin. These meetings, although not frequent, did take place. At that time, in connection with reverses at the front and ruin and famine in the country, we were inclined to explain this in our conversations by the wrong policy of the Central Committee of the Communist Party, the government and the military command. In this connection we spoke about the decisive role Stalin was playing in matters relating to military operations, and therefore a number of reproaches were hurled against Stalin in the course of these conversations. It was during this period that I received a telephone call from Trotsky's secretariat inviting me, on his instructions, to visit him at his home in the Kremlin. I went to see him at once. Trotsky said that Bukharin had informed him that I was now opposed to the policy pursued by the Central Committee of the Party and the government. He told me that to his knowledge a number of ex-"Left Communists" were at present not unwilling to resume the plans which they had outlined in 1918. In characterizing the political situation at that time, Trotsky declared that the situation of the Soviet government as a result of failures at the front, ruin and famine was catastrophic. He declared that the position at the front was such that the surrender of Moscow was inevitable. According to his words, Stalin, who had decisive influence upon Lenin, was to blame for this, and it was therefore necessary to overthrow this government and form a government consisting of people who were prepared to completely share the views of Trotsky and Bukharin. At first he said that he had come to an agreement on this with Bukharin.

Trotsky said that the removal of Stalin must be considered the guarantee or the necessary condition of success. At the same time, he pointed out that he wished to take advantage of one of the conflicts between himself and Stalin regarding questions pertaining to the carrying out of military operations, and during one of his visits to the front, to that section where Stalin was stationed, to effect the arrest of Stalin, using for this his military unit, or, more precisely, Trotsky's personal bodyguard. I recall his words; he said that in such a case Lenin and the Central Committee would capitulate. In reply to my question as to what would happen if they did not capitulate, he said: things will remain the same as in 1918.

After this I also had a meeting with Bukharin and told him of this conversation. Bukharin told me that he was in full and complete solidarity with Trotsky regarding the latter's appraisal of the situation and the steps Trotsky outlined. I spoke of this at the preliminary investigation and I speak of it now.

VYSHINSKY: Consequently, a new attempt was made in 1919 by Trotsky and the "Left Communists" to organize an anti-Soviet conspiracy?

MANTSEV: Yes. Soon after this I had to leave Moscow, and I do not know how the whole affair developed.

VYSHINSKY: But was this affair investigated?

MANTSEV: No, at that time this affair was not investigated.

VYSHINSKY: Why?

MANTSEV: Because I said nothing about it.

VYSHINSKY: But had you no occasion to speak with Trotsky about it?

MANTSEV: It is about my conversation with Trotsky that I am speaking.

VYSHINSKY: Speaking to him about not having to investigate this affair?

MANTSEV: You are speaking of a different occasion, which relates to 1920.

VYSHINSKY: And you are speaking of 1919?

MANTSEV: Yes. Of my conversation with Trotsky in 1919. This was on the eve of the Red Army's offensive and the crushing of Denikin.

VYSHINSKY: You told no one about this and the affair was buried?

MANTSEV: Yes.

VYSHINSKY: And how did things develop later? What took place in 1920?

MANTSEV: At that time I was chairman of the All-Ukrainian Extraordinary Commission and chief of the Special Department of Front Headquarters. When Stalin was leaving Kharkov I was informed by the Chief of the Department of the Transport Cheka of the Kharkov Railway Junction that traces of an attempt on the train and carriage in which Stalin was travelling had been discovered. An investigation was instituted, and investigator Gusakov, who was investigator of the Presidium of the All-Ukrainian Cheka, was assigned to handle the case. Trotsky arrived soon after this. I must say that at that time I was also chief of the area behind the lines. When reporting to Trotsky in his carriage, I mentioned among other things this case. Trotsky smiled and said that it was not worth-while to exaggerate the case because our comrades might suffer. The investigation of this case was not brought to a conclusion, it was referred to the Kharkov Revolutionary Tribunal, where further investigation was discontinued.

VYSHINSKY: So, upon whose direct instructions?

MANTSEV: This I do not know.

VYSHINSKY: But you should have investigated the case?

MANTSEV: The case was referred to the Revolutionary Tribunal on my instructions. The investigation of the case was not completed. Consequently, my guilt and crime consists in that the investigation of the case was discontinued and the case hushed up.

VYSHINSKY: This is precisely what I say. And you did this after a conversation with Trotsky?

MANTSEV: Yes.

VYSHINSKY: Consequently, you did this on his instructions?

MANTSEV: Quite right.

VYSHINSKY: I have no more questions to Mantsev.

BUKHARIN (to the Court): I have a question. Citizen Mantsev declared here that the decision to murder Lenin, Stalin and Sverdlov was made by the leading centre of the "Left Communists." Since these were the words used, I have a right to ask Mantsev, who were then the members of this centre of the "Left Communists"? Mantsev should know this, for he was secretary of the largest organization in Moscow.

MANTSEV: I have already declared in my testimony that the Regional Bureau of the Communist Party was the centre of the practical leadership of factional activities, and later of plotting activities.

BUKHARIN: You speak of a decision of the centre, but are such questions decided by an auxiliary bureau?

MANTSEV: This was the Regional Bureau of the Party, not an auxiliary bureau. The leading group of this Regional Bureau consisted entirely of "Left Communists," including yourself, Yakovleva, Stukov and myself.

BUKHARIN: Was I a member?

MANTSEV: Yes, or in any case you closely participated in all meetings where all questions were decided. The same is true of Ossinsky. All of this took place in the room which was then occupied by the Regional Bureau in a building on Soviet Square.

I must say that at a meeting of the "Left Communist" faction during the Fourth Congress a bureau of the faction was elected, which included you, Lomov, Radek, Ossinsky and Yakovleva. But the fact of the matter is that this bureau of the faction was engaged in working out theses to guide all the practical activities of the "Left Communists." It was under the leadership of the Moscow Regional Bureau of the Party. I do not remember whether you were a member of it, but in any case you participated in the active leadership, you participated in this work just like Ossinsky, who, while not a member of the bureau, participated in the work.

BUKHARIN: In view of the fact that Yakovleva relates all these things to the period preceding the Brest-Litovsk Peace and that during this time I was not even in Moscow and that the centre of leading comrades of the "Left Communist" faction at that time was in Petersburg—Mantsev will not deny it—the Moscow

438

bureau was not the central group, but only one of the central groups. At that time I was also in the leading centre.

MANTSEV: Although you were in Petersburg, and Lomov, Ossinsky and Yakovleva were also in Petersburg, I nevertheless declare here that you, Ossinsky, Lomov and Yakovleva knew about all the plans and practical steps of the Regional Bureau, and, what is more, you not only knew but you sometimes sent a number of decisions from Petersburg. Yakovleva does not deny this here. There was a number of decisions which you sent from Petersburg. They were carried out as decisions of the Regional Bureau. Therefore, what you want to imply by saying that you were in Petersburg, and therefore cannot bear responsibility, is wrong.

Then I also wish to note one circumstance, namely, that prior to the Congress, prior to the conclusion of the Brest-Litovsk Peace, in February, Stukov openly stated that he was speaking on your instructions and was expressing your principles. Later, after the conclusion of the Brest-Litovsk Peace, you confirmed this.

BUKHARIN: I ask whether prior to the Brest-Litovsk Peace, the centre of the leading "Left Communists" was in Petersburg. But you try to picture the thing in such a way that the Regional Bureau adopted decisions and I was informed, that is to say, I directed, that is to say, I was aware of what the Moscow Regional Bureau decided. I am not asking about this, what I am asking about is who belonged to the leading group of "Left Communists" in Petersburg. Reply to this question, and if you cannot reply, then do not reply.

THE PRESIDENT (to Mantsev): But you have already replied to this question?

MANTSEV: Yes, and I once more confirm that, notwithstanding the fact that you were in Petersburg, your views were made known to us, taken into consideration because you were the leader of the faction, the leader of the "Left Communists," and there is no use trying to get away from it.

BUKHARIN: That is true. Permit me to say that there is some big misunderstanding here. I do not deny my leadership. . . .

VYSHINSKY: Were there cases in the practice of your work at that time in this group of "Left Communists" when you adopted decisions independently as the leader?

BUKHARIN: No, there were not. Do you want to help me to put the question which I am unable to formulate?

THE PRESIDENT: Nobody wants to help you, but Comrade the Procurator is asking you a question.

VYSHINSKY: I am asking you, were there cases when you adopted decisions independently?

BUKHARIN: There were no such cases.

VYSHINSKY: May I ask Ossinsky?

BUKHARIN: He will say that he was in the Ukraine.

VYSHINSKY: I ask permission to put a question to witness Ossinsky. (To Ossinsky.) Bukharin has already predetermined your answer. Were there actually such cases?

OSSINSKY: Will you permit me to add something to this?

VYSHINSKY: On the subject?

OSSINSKY: On the subject of the Moscow Regional Bureau and independent decisions. There was a centre of the "Left Communists." I can roughly name its membership, if necessary.

VYSHINSKY: Please do.

OSSINSKY: In addition to myself, it consisted of Bukharin, Yakovleva, Radek, Pyatakov, V. M. Smirnov and perhaps some others. There was a centre of the "Left Communists," which met in Leningrad at the period when I was in Leningrad and then it met in Moscow after the transfer to Moscow. On the other hand, there was the Regional Bureau, the Moscow organization, which consisted of a number of leaders of the "Left Communists." Its relation to the centre of the "Left Communists" was roughly the same as that of the Moscow Party organization to the Central Committee, that is, it was the biggest organization; and it even had greater significance because, as a matter of fact, the Moscow regional organization was the only one in which the "Left Communists" had a majority and any firm ground.

VYSHINSKY: At that time?

OSSINSKY: At that time.

VYSHINSKY: And in Leningrad?

OSSINSKY: In Leningrad they had no ground at all.

VYSHINSKY: That is, there were members of the centre there?

OSSINSKY: There were members of the centre there.

VYSHINSKY: And here?

OSSINSKY: Here there were the practical cadres.

VYSHINSKY: And the situation was that the relative importance of the Moscow group of "Left Communists" was enhanced?

OSSINSKY: Of course. Practically and politically, it was the deciding centre.

VYSHINSKY: And it was only necessary to smash this Moscow group of the organization of the "Left Communists" for its effects to be felt all along the line?

OSSINSKY: Quite so.

VYSHINSKY: And the centre would have ceased to exist?

OSSINSKY: Quite so. Now as regards the centre of the "Left Communists" and its attitude to the question of the adoption of this stand, I am unable to say whether the regional centre discussed this question, because at that time I . . .

BUKHARIN: You were in the Ukraine, of course.

OSSINSKY: I can prove by documents that in the latter part of February I left for Kharkov and returned from there in the early part of March.

VYSHINSKY (to Bukharin): And what do you say?

BUKHARIN: What about?

VYSHINSKY: You just said something about Ossinsky's evidence.

BUKHARIN: I want to say that Ossinsky was in the Ukraine.

VYSHINSKY: But he says he was in Moscow.

BUKHARIN. He said himself that he was in the Ukraine.

OSSINSKY: In the beginning of March I returned from the Ukraine to Leningrad.

VYSHINSKY: Ossinsky says that in March 1918 he left the Ukraine and came to Leningrad.

OSSINSKY: I was in Leningrad.

VYSHINSKY (to Bukharin): Then what are you talking about?

BUKHARIN: I am speaking of a different period, a more interesting one from the point of view of the trial.

VYSHINSKY: Listen to what Ossinsky says and don't interrupt him.

OSSINSKY: I cannot recall that this centre of the "Left Communists" discussed this question in my absence. I am inclined to think that it did not discuss this question, because my conversation with Bukharin, as I have had the honour to relate, showed that Bukharin was undoubtedly undertaking action to extend the bloc already without discussion in the centre, because he said to me: "Since you ask me, and since you are a member of the centre, I shall tell you; but this is a very secret matter and must be known only to a limited number of persons. . . ."

BUKHARIN: But assassination calls for so little secrecy that it was discussed at a meeting?

MANTSEV: Assassination was secret to so little an extent that it was discussed at a meeting at which four persons were present. I do not know whether there was a fifth—Bukharin, but I remember that there were four persons who had the deciding voice in this matter. Hence it seems perfectly clear to me from this that Bukharin, of course, did undertake such independent actions, which he arranged with and spoke about to certain persons at his selection with a view to keeping it extremely secret.

VYSHINSKY (to Bukharin): Was that so?

BUKHARIN: It was not so, and could not have been so.

VYSHINSKY: Yet Ossinsky asserts that there were occasions when you decided certain questions independently and informed certain members of your centre at your own selection from motives of secrecy.

441

BUKHARIN: The times were such, Citizen Procurator, that this would have been absolutely inconceivable.

THE PRESIDENT (to the Prosecutor): Have you any more questions to ask the witnesses?

VYSHINSKY: No.

BUKHARIN: Permit me, I have some questions to put.

THE PRESIDENT: To whom?

BUKHARIN: To Mantsev and Ossinsky.

THE PRESIDENT: What question have you to put to Mantsev?

BUKHARIN: My question to Mantsev is as follows: as far as I understood you, Citizen Mantsev, it follows from your evidence that the question of physical extermination was discussed at a meeting of the centre.

MANTSEV: This question was discussed at a meeting of the Regional Bureau of the Party.

BUKHARIN: You said that this question was adopted upon a decision of the centre?

MANTSEV: I say: at a meeting of the Regional Bureau of the Party, which was actually the centre, because the centre about which Ossinsky spoke (he got the names somewhat mixed) did not guide the practical activities of the "Left Communists." Ossinsky was right here when he said that the cadres were actually in the Moscow regional organization of the "Left Communists." For instance, the Urals maintained communication and received directions from the Moscow Regional Bureau. Similarly, the Moscow Regional Bureau was actually the centre of the activities of the "Left Communists"; and in this Moscow Regional Bureau—I do not know who were the four persons Ossinsky referred to, but I think there were five or six persons who knew about the proposals you made to them and who discussed them. This is what I said.

BUKHARIN: Very well, I have no more questions.

THE PRESIDENT: Comrade Commandant, call the witness Kamkov.

(Witness Kamkov enters the Court.)

THE PRESIDENT: Is your name Kamkov, Boris Davidovich?

KAMKOV: Yes.

THE PRESIDENT: Were you a member of the Central Committee of the party of the "Left" Socialist-Revolutionaries in 1918?

KAMKOV: Yes.

THE PRESIDENT: You have been called as a witness in the case of Bukharin, Nikolai Ivanovich. You are called upon to tell the truth in answer to questions. Comrade Procurator, have you any questions?

VYSHINSKY: Tell us, witness Kamkov, did you have occasion in 1918 to conduct negotiations with Bukharin with regard to the

442

mutual and joint actions of the group of "Left Communists" and the group of "Left" Socialist-Revolutionaries?

KAMKOV: Yes.

VYSHINSKY: To what end? What do you recall? What was spoken about, what was proposed, what plans were made, and so on? Tell us briefly.

KAMKOV: I recall the following. One day in the Smolny Institute, as I left my room to go to the conference hall of the Presidium of the Central Executive Committee, I think it was, I was overtaken by Bukharin. There was somebody with him; I cannot recall who. There was also a comrade with me, a "Left" Socialist-Revolutionary, I cannot recall now who he was either. Bukharin stopped me and said roughly the following: the position in the Bolshevik Party, as a result of the attitude towards the Brest-Litovsk Peace, is getting complicated and has assumed fairly acute forms. He said that they were debating the question of the possibility of creating an anti-Brest government consisting of "Left Communists" and "Left" Socialist-Revolutionaries headed by . . .

VYSHINSKY: Headed by?

KAMKOV: Here the name of Pyatakov was mentioned as the possible Chairman of this new government. Here too it was, I cannot recall exactly in what connection, but I think that it was in answer to my question how carrying this out was conceived, that the phrase was pronounced which was later many times repeated after Bukharin's statement in the press in 1924,[5] when he first informed the broad masses and indeed everybody of it, the phrase about the arrest of Lenin.

VYSHINSKY: Was it you who pronounced this phrase, or he?

KAMKOV: As to the question who pronounced this phrase, I can say the following, namely, that throughout the whole existence of the party of the "Left" Socialist-Revolutionaries, right up to its disappearance, the party has never attempted to shift responsibility on to anybody whatever for the events which developed in connection with the struggle against the Brest-Litovsk Peace. As to me in particular, in the hard times I have gone through, I have never in the course of many years raised this question, although this conversation with Nikolai Ivanovich Bukharin was fairly firmly graven on my memory. And so I did not make any attempt, which might have been rather natural in the position in which I found myself, to shift part of the responsibility for the events which developed in connection with the struggle against the Brest-Litovsk Peace on to anybody whatever. On this basis I think there would have been no sense in my depicting matters otherwise than I did. The very fact of our talk was first published by Bukharin. And I must say that even in 1924 I was extremely surprised when I read of this whole story in the newspapers. What surprised me was not publication of this fact. Perhaps there were profound political motives for this, and perhaps this fact was not a profound secret. What surprised me was that the matter was put in the wrong perspective, that the question was put upside down, that words which had been pronounced by Bukharin were attributed to me.

VYSHINSKY: Consequently, in answer to my question, who put this question, Bukharin or you, you say that the question was raised by Bukharin?

KAMKOV: In reply to this question I say that these words were pronounced not by me but by Bukharin. As to the question, who is telling the truth, inasmuch as our conversation took place twenty years ago, I must say that not only was the matter actually so, as I quite clearly recall, but it could not have been otherwise for the following reasons: in order that I might make a proposal to a member of the Central Committee of the Bolshevik Party that a government should be formed without Lenin, and that Lenin be arrested, I would require some sort of authorization. On the other hand, I would have to be firmly convinced that it would not become known the very next day to the whole Central Committee of the Bolshevik Party, which would involve a number of very unpleasant consequences for us. Moreover, at that time—and I assert this categorically—we had not even any thought of matters taking a turn involving the arrest of the chairman of the government and other members of the government who held the same position as Lenin; we, and I in particular, had no such thought. And so, basing myself on the actual state of affairs, which I definitely remember, basing myself on the fact that nobody had authorized me to conduct such a conversation or to make such a proposal, I could not have acted independently before a member of the Central Committee of the Bolshevik Party. And a third and final argument, also a fairly substantial one. Even in 1924, when I read about this incident in the press, where my name was mentioned and where the initiative was attributed to me, the fairly unpleasant initiative of arresting Lenin, I even then could not understand from what motives the matter was depicted in this way; whether it was purely an error of memory, or whether some political ends were being pursued which I could not know at the time because I was in exile in Chelyabinsk and was cut off from political life and could not know the motives which guided Nikolai Ivanovich Bukharin when he depicted the matter in this way. I at that time applied to the Chairman of the Chelyabinsk Territorial Executive Committee, Paramonov, who also came with this newspaper and asked what it was all about. I said, and put it to him, that I was surprised that the matter was being depicted in a somewhat different way. There was such a talk between us, that is a fact, as it was a fact that it had a political significance; and it was a fact it concerned the questions with regard to which I had ad-

444

dressed myself to the Chairman of the Territorial Executive Committee, thinking that indirectly I might help in some degree to correct the mistake. Summing up this part of my evidence, I must say that I firmly hold to my position and am not mistaken that the proposal to arrest Lenin was made by Bukharin. I do not of course answer for individual words—it was twenty years ago. But I do answer for the substance of the dialogue as it then took place, and I insist that it was uttered by N. I. Bukharin and not by me.

VYSHINSKY: At that time you had contact with the "Left Communists" in connection with the struggle against the Soviet power?

KAMKOV: As regards contact with the "Left Communists" at that period, I would hesitate to say categorically that there was contact. What was there actually at that time? If you will permit me, I shall draw a conclusion so that it may be clear why it happened as it did. The party of the "Left" Socialist-Revolutionaries was formed and split off from the party of the Socialist-Revolutionaries in the fight against the party of the Socialist-Revolutionaries, chiefly on the question of war and peace. In this connection we regarded certain of the theses of the Zimmerwald Conference as dogma which could under no circumstances be repudiated; it seemed to us that this was treachery, not subjective but objective, and therefore there was no more sensitive question for the party of the Socialist-Revolutionaries than the question of war and peace and the tactics of the socialist-revolutionary parties on this question. It is quite natural that when, quite unexpectedly to us, from revolutionary strategic considerations, which, as it subsequently appeared, were fairly correct. . . .

VYSHINSKY: Fairly correct or absolutely correct?

KAMKOV: Absolutely correct—when Lenin proposed to conclude a separate peace with Germany, a peace which he himself called indecent—a peace with indemnities and annexations—this seemed to us absolutely unacceptable.

VYSHINSKY: What measures did you adopt to frustrate this peace?

KAMKOV: We bent every effort to make this peace impossible, to frustrate its development in one degree or another. But being a party which had only just been formed and was still unconsolidated, we would have stopped there, we would not have gone so far, if parallel with this there had not been something else which extremely encouraged us.

VYSHINSKY: What encouraged you?

KAMKOV: This was the existence of the group of "Left Communists," the anti-Brest sentiments within the Party.

VYSHINSKY: The anti-Brest and anti-Lenin sentiments within the Party?

445

KAMKOV: Well, in connection with this, we of course constantly sought some sort of contact with the ' Left Communists."

VYSHINSKY: You sought it and found it?

KAMKOV: I shall answer that presently. We sought contacts with the purpose of a possible joint struggle against the Brest-Litovsk Peace.

VYSHINSKY: Was agreement reached with the ·'Left Communists" about a struggle against the Soviet government, headed by Vladimir Ilyich Lenin?

KAMKOV: I know in this connection . . .

VYSHINSKY: Can you answer my question? Was an agreement reached between the "Left Communists" and the " Left" Socialist-Revolutionaries on certain conditions for a joint struggle against the Soviet government, headed by V. I. Lenin?

KAMKOV: At what period?

VYSHINSKY: At this period, in the period following the Brest-Litovsk Peace, or, if you like, the Brest-Litovsk period.

KAMKOV: You are referring to the period prior to the July revolt?

VYSHINSKY: Yes, prior to the July revolt. Was there an agreement or not?

KAMKOV: As far as I know there was such an agreement.

VYSHINSKY: Was there, or was there not?

KAMKOV: Inasmuch as I myself did not conclude . . .

VYSHINSKY: But you were a member of the Central Committee of the "Left" Socialist-Revolutionaries; you should have known whether there was an agreement or not.

KAMKOV: Such an agreement was reached.

VYSHINSKY: On what conditions? What was this agreement?

KAMKOV: I hesitate to give any details about this agreement, but I can tell you of a conversation I had with Karelin.

VYSHINSKY: Why, was this a personal affair of Karelin's? Are you not responsible for it as a leader of the Central Committee of the "Left" Socialist-Revolutionaries?

KAMKOV: I do not say that I am not responsible for it.

VYSHINSKY: Was it an agreement of Karelin's or of your Central Committee of the "Left" Socialist-Revolutionaries of the time, in which you were one of the leaders, and which acted under your guidance?

KAMKOV: I am not aware of any decision of the Central Committee about such an agreement.

VYSHINSKY: You know that decisions are not taken on everything. You had this conversation with Karelin while you were a member of the Central Committee of the "Left" Socialist-Revolutionaries?

KAMKOV: Yes, as a member of the Central Committee.

VYSHINSKY: You were aware of the matter?

KAMKOV: I was aware of the matter, I was kept informed.

VYSHINSKY: Do you hold yourself responsible for this agreement?

KAMKOV: As a member of the Central Committee, I am of course responsible for the activities of the Central Committee, although this was veiled.

VYSHINSKY: The "Left" Socialist-Revolutionaries gave both organizational and political assistance?

KAMKOV: Yes.

VYSHINSKY: That was so?

KAMKOV: Yes, it was.

VYSHINSKY: And a second question. The Soviet government, headed by V. I. Lenin, Stalin and Sverdlov, was to have been overthrown by the joint action of the "Left" Socialist-Revolutionaries and the "Left Communists" and a new government formed consisting of "Left" Socialist-Revolutionaries and "Left Communists." Is that so or not?

KAMKOV: I hesitate to say exactly.

VYSHINSKY: But the idea?

KAMKOV: The idea is roughly correct.

VYSHINSKY: Was not the revolt of the "Left" Socialist-Revolutionaries in 1918 a development of this agreement?

KAMKOV: I hesitate to answer this categorically, whether it was in the plan.

VYSHINSKY: But it was connected with this agreement?

KAMKOV: If we had been isolated generally, we, the "Left" Socialist-Revolutionaries, would not have gone so far.

VYSHINSKY: You embarked on a revolt relying...

KAMKOV: On the anti-Brest sentiments in the country in general and the anti-Brest sentiments within the Party.

VYSHINSKY: On whose assistance did you rely?

KAMKOV: On the assistance of the "Left Communists."

VYSHINSKY: Did the "Left Communists" know that you were preparing to assassinate Mirbach and to organize the July revolt?

KAMKOV: I attempted to answer this question once...

VYSHINSKY: I am asking you a simple question and I request you to give a simple answer. Yes or no?

KAMKOV: Unfortunately, I cannot answer yes or no to that question.

VYSHINSKY: And how did you answer that question at the preliminary investigation?

KAMKOV: I hesitated to answer then too.

VYSHINSKY: Permit me to read Kamkov's testimony, Vol. XLIV, p. 42 reverse, interrogation of Kamkov by the Pro-

ator of the U.S.S.R., last paragraph: "After this" (i.e., after an account of the agreement and conditions), "the 'Left' Socialist-Revolutionaries organized the assassination of Mirbach and the July revolt." Is that correct?

KAMKOV: It is.

VYSHINSKY: By the way, did you, as a member of the organization of the "Left" Socialist-Revolutionaries take a direct part in organizing the assassination of Mirbach?

KAMKOV: I did.

VYSHINSKY: "The 'Left Communists' were fully aware of the preparations for the assassination of Mirbach and for the July revolt." Do you confirm this?[6]

KAMKOV: I do.

VYSHINSKY: Consequently the "Left Communists" were informed about the July revolt?

KAMKOV: Yes.

VYSHINSKY: Fully?

KAMKOV: Fully, as I testified at the preliminary investigation in accordance with the information I had received from Karelin.

VYSHINSKY: Yes, of course, in accordance with some information or other.

KAMKOV: That is what I wanted to say.

VYSHINSKY: And so it is quite clear. I ask you: was Bukharin in particular, as a leader of the "Left Communists," aware of the fact that the Socialist-Revolutionaries were preparing for a revolt, which then actually broke out in July 1918?

KAMKOV: According to what Karelin told me, he was aware of it.

VYSHINSKY: He was aware of it? Fully?

KAMKOV: Most likely not partially, but fully.

VYSHINSKY: I have no more questions.

BUKHARIN (to the Court): I have a question. I should like to ask Boris Kamkov whether he asserts that at the first meeting in the Smolny I told him that even before my conversation with him the question of the overthrow of the Soviet government, headed by Lenin, was being debated in "Left Communist" circles.

KAMKOV: About the possibility of creating a government of "Left Communists" and "Left" Socialist-Revolutionaries?

BUKHARIN: Yes, that this question was being debated.

KAMKOV: Yes.

BUKHARIN: That is enough for me.

VYSHINSKY: But not for me.

BUKHARIN: If you please.

VYSHINSKY: What does debating the question mean?

KAMKOV: In my opinion, debating means discussing.

VYSHINSKY: And the decision?

KAMKOV: (No reply.)

VYSHINSKY: And your agreement, about which you spoke? The agreement between the "Left" Socialist-Revolutionaries and the "Left Communists," of which Karelin told you?

KAMKOV: If Karelin told me, it must have been so.

VYSHINSKY: An agreement about what?

KAMKOV: That the "Left Communists" would assist in overthrowing the government when we took action.

VYSHINSKY: That means that this was decided, since there was an agreement?

KAMKOV: By whom?

VYSHINSKY: By you and the "Left Communists" jointly.

KAMKOV: I do not understand this question. We decided separately, we did not make any joint decisions. We decided to assassinate Mirbach and frustrate the Brest-Litovsk Peace.

VYSHINSKY: That was decided?

KAMKOV: Yes.

VYSHINSKY: And then a revolt was projected? That was decided?

KAMKOV: It was.

VYSHINSKY: And that is what you did?

KAMKOV: That is what we did.

VYSHINSKY: And so the question was not debated, but decided?

BUKHARIN: But pardon me . . .

VYSHINSKY: I request the accused Bukharin not to interfere in my interrogation. I am restraining myself enough, and I request my opponent to restrain himself. (To Kamkov.) I ask you, was there a decision to overthrow the Soviet power?

KAMKOV: From such an aspect . . .

VYSHINSKY: There is only one aspect, to overthrow the Soviet power?

KAMKOV: We had raised the question of frustrating the Brest-Litovsk Peace, assassinating Mirbach and attempting to create an anti-Brest government by an armed struggle.

VYSHINSKY: Was this decided, or only debated?

KAMKOV: We decided it.

VYSHINSKY: Did you discuss or did you decide on the expediency of concluding an agreement with the "Left Communists"?

KAMKOV: I have already replied. There were no such meetings and discussions.

VYSHINSKY: That is not what I am asking—whether there were meetings or not. What I am interested in knowing is whether a decision had been taken by you, by the centre of the "Left" Socialist-Revolutionaries, in 1918, to wage your struggle against

449

... Soviet government together with the "Left Communists."
Was there such a decision?

KAMKOV: There was no such decision.

VYSHINSKY: But was there such an agreement?

KAMKOV: We had decided to wage a struggle against the Brest government, to begin with the assassination of Mirbach, and to carry the armed collision, which would follow as an inevitable consequence, to a conclusion, with the purpose of creating an anti-Brest government. That was our firm decision.

VYSHINSKY: And in this operation of yours you counted on the "Left Communists"?

KAMKOV: Yes.

VYSHINSKY: Why? Because you already had an agreement?

KAMKOV: Because there was an arrangement, according to what Karelin told me.

VYSHINSKY: And so you did not merely debate joint action between the "Left" Socialist-Revolutionaries and "Left Communists," but reached an agreement. Do I understand you rightly?

KAMKOV: According to what Karelin told me, we regarded the support of the "Left Communists"...

VYSHINSKY: That is, you reached an agreement, about collaboration?

KAMKOV: Quite so.

VYSHINSKY: I have no more questions.

BUKHARIN: I want to put a question. During the confrontation Kamkov stated that this question was not discussed by them at all in the Central Committee of the "Left" Socialist-Revolutionaries. (To Kamkov.) Do you confirm this? The question about an agreement with the "Left Communists" for the purpose of overthrowing the Soviet government?

KAMKOV: I do not remember it.

BUKHARIN: Now I would like to ask . . .

VYSHINSKY: Of whom did the Central Committee of the "Left" Socialist-Revolutionaries consist at that time?

BUKHARIN: I have not finished my question, Citizen Procurator.

VYSHINSKY: But I am putting my question.

BUKHARIN: I stopped in the middle of a sentence. . . .

VYSHINSKY: You asked one question and got an answer.

(To Kamkov.) I ask you of whom did the Central Committee of the "Left" Socialist-Revolutionaries consist at that time?

KAMKOV: Of Karelin, Spiridonova, Mayorov, Proshyan, Trutovsky and myself.

VYSHINSKY: Is that all?

KAMKOV: I don't quite recall just now.

VYSHINSKY: Who was actually the leader of the Committee?

Who of these seven people played the most active and prominent part?

KAMKOV: Spiridonova, I should say.

VYSHINSKY: Next?

KAMKOV: I, Karelin, Proshyan.

VYSHINSKY: A quartet, that is.

KAMKOV: The leading quartet.

VYSHINSKY: Maria Spiridonova, you, Karelin and Proshyan.

Regarding the assassination of Mirbach, was this question decided by the four of you?

KAMKOV: It was not decided in the Central Committee.

VYSHINSKY: Who decided the question regarding the July revolt?

KAMKOV: We did not discuss it separately, but discussed together the question...

VYSHINSKY: Who decided it?

KAMKOV: The Central Committee.

VYSHINSKY: "Although it was not discussed?"

KAMKOV: I say that it was not discussed separately.

VYSHINSKY: What do you mean by "not discussed separately"?

KAMKOV: Since it followed from the assassination of Mirbach, it was part of the same discussion.

VYSHINSKY: Was there a resolution of the Central Committee to raise a revolt? Was there such a resolution of the Central Committee?

KAMKOV: It was not recorded in our resolution, because there was no such resolution.

VYSHINSKY: But there was a decision?

KAMKOV: Yes, there was a decision.

VYSHINSKY: That is, there was no resolution, but there was a decision.

KAMKOV: Either I do not understand you, or we are talking about different things.

VYSHINSKY: I understand you very well.

KAMKOV: But I do not understand you at all.

VYSHINSKY: Was there a resolution?

KAMKOV: No, there was not. We decided as follows: to assassinate Mirbach, and then the members of the Central Committee were to make their way to the headquarter staff in the event of an armed struggle, which was considered likely and perhaps even inevitable—to make their way to the headquarter staff on Arsenievsky Street.

VYSHINSKY: To Popov's staff?

KAMKOV: Yes, to Popov's staff.

451

SHINSKY: That was the decision?

AMKOV: Yes, that was the decision.

VYSHINSKY: And what about the plans as to how to act, in at direction, and so forth?

KAMKOV: That was not discussed by the Central Committee.

VYSHINSKY: No. Then what were they?

KAMKOV: They were reflections about this . . .

VYSHINSKY: They were the reflections of Kamkov and Karelin? Or perhaps Spiridonova thought for all of you?

KAMKOV: I cannot tell you.

VYSHINSKY: Now I want to ask: you said at the preliminary investigation that an agreement was reached with the "Left Communists." I have already read these two points. Who reached this agreement?

KAMKOV: Karelin.

VYSHINSKY: On his own?

KAMKOV: He conducted the negotiations.

VYSHINSKY: On his own behalf?

KAMKOV: I do not think so; he was a member of the Central Committee.

VYSHINSKY: On whose behalf, then?

KAMKOV: He should have conducted them on behalf of the Central Committee, of course.

VYSHINSKY: On behalf of your party?

KAMKOV: It must have been on behalf of the party.

VYSHINSKY: Did it approve of these negotiations of his?

KAMKOV: I have already told you that he did not make a report.

VYSHINSKY: But without a report—can you say anything?

KAMKOV: Undoubtedly.

VYSHINSKY: Am I entitled to draw the conclusion that the agreement between the "Left" Socialist-Revolutionaries and the "Left Communists" about a joint struggle in the two cases of which we have spoken here and about which I shall read later was reached by Karelin with the representatives of the "Left Communists" and was approved by the Central Committee of the "Left" Socialist-Revolutionaries?

KAMKOV: That conclusion may be drawn, but as approval does not signify resolution, it logically follows . . .

VYSHINSKY: You understand the difference between a written resolution and the approval of the most active heads of a given institution? Or must it be said that there was no agreement between the "Left" Socialist-Revolutionaries and the "Left Communists," but that Karelin reached some sort of an agreement on his own account? Can it be put that way?

452

KAMKOV: No, I think that would be wrong.

VYSHINSKY: And so Karelin reached an agreement not on his own account, but on somebody's behalf?

KAMKOV: On behalf of the party.

VYSHINSKY: That means that your party approved it?

KAMKOV: It approved it inasmuch as it did not disavow it.

VYSHINSKY: Right. Consequently, it may be said that the party concluded an agreement?

KAMKOV: It may.

VYSHINSKY: Was it so?

KAMKOV: Since it may be said so, it means that it was so.

VYSHINSKY: I have no more questions.

BUKHARIN: I have only one question. I would like to ask Kamkov whether it was only from Karelin that he learnt that I and my colleagues of the time in the faction of the "Left Communists" knew about the plan to assassinate the German Ambassador, Count Mirbach, and about this July revolt.

KAMKOV: Only from him.

BUKHARIN: And you did not learn this from Proshyan?

KAMKOV: I did not learn it from Proshyan.

BUKHARIN: You heard nothing about it from Spiridonova?

KAMKOV: I heard nothing personally from Spiridonova.

BUKHARIN: You heard nothing?

KAMKOV: No.

BUKHARIN: You heard nothing about it from Trutovsky?

KAMKOV: I heard nothing about it from Trutovsky.

BUKHARIN: I have no more questions.

VYSHINSKY (to Kamkov): Tell us, please, did you have occasion to talk to Spiridonova about this?

KAMKOV: No.

VYSHINSKY: Did you have occasion to talk to Trutovsky about it?

KAMKOV: No.

VYSHINSKY: And that is why you heard nothing?

KAMKOV: Yes.

VYSHINSKY: I have no more questions.

BUKHARIN: Then let me put one question. I meant to put it this way: you did not hear about it because you did not talk about it; but I ask you this: why did you not talk about such an important question to such prominent colleagues of yours in the leadership of your still young and still unformed party?

KAMKOV: You see, the position in our party was not yet such that all questions were necessarily discussed, debated, and so on. There was still at that time a fairly anarchic state of affairs in the Central Committee of the "Left" Socialist-Revolutionaries.

VSHINSKY: As in the group of the "Left Communists"?

KAMKOV: And so it might have happened, let us say, that Karelin conducted negotiations and did not inform the others. But at that time in the given case it was a question of the revolt of the "Left" Socialist-Revolutionaries, a question of the possible support of the anti-Brest elements (at least, that is how I understand it). This question did not become the subject of discussion by our Central Committee.

VYSHINSKY: Permit me in this connection to put a question. Which of you chiefly conducted the negotiations with the "Left Communists" about a bloc?

KAMKOV: Karelin; but I do not know exactly.

VYSHINSKY: Perhaps you know whether Karelin spoke about this to Proshyan or to Spiridonova?

KAMKOV: It is possible.

VYSHINSKY: I have no more questions.

BUKHARIN: Neither have I.

THE PRESIDENT: Comrade Commandant, call in witness Karelin.

(Witness Karelin enters the Court.)

THE PRESIDENT: Is your name Karelin?

KARELIN: Karelin.

THE PRESIDENT: Your name and patronymic—Vladimir Alexandrovich?

KARELIN: Vladimir Alexandrovich.

THE PRESIDENT: You have been summoned as a witness in the case of Nikolai Ivanovich Bukharin. You must tell the Court nothing but the truth.

Comrade Procurator, have you any questions to put to witness Karelin?

VYSHINSKY: Yes. Witness Karelin, did you in 1918, while a member of the Central Committee of the Party of "Left" Socialist-Revolutionaries, have occasion to conduct negotiations with Bukharin? Do you know Bukharin?

KARELIN: I do.

VYSHINSKY: Do you recognize him here?

KARELIN: Yes.

VYSHINSKY: Where is he sitting?

KARELIN: At the far end.

VYSHINSKY (to Bukharin): And do you know Karelin?

BUKHARIN: I do. Why, we were confronted at your office.

VYSHINSKY: Had you seen him before the confrontation?

BUKHARIN: I knew him in 1918 and 1919.

VYSHINSKY: Is it the same Karelin who stands here as a witness?

BUKHARIN: Well, he has changed so much that I would

454

not say that he is the same Karelin; but apparently this Karelin is an evolution of the Karelin of that time.

VYSHINSKY: Everybody changes with age. But my question is meant seriously.

BUKHARIN: I understand, Citizen Procurator, and it was not my intention to make a witticism. I wanted to say that his present content differs very much from what it used to be.

VYSHINSKY: I did not put this question without reason. You see, Karelin has changed. . . .

BUKHARIN: But we had already met in your office.

VYSHINSKY: And I ask you, do you really recognize Vladimir Alexandrovich Karelin, former member of the Central Committee of the Socialist-Revolutionaries, in this witness? Do you remember him?

BUKHARIN: It was difficult for me to recognize him in your office, but after I had seen him in your office I recognized him to be the same person, and I have no doubts about it.

VYSHINSKY: The question is an important one. It is no matter for jesting. It is an important question.

BUKHARIN: I had no intention of joking when I said that.

VYSHINSKY: Well, tell us, Citizen Karelin, did you in 1918, while you were a member of the Central Committee of the Party of "Left" Socialist-Revolutionaries, conduct negotiations or meet Bukharin in connection with his activities as leader of the group of the so-called "Left Communists"?

KARELIN: Yes, I did.

VYSHINSKY: Can you tell us where, when and in what connection you met Bukharin? And, secondly, what was the subject of your conversations during these meetings?

KARELIN: In that case, perhaps you will permit me to deal with the last months of 1917, November and December, because the questions you have put seem to concern these negotiations.

VYSHINSKY: If you please.

KARELIN: I, as a member of the Central Committee of the Party of "Left" Socialist-Revolutionaries, met Bukharin for the first time in the latter half of November 1917. At that period the Central Committee of the "Left" Socialist-Revolutionaries had to decide on its tactics in the immediate future in view of the fact that the question of the conclusion of peace had become very acute. The Central Committee of the "Left" Socialist-Revolutionaries regarded the formation of the group of "Left Communists" as an extremely important item in the prognosis which this party made at that time. And in November, during the period directly connected with the period when Bukharin came from Moscow to Petrograd in order to report to a meeting of the All-Russian Central Executive Committee on the October uprising in Moscow,

I had a conversation with Bukharin regarding the position of the group of "Left Communists," which at that time interested us very much. We then elucidated—I say we, because several members of the Central Committee of the Party of "Left" Socialist-Revolutionaries conducted these negotiations. . . .

VYSHINSKY: Who were "we"?

KARELIN: Kamkov, Proshyan and I. The Central Committee had commissioned us to conduct such negotiations. In this conversation Bukharin adopted a quite definite position. I remember a phrase he uttered to the effect that the group of "Left Communists" —at that time it was organizationally identical with the Moscow Regional Bureau of the Communists—would take the actions of the Central Committee of the Communist Party under its control. The implication was that the rupture of the peace negotiations would be ensured. It was just this question that interested us "Left" Socialist-Revolutionaries. In December these negotiations were already sharply concentrated on the purely practical question. This was just the time when the negotiations were being conducted in Brest-Litovsk. We knew, particularly from information which Proshyan gave us, that differences had become extremely acute within the Central Committee of the Communist Party. We knew that Trotsky had advanced the formula: We neither conclude peace nor conduct war. And we realized that this formula practically meant the rupture of negotiations, and consequently the realization of what was then defined in the form of a slogan as a revolutionary war, that is, rejection of the policy of the immediate conclusion of peace.

And when at the end of December or in the beginning of January the question arose of sending a larger peace delegation to Brest-Litovsk in order to bring about the rupture of negotiations—I was one of the members of this delegation as a member of the government at the time—Natanson,[7] who was also a member of the Central Committee of the "Left" Socialist-Revolutionaries, informed us that it had been definitely arranged with Bukharin that this position would be carried out to the full, that it would be carried out in Brest-Litovsk; that the Brest-Litovsk negotiations would thereby be broken off and the result of this would be a revolutionary war. That was in December. Do you also want to know about the January negotiations, because these negotiations were continued?

VYSHINSKY: How did the bloc between the "Left" Socialist-Revolutionaries and the "Left Communists" arise?

KARELIN: It may be taken that this bloc was already formed in December 1917. In January, the Central Committee of the "Left" Socialist-Revolutionaries displayed definite initiative in negotiations which were being conducted not only with Bukharin, but also with a number of other persons. Negotiations were being conducted with Pyatakov and Radek, and on our side negotiations were being conducted by Natanson, Kamkov, Proshyan and myself. All of us reported on these negotiations to the Central Committee of the "Left" Socialist-Revolutionaries. It was learnt from these negotiations that the position of the "Left Communists" at this period was an extremely trenchant one and that they favoured a change of government. In the negotiations that were conducted in February, the same idea was also stressed by the "Left Communists" regarding the necessity of overthrowing the Soviet government and replacing it by a new one: a coalition government consisting of "Left" Socialist-Revolutionaries and "Left Communists" was conceived. The position of Buhkarin in these negotiations amounted to the fact that his group considered it necessary to await the results of the Seventh Party Congress. The purpose of this waiting position was that the "Left Communists," as represented by Bukharin, reckoned that they would succeed in gaining a majority at the Seventh Party Congress. In this way action was postponed until the results of the Seventh Party Congress became known, although the position of Bukharin at that period was a perfectly definite one, and in the information which Proshyan gave at the meeting of the Central Committee of the "Left" Socialist-Revolutionaries it was said that Bukharin favoured the overthrow of the Soviet government without shrinking even from the physical extermination of the leaders of the Soviet government and of the Party.

VYSHINSKY: That is, without shrinking from the assassination of the leaders of the Party and the government?

KARELIN: Well, yes, from physical extermination, or assassination.

VYSHINSKY: Of whom exactly?

KARELIN: The leaders were spoken of, and Lenin, Stalin and Sverdlov were mentioned personally.

VYSHINSKY: Who informed you of this?

KARELIN: Proshyan.

VYSHINSKY: And who had said this?

KARELIN: He cited Bukharin.

VYSHINSKY: Did Proshyan conduct negotiations with Bukharin?

KARELIN: Yes, he did.

VYSHINSKY: On whose instructions?

KARELIN: On the instructions of the Central Committee of the Party of Socialist-Revolutionaries.

VYSHINSKY: And did you personally speak to Bukharin about this?

KARELIN: Yes, we had a conversation on the subject. I am

referring to a conversation that I had with Bukharin after a meeting of the All-Russian Central Executive Committee in April 1918. At this meeting Vladimir Ilyich Lenin had made his well-known report on "The Immediate Tasks of the Soviet Government."[8] At this meeting, on the instructions of the Central Committee of the Party of "Left" Socialist-Revolutionaries, I made a very trenchant speech, in which I concentrated attention on the points which had been tactically agreed upon between the "Left" Socialist-Revolutionaries and the "Left Communists."

VYSHINSKY: That means that you acted against Lenin in accordance with a preliminary agreement between the "Left Communists" and the "Left" Socialist-Revolutionaries?

KARELIN: Yes, in accordance with a preliminary agreement between the "Left Communists" and the "Left" Socialist-Revolutionaries, although not exactly in connection with this utterance. . . .

VYSHINSKY: But on fundamental questions?

KARELIN: Yes, on fundamental questions, which I accentuated. . . .

VYSHINSKY: Accentuated wherever it was necessary to accentuate?

KARELIN: Yes, and where it followed from the bloc which had been formed at that time.

VYSHINSKY: So there was a bloc?

KARELIN: There was. Of course, it was not represented by any signed document, but it goes without saying that the understanding was a complete one.

VYSHINSKY: Who reached this understanding?

KARELIN: I do not quite understand the question.

VYSHINSKY: Who negotiated and reached an understanding on the part of the "Left" Socialist-Revolutionaries, and with whom on the part of the "Left Communists"?

KARELIN: I consider that those stages of the negotiations which more and more precisely clarified the position which I have related and which was sanctioned by the Central Committee of the "Left" Socialist-Revolutionaries were the actual achievement of this understanding. The "Left Communists" were represented by Bukharin, Pyatakov and Radek, and to some extent by other persons; the "Left" Socialist-Revolutionaries were represented by Kamkov, myself, Proshyan and partly by Natanson.

VYSHINSKY: Did Bukharin at this meeting tell you that it was necessary to resort to the physical extermination of Lenin, Stalin and Sverdlov?

KARELIN: He said that direct action would have to be taken, without shrinking from physical extermination.

VYSHINSKY: Tell us, was the "Left" Socialist-Revolutionary

458

revolt carried out as a result of preliminary negotiations on the subject with the "Left Communists"?

KARELIN: The "Left" Socialist-Revolutionary revolt that took place at the beginning of July 1918 was due to the direct initiative of the Central Committee of the "Left" Socialist-Revolutionaries. It was considered that the relations of the bloc of the "Left Communists" and the "Left" Socialist-Revolutionaries had been definitely established, in particular, the definite mutual information and agreement which existed on this question between the "Left" Socialist-Revolutionaries and the "Left Communists."

At the end of June 1918, when all the dispositions had been made, and when at last a precise organizational plan had been drawn up by the "Left" Socialist-Revolutionary Central Committee, I had conversations with Bukharin, in the latter part of June, in the First House of the Soviets.

VYSHINSKY: What about?

KARELIN: About the impending action.

VYSHINSKY: You spoke about the impending revolt of the "Left" Socialist-Revolutionaries?

KARELIN: It was not said definitely in this case when this action would take place; the date was not mentioned; but in this conversation Bukharin referred to the negotiations which he was conducting at this same period with Proshyan, and about which Proshyan had reported to the Central Committee of the "Left" Socialist-Revolutionaries. In particular, one of the prime links in the organizational plan of the "Left" Socialist-Revolutionary revolt was a terrorist act against the German Ambassador, Mirbach. Proshyan said that in his conversation with Bukharin the latter had said that this plan for the rupture of peace and this act of assassination of Mirbach were in general impressive and effective.

VYSHINSKY: Bukharin said that the assassination of the Ambassador . . .

KARELIN: That the terrorist act against the German Ambassador, Mirbach, would be an impressive and effective step towards a rupture of the Brest-Litovsk Peace.

VYSHINSKY: Did the attempt made on the life of V. I. Lenin by the Socialist-Revolutionary terrorist Kaplan on August 30, 1918, have any relation to the plans for the assassination of Lenin, Stalin and Sverdlov? [9]

KARELIN: Yes. One result of the July revolt of the "Left" Socialist-Revolutionaries was that the "Left" Socialist-Revolutionaries very rapidly proceeded to establish organizational contact with the Right Socialist-Revolutionaries. The split had taken place in October 1917, and during the period from October 1917 to June 1918 the relations were rather strained and at times hostile

459

until the crushing of the "Left" Socialist-Revolutionary revolt in 1918.

The fact that, as a result of the crushing of this revolt, the majority of the party organizations and institutions went underground created a certain basis for joint activity and policy. In addition, here again the premises arose for a bloc, and they began to be realized immediately. And it was at this period that Proshyan, who had charge of the combat organization of the "Left" Socialist-Revolutionaries, in a report he made to the Central Committee of the Party of the "Left" Socialist-Revolutionaries, referred to the fact that the insistence that Bukharin had formerly displayed with regard to a terrorist act had become extremely enhanced. And I must say that, although this has been hidden and concealed for nearly twenty years, the Central Committee of the "Left" Socialist-Revolutionaries was definitely posted on these events.

VYSHINSKY: Posted on what?

KARELIN: On the fact that the Right Socialist-Revolutionaries, through their combat organization, were preparing a terrorist act against Vladimir Ilyich Lenin.

VYSHINSKY: That is, the Central Committee of the Party of "Left" Socialist-Revolutionaries was posted on the preparations for the assassination of Comrade Lenin?

KARELIN: Yes.

VYSHINSKY: And what had Bukharin to do with it?

KARELIN: According to Proshyan, who was conducting negotiations with Bukharin bearing an official character, Bukharin urged that the terrorist act should be expedited. And so, when the "Left" Socialist-Revolutionaries informed the Right Socialist-Revolutionaries, gave them to understand that the Party of "Left" Socialist-Revolutionaries was, as it were, ensuring political support for this act, from this moment it was fully realized that the group of "Left Communists," having been smashed, had adopted the standpoint of a direct fight and did not shrink from the most determined methods, including terrorist acts.

VYSHINSKY: And so you confirm that the preparations of the Right and the "Left" Socialist-Revolutionaries for an attempt upon the life of Vladimir Ilyich Lenin were made in conjunction with Bukharin?

KARELIN: With the "Left Communists." We regarded Bukharin as the leader of the "Left Communists."

VYSHINSKY: You said at the preliminary investigation that the fact that you, in conjunction with the Right Socialist-Revolutionaries and on the insistence of Bukharin, had attempted to murder Lenin has been concealed from the Soviet people for twenty years. Do you confirm this?

KARELIN: I confirm that there was insistence on the part of Bukharin as the leader of the group of "Left Communists." This insistence played a very big part in the perpetration of this crime.

VYSHINSKY (to the Court): Permit me to put a question to Ossinsky. Witness Ossinsky, tell us, please, what information have you about Bukharin's implication in the attempt on the life of Vladimir Ilyich Lenin in 1918?

OSSINSKY: I must first say the following. After the July revolt of the "Left" Socialist-Revolutionaries I left the "Left Communists," and at the beginning of 1918 joined another group, the Democratic Centralism group.[10] My resignation from the group of "Left Communists" was connected with my rejection of the methods of struggle employed by the "Left Communists." Nevertheless, I continued my acquaintanceship with some of the former "Left Communists," including Stukov.

At the end of 1918 I had a conversation with Stukov about the state of Lenin's health after he was wounded by the terrorist Kaplan. In this connection, Stukov said the following: "Do you know that the shot fired by Kaplan was not only the result of the directions given by the Central Committee of the Party of Right Socialist-Revolutionaries, but also a direct result of the measures which had been outlined by the bloc for the overthrow of the government, and especially of the stand on the slaying of leaders of the government?" As at that time I did not consider terrorism permissible as a method of struggle, I spoke very sharply on this subject to Stukov, and this ended the conversation, so that I did not ask him the details. So that I can therefore say nothing about Bukharin personally; but this fact I can tell you.

VYSHINSKY: Consequently, Stukov told you that the shot fired by the Right Socialist-Revolutionary Kaplan at Lenin was the result of the standpoint and the organizational measures which had been drawn up, adopted and carried out, by whom?

OSSINSKY: By the bloc.

VYSHINSKY: Which bloc?

OSSINSKY: From the "Left Communists" to the Right Socialist-Revolutionaries.

VYSHINSKY: And Bukharin acted in this as the leader of the group of "Left Communists"?

OSSINSKY: Quite true.

VYSHINSKY: You were told this by Stukov.

(To Bukharin.) What do you say, accused Bukharin?

BUKHARIN: I say that it is all untrue.

VYSHINSKY: Did you hear the evidence regarding your implication in the attempt to assassinate Vladimir Ilyich Lenin?

BUKHARIN: Yes.

VYSHINSKY: What do you say to it?

BUKHARIN: I categorically deny all connection whatsoever.

VYSHINSKY: About the arrest, you admit?

BUKHARIN: Yes.

VYSHINSKY: There was a plan to assassinate Vladimir Ilyich Lenin?

BUKHARIN: I deny it.

VYSHINSKY: And you deny any definite relation to Kaplan's crime?

BUKHARIN: Absolutely.

VYSHINSKY: Karelin implicates you.

KARELIN: Yes, I confirm it.

VYSHINSKY: Ossinsky spoke on the subject.

BUKHARIN: Ossinsky said that he could say nothing about me.

VYSHINSKY (to Karelin): Do you consider that Kaplan's attempt was a measure to which the way was paved by the plan to fight the Soviet government and to organize terrorist acts by the "Left" and Right Socialist-Revolutionaries and the "Left Communists"?

KARELIN: Stukov told me that.

VYSHINSKY: This was co-ordinated with Bukharin's stand on terrorism?

KARELIN: There was a stand that followed from this.

VYSHINSKY (to Bukharin): Moreover, Yakovleva testifies that in 1918 you held the standpoint and planned the arrest and assassination of Comrades Lenin, Stalin and Sverdlov. Karelin testifies to the same, Ossinsky testifies to the same, and Mantsev testifies to the same. I ask you, who gave you instructions to arrange this crime; what intelligence service gave you these instructions?

BUKHARIN: I deny this fact altogether.

VYSHINSKY (to Karelin): I have no more questions. Be seated.

BUKHARIN: I have a question to ask Karelin.

Firstly, I ask you to tell us, Citizen Karelin, whether you confirm what you said at the confrontation, namely, that in the early period prior to the Brest-Litovsk Peace the initiative of the bloc belonged to the "Left" Socialist-Revolutionaries, and that in the second half, that is, after the Brest-Litovsk Peace, it belonged to the "Left Communists."

KARELIN: I confirm that in the period prior to the rupture of the negotiations in Brest-Litovsk on February 10, that is, when it was still not clear how the talk of peace and the formula "Neither peace nor war," would end—at that period, as a matter of fact, the initiative was the same on the part of both groups. In the period following the rupture, the initiative belonged to the "Left"

Socialist-Revolutionaries, who proposed hastening this action, whereas the "Left Communists," as represented by Bukharin, considered that "there was no harm in trying," that it was better to await the results of the Seventh Congress of the Bolshevik Party; for at that time they believed that they would succeed in gaining a majority at the Seventh Congress. After the Seventh Party Congress and the Fourth Congress of Soviets, which already ratified the BrestLitovsk Peace, the initiative belonged to the "Left Communists."

BUKHARIN: At the confrontation you said that during that conversation, the first one, in the Smolny, which has been referred to, it was the "Left" Socialist-Revolutionaries who spoke about the possible arrest of Lenin. It is about this first conversation that I am asking you.

KARELIN: The first conversation in the Smolny?

BUKHARIN: At that time you spoke in conjunction with Kamkov, while on our side there were Pyatakov and I.

KARELIN: I did not say that.

BUKHARIN: At the confrontation you said that the proposal regarding the arrest of Lenin at that time came from the "Left" Socialist-Revolutionaries, while later, in the period following the Brest-Litovsk Peace, you mentioned that the "Left Communists" said this.

KARELIN: Later, before the Seventh Congress, the proposal to hasten action was made by the "Left" Socialist-Revolutionaries, who displayed the initiative. That I confirm.

BUKHARIN: Permit me to put a second question. Does Citizen Karelin know that during the Moscow revolt of the "Left" Socialist-Revolutionaries one of the chief persons who took part in the practical operations, from the standpoint of combative technique, against the "Left" Socialist-Revolutionaries was the "Left Communist" Bela Kun? [11]

KARELIN: I knew that personally certain "Left Communists"—with regard to Bela Kun, I know that he was a "Left Communist" at the time, a member of this group—took part in crushing the "Left" Socialist-Revolutionary revolt, and, in particular, that Bela Kun led a detachment which fought near the Telegraph Office, which had been seized by a "Left" Socialist-Revolutionary detachment. But this was already at a time when the failure of the revolt was clear. At that time we regarded it as abandoning the sinking ship.

BUKHARIN: Very well. Permit me to put another question. Do you confirm here that Proshyan and other colleagues of yours on the Central Committee reported at meetings of the Central Committee on negotiations with the "Left Communists"?

463

KARELIN: I do.

BUKHARIN: I have no more questions.

THE PRESIDENT (to Vyshinsky): Have you any questions to put to witness Karelin?

VYSHINSKY: I have a question in connection with Bukharin's questions. Was it the regular case that reports were made of all meetings and decisions, that reports were made at the Central Committee of the "Left" Socialist-Revolutionaries, or were there also questions on which no reports were made?

KARELIN: Certain decisions of the Central Committee of the "Left" Socialist-Revolutionaries were sometimes adopted by an inner circle of leaders. This was sometimes done by a canvas of opinion, no special meetings being summoned. After all, the Central Committee was a political group; especially in such a situation as existed at that time, it was hardly possible at once to draw up minutes, properly paragraphed, on every step and on every decision.

VYSHINSKY: I have no more questions to put to Karelin. I have a question to put to Bukharin: When did you arrive from abroad?

BUKHARIN: In what sense?

VYSHINSKY: How in what sense? One can arrive in only one sense.

BUKHARIN: I arrived from abroad—I think it was in April 1917.

VYSHINSKY: When did you begin to form the group of "Left Communists"?

BUKHARIN: "Left Communists"? In 1918.

VYSHINSKY: And where were you in the months immediately preceding the October Revolution?

BUKHARIN: In Moscow.

VYSHINSKY: And during the October Revolution?

BUKHARIN: Also in Moscow.

VYSHINSKY: And after the October Revolution?

BUKHARIN: After the October Revolution, on the instructions of the Moscow Bolsheviks, I left to make a report on the progress of the uprising in Moscow, when we seized power here. I made that report. . . .

VYSHINSKY: Did you begin to form the group of "Left Communists" in Leningrad or in Moscow?

BUKHARIN: In Leningrad.

VYSHINSKY: Was it then, immediately?

BUKHARIN: No, not immediately. First, there was the question of peace. . . .

464

VYSHINSKY: I understand; but this was a question of your tactics.

BUKHARIN: No, not of tactics.

VYSHINSKY: And was there a group of followers with you?

BUKHARIN: No.

VYSHINSKY: Did you reckon on coming to power by peaceful means alone, or with a group?

BUKHARIN: At that time this question had not yet been raised, but the differences began over the question of peace.

VYSHINSKY: I am not asking you about the differences; I am asking you when, at what time you began to form the group of "Left Communists."

BUKHARIN: I think that it was towards 1918.

VYSHINSKY: At the beginning of 1918?

BUKHARIN: I do not remember in what month, Citizen Procurator. It was over twenty years ago.

VYSHINSKY: At any rate, when you started negotiations with the "Left" Socialist-Revolutionaries you did have this group?

BUKHARIN: Quite so.

VYSHINSKY: Consequently, you had already formed your group organizationally, and then you entered into a bloc with the "Left" Socialist-Revolutionaries; or was this interwoven?

BUKHARIN: No, we already had a group, although I would not say that it was already fully formed. Excuse me, Citizen Procurator, but you are putting the question in a very personal way. This trend arose . . .

VYSHINSKY: I am not asking when this trend arose, I am asking when this group was organized.

BUKHARIN: I told you, at the beginning of 1918.

VYSHINSKY: I request you to be more precise: did you start negotiations with the group of "Left" Socialist-Revolutionaries after your group had been organized?

BUKHARIN: I think that it was when it had been already formed in the main.

VYSHINSKY: Tell us, were your sentiments at that time very intensely opposed to the Brest-Litovsk Peace and the leadership?

BUKHARIN: Sentiments were rather intense.

VYSHINSKY: Rather intense?

BUKHARIN: Yes.

VYSHINSKY: So that, given such sentiments, the idea of arrest did not arise by chance?

BUKHARIN: No, you see, I would not put it that way.

465

VYSHINSKY: Why, it is perfectly clear that in an intense and heated atmosphere . . .

BUKHARIN: But I want to say that before the Brest-Litovsk Peace . . .

VYSHINSKY: I am not asking that. . . .

BUKHARIN: Before the Brest-Litovsk Peace this idea, in an affirmative way, had not occurred either to me or to others.

VYSHINSKY: And after the Brest-Litovsk Peace?

BUKHARIN: After the Brest-Litovsk Peace it arose.

VYSHINSKY: That is what I am asking. Were your feelings profoundly rancourous?

BUKHARIN: It was not a question of personal rancour against persons and against leaders.

VYSHINSKY: I ask, was the atmosphere heated enough?

BUKHARIN: Yes, heat along the line of the factional struggle was very great.

VYSHINSKY: The atmosphere was intensely heated?

BUKHARIN: Yes, intensely.

VYSHINSKY: And in such an atmosphere, the idea of arrest, and in the case of some, perhaps, of assassination, was not precluded?

BUKHARIN: As regards arrest, I admit it; as regards assassination, I know nothing whatever.

VYSHINSKY: But the atmosphere was . . .

BUKHARIN: The atmosphere was the atmosphere.

VYSHINSKY: The atmosphere was appropriate for such ideas and plans to arise in certain heated minds?

BUKHARIN: Perhaps they did arise in somebody's mind, but I personally saw no symptoms of it.

VYSHINSKY: And nobody urged you in this direction?

BUKHARIN: No, nobody.

VYSHINSKY: Nobody suggested that Lenin, Stalin and Sverdlov must be removed?

BUKHARIN: No, Citizen Procurator, nobody.

VYSHINSKY: No special organs?

BUKHARIN: Neither organs nor persons.

VYSHINSKY: No special organs gave you instructions?

BUKHARIN: No, they did not.

VYSHINSKY: And you entirely deny this evidence of the witnesses?

BUKHARIN: No, I do not deny it entirely.

VYSHINSKY: But in respect to this?

BUKHARIN: In respect to this I deny it entirely.

VYSHINSKY: But why do both former "Left Communists" and "Left" Socialist-Revolutionaries say so—everybody?

BUKHARIN: No, not everybody: of two "Left" Socialist-Revolutionaries, only one said it.

VYSHINSKY: They say that you, as a traitor to the revolution, were preparing to arrest Lenin, Stalin and Sverdlov.

BUKHARIN: That I admit.

VYSHINSKY: And they added that you were also preparing to assassinate them.

BUKHARIN: With this addition I absolutely do not agree; I categorically deny it.

THE PRESIDENT: No more questions?

VYSHINSKY: No.

THE PRESIDENT: I think the witnesses may leave the Court room.

VYSHINSKY: I still have to make a statement about the expert witnesses.

THE PRESIDENT: Allow me to adjourn the Court for ten minutes. Adjournment for ten minutes.

* * *

COMMANDANT OF THE COURT: The Court is coming. Please rise.

THE PRESIDENT: Please, be seated.

The session is resumed. In order to establish a number of circumstances connected with the killing of Alexei Maximovich Gorky, Valerian Vladimirovich Kuibyshev, Vyacheslav Rudolfovich Menzhinsky and Maxim Alexeyevich Peshkov, and also to elucidate a number of circumstances connected with the attempt to poison Nikolai Ivanovich Yezhov, the Military Collegium of the Supreme Court of the U.S.S.R., at the request of the Procurator of the U.S.S.R., has summoned a commission of experts, consisting of Prof. Nikolai Adolphovich Shereshevsky, Scientist of Merit, Prof. Dmitry Alexandrovich Burmin, Scientist of Merit, Prof. Vladimir Nikitich Vinogradov, Prof. Dmitry Mikhailovich Rossisky, and Vladimir Dmitrievich Zipalov, Doctor of Medicine![12]

The experts summoned are present in the Court room. Prof. N. A. Shereshevsky, Prof. D. A. Burmin, Prof. V. N. Vinogradov, Prof. D. M. Rossisky, and Dr. V. D. Zipalov.

(The experts summoned take their seats.)

VYSHINSKY: The questions the prosecution has to put to the expert witnesses are as follows.

On the first section—the killing of A. M. Gorky.

First question: Was it permissible to appoint a regimen of long walks after dinner, especially when accompanied by exhausting work, for a patient who suffered from acute pneumo-sclerosis, broncho-ectasiae and cavities in the lungs, pulmonary emphysema and deterioration of the cardio-vascular system, and who was subject to severe periodic haemorrhage?

Second question: Might such a regimen, practised over a long period, cause the deterioration of the health of the patient and especially of the cardio-vascular system?

Third question: Was it permissible to place such a patient in an apartment where there were known to be persons suffering from grippe?

Fourth question: Was the care of the patient correct, and were the case history and the treatment of A. M. Gorky properly conducted during his last illness, which lasted from May 31 to June 18, 1936?

Fifth question: Is it permissible in general for prolonged, large doses of heart stimulants, namely, digitalis, digilen (extracts of foxglove), strophanthin and strophanthus, to be administered intravenously, subcutaneously and internally at the same time, and, in particular, in the case of the very sick patient A. M. Gorky, who was sixty-eight years of age, and suffered from the above-mentioned affection of the internal organs?

Sixth question: What may have been the consequences of such treatment of A. M. Gorky during his last illness?

Seventh question: Can it be granted that properly qualified physicians could have adopted such a wrong method of treatment without malicious intent?

Eighth question: May it be regarded as established, on the basis of the sum total of these facts, that the method of treatment of A. M. Gorky was a deliberate act of wrecking designed to hasten his death, the expert knowledge possessed by the accused Levin and Pletnev having been utilized for the attainment of this criminal end?

On the second section—the killing of Comrade Kuibyshev.

First question: Was it permissible to prescribe prolonged administrations of large doses of digitalis (foxglove) to the patient V. V. Kuibyshev, who suffered from attacks of angina pectoris and advanced arterio-sclerosis?

Second question: Might the administration of large doses of extracts of foxglove over a long period (several months) have contributed to increasing the frequency of the attacks of angina pectoris?

Third question: Is it permissible in case of attacks of angina pectoris to allow the patient to move about and to climb stairs, and may a patient suffering from an attack of angina pectoris be left without immediate medical attention?

Fourth question: May it be regarded as established, on the basis of the sum total of these facts, that the method of treatment of V. V. Kuibyshev was a deliberate act of wrecking designed to hasten his death, the expert knowledge possessed by the accused, as well as the fact that V. V. Kuibyshev was deliberately left without medical attention during one of his usual attacks of angina pectoris, being utilized for this purpose?

On the killing of Comrade Menzhinsky.

First question: Was the prolonged administration of extracts of foxglove, especially in conjunction with lysates, which tend to enhance the action of foxglove extracts, permissible in the case of the patient V. R. Menzhinsky, who suffered from arteriosclerosis, accompanied by severe attacks of angina pectoris and infarctions of the myocardium?

Second question: Might such a method of treatment have contributed to the exhaustion of the cardiac muscles and thus have contributed to a fatal issue?

Third question: May it be regarded as established, on the basis of the sum total of these facts, that the accused L. G. Levin and I. N. Kazakov deliberately adopted wrecking methods of treating Comrade Menzhinsky, making it their criminal aim to bring about the earliest onset of death, which did in fact result from their criminal actions?

On the killing of Maxim Alexeyevich Peshkov.

First question: In the case of M. A. Peshkov, who suffered from croupous pneumonia as described in the testimony of the accused Levin, was the treatment conducted properly?

Second question: Might this wrong method of treatment, employed by the accused Levin, have contributed to a fatal issue of the sickness?

Third question: May it be regarded as established that the accused Levin, having set himself the criminal aim of hastening the death of M. A. Peshkov, deliberately adopted a wrecking method of treatment for the accomplishment of his criminal aim?

Finally, the questions to the expert witnesses on the subject of the attempt to poison Nikolai Ivanovich Yezhov.

First question: May it be concluded from the materials submitted to the experts regarding the organization of the poisoning of Comrade N. I. Yezhov that the accused G. G. Yagoda and P. P. Bulanov employed for the attainment of their criminal aim extremely dangerous and highly potent means for the gradual poisoning of Comrade N. I. Yezhov?

Second question: May it be regarded as established that as a result of the methods employed by the accused G. G. Yagoda and P. P. Bulanov to poison Comrade N. I. Yezhov, his health, was considerably impaired and that if the crime had not been discovered in time there was a direct menace to the life of Comrade N. I. Yezhov?

Permit me to hand one copy of these questions to the expert witnesses.

THE PRESIDENT: You may.

(The Procurator hands a list of the questions to the expert witnesses.)

THE PRESIDENT: Have the defence any additional questions to submit to the commission of experts?

COUNSEL FOR DEFENCE KOMMODOV: During the adjournment the Counsel for Defence acquainted themselves with the questions. They consider them to be exhaustive, and have no additions to make.

THE PRESIDENT: Have the accused any additional questions to submit to the expert witnesses?

THE ACCUSED: (Reply in the negative.)

I must explain that the expert witnesses may remain in the Court room, that they may examine all the materials of the case, and as a result of their labours they must submit their findings to the Court strictly in accordance with the circumstances of the case and based on the specialized knowledge the experts possess.

VYSHINSKY: Allow me to make a request to the Court. I request that it be explained to the expert witnesses that their findings should also be based on the explanations which will be given to the Court by the accused in this case and by the witness Belostotsky, and I therefore consider it essential that the expert witnesses should be present in the Court during this time.

THE PRESIDENT: That is what I had in mind. If the experts are present in Court during the interrogation of Levin, Pletnev and Kazakov, they will thus acquaint themselves with their testimony.

Adjournment until 11 a.m. on March 8.

[*Signed*] PRESIDENT: V. ULRICH

Army Military Jurist

*President of the Military Collegium of
the Supreme Court of the U.S.S.R.*

SECRETARY: A. BATNER

Military Jurist First Rank

Summary of Morning Session

MARCH 8, 1938

Examination of the Accused LEVIN:

Levin confirms his preliminary testimony. He met Yagoda in the nineteen twenties while treating the late Dzerzhinsky and Menzhinsky, and regularly at Gorky's house while he was the author's attending physician. Yagoda presented Dr. Levin with a country house and allowed him certain privileges relating to customs duties. In 1933, Yagoda asked, and subsequently forced, him to plot the murder of Gorky's son, M. A. Peshkov. Levin enlisted the aid of Professor Pletnev in the crime. Later Yagoda told Levin it was necessary to bring about the death of Menzhinsky. Levin explained to Yagoda that they would require the help of Dr. Kazakov because he prepared and utilized lysates in his treatment of Menzhinsky.

Kazakov confirms that he was approached by Levin. Yagoda insists that he told Levin to bring about the death of Gorky and Kuibyshev, "and that's all." He adds, "I did not bring about the death of either Menzhinsky or Max Peshkov." Kazakov testifies that Yagoda suggested that he kill Menzhinsky. Yagoda denies having met Kazakov previous to the trial. Kryuchkov then testifies that Yagoda told him it was necessary to remove Peshkov because this would stop Gorky's activities, which were in the way of a certain group (Rykov, Bukharin, and others). Yagoda replies, "It is all lies."

Levin resumes his testimony and states that as a result of their activities Menzhinsky and Peshkov died in May, 1934. He testifies that Yagoda insisted that others, including Gorky, who was devoted to Stalin, must be removed. This would facilitate the formation of a new government headed by Bukharin, Rykov, and Yenukidze. Pletnev and Kryuchkov participated in the murder of Gorky. Yagoda confirms this part of Levin's testimony. Levin adds that Yagoda directed him to arrange the death of Kuibyshev and that Maximov and Pletnev participated in this undertaking. Pletnev, Maximov, and Yagoda confirm Levin's testimony.

Levin then explains how the plotters murdered their victims. Wine was consistently used to weaken Peshkov's resistance; he was later forced by Kryuchkov to lie down without a shirt near a river. Peshkov contracted a fever and pneumonia, and medicines were withheld from his "weakened heart." In the case of Menzhinsky, Kazakov used a mixture of lysates to bring on attacks of angina pectoris, and subse-

471

quently death. Kuibyshev, who suffered from a serious heart ailment, was allowed to work and was not confined to bed. This and the misuse of drugs brought about his death. Gorky's lungs were already in very bad shape. Kryuchkov allowed him to do heavy work and to sit near the fire and exposed him to grippe. Levin and Pletnev treated him with overdoses of the "indicated medicines" (forty injections of camphor, etc.).

After a thirty-minute adjournment, Levin explains in greater detail the use of medicines for "weaking purposes" in the death of Gorky, Peshkov, Kuibyshev, and Menzhinsky. He is questioned about the details of his career by Counsel for Defence Braude. He explains that he did not refuse Yagoda's advances and failed to inform the authorities "from cowardice."

EVENING SESSION, MARCH 8, 1938

COMMANDANT OF THE COURT: The Court is coming, please rise.

THE PRESIDENT: Please be seated. The session is resumed.

Accused Bulanov, do you confirm the testimony you gave at the preliminary investigation?

BULANOV: Yes, I do. A number of facts and particulars, about which I gave information at the preliminary investigation, when interrogated by the Procurator, and of which I shall now speak, are known to me from Yagoda personally, from conversations I had with him or from conversations he had with other accomplices in my presence.

During the years I worked with Yagoda as his private secretary and as secretary of the People's Commissariat, I became accustomed to regard everything through Yagoda's eyes, for many years spending a considerable part of the day in the People's Commissariat, near Yagoda and for Yagoda, and was wholly and completely cut off from Party life, from the Party and from public life. If I might so express it, he was my only light. And in the end Yagoda made of me a man who was thoroughly devoted to him, a man about whom he knew that he would not betray him. And, therefore, neither in conversations with me, nor in conversations with others in my presence, did he keep any secrets from me, there were no elements of secrecy whatever. Hence my knowledge of the crimes, which I learnt about from him.

I must say that approximately in 1931, for the first time, quite unexpectedly for me, apparently considering that I was a man already thoroughly schooled and coached, Yagoda told me that he was a Right. I first heard about the conspiracy from Yagoda in 1934. Gradually, in a series of conversations, Yagoda introduced me to counter-revolutionary work. Cut off from Party life, I blindly trusted him, Yagoda, in everything.

VYSHINSKY: In what year do you say Yagoda told you that he was a Right?

BULANOV: In 1931.

VYSHINSKY: Since when have you worked with Yagoda?

BULANOV: Roughly, since the end of 1929.

VYSHINSKY: Continue your testimony.

473

BULANOV: One day, during a conversation, Yagoda told me that they (that is, he and the people who stood behind him— the Rights) had united with the Trotskyites and the Zinovievites, that there could be absolutely no counting on achieving any success in the normal way, by means of a legal struggle within the Party, and that only one means remained by which they could attain power—that was the violent method of arriving at power by a direct armed coup.

One of the principal roles in the coup, according to him, was to have been played by Yenukidze, and the second, perhaps a no less important role, according to him, fell on his, Yagoda's, shoulders. They had spheres of influence: Yenukidze's was the Kremlin, and Yagoda's the apparatus of the People's Commissariat of Internal Affairs. Yagoda himself on this occasion, and repeatedly, dreamed—true, I should not call them dreams, because he conceived it rather clearly as a reality—that in the event of the coup succeeding, in the future Council of People's Commissars he was to be the Chairman of the Council of People's Commissars.

VYSHINSKY: The Chairman of the Council of People's Commissars?

BULANOV: Yes. Party work, as he envisaged it, would fall to Tomsky, Bukharin and Rykov. And, furthermore, as they presumed and supposed, Tomsky was to retain the role of leader of the trade unions. Rykov and Bukharin were to be the Secretaries of the Central Committee. And Yagoda, moreover, stressed the point that when he became the Chairman of the Council of People's Commissars, the functions of the Secretaries of the Central Committee would be something quite different. What exactly, I could hardly explain.

I recall—I request the Court to bear in mind that what I am testifying was not the subject of any one conversation; I say this from conversations that took place at various times, conversations with me alone, and conversations in the presence of others; Yagoda was not the least embarrassed by my presence—I am summing up all the conversations, and I fully answer for the accuracy of my statements.

In this connection I recall a parallel which Yagoda drew between the future Secretary of the future Central Committee, Bukharin, and Goebbels. I must say that in general Yagoda was very much infatuated with Hitler.

VYSHINSKY: He was infatuated with fascism generally? But in particular?

BULANOV: He was infatuated with Hitler, and said that his book, "My Struggle," was a really worth-while book.

VYSHINSKY: A worth-while book?

474

BULANOV: He repeatedly stressed the fact that Hitler had risen from a top sergeant to be the man he is.

VYSHINSKY: And was not Yagoda himself a top sergeant formerly?

BULANOV: I do not know, but his behaviour differed very little from that of a top sergeant.

If my memory does not deceive me, Yenukidze was slated for the post of Chairman of the Central Executive Committee in the future government.

VYSHINSKY: But what has Goebbels to do with it?

BULANOV: He said that Bukharin would be no worse than Goebbels under him.

VYSHINSKY: He said that about Bukharin?

BULANOV: It must be presumed that when he drew this parallel, as far as I understand and conceive it, he intended to say that he, as Chairman of the Council of People's Commissars, with a Secretary of the type of Goebbels, and with a Central Committee that would be completely obedient to him, would rule as he liked. That is how I understood him. I think that I formed a correct idea as far as he was concerned.

The idea was that Bukharin would be a puppet in his hands and would do whatever he, Yagoda, pleased.

As Yagoda put it, they considered that the armed coup must absolutely be timed to coincide with war. I once said to Yagoda in perplexity: "To tell the truth, I don't understand. War, direct danger, a tense situation, and a government upheaval at such a time—why, it might cause very, very serious damage at the front." To this Yagoda bluntly replied that I was very naive if I thought that they, statesmen of such a big calibre, would embark upon a coup without having come to an arrangement with the probable and inevitable antagonists of the U.S.S.R. in a war. The Germans and Japanese were mentioned as the antagonists. He told me outright that they had a direct arrangement that in the event of the success of the coup, the new government that would be formed would be recognized and military hostilities would cease.

VYSHINSKY: On what conditions?

BULANOV: I hesitate to say exactly, but I have a recollection of concessions and cessions. This was the first time I heard that Krestinsky and Karakhan were absolutely their men, and, moreover, not only responsible men, but men who knew how to work—to work, of course, in a counter-revolutionary sense. It was very much later that I heard mention of the name of Tukhachevsky, who in the future government was to be People's Commissar of Defence.

475

VYSHINSKY: And what can you tell us about connections with the Trotskyites?

BULANOV: I shall come to that later.

To be brief, and at the same time precise, I shall now pass to that part of my crimes in which, on the direct orders of Yagoda, I had an immediate part—the poisoning.

VYSHINSKY: Perhaps you will first tell us of all the criminal connections that existed, and of the agreement that existed, and then about the definite particulars of the poisoning.

BULANOV: Very well, as you please.

VYSHINSKY: Did you know that Yagoda, as a member of the centre of the Rights, was connected with the Trotskyites?

BULANOV: I did.

VYSHINSKV: How did you know that? With whom was he connected, and how was he connected?

BULANOV: It was quite obvious that Yagoda had the closest connections with the leaders of the Rights. He was also connected with the Trotskyites. I judge of this because I was more than once a witness to the direct operative instructions, which he gave in one degree or another to the appropriate persons in charge of definite sections of the work, direct or indirect orders not to proceed with cases against Trotskyites, but, on the contrary, to terminate a number of cases against Trotskyites, as well as Rights and Zinovievites.

VYSHINSKY: That is, he shielded them.

BULANOV: I would say that he not only shielded them but directly assisted their activities.

Not to make unsupported statements, I will cite a number of facts. For example, Yagoda gave orders that in his testimony Uglanov should keep within certain limits.

VYSHINSKY: Do you remember a sinister figure in one of the earlier trials, Dreitzer? [1] What relations did Yagoda have with him?

BULANOV: I recall that, in spite of the fact that the department chief concerned possessed absolutely definite and precise facts about Dreitzer's prolonged Trotskyite activities, Dreitzer was not arrested. And, in general, I must say that Yagoda's line with regard to the Rights, as well as the Trotskyites and the Zinovievites, was most definitely directed towards terminating the struggle with them.

VYSHINSKY: I am interested in definite facts.

BULANOV: That was the general line; and only when there was a Party reminder or a public reminder, when a number of odious figures were openly involved, did he adopt repressive measures; and these repressive measures were quite a matter of form.

476

VYSHINSKY: Yagoda knew of Dreitzer's conspiratorial activities and shielded him?

BULANOV: Absolutely correct.

VYSHINSKY: And do you recall another figure in one of the earlier trials, a no less sinister one, Ivan Nikitich Smirnov? Do you know whether Yagoda was connected with him and whether he shielded him?

BULANOV: Of the particulars regarding Smirnov, I know precisely that when Smirnov was in prison, Yagoda sent Molchanov and through him instructed Smirnov within what limits he should keep in case of necessity, if certain testimony should be demanded of him. That is absolutely so.

VYSHINSKY: And do you know what Yagoda did when Smirnov was brought from prison to Moscow?

BULANOV: I know that Yagoda departed from his usual practice. He did not usually visit prisons, but when Smirnov arrived he went to see him.

VYSHINSKY: In his cell?

BULANOV: Yes.

VYSHINSKY: What did he do there?

BULANOV: I heard him say to Molchanov that he, Yagoda, was easy in his mind about the way Smirnov would conduct himself in Court.

VYSHINSKY: That is, he coached him. What was his attitude to Kamenev after the assassination of Sergei Mironovich Kirov?

BULANOV: When the decision was taken to arrest Kamenev and Zinoviev, Yagoda sent me to arrest Kamenev.

VYSHINSKY: Whom did he send with you?

BULANOV: I went with Pauker.

VYSHINSKY: Who was this Pauker?

BULANOV: Chief of the Operations Department.

VYSHINSKY: And yet, who was he?

BULANOV: A man who was completely initiated into the conspiratorial affairs and one who was exceptionally trusted. He was the connecting link with Yenukidze.

VYSHINSKY: Was not Pauker a German spy?

BULANOV: I learnt later that he was a spy.

VYSHINSKY: A German spy?

BULANOV: Quite so.

VYSHINSKY: Accused Yagoda, did you know that Pauker was a German spy?

YAGODA: Yes, I did.

VYSHINSKY: Be seated. So Pauker and you, Bulanov, were sent by Yagoda to arrest Kamenev. And who was to arrest Zinoviev?

477

BULANOV: I think it was Molchanov and Volovich.

VYSHINSKY: Who was Molchanov?

BULANOV: Chief of the Secret Political Department of the People's Commissariat of Internal Affairs and a member of the organization.

VYSHINSKY: Of which organization? The secret organization of the Rights?

BULANOV: Yes.

VYSHINSKY: And Volovich?

BULANOV: Volovich was Assistant Chief of the Operations Department. It is known that he was implicated in espionage.

VYSHINSKY: Do you confirm, Yagoda, that Volovich was also a German spy?

YAGODA: Yes, I do.

VYSHINSKY: Accused Bulanov, how did Yagoda instruct you when he sent you to arrest Kamenev and Zinoviev?

BULANOV: The instructions were quite simple—to bring them in, but not to make a search. And that is what I did.

VYSHINSKY: And that is what you did. Now continue your story.

BULANOV: I shall proceed directly to the specific crimes in which I personally took part. I know from what Yagoda told me that the decision to assassinate Nikolai Ivanovich Yezhov . . .

VYSHINSKY: Did you know where Rykov's secret files were kept?

BULANOV: Yagoda had them.

VYSHINSKY: The conspiratorial files?

BULANOV: If they were not conspiratorial, Rykov would hardly have sought such a reliable place for them.

I now pass to the attempt on the life of N. I. Yezhov. According to Yagoda, the decision to assassinate Nikolai Ivanovich Yezhov was adopted by them, i.e., by the centre, with exclusively political aims. This was one of the stages, or one of the measures, to ensure them against exposure as participants in the conspiracy, and therefore to preserve the possibility of carrying out the conspiracy itself. The reason that led to the adoption of this decision was that very soon, or rather, after the assassination of Kirov, Yezhov was appointed by the Central Committee of the C.P.S.U. (Bolsheviks) to watch the investigation. And I learnt from Yagoda personally that very soon after this Yagoda became extremely and increasingly alarmed over N. I. Yezhov's work. Yagoda stressed the fact that Yezhov was extremely rapidly, as he put it, digging into and mastering all the special features of the work of the Administration of State Security, and that there was absolutely

478

no certainty that in the end he would not arrive straight at the discovery of the true state of affairs, at the discovery of the conspiracy. Yagoda—this I again know from his conversations with a number of the chiefs of operations departments who were at the same time members of the conspiratorial organization—employed every means he could to misinform N. I. Yezhov. Only those materials, information and records were sent to Yezhov that were picked out by Yagoda and his assistants. Corresponding information and documents were concealed and held back. In general, everything was done to hamper Yezhov's work. Yet in spite of this, at the beginning of the first third of 1936 Yagoda said outright that he not only had absolutely no assurance, no guarantee, that Yezhov would not dig down to the true state of affairs, but that, on the contrary, he was already convinced that he was so far on the right path that resolute measures would have to be adopted to localize a really impending danger.

In the early part of 1936 I first learnt that Yagoda had known at the time how the assassination of Kirov was organized. One day I happened to enter Yagoda's office, as always without being announced, and found him in a state of excitement talking to Molchanov. When Molchanov left, Yagoda, in a state of great irritation, uttered the phrase: "It looks as if Yezhov is also getting at the bottom of the Leningrad affair." Then, pulling himself up, although he usually concealed nothing from me, and warning me of the extremely confidential nature of what he was about to tell me, and once again—for the twentieth or fortieth time—promising, "if anything should happen," to tear my head off, he said that he had known that an attempt on S. M. Kirov was being prepared, that he had had a reliable man in Leningrad who was initiated into everything, Zaporozhetz, Assistant Chief of the Leningrad Regional Administration of the People's Commissariat of Internal Affairs, and that he had so arranged matters as to facilitate the assassination of Kirov by Nikolayev. To put it plainly, it was done with the direct connivance, and consequently with the assistance, of Zaporozhetz. I recall that Yagoda said in passing, incidentally abusing Zaporozhetz for his lack of efficiency, that there was an occasion when the whole affair was nearly exposed, when several days before the assassination of Kirov the guard detained Nikolayev by mistake, and a notebook and revolver were found in his portfolio, but that Zaporozhetz released him in time. Yagoda further told me that Borisov, an employee of the Leningrad Administration of the People's Commissariat of Internal Affairs, had a share in the assassination of Kirov. When members of the government came to Leningrad and summoned this Borisov to the Smolny to interrogate him as a witness in connection with the assassination of Kirov, Zaporozhetz, being alarmed by this

479

and fearing that Borisov would betray those who stood behind Nikolayev, decided to kill Borisov. On Yagoda's instructions, Zaporozhetz so arranged it that an accident occurred to the automobile which took Borisov to the Smolny. Borisov was killed in the accident, and in this way they got rid of a dangerous witness. I then understood the exceptional and unusual solicitude which Yagoda had displayed when Medved, Zaporozhetz and the other officials were arrested and brought to trial. I recalled that he had entrusted the care of the families of Zaporozhetz and Medved to me personally. I recalled that he had had them sent for detention to the camp in an unusual way, not in the car for prisoners, but in a special through car. Before sending them, he had Zaporozhetz and Medved brought to see him.

The danger of exposure was so evident to them and so real that Yagoda decided to adopt more resolute measures. To put it plainly, he decided to assassinate N. I. Yezhov. I know from what Yagoda told me that in the summer of 1936 he instructed other persons, not implicated in the present trial, to have poison laid in the apartment in which Yezhov lived. How, when, by what means and under what circumstances this was done he did not tell me, and I do not know. But that it was done I am certain, because I know that with Yagoda word and deed very rarely diverged.

When he was removed from his post as People's Commissar of Internal Affairs, he directly set about laying poison in the office and in those rooms which adjoined the office in the building of the People's Commissariat of Internal Affairs which Nikolai Ivanovich Yezhov was to occupy. He instructed me personally to prepare a poison, namely, to take mercury and to dissolve it in acid. I know nothing about chemistry or medicine, and perhaps I am mixing up terms, but I recall that he cautioned me against sulphuric acid, against burns, odour and more of the same kind. This was on September 28, 1936. I carried out these instructions of Yagoda and made the solution. The spraying of the office which Yezhov was to occupy and the adjoining rooms, the rugs, carpets and curtains was done by Savolainen in the presence of Yagoda and myself. This was on September 29. Yagoda told me that this spraying must be done five, six or seven times, which was done. Two or three times I prepared large flasks of this solution and gave them to Savolainen. He did the spraying with a spray. I recall that it was a large metallic cylinder with a large bulb. I know this spray; it was kept in Yagoda's dressing room; it was a foreign-made spray. The second and third spraying was done by Savolainen in my presence, the others in my absence. He told me about everything, and reported to Yagoda.

I must also add that on September 28, when this conversation took place, Yagoda took two ampoules from a small cupboard where he kept a lot of various things, particularly phials, and gave them to me; judging by their external appearance, they were not of Russian manufacture. He said that these were poisons which should be sprayed simultaneously with the mercury solution. What it was, how it was called, I do not know. I gave it to Savolainen, who sprayed it together with the mercury solution.

That is all I did in connection with the attempt on the life of Nikolai Ivanovich Yezhov.

VYSHINSKY: Tell us, please, was Yagoda interested in poisons generally?

BULANOV: Exceptionally.

VYSHINSKY: How was his special interest in poisons expressed?

BULANOV: He acquired this interest approximately in 1934. I repeat, Citizen Procurator, that I can judge of this not only from conversations, but also from actions about which I knew. I know, for example, that he formed a very close acquaintanceship with a number of chemists and gave direct instructions to build, or rather to arrange, a chemical laboratory.

VYSHINSKY: What for?

BULANOV: It was always emphasized that it must be under the control of Yagoda, as he had not in his arsenal a sufficient number of poisons as means for definite ends.

VYSHINSKY: What ends?

BULANOV: This was later demonstrated in a very real way.

VYSHINSKY: That is?

BULANOV: For counter-revolutionary ends, for purposes of assassination. I know that he employed a number of people on this work. The setting up of this laboratory was an actual fact. I know this because he ordered me personally to find proper premises and to hand them over to definite persons. This I did. I found the premises and handed them over. It is true that I was never there myself, but I heard from these people that everything was done for the setting up of this laboratory. Yagoda warned me that this matter was so important that the people mentioned must be allowed unlimited funds and that no accounts were to be demanded.

VYSHINSKY: Was this interest in poisons connected with his conspiratorial actions and plans?

BULANOV: Quite definitely. During a private conversation, when the coup d'etat they were organizing was being discussed, Yagoda said that for the achievement of this coup all means would be required—armed action, provocation and even poisons. Because there are times, as he put it, when one must act slowly and extremely cautiously, and there are times, as he said, when one must act quickly and suddenly. The idea was that all means are good means, and that there was no point in being squeamish in the employment of means.

VYSHINSKY: And that poison might play an important part in a coup?

BULANOV: As I recall it, he even said a "decisive" part.

VYSHINSKY: After Yagoda was removed from the post of People's Commissar of Internal Affairs, did you remain working in the People's Commissariat of Internal Affairs?

BULANOV: Yes, I remained working there.

VYSHINSKY: And did you work there long?

BULANOV: Until my arrest.

VYSHINSKY: Approximately until when?

BULANOV: Until the end of March 1937.

VYSHINSKY: And when was Yagoda removed?

BULANOV: At the end of September 1936.

VYSHINSKY: Did the poisoning begin soon after Yagoda left?

BULANOV: The first spraying was done on September 29, the second two or three days later, and the last, if my memory does not betray me, in December. Six or seven sprayings were done in all.

VYSHINSKY: Six or seven sprayings?

BULANOV: Yes.

VYSHINSKY: And at which sprayings were you personally present?

BULANOV: I recall exactly. It was the first, second, third and the last. Four in all.

VYSHINSKY: And who did the in-between sprayings?

BULANOV: They were done by Savolainen.

VYSHINSKY: You knew about it?

BULANOV: Yes, I did.

VYSHINSKY: And who instructed him?

BULANOV: As I have already said, the first spraying was done by Savolainen in the presence of Yagoda and myself.

VYSHINSKY: When was that?

BULANOV: I can say exactly, September 29.

VYSHINSKY: That is?

BULANOV: The day before Yagoda left.

VYSHINSKY: In addition to the dastardly preparations for the poisoning of Nikolai Ivanovich Yezhov, do you know of any crimes of the same kind committed by Yagoda and yourself, or by Yagoda alone?

BULANOV: Yes, I know quite definitely of the killing of Menzhinsky, Alexei Maximovich Gorky and Maxim Alexeyevich Peshkov.

VYSHINSKY: Tell us briefly about these cases.

BULANOV: The killing of A. M. Gorky was undertaken by

482

Yagoda as one of the effective measures for the creation of the conditions for success in case the coup came off. Yagoda said that when the Rights became convinced that Alexei Maximovich not only fully and entirely shared the policy of the Party and the government, but that he himself, with his usual enthusiasm, had joined in the building of the Socialist state, when they saw, heard and observed with what exceptional admiration Alexei Maximovich on every occasion spoke about the role of Stalin in the building of the Socialist state, they came to the unanimous conclusion that in the event of the success of the coup, Alexei Maximovich would publicly raise his voice against them, and that, in view of the prestige which Gorky enjoyed among all sections of the population in the Soviet Union and his exceptional significance in the eyes of culturally thinking people abroad, this revolt—as Yagoda put it—of Gorky's against the new power would be of exceptional consequences. They therefore decided to remove Gorky in good time.

From Yagoda I learnt that Dr. Levin, Prof. Pletnev and Kryuchkov, Gorky's secretary, took part in this crime. I personally several times heard Yagoda instructing Kryuchkov that he must try to give Alexei Maximovich a chill, saying that, in view of the condition of Gorky's lungs, a cold might result in complications, and as to the rest, everything required would be done by Pletnev and Levin. As far as I know, Yagoda drew Levin into, enlisted him in this affair, and in the cases of poisoning generally, by taking advantage of some compromising material he had against him (which, I do not know), and he also bribed Levin. For example, I personally arranged for the country house about which Dr. Levin spoke here. I personally, on Yagoda's instructions, when Levin was going abroad, several times gave Levin money in foreign currency.

VYSHINSKY: By the way, do you remember how much you gave him?

BULANOV: It was on two or three occasions, I hesitate to say exactly, I think that Dr. Levin, who received the money, can tell you more exactly than I, but it was something round about $1,000 on each occasion. I do not answer for the exact sum, but it was round about that figure. On Yagoda's instructions too, I sent orders to the frontier that Dr. Levin should be allowed to pass without customs inspection. And from what Yagoda told me, Kryuchkov did not have to be persuaded particularly, because, he said, Pyotr Petrovich was himself to some extent interested as the literary heir—that is what I understood him to say—of Alexei Maximovich Gorky. From what Yagoda told me, I know that Kryuchkov acted accordingly, that on Yagoda's insistence he had Gorky brought to Moscow at, I believe, an unsuitable time of the year with regard to weather conditions; and that on his arriving here he directed him to his town apartment, where somebody was down with the grippe, that is, to an atmosphere where, in view of Alexei Maximovich's weak state, he was most certain to catch the grippe. And further, in treating him, as I have said, both Levin and Pletnev, by means of deliberately wrong treatment, did their job. That is all I know about the killing of Alexei Maximovich Gorky.

VYSHINSKY: And was Menzhinsky killed on direct instructions, and whose?

BULANOV: On the instructions of Yagoda. And I must say that if in the killing of Gorky the motives were, as he said, exclusively political, here I know from him that there were motives of a personal kind.

VYSHINSKY: That is?

BULANOV: The personal motives of a man who wanted by any means, in any way, to make a career for himself, that is, to hasten the vacation of a post, to make the post of Chairman of the O.G.P.U. vacant, considering, obviously, that in that case he, Yagoda, would be the only candidate for the post of Chairman.

VYSHINSKY: That is your analysis?

BULANOV: Of course, political motives were also operative here. It was more than of interest to the centre of the Rights, and of the conspirators generally, to have their own man at the head of the punitive organ, one of their leaders, that is, to create a guarantee, the almost complete possibility of covering up any tracks.

But Yagoda spoke to me personally about motives of a personal character as well. He several times dwelt on the fact that Menzhinsky had actually not been working for a long time, and that he, Yagoda, had to do the work. He dotted the i's—in 1933, I think it was—when he told me outright that he had decided to expedite it, that is, to put it plainly, to destroy Menzhinsky, that he had put Dr. Levin on to this job, but that for some reason Levin had not managed it. Then I learnt from him definitely that he had enlisted Dr. Kazakov as the direct perpetrator.

VYSHINSKY: By the way, do you know whether Kazakov visited Yagoda in the People's Commissariat of Internal Affairs, in his office, on this matter?

BULANOV: If Yagoda said a while ago that he saw Kazakov here for the first time, then I expect him to say now that he sees me also for the first time in his life. Of course he saw Kazakov, and saw him several times. For example, I personally remember an occasion when Kazakov visited Yagoda in his office. This sticks in my memory because it was a rest day. I cannot answer for the date.

VYSHINSKY: Permit me to ask Kazakov. Accused Kazakov, when was that?

KAZAKOV: On November 6.

VYSHINSKY: What year?

KAZAKOV: 1933.

BULANOV: I distinctly remember that it was on a rest day. We usually observed rest days, but on this day we were in the office. That Yagoda saw Kazakov very often with Menzhinsky is a fact. Kazakov used to visit Menzhinsky very often in his office.

VYSHINSKY: Kazakov used to visit Menzhinsky often in his office?

BULANOV: Yes, very often.

VYSHINSKY: And Yagoda could not help seeing him?

BULANOV: Yes, Yagoda saw Kazakov several times in Menzhinsky's office.

VYSHINSKY: So Yagoda is not telling the truth here?

BULANOV: He is not. Where could I have got it from that Yagoda told me that Dr. Kazakov had also been drawn into this affair—the murder of Menzhinsky—and that he was doing it together with Levin, that Kazakov was employing very intricate drugs that were not only unknown to medicine, but not very well known to Kazakov himself, so that to find any clues after this poisoning would be difficult? This is what Yagoda told me. Where else could I have got it from?

VYSHINSKY: Accused Yagoda, did you hear Bulanov's testimony regarding the poisoning of Menzhinsky?

YAGODA: Yes, I did.

VYSHINSKY: After this testimony, which establishes your part in the poisoning, do you continue to deny it?

YAGODA: No, I confirm my part in it.

VYSHINSKY: You do confirm it?

YAGODA: Yes.

VYSHINSKY: Accused Bulanov, and was the killing of Maxim Peshkov also Yagoda's work?

BULANOV: Of course.

VYSHINSKY: Accused Yagoda, what do you say to that?

YAGODA: I admit my part in the illness of Peshkov. I request the Court to hear this whole question in camera.

VYSHINSKY: I have no objections.

Accused Bulanov, you have drawn a monstrous picture here of a number of crimes you committed under the direction of Yagoda. Who else among the leaders of the "bloc of Rights and Trotsky-ites" had a share in these crimes as far as you know?

BULANOV: Yagoda told me plainly that the decision to poison Yezhov and to kill Gorky was adopted by Rykov, Bukharin . . .

485

VYSHINSKY: And Yenukidze?

BULANOV: And Yenukidze, of course.

VYSHINSKY: In a word, the top leadership of the "bloc of Rights and Trotskyites"?

Accused Rykov, do you know that the "bloc of Rights and Trotskyites" adopted a decision to physically do away with Alexei Maximovich Gorky?

RYKOV: No.

VYSHINSKY: But what did you know about it?

RYKOV: I knew about the extremely hostile attitude towards Alexei Maximovich Gorky that had prevailed among the Trotskyites and among certain circles of the Rights for several years.

VYSHINSKY: Did you have a conversation with Yenukidze at the end of 1935 on this subject?

RYKOV: With Yenukidze? Yes, I did.

VYSHINSKY: What about?

RYKOV: Yenukidze told me that the Trotskyites and Zinovievites were extremely concerned because of the influence which Gorky was acquiring, and because he was a determined supporter of Stalin and the general line of the Party. Therefore, as he put it, they considered it necessary, in view of this significance of Gorky's— and his significance both abroad and in our country required no confirmation—they insisted, as he phrased it, on putting an end to Gorky's political activity.

VYSHINSKY: That is, Yenukidze spoke of the necessity of putting an end to Gorky's political activity?

RYKOV: Yes.

VYSHINSKY: How, and in what sense?

RYKOV: He spoke in such a raised voice, or in such sharply hostile expressions, that it was clear to me (inasmuch as it chiefly came from the Trotskyite-Zinovievite part) that this tone concealed the possibility of the employment of violent measures.

VYSHINSKY: From your conversation with Yenukidze you concluded that it was a question of putting an end to the political activities of Gorky by various methods, including violent measures?

RYKOV: Yes, going to that extent in case of need.

VYSHINSKY: And what does it mean, going to the extent of adopting violent measures? May it also mean murder?

RYKOV: Of course.

VYSHINSKY: So you knew that preparations for Gorky's murder were being made?

RYKOV: Not exactly.

VYSHINSKY: You knew that preparations were being made?

RYKOV: I knew what I have already told you.

VYSHINSKY: And is this not enough to qualify it as such?

RYKOV: For the qualification you are referring to, it is not enough. Perhaps I underrated Yenukidze's words.

VYSHINSKY: Underrated?

RYKOV: Perhaps I had no such conviction or opinion that an attempt was being prepared on the life of Gorky. I had no such conviction.

VYSHINSKY: But that such a problem might arise?

That is to say, in other words, could you gather from the conversation with Yenukidze that there might be no hesitation at the murder of Gorky?

RYKOV: During this conversation with Yenukidze I spoke quite vigorously against these attacks.

VYSHINSKY: You did, but I am asking about the bloc.

RYKOV: That is what I confessed to as one of the members of the bloc.

VYSHINSKY: It is your affair whether you want to confess or not.

RYKOV: I also spoke about my protest against this.

VYSHINSKY: Protest against what?

RYKOV: Against the tone, the expressions, the attacks which Yenukidze used with reference to Gorky. Since it was at the stage when the question could have come up only in this sense, I think that my drastic intervention and determined protest excluded this possibility.

VYSHINSKY: In order to avoid any further arguments about this question, I formulate what you have just said in the following words: first—in 1935 you had a conversation with Yenukidze during which he said in sharp terms that the Trotskyite-Zinovievite bloc insisted on putting an end to Gorky's political activity.

RYKOV: Yes.

VYSHINSKY: Second—from the tone, from the hostile manner, from the viciousness of this conversation it was possible to gather that they would not stop at anything in order to put an end to Gorky's political activity.

RYKOV: Now, after it has happened, it is quite clear.

VYSHINSKY: And how did you picture it to yourself at the time?

RYKOV: I said that I underrated this danger.

VYSHINSKY: That would be a characterization of your attitude to the fact, but I am interested in the fact itself. You confirm that from the conversation with Yenukidze it was possible to gather that, for the purpose of putting an end to Gorky's political activity, as he said, they would not stop at anything.

RYKOV: I would simply say that they might not stop at taking violent measures.

487

VYSHINSKY: So. And, third—it was clear from this conversation with Yenukidze that it might be a question of a terrorist act against Gorky?

RYKOV: Yes. The question could have been put that way.

VYSHINSKY: It was clear. Be seated, please.

THE PRESIDENT (to Bulanov): Have you finished your testimony?

BULANOV: I have.

VYSHINSKY: I have a question to put to Bulanov. Do you know of any cases of Yagoda's sending money to Trotsky?

BULANOV: I know quite definitely.

VYSHINSKY: In what year?

BULANOV: It was not at once that I found out from Yagoda that he was supplying Trotsky with money. In 1934 Yagoda called me in and told me that a man would come to me to whom I was to give $20,000.

VYSHINSKY: $20,000? For what purpose and for whom?

BULANOV: I never asked Yagoda why and for what purpose. I handed the money over to this man.

The next day, when I reported that I had executed the order, Yagoda told me that I would have to hand over to this man further sums of money which he would designate. At the same time he said that this man was his direct contact with Trotsky, that Trotsky was lately very hard pressed for money and that the sums which I handed over to this man and which I would hand over to him in the future were intended directly for Trotsky. As a matter of fact, this man came about four or five times during the period of 1934-36, and each time I gave him money, of course on Yagoda's instructions.

VYSHINSKY: I have no more questions.

THE PRESIDENT: Have Counsel for Defence any questions?

COUNSEL FOR DEFENCE: (Reply in the negative.)

THE PRESIDENT: Have the accused any questions?

RYKOV: Bulanov spoke here about my archives, which were found in Yagoda's possession. I should like him to tell us about what was found, where these archives came from, what their contents are and how he knows about it.

BULANOV: If I knew exactly what they contained and the dimensions of these archives, I would most certainly answer my fellow-accused. Unfortunately, I have no such information at my disposal. I spoke about these archives on the basis of the following. When Yagoda was moving to different premises during the renovation of the building, I do not remember under what circumstances it happened, but, at any rate, I found a pile of documents among some of the things which had been lying for a long time in the safe. I asked Yagoda about it. He said: don't unpack them, these are Rykov's archives. It seems to me that was sufficient ground for me to make this statement.

THE PRESIDENT: Adjournment for thirty minutes.

* * *

COMMANDANT OF THE COURT: The Court is coming, please rise.

THE PRESIDENT: Please be seated. The session is resumed.

Accused Yagoda, do you confirm the testimony which you gave during the preliminary investigation?

YAGODA: I do.

THE PRESIDENT: What do you wish to tell the Court about your crimes?

YAGODA: The beginning of my anti-Soviet activities dates back to 1928, when I joined the anti-Soviet organization of the Rights.[2] This was preceded by conversations with Rykov, with whom I maintained rather friendly personal relations.

The peculiarity of my position in the organization of the Rights consisted mainly in the fact that I, as Assistant Chairman of the United State Political Administration at that time, could not take part in the open counter-revolutionary struggle of the Rights and I was on a status of secrecy. This role of mine in the organization of the Rights was known to a few persons: Rykov, Bukharin, Uglanov, Smirnov A. P. (Foma), Tomsky. During the first stage of the struggle of the Rights against the Soviet government my role consisted in supplying the organization of the Rights—Rykov and Bukharin—with tendentiously selected confidential material of the O.G.P.U., which they, Bukharin and Rykov, used for their struggle against the Party.

Later on, when the Rights adopted illegal methods in their struggle against the Party and the Soviet government, the centre of the Rights entrusted me with the task of guarding the organization of the Rights against exposure. On the strength of this understanding I took all measures, in the course of a number of years, to guard the organization, particularly its centre, against exposure. I must state here with full responsibility that it was my treasonable work in the People's Commissariat of Internal Affairs which must be blamed for the fact that it was not until the years 1937-38 that the Soviet government and the People's Commissariat of Internal Affairs were able to uncover and liquidate the counter-revolutionary activities of the organization of the Rights and the "bloc of Rights and Trotskyites." Had the Soviet intelligence service been free of the counter-revolutionary groups of Rights and spies who, thanks to me, occupied positions in the apparatus of the People's Commissariat of Internal Affairs, the

489

conspiracy against the Soviet government would undoubtedly have been uncovered at its inception.

I fully confess this guilt of mine before the Soviet Court. At the same time the responsibility for all this must be shared by those sitting here in the dock, Rykov and Bukharin in the first place. In 1931, during the period when the illegal activities of the Rights became intensified, when the task of guarding the organization against exposure became more urgent, the leaders of the centre of the Rights demanded of me that I appoint active members of the organization of the Rights to leading posts in the O.G.P.U. I may cite as proof the concrete fact of the appointment of Molchanov, a member of the organization of the Rights, to the post of Chief of the Secret Political Department, which was supposed to carry on the struggle against the Right and Trotskyite organizations. In 1931 Tomsky invited me to his country house, where, besides himself, I found also Foma (Smirnov), and he told me in very categorical terms that I must do this, which I did. Molchanov was appointed Chief of the Secret Political Department of the O.G.P.U. It was then that Tomsky informed me of the plan of the Rights with regard to seizure of power and of the intended bloc of the Trotskyites and Zinovievites with the Rights. It was in connection with this proposition, mainly, I repeat, with the object of directly safeguarding the organization against exposure, that they argued about the necessity of appointing Molchanov, who was a member of this organization. During the same period, in the years 1931-32, I set up in the apparatus of the O.G.P.U. a group of Rights made up of O.G.P.U. officials. Prokofyev, Molchanov, Mironov, Bulanov, Shanin and a number of other officials belonged to this group. In 1932, in connection with the general plan of the Rights to overthrow the Soviet government and to seize power, I established connections with Yenukidze on Tomsky's instructions. These instructions were not fortuitous. At that time the main idea of the Rights and the starting point in the activities of the organization was the stake on a counter-revolutionary coup by means of seizing the Kremlin. I consider it superfluous to explain to the Court here that the very fact that the question was put this way was a result of the bankruptcy of the line for a mass insurrection, in the first place kulak insurrections, which we could hope for to a certain extent during the period of difficulties, that is to say, during the years 1930-31. Towards the end of 1932, when the victory of the collective farm system deprived us of our hopes for mass kulak insurrections, the main stake became a so-called "palace coup." Hence, it is quite clear that my role in the organization, the role of a man who was occupying the post of Vice Chairman of the O.G.P.U. and who had in his hands the technical means for effecting the

490

coup, that is to say, the Kremlin guard, military units, and so forth, became the centre of attention. And that is precisely why, on the instructions of the centre of the Rights, I established connections with Yenukidze (at that time he occupied the post of Secretary of the Central Executive Committee of the U.S.S.R.), who was one of those in charge of the conspiratorial activities of the Rights.

In the beginning of 1933 something happened which introduced serious corrections to our plan. I am referring to the fascists' coming to power in Germany. While up to that period the main line of the Rights was based on the idea of a "palace coup" by our own forces, now, starting with 1933, we began to orientate ourselves on the fascist organization.

Before I answer the question as to what concretely the orientation on fascist Germany meant, I must state the following: when the so-called "palace coup" was discussed, we had in mind to arrest, overthrow the leadership of the Soviet government and of the Party, and, having overthrown the Soviet government, to restore capitalist relations in the country—that which Bukharin did not have the courage to state clearly and explicitly during the course of his interrogation. Did we stake on the overthrow of the Soviet government? I answer this question in the affirmative. What social and political order would we have established in the country after the overthrow of Soviet power? I answer this question as well in plain words—a capitalist order.

I am passing on to a concrete presentation of the facts of my crimes. I established connections with Yenukidze at the end of 1931 or the beginning of 1932. Towards the end of 1932 I was meeting him regularly, and discussed with him on more than one occasion the questions of the so-called "palace coup." From Yenukidze I learnt that a military conspiratorial organization had been set up in the Kremlin and that it was ready to effect the coup at any moment. From him I also learnt about the orientation on German fascism, which came to power in 1933.

In 1933 the centre, the bloc of Trotskyites, Zinovievites and Rights, was organized and took shape. I also found out that, through Rykov, the bloc was connected with the Mensheviks and, through Bukharin, with the Socialist-Revolutionaries. Yenukidze kept me informed about the decisions of the centre. It was from him I learnt that in January 1934 there were preparations for a coup d'état entailing the arrest of the Seventeenth Congress of the Party, which was then in session.[3]

I am passing on to the treasonable activities of the "bloc of Rights and Trotskyites" and its connections with foreign states.

In the first place, I must tell the Court that, under my protection, a group of my followers, a group of spies of various foreign intelligence services, existed in the very apparatus of the O.G.P.U., and later in the People's Commissariat of Internal Affairs. I knew about the espionage activities of Zaporozhetz, Gai, Volovich, Pauker, Vinetsky and others, but, having in mind the interests of the conspiracy, I favoured their work, I considered them a valuable force in the realization of the conspiratorial plans, particularly along the lines of maintaining connections with foreign intelligence services. There is no doubt that through these spies the foreign intelligence services were informed about my belonging to the organization of the Rights and about my part in their organization. They were also well informed about the existence and activities of the entire "bloc of Rights and Trotskyites." I can give the Court the facts corroborating this position at an in camera session. It was precisely through one of these spies, it happened to be Vinetsky, who occupied the post of inspector under Rykov in the People's Commissariat of Communications, that the connections of the bloc, and of Rykov personally, with the foreign centre of the Mensheviks, with Nikolayevsky, were arranged.

Besides this group of spies in the People's Commissariat of Internal Affairs, I was aware of other connections of the "bloc of Rights and Trotskyites" with foreign states. I am referring to Karakhan, one of the participants in the conspiracy, about whose connections I found out in 1935. Karakhan informed me of the foreign political orientation of the "bloc of Rights and Trotskyites," on whose instructions he, Karakhan, was carrying on negotiations with the German fascist circles. "The Germans," Karakhan told me, "will help the bloc to overthrow the Soviet power." Karakhan told me that Trotsky had been conducting negotiations with the Germans for a long time before that and that he had "engaged himself" (I put this in quotation marks) too much, since he had promised, in compensation for assistance in the struggle against the Bolsheviks, a great deal more than was necessary. Trotsky had promised to give the Ukraine to the Germans and the Maritime Region to Japan. According to Karakhan, the bloc instructed him to bargain with the Germans. "Of course, we shall have to make some concessions," Karakhan said. Karakhan demanded that I give him information about the organization of the "bloc of Rights and Trotskyites" all over the Union for his forthcoming conversation with the fascist German circles. I gave him this information about the organization. I know that this meeting with leading fascists took place, and that an agreement was reached about assistance to be given by the Germans to the anti-Soviet bloc, but I am not acquainted with the details of the negotiations, I mean with the details as to the price at which

492

this agreement was reached. At the in camera session I shall name the persons whom he met.

I am passing on to the terrorist activities of the "bloc of Rights and Trotskyites," and my own terrorist activities particularly. Not with the object of mitigating my guilt to any extent, but only in the interests of establishing the true state of affairs, I must declare before the Court that the attempts made by some of the accused in the present case to represent me as a professional terrorist are essentially wrong. I cannot, nor have I the desire to, disclaim any of the charges preferred against me with regard to the terrorist acts committed, but I only want to emphasize that not a single one of these acts was committed by me without instructions having been received from the "bloc of Rights and Trotskyites." How is it to be explained that my name is the first to be connected with these terrorist acts? This is explained very simply: only by the special position I occupied in the organization of the Rights; it is also explained by the fact that I, as former People's Commissar of Internal Affairs, had at my disposal more technical opportunities for carrying out the decisions of the centre than other members of the bloc had. The evidence given in Court has brought to light the facts about the terrorist acts which were committed. I want to dwell on the political aspect of the question.

In the first place, the murder of Kirov. How did the matter stand? In 1934, in the summer, Yenukidze informed me that the centre of the "bloc of Rights and Trotskyites" had adopted a decision to organize the assassination of Kirov. Rykov took a direct part in the adoption of this decision. From this it became quite clear to me that the Trotskyite-Zinovievite terrorist groups were making definite preparations for this murder. Needless to say here, I tried to object, I marshalled a series of arguments about this terrorist act being inexpedient and unnecessary. I even argued that I, as a person responsible for guarding the members of the government, would be the first to be held responsible in case a terrorist act was committed against a member of the government. Needless to say, my objections were not taken into consideration and had no effect. Yenukidze insisted that I was not to place any obstacles in the way; the terrorist act, he said, would be carried out by the Trotskyite-Zinovievite group. Owing to this, I was compelled to instruct Zaporozhetz, who occupied the post of Assistant Chief of the Regional Administration of the People's Commissariat of Internal Affairs, not to place any obstacles in the way of the terrorist act against Kirov. Some time later Zaporozhetz informed me that the organs of the People's Commissariat of Internal Affairs had detained Nikolayev, in whose possession a revolver and a chart of the route Kirov usually took had been found. Nikolayev was released. Soon after that Kirov was assassinated by this very Nikolayev. Thus I declare categorically that the murder of Kirov was carried out on the instructions of the centre of the "bloc of Rights and Trotskyites." It was also on the decision of this centre that terrorist acts were committed against Kuibyshev, Menzhinsky and Gorky.

What was the situation here? Even before Kirov was assassinated, Gorky's son Maxim died. I have already stated before the Court that I admit my part in causing Max's sickness, and I again plead before the Court that my explanations with regard to this matter be left for the in camera session of the Court.

VYSHINSKY: In this connection I have only one question. Do you plead guilty to causing, as you express it, Peshkov's sickness?

YAGODA: I shall give all my explanations with regard to this question at the in camera session of the Court.

VYSHINSKY: Very well. But do you plead guilty to Peshkov's death?

YAGODA: I am speaking explicitly: I shall give all the explanations relating to this question in their entirety at the in camera session of the Court.

VYSHINSKY: Do you plead guilty or do you not?

YAGODA: Permit me not to answer this question.

THE PRESIDENT (to the Procurator): Have you any objections to this question about the death of Peshkov being referred to the in camera session of the Court?

VYSHINSKY: I do not object, because I have in mind that the results of this may be announced at an open session.

THE PRESIDENT: The Court has decided to satisfy the request of the accused Yagoda, and the question of the death of Peshkov will be taken up at the in camera session.

Accused Yagoda, proceed.

YAGODA: Around that time the death of Menzhinsky was brought about. I deny that in causing the death of Menzhinsky I was guided by considerations of a personal nature. I aspired to the post of head of the O.G.P.U. not out of personal considerations, not for careerist considerations, but in the interests of our conspiratorial organization. The decision of the centre on this question was conveyed to me personally by Yenukidze. In both of these cases we resorted to the services of physicians, which meant complete guarantee in the sense that exposure was impossible.

When Yenukidze conveyed to me the decision of the contact centre about the assassination of Kirov, I expressed my apprehension that a direct terrorist act might expose not only myself, but the whole organization as well. I pointed out to Yenukidze that there was a less dangerous method and I reminded him, Yenukidze, how Menzhinsky's death was brought about with the help of physicians. Yenukidze replied that the assassination of Kirov must be carried out the way it was planned, that the Trotskyites and Zinovievites took it upon themselves to commit this murder, and that it was our business not to place any obstacles.

As for the safe method of causing death with the help of physicians, Yenukidze said that in the near future the centre would discuss the question as to who exactly of the leaders of the Party and the government should be the first to be done to death by this method.

Indeed, some time later, during my next meeting with Yenukidze, he told me that the centre had decided to undertake a number of terrorist acts against members of the Political Bureau and, in addition, against Maxim Gorky personally. The decision with regard to Kuibyshev was clear to me, but I could not comprehend the decision about committing a terrorist act against Gorky. Yenukidze explained to me that the "bloc of Rights and Trotskyites," considering that the overthrow of the Soviet government was a prospect of the near future, regarded Gorky as a dangerous figure. Gorky was a staunch supporter of Stalin's leadership, and in case the conspiracy was carried into effect, he would undoubtedly raise his voice in protest against us, the conspirators. Considering Gorky's immense prestige within the country and abroad, the centre, according to Yenukidze, adopted a categorical decision about Gorky being physically put out of the way.

In view of my categorical refusal, Yenukidze asked me to send Levin to him. I did as I was told and, when Levin came back from Yenukidze, I confirmed that this act was to be carried out. Later on I spoke to Levin several times about this myself, and at his suggestion I sent for Pletnev.

I declare that Rykov, Bukharin and the others sitting here in the dock bear full responsibility for these terrorist acts. I declare that these acts were committed on their decision. As to how it was done, the physicians will tell you better than I.

I want to draw the attention of the Court to one more fact. I mean the fact of the attempt of a group of the conspirators to poison Yezhov.

When Yezhov was appointed People's Commissar of Internal Affairs,[4] it became quite clear that all the activity of our group and also of the "bloc of Rights and Trotskyites" would be uncovered. Yezhov had already begun to smash up the cadres of the conspirators and, of course, might get at the centre of the bloc and at me personally.

And thus, in order to save our organization, in order to save Rykov, Bukharin and the others, we decided to murder Yezhov. The poisoning was done by Bulanov. He has told the Court about it. I deny some parts of what he said, but that does not change the facts and the essence of the thing.

I also do not deny the fact that at Yenukidze's request I sent money to Trotsky through Mirov-Abramov.

This is the information which I consider it necessary to place before the Court.

THE PRESIDENT: Have you any questions, Comrade Procurator?

VYSHINSKY: Of course.

Hence, if we sum up your explanations, we may say the following:

First—that you plead guilty to the fact that your participation in the underground work of the Rights was of long standing.

YAGODA: Yes.

VYSHINSKY: Second—that you plead guilty to having been one of the leaders of the underground "bloc of Rights and Trotskyites."

YAGODA: Yes, I do.

VYSHINSKY: Third—that, together with this bloc, you pursued the aim of overthrowing the Soviet government and of restoring capitalism in the U.S.S.R.

YAGODA: Yes, I do. We set ourselves the task of seizing the Kremlin.

VYSHINSKY: That for the purpose of overthrowing the government you chose the method of an insurrection timed primarily for the outbreak of war. Is that so?

YAGODA: No, it is not so. An armed insurrection—that was nonsense. Only these babblers here could think of that.

VYSHINSKY: Well, what were you thinking of?

YAGODA: Of a "palace coup."

VYSHINSKY: That is to say, of a violent coup, carried through by a small group of plotters?

YAGODA: Yes, the same as they did.

VYSHINSKY: Timing it preferably for a military onslaught on the U.S.S.R. by foreign powers, or did you have various plans?

YAGODA: There was one plan, namely, to seize the Kremlin. The time was of no importance.

VYSHINSKY: Was it your point of view that it was expedient in case of war to prepare and secure the defeat of the U.S.S.R.?

YAGODA: That was the point of view of the bloc, and therefore it was mine too.

VYSHINSKY: Do you also admit being guilty of espionage work?

YAGODA: No, I do not admit being guilty of this activity.

VYSHINSKY: But you yourself have said that several spies were at work under your direct leadership.

YAGODA: Yes, I admit that.

VYSHINSKY: Did you know they were spies?

YAGODA: Yes, I did.

VYSHINSKY: Did you know they were fulfilling espionage duties?

YAGODA: Yes, I did.

VYSHINSKY: So you helped them?

YAGODA: I am just as responsible for these spies as . . .

VYSHINSKY: Was Volovich a spy?

YAGODA: Yes.

VYSHINSKY: Are you responsible for Volovich?

YAGODA: Just as Rykov is for Sharangovich.

VYSHINSKY: We shall deal with them separately. Now I am speaking about you. Do you admit that a number of intelligence service agents, German and Polish spies, were under your wing? Is that so, or not?

YAGODA: It is.

VYSHINSKY: Did you know of their espionage activity and did you shield this espionage activity?

YAGODA: Yes.

VYSHINSKY: I consider that since you shielded this espionage activity, you helped them, assisted them.

YAGODA: No, I do not admit being guilty of that. Had I been a spy, I assure you that dozens of states would have been compelled to disband their intelligence services.

VYSHINSKY: That would have been the affair of these states. Was Volovich a spy?

YAGODA: I said he was.

VYSHINSKY: Did you know of that?

YAGODA: I did.

VYSHINSKY: You neither arrested nor shot him?

YAGODA: No.

VYSHINSKY: Were you in duty bound to arrest and shoot spies you had discovered?

YAGODA: Obviously.

VYSHINSKY: So then you did not do that, that is to say, in other words, you helped spies to act as spies.

YAGODA: I shielded them.

VYSHINSKY: Did you help them?

YAGODA: I would have helped if I gathered materials together and passed them on to them.

VYSHINSKY: But were you aware that they passed materials on?

YAGODA: Not always.

497

VYSHINSKY: But sometimes you were?

YAGODA: I was.

VYSHINSKY: So they passed on materials to foreign intelligence services with your knowledge?

YAGODA: No.

VYSHINSKY: Were you informed that they passed on materials to foreign intelligence services?

YAGODA: Undoubtedly.

VYSHINSKY: Since you were informed of it, then it was with your knowledge?

YAGODA: With my connivance.

VYSHINSKY: Very well, with your connivance in what they were doing, and of what you were aware. Is that established?

YAGODA: Yes.

VYSHINSKY: Do you also admit being guilty of having placed state funds at Trotsky's disposal on the instructions of the bloc?

YAGODA: I do.

VYSHINSKY: And do you admit being guilty of organizing and effecting terrorist acts: first—the murder of Comrade Kirov on the orders and instructions of the bloc?

YAGODA: I admit being guilty of complicity in the murder.

VYSHINSKY: Do you admit being guilty of complicity in the murder or in causing the death of Menzhinsky?

YAGODA: I do.

VYSHINSKY: Do you admit being guilty of organizing the murder of Kuibyshev?

YAGODA: I do.

VYSHINSKY: Do you admit being guilty of the murder of Alexei Maximovich Gorky?

YAGODA: I do.

VYSHINSKY: I have no more questions.

THE PRESIDENT: Have Counsel for Defence any questions?

COUNSEL FOR DEFENCE KOMMODOV: Does the accused Yagoda confirm the testimony he gave at the preliminary investigation with reference to his meetings with Pletnev?

YAGODA: I said that.

KOMMODOV: Is the same true as regards meetings with Kazakov?

YAGODA: I confirmed that.

KOMMODOV: I have no more questions.

COUNSEL FOR DEFENCE BRAUDE: Who conceived the idea of death from disease?

YAGODA: I have said—Yenukidze.

BRAUDE: Allow me to ask you, what methods did you employ to secure Levin's consent to commit these terrorist acts?

YAGODA: In any case not such as he described here.

BRAUDE: You yourself went into detail about this at the preliminary investigation. Do you confirm this part of your testimony?

YAGODA: It is exaggerated, but that doesn't matter.

BRAUDE: I have no more questions.

THE PRESIDENT: Have the accused any questions to Yagoda?

RYKOV: I have the same question regarding the archives about which Bulanov spoke.

YAGODA: I had no archives of Rykov's.

VYSHINSKY: I have a question to Bulanov. What archives of Rykov's did you say were in Yagoda's keeping?

BULANOV: I spoke of that in my testimony to the Court. I will repeat. When participating in a change of premises I discovered a number of documents of a personal character, I don't remember what they were. From them it was clear that they were personal documents of Alexei Ivanovich Rykov. I asked Yagoda, who confirmed this to me, but as to what was there, and how much of it, I have said and say now that I do not know.

YAGODA: Allow me to put a question. Perhaps you will recall one document at least, and will say what it was?

BULANOV: Had I remembered, I would already have said.

YAGODA: Rather strange. He establishes that this was Rykov's archive, but by what documents? Just by the name, or what?

BULANOV: In reply to that, I can only say one thing: that Yagoda at one time did not doubt for a single second my ability to find my bearings and appraise things very rapidly in any circumstances. I don't know why he now denies a thing that is unquestionably clear to me; I said what I knew and considered it necessary to say so.

YAGODA: In any case, had the archives really existed, in comparison with the other crimes, the Rykov archives are a trifle.

VYSHINSKY: Accused Yagoda, tell the Court, did you in your criminal activities shield the Mensheviks?

YAGODA: The Mensheviks? In what period?

VYSHINSKY: In 1935, did you shield the underground criminal activities of the Mensheviks?

YAGODA: According to my information, the Mensheviks did not play a particularly active role.

VYSHINSKY: Did they play any role at all?

YAGODA: Almost none.

VYSHINSKY: That is to say, they did play some role?

YAGODA: The most insignificant.

VYSHINSKY: But in any case you shielded this, even very insignificant role of the Mensheviks?

YAGODA: I shall not be able to give you an answer to this question.

VYSHINSKY: Allow me to quote to Yagoda his testimony in Vol. II, p. 135: "Question: You are shown a document from the materials of the People's Commissariat of Internal Affairs, containing a report on the Menshevik centre abroad and on its active work in the U.S.S.R." Do you recall this fact?

YAGODA: Yes, I know, only I shall not be able to give you an answer to this here.

VYSHINSKY: I don't want you to answer. In November 1935 the following inscription was made on this document: "This has long ceased to be a party and it is not worth bothering with it." "Reply: Yes, I wrote that inscription." And there follows your explanation: "this is only one of the manifestations of the fact that I was protecting the Mensheviks from discovery and warding the blow off them, because they were in contact with the Rights." Do you confirm that?

YAGODA: Yes.

VYSHINSKY: Hence the conclusion can be drawn from this that the Rights were in contact with the Mensheviks in underground conspiratorial work, and that you were shielding this underground conspiratorial work of theirs, and warded blow after blow off them? Is that right?

YAGODA: Not quite.

VYSHINSKY: And what was the case? Do you confirm this testimony?

YAGODA: I confirm the testimony, but in order to explain the situation to you, I must say something about this document.

VYSHINSKY: I know. Do you admit your testimony to be correct?

YAGODA: My testimony is correct.

VYSHINSKY: Consequently, in your practical activities the position was as you testified?

YAGODA: It was.

VYSHINSKY: Consequently in your practical activities you protected the Mensheviks from discovery? Is that correct?

YAGODA: It is.

VYSHINSKY: Now that is what I am asking you. Please tell me now, what, according to your information, was the role of the accused Rykov and Bukharin in causing the death of Alexei Maximovich Gorky?

YAGODA: From Yenukidze I learnt that they had taken part in a discussion of this question.

VYSHINSKY: We have already cleared up this question as regards Rykov. He has admitted that in a conversation with Yenukidze they discussed the possibility of a terrorist act. I would like to question Bukharin on this point.

BUKHARIN: I took no part whatsoever.

VYSHINSKY: I have not yet put any questions to you, and you hasten to reply.

BUKHARIN: The words you said were "I would like to question Bukharin on this point."

VYSHINSKY: I said I wanted to question you on this point, but I have not yet put a question to you, and have already practically received a reply.

I wish to ask you, what was the attitude of Alexei Maximovich to Trotsky?

BUKHARIN: A sharply negative one.

VYSHINSKY: And do you know what was Trotsky's attitude towards Alexei Maximovich Gorky?

BUKHARIN: Also a sharply negative one. Am I to speak of this in greater detail?

VYSHINSKY: No, there is no need for that just now. I would like to question Bessonov. Accused Bessonov, do you confirm that Trotsky's attitude to Alexei Maximovich Gorky was a sharply negative one?

BESSONOV: Yes, I do.

VYSHINSKY: On the basis of what facts?

BESSONOV: On the basis of what Trotsky said to me in a personal conversation.

VYSHINSKY: Do you confirm your testimony in Court, to the effect that Trotsky conveyed through you the instructions about the physical destruction of Gorky?

BESSONOV: Yes, I passed on these instructions of Trotsky's to Pyatakov.

VYSHINSKY: Trotsky selected Pyatakov as one of the ringleaders of the bloc? Is that so?

BESSONOV: Yes.

VYSHINSKY: You were connected with Pyatakov in underground conspiratorial work?

BESSONOV: Quite right.

VYSHINSKY: Accused Bukharin, are you aware that this hostile attitude to Gorky was adopted not only by Trotsky, but also by the Trotskyites?

BUKHARIN: Yes, of course, because Trotsky and the Trotskyites are one whole; the plotters obeyed in military fashion.

VYSHINSKY: Are you aware that this negative attitude to Gorky on the part of the Trotskyites was clearly expressed?

501

BUKHARIN: Are you asking me about the conversation I had with Tomsky?

VYSHINSKY: If it is a proof of what we are dealing with.

BUKHARIN: I had one conversation with Tomsky.

VYSHINSKY: Where and when did it take place?

BUKHARIN: In 1935 Tomsky told me that Trotsky was preparing some hostile action or hostile act against Gorky.

VYSHINSKY: You learnt from Tomsky that Trotsky was preparing some hostile act against Gorky and you did not ask Tomsky what the source of his information was?

BUKHARIN: No. I presume that he knew about it from the Trotskyite members of the bloc.

VYSHINSKY: Did he not tell you why the Trotskyites were preparing this hostile action or act against Gorky?

BUKHARIN: He did not; he said that it was an action against the "Stalinite Gorky" as a defender of Socialist construction in general, and of Stalin's Party policy in particular. I think that this referred to the great resonance that every word uttered by Alexei Maximovich found on the international arena in general, and among intellectuals in particular.

VYSHINSKY: Did not Tomsky refer to this in connection with the question of the overthrow of the Soviet power?

BUKHARIN: No, Citizen Procurator.

VYSHINSKY: Do you remember this well?

BUKHARIN: I remember it well.

VYSHINSKY: Allow me to remind you what Bukharin stated at the preliminary investigation, Vol. V, p. 117: "The argument that the Trotskyites put forward, Tomsky told me, in support of their contention was that if the question of the overthrow of the Stalin leadership was to be put seriously, one could not disregard the circumstance that the Right and Trotskyite organization would come up against an active and very influential adversary in the person of A. M. Gorky. Tomsky told me that the Trotskyites categorically insisted on their proposal and that it was being carried into effect."

BUKHARIN: You see, Citizen Procurator, since I was asked what meaning I attached to these cursory remarks of Tomsky, and what impression this conversation left with me, I related it in greater detail, and this was my impression that I recalled when I was asked about my conversation with Tomsky.

VYSHINSKY: Tell me, did Tomsky link up the perpetration of a hostile act against Gorky with the question of the overthrow of the Soviet government?

BUKHARIN: In essence he did.

502

VYSHINSKY: In essence he did?

BUKHARIN: Yes, I have answered.

VYSHINSKY: I am interested in the essence.

BUKHARIN: But you are asking concretely . . .

VYSHINSKY: Did your talk with Tomsky provide reason to believe that the question of a hostile act against Alexei Maximovich Gorky was being linked up with the task of overthrowing the Stalin leadership?

BUKHARIN: Yes, in essence this could be said.

VYSHINSKY: Consequently, you knew that some hostile act against Gorky was under consideration?

BUKHARIN: Yes.

VYSHINSKY: And what hostile act in your opinion was referred to?

BUKHARIN: I gave no thought to the matter at all at that time and I had no idea . . .

VYSHINSKY: Tell us what you did think?

BUKHARIN: I hardly thought at all.

VYSHINSKY: But was it not a serious matter? The conversation was about what?

BUKHARIN: Permit me to explain in a few words. Now, post factum, now, during the investigation, I can say . . .

VYSHINSKY: Not during the investigation but during your conversation with Tomsky.

BUKHARIN: But this was only a fleeting conversation, a conversation which took place during a meeting of the Political Bureau and lasted only a few seconds.

VYSHINSKY: I am not interested in how long this conversation lasted; you could have spoken to Tomsky for a whole hour somewhere in a corner, therefore your arguments are of no importance to me. What is important to me are the facts, and these I want to establish. The facts are as follows: in 1935 (if your statement at the preliminary investigation was correct), at the beginning of 1935, a conversation took place between Tomsky and you. Tomsky informed you that the Trotskyite-Zinovievite part of the "bloc of Rights and Trotskyites" was contriving a hostile act directed against Gorky as against an adherent of the Stalin leadership. Is this so?

BUKHARIN: It can be formulated that way.

VYSHINSKY: Is this a fact?

BUKHARIN: It is a fact.

VYSHINSKY: What was your appraisal of this information?

BUKHARIN: I took no notice of this information.

VYSHINSKY: Took no notice?

BUKHARIN: No.

503

VYSHINSKY: When a hostile act is mentioned, one can understand it to mean very serious hostile acts, even terrorist acts?

BUKHARIN: Yes. Between an article in the press, or an unpleasant conversation, and a terrorist act the range is very great.

VYSHINSKY: And how did you regard this at the time?

BUKHARIN: I did not speak on the subject at all at that time, there was nothing in my mind. . . .

VYSHINSKY: Why, was it such an insignificant statement that it deserved no consideration?

BUKHARIN: It was a cursory remark. . . .

VYSHINSKY: Even if it was cursory. You are told that preparations are under way for a hostile act against Alexei Maximovich Gorky. . . .

BUKHARIN: It was approximately in the following way. I treated it in a serious way during my interrogation because I wanted to recall whether this conversation could not throw some light on the material which the investigating authorities already had at their disposal, and from the angle of this material, everything took on a definite shape. But at that time I did not have this in mind, I did not think about the meaning of this fact.

VYSHINSKY: It is not excluded that precisely at that time the physical destruction, the murder, of Gorky was under consideration?

BUKHARIN: Now I consider that this cannot be excluded.

VYSHINSKY: That means, what Tomsky said gave ground to think that it was a matter of a terrorist act against Gorky?

BUKHARIN: Now I affirm that this is so.

VYSHINSKY: But at that time you did not understand?

BUKHARIN: At that time I understood absolutely nothing.

VYSHINSKY (to the Court): I have no more questions.

THE PRESIDENT (to the accused): Has any one questions to Yagoda?

RYKOV: Yagoda mentioned here the name of Vinetsky as a man who was my accomplice and through whom I maintained connection with someone. I would ask him to state where he got this information and who this Vinetsky is. Does Yagoda know of this from Vinetsky himself or from some other source? Personally, I had no inspectors at my disposal.

YAGODA: Vinetsky was inspector of communications in the People's Commissariat of Communications and simultaneously inspector of communications in the People's Commissariat of Internal Affairs. On one occasion he called me on the 'phone and said that Rykov asked him to deliver a parcel abroad, to Nikolayevsky; he asked me whether he could accept it. I replied: Talk it over with Rykov, if he gives you the parcel, take it. From this I see that Vinetsky was the liaison man between Nikolayevsky and Rykov.

THE PRESIDENT (to Vyshinsky): Have you any more questions?

VYSHINSKY: No.

THE PRESIDENT: The Court has no questions either. Please be seated.

We will now proceed to the examination of the accused Kryuchkov.

Accused Kryuchkov, inasmuch as you have already confirmed the testimony given by you at the preliminary investigation, tell the Court briefly of your criminal deeds.

KRYUCHKOV: I have confirmed my testimony completely. I treacherously murdered Maxim Gorky and his son, Maxim Peshkov. I committed both murders on Yagoda's instructions and under the influence of his threats.

While ordering me to murder Maxim Peshkov, Yagoda informed me of the proposed coup d'état and of his, Yagoda's, participation in it. By accepting this order I became a participant of the counter-revolutionary organization of the Rights.

I cannot hide from the Court, as I have already testified at the preliminary investigation, that my personal interests coincided, were interwoven with the underlying political motive of this crime. I do not wish to minimize the degree of my guilt by referring to Yagoda. I set about undermining Maxim Gorky's health after great hesitation. But in the death of Maxim Peshkov I was interested personally. I calculated that with the death of Maxim Peshkov I would become the only person close to Gorky, a person who in the future might succeed to Gorky's large literary inheritance, which would provide me with means and an independent position in the future.

I made Yagoda's acquaintance in 1928. We established a closer contact in 1931. In 1932 our meetings became more frequent. Yagoda often talked with me, we spoke of Alexei Maximovich, of his role as a political figure, of his proximity to the Party and Stalin. We spoke of the work which Maxim Peshkov was doing for Alexei Maximovich. Yagoda also sounded out my political views. I did not believe in the forces of industrialization of the country, I did not believe in the collectivization of the country's agriculture.

In conversations with me in 1932, Yagoda often hinted to me that he was aware of the fact that I lived rather lavishly and spent relatively large sums for my personal needs.

505

VYSHINSKY: Where did you get the means?

KRYUCHKOV: I embezzled large sums of money belonging to Gorky, exploiting his full confidence in me. And it was precisely this that made me in a certain way dependent on Yagoda. I was afraid that he knew of my embezzling money and committing a felony. Yagoda began to use my services in order to gain access to Gorky's home and become more intimate with Gorky. I helped him in everything.

In the course of one of our conversations, at the beginning of 1933, Yagoda said that Alexei Maximovich might die soon, that he was getting old and that after Alexei Maximovich's death his son Max would be in charge of Gorky's literary heritage. "But you are used," Yagoda said, "to an easy life, and you will remain in the house in the role of a retainer." This remark of Yagoda's embarrassed me and Yagoda noticed my embarrassment. With this our conversation came to an end.

In 1933, I think in the spring, as I have already testified today, Yagoda again resumed this conversation. This time he bluntly urged the removal, or, to be more exact, the murder of Maxim Peshkov.

He spoke to me in the following way: "It is not Maxim Peshkov that matters, it is necessary to lessen Gorky's activity, because it is in the way of the 'big chiefs'—Rykov, Bukharin, Kamenev, Zinoviev." The conversation took place in Yagoda's office. He also spoke to me of the counter-revolutionary coup. As far as I can remember his words, he spoke about a new government soon coming to power in the U.S.S.R., which would fully correspond to my political tendencies. M. Gorky's activity was an obstacle in the way of the coup d'état, this activity must be lessened. "You know how Alexei Maximovich loves his son Maxim; he derives great strength from this love," he said.

I told him that I did not intend to stand in his, Yagoda's, way, and asked what I must do. To this he replied: "Remove Maxim"—and added that Maxim's death would affect Gorky and turn him into a harmless old man. In the course of further conversation he said: "Your task is very simple; make Maxim drink heavily. I have spoken with Dr. Vinogradov and I know what fatal effect wine has on Maxim's constitution."

I was surprised that he had consulted Vinogradov on this subject and gave expression to my surprise. He told me that Dr. A. I. Vinogradov and Dr. Levin had been enlisted for this purpose.

I complied with his orders and set about preparing the murder of Maxim Peshkov. I began to ply him with liquors, receiving them directly from Yagoda in fairly large quantities. But nevertheless Maxim Peshkov's strong constitution would not give

506

way. And then in 1934 Yagoda kept hurrying me; he advised me to get Maxim chilled. Yagoda said: "You should arrange somehow to leave him lying in the snow." In March or April, a short time before Maxim Peshkov's critical illness, I did this, but Maxim Peshkov got off with a light cold. On May 2, after getting Maxim drunk, I left him to sleep for a few hours on a bench in the garden, as Dr. Levin testified here today. It was a cold day and Maxim took ill and died on May 11. On the evening of May 3, Maxim told me he was not feeling well; he took his temperature, which proved to be 39.5, but notwithstanding this I did not summon a doctor. I advised him to warm himself up by drinking some more vodka. Nurse Olympiada Dmitrievna Chertkova, a staunch friend of the Gorky family, was greatly concerned and demanded that a doctor be called immediately. I replied that it could wait till the morning. The following morning I summoned Levin.

Levin arrived and stated that Maxim's ailment was a light form of the grippe. He called me aside and said: "You have achieved what you were aiming at." I was a bit surprised by his words; how did he learn of my complicity in this crime? Previously we had had conversations regarding the state of health of Maxim Alexeyevich Peshkov, but we had never spoken openly as one criminal to another. A few days later, Dr. Badmayev came by chance to see Alexei Maximovich Gorky. Badmayev examined Maxim Peshkov and immediately declared that he was suffering from croupous pneumonia. He asked in surprise: "But didn't Levin examine him?" When Maxim Peshkov learnt that he was suffering from croupous pneumonia, he asked whether A. D. Speransky, who often visited the Gorky family, could not be summoned. Alexei Dmitrievich Speransky was not a practising physician, but Alexei Maximovich was very much attached to him and had high regard for him as a prominent scientist. I informed Levin about this. Levin said: "Under no circumstances should Speransky be called." Levin added that he would soon come together with Dr. A. I. Vinogradov. Towards evening he did arrive together with Vinogradov. Dr. Vinogradov, though he had not yet seen the patient, brought some medicine with him. I recall that there was some sort of clash with Olympiada Dmitrievna Chertkova when Vinogradov gave Maxim some medicine without her knowledge; she was the one who always looked after all patients in Gorky's house and demanded that everything should go through her hands. And she administered some medicine taken from Gorky's family medicine chest.

On May 7 or 8, Maxim Alexeyevich's health improved. I reported this to Yagoda, who indignantly said: "Damn it all, they are able to kill healthy people by their treatment, and here they cannot do the trick on a sick man." I know that after this Yagoda spoke to Dr. Vinogradov and Dr. Vinogradov proposed that Maxim Peshkov be given champagne. Levin said that champagne would be very beneficial because the patient was in a very depressed state. Maxim Alexeyevich was given champagne, and this caused indigestion accompanied by a high temperature.

When this indigestion began, Vinogradov personally—I know this for sure—gave the patient a laxative, and upon leaving the patient's room said: "Any layman knows that with such a high temperature a laxative should not be given."

The medical consultation which was summoned at the insistence of Alexei Maximovich Gorky raised the question of applying blockade treatment according to Speransky's method, but Dr. Vinogradov, Levin and Pletnev categorically objected to this and said that a little more time should be allowed to pass. On the night of May 10 when Maxim was actually dying, and when cyanosis set in, it was decided to apply Speransky's blockade treatment method, but Speransky himself said that it was already too late and there was no sense in doing it.

Thus, Maxim died on May 11. I have already testified that I had a personal interest in the killing of Maxim Peshkov. Yagoda put the dagger in my hand. I killed Maxim on Yagoda's instructions.

I forgot to add that when Yagoda spoke to me about the murder of Maxim Peshkov, he said: "Pyotr Petrovich, I can remove you from Gorky in no time, you are in my hands. The slightest disloyal step on your part with regard to me will result in more than unpleasant consequences for you."

Having committed this crime, I was compelled to agree to a more horrible crime, to the murder of Gorky. Yagoda said bluntly that I was to set about undermining Gorky's health. I wavered; I tried to avoid carrying out this order. Yagoda said that he would not stop short of denouncing me as the murderer of Maxim Peshkov. And Yagoda gave me to understand in no ambiguous way that if I ever thought of bringing his name into it, nothing would come of it. "The investigation will be conducted by my people," Yagoda remarked, and I agreed to perform this crime. Levin explained in his testimony today how I made Gorky catch cold. In this case our actions were co-ordinated; that is, I consulted Levin. Maxim Gorky spent the winter of 1935-36 in Tesseli, in the Crimea. I was staying in Moscow, but I visited him in the Crimea once every three weeks or once a month. I arranged long walks for Alexei Maximovich, I was always arranging bonfires. The smoke of the bonfire naturally affected Gorky's weak lungs. This time, in the period of

1935-36, Gorky did not recuperate in the Crimea; on the contrary, he started on his return trip to Moscow tired out. Gorky's return to Moscow was organized, or, to be more exact, hastened by Yagoda, who both with regard to the murder of Maxim Peshkov and with regard to the murder of M. Gorky was always hurrying me on. While in the Crimea, I spoke to Yagoda on the telephone. Yagoda urged me to make haste; he said it was necessary to bring Gorky back to Moscow, and this notwithstanding the fact that the weather in the Crimea was very warm, while in Moscow it was cold. I spoke to Gorky about returning to Moscow; he agreed and began preparations for the trip. Approximately on May 26, 1936, Nadezhda Alexeyevna Peshkova, the widow of Maxim Alexeyevich Peshkov, informed us by telephone that we should not return under any circumstances—the weather in Moscow was cold, and, besides, Alexei Maximovich's granddaughters, i. e., her daughters, who were in Moscow, were down with the grippe, accompanied by a rather high fever. A day or two after this I again spoke to Yagoda over the 'phone. Yagoda told me that the granddaughters were perfectly well, they had recovered entirely, and it was necessary to persuade Alexei Maximovich to return to Moscow. I told Alexei Maximovich of this, and on May 26 or 27 we left for Moscow. Immediately upon arriving in Moscow on May 31, Alexei Maximovich went to see his granddaughters, who were really down with the grippe and had fever; and Gorky took sick on May 31. Dr. Levin was summoned the same evening. Levin diagnosed Gorky's ailment as a light form of the grippe, but on June 2 Alexei Maximovich, in speaking to me in the morning, asked: "What do the doctors say?" I replied: "The grippe." But he said: "In my opinion, I am developing pneumonia; I see this by the sputum." I then 'phoned Levin. Levin arrived and immediately agreed with the diagnosis given by the patient. After this the "cure" began. Gorky was treated by Professor Pletnev and Dr. Levin. I watched this treatment, and must say that the administration of digalen to Gorky produced a critical effect, about which the Court possesses data. While prior to June 8, 1936, Gorky's pulse was even and reached, I think, 130 a minute, after digalen had been administered his pulse immediately showed sharp fluctuations.

This is my second horrible crime. That is all I have to say.

THE PRESIDENT: Has the Procurator any questions?

VYSHINSKY: No.

THE PRESIDENT: Have Counsel for Defence any questions?

COUNSEL FOR DEFENCE KOMMODOV: No.

COUNSEL FOR DEFENCE BRAUDE: No.

THE PRESIDENT: Have the accused any questions?

THE ACCUSED: (Reply in the negative.)

THE PRESIDENT: Have the medical experts any questions?
COMMISSION OF EXPERTS: (Reply in the negative.)
THE PRESIDENT: The Court is adjourned till 11 a.m. March 9.

510

Summary of Morning Session

MARCH 9, 1938

Examination of the Accused PLETNEV:

Pletnev testifies that he met Yagoda in 1934 and was told that a *coup d'état* involving Yagoda, Yenukidze, and Rykov was maturing. Yagoda recruited him into the plot against Gorky and Kuibyshev. Pletnev verifies Levin's account of the treatment used to murder Gorky and Kuibyshev. In the case of Gorky, the plan was "to tire out the organism and thus lower its power of resistance . . . to bring about . . . death." He admits full responsibility in both affairs, stating that he participated because he was afraid of Yagoda, who was then People's Commissar of Internal Affairs.

Counsel for Defence Kommodov questions Pletnev about his life and Vyshinsky asks him about his alleged attack on a woman patient in 1937.

Examination of the Accused KAZAKOV:

Kazakov testifies that his crimes are connected with the murder of Menzhinsky. He treated the patient correctly until November, 1933, when at the instigation of Yagoda and Levin he began using lysates improperly to bring about the death of Menzhinsky, who suffered from angina pectoris and bronchial asthma. Kazakov reconfirms his guilt when questioned by Kommodov.

Answers of the Commission of Medical Experts to the Questions Submitted by the State Prosecutor:

The Commission, comprised of Professors D. A. Burmin, N. A. Shereshevsky, V. N. Vinogradov, D. M. Rossisky, and Dr. V. D. Zipalov, testifies that Kazakov had sole control over the preparation of lysates and that the employment of lysates by Kazakov led to "the acceleration" of Menzhinsky's death.

Examination of the Accused MAXIMOV-DIKOVSKY:

Maximov testifies that his connection with the Rights and his association with Gaister date back to 1928. In 1929 he entered on the "anti-Party, counter-revolutionary path," but continued to conceal his views and activities. During 1930 and 1931 his connections with the Rights increased and in 1932 Gaister placed him in Kuibyshev's Secretariat. At this time he met Yenukidze, who informed him

511

that the Rights were planning to overthrow the government. In 1934 Maximov was told by Yenukidze that it was necessary to ruin the health of the Party leaders and that he must take part in a terrorist act against Kuibyshev. His role involved allowing Levin and Pletnev to carry on their activities and reassuring Kuibyshev while he was suffering from the effects of maltreatment. Maximov testifies that he was drawn into the plot by Yenukidze and Yagoda; he was told that Bukharin, Rykov, and Tomsky "were taking part in this affair."

Bukharin questions Maximov as to when and how often he met with Yenukidze.

Examination of the Witness DR. BELOSTOTSKY:

Belostotsky states that he was appointed by the Medical Administration of the Kremlin to give Gorky intravenous infusions and that he was present during the last period of Gorky's illness. On one occasion, he noticed that Levin planned to use a dangerous formula of glucose; another time, Pletnev told him that "in such a condition the patient should be allowed to die in peace."

Vyshinsky: Not to save him?

Belostotsky: Not to save him.

Answers of the Commission of Medical Experts to the Questions Submitted by the State Prosecutor:

The Commission examines the medical testimony given at the session and concludes that criminal medical treatment led to death in the cases of Gorky, Kuibyshev, Menzhinsky, and Peshkov. In addition, an analysis revealed that mercury poison had been placed (by Yagoda and Bulanov) in the office of N. I. Yezhov and that "if the present crime had not been discovered in time the life of Comrade N. I. Yezhov would have been in immediate danger." The medical experts are unanimous in their findings.

At this point Vyshinsky questions Rosengoltz about a written prayer found in his pocket at the time of his arrest. Rosengoltz answers that his wife had placed it there for "good luck" several months earlier. Vyshinsky concludes: "And you agreed to become the keeper of a talisman? I have no more questions."

The session is adjourned and resumed *in camera*.

512

THE SESSION IN CAMERA

At the session in camera the accused RAKOVSKY, GRINKO, ROSENGOLTZ and KRESTINSKY gave evidence about their treasonable, espionage connections with certain official representatives of certain foreign states.

The Court established both the exact identity of the representatives with whom the above-mentioned conspirators from the anti-Soviet "bloc of Rights and Trotskyites" were connected, and the states they represented.

At this session in camera the accused G. G. YAGODA gave testimony in which he fully admitted to organizing the murder of Comrade M. A. PESHKOV, stating that he had pursued personal aims as well as conspiratorial aims in committing this murder.

COMMANDANT OF THE COURT: The Court is coming. Please rise.

THE PRESIDENT: Please be seated. The session is resumed. Comrade Vyshinsky, Procurator of the U.S.S.R., will speak for the Prosecution.

VYSHINSKY: Comrades Judges, members of the Military Collegium of the Supreme Court of the U.S.S.R.

In proceeding to make my speech for the Prosecution in the present case, which constitutes an exceptional phenomenon of extraordinary public and political significance, I would like in the first place to direct your attention to certain distinguishing features of this case, to certain of its outstanding peculiarities.

It is not for the first time that the Supreme Court of our country is examining a case involving gravest crimes directed against the well-being of our country, against our Socialist fatherland, the fatherland of the working people of the whole world. But I will hardly be mistaken if I say that this is the first time that our Court has had to examine a case like this, to examine a case of such crimes and such foul deeds as those that have passed at this trial before your eyes, before the eyes of the whole world, a case of such criminals as those you now see in the prisoners' dock.

With every day and every hour that passed, as the Court investigation on the present case proceeded, it brought to light ever more of the horrors of the chain of shameful, unparalleled, monstrous crimes committed by the accused, the entire abominable chain of heinous deeds before which the base deeds of the most inveterate, vile, unbridled and despicable criminals fade and grow dim.

And indeed, what trial of all those that have taken place here—and there have been not a few of them lately due to the conditions of the class struggle and of the furious resistance of our enemies to the cause of Socialism—can compare with the present trial in the monstrosity, brazenness and cynicism of the crimes committed by these gentlemen?

In what other trial was it possible to uncover and expose the real nature of these crimes with such force and depth, with such force to tear the mask of perfidy from the faces of scoundrels, and to show to the whole of our people and all honest people throughout the world the bestial countenance of the international brigands who cunningly and cleverly direct the hand of miscreants against our peaceful Socialist labour that has set up the new, happy, joyously flourishing Socialist society of workers and peasants?

This circumstance alone provides sufficiently clear proof of the tremendous social and political significance of this trial, of the fact that the present trial constitutes an outstanding phenomenon, that the present trial is of historic significance.

What constitutes the historic significance of the present trial? What are some of its distinguishing features?

The historic significance of this trial consists before all in the fact that at this trial it has been shown, proved and established with exceptional scrupulousness and exactitude that the Rights, Trotskyites, Mensheviks, Socialist-Revolutionaries, bourgeois nationalists, and so on and so forth, are nothing other than a gang of murderers, spies, diversionists and wreckers, without any principles or ideals.

Exactly a year ago, when analysing the shortcomings in our work and indicating the measures whereby to liquidate the Trotskyite and other double-dealers, Comrade Stalin said:

"Two words about wreckers, diversionists, spies, etc. I think it is clear to everybody now that the present-day wreckers and diversionists, no matter what disguise they may adopt, either Trotskyite or Bukharinite, have long ceased to be a political trend in the labour movement, that they have become transformed into a gang of professional wreckers, diversionists, spies and assassins, without principles and without ideals. Of course, these gentlemen must be ruthlessly smashed and uprooted as the enemies of the working class, as betrayers of our country. This is clear and requires no further explanation."

A year has gone by. The example of the present trial shows us how profoundly right was Comrade Stalin in his estimation of the Trotskyites and Bukharinites.

The Trotskyites and Bukharinites, that is to say, the "bloc of Rights and Trotskyites," the leading lights of which are now in the prisoners' dock, is not a political party, a political tendency, but a band of felonious criminals, and not simply felonious criminals, but of criminals who have sold themselves to enemy intelligence services, criminals whom even ordinary felons treat as the basest, the lowest, the most contemptible, the most depraved of the depraved.

515

The so-called "bloc of Rights and Trotskyites" is an organ-ization engaged in espionage, acts of diversion and wrecking, political murder and in selling their country to the enemy.

The bloc has no ideals; there is nothing "spiritual," so to speak, nothing ideological about it. That which some of the partici-pants of this bloc once possessed, in some measure or other, has long ago been squandered and lost, has long ago vanished and gone rotten in the foul-smelling, abominable underworld of spies.

True, some of the accused, particularly the accused Bukharin, made attempts on more than one occasion at this trial, as the French say, to keep a straight face while the going's bad, to assume the appearance of people with "ideals," to cover up their bandit criminal activity with all kinds of "philosophical," "ideological" and other chatter.

Bukharin attempted here to reduce the whole nightmare of his heinous crimes to some sort of "ideological lines" about which he attempted to deliver lengthy and pompous speeches. Bukharin spoke here of the division of labour in this spying and wrecking organization, of some sort of "programmatic items," of some sort of "ideological orientation," albeit, he added, an ideological orientation on the kulaks.

Bukharin tried to represent his own role in this gang as that of a "theoretician." On the fourth day of the trial, when the crimes of felonious espionage committed by this so-called bloc had been fully exposed, Bukharin had the effrontery to say literally the following:

"I mainly occupied myself with the problematics of gen-eral leadership and with the ideological side; this, of course, did not exclude either my being aware of the practical side of the matter, or the adoption of a number of practical steps on my part."

Pray appraise the role of this little gentleman who alleges that he was occupied not with the direction of all kinds of crimes, and the most monstrous at that, but with the "problematics" of these crimes, not with the organization of these crimes, but with the "ideological side" of these black deeds. Appraise the role of this little gentleman who does the most rabid work of wreck-ing and destruction, taking advantage, on his own admission, of all the difficulties of the Soviet power, who prepares and engineers black treason, prepares the defeat of his country in war with fascist enemies and hopes to hide his treason with jaunty, cynical chatter about taking advantage of the war which "prognostically stood in perspective." Appraise the role of this garrulous little gentleman who says that the arch-bandit and Anglo-German spy Trotsky in 1932 already threw off his "Leftist uniform"—to employ Bukha-rin's words used here—and that he, Bukharin, together with

516

Rykov and Tomsky armed this gang of criminals with their "ideology."

Caught red-handed in the act, Bukharin calls Hegel himself as witness, hurls himself into the jungle of linguistics, philology and rhetorics, mumbles some sort of learned words, so as to cover up the traces in one way or another. But he does not stand the test, and ends his scientific raving babble with the following admission:

"We all became rabid counter-revolutionaries, traitors to the Socialist fatherland, we turned into spies, terrorists, and restorers of capitalism. We embarked on treachery, crime, and treason. We turned into an insurrectionary band, we organized terrorist groups, engaged in wrecking activities, wanted to overthrow the Soviet government of the proletariat."

To this Bukharin should have added: "We became a police department of the Japanese and German intelligence services, we became shameless barterers of our country."

The bloc is an agency of foreign intelligence services. The members of the bloc and its leaders, such as Trotsky, who is not in the dock here, Bukharin, Rykov, Yagoda, Krestinsky, Rosengoltz, and its rank-and-file members, such as Zubarev, Maximov-Dikovsky and others, are slaves of these intelligence services, they are bondmen of their masters.

What room, then, is there here for ideology, "problematics" or "prognostics," for theory or philosophy?

Philosophy, behind the smoke-screen of which Bukharin tried to hide here, is only a mask wherewith to cover up espionage and treason.

Bukharin's literary-philosophical exercises are a screen behind which he tries to hide from his final exposure.

Philosophy and espionage, philosophy and wrecking, philosophy and acts of diversion, philosophy and murder, like genius and villainy, are two things that do not go together!

I know of no other instances—this is the first instance in history of a spy and murderer using philosophy, like powdered glass, to hurl it into his victim's eyes before dashing his brains out with a footpad's bludgeon.

The historical significance of this trial lies first and foremost in the fact that it has completely exposed the bandit character of the "bloc of Rights and Trotskyites," its ideological sterility, exposed the fact that the bloc—all these Rights, Trotskyites, Mensheviks, Socialist-Revolutionaries, bourgeois nationalists, etc., etc.,—are all hired agents of the fascist intelligence services.

The "bloc of Rights and Trotskyites" is no political grouping; it is a gang of spies, of agents of foreign intelligence services.

This has been proved fully and incontestably. Herein lies the

517

enormous social, political and historical significance of the present trial.

The "bloc of Rights and Trotskyites" now in the dock—as the trial has shown with the utmost clarity—is only an advance detachment of international fascism, is a pack of hangmen and surreptitious murderers, with whose aid fascism is operating in various countries, primarily in Spain and in China.

That is why the exposure of the "bloc of Rights and Trotskyites" as a gang of spies is of enormous importance not only for our Socialist revolution, but also for the whole international proletariat. It is of enormous importance for the cause of peace throughout the world. It is of enormous importance for the whole of human culture, for the fight for real democracy and the freedom of nations, for the struggle against all and sundry warmongers, against all international provocations and provocateurs.

That is why this trial is being followed with bated breath by the working people throughout the world, and particularly in those countries where the people are engaged in a heroic struggle for their freedom, against fascist tyranny.

Under the leadership of Trotsky, under the leadership of the German, Japanese, Polish and other intelligence services, the Bukharins and Rykovs, Yagodas and Bulanovs, Krestinskys and Rosengoltzes, Ikramovs, Khodjayevs and Sharangoviches do their dark deeds by order of their masters not only in our country, but in Spain, in China, and wherever the class struggle of the working people is going on, wherever honest people are fighting for genuine freedom, for genuine democracy, for genuine human culture.

The Bukharins and Rykovs, Yagodas and Bulanovs, Krestinskys and Rosengoltzes, Ikramovs, Sharangoviches, Khodjayevs and others are the very same as the Fifth Column, the POUM, the Ku Klux Klan. They are one of the detachments of the fascist provocateurs and incendiaries of war operating on the international arena.

The smashing of this detachment is a great service to the cause of peace, the cause of democracy, the cause of genuine human culture.

The exceptional importance of the present trial is, however, not limited to what I have said.

Here in the dock is not some one anti-Soviet group, the agents of some one foreign intelligence service. Here in the dock is a number of anti-Soviet groups, the agents of the intelligence services of a number of foreign powers hostile to the U.S.S.R.

Implicated in this "case" are the remnants of all anti-Soviet forces, groups and organizations, and at least, as has been exactly established by the trial, four foreign intelligence services—the Japanese, German, Polish and British—and, it goes without saying, all the other foreign intelligence services which maintain friendly, so-called operative contact with the above-mentioned intelligence services.

Indeed, if we speak of Trotsky, his connections with the Gestapo were proved up to the hilt at the trials of the Trotskyite-Zinovievite terrorist centre in August 1936 and of the anti-Soviet Trotskyite centre in January 1937. Now, however, it has been proved that his connections with the German political police and the intelligence services of other countries date back to a much earlier period, that Trotsky has been connected with the German intelligence service since 1921. This has been stated quite definitely by Krestinsky at the present trial. It is now a proved fact that Trotsky has been connected with the British Intelligence Service since 1926. This has been stated definitely and proved by the accused Rakovsky. The whole bloc headed by Trotsky consisted in its entirety of foreign spies and agents of the tsarist Okhrana.

Through their accomplices Bukharin and Rykov were connected with a number of foreign intelligence services, which they served systematically.

Yagoda was surrounded, as with flies, with German, Japanese and Polish spies whom he not only shielded, as he himself admitted here, but through whom he engaged in espionage work, supplying foreign intelligence services with confidential state information, selling and betraying our country to these foreign intelligence services.

Krestinsky, on his own admission, has been a German spy since 1921.

Rosengoltz, one of the leaders of the Trotskyite underworld, as has been established, began his espionage work for the German General Staff, on his own admission, in 1923, and for the British Intelligence Service, also on his own admission, in 1926.

Rakovsky, one of Trotsky's closest and particularly trusted men, has been, according to his own testimony, an agent of the British Intelligence Service since 1924, and an agent of the Japanese intelligence service since 1934.

Chernov, according to his own testimony, began his espionage work for Germany in 1928, by forming a connection with the German intelligence service on the initiative and with the assistance of the notorious émigré—the Menshèvik, Dan.

Sharangovich was enrolled by the Polish intelligence service, and in 1921 was sent to the U.S.S.R. to carry on espionage work.

Grinko, according to his own words, became a spy of the German and Polish intelligence services in 1932, and prior to this maintained espionage connections with these intelligence services, particularly with the Polish intelligence service.

Ikramov and Khodjayev through their bandit chiefs "worked" under Bukharin's leadership on the establishment of contacts with

519

the resident agents of the British Intelligence Service, to strengthen which the notorious Intelligence Service agent and adventurer Lawrence expended a great deal of energy on the Central Asiatic borders of the U.S.S.R.

Then follow the provocateurs and agents of the tsarist Okhrana—Zelensky, Zubarev, Ivanov—Ivanov being in addition a British spy.

Add to this gang the group of poisoners and murderers—Levin, Pletnev, Kazakov, Kryuchkov, Maximov-Dikovsky and the others connected with them—and then the moral and political countenance of this bloc and of each of its participants becomes clear to the utmost.

That is why we can say that here is a foul-smelling heap of human garbage, who stop at nothing, who have no qualms whatsoever, who are ready for anything—to blow up factories and trains, to destroy cattle, to spoil grain, to engage in murder, espionage and high treason.

It is precisely all these criminal political and moral qualities that made of the Rights and Trotskyites such valuable material for provocation, for kindling the flames of war, for the foulest crimes of fascism. Nobody is so able to mask himself as they are. Nobody has mastered the art of cynical double-dealing to such a degree as they have.

The contemptible, treacherous, bandit activity of the Bukharins, Yagodas, Krestinskys, Rykovs and other Rights and Trotskyites is now exposed to the whole world. They sold their country, traded in the military secrets of its defence, were spies, diversionists, wreckers, murderers, thieves—and all in order to help the fascist governments to overthrow the Soviet government, to overthrow the power of the workers and peasants, to restore the power of the capitalists and landlords, to dismember the country of the Soviet people, to wrest away the national republics and turn them into colonies of the imperialists.

Such were the orders of their masters, which they fulfilled as best they could, exerting all their strength in doing so.

They strove with all their strength to set fire to our native home from all sides; they were in a hurry to open the gates to the enemy so as to clutch at power, even at the price of Judas-like betrayal, so as to destroy the fruits of the heroic labour of our people who have built up the new, the Socialist society, so as to bring back the power of the landowners and capitalists, for whom these traitors worked tirelessly.

Such are these people, such are their plans and calculations, such are their shameful and monstrous crimes.

The accused Bukharin made the boastful statement here that it was they, the Rights, the menials of the capitalists who armed

520

Trotskyism with the "spiritual" weapon of the theory of the restoration of capitalism.

Of what "theory" does Bukharin speak—this hardened political swindler and one of the leading organizers of foreign espionage against the U.S.S.R.?

Bukharin shrinks from the admission of his guilt as the devil from incense. Bukharin denies his guilt here.

But what is his denial of this crime worth in the light of his admission that he is guilty of other most serious crimes organically bound with this crime?

What is this denial worth in the light of the evidence we have against Bukharin?

I would only remind you that at the morning session on March 7, Bukharin and Rykov were shown to be fully guilty of espionage connections and of conducting espionage work for the German and Polish intelligence services. I would briefly call to mind my dialogue with Rykov at the morning session on March 7.

At the investigation Rykov had stated:

"Chervyakov developed exceptionally active work in Byelorussia. In his relations with the Poles, he and those connected with him in illegal activity drew all the practical conclusions from these directions of ours."

Rykov confirmed this in Court as well. He was asked in Court by the State Prosecutor:

"Consequently, Chervyakov and the people connected with you maintained systematic connections with the Poles?

"RYKOV: Yes.

"*Question:* What kind of connection is it?

"RYKOV: There was an espionage connection there, too.

"*Question:* But was there an espionage connection maintained by a part of your organization with the Poles on your instructions?

"RYKOV: Of course.

"*Question:* Bukharin included?

"RYKOV: Of course.

"*Question:* Were you and Bukharin connected?

"RYKOV: Absolutely.

"*Question:* So you were spies?

"RYKOV: (No reply.)

"*Question:* And the organizers of espionage?

"RYKOV: I am in no way better than a spy.

"*Question:* You organized espionage, so you were spies.

"RYKOV: It may be said, yes."

But Bukharin under these conditions speaks of some sort of

521

"theory" in an attempt to give a "theoretical" explanation of the course of events that led the Rights into the camp of the sworn enemies of the Soviet power and the Soviet people. . . .

There is no point in seeking for these explanations in Bukharin's "theory." They must be sought in Bukharin's crimes even though they be cloaked in something like a "theory."

It is just these crimes that explain the real course of developments, the real logic of the events and the struggle that brought two worlds face to face, two blocs—the bloc of traitors, hirelings of foreign capital, now exposed and crushed by the wrath and might of the great Soviet country, the bloc of betrayers covered with eternal contempt, shame and condemnation of millions of working people throughout the world—and the bloc of Soviet patriots, great and invincible in their love for their country, patriots who have won more than one historic battle over their enemies, ready under the leadership of the Communist Party and the great Stalin to give a crushing rebuff to any enemy, under any conditions, at any time, whatever the point from which he may appear, despite all treachery, despite all betrayal.

It goes without saying that the significance of the present trial is also determined by the lessons which must inevitably be drawn from it by all of us, patriots of the Soviet land.

Our country enjoys the happiness of the victory of Socialism, the happiness and joy of labour delivered from the yoke of capitalism.

For twenty years the Soviet state, the Socialist state of workers and peasants, has stood like an indestructible. rock.

For twenty years the great land of victorious Socialism has been the scene of the heroic work of the organization of a new social and state system, free of exploitation, free of the misery and suffering of the millions of people enslaved by the yoke of capitalism in almost all the remaining countries of the world.

For twenty years there has been going on unswervingly and persistently the harmonious work of the numerous peoples united in the fraternal Union of Soviet Socialist Republics, built by the genius of the leaders of the Socialist revolution, Lenin and Stalin.

In these twenty years the once poor and weak country has become a rich and mighty country, a powerful and invincible country.

In these twenty years the Russian state has become a Socialist state.

At the Extraordinary Eighth Congress of Soviets of the U.S.S.R., which adopted the great Stalinist Constitution, Comrade Stalin said:

"Our Soviet society has already, in the main, succeeded in achieving Socialism; it has created a Socialist system,

522

i. e., it has brought about what Marxists in other words call the first, or lower phase of Communism. Hence, in the main, we have already achieved the first phase of Communism, Socialism. The fundamental principle of this phase of Communism is, as you know, the formula: 'From each according to his ability, to each according to his work.' "

In these twenty years, under the leadership of the Party of Lenin and Stalin, our country has attained the final abolition of the exploitation of man by man, the final assertion of public, Socialist property as the firm basis of our Soviet society.

In these twenty years, the whole aspect of our country has undergone a radical change; it has become a rich and mighty proletarian power.

"As a result of all these changes in the sphere of the national economy of the U.S.S.R.," says Comrade Stalin, "we now have a new, Socialist economy, which knows neither crises nor unemployment, which knows neither poverty nor ruin, and which provides citizens with every opportunity to lead a prosperous and cultured life."

Socialism has become part of the everyday life of our people, Socialism has emerged victorious in our country. And there is no force on earth capable of weakening the significance or the grandeur of this Socialist victory. And this despite all the difficulties that have stood and that still stand in our path. And this despite all the efforts made by the foreign powers hostile to us and by the remnants of exploiting classes in our country, which have lived their day and are dying out, to hold back the progressive development of our society, to hinder our Socialist successes, to disrupt our peaceful creative work of building Socialism in the U.S.S.R.

It can be said without any exaggeration whatsoever that in the past twenty years of Soviet history our state and our people have not lived through a single year, month or day when we have not been attacked by enemies—furious, insidious, brutal and seeking revenge for defeats suffered by them at the hands of our workers and peasants, seeking revenge for the "lost paradise" of their economic and political domination.

From the very first days of the Great October Revolution up to the brilliant days of the greatest epoch in history—the epoch of the Stalinist Constitution—the young Republic of Soviets has not emerged from the fire of class attacks by the exploiters and their numerous agents, the Trotskyites, Mensheviks, Socialist-Revolutionaries, Bukharinites, Zinovievites, Mussavatists, Dashnaks, Georgian, Uzbek and other nationalists, members of the "Black Hundreds," Whiteguards, Cadets, priests, kulaks, etc., etc.

This trial has reminded us once again, and has done so with unprecedented force and acuteness, that two worlds face each other as irreconcilable and deadly enemies—the world of capitalism and the world of Socialism.

The logic of class contradictions and of the class struggle urges the remnants of the exploiting classes within the U.S.S.R. and the exploiting classes beyond its bounds to undertake more and more furious attacks against the state of working people, which is paving a broad highway towards a better, a new life for the working people and the oppressed nations of the entire world.

Lenin and Stalin, our teachers, have on more than one occasion pointed to the danger represented by the capitalist encirclement to the cause of Socialism in the U.S.S.R.

At the Eighth Congress of the R.C.P. (Bolsheviks), in March 1919, Lenin said:

"We are living not merely in a state, but in *a system of states*, and the existence of the Soviet Republic side by side with imperialist states for a long time is unthinkable. One or the other must triumph in the end. And before that end supervenes, a series of frightful collisions between the Soviet Republic and the bourgeois states is inevitable." (Collected Works, Vol. XXIV, p. 122.)

"We must remember," Lenin taught us, "that we are at all times but a hair's breadth from invasion." (Collected Works, Vol. XXVII, p. 117.)

Just recently Comrade Stalin once again reminded us of this capitalist encirclement.

"Indeed," wrote Comrade Stalin in his historic reply to Comrade Ivanov, "it would be ridiculous and stupid to close our eyes to the capitalist encirclement and to think that our external enemies, the fascists, for example, will not, if the opportunity arises, make an attempt at an armed attack upon the U.S.S.R. Only blind braggarts or masked enemies who desire to lull the vigilance of our people can think like that. No less ridiculous would it be to deny that in the event of the slightest success of military intervention, the interventionists would try to destroy the Soviet system in the districts they occupied and restore the bourgeois system. Did not Denikin or Kolchak restore the bourgeois system in the districts they occupied? Are the fascists any better than Denikin or Kolchak? Only blockheads or masked enemies who with their boastfulness want to conceal their hostility and are striving to demobilize the people can deny the danger of military intervention and of attempts at restoration as long as the capitalist encirclement exists."

Over a number of years our enemies placed their hopes upon

successful intervention; they organized and inspired various anti-Soviet groups in the U.S.S.R. to struggle against the Soviet power, calculating on being able with the aid of these groups to carry through their predatory designs.

The entire history of bourgeois counter-revolution in the U.S.S.R. is linked up with the active attempts of the most reactionary circles of the international bourgeoisie to overthrow the power of the Soviets. There has not been a single more or less serious plot against the Soviet power in the U.S.S.R. without the direct and most active participation of foreign capitalists and military cliques.

In 1921 Lenin warned us:

"We are surrounded by the world bourgeoisie, which watches every minute of vacillation in order to bring back 'its own,' to reinstate the landlords and bourgeoisie." (Collected Works, Vol. XXVI, p. 348.)

Comrade Stalin is tireless in reminding us of the danger of the capitalist encirclement, he proves that "the resistance of the dying classes in our country does not take place in isolation from the outside world, but finds support from the capitalist encirclement." ("Problems of Leninism," p. 386.)

Was not the famous Shakhty case proof of this?[1] There the main directing role belonged to Polish-French-German capitalists, who had united with the wreckers in the struggle against the U.S.S.R.

Were not the Polish manufacturer Dvorzhanchik, the French shareholders Sanset, Remaux, and Bourose, the German AEG and the military in a number of capitalist countries who supported the first, second and third—were not all of these the inspirers of the Shakhty conspiracy, which aimed, together with the foreign General Staffs, at drowning our land in blood in 1928?

Was not the well-known "Industrial Party"[2] case proof of this, where, side by side with Ramzin and Charnovsky, first fiddle was played by the Whiteguard émigrés Ryabushinsky and General Lukomsky, by the British intelligence service man Colonel Lawrence and the French General Joinville, well-known participant of the Northern intervention in 1919 and military attaché at Kolchak's headquarters?

It is a known fact that those implicated in the Shakhty trial and in the trial of the "Industrial Party" not only engaged in wrecking work and prepared acts of diversion in case of war, but systematically conducted espionage work, and, as the "Industrial Party" trial disclosed, Ramzin even organized, for the conduct of this espionage work, a special commission under the chairmanship of the wrecker Professor Osadchy, at that time assistant chairman of the State Planning Commission. The program of the "Industrial Party" focussed attention on the perpetrating of acts of diversion in Moscow, Leningrad, the Donbas and the Urals by resorting to the blowing up of bridges, the damaging of railways, the blowing up of electric power stations, the stoppage of factories and mills.

Was not the devilish work of the foreign intelligence services in our country also shown by the trial of the British engineers Thornton, MacDonald and others, who were exposed in 1933 as agents of the Intelligence Service, as organizers of wrecking activities and acts of diversion at certain of our electric power stations, as people who were preparing bases for the coming intervention?

Finally, has this not been proved also by the recent trials of 1936 and 1937, which exposed the monstrous crimes of the espionage and terrorist gangs of Trotskyites, Zinovievites and other anti-Soviet elements who enrolled in the service of foreign police Okhranas and became espionage, diversionist and terrorist agencies of Okhranas? Yes, yes. The ghastly crimes of these bandit gangs destroyed by the verdicts of our Soviet Court cry out aloud and provide absolutely convincing proof of this.

The Zinoviev-Kamenev trial, the Pyatakov-Radek trial, the trial of the group of military traitors Tukhachevsky, Yakir and others, have proved that our enemies do not intend quietly to "creep into Socialism," as the accused Bukharin, Rykov and their like preached in order to mask their vile treacherous work, but that our enemies resort to the most extreme, most ferocious means of struggle.[3]

This has also been completely proved by the present trial, in which the chief "heroes" are the organizers and inspirers of the "bloc of Rights and Trotskyites," exposed as inveterate enemies of Socialism, of our country, of our people.

That is why the importance of this trial goes far beyond its ordinary, so to speak, criminal bounds and assumes really tremendous historic significance.

This trial sums up the results of the struggle against the Soviet state and the Party of Lenin-Stalin waged by people who, as has with exceptional clarity and conviction been proved by the Court proceedings, spent the whole of their lives behind masks, people who began this struggle long before the present time, who under cover of the loud phrases of provocateurs served not the revolution and the proletariat, but the counter-revolution and the bourgeoisie, who deceived the Party and the Soviet government in order the more conveniently to do their black work of treachery, in order the longer to remain undiscovered.

By means of deception, hypocrisy and double-dealing these detestable criminals succeeded in postponing the hour of their exposure until very recently. But this hour has arrived, and the criminals stand exposed, exposed completely and to the end.

In the light of the facts established at this trial, the entire criminal work of the Trotskyites and Bukharinites, who employed a cunning guise to hide their real countenance of sworn enemies of the Soviet people, becomes clear and comprehensible. . . .

Their mask has been torn off. Their true colours, their real face are now clear for all to see; their shameful deeds are also clear to all, just as is their miserable and shameful fate.

The trials of Zinoviev and Kamenev and of Pyatakov and Radek completed the exposure of the Trotskyite-Zinovievite scum of humanity as a rabid and unprincipled band of wreckers, diversionists, spies and assassins, acting on instructions of the intelligence services of foreign powers.

The 1937 trial, where the Trotskyite ringleaders Pyatakov, Radek, Sokolnikov and others were in the dock, exposed the political platform of the Trotskyites despite the fact that they stubbornly hid it from the people.

And how could they do other than hide this platform of theirs, woven as it was of treachery, betrayal and perfidy, and subordinated to the one task of ensuring the overthrow of the Soviet power and the restoration of capitalism in the U.S.S.R.?

The present trial has shown that this "program," if you please, was copied by the Trotskyites from the Rights, a point stressed in Court, not without boasting, by the accused Bukharin.

The present trial has completely and utterly exposed as fascist agents not only the Trotskyites, but also the Bukharinites, who cunningly camouflaged themselves over a lengthy period of time, and cunningly avoided being exposed as murderers, spies and provocateurs.

It is now clear to all and sundry what the Rights are, who, like the Trotskyites, long ago ceased to be a political trend, and, like Trotskyism, degenerated into a rabid and desperate gang of felonious criminals.

The entire process of their degeneration into a counter-revolutionary gang, a degeneration that began long ago and was repeatedly exposed by our Party and Comrade Stalin personally, has been completely revealed.

We shall yet dwell specially on the crimes of the accused Bukharin in the year 1918; now we shall mention them only in order in the light of these crimes the better and more graphically to see the path of this degeneration.

And really, could Bukharin, having begun in 1918 with the plot against Lenin as head of the Soviet state, having raised his criminal hand against Lenin in 1918, end in any other way than he has done now, in the shameful prisoners' dock, awaiting the severe but just sentence of the Soviet people, who now pronounce this hated name with imprecations?

Having begun with the quack "theory" of the peaceful growth

of the kulaks into Socialism, and having, during all these last ten years, conducted an underground struggle against the Party and the Soviet people, could Bukharin end his political career in any other way than he is doing now, grimacing and playing the buffoon even now on the threshold of what is perhaps his last hour, the hour of his death?

It was not by chance that Bukharin, Rykov, Yagoda and the other Rights came to the espionage bloc with the Trotskyites. There was nothing unexpected in the fact that such a bloc was constituted and at last, in 1932, took final shape; the entire development of the relations between the Rights and the Trotskyites, who at bottom constitute varieties of one and the same phenomenon, led towards this.

At the Sixteenth Party Congress, in 1930, Comrade Stalin, exposing the duality of Trotskyism, pointed out that this duality . . . "explains the fact that Trotskyism "(masked capitulation)" usually crowns its 'furious' attacks upon the Right deviators by entering into a *bloc* with these capitulators without masks."

The Trotskyites and Rights are capitulators. The former are capitulators behind the mask of hysterical, provocative, "revolutionary" phrases, while the others are capitulators without masks.

At the Seventeenth Party Conference, in his report on the Second Five-Year Plan, Comrade Molotov showed the complete kinship of souls of the Rights and the Trotskyites. The Trotskyites came forward with slanderous counter-theses against the First Five-Year Plan. They were echoed by the Rights, who countered Stalin's Five-Year Plan with Rykov's Two-Year Plan.[4]

The Trotskyites spread slander about the growth of the kulak elements and about the dependence on them of the state economy of the U.S.S.R. Day in and day out, the Rights whined that "for a long time to come the main source of grain will be the individual peasant farms" (i. e., kulak farms) "and therefore go slow with the offensive on the kulaks."[5]

The Trotskyites spat slander about "Thermidor," i. e., about the collapse of our revolution.[6] The Rights echoed them and whined that our industrial plants and factories would soon fall into the hands of the Whiteguards. True, the Rights occasionally fought the Trotskyites, but, as Comrade Stalin has already pointed out, these were "cock-fights" which "the Right deviators usually crown with backstage negotiations for a *bloc* with the Trotskyites." ("Problems of Leninism," p. 421.)

And so from year to year, throughout the whole duration of our revolution, throughout the whole of the existence of the Soviet state.

Wherein lies the explanation of this kinship of the positions of the Trotskyites and the Rights, of their constant attraction one for the other, of their constant search for blocs, and, finally, of the existence of these blocs at the various stages of their struggle against the Party, the Soviet state and Socialist construction?

The explanation, of course, lies above all in the common nature of the social base of the Trotskyites and the Rights. It lies in the fact that both the Trotskyites and the Rights reflect the pressure of the capitalist elements resisting the successes of Socialism, with no intention of departing peacefully and quietly from the historical stage.

The explanation lies, as we now know, in the fact that both were acting on the orders of the very same masters, installed in the General Staffs and intelligence services of foreign powers hostile to the U.S.S.R.

The Trotskyites and Bukharinites found their way into the camp of counter-revolution many years ago. Trotskyism and the Rights turned many years ago into the armour-bearers of bourgeois counter-revolution. For many years already the Trotskyites and Rights have been supplying the counter-revolutionary bourgeoisie with weapons for the struggle against the Soviet state. The Trotskyites and Rights have engaged in one and the same dark work of treachery.

These are the facts which now assume a new meaning in the light of the circumstances that have now been established, completely and with absolute authenticity, at the Court proceedings in the present case.

The facts establish with absolute incontrovertibility both the inevitable and natural character of the bloc concluded between the Rights and the Trotskyites and the degeneration of this bloc into an agency of foreign fascist intelligence services.

The way the Trotskyites and Zinovievites fought against Lenin, against Socialism, against the heroic efforts of the proletarian revolution to build a new Socialist society in the U.S.S.R. was shown with exhaustive completeness by the examples of Pyatakov, Zinoviev, Kamenev, Radek, Smirnov and others at the two preceding trials.

I would now like to remind you of certain facts which characterize from this angle the position and behaviour of some of the heroes of the present trial, and primarily of the accused Bukharin and Rykov.

As I have already said, Bukharin likes to picture himself as a "theoretician," aye, and a Marxist too, and of the most orthodox kind to boot. But the actual state of affairs may be seen from the following brief historical review of the anti-Party activity of Bukharin from 1909 to 1936 inclusive.

Here are several brief data.

The year 1909—Bukharin adhered to the position of "Otzovism."[7]

The years 1914-1917 (the period of the imperialist war)—Bukharin was a "Left Communist," rejected the minimum program, and waged a struggle against Lenin.

The year 1914—he was fussing about a plan for publishing his own paper, as against the Bolshevik press, the Leninist press.

The spring of 1915—Bukharin was a Trotskyite. At the Berne Conference he opposed the slogan of civil war, and advocated unity with the Trotskyite-Menshevik "Nashe Slovo." Lenin wrote the article "About the National Pride of the Great Russians," which Bukharin treated as a manifestation of social-patriotism.

The autumn of 1915—Bukharin came forward with theses rejecting the right of nations to self-determination.

February 1916—Bukharin endorsed the semi-anarchist program of the Dutch Left Social-Democrats.[8]

In 1916 Bukharin expressed anarchist, anti-Leninist views in the magazine "The Youth International" on the problem of the state, against the dictatorship of the proletariat.[9]

In an article entitled "World Economy and Imperialism"[10] (1915), Bukharin openly defended the Trotskyite thesis that isolated actions by the proletariat of individual countries could not result in victory. In other words, as Lenin stated, the Bukharins were postponing Socialism . . . "to the Greek Calends, i.e., forever." (Collected Works, Vol. XIX, p. 221.) Vladimir Ilyich wrote of him in 1916 that he—Bukharin—was "(1) credulous towards gossip and (2) devilishly *unstable* in politics." (Collected Works, Vol. XXIX, p. 229.)

"The war," wrote Lenin, "spurred him on to semi-anarchist ideas. At the Conference that adopted the Berne Resolutions (spring of 1915) he produced *theses* . . . the acme of absurdity; a disgrace; semi-anarchism."

In 1916, as I have already stated, Bukharin, in "The Youth International" magazine, developed anarcho-syndicalist ideas about the proletariat's hostility in principle to the state, the necessity to blow up any state whatsoever.

Subsequently, a year after the death of V. I. Lenin, Bukharin came forward with the brazen assertion that not he, Bukharin, had been wrong on this question, but Lenin.[11]

The years 1916-17—Bukharin, together with Trotsky, edited the Trotskyite paper "Novy Mir" in New York, in which he denied the possibility of the victory of Socialism in a single country.

The year 1917—at the Sixth Congress of the Party, Bukharin came forward with a Trotskyite scheme. During the October days he again and again advocated the idea of the impossibility of the victory of Socialism in Russia.

530

The year 1918—Bukharin was the leader of "Left Communism."
This episode has been most carefully examined at this trial.

On October 8, 1918, Bukharin made a statement at the Plenum
of the Moscow Soviet to the effect that his "Left Communism"
had been a mistake. "In my time I was against the Brest-Litovsk
Peace, but never advocated the disruption of peace, as the 'Left'
Socialist-Revolutionaries did. I now must make the honest and
open admission that we opponents of the Brest-Litovsk Peace were
wrong, while Lenin was right." We know—and Bukharin has had
to admit this at the trial—that in actual fact he carried on an
active struggle to disrupt the Brest-Litovsk Peace.

The year 1919—at the Eighth Congress of the Party, Bukharin
again opposed the recognition of the right of nations to self-
determination. [12]

Then followed the Ninth and Tenth Congresses of the Party,
where Bukharin invariably pursued his "own" line directed against
the Party, against Lenin, against Stalin.

In 1921, in the interests of Trotsky, Bukharin adopted the
position of buffer, [13] treacherously fanning the flame of the discussion, and, to use Lenin's expression, pouring "buffer oil" on it.

Bukharin joined Serebryakov, Radek, Krestinsky, Pyatakov
and other Trotskyites in the anti-Lenin faction.

At the end of 1920 and the beginning of 1921 there took place
the discussion on the trade unions. The country was preparing for
the transition to the New Economic Policy. Bukharin assumed the
role of "buffer," then passed over completely to Trotsky's position. And at the Tenth Congress he declared that "the Republic
hangs by a thread."

In 1923 Bukharin wrote an article in the "Pravda" entitled
"Down with Factionalism," in which he spoke of Trotsky's errors, and vaguely of those of "a number of other comrades," while
keeping silent regarding himself. [14]

In 1922 Lenin was battering Bukharin for his attempt to
disrupt the monopoly of foreign trade. Lenin bluntly exposed
Bukharin as a profiteer, a petty-bourgeois, as a defender of the interests of the kulak upper stratum of the peasantry, opposing the
industrial proletariat. (Collected Works, Vol. XXVII, p. 381.)

In 1923-24 Bukharin formed a bloc with Kamenev and Zinoviev against Comrade Stalin. On the eve of the discussion Bukharin published an article in which he propagated in a veiled form
the theory of the kulaks growing into Socialism.

The year 1925—Bukharin's kulak slogan of "enrich yourselves." [15]
True, in his booklet "Caesarism Behind the Mask of Revolution" and [16]
at the Fourteenth Party Congress, Bukharin admitted the erroneousness of this slogan, but here in Court Bukharin has admitted

that this "repentance" was nothing but a tactical manoeuvre, a fraud.

The year 1928—Bukharin declared at the Plenum of the Central Committee of the Party that he had no differences with the Party, and at the same time engaged in negotiations and reached a secret understanding with Kamenev. He wrote the "Notes of an Economist."[17]

The year 1929—Bukharin made a declaration in "Pravda" regarding the erroneousness of his views. "While admitting these errors of ours, we on our part will exert every effort to wage, together with the entire Party, a resolute struggle against all deviations."[18] Now in Court he has testified that this was also a tactical manoeuvre, that at that time, in 1929, he was also lying. For it was precisely at that time that there was taking shape the underground organization that began, with arms in hand, to oppose the Soviet power.

To avoid unfounded statements, I will remind you of the testimony of Bukharin, Rykov and finally Ivanov as to how Bukharin was fanning the struggle in the North Caucasus, how through his disciple and henchman in this affair, Slepkov, he organized kulak uprisings against the Soviet power, how he sent Yakovenko to Siberia, how they all succeeded in provoking a kulak uprising in the Biisk area and other places. I will remind you that at that very time Bukharin wrote to the press stating that "we will exert every effort to wage together with the entire Party a resolute struggle against all deviations." Bukharin lied here as well.

On December 15, 1929, Bukharin published an article in "Pravda" at the end of which he enumerated and condemned his errors. And at the same time he was conducting secret negotiations with Kamenev.

At the same time, as he has himself admitted here, he joined with Rykov in sending Slepkov to the North Caucasus and Yakovenko to Siberia to rouse kulak uprisings against the Soviet power. In Court Bukharin has admitted that it was they who at that time provoked such-and-such kulak uprisings.

And how did Bukharin behave then?

With the hypocritical mien of a Pharisee, and hiding behind a mask of sincerity, Bukharin began at the very outset of the struggle to engage in base intrigues, secret factional machinations against the Party and its leadership. He concluded a bloc with the worst enemies of Bolshevism, who have been exposed, who had but shortly before, in November 1927, undertaken a hostile demonstration against the Soviet power in the streets of Moscow and Leningrad.[19]

In 1930 Bukharin again handed in a declaration to the Central Committee and admitted his errors. Bukharin wrote about his "unreserved condemnation of every attempt against the unity of the Party, all factional activity, all attempts at surreptitious struggle against the Party leadership, surreptitious defence of another political line differing from that of the Party." But in actual fact, as you have heard from Bukharin's testimony, it was precisely at this moment that he was engaged in negotiations with Semyonov regarding the organization of a terrorist act against the leaders of our Party and government.

In January 1933 Bukharin made a speech at the Joint Plenum of the Central Committee and the Central Control Commission of the C.P.S.U. (Bolsheviks) (see "Pravda," No. 14), in which he demanded "severe punishment of A. P. Smirnov's grouping," spoke of his own "Right opportunist, absolutely wrong general political line," of his "guilt before the Party, its leadership, before the Central Committee of the Party, before the working class and the country," spoke of Tomsky and Rykov as of his "former companions in the leadership of the Right opposition." In general he "criticized" his "former" views.

In actual fact, however, this was the first year of the formation of the "bloc of Rights and Trotskyites," which proceeded to fulfil such tasks as terrorism, espionage, diversion, wrecking, and high treason, the wresting of the national republics from the U.S.S.R.

The beginning of 1934. The Seventeenth Party Congress—Bukharin's speech in which he approved of the "ruthless crushing of all oppositions and of the Right opposition as the main danger, i.e., of the very group to which I once belonged."

And at the same time he was mobilizing all forces in order to intensify the criminal activity of his group, which had already degenerated into a group of genuine spies, murderers, and intelligence service agents.

The beginning of 1936—in an article in the "Izvestia" Bukharin dubbed the Russian people a "nation of Oblomovs." In the issue of the "Izvestia" dated February 14, 1936, Bukharin declared that this assertion of his was erroneous. ("The assertion is wrong," and "I express my profound regret" at this.) [20]

Such is Bukharin, this hypocritical, false, wily creature; this piously rapacious and respectfully malicious person, this "damnable cross of a fox and a swine," to use Maxim Gorky's words about one of the heroes from the gallery of "Those Who Once Were People."

Neither are the others—also "heroes"—any better.

Take the accused Rykov.

Prior to joining the Bolshevik Party, Rykov was a member of the united Party of Socialist-Revolutionaries and Social-Democrats in Saratov.

The years 1909-11—Rykov was a semi-Trotskyite, a semi-Liquidator. In the period of the April Conference, Rykov and Kamenev advocated the unification of the "live forces" of revolutionary democracy, i.e., an alliance with the Socialist-Revolutionaries and Mensheviks.

In October 1917 Rykov, together with Kamenev and Zinoviev, turned deserter.

In December 1917 Rykov croaked about the instability of the Soviet power and declared that "a purely Bolshevik government cannot maintain itself in a backward country while the Socialist revolution has not taken place in Europe."

In 1920 Rykov joined the Sapronovites in opposing Lenin, and in defending collegiate responsibility. [21]

Rykov was against Lenin's GOELRO plan, [22] he sank with his head in philistine "realism," sank to the ears in routine (as Comrade Stalin wrote at the time about him to V. I. Lenin).

And later? Later there was 1928, 1929, 1932—blocs, centres, plots, betrayals.

The other accused are no better.

Here we have the old Trotskyite and German spy Krestinsky, who began his career of treason while Vladimir Ilyich Lenin was still alive. Krestinsky passed on espionage information to the German intelligence service and annually received 250,000 gold marks from the German Reichswehr for the underground work of the Trotskyites.

Here we have an equally inveterate Trotskyite, Rosengoltz, who became a German spy in 1923 and a British spy in 1926.

These are the people who, together with Trotsky, Pyatakov, Yagoda, Bukharin and Rykov, were the chief ringleaders of this bloc, this "centre of centres" of all the anti-Soviet fascist forces in our country.

I consider it necessary to deal briefly with the investigation that took place here of the circumstances of the plot against Vladimir Ilyich Lenin in 1918.

Both at the preliminary investigation and in Court Bukharin was doing everything to wriggle out of the events of 1918, to evade his responsibility before history, before the working class, before all honest mankind for the monstrous crime organized and partly committed by Bukharin, together with the "Left" and Right Socialist-Revolutionaries, together with Trotsky and his group. Bukharin lied disgracefully in October 1918, when he disowned the "Left Communists." Bukharin lied disgracefully in 1924 as well, when under the pressure of circumstances he raised a tiny corner of the curtain that concealed from us the real truth about this heinous and ghastly crime.

Bukharin lied, for example, in 1924 when he denied the existence of a bloc between himself and the "Left" Socialist-Revolutionaries in 1918.

Bukharin does not tell the truth here, in Court, either when he tries to deny facts that have been corroborated here by a number of witnesses.

Yet these facts are extremely important both for finally exposing the treacherous countenance of Bukharin and for the most complete and correct understanding of all the subsequent criminal activities of Bukharin and his accomplices, the ·Bukharinites.

One must recall the facts, the situation and the conditions of the year 1918 in order properly to evaluate the entire profundity of the fiendish crime of Trotsky and Bukharin against the Revolution, the entire abyss of their treachery! . . .

These facts, Comrades Judges, are now, of course, to a considerable extent a matter of history. But they throw full light on the question that interests us, that interests many, and particularly those who are not yet versed in Bukharin's past and in the past of the anti-Soviet groups, namely, how could it happen that Bukharin and Rykov, who for so many years posed as adherents of Socialism, as adherents of the Socialist struggle, proved to belong to the camp of the most inveterate enemies of the Soviet power, to the camp of traitors to and betrayers of the revolution, of the Soviet people and the fatherland.

In the light of the present trial, these facts, already covered with the dust of archives, again revive and begin to speak in the loud voice of an impeacher demanding that the culprits be called to account, if not before a criminal Court restricted by the Statutes of limitation, then, at any rate, before the tribunal of history which knows of no Statutes of limitation, which knows no mercy.

The year 1918—the young Soviet Republic was exerting its entire strength to overcome the gigantic difficulties that had arisen in its path toward the assertion and consolidation of the victory of the Socialist revolution.

In those days the country was literally thrown into dust. It had to be raised to the level of new, supreme historic tasks previously unknown by any revolution of working people.

"From the period of triumphal processions," said V. I. Lenin on this subject, "we had to pass to the period of an extraordinarily difficult and severe position, which could not be brushed aside with words, with brilliant slogans—however pleasant that would have been—because in our disturbed country we had incredibly weary masses who had reached a state in which they could not possibly go on fighting; they had been so utterly broken up by three years of agonizing war that they were rendered utterly useless from a military point of view." (Collected Works, Vol. XXII, p. 318.)

In these conditions the struggle for peace was a struggle for the entire future of the proletarian revolution, the fate of which was literally at stake.

In these conditions the question of war or peace in essence amounted to the one question of whether the Soviet power, the Soviet state, the Land of Soviets, was to be or not to be.

Lenin's brilliant strategy gave a positive solution of this problem. History confirmed the correctness of this solution. It declared: "To be."

Leninism teaches not only the art of advance, but also the art of retreat.

". . . One cannot win," Lenin wrote, "without having learned both how to attack and how to retreat correctly." (Collected Works, Vol. XXV, p. 177.)

Comrade Stalin said in this connection:

"The object of this strategy is to gain time, to disintegrate the enemy and to accumulate forces in order to assume the offensive later.

"The signing of the Brest-Litovsk Peace may be taken as a model of this strategy, for it enabled the Party to gain time, to make use of the conflicts in the camp of the imperialists, to disintegrate the forces of the enemy, to retain the support of the peasantry and accumulate forces in preparation for the attacks upon Kolchak and Denikin." ("Problems of Leninism," pp. 56-57.)

This strategy, the brilliant strategy of Lenin and Stalin, was completely justified. It saved the new Russia and the Soviet power from inevitable doom.

In 1924, Comrade Stalin in this connection reminded us:

" 'Now even the biggest fool,' said Lenin three years after the Brest-Litovsk Peace, 'sees that the "Brest Peace" was a concession that strengthened us and broke up the forces of international imperialism.' " ("Problems of Leninism," p. 57.)

It is well known that Trotsky and Bukharin, along with their adherents, did everything possible to disrupt the Brest-Litovsk Peace.

Trotsky and the "Left" Socialist-Revolutionaries behaved like agents-provocateurs during the negotiations with General Hoffmann. The "Left Communists," headed by Bukharin, raved about the peace policy of the Soviet government, at the head of which stood Lenin, Stalin and Sverdlov, and demanded that negotiations be broken off and that a "revolutionary war" be declared.

536

By their trenchant but at bottom provocateur speeches and slogans, the Bukharinites and Trotskyites tried to divert our Party from the Leninist path.

"'Neither peace nor war!' 'A holy war against the world bourgeoisie!'—such and similar provocateur slogans were issued by the Trotskys, Bukharins and their like,'' as Comrade Voroshilov said in his speech on the occasion of the twentieth anniversary of the Workers' and Peasants' Red Army and Navy, "with the sole purpose of involving our country in an armed conflict with the imperialists at a moment when the Soviet government still did not possess a strong army, and in this way putting an end to the Soviet power and clearing the way for the victory of the bourgeoisie and the complete restoration of capitalism in our country.''

Till now the Bukharinites succeeded in concealing from history the truth regarding this point as well.

Even at the preliminary investigation, in testimony given on June 2, 1937, Bukharin attempted to conceal the real character of his struggle during the period of the Brest-Litovsk Peace against Lenin as the head of the Soviet state.

Bukharin tried to evade this question and, as usual with him, confined himself to general abstract utterances to the effect that he allegedly "did not understand" that "the most concrete of the most concrete questions about the 'moujik' was precisely the question of giving the masses a 'breathing space,' and had substituted for the vital needs of the moment his general literary effusions about the proletarian fatherland having to be defended.''

Bukharin's trick did not succeed. The investigating authorities did not fall into this trap. On the contrary, the investigation exposed Bukharin, and exposed him of much more serious things than any "general literary effusions.''

The investigation established, and I deem it necessary to remind you of this here in its full scope, Comrades Judges, that in 1918, immediately following the October Revolution, in the period of the conclusion of the Brest-Litovsk Peace, Bukharin and his group of so-called "Left Communists," and Trotsky with his group, together with the "Left" Socialist-Revolutionaries organized a conspiracy against Lenin as the head of the Soviet government.

Bukharin and the other conspirators, as can be seen from the materials of the investigation, aimed at frustrating the Brest-Litovsk Peace, overthrowing the Soviet government, arresting and killing Lenin, Stalin and Sverdlov, and forming a new government made up of Bukharinites, who then for purposes of camouflage called themselves "Left Communists," and of Trotskyites and "Left" Socialist-Revolutionaries.

537

During the preliminary investigation, Bukharin was confronted with facts, was brought face to face with five people. And it was then that the accused Bukharin recalled something more serious than "general literary effusions." Bukharin, for example, recalled such a fact as the bloc with the "Left" Socialist-Revolutionaries in 1918, with the aim of struggle against the Soviet government; such a fact as a direct plot against the Soviet government, as preparations for the arrest of Lenin, for the arrest of Stalin and of Sverdlov.

All of this, as you recall, was admitted by Bukharin. But he did so grudgingly.

We remember the witnesses who gave evidence before the Court, we well remember their evidence, we saw them, we heard them. We remember how their words fell like heavy lead on the head of Bukharin, the inspirer of the provocateur struggle against Lenin's Council of People's Commissars—Bukharin, who, as has been fully and clearly established by the Court investigation, had been the organizer of a plot and insurrection against the Soviet state—the instigator of the assassination of the leaders of the Soviet government, Comrades Lenin, Stalin and Sverdlov.

I have every ground for saying—and I base myself upon these facts—that all of this has been exactly ascertained, established with sufficient precision, and sufficiently proved.

Permit me to dwell briefly on the evidence that confirms the correctness of this conclusion. You recall the testimony given here by Kamkov. Kamkov was one of the foremost leaders of the Central Committee of the Party of "Left" Socialist-Revolutionaries. Kamkov testified that he had a conversation with Bukharin in 1918 on the question of the Brest-Litovsk Peace, that the struggle on this question, in Bukharin's words, was assuming extremely acute forms. Bukharin told Kamkov of the acute forms of this struggle, of the fact that among the "Left Communists" the question was being debated about the establishment of a new government. In this connection, said Kamkov, Bukharin mentioned Pyatakov as a possible candidate for head of the new government, and stated that the change of government was proposed to be effected by the arrest of the entire Soviet government, headed by Lenin.

Bukharin did not deny this. True, he said something here about arrest for "twenty-four hours." But this is not a serious statement. As far back as in 1924, Bukharin, writing in the "Pravda," himself explained how real and serious was this plan to arrest Vladimir Ilyich Lenin. But Bukharin disclaims the plan to murder our leaders.

What proofs did he produce to justify himself on this

question? Nothing, except bare denial. He was exposed here by Yakovleva, he was exposed by Ossinsky, he was exposed by Mantsev, he was exposed by Karelin in the corresponding and most essential part of the question, he was also exposed by Kamkov, because, as you remember, Bukharin tried to present even the question of the arrest in such a manner as if the initiative came not from him, but from Kamkov, from the "Left" Socialist-Revolutionaries. Kamkov testified here that the initiative came from Bukharin. I am inclined however to reconcile them, for the initiative apparently came from both of them. This explains the furious struggle carried on by these people against the Soviet government, against Lenin and against his companions— Comrades Stalin and Sverdlov.

Bukharin denies this. But one cannot really accept an absolutely unfounded denial as a proof, all the more since this denial runs contrary to the very logic of things.

Had this fact—the plan to kill Lenin, Stalin and Sverdlov— not existed, then why did Karelin, Yakovleva, Ossinsky, Mantsev find it necessary to speak of this—people for whom the admission of such a shameful and such a terrible fact, such a monstrous crime against our country, is now of no advantage. Yet, according to Karelin's testimony, Bukharin spoke bluntly about the physical destruction of Lenin and Stalin. Yakovleva also says:

"Bukharin expressed to me the idea that the political struggle was assuming ever more acute forms and that matters could not be confined to the mere political formulation of lack of confidence in the Central Committee of the Party. Bukharin declared that a change of leadership was inevitable, and that in this connection the question stood of arresting Lenin, Stalin and Sverdlov, and even of their physical destruction." (Vol. XLIV, p. 77.)

This was also confirmed by Ossinsky, confirmed by Mantsev.

Bukharin was not alone. His viewpoint was shared, as has now been established, by Trotsky as well, about whose role in the plot against V. I. Lenin in 1918 we now have a series of testimonies at this trial, including the testimony of Bukharin himself.

"At that time," testified the accused Bukharin, "the idea again arose of a coup and the arrest of Lenin, Stalin and Sverdlov as the dominant figures in the Party and Soviet leadership. This time it arose on the initiative of Trotsky, to whom the proposal of the 'Left' Socialist-Revolutionaries apparently became known—through Pyatakov, I presume." (Vol. V, p. 124.)

Bukharin does not tell the whole story, and remains true to his tactics of half-admissions.

But there are two witnesses, Yakovleva and Mantsev, who on this question as well speak with such precision as allows of no doubts as to the fairness and correctness of their testimony.

Are not these facts sufficient to permit one to say that the conspiracy of the Bukharinites, Trotskyites and "Left" Socialist-Revolutionaries in 1918 against Lenin, Stalin and Sverdlov has been proved to the hilt?

Bukharin himself has admitted the existence of this conspiracy; Bukharin himself has admitted the existence of a plan to arrest Lenin, Stalin and Sverdlov. Bukharin only repudiates the plan to murder Lenin, Stalin and Sverdlov.

However, the accused Bukharin's first admission regarding the plan for a coup, the plan for the arrest, essentially speaking, confirms also what follows. Indeed, Bukharin admitted that together with his group of "Left Communists," together with Trotsky and his group, and together with the "Left" Socialist-Revolutionaries, they sought to bring about the forcible overthrow of the Soviet government, headed by Lenin, Stalin and Sverdlov, and even the arrest of Lenin, Stalin and Sverdlov.

But does Bukharin know what forcible overthrow means? Does Bukharin know the meaning of arrests connected with the task of forcible overthrow? Does Bukharin know that people embarking on a forcible overthrow and violent arrests are thereby embarking upon violence, are thereby embarking upon murder as well?

Forcible overthrow presupposes, and does not exclude, such a form of violence as physical extermination. Bukharin admits forcible overthrow, but denies physical extermination. This is an obvious falsity, an obvious absurdity; it is obviously illogical. But Bukharin is in a position where one cannot demand logic of him.

The facts established in Court speak more authoritatively and more convincingly than Bukharin imagines or desires. Bukharin, it is true, has now said somewhat more than, for example, in 1924, but nevertheless he has not said everything. This is not the first time Bukharin acts in this way. In 1924, Bukharin told something about this shameful crime, but only something.

In 1938, Bukharin, forced to the wall, was obliged to tell more about this fact. If we want to estimate the degree of falsity, jesuitry and hypocrisy of Bukharin, we have only to compare the text of the letter he published in the newspaper "Pravda" in 1924 with what he said during the preliminary investigation. He concealed a number of facts in this letter, he did not say that there had been a plot, he did not say that there had been a direct understanding between his group and Trotsky, he said nothing about the murder of Lenin, nor yet about the murder of Stalin and Sverdlov. This has now been brought to light. This has now been exposed, it has been divulged, it has been established; the whole world has been informed of it, despite Bukharin's wishes, despite all his resistance to the establishment of this fact. Bukharin admitted—and even so, as you saw during the trial, only half admitted it and only because there was no way of escaping it—that in 1918 he had proclaimed that the Soviet power was a mere formality and had proposed that it should be liquidated.

Lenin exposed the monstrosity of this "thesis" of Bukharin's, pointing out among others the historical examples of France in 1793 and of Prussia in the beginning of the nineteenth century, when the finest people of these countries, in the dark hours through which their fatherland was passing, did not give way to despair, but

". . . signed peace treaties immeasurably more onerous, bestial, shameful and oppressive than the Treaty of Brest-Litovsk; and then were able to endure, staunchly bore the yoke of the conqueror, again fought, again fell beneath the yoke of the conqueror, again signed indecent and most indecent peace treaties, again rose and finally emancipated themselves (not without utilizing the differences between the strongest of the competing conquerors)." (Lenin, Collected Works, Vol. XXII, p. 302.)

But these were the finest people of their country, and not traitors and provocateurs, which the so-called "Left Communists" and their friends from the underground actually proved to be.

But for this it was necessary, as Lenin taught, to love one's country, one's people, and not vilify them, as Bukharin and his henchmen do, rising against Lenin, who bade us love and respect our people.

The trial has established the fact that in 1918 Bukharin and Trotsky concluded a bloc with the Socialist-Revolutionaries for the purpose of waging a joint struggle against the Soviet government, which was then headed by Lenin, Stalin and Sverdlov, that they plotted an armed uprising and that they were prepared to arrest and murder Lenin, Stalin and Sverdlov.

Has this been proved, or not?

It has been proved completely. It has been proved by the testimony of Bukharin himself and by the evidence of Yakovleva and Karelin, Kamkov, Mantsev and Ossinsky.

Bukharin denies the preparations for assassination. But how does he deny them? Comrades Judges, I would request you, in your conference chamber, to examine the records of the appropriate session of our trial in order to recall with complete clarity the method which Bukharin employed to deny this fact.

Here is the dialogue. Bukharin admits that he was one of the organizers of this plot.

He is asked: "Did you speak openly of the arrest of Lenin, Stalin and Sverdlov?"

"BUKHARIN: There was talk of arrest, but not of physical extermination. This was not in the period prior to the Brest-Litovsk Peace, but after. . . . At that time I had one conversation with Pyatakov, when Karelin and Kamkov came and said that they proposed to set up a new government. . . .

"*Question*: When was that?

"BUKHARIN: It was before the Brest-Litovsk Peace. They proposed to form a government by arresting Lenin for twenty-four hours.

"*Question*: And so we may say that prior to the conclusion of the Peace of Brest-Litovsk you had a conversation with the 'Left' Socialist-Revolutionaries, Karelin and Kamkov, about the formation of a new government, that is, by first overthrowing the government headed by Lenin? Was there such a conversation?

"BUKHARIN: There was.

"*Question*: About the arrest of Lenin?

"BUKHARIN: The Socialist-Revolutionaries spoke of that.

"*Question*: As you put it, the Socialist-Revolutionaries spoke about the arrest of Lenin; but the witness Yakovleva affirms that Bukharin too spoke about the arrest of Lenin.

"BUKHARIN: She is mixing it up with another question. She asserts that the conversation took place before the conclusion of the Brest-Litovsk Peace.

"*Question*: I ask you, were there before the conclusion of the Brest-Litovsk Peace negotiations with the Socialist-Revolutionaries about the arrest of Lenin?

"BUKHARIN: Yes."

And so, at first it was the Socialist-Revolutionaries who said this, and then Bukharin testifies that there was such a conversation, and that it was he who conducted it.

"*Quesion*: And were there also negotiations after the conclusion of the Brest-Litovsk Peace?

"BUKHARIN: There were.

"*Question*: What about?

"BUKHARIN: About political contact.

"*Question*: And about arrest?

"BUKHARIN: And about the arrest.

"*Question*: Of whom exactly?

"BUKHARIN: Of Lenin, Stalin and Sverdlov.

"*Question*: Also for twenty-four hours?

"BUKHARIN: This formula was not employed then."

As you see, before it was for twenty-four hours, but now it

is not for twenty-four hours. Then only Lenin was mentioned, but now it turns out that Lenin, Stalin and Sverdlov are mentioned.

"*Question*: And how were they to be arrested? And what for?

"BUKHARIN: In order to form a new government.

"*Question*: And what was to be done with the arrested?" Bukharin hastened to say: "There was no talk of physical extermination." But I had not asked him that yet.

"*Question*: When a government is overthrown and arrested, are not forcible methods resorted to?

"BUKHARIN: Yes.

"*Question*: Did you envisage adopting forcible methods when making the arrest? Is this true or not?

"BUKHARIN: It is.

"*Question*: But what do forcible methods involve? Did you determine that precisely?

"BUKHARIN: No, we did not.

"*Question*: And so you decided to act as circumstances permitted and dictated?

"BUKHARIN: Just so.

"*Question*: But circumstances might dictate very decisive action?

"BUKHARIN: Yes."

The conclusion is a simple one: it was proposed to overthrow the government, for this purpose to arrest the government—Lenin, Stalin and Sverdlov—and to adopt all measures that might be dictated by circumstances and by the conditions of the struggle that was being waged for the purpose of overthrowing the government. The struggle was of a most acute kind, and while there was no talk of assassination—if we assume that what Bukharin says is true—why, the very fact, the very aim of overthrowing the government, the very necessity of arresting the leaders of the government which the conspirators had made it their aim to overthrow, quite naturally shows that they could not have repudiated and renounced the assassination of the leaders, the proposed assassination.

The whole logic of events, the whole meaning of this struggle, the whole ferocity of the atmosphere in which this struggle was waged, the whole acuteness of the question itself—whether there should be a Brest-Litovsk Peace, that is, whether there should be a Soviet country, a country building a Socialist society, or whether there should not be a Brest-Litovsk Peace, whether there should not be a Soviet land, which they, considering it a "formality," proposed to surrender to the tender mercies of the enemy— all this indicates in the most serious manner that it was a question of a real struggle, which in all such cases is associated with the

543

inevitability of measures which lead to death, to assassination. That is why I say that to me, not from the standpoint of criminology—for today, twenty years after this crime, we are not bringing any independent charge against Bukharin—this is important because it enables us to form a judgment of the connection which exists between the conspiratorial activities of the assassin and counter-revolutionary Bukharin and his accomplices, and what they have been doing subsequently. All this is of importance in showing that on a question of historical interest and significance, Bukharin even to this day is unable and unwilling to confess all the crimes which he in reality committed against the Soviet country, against the Soviet power and against the Soviet people.

Bukharin wrote on this subject in 1924:

"I consider it my Party duty to tell about the proposal made by the 'Left' Socialist-Revolutionaries at a moment of bitter factional struggle so as to paralyse that idyllic varnishing of the events of the Brest period which has been practised by the comrades of the opposition. ..."

He is referring to the arrest of Lenin and the overthrow of the Soviet power. Thus, in 1924 Bukharin admitted that it was a moment of bitter struggle.

And further:

"They depicted the Brest period in the Party as 'the height of democracy.' I know very well that this was a period when the Party was within a hair's breadth of a split, and when the whole country was within a hair's breadth of its doom."

At such a time, a time of bitter struggle, could people who were prepared to arrest Lenin, to arrest Stalin and Sverdlov, the leaders of our Party and of our government, could such people have stopped short at the prospect of annihilating their opponents, of murdering our leaders? That is absolutely incongruous, it is absolutely inconceivable. This is the policy of not telling the whole truth, an attempt, it seems to me, which has been completely exposed here by the evidence of witnesses and by the very logic of the historical events that were unfolding at that time.

The monstrous crime that was committed on August 30, 1918, has now also been completely revealed. I am referring to the attempt made on the life of Vladimir Ilyich Lenin on August 30, 1918, by the Socialist-Revolutionary terrorist Kaplan. The evidence of Karelin and Ossinsky enables us to judge how this attempt was in reality organized. Karelin declared here that for twenty years every effort was made to keep this terrible crime secret, not to reveal its real and genuine meaning and significance. Karelin has affirmed here that the question of a terrorist attempt on the life of Lenin was raised in 1918 by no other than Bukharin himself.

Karelin has affirmed that Proshyan reported on the subject to members of the Central Committee of the Party of "Left" Socialist-Revolutionaries. Karelin has affirmed that "a demand of this kind from the 'Left Communists' made by Bukharin, their ringleader, played an important part in expediting the terrorist act committed against Lenin by the Central Committee of the Right Socialist-Revolutionaries." This monstrous crime is a fact.

Ossinsky, on the authority of Stukov, has testified that the latter was of the same opinion and had the same idea of the crime of August 30, 1918.

"At the end of 1918," Ossinsky has testified here, "Stukov, who together with Bukharin was connected with the Socialist-Revolutionaries, told me that the shot fired at Lenin by the Right Socialist-Revolutionary Fanny Kaplan was the result not only of the instructions of the leadership of the Right Socialist-Revolutionaries, but also of measures that had been outlined by the bloc of 'Left Communists' with the Socialist-Revolutionaries aiming at the physical extermination of Lenin, Stalin and Sverdlov." (Vol. XLIV, p. 89.)

This evidence is a sufficiently convincing testimony of the vile, treacherous and diabolical work performed by Bukharin, that chartered hypocrite and jesuit.

To conclude my appraisal of the conduct of Bukharin and of Bukharin himself, it must be said that the hypocrisy and perfidy of this man exceed the most perfidious and monstrous crimes known to the history of mankind.

He has completely exposed himself in this Court.

We have followed the political life of Bukharin step by step, year by year.

How many times has Bukharin sworn by the name of Lenin, only the better to deceive and betray the Party, the country and the cause of Socialism right afterwards!

How many times has Bukharin kissed the great teacher with the kiss of Judas the traitor!

Bukharin reminds us of Vasily Shuisky[23] and Judas Iscariot, who betrayed with a kiss.

And the manners of Nikolai Ivanovich Bukharin are just like the manners of Vasily Ivanovich Shuisky, as depicted by the famous writer Ostrovsky:

> "Vasily, love, Ivanich,
> Whatever he does is holy!
> When clearly preparing for knavery,
> Or patently planning some roguery,
> See how he sighs and piously smirks,
> And says 'Tis a sacred cause, brethren!' ...''

And so with Bukharin—he organizes wrecking and diversive

acts, espionage and murder, but his look is meek and mild, almost saintly, and it is as though you hear from the mouth of Nikolai Ivanovich the meek voice of Vasily Ivanovich Shuisky, "'Tis a sacred cause, brethren!'"

Here is the acme of monstrous hypocrisy, perfidy, jesuitry and inhuman villainy.

The trial has exposed and proved absolutely definitely the fact that the "bloc of Rights and Trotskyites" represented a veritable agency of the intelligence services of certain foreign states, which through this bloc, through this conspiratorial group, were effecting espionage, wrecking and diversive acts, terrorism, the undermining of the military power of the U.S.S.R., that this "bloc of Rights and Trotskyites" attemped to provoke armed attack of these states on the U.S.S.R., with the aim of overthrowing the Socialist system existing in the U.S.S.R., restoring capitalism and the power of the bourgeoisie in the U.S.S.R., dismembering the U.S.S.R. and severing from it the Ukraine, Byelorussia, the Central Asiatic Republics, Georgia, Armenia, Azerbaijan and the Maritime Region for the benefit of the states mentioned.

It has been established at this trial that the real masters of this bloc were Trotsky and the foreign intelligence services, that all its criminal activities were carried on under the immediate direction and in accordance with plans drawn up by the General Staffs of Japan, Germany and Poland.

Take the testimony of Chernov. Chernov forms connections with the police, or, through a police official in Berlin, with Oberhaus. Oberhaus, Chernov says, told him that the German intelligence service was taking proper measures for the overthrow of the Soviet power. And he further said to Chernov: "Well, you regard yourself as the opposition in the Soviet Union, you should unite to form an organizing force. If you want to seize power, you must not be squeamish about methods of struggle." Speaking of methods of struggle, Oberhaus proposed that closer connections be formed between the Rights and the German intelligence service. He said that the whole organization of the Rights could be made to serve the ends of the German intelligence service.

When asked here in Court who his masters were, Chernov replied: "None except Rykov and the German intelligence service." Is it not clear that the organization of this so-called "bloc of Rights and Trotskyites" was nothing but an espionage agency of the intelligence services of certain foreign states?

The accused Sharangovich has fully confirmed here his connection with the Polish General Staff. He confirmed that, as the head of the local Byelorussian bourgeois-nationalist underground organization, he set himself the task of serving the interests of the Polish intelligence service and the Polish General Staff. He said that he had received a proposal on behalf of a certain consul that he should establish close connections with a number of persons belonging to the leadership of the national-fascist organization in Byelorussia, including Benek. He said that he was told to transmit various kinds of information required by the Polish intelligence service; he was instructed to form such close connections with the Polish General Staff that the latter, in its work against the Soviet state, might be able to rely upon this contemptible gang of traitors of the Byelorussian national-fascist organization.

What were the chief aims of this organization? Sharangovich has himself formulated them briefly: the overthrow of the Soviet power, the restoration of capitalism, and the severance of Byelorussia from the Soviet Union in the event of a war with fascist states. He said that the necessity was stressed of establishing close connections with the Polish General Staff for the achievement of this goal. This was one of the chief aims pursued by the bourgeois-nationalist organization in Byelorussia in accordance with the instructions of the centre of the "bloc of Rights and Trotskyites." Who needed this? This was needed by the Polish intelligence service, this was needed by the Polish General Staff, which reckoned that in case of need its success would be ensured by this small but dangerous Fifth Column being at its disposal on the territory of the U.S.S.R.

That is why Rykov was quite right when he said here that the Byelorussian organization of the Rights was virtually an espionage agency of the Polish General Staff. Rykov told us that he was aware that Karakhan had conducted negotiations with the German fascists as early as 1933; that the German fascists, as the accused Rykov expressed it here, were quite favourable to the prospect of the accession to power of the Rights, and promised to welcome and support their accession to power in every way.

The favourable attitude of the German intelligence service was of course dictated exclusively by its own interests: the Rights and their organization, after all, were a fascist agency. Having a group of traitors at their disposal, and relying on them, German fascism could at a lesser cost accomplish its villainous plan of military intervention in the U.S.S.R. And what were the aims? The aims were not only those which Sharangovich mentioned. Rykov very clearly indicated another highly characteristic feature which thoroughly exposes the "bloc of Rights and Trotskyites" as an agency of certain foreign intelligence services. Questioned on the subject of the dismemberment of the U.S.S.R., the severance of a number of republics from the U.S.S.R., and asked, "Was there also the aim of preparing a base for the fascists, for their attack upon the U.S.S.R. and for their victory?"—Rykov replied: "Yes, that is unquestionably so."

It is quite obvious that the aim of preparing a base for an attack upon the U.S.S.R. and of ensuring victory over the U.S.S.R. in the event of such an attack was set by the German, Polish and other intelligence services to the "bloc of Rights and Trotskyites" as to a direct agency of the fascist intelligence services. It shows that Chernov was right when he said that, apart from Trotsky, the real masters of the "bloc of Rights and Trotskyites" were indeed the intelligence services of certain foreign states.

Lastly, we recall the testimony of Krestinsky. Like a mouse in a trap, he during the trial scurried hither and thither, trying to find a possible way of escape, but in vain. Krestinsky admitted that as far back as 1920-21, on instructions from Trotsky, he, Krestinsky, together with other Trotskyites, conducted negotiations with General Seeckt and with the German Reichswehr, and that for 250,000 gold marks per annum he sold espionage information to the German General Staff and ensured the unhampered admission of German military spies into the U.S.S.R.

What then was the intention, if not to transform the U.S.S.R. into a colony of German fascism? The essence of this agreement with the Reichswehr, the threads of which led to the treason and treachery of the so-called "bloc of Rights and Trotskyites," was exposed by Krestinsky himself. Permit me to recall it briefly.

"We were receiving," he said, "a small sum of money and they were receiving espionage information which they would need during an armed attack. But the German government," Krestinsky goes on to say edifyingly, thus revealing his own cards, "Hitler particularly, wanted colonies, territory, and not only espionage information. And he" (that is, Hitler) "was prepared to be satisfied with Soviet territory instead of the colonies for which he would have to fight England, America and France."

Here you have the nakedly cynical attitude, reaching the very limit of human vileness, which quite definitely shows how certain intelligence services, including the German, and certain of the most reactionary, principally military, circles of certain foreign states regarded the activities of this so-called "bloc of Rights and Trotskyites." They looked upon them as their slaves and captives. They regarded them as masters regard their servants. They sought the aid of these traitors because these traitors held the keys, at least in their own imagination and partly by taking advantage of their official positions, to the gates of our frontiers. They were fitted for the purpose of opening the gates to the enemy. Although twisting and squirming and trying to cover up his tracks, the accused Bukharin cynically admitted this in the end. In a conversation with Rykov and Tomsky, Bukharin said that the front must be opened to the Germans. The question is as clear as clear can be. Marked though they are, the cards have been completely uncovered. They said: "We will not only supply you with secret information, but at the right moment we will open the front. In return, pay us money, with which we will conduct our criminal, underground Trotskyite activities. Why should you fight England, America and France for colonies? You can transform the U.S.S.R. into your colony—at least its flourishing border republics, such as the Ukraine. Why should you fight America, England and France for colonies, when we, your obedient servants, are prepared to sell Soviet land to you for those gold marks by which you would help us to carry on our underground work?"

That is the meaning of this agreement.

Does the existence of such an agreement indicate that the "bloc of Rights and Trotskyites" was a political group of any kind? No. The "bloc of Rights and Trotskyites" is not only a gang of wreckers, diversionists, assassins and spies, without any ideology or principles; it is a mere gang of agents of foreign intelligence services in the real meaning of the word. They open the gates to the enemy, fire on the streets from secret loopholes, assist the enemy who has invaded town and village, and help to bring about the defeat of their country.

Krestinsky said: "We were prepared to restore capitalist relations in the U.S.S.R. and to make territorial concessions to the bourgeois states with which we had already come to an agreement."

And this, actually speaking, is the whole meaning of the criminal activities of the bloc.

Grinko does not fall short of Krestinsky in the cynicism of his testimony. Grinko bluntly stated that the task set them by their masters, the foreign intelligence services, was chiefly to aid the foreign aggressors. This, Grinko said here, was the common position of the Trotskyites, the Rights, the bourgeois-nationalist organizations, and, in particular, the Ukrainian national-fascist organization.

This meant undermining the power of defence of the Soviet Union, sabotage in the army and in the defence industry, opening the front in case of war and provoking this war.

An honourable task, say what you like!

The very enumeration of these criminal aims thoroughly exposes this bloc as a sheer gang of spying and intelligence organizations of certain foreign states.

Ikramov has told us here how the ringleaders of the "bloc of Rights and Trotskyites," and in the first place Bukharin, persuaded him to do everything he could to become a real agent of foreign intelligence services.

549

The Moscow ringleaders of the "bloc of Rights and Trotskyites" informed Ikramov of the Japanese-German "orientation," as they called it, of their connections with the Germans and Japanese. For what purpose? For the very purpose that was so clearly depicted by both Grinko and Krestinsky.

The second meeting was devoted to a discussion of wrecking activities. The third meeting was devoted to the question of connections with England. The accused Khodjayev spoke about this here very circumstantially and fully.

What did Bukharin tell him? He told him that they must orientate themselves on England, that if war did not break out at once, if intervention did not take place soon, it was all up with them. Bukharin said to Ikramov: "They will bag us all, yet we cannot expedite war because of England, which in certain respects is an international arbiter."

This idea of the conspirators, who placed all their hopes in an armed attack on the U.S.S.R., that England was a sort of international arbiter is interesting. It is well known, Bukharin said, that the British have long had their eyes on Turkestan as a choice morsel. If such offers are made, the British perhaps will sooner come over to the side of an aggressor against the Soviet Union.

Actually speaking, Bukharin did not deny this conversation here. He spoke about certain details, argued over certain words, said that it had been formulated differently, but in the main Bukharin confirmed that there had been such talk, that there was an "orientation on the British arbiter," who was prepared to receive a "choice morsel" in the shape of Turkestan. This was also confirmed by another of the accused, Khodjayev, who admitted that Bukharin had talked to him, organizing activities in Central Asia which may be fully and completely described as high treason, as working for the defeat and dismemberment of the U.S.S.R. They regarded the severance of whole regions, and even of Union Republics, from the U.S.S.R. as a recompense for the help which a military aggressor was prepared to give the bloc in its criminal fight for the seizure of power and for the overthrow of the lawful Soviet government in our great country.

I have already said that all the circumstances that were so exhaustively revealed at this trial go to show that the "bloc of Rights and Trotskyites" was nothing but an agency of foreign intelligence services. This circumstance also determined the whole character and nature of the mutual relations that arose and existed between this so-called "bloc," on the one hand, and certain foreign intelligence services, who were the real bosses of these criminals, on the other.

550

The character of the relations that existed between the foreign intelligence services and the bloc can be judged by a number of facts which have been incontrovertibly established in the present trial.

I would remind you of the interrogation of the accused Rykov. Asked about the nature of the bourgeois-fascist organization that was active in Byelorussia under the direction of Goloded, Chervyakov and Sharangovich, Rykov was obliged to admit that even the appointments to leading posts of any importance in Byelorussia received the preliminary sanction of the Polish intelligence service.

This fact, in itself, sufficiently vividly illustrates the true nature of the relations that existed between the "bloc of Rights and Trotskyites" and the Polish intelligence service. If the Polish intelligence service decided who was to be appointed to the most important posts, it is obvious that the real and true master of the fate of the "bloc of Rights and Trotskyites" and of all its criminal activities was the Polish intelligence service. This "bloc" had also other masters—the intelligence services of other states, with which individual members of this criminal conspiratorial organization maintained criminal connections and relations on the instructions and with the knowledge and consent of the leaders of this "bloc."

I would remind you of the testimony of the accused Ivanov, who has already told us here that sometimes the members of the bloc could not distinguish between the activities of the Rights and those of the foreign intelligence service, so closely were they intertwined. I would also remind you that, according to Ivanov, Bukharin advised him to form connections with the British Intelligence Service. Bukharin said that England had very great interests in the Northern Territory. He said that the Right centre had an agreement with that country about helping the Rights to overthrow the Soviet power, and that this agreement included a guarantee of the interests of British timber firms in the forests of the Northern Territory.

Here too we find clearly expressed the specifically business concern of the intelligence service with which Bukharin recommended the accused Ivanov to form connections, and with which the accused Ivanov did form connections in fulfillment of Bukharin's behest. Ivanov stated that Bukharin recommended him to arrange matters in such a way as to prove to the British bourgeoisie that the Rights were willing to satisfy all the economic and financial interests of the British bourgeoisie, and recommended him to give advances to the British bourgeoisie in order, on the one hand, not to lose their support and, on the other, not to forfeit their confidence.

It is perfectly clear that this "confidence" was based on one

551

thing only, namely, the ability of these plotters to pay in cash —in Soviet land and Soviet blood for their treasonable activities, for the assistance which the foreign aggressors were prepared to grant the plotters in the achievement of their criminal aims.

It was essentially of this that Rakovsky spoke when he testified how often the "honest" agents of the foreign intelligence services, like this nice old gentleman sitting here before you in the dock, found themselves in a contradictory situation. The position of those spies who simultaneously served several intelligence services, and there are such among the accused, was very, very difficult. Rakovsky himself was an expert of this kind, who at one and the same time served both the Japanese and the British intelligence services and, with Yurenev, landed in a "difficult" situation.

"We," said Rakovsky here, quoting Yurenev's words, "have gotten into such a mess that sometimes one does not know how to behave. One is afraid that by satisfying one of our partners we may offend another. For instance, here at present, antagonism is arising between Great Britain and Japan in connection with the Chinese question, while we have to maintain connections both with the British and Japanese intelligence services. . . ."

A hard situation for a spy! A hard situation for a British and Japanese spy!

". . . We Trotskyites," said Rakovsky, "have to play three cards at the present moment: the German, Japanese and British."

We see that this game can end in no good for the gamblers.

". . . It was not quite clear to me, at that time at least, what the German card promised."

Although it was sufficiently marked.

". . . Personally I thought that . . . Japan . . . was a potent aggressor against the U.S.S.R."

And he goes on to say:

"For us Trotskyites the Japanese card was extremely important, but, on the other hand, we should not overrate the importance of Japan as our ally against the Soviet government. Even if Japanese aggression could force its way into the territory of the U.S.S.R., it would be lost in the vast spaces, and in the taiga. As for Great Britain, the situation was rather more serious. At that moment Great Britain was antagonistic to Japan. . . . It should not be forgotten that England once headed a coalition against the French Revolution and fought on for twenty-five years."

It turns out that the most valuable card was that of the British Intelligence Service. But it is not my purpose to examine the value and distinguishing features of all these "cards." I only wanted to show how hard was the lot of those gentlemen who managed to worship three gods at once, to serve three intelligence services at one and the same time. We cannot but humanly sympathize with them, but we can help them in only one way—by depriving them of the opportunity of playing any cards at all, however valuable these cards might seem to them.

On the subject of connections with the British aggressors, the accused Rakovsky testified that the bloc worked for the defeat of the U.S.S.R. and systematically engaged in spying.

Reference must be made in this connection to Bukharin, who wanted to prove here that, actually speaking, he did not favour the defeat of the U.S.S.R., that he did not favour espionage, nor wrecking, nor diversive activities, because in general he was not supposed to have any connection with these practical matters, for he was a "theoretician," a man who occupied himself with the problematics of universal questions. But even Bukharin was obliged to dot all his "i's." He said:

"In short, as one of the leaders of the Right centre, it was my duty to communicate our line to one of the leaders of the periphery centre."

What was this line?

"Briefly, this line was that in the fight against the Soviet power it is permissible to utilize a war situation and to make certain concessions to capitalist states for the purpose of neutralizing them, and sometimes for the purpose of obtaining their assistance."

If this involved and intricate statement of Bukharin's is deciphered, it means downright treason, desertion to the enemy, depending upon military circumstances and war conditions, in order to utilize assistance of these enemies for the achievement of one's criminal ends.

When Bukharin was asked: "In other words, orientation towards assistance from certain foreign states?"—he replied: "Yes, it can be put that way." He does not want to give a direct answer, but says: "Yes, it can be put that way."

It can and should be put that way, because it corresponds to the facts. When asked: "In other words, orientation towards the defeat of the U.S.S.R."—Bukharin remained true to his nebulous verbal acrobatics, and said: "In general, summarized, I repeat, yes."

And so, "summarized," Bukharin admits the orientation on the defeat of the U.S.S.R.; and in the specific conditions in which he, as a leader of the "bloc of Rights and Trotskyites," found himself, this "summarized" meant: "We were working for the defeat of the U.S.S.R.; we were prepared to open the gates to the enemies."

"To open the front to the enemies"—this is what Rykov confirmed, and what Bukharin could not escape confirming.

Comrades Judges, I would like in this connection to draw your attention to the manner in which here, too, Bukharin tried to get off unscathed, and, while admitting his connections with the military conspiratorial organization of Tukhachevsky and Yakir, he tried to make play of the phrase "was to" open the front, and the manner in which he tried to evade a direct answer to this question which was highly unpleasant to him.

But however Bukharin exerted himself in juggling with words and phrases, however much he tried to assure us that the concept "was to," although expressed by one term, has various meanings—we have a clear idea of Bukharin's real attitude to this question.

It was not a trifling matter that Bukharin, Rykov and Tomsky were organizing, but a very serious one, the overthrow of the Soviet government and the Soviet power, without shrinking from any means whatever. Having lost all support within the U.S.S.R., and placing all their hopes on foreign states hostile to the U.S.S.R., they arranged with them about opening the front, about their joint intention of smashing the Soviet people, the Soviet state, in order by treasonable means to clamber into power, which they would at once hand over entirely, unreservedly and completely to the fascists, to their real masters.

Enough of word play! Enough of acrobatics and "philosophy"! It was high treason that was involved, desertion to the enemy, opening the front, bringing about the defeat of the U.S.S.R., and the rout of our fatherland.

The whole espionage work of individual participants in this plot on all sectors was directed by Bukharin and Rykov. All secret information was transmitted to the appropriate organs by channels, through means and contacts, which were under the control of Rykov, Bukharin, Yagoda and their accomplices.

Here in Court the connections of Rykov, Bukharin and Yagoda with the intelligence services of a number of foreign states were fully revealed. In conjunction with the Mensheviks, with Dan, with the Second International, with the Socialist-Revolutionaries, with Maslov, with foreign intelligence services abroad, and together with aggressors, they tried to overthrow the Soviet power and to restore the rule of real capitalism, inveterate, one hundred-per cent capitalism, and the real domination of the landlords and manufacturers.

All these acts of wrecking, treason and betrayals were combined with the systematic supplying of foreign intelligence services with secret information and various kinds of material. Krestinsky, Rosengoltz, Ivanov, Sharangovich, Chernov, Rakovsky, Yagoda and others systematically transmitted Soviet state secrets to foreign intelligence services.

We have authentic information that the plotters of the "bloc of Rights and Trotskyites" regularly performed services for foreign intelligence services. I shall quote an excerpt from the Tokyo newspaper "Miyako" of February 20, 1937, which reports a secret meeting of what is known as the Planning and Budget Commission. Deputy Yoshida asked General Sugiyama, Minister of War, whether he and the army had any information about the carrying capacity of the Siberian Railway. The Minister answered this question in the affirmative and said that the carrying capacity of the Siberian Railway was known to them, that they were in receipt of systematic information about the capacity of the Siberian Railway from elements in Russia who were in opposition to the present Soviet government. Japan received information about the Siberian Railway through them.

Here you have these elements, here you have these scouts, spies, servitors of imperialism, who trade in the interests of our country. Here you have them—these agents of the Minister of War who is mustering his forces on the borders of our country for an attack upon our sacred frontiers.

I cannot refrain from citing another fact. The "Japan Times," organ of the Japanese Ministry of Foreign Affairs, stated in an editorial article in January 1937:

"That both countries, Japan and Germany, naturally seek to obtain all information in regard to Soviet Russia that might be of military value, must be accepted as a fact. If they did not do this they would be both foolhardy and failing to perform their duty to the State and the people. The possibility of an armed clash with Soviet Russia at some future date cannot safely be precluded, although it is to be hoped that it never comes, and it is the obligation of those nations which face such a prospect to prepare in every way possible for gaining the victory."

Gentlemen the accused, do you want proofs of your criminal, provocative, prying and spying activities, apart from your testimony? Then look for them in the pages of the organ of the Japanese Ministry of Foreign Affairs, look for them in the pages of the Tokyo newspaper.

Far from concealing their aspirations in the matter of espionage, when, as in the present case, it concerns the U.S.S.R., the Japanese aggressors eulogize espionage as a supreme patriotic virtue. It is clear that we must treat the "virtuous" people now sitting in the dock in the way the quality and profundity of their spy "virtue" merits.

Bukharin, Tomsky, Rykov and Yagoda were preparing to open the front. But here, as everywhere, as in all their treacherous work, they acted like provocateurs. And this is not fortuitous, for it is

555

characteristic of the method by which these gentlemen work. They were preparing to open the front, but they wanted to make the workers and peasants of our country, our whole people, believe that it was not they who opened the front, but somebody else, and that, quite the contrary, they were against opening the front, against treason. They even agreed among themselves to bring to trial those who opened the front at their own orders, in order, as Bukharin cynically expressed it, to play on patriotic slogans. I have no doubt that Bukharin will take advantage of his speech in defence or of his last plea in order, with the help of the most preposterous circus acrobatics, to try once more to attach a special meaning to this, other than the meaning I, the State Prosecutor, attribute to it at this trial. But it seems to me that no other meaning can be attributed to it.

At one of the sessions of the Court I quoted the testimony of Bukharin in which he speaks of the high wave of Soviet patriotism which would never allow anybody to gamble with his country, and which for every act of treachery would demand the head, the life of the traitors.

Bukharin and his pals fully realized and appreciated the significance of this supreme and genuine patriotism of the people, the high level of patriotism which is shared by the whole country, where every man, old and young, is prepared in the hour of need to lay down his life in defence of his motherland against the intrusion of foreign invaders. They realized this, they knew and understood that it would be dangerous to trifle with the love cherished by the people for their native land. And realizing this, they built up this whole system of provocation and treachery. They were prepared to open wide the gates to foreign intervention, but they wanted to depict it as being the work of others, against whom these jesuits and pharisees, these Judas Iscariots and Vasily Shuiskys allegedly raised their "patriotic" voices. Bukharin said that they intended to bring to trial those guilty of opening the front, and thus play on patriotic slogans.

The game has been exposed. The masks have been torn from the traitors' faces, once and for all. Not one of the accused dared to deny that he criminally worked for the defeat and dismemberment of the U.S.S.R. Some of them spoke of it plainly, coarsely, cynically; others—I am again referring to Bukharin and Rykov— jesuitically veiled their confessions. But in the end even they dared not and could not deny this crime in the open Soviet Court. The proofs are too damning, the evidence too convincing!

It was established in previous trials, and once again confirmed in this trial, that Trotsky had come to an agreement with the German and Japanese intelligence services to wage a joint struggle against the U.S.S.R. and the Soviet power. At this trial, too, we have the circumstantial testimony of one of the accused, Besson-ov, on this subject. He said that the agreement was concluded on the basis of the five points he had mentioned in his testimony. They were, firstly, the mutual sabotage of all official relations, sabotage of the normalization of relations between the U.S.S.R. and Germany. What does this mean?

It means a system of provocation in international relations. And this, of course, was not an empty word, because we know that the Trotskyites, masked by their duplicity, were able to worm their way into a number of fairly important posts, where our foreign policy is put into practical effect. The Rakovskys, Krestinskys, Yurenevs and the others, the Bessonovs and their like, are all people who acted as the authorized diplomatic representatives of the U.S.S.R. in foreign relations. This, incidentally, increases the gravity of their guilt and of their responsibility before the Soviet state and the Soviet people.

Sent to represent the interests of our state, in reality they combated these interests in every way. These gentlemen utilized their official positions—and they all, Rakovsky, Grinko and Krestinsky, acted in this way—in order to thwart the cause of peace, in order by every means to provoke conflicts in the interests of the imperialists.

The second point of the agreement was all-round collaboration between the Trotskyite organizations in the U.S.S.R. and the German secret and espionage organizations and their agents. What for? In order to undermine the military and economic might of the U.S.S.R. and to hasten the defeat of the U.S.S.R. in war.

The third point was that German fascism was to help the coup d'état in the U.S.S.R. with the object of transferring power to the "bloc of Rights and Trotskyites."

The fourth point was that intervention should be accelerated and peace immediately concluded with the new government after it had come to power—a natural step in the plan of these gentlemen's treasonable work.

The fifth point was the severance of the Ukraine from the U.S.S.R. in favour of Germany, the severance of the Maritime Region in favour of Japan, the severance of Byelorussia in favour of Poland, the dismemberment of our whole Soviet Union by severing regions and republics from it and placing them at the disposal of foreign imperialists.

Bukharin was obliged here to admit that the conditions on which this so-called alliance—it was not an "alliance" at all, it was actually a master-and-servant agreement—was concluded were the dismemberment of the U.S.S.R. and the severance of the Ukraine, the Maritime Region and Byelorussia from the U.S.S.R. I asked Bukharin: "In whose favour?" And he answered: "In favour of Germany, in favour of Japan, and partly in favour of England." This is Bukharin's own admission, which he cannot get away from, and will not get away from.

The Trotskyites and Rights in fact acted in accordance with this agreement. Grinko has related what the Ukrainian national-fascists did in fulfillment of this agreement. Krestinsky confirmed what they did in fulfillment of this agreement. As Trotsky had instructed them, they planned diversive, espionage and wrecking activities, the activities of the Hitlerites and Trotskyites within the U.S.S.R.

A prominent place in the anti-Soviet "bloc of Rights and Trotskyites" was held by the bourgeois-nationalist groups, which were formed in certain of the national republics under the direct influence of the agencies of these same foreign intelligence services and under the direct guidance of the so-called centre of the "bloc of Rights and Trotskyites."

The traitors Grinko, Khodjayev, Sharangovich and Ikramov are hardened and inveterate counter-revolutionaries of various hues with counter-revolutionary records of long standing, from the Borotbists, the "Milli-Istiklal" and "Milli-Ittikhad" to the "bloc of Rights and Trotskyites."

Rykov assured Khodjayev that, under the guidance of the Rights, the Uzbek nationalist organization could secure the "independence" of the Uzbek Republic.

Khodjayev was obliged to admit—you have seen Khodjayev and you know that he is a fairly educated man, who perfectly understands all the subtleties and variations of the struggle in which he took part—Khodjayev was obliged to admit that he fully realized the falsity and hypocrisy of this slogan of the so-called independence for the Uzbek Republic; he understood perfectly well that this slogan really served to mask the dependence of the Uzbek nation on the exploiters of the capitalist country which would help the republic to achieve this phantom of independence.

Bukharin worked in the same direction as Rykov. According to Khodjayev, Bukharin eulogized German fascism and stated that fascist Germany was now working with all its might to make Germany the hegemon of Europe, and that an agreement between Japan and Germany to fight the U.S.S.R. was likely.

Bukharin persuaded Khodjayev to find ways of getting into contact with the British Intelligence Service through the kur-bashis, to whom Khodjayev referred here. Bukharin advised him to get in touch with British circles and to promise something to England. He said: "Uzbekistan with its 5,000,000 population cannot become an independent state between two colossuses—the Soviet Union on the one side and Great Britain on the other. We must make fast on some shore." And Bukharin prompted Khodjayev, who, incidentally, was quite prepared for it as it was, to make for the shore of bourgeois counter-revolution.

Bukharin spoke about the stabilization of capitalism, and said that fascism, especially German fascism, had played an important part in this. Like a true watchdog of fascism, he barked joyfully expressing his admiration for German fascism.

Bukharin worked upon Ikramov, too, for the same purpose, although Ikramov is also a type that does not require to be spoon-fed. Bukharin told lies about Lenin; he said that colonial countries cannot arrive at Socialism with the support of the proletariat of the U.S.S.R. and avoiding the stage of capitalism, and so on. To drive it home to Ikramov, Bukharin preached the theory and practice of the restoration of capitalism not only in Uzbekistan, but throughout the U.S.S.R. He said: "Your methods are petty. You want to wait until the U.S.S.R. is in difficulties, and then act. No, you must act in a better way. We approve your actions in the matter of the severance of Uzbekistan. On this subject the Rights have an understanding with the Ukrainian nationalists, the Byelo-russian nationalists and the nationalists of other republics."

The Right-Trotskyite and bourgeois-nationalist traitors wanted, in the interests of their capitalist masters, once more to place the capitalist yoke on the nations of our fraternal Union Republics, which had been formerly oppressed by tsardom and the landlords and capitalists, and which had been liberated by the Great Socialist Revolution. Not daring to speak openly of their treacherous plans for the enslavement of the nations which had made tremendous progress as the result of the national policy of Lenin and Stalin, which had progressed culturally, politically and economically, these traitors uttered their treasonable, lying and fraudulent slogans and speeches about the independence of these republics.

As though there is any country in the world except the U.S.S.R. in which genuine national independence, genuine and complete national culture, and the genuine prospering of the millions are really guaranteed! There is no such country in the world except the U.S.S.R! While in the colonies of capitalist countries—in India, Algeria, Tunis, Morocco, in the Oriental countries—the nations are languishing beneath the dire yoke of capitalist oppression, where poverty and want are on the increase, where the masses are starving, where syphilis and tuberculosis are rampant, and ruin and pauperism becoming ever more widespread, in the U.S.S.R., in its glorious eleven Union Republics, the standard of living of the people is steadily rising, culture, national in form and Socialist in content, is steadily progressing, and ever more brightly and joyfully above the rich and boundless expanses of these republics shine the great and beneficent rays of the new, Socialist sun, the sun of un-

559

fading glory of the indestructible fraternal union of the nations of the Union of Soviet Socialist Republics.

The provocateurs, spies and fascists strove, of course, to sever the Union Republics from our Union. Why? Because, as Comrade Stalin said eighteen years ago, the severance of the border regions would undermine the revolutionary might of Central Russia, which stimulates the movement for emancipation in the West and East. ". . . The border regions that seceded," Stalin said, "would inevitably fall into bondage to international imperialism." The genuine independence of the national republics is ensured only in the conditions of a Soviet state, in the conditions of victorious Socialism, and on the basis of the great Stalinist Constitution.

This gang of traitors employed criminal methods which are already well known and which have frequently been exposed in Court: methods of wrecking, diversion, espionage and terrorism. The wreckers, diversionists and spies wormed their way into a number of branches where they took possession of key positions. Such was the case with Chernov, who held the important post of People's Commissar of Agriculture of the U.S.S.R.; such was the case with Grinko, who held the important post of People's Commissar of Finance of the U.S.S.R.; such was the case with Rosengoltz, who held the important post of People's Commissar of Foreign Trade of the U.S.S.R.; such was the case with Zelensky, the former Chairman of the Centrosoyuz; and such was the case with a number of others. These criminals, of course, had opportunities for the widest and at the same time the most carefully masked and most dangerous wrecking activities, such as have rarely been enjoyed by criminals.

The chief aim of the sabotage and wrecking of this "bloc of Rights and Trotskyites" was to undermine the economic might of the U.S.S.R. in every way. To liquidate the Soviet, Socialist system, to enfeeble the defensive power of the U.S.S.R. and the defence industry, to shatter agriculture by abolishing the collective farms and state farms, and to disrupt transport, which is of enormous importance to the economic life of the country—such were the monstrous aims the criminals set themselves.

They set themselves the aim of timing all these fatal consequences for the moment of armed attack by foreign aggressors upon the U.S.S.R.; and not only to time them for the moment of attack, but also to strive to have these criminal actions play an independent role as a definite means of weakening the might of the Soviet state.

While pursuing their fundamental aim of overthrowing the Soviet power, the "bloc of Rights and Trotskyites"—as our trial has shown—did not shun the most sordid and cynical methods to undermine the confidence of the masses in the organs

560

of the Soviet power, to sow discontent with the Soviets among the population, and as far as possible to rouse the people against the Soviet power.

These provocateur activities, pursued by each of the accused wherever he was working, represented a tremendous, general political danger. This is particularly borne out by such facts as the Lepel affair, which was mentioned in this Court—arbitrariness and lawlessness practised by conspirators and criminals at the instigation of this bloc and aimed at discrediting the Soviet power in the eyes of the broad masses of the population by the practice of unlawful acts.

The trial and the preliminary investigation have shown how unscrupulously cynical and monstrously criminal were the means and methods employed by the bloc for the achievement of its aims. This work of wrecking and sabotage was particularly dangerous in view of the extremely important positions occupied by a number of the accused in the Soviet state system.

Take the finances. The chief line of the wreckers in the sphere of finances—as formulated by Rykov, in agreement with Bukharin—was "to strike at the Soviet government with the Soviet ruble." This is a paraphrase of the old Trotskyite slogan, made known to us in other trials through Pyatakov, namely, "to strike with the most effective means at the most sensitive spots."

"To strike at the Soviet government with the Soviet ruble"—such were the directions which determined all the activities of Grinko, the former People's Commissar of Finance, who at the same time acted as an agent of the German and Polish intelligence services and as Bukharin's and Rykov's right-hand man. It was these directions, this decision of the "bloc" that he endeavoured to carry into effect in all conscience, a rotten conscience though it was.

Moreover, we know that finances are not self-contained, but determine the direction and development of all branches of industry. And this was taken into account by the criminal bloc of wreckers. Wrecking in the financial sphere spread to various branches of economy. In agriculture, which is of tremendous importance to the U.S.S.R., the wrecking work was designed as far as possible to frustrate the task set by the Party and the government of achieving a harvest of seven to eight billion poods.

Grinko has mentioned the wrecking work he performed in the sphere of taxation and in the savings banks, where he tried in every way to incense the public. We all know how abominably the savings bank business was organized under Grinko, when depositors had to waste an enormous amount of time and encountered endless unpleasantness and insolence, rudeness and lack of attention, and when every attempt was made to incense the public and to scare them away from the savings banks.

561

Grinko has now frankly explained the secret. The secret was the deliberate attempt to exasperate the depositors and to undermine the savings bank business. This business was put in charge of such a cut-throat, as Grinko himself called him, as Ozeryansky, who at the same time was preparing terrorist acts against the leaders of our Party and government.

I will not deal with other facts that show that in Grinko we have an old and ingrained enemy of the Soviet power, who had entirely and completely sold himself to the German intelligence service, who actively strove by means of wrecking, diversion, treachery and terrorism against the Soviet power to bring about the restoration of capitalism.

Take another spy, Chernov, an undoubtedly "talented" individual, because in one evening he managed to visit Dan and Kibrik, to get into a scrap with the police, to land in the Polizeipräsidium and to become a German spy.

However, there is nothing improbable in this. That is how it happens in life with people like Chernov. He has only now acquired that more or less fresh and healthy look. Confinement has done him a lot of good. He had a different look when he was free, the haggard look of a toper, who drank more than he worked. He suffered from a social disease—alcoholism. And here he goes abroad on government business. But at the same time he accepts a commission from the "bloc," which takes advantage of his accidental trip abroad to send him to establish connections with Dan. He gets to Dan and Kibrik. Dan and Kibrik are German spies, that is clear. It can be seen from the mere fact that the conversation he had with Dan and Kibrik immediately became known to the intelligence service of the Polizeipräsidium.

It is said that walls have ears. But there are walls that have eyes, walls through which not only everything can be seen, but through which even a camera can pierce. And so, while Chernov drank and ate with Dan and Kibrik, a camera clicked and perpetuated this "meeting of friends"—Chernov and Dan. The Polizeipräsidium got possession of a document which might spoil Chernov's whole career. He had gone on government business, but got himself tied up with such inveterate Mensheviks as Dan and Kibrik and carried on a love intrigue with them. This might cost Chernov something more than his political career. And the German intelligence service played on this. It did not consider Chernov important enough to waste a taxi ride on him—a trolleybus would do. But the trolleybus is boarded by people who start a scrap, a row, which ends in the police station. A fine picture this—a People's Commissar who starts a row and slaps a policeman's face. Add to this the compromising photos, and Chernov was "cooked." Chernov had either honestly to break and make a full right-about face, or swim with the current he had got into. It should be added that Chernov is a former Menshevik and stuck to his Menshevism to the last minute. Consequently, like Rosengoltz, he could repeat the prayer—"Let his enemies be scattered." Even Rykov poked fun at Chernov, saying that he managed in one evening to land in the police station and to become a spy.

But is the recruiting of intelligence service agents done otherwise? We know from the abundant material that has been recently published that they are caught in dance halls, in private conversations, in love affairs, when members of the charming sex are specially introduced and play the part of far from charming representatives of far from charming institutions. We know that they are caught by card games and by a bottle of brandy. They are caught like moths attracted by a candle.

We learnt in the last trial how skilfully the German intelligence service, to give it its due, recruited Stroilov. Rakovsky, a man of great experience in the world, told us here how he was recruited by the British and Japanese intelligence services, and how a certain Armstrong or a certain Leckart turned him into a British spy.

So this Chernov acts on instructions of the German intelligence service and bluntly tells us that "the German intelligence service made a special point of the organization of wrecking activities in the sphere of horse-breeding," the purpose being, as Raivid said, not to provide horses for the Red Army. The matter is clear. It is not difficult for Chernov to fulfil this commission, and he proceeds to fulfil it. This man specially selects three factories: Kashintsevo, Orel and Stavropol. What for? In order, as he put it here, to prepare "serums with virulent bacteria." He does this in order to disrupt horse-breeding, to destroy horses, and to undermine stock-breeding in general.

Who, of course, can do this better than a man who occupies such a high post as Chernov? Who else could set up factories specially for the preparation of infectious serums? He alone. And he did it. He has himself told us here that 25,000 horses were destroyed at his behest. A large number of horses were exterminated in regions like Siberia. They deliberately infected pigs with erysipelas and the plague. They did this in the Voronezh Region, in the Azov-Black Sea Territory and in the Leningrad Region.

The purpose was plain—to sap the defence efficiency of the Red Army. This is not mere wrecking, it is espionage wrecking, it is the scouts of the war-time enemy, who had decided to take his cue from the Iliad and the Odyssey, and to smuggle a Trojan horse into the city, so that if need be this horse might serve as a base of support against the defenders of the fatherland.

Rosengoltz also acted in a way that served the interests of the Germans and Japanese. He specially signed an oil agreement that furthered the interests of these foreign states. He specially organized the sale of gold tailings in a wrecking way, to serve the interests of these same states and in direct violation of the interests of his own fatherland. He organized in a wrecking and criminal way the export of iron to Japan, so that this iron might be used to make the shells with which the Japanese military are preparing, if not to bombard, at least to intimidate our country. He retarded imports for defence purposes in every way. He acted just as he was told to by the intelligence service, utilizing his high post, playing a game of deceit and perfidiously betraying his duty to the state.

Ikramov and Khodjayev did not lag behind their central "colleagues" in wrecking work. Ikramov himself testified here on wrecking work in Namangan, in the silk mills, in the cotton-ginning plants, and in cotton growing. According to their testimony, Rykov and Bukharin played a perfectly definite role in the organization of this wrecking and sabotage—a role which may be described as a leading one.

Take Zelensky. I shall only refer here to the most abominable practice of mixing glass and nails with foodstuffs, butter in particular, which hit at the most vital interests, the health and lives of our population. Glass and nails in butter! This is so monstrous a crime that, in my opinion, all other crimes of the kind pale before it.

In our country, rich in resources of all kinds, there could not have been and cannot be a situation in which a shortage of any product should exist. It was just for this reason that this whole wrecking organization made it its task to create a shortage of things which we possess in superabundance, to keep the market and the consumption of the population in a strained state. I shall only recall one episode in the activities of Zelensky, the case of the fifty carloads of eggs which he deliberately destroyed so as to create a shortage of this necessary food article in Moscow.

It is now clear why there are interruptions of supplies here and there, why, with our riches and abundance of products, there is a shortage first of one thing, then of another. It is these traitors who are responsible for it. And it enabled them to stir up feeling against the system of our economic administration, against the whole system of the Soviet power. Striking at the daily needs of the population is in fact complying with the old instructions of Ryabushinsky, who wanted to strangle the proletarian revolution with the gaunt hand of famine. But he did not succeed![24]

In organizing this wrecking work, all these Rykovs and Bukharins, Yagodas and Grinkos, Rosengoltzes and Chernovs, and so on and so forth, pursued a definite aim, namely, to try to strangle

Rosengoltz also acted in a way that served the interests of the Germans and Japanese. He specially signed an oil agreement that furthered the interests of these foreign states. He specially organized the sale of gold tailings in a wrecking way, to serve the interests of these same states and in direct violation of the interests of his own fatherland. He organized in a wrecking and criminal way the export of iron to Japan, so that this iron might be used to make the shells with which the Japanese military are preparing, if not to bombard, at least to intimidate our country. He retarded imports for defence purposes in every way. He acted just as he was told to by the intelligence service, utilizing his high post, playing a game of deceit and perfidiously betraying his duty to the state.

Ikramov and Khodjayev did not lag behind their central "colleagues" in wrecking work. Ikramov himself testified here on wrecking work in Namangan, in the silk mills, in the cotton-ginning plants, and in cotton growing. According to their testimony, Rykov and Bukharin played a perfectly definite role in the organization of this wrecking and sabotage—a role which may be described as a leading one.

Take Zelensky. I shall only refer here to the most abominable practice of mixing glass and nails with foodstuffs, butter in particular, which hit at the most vital interests, the health and lives of our population. Glass and nails in butter! This is so monstrous a crime that, in my opinion, all other crimes of the kind pale before it.

In our country, rich in resources of all kinds, there could not have been and cannot be a situation in which a shortage of any product should exist. It was just for this reason that this whole wrecking organization made it its task to create a shortage of things which we possess in superabundance, to keep the market and the consumption of the population in a strained state. I shall only recall one episode in the activities of Zelensky, the case of the fifty carloads of eggs which he deliberately destroyed so as to create a shortage of this necessary food article in Moscow.

It is now clear why there are interruptions of supplies here and there, why, with our riches and abundance of products, there is a shortage first of one thing, then of another. It is these traitors who are responsible for it. And it enabled them to stir up feeling against the system of our economic administration, against the whole system of the Soviet power. Striking at the daily needs of the population is in fact complying with the old instructions of Ryabushinsky, who wanted to strangle the proletarian revolution with the gaunt hand of famine. But he did not succeed!

In organizing this wrecking work, all these Rykovs and Bukharins, Yagodas and Grinkos, Rosengoltzes and Chernovs, and so on and so forth, pursued a definite aim, namely, to try to strangle

565

arriving at power in any other way, the adoption of terrorist methods, in the opinion of the centre, held out some prospects."

Rykov has given in Court a full and consistent account of the way the organization of the Rights was secretly formed and the way it was passing to ever sharper forms and methods of struggle. Rykov dates the growth of terrorist tendencies back to the period preceding 1930. Approximately in 1932, according to Rykov's testimony, there definitely formed what he called a positive attitude towards the use of terrorism as a method of struggle for power. Rykov here made a certain philosophical digression to stress the fact that he did not conceive terrorism in theory only, without practice. And, indeed, having adopted the position of terrorism, Rykov at once proceeded to organize terrorist acts and to prepare for such acts. He prepared for the assassination of our leaders with all the pedantry and with all the calmness with which he gave his explanations here in Court, and with which, apparently, he at one time signed his orders in the Commissariat of Post and Telegraph.

The chill and stench of death breathes in the testimony of Rykov and the other Right and Trotskyite fascist conspirators.

Terrorism is in full swing. The whole bloc systematically and pedantically devotes itself to terrorism.

Bukharin also favoured terrorism, although, as he says, he orientated himself rather on mass revolts than on terrorism. Well, how he orientated himself it is his business to explain; but we know that a very long time ago—it can now be considered fully proved—in 1918, he took part in the organization of the terrorist acts of Kaplan, the "Left" Socialist-Revolutionaries, the Trotskyites and the Right Socialist-Revolutionaries. He himself says quite openly that later, in 1932, he conducted negotiations with Semyonov, a former Socialist-Revolutionary, organizer of terrorist acts and leader of Socialist-Revolutionary action squads; he negotiated with him for the organization of a terrorist fight against Comrade Stalin and Comrade Kaganovich. In 1932, through Pyatakov and Sedov, Bukharin conducted negotiations about the conditions, the directions, or, as he called it, the line of Trotsky, which was that terrorist methods must be adopted. And it is characteristic that Bukharin at once proceeded to the practical execution of this line. It is now clear that Bukharin's position on this question was anything but theoretical: he acted like a real practical worker, for it was he who conducted negotiations with Semyonov and it was he who commissioned Semyonov to organize a terrorist act. It was he who, although somewhat later, entrusted the organization of an armed and bloody kulak revolt to his disciple, Slepkov, and others. The conspiratorial bloc widely developed the organization of terrorist groups, which made the practical preparations for terrorist acts, for the assassination of Kirov. This assassination was fully revealed and unmasked in the preceding trial, but it has only now been established that the activities of the Trotskyite-Zinovievite centre which murdered Sergei Mironovich Kirov were not of an independent character. It has now been established that Kirov was assassinated by decision of this very Right-Trotskyite centre, of this bloc, which may be called the centre of all centres.

The accused Yagoda confirmed in Court that Kirov was assassinated by direct decision of the "bloc of Rights and Trotskyites," that this decision was carried out by Yagoda, to whom this shameful duty was entrusted. And Yagoda performed this duty. He gave orders to Zaporozhetz, assistant chief of the Regional Administration of the People's Commissariat of Internal Affairs in Leningrad, to do all he could to have this assassination committed. Some two months before the assassination, Leonid Nikolayev was detained and brought to the Regional Administration. He was found to be in possession of a revolver and cartridges and a chart of the route that Kirov used to take. This made it perfectly clear that this scoundrel was preparing to commit a monstrous crime. But observing the direct orders of Yagoda, Zaporozhetz released this scoundrel, and two months later Nikolayev assassinated Kirov, committing this dastardly act with the direct participation of the contemptible traitor Yagoda, whose duty it was at that time to protect the persons of members of the government.

Yagoda confirmed in Court that Rykov and Bukharin had taken part in the adoption of this decision; that Rykov and Yenukidze had participated in the meeting of the centre where the question of assassinating S. M. Kirov was discussed, and that therefore Rykov and Yenukidze had taken a direct part in discussing the question of the assassination of Sergei Mironovich Kirov. In reply to my direct question whether Bukharin and Rykov were telling the truth here when they declared that they knew nothing about this assassination, Yagoda stated that this could not be so, because when Yenukidze told him that the "bloc of Rights and Trotskyites" had decided at a joint meeting that a terrorist act should be committed against Kirov, he, Yagoda, refused to have anything to do with it for certain "tactical" and conspiratorial reasons, but he was, nevertheless, aware that this was a decision of their centre and not the action of a guerilla band of conspirators, that this decision emanated from the "bloc of Rights and Trotskyites," in which Bukharin and Rykov had taken an active part.

It has now been definitely established that Yagoda had an immediate part in the assassination of Comrade Kirov. I also consider it proved that Rykov and Bukharin had an immediate part in the assassination.

What are my proofs?

If we assume that Rykov and Bukharin had no part in this assassination, then it must be admitted that for some reason or other two of the principal leaders of the "bloc of Rights and Trotskyites" that adopted the decision to assassinate Kirov held aloof from this dastardly act. Why? Why did people who had organized espionage, who had organized insurrectionary movements and terrorist acts, and who, on their own admission, had received instructions from Trotsky on terrorism, suddenly, in 1934, stand aloof from the assassination of one of the greatest comrades-in-arms of Stalin, one of the most prominent leaders of the Party and the government?

Bukharin and Rykov did know about it! Such important leaders of this "bloc of Rights and Trotskyites" as Rykov and Bukharin could not but know about this important terrorist act. It would have been anomalous if they had not known it, it would have been entirely illogical.

Bukharin and Rykov have admitted that the assassination of leaders of the Party and the government, of members of the Political Bureau, was part of their plans. It was this, too, that Bukharin talked about with Semyonov, or Semyonov talked about with Bukharin. Why should we assume that, having entered into negotiations with Semyonov for the organization of the assassination of members of the Political Bureau, Bukharin deletes from this list of persons who are to be slain one of the most influential members of the Political Bureau who had distinguished himself by his irreconcilable fight against the Trotskyites, Zinovievites and Bukharinites? Where is the logic in such behaviour? There is no logic in it.

Finally, Rykov admitted that in 1934 he instructed Artemenko to keep a watch on the automobiles of members of the government. For what purpose? For terrorist purposes. Rykov was organizing the assassination of members of our government, of members of the Political Bureau. Why should Rykov make an exception in the case of Sergei Mironovich Kirov, who nevertheless was assassinated on the decision of this accursed bloc? He made no such exception!

Yenukidze and Yagoda were members of the centre and closest associates of Bukharin and Rykov. How can we believe that Yenukidze and Yagoda—who had a share in the assassination of Sergei Mironovich Kirov, who were closest associates of Rykov and Bukharin, and who were the centre of the whole system of terrorist acts against leaders of the Party and the government—how can we believe that Rykov and Bukharin did not know what was known to Yenukidze, the immediate friend, accomplice and coadjutor of Bukharin and Rykov, and what was known to

Yagoda, the closest friend, accomplice and coadjutor of Bukharin and Rykov?

These are the circumstances which completely prove the participation of Rykov and Bukharin in the organization of the assassination of Sergei Mironovich Kirov.

But, as the Court proceedings have established, the terrorist activities of the Right and Trotskyite traitors were not confined to the assassination of Kirov.

As the investigation has established, Alexei Maximovich Gorky, Vyacheslav Rudolfovich Menzhinsky and Valerian Vladimirovich Kuibyshev fell victims to the terrorist acts committed on the instructions of this same "bloc of Rights and Trotskyites." M. Peshkov, the son of A. M. Gorky, was also the victim of assassination. In this connection Yagoda testified as follows:

"I declare categorically that the murder of Kirov was carried out on the instructions of the centre of the 'bloc of Rights and Trotskyites.' It was also on the decision of this centre that terrorist acts were committed against Kuibyshev, Menzhinsky and Gorky."

This was also confirmed by the persons who took a direct part in these assassinations. The dastardly design of the chief of the murderers, Yagoda, was executed in the most perfidious, dastardly and jesuitical fashion. Yagoda at first tried to deny all share in the organization of the murder of Maxim Alexeyevich Peshkov. He then admitted it in camera. He fully confirmed, as the records of the trial show, the testimony he gave in the preliminary investigation; he confirmed the fact that he had organized the murder of Maxim Peshkov, explaining that his unwillingness to speak of it was due to the fact that the motives of the murder were of a strictly personal character.

But Yagoda spoke about the murder of Menzhinsky in open session, denying, however, that there had been any personal or careerist motives for it. He explicitly said:

"I deny that in causing the death of Menzhinsky I was guided by considerations of a personal nature. I aspired to the post of head of the O.G.P.U. not out of personal considerations, not for careerist considerations, but in the interests of our conspiratorial activity."

This is very probable, but the one does not exclude the other. That Yagoda is capable of murder for personal reasons is shown by his own confession regarding the murder of Maxim Peshkov. He explicitly stated that the motives were personal ones. The possibility is therefore not excluded that Yagoda was guided by personal motives here too.

He said that there was a special decision of the centre on this question, which decision was transmitted to him by Yenukidze.

569

It envisaged recourse to doctors, which furnished a perfect guarantee against exposure.

As we see, Yagoda is not a simple murderer. He is a murderer with a guarantee against detection. But here too his expectations have not been justified. The guarantee proved to be worthless, it failed. Yagoda and his vile and criminal activities have been exposed, exposed not by the treacherous intelligence service which was organized and directed against the interests of the Soviet state and our revolution by the traitor Yagoda, but by that genuine and truly Bolshevik intelligence service which is guided by one of Stalin's most remarkable comrades-in-arms—Nikolai Ivanovich Yezhov.

Yenukidze and Yagoda discussed what, from the standpoint of the guarantees that Yagoda sought, would be the best way of despatching Menzhinsky and the other victims they had selected. Yagoda advances his crafty idea, namely, to cause death, as he says, by illness, or, as he put it here in Court: "I admit my guilt in the illness of Maxim Peshkov." This, by the way, is not as paradoxical as it might at first seem. It is not so paradoxical to create the conditions under which a weak and undermined organism would fall sick, and then to devise a method of treatment, or, as Pletnev put it, to foist on the weakened constitution some infection—not to combat the illness, to help not the patient but the infection, and thus to bring about the death of the patient.

Yagoda has mastered the technique of slaying by the most crafty means. His was the last word in bandit "science," way beyond most other criminals, to whom the scope and depth of Yagoda's criminal designs would have been incomprehensible.

Yenukidze rejected Yagoda's proposal to kill Sergei Mironovich Kirov by illness. He said that Kirov was to be assassinated in the way the centre had decided. But, as Yagoda tells us, he promised that next time they would adopt the method and means proposed by Yagoda.

This time came when the next murders were discussed.

"When Yenukidze conveyed to me the decision of the contact centre about the assassination of Kirov," Yagoda said, "I expressed my apprehension that a direct terrorist act might expose not only myself, but the whole organization as well. I pointed out to Yenukidze that there was a less dangerous method, and I reminded him, Yenukidze, how Menzhinsky's death was brought about with the help of physicians. Yenukidze replied that the assassination of Kirov must be carried out the way it was planned, that the Trotskyites and Zinovievites took it upon themselves to commit this murder, and that it was our business not to place any obstacles.

"As for the safe method of causing death with the help of physicians, Yenukidze said that in the near future the centre would discuss the question as to who exactly of the leaders of the Party and the government should be the first to be done to death by this method."

Could anything surpass the cynicism and perfidy of these people who with revolting calmness and coolness discussed which of the leaders of the Party and the government it would be best to murder, and what method should be adopted in order to avoid detection?

Yagoda further said:

"Some time later, during my next meeting with Yenukidze, he told me that the centre had decided to undertake a number of terrorist acts against members of the Political Bureau and, in addition, against Maxim Gorky personally.... Yenukidze explained to me that the 'bloc of Rights and Trotskyites,' considering that the overthrow of the Soviet government was a prospect of the near future, regarded Gorky as a dangerous figure. Gorky was a staunch supporter of Stalin's leadership, and in case the conspiracy was carried into effect, he would undoubtedly raise his voice in protest against us, the conspirators."

That is why the question of killing Alexei Maximovich Gorky was raised and finally decided by this bloc.

Another decision was to remove Valerian Vladimirovich Kuibyshev, who was one of the active members of the Leninist-Stalinist Political Bureau.

Thus, in the course of this brief period three victims, three remarkable men, met an untimely death by decision of the "bloc of Rights and Trotskyites." Three of the finest people of our country, true sons of their fatherland, fell victim to a shameless conspiracy of traitors. And among them was the pride of Russian and world literature, the great Russian author and literary genius, Alexei Maximovich Gorky.

Every line of his songs and stories, of his novels and tales, breathes the spirit of nobility and the ardour of revolutionary action. It was not without good reason that he bound up his life with the great Lenin and the great Stalin, as one of their best and closest friends. It was not without good reason that Lenin several times wrote that Gorky was a man of great artistic talent who had done and would do much for the world proletarian movement.

It was not without good reason that Lenin wrote that Gorky was undoubtedly the greatest representative of proletarian art, who by his great artistic productions had formed firm ties with the working class of Russia and the world. Gorky sensed the coming storm, he foretold the victory of our movement, the triumph of the bright intellect of the proletariat over the murk and vileness of capitalism.

One of the finest friends of toiling mankind perished from the treacherous blows delivered at the sick heart of this great man. One of the brightest and mightiest beacons of human reason and human beauty was extinguished. This beacon was extinguished by these traitors, by these beasts in human form, who coldly and treacherously stopped forever the ardent and noble heart of this great man.

Everything has now been brought to light. We now know not only how the murders were committed, but the motives for the murders and the murderers themselves. Bessonov said that when in Paris in July 1934 he met Trotsky, who always rancorously hated Gorky, as also Gorky hated Trotsky, the super-bandit of international espionage and treachery, Trotsky then said that Gorky must be removed at all costs, that Gorky was widely popular as a close friend of Stalin's and as a champion of the general line of the Party. Trotsky gave Bessonov direct orders to convey to Pyatakov. As Bessonov tells us, this message was couched in the most categorical form, namely, to physically destroy Gorky at all costs. And this order of the enemy of the people and super-bandit Trotsky was brought by Bessonov to this country, to the U.S.S.R., and transmitted to Pyatakov, transmitted to the bloc, which, as Yagoda has testified, and as I shall prove later, accepted this order and adopted the decision to murder A. M. Gorky. This is so monstrous a crime that I consider it necessary to dwell upon it particularly and specially at greater length.

The first question I should like to raise is whether Rykov and Bukharin took part in this affair, whether they knew that preparations were being made for this monstrous villainy. To this question I answer firmly and unhesitatingly: yes, they did know; yes, they did take part in it. I do not wish to use any other evidence, and particularly the evidence of Yagoda. I will use (1) the testimony of Rykov and Bukharin themselves, and (2) what I call the logic of things. What is the position? Just see what Rykov says on this subject. Rykov stated that he had had a talk with Yenukidze, that is, one of the most active members and organizers of the conspiratorial bloc. We have the evidence of Maximov-Dikovsky to show how active Yenukidze was in the organization of the assassinations. Yenukidze repeatedly summoned him and instructed him how best to cause the death of Valerian Vladimirovich Kuibyshev. Yenukidze and Yagoda had charge of this "job." And it is with this Yenukidze that Rykov talked. What about? Let us take only what Rykov himself said: "Yenukidze told me that the Trotskyites and Zinovievites were extremely concerned because of the influence which Gorky was acquiring and because he was a determined supporter of Stalin and the general line of the Party." This is just what Bessonov was told by Trotsky in 1934, and what he brought here in the autumn of 1934 and transmitted to the bosses, the heads, the ringleaders of this bloc.

And so there follows from Rykov's testimony the first incontrovertibly established circumstance: in 1935 Rykov and Yenukidze had a conversation about Gorky; they talked about the tremendous influence which Alexei Maximovich Gorky wielded over public opinion as a true friend and supporter of the general line of the Party, and as a true friend and supporter of the Stalin leadership. And this is what worries the Trotskyites and Zinovievites, it worries them just as they were worried when they discussed the assassination of Sergei Mironovich Kirov. For they selected Sergei Mironovich Kirov as a victim of their villainy for the same reasons. And here you have the complete coincidence, the full historical logic of this conspiracy.

What came next? "They" (the Trotskyites and Zinovievites) "considered it necessary," said Rykov, "in view of this significance of Gorky's—and his significance both abroad and in our country required no confirmation—they insisted, as he phrased it, on putting an end to Gorky's political activity." If Rykov had said only that, it would have been enough. Even a child could have understood what this implied. How can the political activity of a grown man be put an end to in our country? How could Gorky be compelled to stop being politically active in the direction he had displayed himself, as a champion of the Bolshevik, Leninist-Stalinist truth? How could he be compelled to do this?

Men like Al Capone in America organize gangster raids, kidnap people or their children, and then demand ransom. But this is impossible in our country, because we make short shrift of Al Capones. How in our country, in the conditions that exist in the Soviet state, could it be made impossible for Gorky to display political activity except by taking his life? And in reply to my question, Rykov explicitly stated: "He," that is, Yenukidze, "spoke in such a raised voice, or in such sharply hostile expressions, that it was clear to me that this tone concealed the possibility of the employment of violent measures." Consequently, I consider it quite definitely established that in 1935 Yenukidze and Rykov talked in a tone menacing to the life of Gorky. And it was quite clear to Rykov that measures of violence against Gorky were intended. And I again asked the same question: "What were these violent measures? Did you count on isolating Gorky, did you count on keeping him in some sort of confinement? How could that be done in our country, in the country of the proletarian dictatorship?'' This could be done in only one way, by slaying Gorky. Rykov understands that only this could have been implied, and only in this way are we entitled to interpret this criminal conversation, which amounted to nothing else than that Yenukidze was informing Rykov of the preparations for the assassination of Alexei Maximovich Gorky.

And finally, in reply to my last question during the Court investigation: "What does 'going to the extent of violent measures' mean? May it also mean murder?''—Rykov explicitly answered: "Of course.''

I asked Rykov: "You knew that preparations for Gorky's murder were being made?'' How would Rykov have answered this question if he had known nothing about the crime? He would have answered: "I did not know.'' But what did Rykov say? Here is the stenographic report. He said: "Not exactly.'' Not exactly, but he did know!

I regard as fully proved and established the following facts, from which only one conclusion follows, namely, that Rykov took part in the preparations for the murder of A. M. Gorky. Firstly, Yenukidze and Rykov spoke in 1935 about the particular rancour which the bloc entertained against Alexei Maximovich Gorky. It is true that they tried to lay this at the door of the Trotskyite-Zinovievite part of the bloc; but this does not change the situation in any way. Secondly, they expressed this rancour in tones which implied preparations for violent measures designed "to put an end to Gorky's political activity.'' And thirdly, the idea of putting an end to Gorky's political activity included even the adoption of violent measures against Gorky.

Fourthly, these violent measures included the assassination of Alexei Maximovich Gorky. Rykov and Bukharin knew about these violent measures. They knew that preparations were being made for the assassination of Gorky, they organized this assassination, they shielded this assassination. Rykov and Bukharin were therefore participants in this vilest assassination of A. M. Gorky.

And Bukharin—that damnable cross of a fox and a swine— how does he behave here on this question? As befits a fox and a swine. He squirms and wriggles. But in the end Bukharin virtually says the same as Rykov. Let us take this part of Bukharin's testimony. Allow me to refer to the following part of his testimony: "In 1935 Tomsky told me that Trotsky was preparing some hostile action or hostile act against Gorky.''

How did Tomsky know about this? He of course knew about it from Bessonov, who had brought these instructions from abroad. And what were Trotsky's instructions? To destroy Gorky, to destroy him physically. Bukharin testifies: "Tomsky said that Trotsky was preparing a hostile action or a hostile act against Gorky.''

I ask, through whom was Trotsky preparing this hostile action? Through this bloc, of course, which was in the hands of Trotsky, through the bloc in which were intermingled Rights and Trotskyites, Mensheviks and Socialist-Revolutionaries, bourgeois nationalists and just scoundrels of all shades, degrees and categories.

This fact has been established. Bukharin himself admitted that in 1935, a year before Gorky's death, Tomsky had informed Bukharin that Trotsky was preparing a hostile act against Gorky. This is exactly what Rykov said when he reported his conversation with Yenukidze, and this, in its turn, is what was said by Bessonov when reporting the conversation he had had with Trotsky in Paris in July 1934. There are no divergences here at all.

Let us examine the second question: What exactly was this hostile act, what did this hostile act represent? It is not so easy to get a direct reply to a direct question from Bukharin.

I asked Bukharin: "What did this hostile act consist in?" He gave no direct answer. He said: "Action against the 'Stalinite Gorky,' as a defender of Socialist construction in general, and of Stalin's Party policy in particular." That is what they had in mind. "This referred to the great resonance that every word uttered by Alexei Maximovich found on the international arena in general, and among intellectuals in particular."

Here again we have complete coincidence of the facts of which Rykov spoke, of which Bessonov spoke, of which Yagoda knew and spoke, and of which Bulanov knew and spoke. Here everything is organically connected.

I asked: "Did Tomsky link up the perpetration of a hostile act against Gorky with the question of the overthrow of the Soviet government?" Bukharin answered that "in essence he did." Consequently, it was not merely a question of causing Gorky some personal unpleasantness, or as Rykov, in his involved way, said, "putting an end to his political activity," but of committing such a hostile act against Gorky as would directly represent one of the elements in the overthrow of the Soviet power.

Clearly, when put in this way, the intention was not to deprive Gorky of the possibility of writing articles or giving lectures, although even that is beyond your power, gentlemen murderers. Consequently, we must here recognize what Bukharin confirmed, namely, that the hostile act against Gorky was associated with the aim of overthrowing the Soviet power and was one of the acts in the struggle against the Soviet power.

We know how the plotters conceived the struggle against the Soviet power. Their methods were terrorism, treason, etc.

575

Bukharin said that when one speaks of a hostile act it may mean anything, including a terrorist act; the amplitude is here very great. Bukharin admits that at the time, the murder of Gorky was not precluded. This is a veiled admission, which completely incriminates Bukharin.

I have already spoken of the method by which were committed the three terrorist acts—against Menzhinsky, against Kuibyshev and against Alexei Maximovich Gorky.

The method by which these murders were committed is worthy of attention. It is the method of killing by degrees, "murder with a guarantee," as Yagoda put it—it is the method of murdering with the help of the expert knowledge of accomplices. Not a bad idea! Levin, Pletnev, Kazakov, Maximov-Dikovsky, Kryuchkov and Bulanov—this gang of murderers, of specially trained murderers, had a hand in this "affair." I should like to draw your attention to the particular method employed and the particular role played in the commission of this murder by the accused physicians Levin, Kazakov and Pletnev. But first I would like to make a few remarks. We know from the history and chronicles of criminal murder that during the last few decades poisoning through the aid of professional murderers has practically ceased.

The place of these poisoners has been taken by doctors. If you examine the handbook on medical jurisprudence by Dr. Karl Emmert, Professor at the University of Berne, you will find some extremely edifying remarks. Emmert says:

"Murder by poisoning has become rarer than in former times, partly because it has become more difficult for laymen to obtain poisons. The professional poisoner is therefore not to be met with as frequently as in the old days. Such as there are are frequently members of the medical profession."

It is therefore with good reason that Yagoda chooses precisely doctors for his monstrous design and its realization. He reckons with historical circumstances, so to speak.

There are a number of historical examples which show that all murderers who employ poisons of any kind exert every effort to escape detection. It is highly characteristic that in a number of cases poisoning is performed in such a way that the very poisoning may—as Yagoda had planned—be represented as natural death from disease.

It must first be explained that poisoning effected in accordance with the modern scientific view is one of the varieties, and the most dangerous variety, of what is known to science as treacherous murder, the danger of which lies in the fact that it does not require the use of any specific substances fatal to human life, and that any substance may be used for this criminal purpose. History teaches us that all that is required for such a poisoning is to introduce into the organism any substance capable of curtailing the duration of life, or of causing death. And these substances are not always what are specifically termed poisons. There are a number of medicinal substances which by their very nature and character are suitable for this, and criminals often take advantage of the fact.

From history, from Tacitus, for example, we know of such cases as the murder of Seanus by a poison which made it appear that Seanus died from an ordinary ailment. It is in this that the art of crime consists. It is a known fact that Philip II made very wide use of a poison which could not be detected even by the most scrupulous investigation, a poison which he named "Requiescat in pace" (may he rest in peace). We know that John of Castile was done to death by means of poisoned footwear. Finally, we know that Pope Clement II was killed by the fumes of a poisoned candle. Consequently, it is a known fact that people were killed by murderers who took advantage of their privileged position and a knowledge of chemistry, medicine and pharmacology, and who employed the most varied methods in committing their murders.

We remember the famous case of Buturlin. Buturlin's murderer was none other than Dr. Panchenko, who was very widely known in pre-revolutionary Russia and who engaged in the distribution and application of a medicine known as "Pel's Spermine." Dr. Panchenko, pretending that he was using "Pel's Spermine," inoculated the patient with diphtheria bacilli and killed him with diphtheria.

This was exposed quite by accident. Had it not been for Dr. Panchenko's confession, Buturlin's murder would probably never have been disclosed. Had it not been for Levin's confession, it is possible that the minutely elaborated criminal plan of the murder of Comrades Menzhinsky, Kuibyshev and Gorky would not have been disclosed.

Finally, I may mention the famous case of Prochar, who caused his victim to suffer from a chronic gastric catarrh and in this way brought about her death. And lastly, the case of Dr. Palmer, who poisoned his victim with arsenic and strychnine, which he used in doses permitted by medical science. Here, finally, we have an example which tells us that when we speak of poisoning we must not think that only potassium cyanide, arsenic, and so forth, has to be used. No, very frequently murderers use physicians and medical science ostensibly in order to effect a cure, but in reality in order to achieve their criminal purpose.

The cases of Palmer, Prochar, Panchenko and numerous other historical examples could be cited in proof of the fact that the path which Yagoda selected was a path suggested by a detailed study of the history of crime, of the history of murders which were perpetrated in various countries by various monsters in human shape.

Finally, I must say that it was precisely on these lines that the criminal murderers planned a terrorist act against Nikolai Ivanovich Yezhov. For this murder was also planned very craftily—by means of poisoning the air which Nikolai Ivanovich Yezhov was to breathe in his office, by poisoning the air with mercury dissolved in an acid. Moreover, Yagoda warned that under no circumstances was sulphuric acid to be used, because sulphuric acid leaves traces and could burn the window shades and curtains, which, on Yagoda's instructions, were to be saturated, so that by inhaling this air Nikolai Ivanovich Yezhov might die.

Comrades Judges, I want to recall to your minds some of the findings of the experts with regard to this question, which leave no room whatever for doubt as to the fact that this very crafty, perfidious and dastardly plan was conceived by Yagoda with the knowledge and approval of the Right and Trotskyite centre, particularly in respect of Kuibyshev, Gorky and Nikolai Ivanovich Yezhov, whom they wanted to get out of the way in order to escape exposure.

First of all, I draw your attention to the fact that the commission of experts was made up of foremost representatives of Soviet and world medical science. I also draw your attention to the fact that this commission of experts arrived at a unanimous conclusion: the commission of experts confirmed that the means which the murderers used in bringing about the death of A. M. Gorky, V. V. Kuibyshev and V.R. Menzhinsky were in fact minutely planned and that they resulted in the death of these foremost people, which these gentlemen were striving to bring about.

In the case of the death of Gorky, the following questions were put to the commission of experts:

"Can it be granted that properly qualified physicians could have adopted such a wrong method of treatment without malicious intent?"

The reply was: "It cannot."

Another question put to the commission of experts:

"Is it permissible in general for prolonged, large doses of heart stimulants, namely, digitalis, digalen (extracts of foxglove), strophanthin and strophanthus, to be administered intravenously, subcutaneously and internally at the same time, and, in particular, in the case of the very sick patient A. M. Gorky, who was sixty-eight years of age, and suffered from the above-mentioned affection of the internal organs?"

The reply of the commission of experts: "Absolutely impermissible."

Another question: "May it be regarded as established, on the ba-

578

sis of the sum total of these facts, that the method of treatment of A. M. Gorky was a deliberate act of wrecking? . . ."

The reply of the commission of experts: "Yes, it can be taken as established beyond doubt."

And we have the same findings in the other cases.

Therefore I make bold to state that the charges contained in the indictment and sustained by me as the State Prosecutor may be considered as fully proved in this part also. The charge is here also entirely and fully corroborated by the findings of a most authoritative commission of medical experts which thoroughly investigated all the materials that were placed at its disposal. Neither, it is clear, can we discard the confessions of the accused.

In speaking of this part of the charges I want to dwell particularly on two of the accused—Yagoda and Levin.

With regard to Yagoda there is not much to say. Yagoda was the main organizer and inspirer of these monstrous crimes. His responsibility is all the greater and graver since, after all, Yagoda is not just Yagoda, but the man who at that time was Assistant Chairman of the O.G.P.U., actual Chairman of the O.G.P.U. He is the man whose duty it was to protect the safety of the state. If Yagoda had committed only a millionth part of the crimes which he did commit, and to which he confessed, even then I would be justified in demanding from the Court that Yagoda be shot.

Levin also played a very important part in these murders. Levin was the main organizer of the murders which had been conceived by Yagoda; he enlisted the services of both Kazakov and Pletnev for these purposes; he was, I might say, Yagoda's right hand in this business, just as Bulanov was Yagoda's right hand in all of the latter's crimes in their entirety.

When Alexei Maximovich Gorky perished at the hands of Levin, Levin, Doctor of Medical Sciences, published an obituary in the newspapers: "The Last Days of Alexei Maximovich Gorky." In this obituary he wrote, he sighed, he sobbed over the death of the great man. "Great men," he wrote pharisaically, hypocritically, with duplicity, "live and die like great men." "Live and die like great men!" Levin did not add: "by the hand of the author of this obituary, one of the dastardly murderers"!

If we should now consider this article in connection with the findings of the commission of experts, it would present a certain, in my opinion, considerable interest for the estimation of Levin's part in this murder.

In the first place, we find here an exposure of the technique of bringing about Alexei Maximovich's death, which has now been revealed to the full. It is the technique which was primarily directed at the therapeutical preparation of the murder of Alexei Maximovich.

579

Levin wrote in this obituary:

"In the ten years during which Alexei Maximovich was under my medical observation this was the sixth time he fell ill with the grippe. Each time the grippe invariably caused complications of bronchitis and catarrhal pneumonia."

Hence Levin was already well aware in what direction to look for complications in this struggle of Alexei Maximovich Gorky with his ailment.

"At each attack of the illness this indomitable fighter suffered severely under it, each time there was cause for alarm from the very first days of his illness. When people asked me during the good calm periods of Alexei Maximovich's life about the state of his health, I always answered:

" 'Comparatively well, but only till the first grippe.' "

And further:

"I knew from experience what a severe course the grippe takes in the case of Alexei Maximovich, how rapidly it affects his lungs—the place of least resistance in his system—and how frightful it is with his lungs transmuted owing to an old tubercular process and with his sick heart. Thus, his powerful constitution made it possible for us to emerge victorious for five times, and Alexei Maximovich's constitution was powerful indeed. Gorky was of those people who live to be a hundred, and he would undoubtedly have lived to be a hundred if not for the vicious tuberculosis."

The murderer is giving away the secret of the murder. It is precisely here where the place of least resistance lies—physicians call it *locus minoris resistentiae*—and it was to this spot that the perpetrators of the murder directed their main blow aimed at the sick A. M. Gorky.

Shameful duplicity, perfidy, hypocrisy are here rivalled by the shamelessness of the poisoner, who weeps at the bed of the victim of his so-called "treatment."

That is the kind of man this Levin represents! Not so much difference between him and Yagoda!

In conclusion, I should like to remind you of Yagoda's evidence, in which he shows his real moral and human, if this expression could be used here, countenance. Here are extracts from Yagoda's evidence, on p. 58 of the record.

"All my life I wore a mask, I posed as an irreconcilable Bolshevik. Actually, I never was a Bolshevik in the real sense."

And further:

"My petty-bourgeois origin, lack of theoretical training—all this brought it about that from the very beginning of the organization of the Soviet power I had no faith in the final victory of the cause of the Party.". . . .

"I did not share the views and the program of the Trotskyites, but still I followed the course of the struggle with great attention, having made up my mind beforehand that I would join the side which emerged victorious from this struggle. Hence the special line which I pursued during that period in the fight with Trotskyism.

"When measures of repression began to be taken against the Trotskyites, the question as to who would come out the victor (the Trotskyites or the Central Committee of the Communist Party of the Soviet Union) was as yet not finally settled. In any event, that was what I thought. Therefore I, as Assistant Chairman of the O.G.P.U., in carrying out the punitive policy, did it in a way that would not arouse the anger of the Trotskyites against me. When I was sending Trotskyites into exile, I created for them such conditions in their places of exile as enabled them to continue their activity.

"Things took the following shape: on the one hand, my conversations with Rykov determined my personal sympathy for the program of the Rights. On the other hand, from all that Rykov told me about the Rights, about the fact that, besides himself, Bukharin, Tomsky and Uglanov, the Rights had on their side the entire Moscow organization, the Leningrad organization and the trade unions—all this created the impression in my mind that the Rights might win in the struggle with the Central Committee. And since at that time they already raised the question of changing the leadership of the Party and of the Soviet government, it was clear that the Rights were heading for power.

"It was precisely for the reason that to my mind the Rights seemed a real power that I told Rykov that I was on their side.

"That is why I came to an understanding with Rykov about the special position which I was to occupy among the Rights."

So it turns out that Rykov quite definitely influenced even Yagoda. For, essentially, what Yagoda is speaking about is the old school of treachery and duplicity, the school of a political careerist and infamous scoundrel; it is the system of Joseph Fouché. I cannot refrain from citing only a few lines from Stefan Zweig's well-known book "Joseph Fouché."

"Among the seven hundred and fifty who solemnly entered the hall of the dethroned king, silently, with a tri-colour band across his breast, enters the people's representative, Joseph Fouché, deputy for the city of Nantes. His tonsure al-

581

ready grown over with hair, the clerical garb discarded long ago, like everyone else here, he wears civilian clothes, without any decorations.

"Where will Joseph Fouché take his seat? Among the Radicals, on the Mountain, or with the Moderates, in the Valley? Joseph Fouché does not hesitate too long; he recognizes only one party, to which he will remain true to the end: the party which is the strongest, the party of the majority. And this time, too, he weighs the pros and cons and counts under his breath the number of votes; he sees that at the present moment the power is still with the Gironde, with the Moderates. And so he takes his seat on their benches, next to Condorcet, Roland, Servan, to those who hold ministerial posts, influence all appointments and distribute the spoils. In their midst he feels himself at ease, that is where he takes his seat."

That is the source from which Yagoda drew his spiritual strength, if ever he was acquainted with the life and activities of Joseph Fouché. I doubt it, because in the testimony and in the records of the case we find only one mention of his acquaintance with literature, and that refers to Alexandre Dumas' "The Three Musketeers," who were Yagoda's ideal, for, as it appears from the testimony given by Bulanov, Yagoda used to say that, in order to ensure success in seizing power, it was necessary to select a few dozen dashing fellows like the three musketeers, with whose help one could do anything one liked.

Such is Yagoda, who occupies a position of importance in the dock next to Bukharin and Rykov. He is one of the biggest plotters, one of the foremost enemies of the Soviet power, one of the most brazen traitors, a man who tried to organize a group in the very People's Commissariat of Internal Affairs and who partly organized one, consisting of the traitors Pauker, Volovich, Gai, Vinetsky, and others who turned out to be Polish and German spies and intelligence service agents. Such a one was Yagoda himself, who instead of directing our glorious intelligence service to promote the interests of the Soviet people, the interests of Socialist construction, tried to turn it against our people, against our revolution, against Socialism.

The attempt failed, it miscarried! Yagoda was exposed, he was thrown out of our state apparatus, put in the dock, disarmed, and now he must be thrown out, he must be completely eradicated from life.

I am coming to the end. In conclusion I want to raise a few questions which I would describe as legal questions.

First of all, the question of complicity. The Court investigation has shown that not all the accused participated to an equal extent in the crimes which were reviewed at this trial.

Hence the question: To what extent and in what degree can and should each of the accused be held answerable for the charges preferred against them in the indictment?

The second question: To what extent and in what degree have the charges preferred against the accused been proved?

And the third question: What punishment do the accused deserve?

I shall answer the second question first. Have the crimes committed by the accused been proved, and in what degree? I think that in your verdict, Comrades Judges, you will reply to this question in the affirmative: Yes, they have been proved. They have been proved by the confessions of the accused themselves, they have been proved by the witnesses who appeared before the Court, they have been proved by the findings of the medical expert investigation, they have been proved by material evidence.

We have here the sum total of proofs conceivable in criminal proceedings; it is now at the disposal of the Court. On the basis of these proofs the Court will be able to pass its final decision with regard to the degree of guilt of one or the other of the criminals who committed these crimes.

But there is one more very important proof, and that is the logic itself of the circumstances of the case.

The main charge preferred against the accused in the present case is covered by Articles 58[1a] and 58[11], dealing with the organization of treasonable conspiracy. This charge has been proved by the confessions of all the accused, including those who did not admit their guilt in full or who admitted only part of their guilt in another crime. This must be said with regard to all the accused.

Secondly, according to our law, to what extent must each of the accused be held answerable for the aggregate of the crimes committed by this gang of conspirators. To this question I answer: Fully. Why?

Each of the accused must be held answerable for the sum total of the crimes as a member of a conspiratorial organization whose criminal objects and aims, and whose criminal methods of carrying out these aims, were known to, approved of and accepted by each of the accused. Here we observe only a peculiar "division of labour" in criminal activities, depending on the special qualities and means which each member of the gang possessed. This is entirely natural and logical from the point of view of the conspiracy as a whole.

There is an opinion current among criminologists that in order to establish complicity it is necessary to establish common agreement and an intent on the part of each of the criminals, of the accomplices, for each of the crimes. This viewpoint is wrong. We cannot accept it and we have never applied or accepted it. It is narrow and scholastic. Life is broader than this viewpoint. Life knows of examples when the results of joint criminal activity are brought about through the independent participation in such activity by individual accomplices, who are united only by a single criminal object common to all of them.

To establish complicity, we must establish that there is a common line uniting the accomplices in a given crime, that there is a common criminal design. To establish complicity, it is necessary to establish the existence of a united will directed toward a single object common to all the participants in the crime. If, say, a gang of robbers will act in such a way that one part of its members will set fire to houses, violate women, murder and so on, in one place, while another part of the gang will do the same in another place, then even if neither the one nor the other knew of the crimes committed separately by any section of the common gang, they will be held answerable to the full for the sum total of the crimes, if only it is proved that they had agreed to participate in this gang for the purpose of committing the various crimes.

In this case, Comrades Judges, we are dealing with a conspiratorial group, with an agency of foreign intelligence services, united by a will common to all its members, by a criminal aim which is the same for all of them. The concrete crimes which were committed by the individual criminals were only particular cases of putting into effect this plan of criminal activities, which was common to all of them.

This community of criminal activity is legally expressed in the charge preferred against all the accused and dealt with in Article 58[11] of the Criminal Code of the R.S.F.S.R.

This, however, does not mean that all must answer to the same extent. This does not preclude the obligation for the Court to individualize the punishment according to the concrete part of each of the accused in the present case.

From this point of view, I think that of all the accused, two should be singled out—I refer to Rakovsky and Bessonov. I think that Rakovsky, although he committed very grave crimes against the Soviet state, against the Soviet power, still, owing to his entire position in this conspiracy, owing to the fact that he was in a certain way, if one may say so, isolated from the most important crimes committed by the "bloc of Rights and Trotskyites," deserves that with regard to him a less severe measure of punishment should be applied than with regard to the rest of the accused.

To a certain extent the same may be said about Bessonov, who, of course, differs from Chernov, Rosengoltz, Krestinsky or Rykov, even if for the reason that his part was confined to the role of a liaison man, which, although it is also criminal, must be considered

584

EVENING SESSION, MARCH 11, 1938

COMMANDANT OF THE COURT: The Court is coming, please rise.

THE PRESIDENT: Please be seated. The session is resumed. Comrade Braude, member of the Collegium of Defence, will now speak.

BRAUDE: Comrades Judges! The characteristic feature of present-day conspiratorial counter-revolutionary organizations is that they have no mass support.

At the Plenum of the Central Committee of the C.P.S.U. held in March 1937 Comrade Stalin said: "The present-day Trotskyites are afraid to show their real face to the working class, are afraid to reveal to it their real aims and objects, carefully hide their political face from the working class, fearing that if the working class learns about their real intentions it will curse them as people alien to it and drive them away."

We see, Comrades Judges, that for the technical fulfilment of their wrecking designs these conspirators have only their own insignificant forces and foreign intelligence services on which to count. Only by deception, double-dealing and blackmail did they succeed in drawing into their villainous crimes individual persons whose outlook has nothing in common with them.

Indeed, Levin, an old doctor, an individual who is far from a counter-revolutionary outlook and from counter-revolutionary aims, was drawn through the enemy Yagoda into the organization of Rights and Trotskyites to commit monstrous crimes while Yagoda himself wanted to stand aside.

And today, Comrades Judges, I have to defend this old man, Dr. Levin, who towards the end of his life has come to be technical executor of the specific designs of the "bloc of Rights and Trotskyites," about the very existence of which he had hardly any idea, and not only the technical executor, but, as the Procurator correctly stated today, one who also undertook a certain organizing role. How could it have come about, how could it have happened, that a doctor of forty years' standing, a man who was close to Maxim Gorky, the doctor of Kuibyshev and Menzhinsky, should become the murderer of his patients?

In studying the materials of the preliminary investigation, of

587

the examination of Bulanov, Yagoda, Levin and the other accused. I saw that the investigating authorities themselves had taken an interest in how Levin could have undertaken such horrible commissions, in what it was that held him back from offering the necessary resistance to Yagoda. The Procurator asked Levin here: "Why did you not attempt to resist Yagoda?" And, formulating Levin's reply, the Procurator said: "You had no support within yourself, and you did not seek for it from without."

But such a reply does not solve the question as to why he had no support within himself, and why Levin did not seek for it from without.

In order to attempt to reply to this question, it seems to me that it is necessary to go somewhat into the past of our intelligentsia.

I think I shall not be committing a big error if I say that in casting a retrospective glance over the past and analysing the present of this intelligentsia, one may divide it into three groups.

The first group is the insignificant, small section of that bourgeois intelligentsia that occupied key positions with the capitalists in the past, and that later had to work with the Soviet power. Over a number of years this small group manifested itself by engaging in counter-revolutionary wrecking in all spheres of our economy, as one of the forms of the class struggle. This wrecking assumed the most varied forms. Call to mind the Shakhty wreckers, call to mind the case of the Industrial Party.

The wrecking organizations were crushed by the organs of the People's Commissariat of Internal Affairs, by our Court authorities, but individual remnants of them maintained their existence here and there, escaped destruction and continued to manifest themselves from time to time. The anti-Soviet sentiments of individual representatives of this section of the intelligentsia constitute a field for the work of counter-revolutionary organizations and for foreign intelligence services.

There is a second group, which is also not such a big one, made up of that section of the petty-bourgeois intelligentsia that took no part in sabotage, and that worked honestly together with the Soviet power for a number of subsequent years. But these people remained mere specialists in their own line and did not merge organically either with the Party or with the working class. They imagined that to have the right to be called Soviet specialists it was sufficient for them to work only at their own specialities. They bear all the features of philistines, of petty-bourgeois, and experienced agents of the enemy frequently make use of these features of theirs to recruit them into their ranks.

And finally, there is the third group—of the real Soviet intelligentsia, which constitutes the greatest part of our intelligentsia, its overwhelming majority. This is the new Soviet intelligentsia which has come from the midst of the working class, which has enriched itself with the treasures of the old and the new cultures, which has passed through the severe schooling of the class struggle. To this group belongs, in particular, a considerable section of the old specialists, who have merged organically with the working class and adopted its splendid features, its vigilance and ability to discern class enemies. These are the people who have the right to the honoured title of "non-Party Bolsheviks."

Had Yagoda approached one of the representatives of this really Soviet intelligentsia, which constitutes the majority of intellectuals in our country, with his base suggestions, he would immediately have been exposed, and the counter-revolutionary, criminal, bandit organization would have been uncovered several years earlier.

The three doctors now in the dock cannot, of course, be classed in the category of representatives of the real Soviet intelligentsia.

I am defending Dr. Levin. Prior to 1934 Dr. Levin worked very conscientiously, showing great professional knowledge, in various hospitals, medical organizations, scientific societies. He treated Lenin and was a close acquaintance of Gorky. He enjoyed the confidence of Kuibyshev. He sincerely imagined that this proximity gave him the right to call himself an honest Soviet specialist. But he did not understand that this proximity was a mechanical one, that politically he was far from them. Levin was apolitical. He does not even have a clear notion as to what the Mensheviks are. In answer to a question as to his party affiliations, he replied here in Court that he belonged to the physicians' party. His reply brings out all his craft isolation from the working class. In reply to a question from the Procurator he stated that he was a coward, and the materials in the case, unfortunately, allow of no doubt on this point. Add to this that he is very wishy-washy, and inclined towards panic, and you will have a portrait of Levin as of a specialist belonging to the second group of the intelligentsia that I mentioned.

In recruiting the doctors according to the recipes of the fascist intelligence services, Yagoda adopted an individual approach to each one of them. Let us see what Yagoda himself said about this at the preliminary investigation. His attitude towards Pletnev was that of an outright bully: he collected compromising material about him. According to him, "Pletnev belonged to some sort of anti-Soviet grouping, and was an anti-Soviet person generally." Yagoda made use of this.

He influenced Kazakov through intimidation, and at the same time aroused the hope in him that he would render him some aid in his struggle against a group of doctors.

Yagoda took advantage of Kryuchkov's mercenary traits,

inspiring him with the hope that after Maxim's death he would become Gorky's literary heir, and, on the other hand, he also intimidated him by pointing out that he, Yagoda, was aware of the fact that Kryuchkov had embezzled money belonging to Gorky. And he had Kryuchkov under his thumb.

The Procurator stated that Levin was Yagoda's right hand—that he, together with Yagoda, was the organizer. Formally, this is correct. But if Levin was Yagoda's right hand, it must not be forgotten for a moment that the brain guiding this right hand was Yagoda. And the fact that Levin came to be Yagoda's right hand was simply a matter of chance. Yagoda knew Levin. Levin had the entrée to the sick, to the splendid people whom the "bloc of Rights and Trotskyites" was interested in removing. Yagoda worked over Levin for a long time, and did so very cunningly and subtly.

There was nothing shady in Levin's past history, no anti-Soviet sentiments; he had forty years of irreproachable work to his credit. Prior to his conversation with Yagoda he had been devoted to the Soviet government and probably had been attached to Gorky. Yagoda had to overcome Levin's internal resistance, and Yagoda spent a long, a very long time, in the endeavour to win him over, employing subtle methods which outdo the Jesuit methods of Ignatius Loyola. With the cunning of a foreign intelligence service agent he played on Levin's faint-heartedness, irresoluteness, vanity, credulity and timidity.

Yagoda himself testified that Levin was Peshkov's family physician and frequented Gorky's place; he naturally encountered Levin on more than one occasion. That is just why Yagoda directed his attention towards Levin and made him his right hand. He knew him, frequently came in contact with him in particular, and not with Pletnev or Kazakov.

Levin was needed to carry through criminal designs, and so Yagoda began to develop a closer interest in him and to pay attention to him. How was this attention expressed? Levin himself and Bulanov have spoken of it: French wine, flowers, facilitating customs formalities, dollars for a trip abroad. All this took place as a gradual process of winning Levin over, extending over many months, and perhaps many years, for Yagoda had been charged by the "Right and Trotskyite centre" long ago. Therefore these efforts to win him over extended over a prolonged period of time prior to the outright commission of the crime.

Levin, of course, did not and could not understand what it was all about. He naively imagined that Yagoda was doing this out of respect for his personal merits and qualities as a doctor. This agreeably tickled his sense of vanity—and Levin does not hide the fact that he was vain.

But Yagoda took excellent stock of this. Together with his

gratitude for the generosity and attentiveness of Yagoda, Levin began to feel a certain peculiar sort of dependence, which is just what Yagoda was aiming at.

The hour arrived for the carrying through of Yagoda's nefarious designs against Max Peshkov. I must tell you, Comrades Judges, that as I listened to Yagoda's explanations about the reasons for the murder of Max Peshkov, I came to the conclusion that the reasons here were of a twofold nature: Yagoda's profoundly base reason, and the commission given by the "bloc of Rights and Trotskyites" to inflict such a psychological blow on Gorky through the murder of his beloved son as would still further weaken the physical power of resistance of the great writer in his struggle against his illness. Yagoda's base personal motives undoubtedly coincided with the line of the "bloc of Rights and Trotskyites."

What does Yagoda say about this? At one point in his testimony he says literally the following: "I fostered within myself the idea of physically murdering Max Peshkov. He was in my way." At first there was the idea of murdering Max Peshkov with the aid of bandits, but it appeared dangerous to draw many people into such a crime, and the idea arose among the ringleaders of the "bloc of Rights and Trotskyites" that the best way to bring about the death of Max Peshkov was "death from disease."

I draw the attention of the Court to the fact that the idea of "death from disease" did not enter into or originate in the minds of the doctors. This idea originated with Yagoda, with the "bloc of Rights and Trotskyites." And he forced it on the doctors. While still under examination by the investigation authorities, in reply to a question as to "how is this to be understood?"—Yagoda said, "Very simply. A person naturally falls ill; he is sick for some time; those who surround him become accustomed, as is also natural, to the idea of the patient's either dying or recuperating. The physician who treats the patient can facilitate either the recovery of the patient or his death. . . ." ". . . Well, and all the rest is a matter of technique."

A doctor was needed to put this idea into effect. It was convenient to accomplish this black deed with the hands of others, with the hands of a doctor, while himself remaining aside.

Yagoda also employed theoretical arguments to win over Levin. Yagoda unfolded to Levin a peculiar "theory" which bore traces of the influence over him of the German fascist advocates of sterilization. Yagoda himself has testified that in the effort to win Levin over he employed theoretical arguments acquired from outside sources, as to the right of a doctor to put an end to a patient's life. "In a talk with Levin I began with the abstract question as to whether a doctor should assist in bringing about the death of his patient. On receiving a positive reply, I asked him whether he understood that patients are sometimes an obstacle to people around them, and that the death of such patients would be met with joy. Levin said that this was a debatable question, that a doctor had no right to put an end to the life of a human being, of a sick person. But I argued with him and pointed out that he was backward, and that 'we' (this should be understood as meaning modern people) held another point of view. I had several conversations with Levin on this subject."

But this proved to be insufficient. Levin apparently did not accept these "theoretical inoculations." Then Yagoda endeavoured to present the plan for murdering Maxim Peshkov as an act necessary in the interests of the state, and primarily in the interests of Gorky himself. He pointed out how fatal was Peshkov's influence over his father. In further conversations he stressed the point that the instruction to put an end to Maxim Peshkov was not his, Yagoda's, instruction, but that of a group of most responsible leading officials. In proof of this, in order that no doubts should be left in Levin's mind, he arranged a meeting between him and Yenukidze, who at that time occupied the post of Secretary of the Central Executive Committee of the U.S.S.R. and who personally expressed to Levin approbation of the plan of murder by "death from disease."

Why did not Levin expose this fascist gang? I have already spoken of his apolitical, irresolute nature and lack of character. But here, of course, the main role was played by the combination of methods employed against him by Yagoda. Levin was certain that Yagoda would stop at nothing.

At one point in his testimony Levin said with a shudder: "On every occasion I would call to mind Yagoda's terrible face and threats. Yagoda's speech made a terrible impression on me." Levin, this wishy-washy intellectual, this old, non-Party, credulous doctor, devoid of will power, trembled not so much for himself as for his family, which Yagoda had threatened to destroy.

Am I not entitled, Comrades Judges, to say that Levin was mentally terrorized by Yagoda, and that this also explains the role he played in these ghastly murders? Levin testified: "I felt myself enslaved by Yagoda; it was clear to me that at the first attempt to refuse to fulfil the tasks set by Yagoda or even should there be accidental failure threatening to lead to discovery, not only would I perish, but so would my family." He spoke of this. He took part in bringing about the death of Maxim Peshkov and then began the chain of the subsequent horrible crimes; Maxim Peshkov was followed by Kuibyshev, Kuibyshev by Maxim Gorky and Menzhinsky. What, then, were the motives impelling Levin to carry out these further awful charges of the "bloc of Rights and Trotskyites"?

592

An old Russian proverb says: "Once the claw is caught, the whole bird is lost." Having committed one crime, feeling himself bound to Yagoda by bonds of crime, it was still more difficult for Levin to get away from his influence.

Yagoda understood this, and his tone towards Levin changed sharply. He began to talk to him bullyingly, in a threatening language. With cynical candour he put his cards on the table before Levin, explained to him in whose interests Levin was acting, and the apolitical, non-Party Levin willy-nilly became a politician.

While not sharing the convictions of these gentlemen, Levin was in fact with them. He understood that, having become their accomplice, he could not but fulfil their instructions. Having bound himself up with counter-revolution and the criminal deeds of the organization, he shared Yagoda's fate. Such is the logic of counter-revolution.

But, Comrades Judges, did Levin really yield to Yagoda in his awful commissions without any internal resistance, without a mental struggle? I allow that Levin's epically tranquil relation here of his crimes could produce the impression of his being a dull-witted vivisector, when taken in connection with the letter to the press published by Levin after Gorky's death. But this letter was not Levin's creation, it was written at the time when Levin was completely under Yagoda's influence, and as far as I am concerned I have no doubt but that it was written at Yagoda's dictation. The jesuitic and pharisaic character of this letter must be placed entirely to the account of Yagoda.

If one examines Levin's testimony and letters, one can become convinced that he underwent a profound mental strain. He lived in a torment of frenzy. While in custody, he wrote a letter to Comrade Yezhov in which he made a clean breast of everything, wrote that the memory of his awful misdeeds weighed heavily on him. He wrote: "During these years I felt that I was cut off from my past life by heavy gates which Yagoda held to with an iron hand and which I was unable to open. In the autumn of 1936," he wrote in a letter, "I learnt that Yagoda was no longer People's Commissar of Internal Affairs and experienced a feeling of supreme happiness; I decided to devote the rest of my life to my former honest work, to devote my remaining strength to the happiness of the peoples, to devote all my strength, knowledge, experience and love to the sick, to the further prosperity of our splendid fatherland, for the happiness and well-being of which I could contribute a mite of labour. But the tormenting memory of my great crimes burdened my soul like a rock. Now, in prison, having related all that has taken place in my mind, I have felt a profound relief."

I am profoundly convinced that when he wrote this confession, laying his soul bare to Comrade Yezhov, he could not but feel relief, feel liberated of the infinitely heavy burden he had hidden till then. And when he spoke of his crimes here, before the Court of the people, before the Court of the working class he continued to feel this relief.

I am drawing to a close, Comrades Judges.

What should be done with Levin? I will not hide from you that at this moment, when I raise the question as to what should be done with Levin, the infinitely dear features of Maxim Gorky, the great writer, our national pride, the pride of the whole of toiling mankind, appear before my mind's eye, as do the features of that ardent Bolshevik, Comrade Kuibyshev, and of that uncompromising fighter against the enemies of the people, that man of encyclopaedic erudition, Comrade Menzhinsky. Had it not been for the crimes of the "bloc of Rights and Trotskyites," committed through the hands of Levin and two other doctors, these great people would have been alive now, and by their active, creative and splendid lives would have brought no small benefit to the cause of the building of Socialism, which they served all their lives and which, is served by all the politically mature people of our country.

But nevertheless, Comrades Judges, I still say that despite the weight of these thoughts, Levin should remain alive, although he should be given a very severe punishment. Your sentence is now awaited by these gentlemen in the prisoners' dock, who have committed a series of the most heinous crimes, who from the day of the revolution have fought against their people, against the working class, against the Party, against the independence of their country. They are the actual murderers of Gorky, Kuibyshev and Menzhinsky, but they are also guilty in that three doctors became murderers. This also lies at their door. They are the murderers of these doctors. For their nefarious ends they made murderers of people foreign to their criminal views, to their criminal activity. They transformed the art of an old doctor in helping suffering mankind into a weapon of death in his hands. Had Levin not met them, he would have lived peacefully to the end of his days, rendering aid to sufferers.

So, then, can an equal sign be placed between Levin and these gentlemen, however heinous his personal crimes? And while they, these gentlemen, are useless and worthless in the coming struggle for the happiness of mankind, old Dr. Levin can still live the few years which remain him, and attempt to expiate at least a part of his crimes by helping suffering mankind. I ask you to spare Dr. Levin his life.

THE PRESIDENT: Comrade Kommodov, member of the Collegium of Defence, will now speak.

COUNSEL FOR DEFENCE KOMMODOV: I think, Comrades

Judges, that there is no need for me to tell you how difficult is the task of Defence Counsel in the present case. This difficulty is rendered greater by the stern demand of the State Prosecutor, which has met with universal endorsement by Soviet public opinion.

But as far as our abilities and strength permit, it behooves us to gather at least bit by bit the arguments that will make it possible for us to ask, and for you perhaps to satisfy our request, and to depart from the stern demand that rang out from the lofty tribune of the State Prosecutor in relation to our clients.

The crimes of Levin, the crimes of Kazakov, the crimes of Pletnev are undoubtedly one link in a very long chain of crimes, which in their sum total characterize the methods, modes and means of struggle employed against the Soviet power by its enemies throughout the course of these twenty years.

This struggle died down at times only to burst forth again with greater force. Especially has it revived in recent years—a fact that must undoubtedly be connected with the advent to power of fascism, which found loyal allies in the shape of all the counter-revolutionary parties within the Union.

Fascism as a form of government is based on the degradation of mankind and cannot reconcile itself with the existence of a country where the system of social life is based on the principle of social justice and respect for human dignity. That is why the struggle against the Soviet Union has been placed on the order of the day by fascism as a most urgent task. And, as a matter of fact, they do not hide this. Bring to mind, Comrades Judges, the September 1936 Nuremberg Congress, the leaders of the fascist party, who openly and cynically preached a crusade against the Soviet power.

Several months prior to this, an article was printed in the Polish paper "Bunt Mlodich" ("Revolt of Youth") which stated: "We consider the main thing for modern Poland to be the need to smash the Germano-Russian pincers in which Poland finds itself today. In view of the fact that the struggle of over-populated Poland against over-populated Germany is simply absurd, we must destroy Russia . . . deprive her of her hegemony in the East, and acquire the land we need for colonization at the expense of Russia."

In printing this item, "Pravda" correctly called these young people brainless. But it is characteristic that the struggle against the Soviet Union is carried on openly through the press. To this should be added an item in the Japanese newspaper "Reki-si-Koren," which was reprinted by "Pravda," and in which a Japanese official, Sigotomi, discusses the idea of the same food for horses and for men in the future war. And his point of departure was as follows: the rice required by the Japanese will not grow at the war fronts, while the available food reserves will freeze there.

It is absolutely clear that what is referred to here is not a war in Singapore, but a war in cold Russia; it is clear that they are openly and cynically preaching a crusade against the Soviet Union.

Thus the struggle against the Soviet Union by fascism has been placed on the order of the day as an urgent task. What means do they employ in the fight against us? I would say—all means by which in their opinion they can weaken the Soviet Union and lead to the destruction of the Soviet Union, which help or can help them in the coming war. Do not seek, Comrades Judges, for scruples as to the means of struggle. One of the characteristic features of the advent of the fascists to power is the complete corruption of public morals. The methods of struggle against the Soviet Union are espionage, wrecking, acts of diversion and murder, support for armed gangs, terror, etc.—an entire assortment of means designed to bring about the weakening and crushing of the Soviet Union. The Procurator has cited here to you innumerable cases of espionage, wrecking and terror. The forms of wrecking have changed somewhat in recent times; I would say they have become more subtle and more dangerous.

Remember the wrecking activities spoken of by Chernov, former People's Commissar of Agriculture, and by Khodjayev—the wrecking in agriculture and in sericulture. The accused Chernov related how on his instructions a plague bacillus was cultivated without its virulence being destroyed. Whole factories were set up which supplied these preparations as prophylactic means, whereas actually they were a means of spreading infection.

As far as I am concerned, it is clear to me that with such wrecking work carried through on the instructions of Chernov and Khodjayev, there were also undoubtedly people who suffered innocently.

Khodjayev said here literally the following: we hit and hit hard at those who opposed the operation of these wrecking measures. To use Khodjayev's words, they carried through these wrecking measures under the guise of mechanization, and those who resisted them they accused of anti-Soviet sentiments and dealt with them. And so it seems to me that many local officials suffered thereby; many local officials who did not suspect all the monstrous designs of the enemy were the victims of these individuals.

In terrorist activity new methods of removing political leaders have also appeared. It should be stated that in the fascist countries terrorism is particularly widespread. It is valued there not only as a means of removing unwanted people, but mainly as a means of provoking war as well. I will say more—there are theoreticians who have found an ideological basis for justifying terrorism as a means of struggle against the Soviet Union. Very characteristic in this connection is the report of a certain Professor Radulescu at the Fourth Conference for the Unification of Criminal Legislation, held in Paris. At this conference Professor Radulescu was the official reporter on the question of terrorism. And it is interesting how this professor disclosed the meaning and content of this international delictum in his report: "It is a matter of attempts undertaken either with the aim of violently destroying all political and legal organization of society, attempts characteristic of the anarchists, or with the aim of violently overthrowing the economic and social order of the majority of the modern states, attempts characteristic of revolutionary Communism. Revolutionary Communism," continues Radulescu, "in our days constitutes one of the most dangerous threats to public order in general."

I repeat, he was the official reporter on the question of terrorism, quite openly and cynically preaching terrorism against the leaders of Communism, against the revolutionary movement.

One could point further to the attempt at the Brussels Conference of the fascist criminologist Garofolo, to place the actions of the working people fighting for liberation from the yoke of exploitation, from the capitalist yoke, on a par with those of international thieves and counterfeiters. With such an understanding of terrorism, ideologically justified against the Soviet Union, and not only against the Soviet Union, but against the leaders of the Communist movement in general, what is there surprising, then, in the fact that terrorist activity has revived in all countries of the world, and terrorist acts are occurring in all parts of the globe? This activity has revived in our country as well. There has also been a refinement, I would say, in the methods and modes of terrorist acts, and the method employed in the present case, in relation to Comrades Menzhinsky, Kuibyshev and Gorky, is a fundamentally new one.

You remember, Comrades Judges, the period of kulak terrorism which existed in the years 1929-30-31, when many honest and active Soviet workers, village librarians, village newspaper correspondents, perished. You remember that the usual means employed in committing these terrorist acts was the sawed-off shotgun, the axe, the dagger, the knife. Later on we see how terrorist acts were carried through according to a definite, organized plan. Call to mind the murder of that people's tribune, Sergei Mironovich Kirov. From the Pyatakov trial and the present trial we know that terrorist groups were organized throughout the Soviet Union.

One of the methods of murder in the present case is the method characterized by Yagoda as "death from disease." I must say that the history of human malefactions does not know of such a method. Comrade the Procurator cited cases of numerous poisoning by doctors, characteristic of the Middle Ages. Quite right. The entire history of the Florentine Republic during the days of the Borgias and Medici, was full of cases of poisoning. Frequently they too resorted to the aid of physicians. Pope Alexander VI, having poisoned Cardinal Orsini with the assistance of doctors, cynically told the College of Cardinals that "we placed him in the hands of the very best doctors." At that time poisoning, as a means of doing away with people, was usually practised through some medium such as gloves, books, flowers, perfumes, furniture.

But what Yagoda devised bears a far more subtle character. I know of no such example in Russian practice. I have read in Stendhal's novels of something like it in the days of the Medici, but I know of no other examples. At first Pletnev also understood this method as a proposal to use poison, but Yagoda told him, "No, that is crude, too crude and dangerous; the thing to do is to employ a suitable method of treatment to hasten the end of the people whom you will be called on to treat."

Any employment of poison is undoubtedly more dangerous than the method that has begun to be employed in recent times, particularly in the present case. Although there are poisons which vanish rapidly they leave traces of pathological or anatomical changes in the organism.

Defence Counsel Braude has spoken of how Yagoda explained the idea of death from disease to the investigating authorities. I must say that one cannot read these words in the formulation used by Yagoda himself to describe it without shuddering.

It is very simple, says Yagoda. A person falls ill, and everybody becomes accustomed to his being sick. The doctor can facilitate his recovery, but the physician can also facilitate his death. This is the gist of the idea. "And all the rest," adds Yagoda, "is a matter of technique." According to Yagoda, when he told this to the old man Levin, the latter was stupefied.

There are many, very many cruel methods of killing. But I must say that not a single one of these methods is so heartrending, so nerve-racking as the method described in the present case, even though the individual does not die in a ravine with a broken head, but at home in his bed, surrounded by the solicitude of all. No other method of killing can arouse such public indignation as this one.

It is an insult to all the ethical principles of the doctor, who even on the battlefield must render aid to the enemy. This method kills the confidence of patients in physicians.

That is why it shocks public opinion so. It is so horrible that it leaves a sort of depressed feeling in the mind when you learn of it.

The question arises, how could doctors each of whom has forty years of medical practice to his credit, and who have grown grey in their profession, resort to such a method of murder?

Comrades Judges, every profession undoubtedly gives rise to definite instincts, as for instance the profession of Defence Counsel gives rise to an instinct of defence; the same is true of physicians. To resort to such a method of killing, one must uproot this instinct, kill oneself as a doctor and then undertake the murder of a human

598

being. How could they commit such a crime? This is a question which cannot but agitate people, a question which everybody is raising, a question which perhaps prevents many people from sleeping peacefully. And it is our task to explain this difficult problem.

An explanation easily arises in the sense that perhaps it was assisted by personal sentiments, or anti-Soviet sentiments. I think that is not the explanation, and I shall take the liberty of saying why. Had Pletnev's anti-Soviet sentiments been a sufficient stimulus for him to resort to such a crime, Levin would not have needed the assistance of Yagoda, who had to exert pressure on Pletnev before he resorted to such a crime. It would have been sufficient for Levin alone to have said the word and Pletnev would readily have agreed.

But what do we see? We see the opposite. Levin told Kazakov, Levin told Pletnev, but before the meeting with Yagoda neither the one nor the other had committed any wrecking. More than that, on November 6, Kazakov was with Menzhinsky; at that time Menzhinsky had moved to Moscow, to his residence in Meshchanskaya Street—and when Kazakov saw that the air was heavy, polluted, one in which the very sick Comrade Menzhinsky found difficulty in breathing, he gave instructions for all the rooms to be aired, for Menzhinsky to be brought onto the balcony. And that day he went to Yagoda who met him with the words: "Why are you fiddling about, why don't you act?"

What is the significance of the very summons to Pletnev and Kazakov to go to Yagoda? It signified that Levin did not count on being able by a mere talk, or by playing on Kazakov's base feelings and Pletnev's anti-Soviet sentiments, to spur them on to monstrous crimes. And this is understandable, because before undertaking this crime both the one and the other had to change his nature and uproot the instinct that had arisen as a result of forty years of medical activity.

That also was not enough. Yagoda attempted to draw Pletnev into this crime by playing on his anti-Soviet sentiments. He spoke of the unification of all anti-Soviet forces, asserting that he, Yagoda, would help them in their counter-revolutionary action. But he himself did not hope that his assertions would produce favourable results, that was why he demanded to be given compromising material affecting Pletnev. But even when Pletnev saw the compromising material that had been gathered against him by Yagoda he still did not agree.

Then Yagoda resorted to the most effective means; he threatened, and said: "I shall not stop at the most extreme measures to compel you to serve me." Read the following in Yagoda's testimony of this conversation with Kazakov: "Why are you fiddling about? Why do you do things on your own account which you

599

should not do?" When Kazakov began to justify himself, says Yagoda, "I threatened him, I hurled a volley of threats at him, and he agreed."

Thus that old man Levin was right when he said: "Fear of threats, fear of Yagoda, spurred me on to this crime." And he was right not only as regards himself, but also as regards his fellow accused, Pletnev and Kazakov.

Allow me to dwell on this moment. It was the most terrible moment in their lives, it was more terrible than the trial and the sentence. For that reason allow me to dwell upon it.

Comrades Judges, blackmailing by threats of death is no joke. It breaks down not only men of flaccid old age but sometimes even strong, powerful, healthy young men. In 1880 at the trial of the "Sixteen" young Okladsky said in his last plea: "I do not ask the Court for clemency. Any clemency whatsoever would be humiliation to me." But in a few months' time he became a traitor. What took place in this period? Merely an interview with Sudeykin, who said to him: "Death or treachery." And he chose the second. Blackmailing by threats of death is no joke. But how else could both Pletnev and Kazakov take Yagoda's threat? How else could Yagoda's threats be taken by Pletnev, to whom Yagoda stated: "I shall not stop at the most extreme measures both in relation to yourself and in relation to your family, to compel you to serve me." How else could Yagoda's threats be taken by Kazakov, to whom Levin said when blessing him as he was about to see Yagoda: "You must understand that this man will stop at nothing, this man forgets nothing." And was Levin not right? Did the law keep Yagoda back from committing monstrous crimes? Did conscience keep Yagoda back from engaging in unheard of infamy? Did reason hold him back from committing desperate acts? What else could have held him back? The lack of opportunities? But you know the degree of authority with which Yagoda was invested. What could have prevented him from achieving his nefarious aims? The lack of will power? Weak nerves? Who can believe this!

What tenacity one must possess, what craftiness one must possess to enable one, while occupying such a responsible post, being in the public eye, and having as his main task the struggle to preserve and protect the Socialist state over a number of years, to carry on work daily to bring about the defeat of the state and to go unpunished!

In the last analysis, both Yagoda and his accomplices miscalculated. They did not understand one thing, the chief thing. If there are dozens of unscrupulous people sapping the foundations of the Soviet Union, there are millions of honest people protecting it by their vigilance and devotion.

That is why the ruin they were preparing for the Soviet Union and at the same time for each one of us descended on their own heads. He who sows the wind reaps the whirlwind.

But it is not they who are important to me just now. What is important to me is the behaviour of Pletnev and Kazakov at that ill-fated moment when they were face to face with Yagoda in his office. The question was put to them bluntly. They understood quite well that the menace facing them was a real one. What is more, both Kazakov and Pletnev understood perfectly well that Yagoda could not but carry out his threats. This was dictated by the position of Yagoda himself. After Yagoda had spoken of the conspiracy, after Yagoda had stated that he himself was a participant in the conspiracy, after he had made the proposition to them to commit this monstrous crime, he could not but carry out his threats.

In what way could he safeguard himself against Kazakov and Pletnev as witnesses of his conversation with them?

There were two ways: either at all costs to win them as accomplices in the crime, and then they would be silent, or else to compel them to be silent, even at the price of destroying them. It is impossible to invent any third way. These were the conditions under which the question was raised before Pletnev and Kazakov.

Comrades Judges, under these conditions they had to give a reply without delay. There was no way for them to escape. There was no time to think the matter over. Here was a moment when the fate of a man was being decided. And at that moment Yagoda was eyeing them with his evil, piercing glance. I can imagine that this fatal, piercing glance crushed their consciousness, paralysed their will, killed their feelings. Reason, when shaken, Comrades Judges, often does not bear up under its own weight and goes mad, and a free man is broken.

Perhaps I do not possess the necessary words capable of enabling you to feel the whole horror of the moment through which Pletnev and Kazakov passed. If I had had these words at my command, I would not be in the least uneasy as to their lives.

The horrible thing is frequently not in what an individual does but what he becomes afterwards. What did they become after this moment of their fall? Before they became the murderers of others they morally murdered themselves. This was a moment which killed them themselves. They made their conscience, the conscience of physicians, black as the conscience of a tyrant. They bespattered the name of professor with the filth of unbelievable crimes, they cast shame on the halo surrounding men of science, they trampled upon the name of man. Only a great psychologist can describe such moments.

All the rest is the consequence of this moment. The moment Yagoda broke them, the moment they gave their consent, they became moral corpses, they killed themselves. And you, Comrades

Judges, know who it was that spurred them on first to moral suicide and then to the murder of others.

That is why I request clemency for them. That is why the Counsel for Defence asks that they not be placed on the same level in punishment as those who were their murderers.

There is yet another argument for the defence. When speaking here of participation in crimes, the Procurator theoretically correctly developed the thought that a member of an organization is responsible for all the crimes committed by that organization. But as a practical man, as the State Prosecutor, he told you, Comrades Judges, that in each specific case one must judge how closely one or another criminal was implicated in the commission of the crime. This gave him grounds for departing from the severe demand of punishment in relation to the accused Rakovsky and Bessonov.

According to this standard, have Pletnev and Kazakov less grounds for clemency? They were drawn into the chain of these great crimes later. Others of the accused are guilty of crimes extending from the year 1918 to the present time. My clients did not know of this, were not privy to this.

We believe, Comrades Judges, that you will take these arguments of the defence into account, and that despite the series of ghastly and unparalleled monstrous crimes committed by Pletnev, Kazakov and Levin you will find it possible to spare their lives. And if they are destined to live, after your sentence, then let them remember the words of a certain public figure of the Great French Revolution who said: "Mercy can also be insulted if it is given to the unworthy." Their task will be to use the rest of their lives to prove that they were worthy of the mercy extended to them by you. They have admitted their guilt. They have stated: "We repent." And I believe them, Comrades Judges. Woe wears no mask.

When Pletnev wrote in his statement to Comrade Yezhov that after confessing he felt relief, when Kazakov said the same thing, they were not being hypocritical. In their position, their conscience, the trial, the punishment and the mental suffering are all that can reconcile them to themselves, at least to some extent. At times distress is the only form of truth, and they well understand it.

I have said that the task before them, if they are destined to live, is to prove that they are worthy of mercy. How can they do this? They must forget themselves, and give everything they possess—knowledge, experience, practice, theory—to the fatherland that they betrayed. And they do have something to give. Forty years of Pletnev's medical, clinical, professorial, and pedagogical activities have given him great scientific treasure. He is capable of work, even while under detention he has been engaged on his scientific works. Kazakov has a medical, chemical and agronomical education. Thirty years of research work have undoubtedly enriched Kazakov and he must pass on this wealth to others.

They must give themselves to their fatherland without stint. This is the demand made on them by their defence if they are fated to live. And to you, Comrades Judges, I address only one appeal—spare them their lives.

THE PRESIDENT: Adjournment for 20 minutes.

* * *

COMMANDANT OF THE COURT: The Court is coming, please rise.

THE PRESIDENT: Please be seated. The session is resumed. Accused Bessonov, inasmuch as you have declined Counsel, you are entitled to make a speech in your defence, or perhaps you wish to combine your speech in defence with your last plea?

BESSONOV: Yes.

THE PRESIDENT: Accused Grinko?

GRINKO: I waive the speech in defence, I shall combine it with my last plea.

THE PRESIDENT: Accused Chernov?

CHERNOV: I waive the speech in defence. I shall say everything in my last plea.

THE PRESIDENT: Accused Ivanov?

IVANOV: I waive it. I shall defend myself in my last plea.

THE PRESIDENT: Accused Krestinsky, do you wish to avail yourself of your right to a speech in defence?

KRESTINSKY: No, only my last plea.

THE PRESIDENT: Accused Zubarev?

ZUBAREV: I waive the speech in defence.

THE PRESIDENT: Accused Rykov?

RYKOV: I shall only make a last plea.

THE PRESIDENT: Accused Sharangovich?

SHARANGOVICH: I do not intend to defend myself, therefore I waive the speech in defence, I shall only speak in the last plea.

THE PRESIDENT: Accused Khodjayev?

KHODJAYEV: I also waive it.

THE PRESIDENT: Accused Zelensky?

ZELENSKY: I waive it.

THE PRESIDENT: Accused Ikramov, do you wish to avail yourself of your right to a speech in defence?

IKRAMOV: I waive it.

THE PRESIDENT: Accused Rakovsky?

RAKOVSKY: I waive the speech in defence, I shall only avail myself of my last plea.

THE PRESIDENT: Accused Rosengoltz, do you wish to avail yourself of your right to a speech in defence?

ROSENGOLTZ: No, I shall avail myself only of the last plea.

THE PRESIDENT: Accused Bukharin?

BUKHARIN: I waive a special speech in defence, but shall combine defence on certain points of the accusation with my last plea.

THE PRESIDENT: Accused Bulanov?

BULANOV: I shall only avail myself of the last plea.

THE PRESIDENT: Accused Yagoda?

YAGODA: Only the last plea.

THE PRESIDENT: Accused Kryuchkov?

KRYUCHKOV: Only the last plea.

THE PRESIDENT: Accused Maximov-Dikovsky?

MAXIMOV: I shall avail myself of the last plea.

THE PRESIDENT: In that case we shall pass on to the last pleas. Accused Bessonov, you have your last plea.

BESSONOV: Citizens Judges, together with the other accused I answer here before the proletarian Court for the very grave crimes against the state, committed by the "bloc of Rights and Trotskyites" and by myself personally as one who actively participated in it. Of these crimes the most terrible, tremendous, is the treason to the fatherland of which I am guilty. I was an intermediary in and participant of the criminal negotiations between the "bloc of Rights and Trotskyites" and fascist circles in Germany. In these negotiations there culminated the criminal collaboration begun long ago between the "bloc of Rights and Trotskyites" and the fascist agency abroad, a collaboration designed to undermine the military and economic power of the U. S. S. R., to hasten a fascist attack on the land of victorious Socialism.

In these negotiations the war incendiaries from both sides elaborated a monstrous line for the defeat of the U.S.S.R., outlined a plan of huge territorial concessions to the enemy.

The stern hand of proletarian justice was timely in uncovering the ghastly ulcers of treason and treachery, in exposing the monstrous plot and placing its participants, including myself, before the relentless responsibility of Soviet law.

I was also an intermediary and participant in the criminal connections between the "bloc of Rights and Trotskyites" and the whiteguard émigré section of the so-called "Trudovaya Krestyanskaya Partia." Deprived of all support whatsoever within the country, spurred on by their fascist masters, the leaders of the "bloc of Rights and Trotskyites" strove to gather under their wing all the agents of fascism within the U.S.S.R., including the so-called "Trudovaya Krestyanskaya Partia." Proletarian justice dealt a crushing blow to this miserable effort, too.

Not all the crimes of the "bloc of Rights and Trotskyites," of which I personally am also guilty, such as the execution of the heinous design to destroy the great writer of the working class, the treacherous killing of several outstanding figures of the Soviet country could be prevented by justice. But apart from the crimes spoken of in the Indictment and in the speech of Citizen the State Prosecutor, I must admit yet another crime against proletarian justice, which has not been spoken of at the trial.

In the year that has passed since I was arrested, I have already on one occasion faced a proletarian Court, and hid from it the facts of my anti-Soviet activity of which I am accused at the present trial.

I was arrested on February 28, last year. The investigation on my first case lasted five and a half months. Extensive material was collected by the organs of the People's Commissariat of Internal Affairs, a large number of witnesses was examined, several confrontations took place, references were collected with regard to me and my connections from all places where I had worked. Everything was checked up. A year has gone by and what then?

Making use of the fact that the testimony given about me by individuals not participating in the present trial did not completely reflect the real state of affairs, I stubbornly denied the main charges preferred against me, namely, that I belonged to an illegal anti-Soviet organization.

On August 13, last year, I faced the Military Collegium of the Supreme Court which was 'composed of almost the same people as in the present trial, but sat in camera, and applied the law of December 1,1934.[1] The Military Collegium subjected all the accusations made against me to a careful examination. I was enabled to give an extensive explanation on all the questions put to me. However, in Court as well, I continued the same tactics of disavowal that I had mastered at the investigation. After a thorough investigation of the case, the Military Collegium did not consider it possible either to acquit me or to pass sentence on me, and sent my case for further examination.

An additional four and a half months passed by. During that time the organs of the People's Commissariat of Internal Affairs discovered several threads capable of leading to the discovery of my illegal anti-Soviet activity. And it was only at the end of last year that there was discovered for the first time the thread that led from Krestinsky to me. On October 28, last year, exactly ten months after my arrest, I was shown that part of Krestinsky's testimony which exposed me as the liaison man between the "bloc of Rights and Trotskyites" and abroad and Trotsky. Since Krestinsky, after Pyatakov, was the only person who knew everything about my anti-Soviet activity, I no longer had the energy and did not attempt to maintain my former position of disavowal, I only asked for a few days in which to think things over, and these were granted to me. I was faced with the choice: either to continue my former tactics of disavowal with immeasurably smaller chances of success, in view of the fact that the investigating authorities possessed far greater materials about my anti-Soviet activity and were on the unerringly correct road, or else, to make a clean breast of everything that I knew to the investigation authorities.

Only on December 30 of last year did I state to the investigating authorities that I was breaking resolutely and utterly with my criminal past, and that I would begin to give testimony frankly and thoroughly. I did not prevaricate nor did I deny things. The break with the criminal past—and I very clearly understood this—could only assume one form, the form of complete, frank detailed testimony. I testified absolutely everything I knew both of the facts that were wholly or partly known to the investigating authorities, and of facts that were not known to the investigating authorities. I mention this circumstance not because I wish to see in it any circumstance mitigating my guilt, but only in order by this touch to complete the picture of the ten months of fruitless struggle against proletarian justice, a struggle that has the sad advantage of being outstandingly long even at the present trial.

Citizens Judges, lofty words are out of place and not very convincing on the lips of a person accused, as I am, of very grave crimes against the State. It is late to beat one's breast, and—to repeat the words of Citizen the State Prosecutor—to unmask one's own crimes. But there is one circumstance on which I cannot but touch. Not because I see in it the mitigation of my tremendous guilt, but because it alone has given me the strength to avail myself of the right of accused to make a last plea. My criminal activity took place in the conditions of work carried on abroad. My lengthy detachment from Soviet realities also explains to a considerable degree the fact that I took the criminal path. The more than six years of my sojourn in a directly capitalist environment had a fatal effect on my political behaviour.

But there is another side to this fact of my stay abroad to which I would like to devote a couple of words. Had I been a consistent betrayer of my country, nothing, it would appear, would have prevented me remaining on the other side of the border, particularly after the trial of January, 1937, when Pyatakov—the immediate leader of my criminal work, about whose possible testimony against me I could build the most gloomy conjectures was exposed and sentenced, and yet, at the first call in February 1937, I appeared in Moscow to answer before the fatherland. Now it is this, at first glance, inexplicable inconsistency, which drove me to my country, while criminal logic apparently should

606

have dictated the opposite to me, that gives me the right to say now: whatever the sentence of the proletarian Court, it will be the sentence of my country, and I shall accept it with resignation.

THE PRESIDENT: Accused Grinko, you may avail yourself of your last plea.

GRINKO: I am making my last plea not in order to defend myself before the Supreme Court. I have nothing to say in my defence. Nor shall I make use of this plea in order to ask for a mitigation of the sentence. I have no right to a mitigation of the sentence. I am wholly and completely in agreement with the qualification and political estimation, both of our crimes in general and of my crimes in particular, as given in the speech of the Procurator of the U.S.S.R. Yes, that is how things stand.

I face the Supreme Court as a traitor to the country, as an active participant of the plot of the Rights and Trotskyites against Socialism victorious in the U.S.S.R., as an ally and agent of capitalism in its mortal struggle against Socialism, as an offender against the state who had set his hand to the preparation of the provocation of war, of the dismemberment of the U.S.S.R. for the benefit of fascism, who had set his hand to the preparation of the murder of the best people of our country and to the violent overthrow of the Socialist state and public order in the U.S.S.R.

There is nothing to be added to this list of crimes. Many facts and criminal deeds of the "bloc of Rights and Trotskyites" became known to me, as apparently to several others of the accused, for the first time in the Court itself. But I must say to you outright that the most monstrous of these crimes—the monstrous murders of the best people of our country as outlined by Yagoda, facts that I was unaware of before—have not surprised me, for in them I have beheld the countenance and handiwork of the plot of Rights and Trotskyites; in them I have beheld the line of the "bloc of Rights and Trotskyites" and its leaders. Our former leaders would have done better had they not made any attempt at all in Court to mitigate in any way whatsoever their direct responsibility for all these deeds. None of us can or should avoid this responsibility.

Like some others of the accused, I face the Court as a direct agent and spy of fascist powers and their intelligence services, as a direct ally of fascism in its struggle against the U.S.S.R.

But it was not fascism that made me such. Fascism gathered for itself the ready fruits of the many years of struggle by the Trotskyites and the Rights against the Party and the Soviet power. It is to Trotsky and Bukharin that I am obliged for the "ideology," pardon the expression, and the school of monstrous double-dealing led us all to outright fascism.

I face the Court as a Ukrainian bourgeois nationalist and at the same time as a participant in the "bloc of Rights and Trotskyites."

607

This is no chance combination. The hunting after bourgeois nationalists and the political corruption of unstable political elements in the national republics are old-established stubbornly conducted tactics of the Trotskyites and the Rights.

It was along the criminal treasonable path that the Ukrainian national-fascist organizations came to join the forces of the counter-revolution united in the "bloc of Rights and Trotskyites." This Ukrainian national-fascist organization operated at one and the same time both on the instructions of the "bloc of Rights and Trotskyites" and on the instructions of the fascist intelligence services.

My very grave crimes, as a participant in the plot of Rights and Trotskyites are to a tremendous degree aggravated by the following circumstances.

Firstly, as one of the organizers of the Ukrainian national-fascist organization, I operated particularly in the Ukraine, that is to say, at the main gates through which German fascism is preparing its blow against the U.S.S.R.

At the orders of the "bloc of Rights and Trotskyites" and of the German intelligence service, the Ukrainian national-fascist organization, including myself, conducted a tremendous amount of work to undermine the western border of the U.S.S.R. And it seems to me that it is only the absence of the desire to tell the complete truth to the Court that explains the fact that while both Rykov and Bukharin admit personal contacts with me, as a participant of the "bloc of Rights and Trotskyites" they deny contact through me with the Ukrainian national-fascist organization which was an important card in the anti-Soviet struggle of the "bloc of Rights and Trotskyites."

This Ukrainian national-fascist organization—Lyubchenko, Poraiko and others—completes the last link in the long chain of criminal deeds committed against the Ukrainian people, by various factions of Ukrainian bourgeois-nationalism from the very beginning of the revolution.

The Procurator of the U.S.S.R. was right when he said that under the leadership of the Bolshevik Party and the Soviet government, the Ukrainian people, advancing along the road of the national policy of Lenin and Stalin, have been raised to such a high level as never before in all its previous history. The Bolshevik Party and Soviet power have created the Ukrainian state, they have made the Ukraine a very rich industrial and collective farming country, they have raised Ukrainian national culture to an unprecedented high level. And this Ukrainian national fascist organization, which it is my sad lot to represent before the Court, was, by resorting to bogus slogans of national "independence," leading the Ukrainian people to the yoke of German fascists and Polish gentry.

The second circumstance which makes my guilt, as a participant in the plot of Rights and Trotskyites, more grave is that for over two years I knew of the conspiracy in the Red Army, I was personally connected with a number of the outstanding military conspirators who were undermining the defensive power of the U.S.S.R. and preparing its defeat. I knew and was connected, with people both in the Ukrainian organization as well as in the Red Army, who were preparing to do what was spoken of at this trial, to open the front to the enemy.

The third circumstance which adds to the gravity of my guilt before the peoples of the U.S.S.R. is that in the course of several months I knew not only of the general terrorist line of the centre of Rights and Trotskyites, but I also knew about the fact that two terrorist groups, day after day, kept trailing Stalin and Yezhov, with the aim of assassinating them. In other words, I raised my hand against Stalin, who is honoured by the working people of the entire world as the genius of liberated humanity, and against Yezhov, who personifies the great determination of the Party to crush the enemies of the U.S.S.R.

Finally, my guilt is made more grave by the high station which I occupied, by my high post and by the confidence shown in me by the Central Committee and Stalin.

The Party raised me from the petty-bourgeois mire, it placed me in a high post in the government, a high station, entrusted me with State secrets and with control over the State finances of the U.S.S.R. I betrayed these secrets. I permitted, I collaborated in the utilization of State funds, public funds of the U.S.S.R. to finance an unparalleled conspiracy against the peoples of the U.S.S.R.

I recall one episode of my life. In 1933, when the Ukrainian nationalist organization was destroyed and several of my closest pals were arrested, I was seriously compromised by my personal contact with them. My Party organization recoiled from me. I was alone and isolated. And I wrote a personal letter to Stalin about this. On the very same day, on the very same evening I received over the telephone from the leadership of the Central Committee a very warm message of comradely encouragement and support which put me at ease. And within a few months I was shown such confidence as is the dream of every Party member. I was elected to the Central Committee of the C.P.S.U.

And to all of this I replied by betrayal, by darkest betrayal, of the Party, the fatherland and Stalin.

And it is in conditions like these, members of the Supreme Court, that I must tell you of my remorse. I very well understand with what scorn and contempt every Soviet person will meet these words of repentance coming as they do from me. Nevertheless, I must say this because it corresponds to the truth, because there is no one else to whom I can address these words. In the situation in which I found myself there was only one way open to me to prove by my deeds that I have repented, and that was to disclose all the facts of the conspiracy and all the participants in the conspiracy known to me to the investigating authorities and the Court. I have done this to the end. In my testimony I did not spare myself, did not spare any of my confederates. I named all the facts and all the plotters known to me. I must confess that I did not do this at once. But was it possible for me at one blow to overcome the inertia of many years of stubborn and dangerous underground struggle against the Soviet government, to suppress the feeling of friendship for accomplices, to destroy the ulcer of double-dealing, to suppress the feeling of shame? In a word, could I at once lay bare my soul, the soul of a traitor, the like of which the world has never seen? But I have done this to the very end and the Court has had the possibility of verifying this.

In my situation there is still another form in which to express repentance. Unfortunately this is a form which cannot directly be checked by the Court but nonetheless this form does not cease to exist because of this. I refer to my inner feeling of satisfaction. I make bold to speak of my happiness at the fact that our villainous conspiracy has been discovered and that the unexampled calamities, which we were preparing and partially carried out against the U.S.S.R., have been averted. The People's Commissariat of Internal Affairs, given new vitality, wiped out the plot of Rights and Trotskyites in their last lair. I am glad of this.

I will accept the most severe verdict—the supreme penalty— as deserved. I have only one wish: I wish to live through my last days or hours, no matter how few they may be, I wish to live through and die not as an enemy taken prisoner by the Soviet government, but as a citizen of the U.S.S.R. who has committed the gravest treachery to the fatherland, whom the fatherland has severely punished for this, but who repented.

THE PRESIDENT: Accused Chernov, you may make your last plea.

CHERNOV: Citizens Judges, I am taking advantage of my right to the accused's last plea not in order to defend or exculpate myself. The heinous crimes which I committed against the great Soviet country can neither be exculpated nor defended.

I am a traitor to the Socialist fatherland. I was selling the interests of the fatherland to fascism, that enemy of the working class and of the whole of humanity. I am a spy in the employ of the German intelligence service, an active member of the counter-revolutionary organization of Rights, an organization of wrecking and diversion. I am an active participant of the "bloc of Rights and Trotskyites," which had for its aim the overthrow of the Socialist social and state system existing in the U.S.S.R. and the restoration of capitalism, the restoration of the power of the bourgeoisie. I am an active participant of the bloc which undertook crimes unprecedented in their monstrosity in order to achieve its aims— the restoration of capitalism, and utilized the whole arsenal of banditry for this purpose.

The crimes which I committed, I repeat, can be neither defended nor exculpated. They merit the most severe punishment.

How could it come about that I, in whom the Party placed the greatest confidence, could betray the Party and fatherland and become a spy in the employ of the German intelligence service and a member of a counter-revolutionary organization?

As I have already testified in Court, I had been a Menshevik in the course of a long period, and not a rank and file member of the Menshevik Party but the leader of one of its organizations, the Ivanovo-Voznesensk organization. I possessed sufficient education and political understanding to accept Menshevism conscientiously and fight for its program of the defence of capitalism.

I joined the Communist Party at a time when the forces of counter-revolution in the country were already smashed and when the working class under the leadership of the Bolsheviks emerged victorious from the civil war.

The time of my entry into the Communist Party coincides with the beginning of the New Economic Policy.[2] I did not appraise this policy in the way it was accepted by real Bolsheviks, but in my own, Menshevik way. Therefore, when the Party proceeded from its policy of limiting the kulaks and the capitalist elements in the cities towards the policy of an offensive and routing of them, my Menshevik soul could not reconcile itself to such a policy and I began to look around, in the anti-Soviet groups and parties, for people whose views corresponded to my Menshevism and whose practical aims implied the struggle for the overthrow of the Soviet government and the restoration of capitalism.

I found people with these views in the counter-revolutionary organization of the Rights. The views and practical aims of this organization fully and completely coincided with my own Menshevik views. In those days of 1928 I was yet a person of little importance in the Party. In saying this I have not the slightest desire to minimize my guilt or belittle my crimes. My crimes are boundless and monstrous. People like Rykov, Bukharin and Tomsky stood at the head of the counter-revolutionary organization of the Rights, and the fact that they arrived at the aim of overthrowing the Soviet government and restoring capitalism, that is to say they arrived at Menshevism, strengthened me in my Menshevik stand. This played a definite role in my joining the counter-revolutionary organization of the Rights.

Dan played an important role in my entering upon the path of a German spy. In his meetings with me Dan used to argue the necessity for the Rights to struggle against the Soviet power and to render assistance to capitalist states in the latter's struggle for the common aim, that is, for the overthrow of Soviet power. The fact that Dan himself, as I became convinced later, was an agent of the German intelligence service, was of great importance in my consenting to become a German spy. In enumerating the reasons which led me to espionage, I must also add my moral instability, namely, excessive drinking.

Upon my return to the Soviet Union from Germany it was my duty, not only as a member of the Party but as a citizen of the Soviet Union, to tell of the criminal contact which I had established with the German intelligence service. In doing so I would have reinstated myself in the ranks of honest citizens. I did not do this. I preferred to remain a traitor to the fatherland. During 1929 through Paul Scheffer and in the subsequent period up to my arrest, through Raivid, I served the German intelligence service and helped it in its struggle for the dismemberment of the Soviet Union and for the defeat of the U.S.S.R. in war.

The commissions I received from the German intelligence service, namely, to perform acts of wrecking and diversion coincided with the instructions which I received through Rykov from the centre of my counter-revolutionary organization of Rights. Essentially speaking there was no difference between the two. Both of them acted in one and the same direction, namely, striving to undermine the economic might and defence capacity of the Soviet Union and in this way to secure the latter's defeat in war, the overthrow of Soviet power and the restoration of capitalism.

This coincidence in the aims and practical instructions of the German intelligence service and of the centre of the Rights served as an extra inducement for me to continue espionage work and organize wrecking and acts of diversion.

In the course of my criminal activities, as an active participant of the counter-revolutionary organization of Rights and as a German spy, I carried out wrecking and diversion actions of a monstrous character and on a large scale. I gave detailed testimony on this at the preliminary investigation and spoke of it in Court.

The Party had shown me the greatest confidence by placing me at the head of the People's Commissariat of Agriculture. But I used this confidence against the Party, I used it against the fatherland. It was not the directions of the Party, aimed at consolidating the collective farming system, fostering the might of the collective farms and enhancing the well-being of the collective farmers, that I carried out; I carried out the directions of the centre of the counter-revolutionary organization of Rights and of the German intelligence service, tending to destroy the collective farming system, to undermine the collective farms. Rykov tried to deny here that he gave me instructions to organize wrecking activities in agriculture. I recall this not in order to lessen my guilt or shift the blame onto someone else. I do this with the sole purpose of establishing the truth.

Rykov wishes to depict matters as though he supplied only "ideological" advice on wrecking activities but took no part in the organization of these activities. This is not true. Or, to be more precise, this is only half of the truth, and a half truth is already a lie. On behalf of the centre of Rights, Rykov, side by side with the German intelligence service, directed all my activities in wrecking and diversion in agriculture.

On the very first day of my arrest, at the very first interrogation, I gave sincere and truthful testimony to the investigation authorities regarding my criminal activities as an active participant of the counter-revolutionary organization and as a German spy.

I also gave testimony to the investigation authorities regarding the people with whom I was connected in my counter-revolutionary and espionage work. I equally sincerely and truthfully testified in Court.

What prompted me to give truthful testimony immediately after my arrest?

The smashing of the counter-revolutionary organization of Rights began in 1937. The ringleaders of the organization, Rykov, Bukharin and others, were arrested, the counter-revolutionary organization of the Rights in the People's Commissariat of Agriculture was routed. Raivid, the above-mentioned resident agent of the German intelligence service, was arrested in the summer of 1937. All of this made me ponder over the question of whether the continuation of the struggle would be of any use. The reply could be only in the negative. The might of the Soviet state is invincible!

What was our counter-revolutionary organization? It was a gang of frenzied bureaucratic officials, it had no roots in the people. Agreements with the fascist governments formed its basis.

The Soviet people, despite all our machinations, the machinations of counter-revolutionaries, have built Socialism and have achieved an unprecedented victory. The realization of this might of the Soviet power and Soviet state led me to down arms immediately after my arrest and give sincere and truthful testimony.

My crimes are great and monstrous. Any punishment which

the Court deems necessary to mete out to me would be inadequate as against these crimes.

And nevertheless I make bold to plead to the Court and ask that it spare my life.

Should the Court find it possible to do so and should my life be spared, I will devote all my strength to the service of the great Soviet people.

I cannot expiate my crimes—they are too great. By my honest work in the future I shall try to make up if even for a very small particle of these terrible crimes against the fatherland, against the great Soviet country.

THE PRESIDENT: The Court is adjourned till 11 a.m.

[*Signed*] PRESIDENT: V. ULRICH

Army Military Jurist

President of the Military Collegium of the Supreme Court of the U.S.S.R.

SECRETARY: A. BATNER

Military Jurist First Rank

614

MORNING SESSION, MARCH 12, 1938

COMMANDANT OF THE COURT: The Court is coming, please rise.

THE PRESIDENT: Please be seated. The session is resumed. The accused Ivanov may make his last plea.

IVANOV: Citizens Judges, in my last plea I wish to tell the Court that I have fully and sincerely revealed the history of my criminal struggle against the Party and the Soviet power, against the Soviet people. I have hidden nothing, I have concealed nothing, either as regards my counter-revolutionary treasonable activities, or as regards the activities of the "bloc of Rights and Trotskyites," of which I was an active member.

I waived my speech for the defence because I fully admit and painfully realize my profound* guilt before the Soviet land, and have nothing to say in my defence.

The only thing that supported me in these dark days, the days of my public disgrace, was the thought that I had at last broken with that accursed and criminal past which bound me, that I had broken once and for all and had left it behind me.

When I was drawn into this criminal business of provocation, I was just a raw lad, without any experience in life. I did not stand the first test; I acted like a coward, took the first step along the path of treachery, and then slipped down the inclined plane and was sucked into the quagmire of treachery. And treachery has its own logic. I experienced its full power after the October Revolution. It would be false and a superfluous exaggeration if I were to say that I felt no sympathy at all for the October Revolution, that I did not accept it. The power of the proletarian party, the power of the Revolution is such that a man whose status in life is close to the working class—as I was—feels its influence even while fulfilling such a role as I was before the victory of the working class. In the period of the October Revolution I experienced both joy and fear: joy, together with the victorious masses, and fear at the menace of exposure. I must say that even then I did not have the courage to come and openly confess my treachery. And the fact that I did not do so was decisive, as my whole subsequent history shows. As time went on I came more and more to resemble a man who had been flung into the water with a weight tied to his feet, a man who passionately desires to reach the shore, while the weight steadily drags him to the bottom. And this bottom was the "Left Communists," and later my enlistment into the ranks of the organization of the Rights by Bukharin.

I believed that the menace of exposure of my provocateur activities would be removed only if the power of capitalism were restored. This constantly impelled me to seek for hostile forces of restoration, so that I might join them. I looked for people who desired what I did, who desired a bourgeois system. I sought for these people, and I found them in the organization of the Rights. It is therefore clear that I sympathized with all the actions and activities of the Rights, and of Bukharin, with whom I maintained anti-Soviet connections as the leader of the "Left Communists." It required no effort at all in 1928 to enlist me into the organization of the Rights. And then the whole subsequent development of my anti-Soviet activities was influenced by Bukharin, who led me step by step down the ladder of crime.

On Bukharin's instructions, I endeavoured in 1928 to organize a kulak insurrectionary "Vendée" in the North Caucasus. In 1932, again on his instructions, I associated myself with an uprising for the overthrow of the Soviet power in the North Caucasus, where I was working at that time. In 1934 Bukharin spoke to me of the need for defeat in war, of the necessity to base our plans on the aggressive fascist countries, on Germany and Japan in the first place. Accordingly, a group of Rights in the Northern Territory began to engage under my guidance in terrorist, diversive and espionage activities. After all this, it was strange to hear Bukharin declare here that he was a "pure theoretician" who concerned himself only about problematics and "ideology." Citizens Judges, the fact that I have laid down my arms and have repented would not be worth a brass farthing if in my last plea I did not raise my voice against this blatant untruth. According to Bukharin, the organization of the Rights comprised, on one hand, so-called pure theoreticians, leaders, who were not responsible for the specific crimes and who occupied themselves with the delicate and "noble" business of ideology; and, on the other hand, dirty practical men, who did all the damage, who were responsible for everything, who placed before Bukharin specific questions of terrorism, wrecking, diversion and espionage, while he, Bukharin, only listened and remained silent

Only in trials of counter-revolutionaries is such a thing possible, that the leaders lay the whole blame on the practical executors, and try to escape it themselves. Yes, I have committed monstrous crimes, and I am answering for them. But I committed them jointly with Bukharin, and we must answer for them jointly. And what ideology, indeed, could there be here? Hatred for the

Soviet power and the Party, calumny against its leaders—that was the whole of our ideology. And just because I, as an active participator, bear responsibility not only for my own activities but also for the activities of the whole organization of the Rights, I must firmly and clearly declare, Citizens Judges, that Bukharin has not told everything here, that he has concealed many of the threads and connections, and has tried to evade responsibility for his grave crime. Bukharin was not our ideologist. We conspirators needed no ideologists. Bukharin was the organizer of the Right conspirators; he selected people and placed them, gave them instructions and demanded account of them. Bukharin was the initiator of the practice of terrorism, wrecking and diversion, and of the whole system of defeatist measures. He was the principal leader of the espionage activities, and he it was who held in his hands the most important connections with the intelligence services of the fascist countries.

As such, and only as such, do I know him. That is what I took him to be; and, moreover, that is what all the other members of the organization took him to be. Bukharin directed the organization of the Rights by the same means and methods as Trotsky directed the whole "bloc of Rights and Trotskyites."

Why has not Bukharin told the whole truth? This question arises in my mind, and cannot but arise in my mind, when we are being called upon to answer before the people for our heinous crimes, crimes which are without precedent in the history of the revolutionary working class movement. The reason, I think, why Bukharin has not told the whole truth here is because throughout the whole period of the revolution he has fought the revolution and to this day has remained its enemy, and because he wants to preserve those remnants of the hostile forces which are still lurking in their dens.

I, as a man who, although he did not belong to the central nucleus of the leadership of the Rights, nevertheless was an active conspirator, as a man who knows Bukharin well, consider it my duty to declare here that after the collapse of our hopes for a kulak uprising, the only hope that remained to us was the hope for the defeat of the Soviet Union in war. I was unable in my testimony to bring out in sufficient relief how profoundly defeatism had become part of the very bone and marrow of our organization. The point must be stressed that we, the members of the "bloc of Rights and Trotskyites," became as strongly possessed by the idea of defeatism as by duplicity; like duplicity, defeatism literally became part and parcel of the psychology of every one of us. Wherever I happened to meet a member of our organization, the talk would invariably turn to the subject that war was bound to break out in the near future, and that the defeat of the Soviet Union, for which we were paving the way, would radically alter our position. I wanted war, I longed for it. I recall that every diplomatic success of the Soviet Union which tended to postpone war, that every success of the united front in the struggle against fascism and war, caused despondency and dejection in all of us.

One must lose the last remnants of conscience to deny that we placed our stake on defeat and on the establishment of a fascist dictatorship.

In connection with defeatism, I recall another characteristic detail, a conversation I had with Bukharin in 1936. Bukharin asserted that it was essential, by means of a series of diversive and terrorist blows, to destroy the defence of the country; he said that the Rights in the Northern Territory were very slack in mustering insurrectionary cadres. And he added the following: of course we would have to pay for assistance by cessions of border territories, you will get nothing for nothing, no help; but, after all, it is not indispensable that Russia should constitute one-sixth of the world—she may be one-tenth. That is not the important thing, Bukharin said, and it is only people who feared terrible words who cannot understand it.

I am not concealing the truth, I am not sparing myself. Neither can I avoid telling the truth to spare my accomplices. I was a defeatist and a spy, and so was my leader, Bukharin.

In order to give a clear idea of my state of mind by the time of my arrest I would like to say a few words about the poisonous, asphyxiating atmosphere that prevailed in our counter-revolutionary underground organization.

We, the members of the underground organization, regarded the masses of the toilers with misgivings and rancour. We conspirators hounded honest people, and tried in every way to drag honest people into our quagmire. We played a game of duplicity. We tried to lure every novice into some wrecking act so as to get him into our power by the threat of exposure. In recruiting cadres we widely resorted to various forms of provocation. The conspirators held these novices firmly in their hands.

As I have already stated in my testimony, there were many moments when my heart was torn by repentance, and the thought throbbed insistently in my mind to go and tell about the organization of the Rights. But I did not do so.

It is especially painful for me to stand before the people, the broad masses, as a betrayer of my country, as a traitor. But I must say that I have now made a clean breast of my crimes to the Court. When I begin to analyse my crimes and wish to find mitigating circumstances, I cannot, amidst my dastardly crimes, find anything to mitigate them. It was only after my arrest that I felt relief, that I felt that I was really through with my dastardly deeds. I felt that only one path now lay before me to the end. I felt that I now stood alone, with the whole people against me.

I could fight no more. It became clear to me that we had suffered a debacle, that my struggle against the Soviet power was over, and it became clear to me that it was impossible to continue the struggle. That is why I told the whole truth at the preliminary investigation and in Court, without any concealment. I have told everything to the very end. I am now in a position where burdensome crimes weigh down upon me: treason, treachery, terrorism.

I now feel much easier at heart, because I have completely divulged my crimes.

Citizens Judges, I now experience a dual feeling with regard to the sentence. It is hard to go on living when you have been through a black and stinking cesspool. When I pondered whether there was anything to lessen my guilt, whether there was any crime about which I could say that I had not committed it, I could find nothing.

My crimes included provocation, active participation in the "bloc of Rights and Trotskyites," treason to the fatherland, wrecking, diversion and insurrection. It is hard to live, comrades, with such a record. But on the other hand, I experience the contrary feeling. Citizens Judges, I must say that I shall accept the most severe sentence, but I find it inexpressibly hard to die when I have at last cleared myself of this filth, of this abomination. If I am given the opportunity to prove my loyalty, I shall work honestly and devotedly for the benefit of the people.

I plead with the Soviet Court to give me this opportunity. I plead with the Soviet government for mercy.

THE PRESIDENT: The accused Krestinsky may make his last plea.

KRESTINSKY: Citizens Judges, in this dock I am one of those who have the longest records of active participation in political life. I began my revolutionary career as an eighteen-year old youth, in 1901, and for twenty years, until 1921, that is, until the moment when I, in conjunction with Trotsky, began my struggle against the Party and the Soviet power, the struggle which finally led me into the dock, I worked as an honest Bolshevik.

During the preliminary investigation and the Court investigation I did not say a single word about this, I made no reference to the period of revolutionary struggle in my life, because I considered that in the dock I must answer for my counter-revolutionary actions, and not indulge in repentance.

And only now, in my last plea do I find it possible, before proceeding to recount and severely judge my monstrous crimes, to deal briefly with these periods in my life as well, inasmuch as the purpose of the last plea is to give the Court a complete idea of the criminal, including the time when he had not yet committed criminal deeds.

The first stage in my revolutionary activities, 1901-06, was connected with the first revolution of 1905. These years I spent partly in St. Petersburg, but chiefly in the North-Western Territory. Being one of the active leaders in the territory, I worked in practically every town of the North-Western Territory, was several times arrested in St. Petersburg and various regions, was deported, and towards the end of 1906 was unable to remain in this region where the possibility of illegal work was closed to me.

I removed to St. Petersburg, where I established connections with Lenin, Nadezhda Konstantinovna Krupskaya[1] and Mikhail Ivanovich Kalinin,[2] who worked in the Vasily-Ostrovsky organization and in the trade unions. At that time I worked on the "Zvezda" and on the "Pravda." In this work I had the constant guidance of Stalin and the guidance of Lenin, who sent articles and letters to the "Pravda" almost daily. I took part in the election campaign and was nominated as candidate to the Fourth State Duma. I had charge of insurance work. And finally, I worked in the Fourth State Duma, in the Bolshevik group in the Duma, which was virtually the Russian Bureau of the Central Committee. More exacting demands were made on me, and I developed in this work. At that time Lenin was confined in an Austrian prison; Stalin and Sverdlov were in exile in Turukhansk. During the war period we defined our position as defeatists, as advocates of the transformation of the imperialist war into civil war. I went to the Urals, then to Sverdlovsk, then to the remote town of Kungur.

At the conference of Bolsheviks which took place in March under Stalin's guidance, I fully and completely supported Stalin in his fight against all vacillations and waverings. In 1917 I was transferred to the Urals and put in charge of the work there. In 1918 I was transferred to the centre, and after the revolt of the "Left" Socialist-Revolutionaries, was made People's Commissar of Finance. Later, after the death of Sverdlov, I was appointed secretary of the Central Committee. I was Lenin's organizational assistant. The daily current work of the Central Committee passed through my hands.

On all the fundamental economic and political questions during the period of the civil war, I shared the political line of Lenin and Stalin and wholeheartedly supported them.

The political rapprochement with Trotsky, which led me to take up hostile activities against the Soviet system, took place under the following circumstances.

Just before the Tenth Party Congress I had taken part in the trade union discussion, siding with what was known as the Tsektran opposition,[3] the Trotskyite opposition, as one of its leaders. Unlike Trotsky, I considered the differences on this question to be temporary and transitory differences on one specific question of tactics. I assumed that after the Congress I would be able loyally to continue my Party work. As a matter of fact, the Central Committee adopted a decision to the effect that, after my vacation, I was to be transferred, at my own wish, to the Urals as a member of the Urals Bureau of the Central Committee, for the purpose of conducting Party work in the Urals. But when, while I was away on vacation in Germany, the question was reconsidered and a decision taken to appoint me ambassador in Germany, Trotsky, on my return to Moscow in the autumn, began to instill the idea into my head that I, who was not acquainted with foreign countries, and who did not know foreign languages, was not a suitable man for diplomatic work, that my appointment was not caused by practical considerations but by the desire to keep me away from Party work, and that I would never be able to return to leading Party work by normal means.

In 1921 I accepted Trotsky's proposal to take part in the illegal Trotskyite work which he was then commencing, mustering forces and cadres for subsequent open action.

A bureau was formed right then, consisting of Trotsky, Serebryakov, Preobrazhensky, Pyatakov and myself. This was in October 1921. My illegal struggle against the Party dates from this moment.

In the spring of 1922, when I arrived for the Eleventh Party Congress, Trotsky broached the subject of securing funds for the internal Party struggle, for the struggle against the Central Committee, which, as he visualized it, would be a prolonged and acute one. Victor Kopp, who was present, proposed that an attempt be made to secure funds from the German Reichswehr. This proposal at first gave rise to certain vacillations on my part, but I afterwards accepted it and played an active part in the conclusion of a treasonable agreement with the Germans.

Towards the end of 1923 an open attack of the Trotskyites on the Party took place. The defeat which we Trotskyites suffered only served to intensify our resentment and to aggravate the struggle.

In 1926-27 the Trotskyites launched a number of attacks on the Central Committee. Simultaneously, a Trotskyite struggle began in the Western Communist Parties as well. Taking advantage of the situation, the Reichswehr demanded that we should not only intensify our espionage activities, but also give certain political promises of future grants of economic concessions in the Ukraine in case we came to power. Trotsky and I, fearing to lose a source of funds at a moment of acute struggle, agreed to it and consented to deepen this treasonable agreement.

At the end of 1927 Trotsky flung all his forces into the struggle, but suffered smashing and utter defeat. The Trotskyites were expelled from the Party. The majority of their leaders were exiled.

The masses were against us, and an open struggle offered no prospect of success. Accordingly, Trotsky gave instructions to all who had been expelled or exiled to get themselves reinstated in the Party by submitting double-dealing statements to the effect that they had renounced their views. At the same time he gave instructions for the restoration of the illegal Trotskyite organization, which now was to bear a purely conspiratorial character.

Its method of struggle was to pave the way for an armed coup. The means to this end were terrorism, wrecking and diversion.

The change in the tactical line was accompanied by a change of program. We had always considered that the building of Socialism in the U.S.S.R. alone is impossible inasmuch as the bourgeois-capitalist system was still preserved in the other countries, and the fascists had come to power in some. We deemed it necessary to adopt the policy of permitting capitalist relations in the country, and then, as our connections with the foreign bourgeoisie became more extensive, we in this way arrived at the policy of direct bourgeois restoration.

During the meeting in Meran in October 1933, Trotsky expounded to me at length the bourgeois-restorationist program of our conspiratorial organization and the program for the overthrow of the Socialist social system existing in the country, adopting for this purpose methods of terrorism, wrecking and diversion, and envisaging the subsequent dismemberment of the Soviet Union and the severance from it of the Ukraine and the Maritime Region.

I accepted the program proposed by Trotsky, and also agreed to the new methods of struggle. And from that moment I bear complete political and criminal responsibility for all these methods of struggle.

In February 1935 Pyatakov informed me that an agreement on a joint armed coup had been reached between the Trotskyites, the Rights and Tukhachevsky's military group. From that moment I bear responsibility not only for the actions of the Trotskyites, but for the actions of the Rights and of the military conspirators as well.

I cannot, however, refrain from saying that my personal counter-revolutionary activities until the beginning of 1937 were of a strictly limited character and consisted, firstly, in the establishment and maintenance of illegal connections between the Trotskyite centre in the U.S.S.R., as represented by Pyatakov, and Trotsky, who was abroad; and, secondly, in the carrying out of our treasonable agreement with the Reichswehr down to the end of 1930, and, from the end of 1935, in the selection of cadres for the government apparatus which was to come to power as the result of the counter-revolutionary coup. In this counter-revolutionary work of mine I was connected with Pyatakov, as the leader of the Trotskyite centre, with Rosengoltz, who was carrying on the same sort of

622

work, with Rudzutak, the representative of the centre of the Rights, and with Tukhachevsky, the leader of the military conspiratorial organization.

I dwell on this limited character of my personal counter-revolutionary activities not because I want to disclaim my responsibility for terrorism, wrecking and diversion and for immediate preparations for armed action. I have already said that since the end of 1933, and then since the end of 1935, I bear responsibility for all these forms of counter-revolutionary work. But for the purpose of determining the degree of my personal responsibility, as Citizen the Procurator has said, it is important to know what counter-revolutionary activities I personally performed and what counter-revolutionary acts performed by other participators in the conspiracy were known to me.

I therefore consider it necessary to stress the fact—the Court knows this from the records of the preliminary and Court investigations—that up to the beginning of 1937 I was not a leader either of the Trotskyite organization or of the Right-Trotskyite centre. And only in February 1937, when I, Rosengoltz and Gamarnik took it upon ourselves to unite all the illegal work of the Trotskyites, and when Rosengoltz and I joined the centre of the "bloc of Rights and Trotskyites," did I begin to occupy myself directly with the preparations for an armed coup and joined in the organization of terrorist acts.

I consider it necessary to stress the fact that I had absolutely no knowledge of the terrorist acts enumerated in the second section of the Indictment, and that I learnt about them only when I was handed a copy of the Indictment.

I further consider it my duty to inform the Court—although this rather enhances than lessens my responsibility—that for two years prior to my arrest doubts often arose in my mind as to the correctness of this counter-revolutionary, criminal path which I and the other Trotskyites were following. I stood at the centre of government work, and I could not but see how the might and wealth of the Soviet Union were growing, how the standard of living of the working people was rising and what tremendous cultural progress was taking place in our country.

After the arrest of Pyatakov and Radek and the exposure of the Trotskyite organization, I felt that an end must be put to this: I must either go and tell about my criminal activities, or the coup must be expedited. I sank to the latter alternative, and embarked on crime. This, of course, corresponded with the urgings of Tukhachevsky and Trotsky, and I began to make intensive preparations for a coup d'état in the very near future.

And it was not until after my arrest that I made a critical survey of my counter-revolutionary activities. I became convinced of the shadowiness of our hopes, and I realized the utter hopelessness and

623

criminality of our struggle. I drew the conclusion from this, and immediately, at the first interrogation, told the investigating authorities what had weighed most on my mind during the past fifteen years, what was the darkest and most shameful fact in my life, namely, my connections with the German military intelligence service. But at that time I did not draw all the conclusions to the last one. I did not relate everything, I did not expose the Trotskyite organization, I said nothing about my criminal activities. I did not name all my confederates. It was not because I wanted to enable the organization to continue its counter-revolutionary struggle that I did not do so. On the contrary, if I had believed that the organization had not been smashed, that terrorist or diversive acts might still be made, I would have at once told about it all, because from the very first day of my arrest I realized the utter criminality of our struggle. But I believed that the organization was smashed, destroyed, that it was incapable of further action, and that therefore it was a question of exposing the shameful past activities of the organization with which I had been connected for fifteen years, and of naming my confederates, people who had already been smashed and actually no longer represented any danger. Old habits of thought, old personal connections prevented me at the time from doing this; and another four months were required—during which I came to realize and suffer from the consciousness of my criminal activities—before I related to the investigating authorities at length all my counter-revolutionary work, the work of the organization with which I had been connected, and named my confederates. Of course, I was unable to give the investigating authorities a complete picture of the work, I was unable to name all the Trotskyites belonging to the organization; but this was only because I myself did not know everything and everybody, because I had assumed the leadership of the organization only three months prior to my arrest, so that nobody had initiated me into the affairs and the connections of the organization, and I had begun to muster the forces of the organization on my own initiative. I hope that the sum total of my testimony and the testimony of other arrested Trotskyites have placed the necessary threads into the hands of the investigating authorities, and that the Trotskyite organization has now been definitely liquidated. After that, five months elapsed before the trial began. I continued to suffer painfully from the consciousness of my criminal activities. I not only laid down my arms, ceased to be an enemy, but re-armed myself; I became another man, and nothing remained within me of the old collaborator of Trotsky who had conducted an active struggle against the Soviet power.

This, Citizens Judges, is not contradicted by my conduct on the first day of the trial. I admit that my refusal to plead guilty was objectively a counter-revolutionary act but subjectively, it was not a hostile sally on my part. The fact is that in the days just preceding the trial I was under the painful impression caused by the gruesome facts I had learnt from the Indictment, and especially from its second section. My disapproval of the criminal past was only heightened, and not diminished, by the knowledge of these facts, but it seemed to me beyond my powers to admit my guilt to the whole world, to all working people. It seemed to me easier to die than to give the world the idea that I was even a remote accessory to the murder of Gorky, about which I actually knew nothing.

I conclude. My crimes against my country and the revolution are immense, and I shall accept, as fully merited, whatever verdict you pass, however severe it may be. I request you, Citizens Judges, in passing verdict, to bear in mind that I myself, voluntarily, without confrontations and without being presented with other incriminating evidence, frankly and fully related my criminal activities and the activities of my organization. I beg you to bear in mind that I did not take a direct part in the most acute forms of struggle—terrorism, diversion and wrecking—and did not specifically know about these actions. I beg you to remember my former really revolutionary work, to believe me when I say that during these nine months I have undergone a radical change, and, by sparing my life, to give me the opportunity to expiate my grave crimes in any way, even if only partially.

THE PRESIDENT: Accused Zubarev, you have your last plea.

ZUBAREV: Citizens Judges, I fully and completely admit and confirm the charges brought against me of crimes against the Soviet power. I was one of the organizers and leaders of the counter-revolutionary underground organization of the Rights in the Urals, and directed the wrecking work in the sphere of agriculture both in the Urals and here, in Moscow, when I worked in the People's Commissariat of Agriculture. I was one of the leaders of a terrorist group and carried on espionage and provocateur activities. I realize the profound depths to which I have fallen and the full gravity of the crimes I have committed. I also realize the utter gravity of my responsibility before the proletarian Court. I fully and entirely agree with the speech of the State Prosecutor, with the description he gave of my criminal activities, and with his demand for the supreme penalty. The penalty he demands would be a merited punishment for the gravity of those crimes I have committed. And there is no punishment which the gravity of these crimes does not warrant.

Realizing my responsibility, I cannot, and have no wish to, defend or acquit myself. It would be ridiculous and false to declare to the Court that I am an unfortunate victim of inexperience or ignorance, and that I was led astray by some other hand. But, without defending or acquitting myself, I want to declare, Citizens Judges, that I have said everything down to the last detail both about my activities and the activities of those of my confederates whom I knew personally.

In my position, of course, I cannot cite any facts or material evidence to bear out the sincerity of my repentance, or to corroborate that I have said everything there is to say about my criminal activities. I have only one single argument, if it may serve as an argument and reason at all, namely, the materials of the preliminary investigation and my honest behaviour and confession of all my crimes in Court. And if, Citizens Judges, this sincerity may in any degree serve to lessen the gravity of my crimes and to mitigate the sentence of the Court, if my life were preserved, I would, in practical work, justify not only in words, but also in deeds, the confidence of the Court.

THE PRESIDENT: The accused Rykov may make his last plea.

RYKOV: In my last plea I confirm the admission of my monstrous crimes which I made during the trial. I have betrayed my country. This betrayal was expressed in my relations with the accursed enemies of the Soviets, in my stake on defeat. In its struggle, the "bloc of Rights and Trotskyites" resorted to the whole arsenal of all means of struggle that have ever been employed by conspiratorial organizations.

I was not a secondary figure in this counter-revolutionary organization.

We were preparing for a coup d'état, we organized kulak insurrections and terrorist groups, and adopted terrorism as a means of struggle. Nesterov and I formed a special terrorist organization in the Urals. In 1935 I gave instructions regarding terrorist acts to Kotov, who headed the terrorist organization in Moscow, and so on and so forth.

But the State Prosecutor has charged me with something in which I had no direct part, and which I cannot admit. He has charged me with adopting a decision, or with giving directions for the murder of Kirov, Kuibyshev, Menzhinsky, Gorky and Peshkov. It is absolutely unquestionable that our adoption of terrorism, our advocacy of terrorism, was bound to exert some influence on the perpetration of these murders. If terrorism had not been accepted as a method, if we had not advocated it, the murder of these people would not have occurred. In this respect, I must bear responsibility.

The evidence brought against me in this connection has been set forth here in detail; it is based upon the statements of Yagoda, who refers to Yenukidze. Nothing more incriminating was brought against me at the trial. The Court possesses no other material. Some of the people, members of the organization, who were directly concerned in these murders, met me from time to time. I ask myself why, if they knew that I had given instructions or participated as the guiding spirit in these murders, did not a single one of them ever say a word to me on the subject? And nothing was ever said.

The assassination of Kirov has formed the subject of two trials. Both the direct perpetrators and the organizers and leaders of this assassination have appeared in Court. I do not recall that my name was mentioned then.

In the second part of his charge against me on this score the State Prosecutor came to the conclusion that my participation in these assassinations has been proved by the testimony of Yagoda.

I must say that I cannot deny that on the basis of the sum total of my counter-revolutionary activities, the State Prosecutor has grounds for suspecting me of these assassinations. But it seems to me that logical deductions alone are not enough to accuse a man—it is true, a man who has been incriminated, against whom there is evidence of unusually serious crimes—of these assassinations as well.

The question was examined here of the bloc of the "Left" Socialist-Revolutionaries and "Left Communists," which dates back twenty years. And even this episode in the counter-revolutionary struggle—an episode which had important consequences, leading to the assassination of Mirbach, to the shot fired by Kaplan and the wounding of Lenin, but which nevertheless happened as long as twenty years ago—despite its rather historical significance, was examined, it seems to me, in a most exhaustive manner, not leaving room for any doubts. There were confrontations, direct and immediate witnesses, both "Left" Socialist-Revolutionaries and "Left Communists," who were eye-witnesses and participators in this entire affair. Why, then, on the question of my participation in the assassination of five most important political figures, should a decision be taken on the basis of indirect evidence?

This, it seems to me, would be incorrect. At any rate, I deny any charge of my participation in these five assassinations.

Until my arrest I believed that Gorky had died a natural death. But during my confinement I recalled all the conversations I had had with regard to Gorky not only with Yenukidze but also with Averbach, approximately from 1928 to 1930.

I had underrated my conversation with Yenukidze, I had underrated the menace to the life of Gorky which lurked in this conversation. But Yenukidze spoke only about the liquidation of Gorky's political activities; he spoke with unusual sharpness. I did not get the impression from the conversation with Yenukidze that any danger was threatening Gorky. For this underestimation I am undoubtedly to blame. It is quite clear to me now that this was a sort of signal that an attempt on Gorky's life was in preparation.

When we discussed terrorism, we regarded it as a means of inflicting a blow on the most important and most powerful link of the Party. When we spoke of it, before us there always loomed such figures as Stalin, Voroshilov, Molotov and Kaganovich. In this connection I must undoubtedly admit the responsibility that falls upon us for the assassination of Menzhinsky, Kuibyshev, Maxim Peshkov and Gorky—assassinations that corresponded with the stand of our organization on terrorism as one of the methods in our struggle against the Party—and for this I worked no less than any other member of the counter-revolutionary organization. At the investigation I endeavoured as fully as possible to tell everything that remained in my memory about the counter-revolutionary activities of the members of our counter-revolutionary organization. This was not easy to do: it was a question of long periods of time—eight or nine years—and of a large number of people, of a very secret conspiratorial organization, so secret that it was only at this trial that I first learnt of such members of our counter-revolutionary organization as Ivanov. So that I cannot, nor can any of the members of the centre, reproduce the whole picture in full. Here certain discrepancies in the evidence of individual leaders of the counter-revolutionary organization are possible. It seems to me that these discrepancies are of no great moment. But in the course of the trial there were several passages-of-arms between my fellow-accused, Chernov, and myself. I touch upon this subject not because it has any great significance, or because any principle is involved. I touch upon it merely in order to avoid the charge of insincerity, the charge of having concealed something. It seems to me that the rejoinder Chernov made was incorrect. Of course, any man's memory may deceive him in some cases, but in this case I cannot admit that I could have forgotten that I directed in a practical way Chernov's counter-revolutionary wrecking work in the People's Commissariat of Agriculture. That could not be forgotten. I do not recall it. Where there were wrecking activities, activities no less serious than in Byelorussia, I completely admit my guilt. It seems to me suspicious that Chernov should try in every way to magnify my authority and to minimize his own role in these wrecking activities, to picture it as being as small as possible. I must say that this is not true. Already during my first meeting with Chernov in 1928, when I wanted to recruit him for the counter-revolutionary organization, I found him to be a full-fledged counter-revolutionary, who had fully developed to, and had even developed beyond, the counter-revolutionary convictions which I held, without any assistance on my part. So that his independent counter-revolutionary development cannot be denied by any means. It cannot be denied that he carried on counter-revolutionary work in the People's Commissariat of Agriculture independently, that he did not necessarily wait for instructions from me or from the German fascists. He wants to make himself out to be smaller than he actually is.

As regards Grinko, it is possible that either he or I have forgotten. I grant that it is possible, but I draw your attention to the fact that we are referring to something that happened in 1936. He also respects my authority very highly. Of course, my advice or directions were bound to have some effect, but wrecking work in the People's Commissariat of Finance, and Grinko's relations with the Germans, existed before 1936. That is the most essential thing in Grinko's evidence.

I should like to say a few words about Bukharin. The State Prosecutor reproached me with wanting to shield my pal. The State Prosecutor was quite right in calling Bukharin my pal, because Bukharin and I were really very intimate. But I would like to say that Bukharin's reference to some sort of division of labour is of course wrong. He says that he bore an additional duty as a writer. There was absolutely nothing in which he was less active than we were. I might mention a sphere in which, I think, the initiative belonged to him and in which he played the leading role from the very beginning, namely, the building up of the bloc. With Bukharin this arose from the fact that he had occupied a specific position even during the period of the struggle against Trotsky, and used to say that they must become used to each other while fighting each other. This was one of Bukharin's typical, verbose somersaults, but it signified his desire not to lose Trotsky. From the very beginning of the organization of the bloc it was Bukharin who was the most active; and sometimes he confronted me with an accomplished fact. Of course, I do not want to deny responsibility for the formation of the bloc. I am too old a man to claim that Bukharin led me one way or another, but the initiative and the most active role in this respect undoubtedly belonged to Bukharin.

The State Prosecutor was quite right about Bukharin and me when he said that we must answer for the sum total and for all the consequences of our counter-revolutionary activities. That is quite true, and that is why I, as one of the founders of the counter-revolutionary organization of the Rights, who enjoyed certain, sometimes considerable influence among the Rights, of course answer not only for what I did personally and for what was done on my instructions, and about which I knew, but also for the consequences. Of course, there may be varying degrees of responsibility for one thing or another, but—the State Prosecutor is quite right there—I must answer for what arose on the monstrous counter-revolutionary foundation, in the laying of which I, of course, played no little part. And this responsibility of mine of course transcends all the discrepancies

629

which still remain regarding certain facts and certain details. That roughly is all that I wanted to say in my last plea. Perhaps I am living my last days, and perhaps my last plea is my last utterance in the literal sense of the word.

I would, in conclusion, like to take advantage of my last plea in order to try with all my might to influence those of my former supporters who perhaps have still not been arrested and have still not laid down their arms, and whom I did not know or have forgotten. As I enjoyed—true, not quite the influence which Chernov says I did—but a certain amount of influence, I have no doubt that if these words are published they will be read, and perhaps some of my former supporters will be influenced by them. And so I want, to this end, firstly, that my former supporters should know that I have given away—as we say in the underground movement—exposed all of them whom I could remember.

I would like those who have not yet been exposed and who have not yet laid down their arms to do so immediately and openly. I would like my example to convince them of the inevitability of their being disarmed, and that they should lay down their arms at all costs and at the earliest moment, that they should realize that only by laying down their arms, even at the risk of certain privations and even arrest, can they secure any sort of relief and disencumber themselves of the monstrous burden which has been revealed by the present trial.

Salvation lies only in laying down their arms. Their only salvation, their only escape lies in helping the Party, in helping the government to expose and liquidate the remnants, the dregs of the counter-revolutionary organization, if any still happen to remain in any part of the territory of the Soviet Union.

THE PRESIDENT: The accused Sharangovich has his last plea.

SHARANGOVICH: Citizens Judges, I do not intend to say anything in my defence. I have committed loathsome, vile and heinous crimes against the country and the people, and I perfectly realize that I must fully answer for them before the proletarian Court. I have betrayed my country, and as a traitor I deserve no mercy.

For a long period, ever since 1921, I was a Polish spy and carried on espionage activities on behalf of the Polish intelligence service. During these years, on the instructions of the Polish intelligence service, I actively carried out espionage and treasonable tasks, directed toward undermining the power of the Soviet Union and bringing about the defeat of the Soviet Union in a war with fascist states. I was one of the leaders of the national-fascist organization in Byelorussia which waged a struggle against the Soviet power, a struggle for the overthrow of the existing Soviet system in the country. Guided by the direct instructions of the "bloc of Rights and Trotskyites" and of Rykov and Bukharin personally, on the one hand, and by the orders of the Polish General Staff, on the other, our organization strove by its counter-revolutionary activities to bring about the overthrow of the Soviet power and the establishment of a capitalist system in its place. We attempted to achieve the severance of Soviet Byelorussia from the Soviet Union and to place the working people of Soviet Byelorussia under the yoke of the Polish landlords and capitalists. We desired the defeat of the Soviet Union in a forthcoming war with the fascist states, with whose help the "bloc of Rights and Trotskyites," and we too, under its leadership, worked to bring about the overthrow of the Soviet power. I admit that I am guilty of this too, and I once more declare to the proletarian Court that I am guilty and must be held fully responsible.

I am guilty of the fact that I personally, and the national-fascist organization of Byelorussia under my guidance, directed by the centre of the Rights, carried on extensive wrecking and diversive activities in all branches of economic and cultural life. Together with my accomplices, I undermined agriculture, destroyed horses, deprived collective farmers of household land, muddled the planning of crop areas and endeavoured, from provocateur motives, to incense the collective farmers against the Soviet government.

In the industry of Byelorussia, we undermined the fuel base, the power industry, retarded the speed of new construction work and committed a number of wrecking and diversive acts.

We endeavoured in every way to provoke, to discredit the national policy, the national policy of Lenin and Stalin; and with this object in view, we developed extensive wrecking activities on the principal sectors of the cultural front—in the schools, the Academy of Sciences, the higher educational establishments, and so forth.

We scorned no means in our struggle against the Party and the Soviet power; we took the path of the physical extermination of the leaders of the Party and the government.

I once more wish to tell the Court of the terrorist activities in which I and our underground organization engaged on the instructions of the "bloc of Rights and Trotskyites" and of the Polish General Staff.

I am fully responsible for the creation of a terrorist group and for the preparation of terrorist acts against the leadership of the Party and the government. In the chain of crimes committed by me against the Soviet power I am, of course, many times guilty.

I was mature and politically developed, and I cannot,

I have not the right to advance my sentiments or my ignorance as an excuse—that would be a lie, it would be an untruth.

I understood what our aim, the severance of Soviet Byelorussia from the Soviet Union, meant. And not only did I understand it, but I saw close at hand an example of what such severance meant, what a protectorate meant. That example was Western Byelorussia, where the working people languish under the yoke of the Polish landlords and capitalists.

I understood this, yet I embarked on the commission of these crimes. I understood that by consenting to become a Polish spy and to work for the Poles, I was betraying my country. I am sensible of these grave and treasonable crimes. I committed them, and I admitted them at the preliminary investigation and to you. I deserve the most drastic sentence of the Soviet Court.

I do not want in my last plea to dwell on all my vile and treacherous activities and the treacherous activities of my accomplices who are sitting here in this dock, and of our leaders in the first place, some of whom, instead of sincerely admitting their despicable, bloody and treasonable crimes, are trying with the help of theoretical phrases to hide behind the backs of their accomplices, and to escape answering to the proletarian Court. I think the Court will see through this and its verdict will be a just one. Of this I am profoundly convinced.

I have come to understand the full horror of the treasonable and treacherous crimes I have committed against the Soviet people and the Soviet country. I declare to the Court that both at the preliminary investigation and here in the Court I have sincerely told everything, down to the last detail. I desire only one thing, namely, that my crimes, which I have frankly recounted, may serve as a warning to those who are still trying to carry on, or who are carrying on treasonable activity against the Soviet Union and against the Soviet people. They will all, like me, undoubtedly be crushed by the whole might of the Soviet power.

I do not plead for clemency, Citizens Judges, because I am not fit to plead for it. I have told all there is to tell about my crimes, and I request the proletarian Court to take this into account.

THE PRESIDENT: Adjournment for half an hour.

* * *

COMMANDANT OF THE COURT: The Court is coming, please rise.

THE PRESIDENT: Please be seated. The session is resumed. The accused Khodjayev may have his last plea.

KHODJAYEV: Citizens Judges, at the preliminary investigation and here, before you, I have related in detail all the grave crimes which were committed by the nationalist organizations of Uzbekistan under my direction. I have related to you in detail the grave crimes which I have committed both as an active member of the bourgeois-nationalist movement and as its leader in Uzbekistan, and as an ally and member of the Right counter-revolutionaries and, through them, of the whole Right-Trotskyite counter-revolutionary bloc.

From the first moment of my arrest I began to make sincere confession of the misdeeds I had committed. I did this because I realized the utter loathsomeness of what has been done by the bourgeois nationalists in Uzbekistan. I understood what tremendous damage, what severe blows had been inflicted at various periods of the revolution by this bourgeois-nationalist movement and by the actions of its leaders. I understood that, as one of the leaders of this bourgeois-nationalist movement, as a deserter to the side of the counter-revolutionary Rights and the "bloc of Rights and Trotskyites," I had committed grave crimes against the proletarian state, against the peoples of the Union of Soviet Republics and against the Uzbek people.

Having decided to make a clean breast of my crimes, I was guided by only one consideration, namely, by my sincere confession to help the investigating authorities to bring to light all the black, counter-revolutionary elements with which I had been connected, which had bound me, and which were a source of putrefaction that might later constitute a danger of infection. I spared neither myself nor the other participants in my counter-revolutionary actions, in order to make it easier for the Soviet people's power and the Party to eradicate this evil. I waived my speech in defence, for I cannot find a single argument, not even a single word, in any sort of justification of my conduct, my actions and the crimes I have committed. I have nothing to say in my defence and I cannot defend myself. Too much evil has been done, too serious are the crimes that have been committed, for anything to be said in justification, or for any words to efface them.

But I decided to make a last plea, and to utilize it to tell the proletarian Court once more, and our whole country that I have sincerely and honestly repented, and to convey my repentance through the proletarian Court to our Soviet people, the Party and the government.

Citizen the Public Prosecutor has given an annihilating description of the actions of the "bloc of Rights and Trotskyites." He has also dwelt on the character of the activities of the bourgeois-nationalist groups. He has referred to the results of the national policy of Lenin and Stalin, and to the achievements of the peoples of the Soviet Union.

I stand here in the dock—I am a criminal. Perhaps it is hardly appropriate coming from my lips, but I would like to cite the vivid example of the Republic which I once represented. I am referring to Uzbekistan.

People who knew Uzbekistan before the revolution, or who were there ten years ago and have seen it in recent years, have found the country unrecognizable. Why? Because it has completely changed. Tremendous progress in economic and cultural life, the huge growth of the political activity of the broad masses of the people—all this has been achieved in relatively so brief a period as ten or twenty years only thanks to our proletarian revolution, to the Leninist-Stalinist national policy. In 1917 only $1^1/_2$ per cent of the population of Uzbekistan was literate, while today the population of the country is almost universally literate.

Formerly the country had absolutely no industry, but now it has hundreds of big plants and hundreds of thousands of working men and women.

The once backward and poverty-stricken agriculture of Uzbekistan is today one of the foremost in the Soviet Union.

During the past five years the standard of living of the broad masses of the working population, especially of the dekhkan collective farmers, has reached such a level that a return of 20 to 30 rubles per work-day of the collective farmer no longer surprises anybody in Uzbekistan. This is all the result of the beneficent effect of the revolution, of the correct application of the national policy of Lenin and Stalin, and of the tremendous help which has been and is being given by the Russian working class to the workers and peasants of Uzbekistan.

This will be clear to anyone from even the briefest analysis of the general conditions prevailing in Uzbekistan. And I have to tell the proletarian Court that the policy which was pursued by the bourgeois-nationalist organization to which I belonged, and the counter-revolutionary activities of which I directed, meant for the working masses of Uzbekistan a return to the past. Now that I have realized the utter criminality of my deeds, now that I have realized into what an abyss I have fallen, it has become more clear to me, more obvious against the background of the deeds of the "bloc of Rights and Trotskyites" unfolded at this trial, that the victory of this counter-revolutionary line would have meant for Uzbekistan the victory of the blackest reaction, the restoration of feudal and capitalist relations and, consequently, a new bondage for the workers and peasants and the broad masses of the peoples of Uzbekistan. Both in economic development and cultural life, Uzbekistan would have been flung back many scores of years. It is particularly hard for me to talk about this side of the matter, because I now realize it quite clearly, I understand it and am sen-

634

sible of the depths to which I have fallen, of the full horror of my disgrace and the full gravity of my misdeeds. Nevertheless, having decided to make an open confession of all my misdeeds, I was obliged to state this too before the proletarian Court and before public opinion of our country.

Yes, Citizens Judges, I was a bourgeois nationalist; I have committed many crimes. Unfortunately, I cannot obliterate them now, at this late date, by this belated repentance. They remain hanging over me. But I became ever more horrible in my own eyes from the time I realized all my crimes and villainies, after the agreement with Rykov and Bukharin, after the circumstances which I have recounted in detail here in Court, and after I joined this conspiracy. Why, even in the period when I was a nationalist, when I also engaged in anti-Soviet activities and worked against the Soviet people, even then I was not an organizer of insurrectionary groups, I was not a member of terrorist groups. I became such, as I have told you, Citizens Judges, only after I had adopted the position of the Right counter-revolutionaries and through them found myself in the camp of the "bloc of Rights and Trotskyites." In this way I became a participant in the acutest methods of struggle against our country, against the peoples of our great Union, against the Party and the government. This is what I find it hardest of all to bear, this is what weighs most on my mind.

The state independence of Uzbekistan which was held out in prospect by the Right restorers of capitalism, even if it became possible at the price of black treachery, at the price of treason to the fatherland, the dismemberment of the great Union of Soviet Socialist Republics and by means of preparing its defeat in the future war, that is, by means that are absolutely impermissible to people who have preserved even a shadow of their human shape, even if, I say, this proved possible at first, it goes without saying that this fictitious state independence would have been a new disaster to the peoples of Uzbekistan. I have already spoken of this partially when I gave my testimony. I was then answering the questions put by the State Prosecutor. When I said that having left one shore we would naturally have to make for another shore, I had nothing else in mind than the shore where the capitalist countries are located, imperialist capital, which crushes and oppresses hundreds of millions of working people. And so in this case, too, the victory of this line, even if the black and disgusting conspiracy succeeded, would only entail new hardships for the working people of Uzbekistan.

I stand disgraced. The nationalist organizations have been smashed. The accused "bloc of Rights and Trotskyites" has been smashed. This is to the glory of our country, to the benefit of the peoples of our great fatherland, and to the happiness of the peoples of Uzbekistan. And this thought to some degree alleviates these last days of my severe, incredibly severe, mental sufferings.

Characterizing the "bloc of Rights and Trotskyites" and its deeds and people, Citizen the State Prosecutor said that all the participants in this bloc must be held jointly responsible for all its misdeeds. I cannot help agreeing with the definition given by Citizen the State Prosecutor. I consider this definition absolutely correct, although I personally knew nothing of the existence of a contact centre and knew nothing about many of its misdeeds until I was imprisoned and began to give testimony. I personally have never been a provocateur or an assassin. But of what significance is this when I was anyway a member of this bloc which engaged in provocation, espionage and assassination. Hence, I must answer for all its misdeeds.

Citizens Judges, not only have you had the bloc before you, not only have its deeds been demonstrated to you, but all of us, its participators, have passed before you. It is for you, Citizens Judges, to determine what measure of responsibility each of us must bear. It is for you to apply or not to apply to us that drastic, but justified, absolutely justified demand of Citizen the State Prosecutor.

I knew what I was heading for when I discussed matters with Rykov, when I discussed matters with Bukharin, although much that was revealed to me in Court caused even me, a criminal, to shudder at the horror of it.

Is not the very fact of the conspiracy, the very decision that the Rights should come to power and the bourgeois-nationalists receive independence—which they wanted to receive at the cost of the defeat of the Soviet Union and by paving the way for this defeat—is not this enough to completely justify the application to us of the drastic measure of punishment which Citizen the Procurator has demanded?

And yet, Citizens Judges, standing here in the dock, answering for my crimes, I cannot adopt a false pose, for that would merely be proud words. I cannot say that I do not ask for clemency. I cannot say that. Perhaps there are some who think that the words, "I do not ask for clemency," would sound proud and well. But not on my lips, not on the lips of a man who is nailed to the pillory, who stands in this dock. Words of pride would be out of place on the lips of such a man. There is no ground for pride! We shall not go down in history as men who rendered any services to the people, with any good deeds to show. If we go down in history at all, it will be as hardened criminals, as heroes of bandit deeds, as people who have sold their honour and conscience. The word "pride" sounds fine on the lips of a man, a real man, of whom Gorky, the great writer and great man of our country, wrote. But on the lips of people who either themselves had a hand in the murder of Gorky, or were in some way implicated in it, on the lips of people who have brought about the death of this man, on the lips of people of our type, such words sound false. Yes, I would be a liar were I at this last hour to say that I did not crave clemency. I want to live. I want to live because I have realized the full depth of my fall, I have realized the full gravity of my crimes. I have learnt a severe lesson, but then I have learnt something else. It seems to me that I have really learnt how a real man, a real citizen of our great fatherland should serve his people, his country. And having realized this, having fully and completely laid down my arms, I cannot but ask for your indulgence, Citizens Judges, because, if it is possible, I should like my life to be preserved. I should like under any conditions, in any form, in any place, now or in the future, to wash away the disgrace which now lies upon me.

I ask for life so that perhaps, in the remainder of my days, I might obliterate at least some particle of my crimes and my profound guilt. I want to live so that somehow, somewhere, I may again prove useful to our great country and serve the great cause of the building of Socialism, to which all the thoughts and all the strength of the finest people of our great Union of Soviet Socialist Republics are devoted.

THE PRESIDENT: The accused Zelensky may have his last plea.

ZELENSKY: Citizens Judges, I take advantage of my last plea not to say anything in defence or excuse of my grave crimes. Such crimes, and such criminals as I, have no right to defence or exoneration.

My grave crimes against the Party, the country and the revolution have brought me into the dock as an enemy of the people and as a member of the "bloc of Rights and Trotskyites." There can be nothing more heinous than this.

Citizen the State Prosecutor has correctly described the criminal activities of the "bloc of Rights and Trotskyites" and my own crimes as one of its members.

I am guilty of treason and of treachery to the revolution, of having served in the tsarist Okhrana; I am guilty of having for many years concealed these crimes from the Party. I am guilty of having in 1929 joined the counter-revolutionary organization of the Rights, and of having, through it, joined the "bloc of Rights and Trotskyites."

I am guilty of having wormed my way into high posts that demand the particular confidence of the Party, by playing a double game and by camouflage. I utilized the confidence shown in me in order to deceive the Party; I carried on undermining, wrecking, counter-revolutionary activities, stirring up discontent among the population against the Soviet power.

Addressing the accused in the dock, Citizen the State Prosecutor

637

spoke yesterday of the sincerity which each of us should display on the threshold of our last hour.

On the threshold of my last hour, I would like first of all to relate how I came to fall. I want to relate this in order that my example might serve to warn those who are still vacillating, who are still discontented, wavering, and who harbour doubts in the Party leadership and in the correctness of the Party line. I want to speak of this not in order to exonerate myself or mitigate my lot, but in order to show how people sink to such shameful depths.

What led me onto the path of treason and treachery? It was a petty-bourgeois disbelief in the forces and victory of the revolution. Cowardice impelled me in my youth to become a traitor, provocateur and servitor of the tsarist Okhrana. This fact was enough to cripple me as a man and to destroy me as a revolutionary. My past crimes weighed upon me for many years; my past activities as a provocateur determined a certain aloofness on my part from honest members of the Party.

The difficulties of collective farm development engendered in me a disbelief in the strength of our working class, a disbelief in the strength of our state, and this pre-determined my joining the counter-revolutionary organization of the Rights. Even when I joined the organization of the Rights I did not immediately become a wrecker. I endeavoured to advocate my ideas, to carry them into effect, but the wrecking character of my proposals was immediately exposed. I had either to renounce my Right views and to work honestly in my Soviet post, or to go underground, to engage in wrecking and to recruit followers for this purpose. I chose the second path, the path of struggle against the Party and the government, the path of wrecking, which has led me to this shameful dock. I continued to play a double game, and for doubledealers there is only one path—the path of underground counter-revolutionary activities. And it is to such counter-revolutionary activities that I sank. In 1933 I became a wrecker and began to recruit supporters for the Rights. But I succeeded in recruiting for the Rights only people who had committed crimes against the Party, or who were careerists, self-seekers, and the like. The shameful example of my fall shows that the slightest rift with the Party, the slightest insincerity towards the Party, the slightest hesitation with regard to the leadership, with regard to the Central Committee, is enough to land you in the camp of counter-revolution.

I engaged in wrecking activities in the consumers' co-operative societies. Citizen the Procurator characterized my wrecking activities as having been directed against the growth of trade and the development of the trading system, and towards undermining the normal supply of commodities to the population. He is right; I have nothing to

638

add and no objections to make to this conclusion. I have told the Court what sectors have been affected by the wrecking activities carried on by myself and my accomplices. I have told the Court what damage was caused to the state and to the people by my wrecking activities. I must say that my wrecking activities grew much more intense beginning with 1935 on the direct instructions of Antipov. Wrecking activities caused a good deal of damage and really did hamper the development of trade and the trading system, and thus disrupted the supply of commodities to the workers and collective farmers. I endeavoured in my testimony to reveal the hotbeds of wrecking and the methods of wrecking work, with the object of facilitating the earliest possible liquidation of the consequences of these wrecking activities. I did this in order that my self-exposure might help in some degree to correct the tremendous harm that was caused by my wrecking activities.

I must say here that the Soviet co-operative movement has very often been subjected to, and is still being subjected to, the attacks of bourgeois capitalist co-operators. The bourgeois co-operators of capitalist countries, those who, like us, the counter-revolutionaries, are in the service of the bourgeoisie, try to discredit the Soviet co-operatives, utilizing the false information we supplied and our wrecking activities in order to prove the impossibility of the development of the Soviet co-operatives. I must say that despite our wrecking activity, despite our undermining work, the Soviet co-operatives steadily grew in strength; and when we counter-revolutionaries, wreckers are removed, it will progress further.

We endeavoured to win recruits among the rank and file. We wanted to extend our base in the countryside by relying on the kulak elements. I must say that the rural co-operative workers very rapidly detected our criminal efforts and that we met with a severe rebuff from the overwhelming part of the rank-and-file co-operative workers, who are honest and devoted to the Soviet power. These masses rejected every attempt at the restoration of capitalism, and us, who made the attempts. The elimination of wrecking activities, and the eradication of all the participators in our despicable activities will lead to the extremely rapid growth of trade and the trading system.

Citizens Judges, I must say that the sum total of our crimes, our vile and treacherous activities, is horrifying. Judging these activities, and endeavouring to switch to Soviet lines, I can find only one honest thing which we could do in the course of the investigation, the interrogation. This only honest thing open to us was relentlessly and thoroughly to expose to the country, to the revolution, to the revolutionary people, all our vile actions and crimes, all our accomplices and confederates, all the monstrous criminal activity of the "bloc of Rights and Trotskyites," the undermining work which I had engaged in from the very outset.

The testimony I gave about my crimes, and my exposure of my accomplices followed from my realization of my criminality, falsity and treachery.

It is painful, extremely painful, to feel that you are an enemy of the people, to see and know that you are in the wrong, to see and feel that the people are against you, to be always a counterfeit, and to act covertly.

Long before my arrest I had already lost faith in the Rights and realized the hopelessness of their struggle. That is why I immediately gave frank testimony to the investigating authorities. This is the only thing that could reinstate me in the ranks of Soviet people, if not to live, then at least to die as a Soviet man.

I had clearly foreseen the collapse of the Rights long ago. Why did I not break with them, why did I not expose myself and my criminal associates? This question might legitimately be put to me by the Court and the State Prosecutor. I must say that having every opportunity to do so, I should have done so; but I was in the hands of the Rights, having committed crimes. I feared the exposure of my past. I did not expose the gang of bandits, I did not give away my accomplices—that shows the depths to which I had fallen.

I clearly foresaw the collapse of the "bloc of Rights and Trotskyites" when we, the Rights, attempted to frustrate the campaign against the kulaks, the rout of the kulaks, that last of the exploiting classes. And when this failed, I, together with the Rights, became a direct fascist agent, became a wrecker; and I must admit that my wrecking activities thereby became part of the general plan of disruptive work of the "bloc of Rights and Trotskyites," which was performed on the instructions of foreign agents, and the purpose of which was to bring about a coup d'état in our Union.

Monstrous deeds and monstrous crimes—a sample of our vile Right-Trotskyite work, of our vile Right-Trotskyite underground activities, in which to my shame, disgrace and misfortune, I participated. I must, however, say that even for me, a participant in this underground activity, much of what has been revealed in the trial was new, unknown and dumbfounding.

The talk of Bukharin, the leader of the Rights, about the treachery and criminality of provocateurs and spies is valueless. For, Bukharin, you yourself are a past master in this art, you have shown a chain of crimes and treachery against the Party and the government by your actions, by your behaviour in Court. We are puppies compared with you. You, Bukharin, want to come out of it unblemished. But you will not succeed. You will go down in history with us, branded with the shameful stigma that marks the foreheads of all of us. I have heard speeches made here, and at the preliminary investigation and in the last pleas of the Trotskyites and Bukharinites. I had expected that they would really expose everything to the very end. I expected that the Trotskyites and Bukharinites would open up one other page of their crimes against the Soviet power, against the Party, against Lenin, crimes committed in 1921. They should have done so, if only to destroy the legend that Trotsky's attack in 1921 was a sort of legal discussion. Nothing of the kind! I take advantage of my last plea to do it for them. I want to help the Court and the investigating authorities to reveal these crimes. I want to elucidate facts which cast a vivid light on the activities of the Trotskyites against the Party in 1921. These facts are very little known to the public. I now affirm, in the light of the events of 1918 revealed by the investigation in this Court, that what confronted the Party in 1921 was not a discussion but a conspiracy. I affirm this on the basis of the following facts. The actions in Moscow in the beginning of 1921 of the Trotskyites, of Bukharinites like Boguslavsky, Drobnis, Sosnovsky, Rafail and other Mensheviks who then joined the Party, and Mensheviks who remained outside the Party and who continued to come out openly as Mensheviks, and the actions of the counter-revolutionaries who had formed a bloc with Trotsky, did not differ from each other in any way and all bore a Kronstadt character. All these anti-Party, anti-Soviet elements acted in concert; developing furious activity in January and February 1921, utilizing the food and fuel difficulties, they attacked the Central Committee and Lenin, endeavouring to organize strikes and to bring the workers out on the streets. I have no time now, and my position does not permit me to dwell on this in detail. I only say this because those who endeavoured to provoke the workers to strike, and who partially succeeded in this, endeavoured to penetrate to the Khamovniki barracks, to get possession of arms and to gain the following of the Red Army men. The attempt failed. These facts and documents are to be found in the archives of the Moscow Soviet and the Moscow Party Committee. Simultaneously with the collapse of this attempt, a plot was discovered in a Rifle Division in Zamoskvorechye, a plot of Whiteguard officers and Mensheviks. The commander of the Moscow military area, Petrayev, a former lieutenant of artillery and a protegé of Trotsky's, was dismissed on suspicion of being implicated in this plot. Trotsky objected to the dismissal of Petrayev just because he knew that Petrayev was implicated in the plot. It can now be said with certainty that Trotsky at the time employed his double-dealing method: while formally adhering to the platform of the October Revolution, he mustered his followers within the Party for the purpose of blowing up the Party from within. I affirm this. I also affirm that the armed force of this planned coup was a military conspiracy. Under these circumstances, the attempt to penetrate into the Khamovniki barracks was a signal for action to the plotters. About this you have said nothing, Messrs. the Trotskyites and Bukharinites. I am convinced that a detailed investigation of the facts will supply rich material about this plot and put an end to the legend that what took place in 1921 was a mere discussion. As a member of the "bloc of Rights and Trotskyites," I cannot but bear responsibility for its vile, treacherous and brigand activities. I also bear responsibility for the crimes which I committed myself.

My guilt is aggravated by the fact that I for a long time deceived the Party, betrayed the confidence it placed in me; I wormed my way into high and responsible posts. I need hardly mention that I repent. The proof of my repentance is the testimony, the exposure of myself and my accomplices which I made in Court and at the preliminary investigation.

I am making my last plea. It will most likely be the last utterance in my life. I find it hard to ask and expect that my words be credited. But I declare to the Court that I did not know, that I took no part, that I dissociate myself from such crimes as the preparations for a coup by means of a military conspiracy; that I did not know about the criminal decision of the centre to assassinate Kirov, that I knew nothing about espionage matters and connections and had no relations with foreign intelligence services; that I had no relation whatever to the negotiations with foreign states regarding the severance of national republics and regions from the Soviet Union, nor did I have any relation to the terrorist acts committed by Yagoda and others. This is also borne out by the material of the investigation.

I say this not in order to evade responsibility for these crimes. I cannot but bear responsibility for these crimes just as much as Bukharin and Rykov and the direct perpetrators of these misdeeds. I know that as a member of the "bloc of Rights and Trotskyites" I bear the stigma of these shameful deeds as well and that nothing will remove this shameful stigma from me.

My crimes against the Party, the country and the revolutionary people are great indeed. That is why I can find no reasons, no grounds, to seek for mitigating circumstances for my crime and my guilt. My repentance and confession of my crimes have come too late. They would have been of value if they had come before my arrest. That is why I cannot ask for any mitigation of my lot. I shall accept the verdict of the proletarian Court as a just retribution meted out to me by the Socialist state, the people and the Party for my crimes.

THE PRESIDENT: Accused Ikramov may make his last plea.

IKRAMOV: Citizens Judges, I waived my speech in defence not because I did not want to say anything in my defence. If I were to say that I could say something in my defence, but do not want to, that would be a pretence, a continuation of the phariseeism and duplicity by which I was affected right down to my arrest and to the time I began to testify. This is not the hour, this is not the moment, for me to pretend, or to continue to play the pharisee and double-dealer. I could not find even words, let alone arguments, to justify and defend my crimes. Criminals like the participators in the Right and Trotskyite nationalist bloc, and not only participators, but active participators like myself, can scarcely find words in any language to say in their defence. That is why I was obliged to waive my defence. I cannot say anything in my defence, all the more that I am not a political infant, nor a dotard, an "old shoe," as they say; I am neither the one nor the other. I spent half my life (I am forty years old) in politics, that is, twenty years, and I therefore cannot plead youth and inexperience in my defence. I cannot, nor have I any desire to, hide behind the back of Bukharin or of anybody else. This is not bragging. I may be ignorant of theory, but politics I understand, and understand them no worse than Bukharin. I say this not in boast, but in order to expose the depths of my crime. That is why I say it.

When I spoke here of how Bukharin won me over, or of the instructions which I received from the Right-Trotskyite centre through Bukharin or Antipov, I had no desire, not the least desire, to shift the blame on anybody else. No, I only recorded the fact of my participation and the receipt of various instructions given by the Right leaders to us, the members of the Right-Trotskyite nationalist anti-Soviet bloc.

In my testimony both at the preliminary investigations and here I have concealed nothing, I have told everything. I bear responsibility, and not only for the crimes I myself committed, or which were committed by the nationalist counter-revolutionary organization which existed in Uzbekistan—I also bear full responsibility for such actions of the "bloc of Rights and Trotskyites" as espionage or the dastardly murder of such famous people of the Soviet country as Alexei Maximovich Gorky, Kuibyshev and Menzhinsky, and for the participation in the assassination of Sergei Mironovich Kirov. Nevertheless, it is a relief to me that I, a participator in this conspiracy, an active participator, bear full responsibility on all the points which were here published, both as these crimes are reflected in the criminal code and as these facts were revealed at the trial.

The counter-revolutionary organization which existed in Uzbekistan, which was directed by me, and which formed close contacts with the "bloc of Rights and Trotskyites," called itself a "nationalist" organization. This term "nationalist" might give some people the impression that we wanted to do something for the benefit of our nation. But we betrayed the interests of our nation. I then realized to what depths I had sunk, how far I had fallen. Just see, the nationalists claimed that they wanted to work for the benefit of their nation, but what actually came of it? Actually, they engaged in wrecking activities in municipal enterprises, they engaged in wrecking against the people, they engaged in wrecking against the improvement of living conditions and they engaged in wrecking in agriculture, all in order to frustrate the measures of the Soviet government and the Communist Party, when the Soviet government and the Communist Party were improving the condition of the nation. The nationalists pretended to be striving for "independence," but what they were actually striving for was dependence. The nationalists, in striving for "independence," were striking at the pocket of the working people, at their standard of living.

This disgrace cannot be justified in the eyes of the Court, in the eyes of the workers, and it cannot be justified in the eyes of the nation of Uzbekistan in particular.

Citizen the State Prosecutor has vividly described the rising standard of living and culture of the nations of the Soviet Union. I think, I am convinced, that Uzbekistan may serve as one of the most striking examples of this, especially the rate of progress it is making.

We were only a hindrance and an obstacle to this progress. Were it not for us, Uzbekistan would have attained far greater and much finer achievements.

Everybody knows that before the revolution famine often raged in Uzbekistan, malaria was prevalent, and people perished from these and other maladies. People perished from starvation and malaria. But the Soviet power put an end to all this.

Our nationalist counter-revolutionary organization only tended to foster these diseases and to bring about starvation and death. That is why my guilt, my crimes are so grave.

The nationalists wanted to drown Uzbekistan in the blood of the workers and dekhkans. They pretended that they wanted "independence," but the logic of the struggle would have led to this "independence" being transformed into dependence.

Now the Uzbek nation, like all the other nations of the Soviet Union, is dependent on nobody; it is dependent only upon its collective will, its collective decision. Only in this is it dependent; in all else it is independent.

The "bloc of Rights and Trotskyites" wanted to deprive the Uzbek nation of its independence and to make it dependent on imperialist states, on beks, bais, plutocrats and parasites. It is a good thing that the "bloc of Rights and Trotskyites" was not victorious. If the "bloc of Rights and Trotskyites" were victorious there would be a veritable massacre the very next day, conflict would at once break out between the Trotskyites and the Rights in the Ukraine, Byelorussia, Uzbekistan and other republics. The ideology of the Rights, if they had any ideology left, was the restoration of capitalism. The ideology of the nationalists was the ideology of the kulaks, the ideology of the capitalists.

And in spite of this, such a union of forces took place. In spite of this unprincipledness, principles for a union were found. This only aggravates the disgrace of the participants in this "bloc of Rights and Trotskyites." We were all united by only one principle—the struggle against the Soviet power.

Realizing all these crimes, all these shameful deeds, I can find no grounds to ask for clemency. I thought, I too am one of the people who gave evidence, not after eight or ten months, as some said, but on the sixth or seventh day of the investigation. I thought that this might mitigate my crimes. But I have lost all grounds for asking for clemency. I behaved very criminally before my arrest. Some have mentioned here that they enjoyed confidence, that the attitude of the Party and the government towards them was a good one. This was very painful for me to hear; it was the worst, the keenest internal punishment for me to hear people speaking of confidence.

What should I have said to justify the confidence which was placed in me by the leaders of the Party and the government? Instead of justifying that confidence, I abused it.

In 1930, when Zelensky proposed that I should be removed from my post in Uzbekistan, he was instructed by the Central Committee to show to Ikramov all the material incriminating Ikramov, to acquaint him with it. The Central Committee expressed complete confidence in me. A month or a month and a half later I received another telegram, from which I learnt that in order to support Ikramov, the Central Committee had appointed him Secretary of the Central Asiatic Bureau of the Central Committee of the C.P.S.U. Instead of responding to this confidence with sincerity, I played a double game. What can I say now in my defence, what words, what arguments can I use in pleading for clemency?

I have said this in passing. I do not know whether anybody sitting here in this shameful dock, whether any of these creatures who once were men, enjoyed as much confidence as I did before my arrest.

Before I was arrested I was shown a heap of material collected by the People's Commissariat of Internal Affairs. This was the testimony of people given in 1937, it was material that concerned me. I was told to read it and say whether it was true or not. I must say that in this respect I was treated very considerately by Nikolai Ivanovich Yezhov, who spoke to me four times. And what did I do? I denied everything point-blank. This disgrace therefore cannot in any way be mitigated by the fact that on the sixth or seventh day I changed my mind and began to give sincere and honest testimony. This does not in any way diminish or mitigate the seriousness of my fall.

I must further say that I have not the least desire to shield myself behind Bukharin or the "bloc of Rights and Trotskyites," but I must say that our nationalist program was greatly enriched and activized in counter-revolutionary deeds thanks to the participants in the "bloc of Rights and Trotskyites" sitting here with me in the dock, and especially its Right section, headed by Bukharin and Antipov. We borrowed the acute methods of struggle from them, and we not only borrowed them, but realized what we were doing. And they kept on spurring us on, reproaching us for working badly, for wrecking inadequately, for organizing revolts badly, and so on. Sometimes we asked why this new point had appeared in our struggle against the Party. The reply usually was that the logic of the struggle now demanded the employment of this method. But the logic of the struggle has led us to this shame, from which, whether we live or die, we can never free ourselves. We have been quite rightly called enemies of the people, traitors to the fatherland, spies and assassins.

These shameful stains we cannot obliterate, do as we will.

In connection with this, Citizens Judges, I must say that when I repented, when I came to realize the full gravity of my crimes, I found it very hard to come here and answer for my crimes publicly, before the Court. You know that when your conscience is stirred, it is very difficult to stand up before the people and to look them in the face. When I gave my testimony I very much feared to have to meet the people sitting here.

Fully admitting all the crimes committed by me and by the nationalist organization in Uzbekistan which I directed, admitting my crimes as a participant in the "bloc of Rights and Trotskyites," I have told all I knew, named all the accomplices in the crimes, and have laid down my arms. And so, if there is anything that can be said in my favour when asking for mercy, for clemency, it is that I, a beast in man's shape, stand absolutely naked. I have told everything I know. I have lanced the ulcer within me. And I now feel greatly relieved. I thought that if I told all this to the Court the people would know, the people would know that this Ikramov, even if in the last hour of his life, abandoned and renounced the position which is called treachery, espionage, enemy of the people and the fatherland; they would know that he abandoned this position and died an honest Soviet citizen. This is a gr^at relief to me. And if it is to be so, this will be a certain consolation to me.

I only recently realized how painful it is to be an enemy of the people. All the more painful is it to be an enemy of such a country as the land of the Soviets.

I do not say all this so as to save my vile skin. I say this so that every citizen of the Soviet Union may know what criminals we are, what the nationalists were making for, and whither they would have led the peoples of Uzbekistan. Our path was the path of oppression, the path of enslavement for the peoples of Uzbekistan.

The path of the Communist Party leads to freedom, to a prosperous, cultured and contented life. I say this so that all may know that the bourgeois-nationalist talks of the nation only in order to deceive the people, and so that not a single nationalist who still remains undiscovered may be able to speculate on national matters in Uzbekistan. That is why I have related all my crimes here and spoke about them at length at the preliminary investigation.

Any verdict the Court may pass I shall consider absolutely just and right. But I would simply like to say that I do not want to die, still less do I want to die an enemy of the people, and that I would like anywhere, in any place, to atone for the grave crimes which I have committed in company with these people.

THE PRESIDENT: Accused Rakovsky.

RAKOVSKY: Citizen President of the Court, Citizens Judges, yesterday I listened with great and rapt attention to the speech for the prosecution delivered by the Procurator of the Union, not because I intended to enter into a controversy with him. I have no such intention. I confessed to all my crimes. What would it matter for the substance of the case if I should attempt to establish here before you the fact that I learned of many of the crimes, and of the most appalling crimes of the "bloc of Rights and Trotsky-ites," here in Court, and that it was here that I first met some of the participants? It is of no import whatever. I am connected with the "bloc of Rights and Trotskyites," of course within the limits defined by the Criminal Code, by that complicity, both political and juridical, which follows from the fact that I belonged to this bloc.

Like a galley-slave fettered to his galley, I am fettered to the "bloc of Rights and Trotskyites" with the heavy chain of my crimes. I participated in the underground counter-revolutionary Trotskyite organization up to the last moment, to the moment of my arrest.

647

I was an active member of the "bloc of Rights and Trotskyites." I committed the gravest crimes against the state. I am doubly a spy. In 1924 I established criminal connections with the British Intelligence Service, and in 1934 I established criminal connections with the Japanese intelligence service. In 1927 I carried on negotiations with some of the Right capitalist circles in France, the object of these negotiations being in the long run also directed against the Soviet Union. In 1935 I took advantage of the fact that the French Minister Laval was on a visit in Moscow, accompanied by French journalists, in order to attempt in a conversation with one of them (I mentioned his name) to hinder, to disrupt, the Franco-Soviet rapprochement. Citizens Judges, I informed you about Trotsky's letter of July 1934, in which he wrote of the necessity of isolating Stalin internationally, that is to say, of strengthening, consolidating the capitalist encirclement around the Soviet Union. I belonged to the so-called "Fifth Column" of which the Procurator spoke yesterday, and I have deserved all those maledictions which are now sweeping from all corners of the Soviet land against us sitting here in the dock, maledictions of which the speech for the prosecution delivered by the Procurator, however severe and trenchant it was with regard to us, was perhaps but a weak reflection.

Citizens Judges, I share the State Prosecutor's regret that enemy of the people Trotsky is not here in the dock alongside of us. The picture of our trial loses in completeness and depth because of the fact that the ataman of our gang is not present here. Nobody will suspect me of saying this from a selfish desire, from a base motive to shift on to Trotsky a part of that guilt and that responsibility which I myself bear. I am older than Trotsky both in years and in political career, and I probably have no less political experience than Trotsky. I regret his absence here for considerations of a political nature. I am sorry, because Trotsky's absence in this dock means that no matter how his opportunities may be limited, his activities will continue, and this presents a danger, even if a small one, for the international labour movement. It is true that even beyond the Mexican meridian Trotsky will not escape that complete, final, shameful ignominy which we all are undergoing here.

This, in substance, covers everything relating to the legal, juridical aspect of my case, and I would have even foregone my last plea had I not considered it necessary, after what was said here by the Procurator, to try in my turn to point out the exceptional political importance of the present trial. But it seems to me that Citizen the Procurator dwelt on only one aspect of the case. Yes, he stressed the monstrosity of the crimes which we committed, but I should like to turn your attention,

648

Citizens Judges, to the fact that the monstrosity of this is also determined by the persons who committed these crimes. Who were those who committed espionage, wrecking, acts of diversion, terrorism, murder? They were committed not by candidates for criminal court records, people living in slums and cellars. The criminals sitting here had to be taken from the house of the government. And thus the question which arises and to which I, as one of those involved, feel the necessity to find an answer, is the question as to how former members of the Central Committee, former members of the government, former ambassadors have ended up here. What form of insanity brought them to this dock of political infamy? I think that this is all the more necessary since this question faces every one of us and every one is searching for an explanation. I shall mention one explanation which is widely current. After all, this is not the first trial. I remember how this question was answered in connection with the other trials. People are satisfied with the trite and shallow bourgeois explanation, according to which all revolutions finish by devouring their own children. The October Revolution, they say, did not escape this general law of historical fatalism.

It is a ridiculous, groundless analogy. Bourgeois revolutions did indeed finish—excuse me if I cite here some theoretical arguments which, however, are of significance for the present moment—bourgeois revolutions did indeed finish by devouring their own children, because after they had triumphed they had to suppress their allies from among the people, their revolutionary allies of the Left.

But the proletarian revolution, the revolution of the class which is revolutionary to the end, when it applies what Marx called "plebeian methods of retaliation," it applies them not to the advanced elements, it applies them to those who stand in the way of this revolution, or to those who, as ourselves, were with this revolution, marched along with it for a certain time, and then stabbed it in the back.

And I, an active Trotskyite, a very close personal friend of Trotsky (the Procurator has established that our friendship was of 34 years' duration), a man who after many had returned (true, with duplicity) into the Party, continued for many more years to carry on an open struggle against the Party leadership. I want to answer this question. Permit me to share with you my thoughts on this subject.

Citizens Judges, why indeed did it happen that I turned against my Party and in the end sank to the status of a criminal? What did we Trotskyites represent in the Party? We were what is known as an alien body in the living Party organism. Trotsky joined the Bolshevik Party only a few months before the October

649

Revolution, his ideology took shape in the fight against Bolshevism. I joined the Party at the end of 1917, after I had belonged for more than a quarter of a century to the Second International, which developed under entirely specific conditions, under the conditions of peaceful development of capitalism, and, although I belonged to its Left wing, I was permeated by its opportunism. If you trace back the history of other Trotskyites, if I take Radek, Pyatakov, Preobrazhensky as examples, you will find that both before the October Revolution and after the October Revolution every one of them was guilty of a number of serious deviations.

And it must be said that from the very first moment we Trotskyites adopted the attitude of antagonists of the Party leadership. From the very first moment. Brest-Litovsk. I shall not refer here to the testimony (you know it) which clarifies Trotsky's role during the period of the Brest-Litovsk negotiations. The discussion about the trade unions. What was that? It was a trial of forces. The accused Zelensky mentioned facts here which will perhaps reveal that there was in general another attempt there, only, as far as I remember, all the persons whom he mentioned did not belong to the Trotskyite faction, but to the so-called D. C. faction, the faction of Democratic Centralism. We suffered defeat and immediately adopted an orientation toward foreign states. It is sufficient just to remind you of the fact which was here established. We suffered defeat in 1921 in the discussion on the trade unions. The Party in its striving to consolidate its internal unity removed a number of Trotskyites from the Central Committee.

In 1921 Trotsky already gave his first instruction about establishing criminal connections with the German intelligence service. In 1926 came the second instruction. The first instruction was given to Krestinsky, the second to Rosengoltz. At the end of 1924 a recruiting agent of the intelligence service called on me; I could have thrown him down the stairs, because he resorted to blackmail. But when he said: "Do not forget that we obtained the agrément for you because we learnt that you were a Trotskyite," this touched the Trotskyite strain in me. I gave no answer at the time, I talked it over with Trotsky. We knew the position we were in. I had been removed from the Ukraine, some had been removed from the Central Committee, Smirnov had been removed from the Siberian Revolutionary Committee, Radek and Pyatakov were also at a loose end, and Trotsky was saying that in the very near future, within the next few days, he would have to quit the Revolutionary Committee, unless he wanted to be ousted from it with a bang.

I am arraying all these facts so that the picture may become clear. In 1926 we already established connections with the foreign intelligence service. In 1927 it became apparent that we were suffering defeat, and that it would be a defeat after which no manoeuvre

650

would succeed, because before that defeat the Zinovievite-Trotskyite opposition stood at attention before the Party and remained in the Party while continuing to work against the Party; we knew that at the Fifteenth Congress of the Party, at the very latest, we would be expelled, if not all of us, at any rate Trotsky. Now we had to pass on to work in secret. After that I left for France. In August and September I carried on negotiations about uniting the opposition and about what we could obtain from certain French circles in order to gain victory.

I shall not relate the history of Trotskyism, it is well known. I only want to speak about the formation of the "bloc of Rights and Trotskyites." The formation of the "bloc of Rights and Trotskyites" was, if we may put it that way, "a marriage of convenience," each party contributing its dowery. We Trotskyites contributed our connections with foreign intelligence services, the Rights contributed their cadres, their connections with the nationalist, Menshevik, Socialist-Revolutionary and other elements, their connections with the kulaks. Of course, in addition to this fixed capital of ours, each could contribute something else. We did not hesitate before perfidy, before deceit, treason, bribery, murder by means of poison or the revolver instead of the traditional dagger.

I shall not speak of any ideology of this bloc. You heard here the platform of my fellow-accused in this trial, N. I. Bukharin. This, of course, represents restoration of capitalist relations in two leaps, through opening the sluices for free trade with abroad, through the return of the kulaks, through the liquidation of the collective farms, through opening the doors wide for concession capital. We calculated that we would achieve the complete triumph of capitalism in an extremely short period of time.

Ours was, of course, a counter-revolutionary ideology. We wanted to rely for support on the elements which had already been doomed by the Five-Year Plans, the elements which had been swept away, cast out. Of course there is nothing surprising in the fact that these old ruins came down with a crash and we found ourselves buried under the debris. I think that this is not enough. In my opinion, there is no precedent of politically minded people, people who had a definite political past, experience, and so forth, displaying such naiveté, such self-delusion, such illusions as those which held sway over them. Yes, it was raving, real raving, the ravings of a madman to think that way, but we did think that way. We thought that with our insignificant forces, not only without any base of support, but with the working class against us, with the Party against us—we thought that we could achieve some results. These were ravings, calculating on some kind of foreign assistance. Ravings in what sense? This foreign assistance would utilize us and then throw us overboard. From a political force, we became a tool.

651

Ravings in every respect. Our misfortune was that we occupied responsible posts, that power had made us dizzy. We were blinded by that passion, by that ambition for power. This cannot be explained by "ideology" alone. These two factors, taken together and acting in combination, brought us to the dock.

We considered ourselves to be people sent by providence; we consoled ourselves with the thought that we would be summoned, that we were needed. This is what both the Trotskyites and the Rights said. We did not notice that the entire development of the Soviet Union swept over us, that the peaceful revolution which transformed our countryside swept over us, that this immense growth of the cultural and political level of the masses of the people and the creation of new cadres of politically trained people from among the Stakhanovites[5] swept over us. All this swept over us, unnoticed by us.

The sobering moment had to come. Perhaps I will somewhat contradict what the Procurator said, but I am of the opinion that the "bloc of Rights and Trotskyites" was doomed to disintegration. Of course, this does not absolve the bloc of the responsibility for the crimes which were committed.

There was no political future whatever in store for us. For many of us the moment of sobering had not arrived, because it began only after we had been arrested.

Citizens Judges, I told everything that I committed, without concealing or holding back a single fact. Both during the Court investigation, during the preliminary investigation, and during the trial (I think I will not be mistaken if I say so) I was not found guilty of a single contradiction or of concealing any fact.

I think that this proves that I revealed myself before you fully and entirely, that I stand fully and entirely exposed.

I wish to make one appeal to you, an appeal which would never have escaped my lips if this were a different court. But I make this appeal to you because I see in your persons the Soviet Court, the proletarian Court. It is an appeal for mercy. Yesterday the State Prosecutor made this task in a certain sense easier for me, inasmuch as he did not demand the supreme penalty for me. But I must say that in the gradation of the minimum and maximum which the Citizen Procurator mentioned here, there is a certain limit which exceeds the limits of my age. I want to mention this only: that, in applying the appropriate articles of the law to me, you may consider this circumstance and form your decision in accordance, so to speak, with the physiological limitations of the accused who stands before you.

Citizens Judges, from my young days I honestly, truthfully and devotedly performed my duty as a soldier of the cause of the emancipation of labour. After this bright period a dark period set in,

652

the period of my criminal deeds, of treason to the fatherland, a series of dark crimes which I briefly summed up before you today. I told you all I knew, I told everything, I concealed nothing, I held back nothing, I repent deeply and sincerely, and I ask you to give me the opportunity to redeem even if an insignificant part of my guilt, even by the most modest work, no matter under what circumstances. I have finished.

THE PRESIDENT: The accused Rosengoltz may make his last plea.

ROSENGOLTZ: After the description given me by the Prosecution, I should like in my last plea, in my last address to people, to recall to myself and also to others those pages in the story of my life which I may call bright and which raise no suspicion on anybody's part. First of all, a few words about my biography. I want to speak of it all the more that I have never engaged in writing reminiscences or memoirs.

During the years of my tenderest childhood I was brought up by a woman who was a professional revolutionary, a Social-Democrat.

My very earliest recollections are searches made by gendarmes. When I was only ten years old, my hand, the hand of a child, was used to hide illegal literature during the night and to recover it in the morning from a place where the hand of a grown-up could not reach.

I joined the Bolshevik Party when I was only fifteen or sixteen years old. I was first arrested when I was sixteen years old. At the age of seventeen, I was nominated by a Bolshevik group as delegate to the Unity Congress of the Party under the pseudonym of "Stepan," which was the pseudonym under which I carried on my work.

During the difficult years of tsarist reaction I did not desert the Party. During the imperialist war I actively championed the Bolshevik defeatist stand. In Moscow in particular I carried on a campaign in opposition to Chkheidze;[6] I was one of the organizers and chairmen of a meeting of workers' representatives in Moscow which was held in 1915. During the tramwaymen's strike we seized the hall of the City Duma in carrying out measures to support this tramwaymen's strike.

Do not think that I want to engage in bragging, but, still, I should like to recall what was good in my life, what was unquestionably good.

During the October Revolution I brought the first military unit, the Cyclists' battalion, to the Moscow Soviet. I think that I can also feel more or less gratified with my active role as member of the Revolutionary Committee. During the Civil War, the Central Committee of the Party sent me from one army to another, to the more difficult sectors. The confidence which the Central Committee then placed in me found expression even in the fact that I held a mandate, issued by Lenin and Sverdlov, which gave me the right of expelling members from the Party by my own decision. This was in 1918. I may say that I did not then betray the confidence which was placed in me by this mandate. I was sent by Vladimir Ilyich personally to a number of armies—to the Seventh Army and to the Thirteenth Army, to the Leningrad front and to the Southern front. It is with a warm feeling that I recall now the attitude which I always met on the part of Vladimir Ilyich when I came to Moscow from the front. I recall the great support which Stalin always gave me during the Civil War. I recall that during the period of the struggle in the Thirteenth Army on the approaches to Tula, Stalin, on his own initiative, insisted that Pyatakov be removed from that army, and that I become the head of the army on this most important sector of the front. I recall that in the Seventh Army, near Leningrad, a month before Yudenich's offensive, Stalin, who came there at the request of Vladimir Ilyich, defended me against the campaign which was carried on against me in the course of a number of controversies on strategical problems, and he insisted (I consider it necessary to mention it here, because it has also a certain historical significance, it is a fact that is little known), Stalin insisted and brought about the dispatch of considerable military forces to Leningrad, which forces arrived just before Yudenich began his offensive.[7] If Stalin had not brought this about with Vladimir Ilyich's support, Yudenich's offensive might have encountered quite a different picture.

If I recall these various episodes of the Civil War, if I recall with satisfaction my work in the army, I mention this not for the purpose of mitigating the sentence. I want to explain the reason. A simple human reason: after all that I have lived through, after the feeling of shame which I experienced during this trial, after the monstrous crimes which I committed, I have no incentive or desire to ask for the mitigation of my sentence.

This is not a rhetorical figure. This does not mean that it is without a feeling of pain that I part with the beautiful land of the Soviets. We have beautiful new shoots now, a new generation reared by the Bolshevik Party. We have such an upsurge in the Soviet Union as no other country in the world can boast. The pain of parting is intensified by the fact that we already have absolutely real results of socialist construction. For the first time now we have a life, a full-blooded life, scintillating with joy and colour. Millions, tens of millions of people, children and citizens of the Soviet Union, including my own children, sing the song:

"Native land of mine, so beautiful . . .
There is no other land the whole world over
Where man walks the earth so proud and free."
And I repeat these words, I, a prisoner, repeat these words:
There is no other land the whole world over where there is
such enthusiasm of labour, where such gay and joyous laughter
rings, where song and dance resound so free, where there is such
beautiful love; and I say: "Farewell, my native land, my own!"
I want people to believe me. I want nothing from the Court, nor
from people. I do not want and cannot permit myself a single word
of falsehood in this, my last address to people.

There is not a single man in the world who brought so much
sorrow and misfortune to people as Trotsky. He is the vilest agent
of fascism. The Procurator was right, and Rakovsky was right when
they said that here, in the dock, it is Trotsky in the first place who
is missing.

Trotskyism is not a political current but an unscrupulous dirty
gang of murderers, spies, provocateurs and poisoners, it is a dirty
gang of henchmen of capitalism. This is the function which Trotskyism is performing everywhere, in all countries, including the Soviet Union.

The lesson and the conclusion which must be drawn from this
trial by the vast masses in the Soviet Union consists, in the first
place, in the fact that the general line of the Bolshevik Party must
be kept undeviatingly pure. Woe and misfortune will betide him
who strays even to the smallest extent from the general line of the
Bolshevik Party. I want you to believe me, to believe in the
sincerity of the words which I now utter.

I say: Long live, flourish and grow in strength the great, mighty,
beautiful Union of the Soviet Socialist Republics, advancing from
victory to victory, and over which shines the magnificent sun of
Socialism.

Long live the Bolshevik Party with the best traditions of enthusiasm, heroism, self-sacrifice, which can only be found in the
world under Stalin's leadership. In the inevitable clash of two
worlds, Communism will emerge victorious. Long live Communism
throughout the world!

THE PRESIDENT: The Court is adjourned until 6 p. m.

[*Signed*] PRESIDENT: V. ULRICH
Army Military Jurist
President of the Military Collegium of
the Supreme Court of the U.S.S.R.

SECRETARY: A. BATNER
Military Jurist First Rank

655

THE COMMANDANT OF THE COURT: The Court is coming, please rise.

THE PRESIDENT: Please be seated. The session is resumed. Accused Bukharin, you may make your last plea.

BUKHARIN: Citizen President and Citizens Judges, I fully agree with Citizen the Procurator regarding the significance of the trial, at which were exposed our dastardly crimes, the crimes committed by the "bloc of Rights and Trotskyites," one of whose leaders I was, and for all the activities of which I bear responsibility.

This trial, which is the concluding one of a series of trials, has exposed all the crimes and the treasonable activities, it has exposed the historical significance and the roots of our struggle against the Party and the Soviet government.

I have been in prison for over a year, and I therefore do not know what is going on in the world. But, judging from those fragments of real life that sometimes reached me by chance, I see, feel and understand that the interests which we so criminally betrayed are entering a new phase of gigantic development, are now appearing in the international arena as a great and mighty factor of the international proletarian phase.

We, the accused, are sitting on the other side of the barrier, and this barrier separates us from you, Citizens Judges. We found ourselves in the accursed ranks of the counter-revolution, became traitors to the Socialist fatherland.

At the very beginning of the trial, in answer to the question of Citizen the President, whether I pleaded guilty, I replied by a confession.

In answer to the question of Citizen the President whether I confirmed the testimony I had given, I replied that I confirmed it fully and entirely.

When, at the end of the preliminary investigation, I was summoned for interrogation to the State Prosecutor, who controlled the sum total of the materials of the investigation, he summarized them as follows (Vol. V, p. 114, December 1, 1937):

Question: Were you a member of the centre of the counter-revolutionary organization of the Rights? I answered: Yes, I admit it.

Second question: Do you admit that the centre of the anti-Soviet organization, of which you are a member, engaged in counter-revolutionary activities and set itself the aim of violently overthrowing the leadership of the Party and the government? I answered: Yes, I admit it.

Third question: Do you admit that this centre engaged in terrorist activities, organized kulak uprisings and prepared for White-guard kulak uprisings against members of the Political Bureau, against the leadership of the Party and the Soviet power? I answered: It is true.

Fourth question: Do you admit that you are guilty of treasonable activities, as expressed in preparations for a conspiracy aiming at a coup d'état? I answered: Yes, that is also true.

In Court I admitted and still admit my guilt in respect to the crimes which I committed and of which I was accused by Citizen the State Prosecutor at the end of the Court investigation and on the basis of the materials of the investigation in the possession of the Procurator. I declared also in Court, and I stress and repeat it now, that I regard myself politically responsible for the sum total of the crimes committed by the "bloc of Rights and Trotskyites."

I have merited the most severe punishment, and I agree with Citizen the Procurator, who several times repeated that I stand on the threshold of my hour of death.

Nevertheless, I consider that I have the right to refute certain charges which were brought: a) in the printed Indictment, b) during the Court investigation, and c) in the speech for the Prosecution made by Citizen the Procurator of the U.S.S.R.

I consider it necessary to mention that during my interrogation by Citizen the State Prosecutor, the latter declared in a very categorical form that I, as one of the accused, must not admit more than I had admitted and that I must not invent facts that have never happened, and he demanded that this statement of his should be placed on the records.

I once more repeat that I admit that I am guilty of treason to the Socialist fatherland, the most heinous of possible crimes, of the organization of kulak uprisings, of preparations for terrorist acts and of belonging to an underground, anti-Soviet organization. I further admit that I am guilty of organizing a conspiracy for a "palace coup." And this, incidentally, proves the incorrectness of all those passages in the speech for the prosecution made by Citizen the State Prosecutor, where he makes out that I adopted the pose of a pure theoretician, the pose of a philosopher, and so on. These are profoundly practical matters. I said, and I now repeat, that I was a leader and not a cog in the counter-revolutionary affairs. It fol-

657

lows from this, as will be clear to everybody, that there were many specific things which I could not have known, and which I actually did not know, but that this does not relieve me of responsibility.

I admit that I am responsible both politically and legally for the defeatist orientation, for it did dominate in the "bloc of Rights and Trotskyites," although I affirm:

a) that personally I did not hold this position;

b) that the phrase about opening the front was not uttered by me, but was an echo of my conversation with Tomsky;

c) that if Rykov heard this phrase for the first time from me, then, I repeat, it was an echo of my conversation with Tomsky.

But I consider myself responsible for a grave and monstrous crime against the Socialist fatherland and the whole international proletariat. I further consider myself responsible both politically and legally for wrecking activities, although I personally do not remember having given directions about wrecking activities. I did not talk about this. I once spoke positively on this subject to Grinko. Even in my testimony I mentioned that I had once told Radek that I considered this method of struggle as not very expedient. Yet Citizen the State Prosecutor makes me out to be a leader of the wrecking activities.

Citizen the Procurator explained in the speech for the prosecution that the members of a gang of brigands might commit robberies in different places, but that they would nevertheless be responsible for each other. That is true, but in order to be a gang the members of the gang of brigands must know each other and be in more or less close contact with each other. Yet I first learnt the name of Sharangovich from the Indictment, and I first saw him here in Court. It was here that I first learnt about the existence of Maximov, I have never been acquainted with Pletnev, I have never been acquainted with Kazakov, I have never spoken about counter-revolutionary matters with Rakovsky, I have never spoken on this subject with Rosengoltz, I have never spoken about it to Zelensky, I have never in my life spoken to Bulanov, and so on. Incidentally, even the Procurator did not ask me a single question about these people.

The "bloc of Rights and Trotskyites" is first and foremost a bloc of Rights and Trotskyites. How then, generally, could it include Levin, for example, who stated here in court that to this day he does not know what a Menshevik is? How could it include Pletnev, Kazakov and others?

Consequently, the accused in this dock are not a group. They are confederates in a conspiracy along various lines, but they are not a group in the strict and legal sense of the word. All the accused were connected in one way or another with the "bloc of Rights and Trotskyites," some of them were also connected with intelligence services, but that is all. This, however, provides no grounds for asserting that this group is the "bloc of Rights and Trotskyites."

Secondly, the "bloc of Rights and Trotskyites," which actually did exist and which was smashed by the organs of the People's Commissariat of Internal Affairs, arose historically. It did really exist until it was smashed by the organs of the People's Commissariat of Internal Affairs. It arose historically. I have testified that I first spoke to Kamenev as far back as 1928, during the Sixth Congress of the Comintern, which I at that time directed.

How then can it be asserted that the bloc was organized on the instructions of fascist intelligence services? Why, this was in 1928! By the way, at that time I narrowly missed death at the hands of an agent of the Polish "Defensiva," a fact very well known to everybody who stood close to the Party leadership.

Thirdly, I categorically deny that I was connected with foreign intelligence services, that they were my masters and that I acted in accordance with their wishes.

Citizen the Procurator asserts that I was one of the major organizers of espionage, on a par with Rykov. What are the proofs? The testimony of Sharangovich, of whose existence I had not even heard until I read the indictment.

The record of Sharangovich's testimony was submitted to me, from which it appears that I practically drew up the plan for wrecking.

SHARANGOVICH: Stop lying, for once in your life at least. You are lying even now in Court.

THE PRESIDENT: Accused Sharangovich, don't interrupt.

SHARANGOVICH: I could not restrain myself.

BUKHARIN: Take Ivanov. Generally, what I have to say about his testimony is the following. Certain persons, who were connected with the Okhrana in the past, testified that from fear of exposure they decided to wage a struggle against the Soviet power, and that they therefore joined the Rights, the underground organization, which orientated itself on terrorism. But where is the logic? Fine logic, indeed. From fear of possible exposure they joined a terrorist organization, where they ran the risk of being caught the very next day. This is hard to imagine; I at least cannot imagine it. But Citizen the Procurator believed them, although all of it sounds very unconvincing.

Khodjayev asserts that I advised him to get in contact with the British resident agent, while Ikramov says that I told him that Turkestan was a choice morsel for England. In reality, this is far from the truth. I told Khodjayev that advantage should be taken of the antagonisms between the imperialist powers, and in a vague form I supported the idea of the independence of Turkestan. Not a single word was said about any resident agents. Citizen

659

the State Prosecutor asked: But did you see Khodjayev? I did. Was this in Tashkent? It was in Tashkent. Did you talk to him about politics? About politics. That means that you spoke about the resident agent. Such conclusions were drawn several times; and when I protested against them, Citizen the Procurator accused me of not telling the truth, of trying to wriggle out of it, of wishing to conceal the truth, and so on; and in this he was supported by a number of my fellow-accused. But it seems to me that in this case real logic is wholly on my side. Citizen the State Prosecutor declared on the basis of these materials that all the espionage connections proceeded through the channels of Rykov and Bukharin. Yet Citizen the Procurator said that every word was important here. The speech of Citizen the Procurator contained references to two Japanese newspapers. But why does it follow that these reports refer precisely to me and the Rights?

I, however, admit that I am guilty of the dastardly plan of the dismemberment of the U.S.S.R., for Trotsky was negotiating about territorial concessions, and I was in a bloc with the Trotskyites. This is a fact, and I admit it.

I categorically deny my complicity in the assassination of Kirov, Menzhinsky, Kuibyshev, Gorky and Maxim Peshkov. According to Yagoda's testimony, Kirov was assassinated in accordance with a decision of the "bloc of Rights and Trotskyites." I knew nothing about it. But what Citizen the Procurator calls logic comes here to the aid of the factual content. He asked whether Bukharin and Rykov could have stood aside from these assassinations; and he answered that they could not have stood aside because they knew about them. But not standing aside and knowing are one and the same thing. This is what in elementary logic is called tautology, that is, the acceptance of what is yet to be proved as already proven. But what is the real explanation? It might be said: Well, then, you villain, how do you explain these facts? Can you deny that some decision was adopted by some section or other with the knowledge of Yenukidze and Yagoda, or you deny even that? I cannot deny it, Citizens Judges. But if I cannot deny it, and at the same time cannot affirm it, I can make a certain conjecture. After all, you must bear in mind the secrecy of the work. The centre did not hold meetings: matters were discussed as occasion arose, and given such secret methods of communication and connections with each other, such things are quite possible.

As to Maxim Peshkov. Yagoda himself says that this assassination concerns him personally. I have no right to intrude into this sphere. But this is Yagoda's statement, fortified by so fundamental a fact as his request to have the matter heard in camera, a fairly weighty consideration. Yet Kryuchkov says that it was done in order to lower Maxim Gorky's buoyant life tonus. And, if

I am not mistaken, one of the Counsel for Defence also adopted this viewpoint. But this can be seen through. This argument is countered by so weighty a fact as Yagoda's personal statement, which is corroborated by the fact that this point was referred to the session in camera.

As to Menzhinsky. Bulanov testified to personal motives here too. Menzhinsky was already ill, he could not have injured the "bloc of Rights and Trotskyites" in any way.

Why, then, can this be regarded as likely?

I will dwell on Bulanov's testimony.

The most painful and most horrible thing is the death of Alexei Maximovich. What testimony did I give, how did I give it, and under what circumstances? I was asked (apparently the investigation had already furnished material on the subject) whether I did not recall anything that could throw light on the hostile attitude of the Right and Trotskyite parts of the bloc towards Gorky. I recalled the conversation with Tomsky which I mentioned here in Court and about which the Procurator interrogated me. The substance of this conversation was that Tomsky cursorily remarked that the Trotskyites were preparing to commit hostile acts against the Stalinist, Gorky. It absolutely did not occur to me at the time that he could refer to a terrorist act. I turned a deaf ear to it. During the interrogation I recalled this conversation with Tomsky. To the insistent demands of Citizen the Procurator I steadily replied that the thought of a terrorist act had not occurred to me at the time. Here in Court, in reply to one of the questions of Citizen the Procurator, I said: "But now I see that it was to this he was referring." Citizen the Procurator drew the following conclusion from this; he said: "What is this, if not a veiled admission?" A veiled admission of what? What is admitted? The fact that I had learnt in Court a number of new facts which had not been known to me, and that therefore the conversation I had had with Tomsky might retrospectively be regarded in an entirely different perspective. I consider that the argumentation of Citizen the State Prosecutor in this case cannot be regarded as adequate.

Take the year 1918. Citizen the Procurator declares that in 1924 I was compelled to make a confession regarding such and such a conversation in the Smolny. I was not compelled; I experienced absolutely no pressure on me to do so; nobody but myself even hinted at it, and I published this example in order at that time, 1923-24, to show the utter harm of the factional struggle, and what it was leading to. So that first of all I would like to clear up this misunderstanding.

Citizen the State Prosecutor said that Bukharin cited nothing in refutation of the evidence of the five witnesses, who stood here in this Court before us all, before Citizens the Judges of this case, who asserted that I had the design, the thought, the idea, which I insistently advocated, of arresting Lenin and physically destroying him, and, moreover, to Lenin were added two other prominent figures in the Party—Stalin and Sverdlov. But it is not true that I cited no arguments in refutation. Citizen the Procurator may consider them untrue, feeble, unconvincing, but it cannot be said that I cited nothing in refutation. I cited a number of arguments.

The chief witness was Varvara Nikolayevna Yakovleva. Varvara Nikolayevna Yakovleva dates this whole incident about the preparations for the conspiracy with the "Left" Socialist-Revolutionaries against Lenin, Stalin and Sverdlov, for their arrest and supposed murder, etc.,—she dates all this in her evidence, and then at the confrontation and during the trial—to the period prior to the Peace of Brest-Litovsk. I said at the confrontation, at the preliminary investigation, and in Court, that it is not true. It is not true that before the Brest-Litovsk Peace the "Left Communists" and the Trotskyites wanted to effect a coup d'état by forcible means; it is untrue because the Trotskyites and the so-called "Lefts" had the majority in the Central Committee, and if the Trotskyites had not capitulated at the decisive moment when the vote on the question of the Brest-Litovsk Peace was taken, the Trotskyites and the "Lefts" would have had the majority in the Central Committee. That being the case, how can it be supposed that they then capitulated in order to resort to conspiratorial methods? Everybody who lived through that period remembers perfectly well that the feelings of the "Left Communists" at that time, before the Brest-Litovsk Peace, were such that they hoped to win a Party majority at the next Party Congress. That being the case how could there have been any talk about that of which the witness Varvara Nikolayevna Yakovleva now speaks? But I cited another example. Varvara Nikolayevna Yakovleva asserted that the Moscow Regional Bureau was the factional centre of the "Left Communists." I then took the liberty of mentioning several names, several respected members of the Party. I only wanted in this way to discredit the argument of Varvara Nikolayevna Yakovleva. It is well known that a number of prominent people—Kuibyshev, Emelyan Yaroslavsky, Menzhinsky and others—were at that time supporters of the "Left Communists," belonged to my "Left" group. The relative importance of these people was far greater than that of the Mantsevs, Stukovs and the rest; and by political temperament and political activity they were more efficient than the persons mentioned. And so until the Brest-Litovsk Peace the central group in Leningrad comprised the persons mentioned. And so I ask, how could there have been a plan of revolt if these people held the key position in the central group? It is inconceivable, it is impossible. And here Varvara Nikolayevna

662

Yakovleva, the principal witness against me, is mixing things up with an entirely different period, the period following the Brest-Litovsk Peace, the Moscow period.

I beg your forgiveness, Citizens Judges, for fixing your attention on this point: but as it is a very grave matter and a very interesting one, and as so much attention was devoted to it in the Court, I took the liberty of repeating what I have already said. Yet Citizen the State Prosecutor asserted that I cited nothing to exonerate myself on this point.

I will not dwell on other things, because I do not want to take up your time. I admit that there was one conversation with Karelin and Kamkov; and the initiative with regard to the arrest of Lenin for twenty-four hours and the subsequent bloc with the "Left" Socialist-Revolutionaries proceeded from the "Left" Socialist-Revolutionaries. But in the first conversation the reply was negative in a rude form. And as regards the fact that negotiations were subsequently conducted through Pyatakov with the "Left" Socialist-Revolutionaries—and this may be considered, as Citizen the Procurator, if I am not mistaken, formulated it, an attempt to overthrow the Soviet power by forcible means—this I admit; it was the case. As to the plan of physical extermination, I categorically deny it, and here the logic to which Citizen the State Prosecutor referred, namely, that forcible arrest implied physical extermination, will not help in the least. The Constituent Assembly was arrested, but nobody suffered physically. We arrested the faction of the "Left" Socialist-Revolutionaries, yet not a single man of them suffered physically. The "Left" Socialist-Revolutionaries arrested Dzerzhinsky, yet he did not suffer physically. And I say—and this was omitted from the speech of the State Prosecutor—that in these criminal and dastardly conversations, it was specifically stipulated that not one hair of the persons concerned should be injured. You may think what you like, but it is a real fact.

This episode after the Brest-Litovsk Peace generally took up an extremely short space of time, because very soon afterwards the "Left" Socialist-Revolutionaries began to act. We had to arrest the faction of "Left" Socialist-Revolutionaries. I myself took part in this operation, I myself took part in directing the arrest of the faction of "Left" Socialist-Revolutionaries. After this we had nothing more to do with the "Left" Socialist-Revolutionaries generally. I went abroad on revolutionary work, then returned, then, I repeat, I was wounded by a "Left" Socialist-Revolutionary bomb. I do not deny that it was not thrown at me personally, as the witness Mantzev stated, but I want to say that everybody knew that I was to deliver a lecture in the building of the Moscow Committee, and it was at this moment that the attempt was made and I was slightly wounded. A number of leading figures in the Party were killed. As is known this attempt was made by the bloc of the "Left" Socialist-Revolutionaries, headed by Cherepanov and his wife, Tamara, with the so-called underground anarchists.

I mentioned Mantsev because Cherepanov was arrested by the "Left Communist" Mantsev, as he was not an ally of Cherepanov. It is not true that Bela Kun encouraged the "Left" Socialist-Revolutionaries.

I want to say that there was one brief period of criminal conspiracy between the "Left Communists" and the "Left" Socialist-Revolutionaries which quickly collapsed after their action, in the suppression of which a number of "Left Communists" took an active part.

To support his speech, the State Prosecutor advanced a number of other points which were to provide a base for a period, a black period, in my life.

There are a number of mistakes here. First of all, I was never an Otzovist, although the State Prosecutor says I was.

The State Prosecutor accuses me of the fact that I worked with Trotsky as an editor of the magazine "Novy Mir," and that I had a bloc with Trotsky. I object to this.

The State Prosecutor accuses me of having opposed Comrade Stalin in 1924. I do not remember any such case. I now conclude my objections to certain charges which the State Prosecutor brought against me in the course of the trial, and I will return to the crimes I actually did commit. I have already enumerated them twice. The gravity of these crimes is immense. I think it is unnecessary to repeat how grave these crimes are; it is clear enough as it is.

I only want to say that the Trotskyite section on more than one occasion acted separately, and it is possible that individual members of the bloc, like Yagoda, may also have acted separately, because Yagoda, as Bulanov testifies, regarded Rykov and myself as his secretaries, and he himself in this Court has called me a chatterbox who organized idiotic mass uprisings when it was a question of a coup d'état. But I am connected with the "bloc of Rights and Trotskyites," and it is quite natural that I politically answer absolutely for everything.

The extreme gravity of the crime is obvious, the political responsibility immense, the legal responsibility such that it will justify the severest sentence. The severest sentence would be justified, because a man deserves to be shot ten times over for such crimes. This I admit quite categorically and without any hesitation at all.

I want briefly to explain the facts regarding my criminal activities and my repentance of my misdeeds.

I already said when giving my main testimony during the trial, that it was not the naked logic of the struggle that drove us, the

664

counter-revolutionary conspirators, into this stinking underground life, which has been exposed at this trial in all its starkness. This naked logic of the struggle was accompanied by a degeneration of ideas, a degeneration of psychology, a degeneration of ourselves, a degeneration of people. There are well-known historical examples of such degeneration. One need only mention Briand, Mussolini and others. And we too degenerated, and this brought us into a camp which in its views and features was very much akin to a kulak praetorian fascism. As this process advanced all the time very rapidly under the conditions of a developing class struggle, this struggle, its speed, its existence, acted as the accelerator, as the catalytic agent of the process which was expressed in the acceleration of the process of degeneration.

But this process of degeneration of people, including myself, took place in absolutely different conditions from those in which the process of degeneration of the international labour leaders in Western Europe took place. It took place amidst colossal socialist construction, with its immense scope, tasks, victories, difficulties, heroism. . . .

And on this basis, it seems to me probable that every one of us sitting here in the dock suffered from a peculiar duality of mind, an incomplete faith in his counter-revolutionary cause. I will not say that the consciousness of this was absent, but it was incomplete. Hence a certain semi-paralysis of the will, a retardation of reflexes. It seems to me that we are to a certain extent people with retarded reflexes. And this was due not to the absence of consistent thought, but to the objective grandeur of socialist construction. The contradiction that arose between the acceleration of our degeneration and these retarded reflexes expressed the position of a counter-revolutionary, or a developing counter-revolutionary, under the conditions of developing socialist construction. A dual psychology arose. Each one of us can discern this in his own soul, although I will not engage in a far-reaching psychological analysis.

Even I was sometimes carried away by the eulogies I wrote of socialist construction, although on the morrow I repudiated this by practical actions of a criminal character. There arose what in Hegel's philosophy is called a most unhappy mind. This unhappy mind differed from the ordinary unhappy mind only by the fact that it was also a criminal mind.

The might of the proletarian state found its expression not only in the fact that it smashed the counter-revolutionary bands, but also in the fact that it disintegrated its enemies from within, that it disorganized the will of its enemies. Nowhere else is this the case, nor can it be in any capitalist country.

It seems to me that when some of the West European and American intellectuals begin to entertain doubts and vacillations in connection with the trials taking place in the U.S.S.R., this is primarily due to the fact that these people do not understand the radical distinction, namely, that in our country the antagonist, the enemy, has at the same time a divided, a dual mind. And I think that this is the first thing to be understood.

I take the liberty of dwelling on these questions because I had considerable contacts with these upper intellectuals abroad, especially among scientists, and I must explain to them what every Young Pioneer in the Soviet Union knows.

Repentance is often attributed to diverse and absolutely absurd things like Thibetan powders and the like. I must say of myself that in prison, where I was confined for over a year, I worked, studied, and retained my clarity of mind. This will serve to refute by facts all fables and absurd counter-revolutionary tales.

Hypnotism is suggested. But I conducted my own defence in Court from the legal standpoint too, orientated myself on the spot, argued with the State Prosecutor; and anybody, even a man who has little experience in this branch of medicine, must admit that hypnotism of this kind is altogether impossible.

This repentance is often attributed to the Dostoyevsky mind, to the specific properties of the soul ("l'âme slave" as it is called), and this can be said of types like Alyosha Karamazov, the heroes of the "Idiot" and other Dostoyevsky characters, who are prepared to stand up in the public square and cry: "Beat me, Orthodox Christians, I am a villain!"

But that is not the case here at all. "L'âme slave" and the psychology of Dostoyevsky characters are a thing of the remote past in our country, the pluperfect tense. Such types do not exist in our country, or exist perhaps only on the outskirts of small provincial towns, if they do even there. On the contrary, such a psychology is to be found in Western Europe.

I shall now speak of myself, of the reasons for my repentance. Of course, it must be admitted that incriminating evidence plays a very important part. For three months I refused to say anything Then I began to testify. Why? Because while in prison I made a revaluation of my entire past. For when you ask yourself: "If you must die, what are you dying for?"—an absolutely black vacuity suddenly rises before you with startling vividness. There was nothing to die for, if one wanted to die unrepented. And, on the contrary, everything positive that glistens in the Soviet Union acquires new dimensions in a man's mind. This in the end disarmed me completely and led me to bend my knees before the Party and the country. And when you ask yourself: "Very well, suppose you do not die; suppose by some miracle you remain alive, again what for? Isolated from everybody, an enemy of the people, in an inhuman position, completely isolated from everything that

666

constitutes the essence of life . . ." And at once the same reply
arises. And at such moments, Citizens Judges, everything personal,
all the personal incrustation, all the rancour, pride, and a number
of other things, fall away, disappear. And, in addition, when the
reverberations of the broad international struggle reach your ear,
all this in its entirety does its work, and the result is the complete
internal moral victory of the U.S.S.R. over its kneeling opponents.
I happened by chance to get Feuchtwanger's book from the prison
library. There he refers to the trials of the Trotskyites. It produced
a profound impression on me; but I must say that Feuchtwanger
did not get at the core of the matter. He stopped half way, not
everything was clear to him; when, as a matter of fact, everything
is clear. World history is a world court of judgement: A number of
groups of Trotskyite leaders went bankrupt and have been cast
into the pit. That is true. But you cannot do what Feuchtwanger
does in relation to Trotsky in particular, when he places him on
the same plane as Stalin. Here his arguments are absolutely false.
For in reality the whole country stands behind Stalin; he is the
hope of the world; he is a creator. Napoleon once said that fate
is politics. The fate of Trotsky is counter-revolutionary politics.

I am about to finish. I am perhaps speaking for the last time
in my life.

I am explaining how I came to realize the necessity of capitulat-
ing to the investigating authorities and to you, Citizens Judges.
We came out against the joy of the new life with the most criminal
methods of struggle. I refute the accusation of having plotted against
the life of Vladimir Ilyich, but my counter-revolutionary confederates,and I at their head,endeavoured to murder Lenin's cause,which
is being carried on with such tremendous success by Stalin. The logic
of this struggle led us step by step into the blackest quagmire.
And it has once more been proved that departure from the position
of Bolshevism means siding with political counter-revolutionary
banditry. Counter-revolutionary banditry has now been smashed,
we have been smashed, and we repent our frightful crimes.

The point, of course, is not this repentance, or my personal
repentance in particular. The Court can pass its verdict without it.
The confession of the accused is not essential. The confession of the
accused is a medieval principle of jurisprudence. But here we also
have the internal demolition of the forces of counter-revolution.
And one must be a Trotsky not to lay down one's arms.

I feel it my duty to say here that in the parallelogram of forces
which went to make up the counter-revolutionary tactics, Trotsky
was the principal motive force. And the most acute methods—terrorism, espionage, the dismemberment of the U.S.S.R. and wrecking—proceeded primarily from this source.

I may infer a priori that Trotsky and my other allies in crime, as well as the Second International, all the more since I discussed this with Nikolayevsky, will endeavour to defend us, especially and particularly myself. I reject this defence, because I am kneeling before the country, before the Party, before the whole people. The monstrousness of my crimes is immeasurable especially in the new stage of the struggle of the U.S.S.R. May this trial be the last severe lesson, and may the great might of the U.S.S.R. become clear to all. Let it be clear to all that the counter-revolutionary thesis of the national limitedness of the U.S.S.R. has remained suspended in the air like a wretched rag. Everybody perceives the wise leadership of the country that is ensured by Stalin.

It is in the consciousness of this that I await the verdict. What matters is not the personal feelings of a repentant enemy, but the flourishing progress of the U.S.S.R. and its international importance.

THE PRESIDENT: The accused Levin will make his last plea.

LEVIN: Citizens Judges! In my last plea I want to reaffirm my guilt once more.

The State Prosecutor has disclosed my entire guilt with exhaustive comprehensiveness and objectivity and has drawn a vivid picture of the gravity of the crimes I committed. I have always realized the gravity of these crimes, even during the years when they were being committed under the irresistible, as it seemed to me, pressure of the cruel threats and criminal instructions of Yagoda, and thereafter right up to recent days. And if as my Counsel said yesterday the testimony which I gave a few days ago savoured of epic tranquillity, this tranquillity must not be ascribed to the fact that I remained calm when I spoke of this, but to the fact that I, first of the group of doctors to speak, had to give the Court a detailed, clear and complete picture of the crimes that have been executed and realized, had to do this in such a way that everyone would understand; and in order to tell the whole story in a composed manner, in order to overcome the agitation which was so natural under the circumstances, I had to summon all my strength, all my self-possession and try to maintain a calm tone. Furthermore, it seemed to me that in the situation in which I now find myself, I should not speak of my personal emotions, my distress and my sufferings—this is useless now and this would not have struck a chord in anyone. These are the two reasons which perhaps created the impression about which the Counsel for Defence spoke yesterday—an impression of epic tranquillity in my terrible testimony. Of course, there is no tranquillity, there was none, and there will be none. I always felt the gravity of my crimes, and I feel it now. But I felt it all especially keenly only in the very last

668

days in prison, in the short time before the beginning of the trial, when I first had the opportunity of reading the Indictment, when for the first time I learnt from this Indictment what I had never known, had not surmised, could not have surmised, could not have imagined, when I learnt from this Indictment what a criminal Yagoda already was in 1932, when I learnt in whose interests I had been compelled to commit my crimes and onto what criminal path Yagoda had thrown me.

Sitting here in the dock, listening to all the frightful stories which have been told here by human beings, listening to stories of General Seeckt and such like, Trotsky, the Japanese, Germans, British, Poles, who were supplied with secret information, to whom our richest regions and republics were being sold in exchange for some future services, listening to the frightful stories of glass in butter, the destruction of cattle, the destruction of foodstuffs constituting prime necessities for the population, the preparation of defeat in the forthcoming war which they themselves were provoking, listening to all this horror and imagining all this to myself as a sort of satanic orgy, I only here realized into what an abyss the evil genius Yagoda had precipitated me, what forces he had made me serve, for what and with what end he had pushed me from the straight and honest path of labour which I had been treading for forty years, and in my sixty-eighth year put me in this disgraceful dock, together with him.

My guilt is very great, Citizens Judges. My guilt is such that punishment must, of course, be very severe, I do not doubt this. Today or tomorrow you will decide my fate, and perhaps while deciding this fate you will nevertheless wish to consider that the crimes committed by me were committed not of my own evil intent, not of my own personal ambitions, my personal political views, but were committed exclusively at the evil will and instructions of Yagoda.

I have a medical experience of forty-two years, and in the course of this time I never committed any crimes whatever, nor did I ever commit them after 1936 when I was free from the ghastly instructions of Yagoda. I am not saying this in order to hide behind Yagoda's back. There would be no point in that. But, Citizens Judges, I long to tell you, and to tell the country through the walls of this building, that if there had been no Yagoda, I would never have been a criminal. To the end of my life I would have remained the devoted and honest man which I have been all the forty-two years of my working life. I absolutely must emphasize this. I must say once more that I committed my crimes not because of criminal convictions or designs on my part, but because of Yagoda's demands with which he beset me and which I thought had to be obeyed.

669

From the very beginning of the October Revolution I joined in the work and did a great deal, a very great deal of strenuous work in the sphere of Soviet health protection. Both before and after the revolution I did a lot of work in hospitals; I worked, took part in the scientific public life of Moscow. I was one of the oldest members of the therapeutical society, I was on the boards of directors of two medical societies, I was a charter member of the Society of All-Union Congresses, I was a member of the organizational bureau of two or three congresses, one international congress, and so on and so forth. I read papers and took part in conferences, in short, while I did a great deal of practical work I was not in arrears with scientific and public life. And, of course, the savage, absolutely absurd, ghastly thought of causing even the slightest harm to any of the leaders of the Party and the government, the majority of whom I had the fortune of knowing personally, could never have occurred to me personally, of my own volition, on the background of this work of mine which was always enormous. Never could the savage, ghastly thought have entered my head of causing any harm to, let alone the death of, Alexei Maximovich Gorky, of whom I was ardently fond, as everyone knows, with whom I was closely associated, whom I estimated highly as one of the greatest writers of our country and of the whole world.

THE PRESIDENT: Cannot you refrain from blaspheming in your last plea?

LEVIN: Pardon me. In his speech yesterday my counsel advanced arguments on the basis of which he considered it possible to ask the Court to accord me clemency, to spare me my life. At this moment one can tell only the truth. And I would be telling an untruth if I would say that now, at this moment, I look death in the face easily and calmly. Death is easy for a political fighter who dies for his ideas, who goes to the block, to the guillotine, with his head proudly up. But it is, of course, hard to die a disgraceful death. And I will not conceal from you, Citizens Judges, that the thought of death is, of course, hard for me. As I have already said, I am sixty-eight years of age. In any case I have not long to live, and if you find it possible to agree with the arguments of my counsel and with what I have said here, perhaps you will give me the opportunity of devoting what still remains of my life to my country and of expiating at least a part of my crimes by honest work, of living out what is left of my life honestly, and of ending this life in my good, working, Soviet family. Of the crimes I committed, I repent, painfully repent, bitterly repent, sincerely and with my whole heart. Admitting all my guilt, with my heart filled with repentance before you, I ask you to grant me my life.

THE PRESIDENT: Adjournment for twenty minutes.

* * *

670

COMMANDANT OF THE COURT: The Court is coming, please rise.

THE PRESIDENT: Please be seated. The session is resumed. Accused Bulanov you may make your last plea.

BULANOV: Citizens Judges, I will not speak of the crimes I have committed because they are known and proven to the full, if, of course, there is any need to prove the facts, because my crimes are stark facts, demanding at the best mere registration, and not proof of any kind.

There are no excuses in my case, no circumstances mitigating my crime. My crimes are too great.

Before I met Yagoda I was neither a Right nor a Trotskyite. Yagoda made me both a Right and a Trotskyite, in short, an enemy of the people. I have no lengthy experience of duplicity and deceit. That is why when I was arrested and later on in Court I simply related everything that I had done because these were facts.

I heard Bukharin here developing a sort of theory about confession, but, as a matter of fact, it is a very simple thing. Neither I, nor Bukharin, nor my other fellow-accused have any excuses whatever, and there can be no circumstances lessening our guilt, because to add any mitigating circumstances would in effect be to excuse to some extent the crimes that we committed.

When I heard the testimony of my fellow-accused, the last pleas of some of the accused, I think, perhaps I am mistaken, that some of them showed signs of wanting to deceive the Party even now, although each of them invariably began by saying that he fully and entirely shares responsibility, pleads guilty and is answerable. But this was a matter of form, general declarations. In a number of cases they tried to deny their guilt by pleading ignorance of some point. It is not for me, of course, to aggravate the severity of the charge against my fellow-accused, but I think that since I landed here in the dock as an enemy of the people because of these leaders, I have the right here to declare that some of them in my opinion have taken a course of continuing the struggle against the Soviet power—a course of provocation. I am used to calling things by their proper names, just as they are.

Two or three days after my arrest, during the preliminary investigation, and at a confrontation, Yagoda quite brazenly persisted in denying a number of circumstances. Facts can be denied for five or ten minutes, for a day, for two days, but it is folly.

Here at the Court session he denied any complicity whatsoever in two murders. He is the organizer of all the murders I know. What do we find—Bukharin knew nothing, Rykov knew nothing, Yagoda knew nothing. So it was Bulanov that poisoned Nikolai Ivanovich Yezhov? So Gorky was murdered by Kryuchkov and Levin, so Kuibyshev was murdered by Levin, so Menzhinsky was murdered

671

by Kazakov and Levin? And Bukharin, Rykov, Yagoda had nothing to do with it?

But now I think, the countenance of these so-called leaders is perfectly clear not only to you Citizens Judges but to us also. It is too late, but I must say this. I think it will not sound so grotesque and false coming from me, so blasphemous, as it did from Rosengoltz, if I say that the Russian worker, the Russian collective farmer are fortunate that Nikolai Ivanovich Yezhov caught us in time and put us in the dock in time. If these men and I among them, could not have actually let the enemy in, they could in any case have created conditions for the German and Japanese hordes to invade the territory of the U.S.S.R. with the greatest ease, with all the ensuing consequences.

I imagine, if we suppose for a minute that a conspiracy of such men, such "leaders," who are not ashamed here in the dock, who do not hesitate, to drown their own accomplice—the cog in the wheel (Bukharin says he is a leader, not a cog in the wheel, and I am not a leader but a cog in the wheel), who are not ashamed to sell him body and soul in order to get clear themselves even for the thousandth part of a second—what it would be if these leaders had really managed to crash through to power, because the logic of the struggle, which Bukharin denied, this logic in my opinion, in plain words, is the logic of struggle for power. They had a shop on the signboard of which there were the Rights, Trotskyites, Socialist-Revolutionaries and Mensheviks, but they had one and the same assortment of goods: murder, espionage, acts of diversion, treachery in all its forms.

If they had actually crashed through to power I think that Hitler, whom Yagoda considers his model, would soon have been green with envy. For Bukharin's benefit I confirm and repeat that Yagoda told me that Bukharin would be Yagoda's minister of propaganda, and I answer for my words. We know how Hitler dealt with people who did not please him. So I would not have been surprised if under Yagoda, Chairman of the Council of People's Commissars, you Bukharin, the first minister of agitation and propaganda, would turn out to be the first chicken in Yagoda's path.

Citizens Judges, my crimes are grave, and, I repeat, I have no excuse. Grave in particular are my personal crimes against Nikolai Ivanovich Yezhov. I would like my last word, apparently the last in the literal sense, to reach him somehow. I would like to ask Yezhov to forgive me, ask him not as one of the leaders of the Party and Commissar-General of State Security but ask him for this as an individual.

You, of course, are not and cannot be concerned in the slightest with my personal emotions, but here too I ask you to believe that it is particularly hard for me to quit life in the knowledge that I am

672

dying in an unrighteous cause, that I am quitting life because of these people whose countenance is plain to the whole world and although unfortunately too late, has become plain to me also.

THE PRESIDENT: The accused Yagoda may make his last plea.

YAGODA: Citizens Judges, I want to tell the Soviet Court and the Soviet people how a man who spent thirty years in the Party and worked a great deal, stumbled, fell and landed in the ranks of spies and provocateurs.

The Procurator is not right when he says that I have never been a Bolshevik. I would not dwell on the details of my life if he had not made this remark.

Here is my life in two words: From the age of 14 I worked as a compositor in an underground printing press. This was the first underground printing press in Nizhni-Novgorod. We were three brothers. One was killed at Sormovo during an insurrection, the other was shot for taking part in a mutiny of a regiment during the war. I can only envy their death. At the age of 15 I was in a fighting squad during the Sormovo insurrection. At the age of 16 or 17 I joined the Party, the Nizhni-Novgorod organization knows this. In 1911 I was arrested and sent into exile. In 1913-14 I returned to Leningrad. I worked at the Putilov Works in the sick benefit society on insurance together with Krestinsky. Then I went to the front, where I was wounded. The Revolution of 1917 found me in Leningrad, where I was taking an active part, was a member of the military organization, and was setting up Red Guard detachments. In 1918—the Southern and Eastern fronts, in 1919—the Cheka.

Irrespective of how grave my crimes against the people, against the Party, I nevertheless have the temerity to say that even in the years when I was a member of the counter-revolutionary organization I was tortured by my duality. And it is clear why. For me, the former leader of the Soviet intelligence service, having my finger on the pulse of the whole country, the utter futility, the utter hopelessness of any attempts on our part to overthrow the Soviet power was clearer than to any of the prisoners here in the dock. I knew better than all of them that the Soviet people in its many millions would never allow anyone to put the yoke of capitalism on its neck. I knew better than anyone that no intervention, from whatever quarter it came, could break the urge of the Soviet people towards Communism. I, as chief of the Soviet intelligence service, knew the enemies of the Soviet Union very well, I knew the real forces of German and Japanese fascism. But I also knew the strength of the Soviet country well. That is just why I could never count on the success of our counter-revolutionary affairs. That is why I put in the remark about chatterboxes. I lacked the Bolshevik courage to make a final break with the Rights, with this damned counter-revolution,

673

and to give away the whole thing. Were there such attempts on my part? Yes, there were, but I never carried them to the end. I will cite one fact, not to make my lot lighter—for there is no need of that—but to show the duality in my life. The case with Yenukidze in 1935. I exposed him, but far from completely. I should have arrested him; I did not do this because I myself was a conspirator. I repeat, I have not cited this example in my own defence nor am I putting it as a merit of mine, but as an illustration of my duality. There are other facts too; I will not dwell on them. All this was half-hearted and criminal. I understood and understand perfectly well what should have been done. Of course, it would have been best if I had come to the Central Committee and given myself up with the whole organization. Perhaps the result would have been different. I have told about my heinous crimes, I shall not dwell on them a second time.

Disgraced, thrown in the dust, leaving life I want to recount my sad, tragic career, which should serve as a lesson for all those who vacillate, who are not wholly devoted to the cause of the Party of Lenin and Stalin. I also began with waverings. This was in 1929. At that time I made the mistake of thinking that it was not the Party that was right, but Bukharin and Rykov.

My fall began from the moment when Rykov, having learnt of my sympathy for the Rights, told me to conceal my Right views from the Party. And I agreed to this. I became a double-dealer. My duality began. Unfortunately, I lacked the Bolshevik courage to stand up against the masters of duplicity.

This crime of mine affected all my subsequent life and work. I became two men. One was Yagoda—the Party member, in daily contact with the greatest people of our era, and the other Yagoda was a traitor to his country, a conspirator. The first Yagoda saw the gigantic growth of the country, its flourishing under the leadership of the Stalinist Central Committee; he also saw the utter loathsomeness and filth of the Right-Trotskyite under-world, and the second Yagoda was chained to this very under-world as a convict to his wheelbarrow, committing those monstrous crimes which have been analysed here with all clarity.

This is what just one attempt to go against the Party leads to. This is where people who raise their hands against the Party get to. This is life, this is the logic of a fall.

I want to correct the Procurator and make an objection on a part of the charges which he has made. They mean nothing in so far as the decision of my fate is concerned, but the Procurator is not right in considering me a member of the centre of the bloc. I am not a member of the centre of the bloc. For me it is important personally perhaps that I did not take part in the decisions of the bloc. I did not take part in this and I did not take part in the de-

674

cisions on terrorist acts. I was informed post factum and told to carry out the decisions. In all cases they were made without me. This does not lessen my guilt, but the bloc consisted of definite persons; these persons passed the decisions. Rykov was a member of the centre of the bloc, he made decisions.

A second point—the Procurator announced it proved beyond doubt that I was a spy. This is not true. I am not a spy and have not been one. I think that in the definition of a spy or espionage we will not differ. But a fact is a fact. I had no direct connections with abroad, there are no instances of my directly handing over any information. I am not jesting when I say that if I had been a spy dozens of countries could have closed down their intelligence services—there would have been no need for them to maintain such a mass of spies as have now been caught in the Soviet Union.

It is not only untrue to say that I was an organizer but it is untrue to say that I was an accomplice in the murder of Kirov. I committed an extremely grave violation of duty—that is right. I answer for it in an equal measure, but I was not an accomplice. Citizen Procurator, you know what complicity is just as well as I do. The entire material of the Court proceedings and the preliminary investigation has failed to prove that I was an accomplice in this vile murder.

My objections on these points are not an attempt to belittle the significance of my crimes. My defence would have no practical meaning here, because for each millionth part of my crimes, as the Procurator says, he wants my head. I staked my head and I surrender it, but I want to reduce my enormous debt to the Procurator. I know what my sentence will be, I have been awaiting it for a whole year. In the last hours or days of my life I do not want to play the hypocrite and say that I want to die. This is not true. I have committed heinous crimes. I realize this. It is hard to live after such crimes, it is hard to sit in prison for tens of years. But it is terrible to die with such a stigma. Even from behind the bars I would like to see the further flourishing of the country which I betrayed.

Citizens Judges! I directed vast construction jobs—the canals. Now these canals are the adornments of our era. I do not dare to ask to be sent there even for the most arduous work. Citizens Judges! Our laws and our Court differ greatly from the laws and the courts of all bourgeois countries. I remember how Frick, Minister of Justice in Germany, declared at a conference of judges: "The laws of fascist countries are laws of revenge and not of correction. . . ." Our laws are based on a different principle, our Court is a different court. The Soviet Court differs from bourgeois courts in the fact that this Court, when trying a criminal case, does not base itself on laws as on a dogma, but is guided by revolutionary expediency.

675

Our country is mighty, strong as never before, purged of spies, diversionists, terrorists and other scum, and I ask you, Citizens Judges, in passing your sentence on me, to consider whether there is revolutionary expediency in my execution now? I would not dare to ask for mercy if I did not know that the present trial is the apotheosis of the defeat of counter-revolution, that the country has destroyed all the hotbeds of counter-revolution and that the Soviet country has won, has routed counter-revolution completely. The fact that I and my fellow-accused are here in the dock and answering for what we have done, is the triumph, the victory of the Soviet people over counter-revolution. I address myself to the Court with the plea: forgive me if you can.

THE PRESIDENT: The accused Kryuchkov may make his last plea.

KRYUCHKOV: Citizens Judges, there are no human words which I could say in extenuation of my treacherous crime. My crime against the Soviet people, against young Soviet culture is great. In admitting my guilt to the full I would like once more to confirm to the Court that the "bloc of Rights and Trotskyites" through the medium of one of its members, Yagoda, utilized me for their counter-revolutionary purposes of conspiracy against the Soviet people, against the proletarian state. Yagoda gave shape to my criminal thoughts and put them into life, drew me into this "bloc of Rights and Trotskyites," I became the murderer of Gorky, who was so loved by the people and who returned the same great love to the people, its Party, its leader—the mighty Stalin, as Gorky often called Stalin. Yagoda knew about this great love of Gorky's; he also knew how ruthlessly Gorky hated all enemies, and particularly as Gorky expressed it, the self-satisfied animal Trotsky and all of his ilk—the Bukharinites, Zinovievites, Kamenevites and Rykovites.

"The bloc of Rights and Trotskyites" feared the prestige of Gorky, and, knowing to a certainty that he would fight to the end of his days against conspirators and their criminal plans, decided to murder Gorky. Yagoda, not stopping at threats, made me the direct perpetrator of this crime. I ask the Court to believe me when I say that it was not only my personal motives, which were interwoven with the political background of this terrible affair, that were decisive in this crime. I sincerely repent. I suffer burning shame, particularly here in Court when I learnt of and understood the entire counter-revolutionary baseness of the crimes of the gang of Rights and Trotskyites, in which I was a hired assassin. I ask you, Citizens Judges, for a lenient sentence.

THE PRESIDENT: Accused Pletnev.

PLETNEV: Citizens Judges, everything has been said and I will be brief. I stand before you as a man who repented of his crim-

676

inal activities. I am an old scientist. I have worked all my life until recently. My best works belong to the period of Soviet medicine, and when they appeared in West European literature they served to prove the fact that the old-time scientists, despite their not infrequent anti-Soviet tendencies, had been given the opportunity to display their creative faculties. And here in custody I requested the leadership of the People's Commissariat of Internal Affairs to give me books, and over twenty books of my own choice in four languages were brought from my library. In this period I managed to write in prison a monograph ten or twelve signatures long. I say this to explain that here I have been given trust and opportunity and I want to hope that by this I have also shown that I want to work and can work, because to work in these conditions, with such a state of nerves, is not so simple as to work at home. I ask you to take into consideration that if I had not met one of the persons sitting here, about whom the Counsel for Defence recently spoke, and who threatened me, blackmailed me with death, all the subsequent deeds could not have taken place. I became acquainted with the deeds of the bloc only from the Indictment and during the progress of the trial, and I think this gives me the right to believe that I cannot share its responsibility fully. If the Court finds it possible to grant me my life, I will devote it wholly and entirely to my Soviet country, the only country in the world where labour in all its fields is given a place of honour and glory such as it has nowhere else and has never had before.

THE PRESIDENT: The accused Kazakov may make his last plea.

KAZAKOV: Citizens Judges, I stand before you as the worst of criminals, as the murderer of the Chairman of the O.G.P.U., Vyacheslav Rudolfovich Menzhinsky.

It is hard for me to talk of my crime, because as a physician my calling is naturally to cure people, to restore their health. I blackened the calling of physician and trampled on the most valuable thing—the bond between patient and physician, the confidence owing to which the patient fully entrusts his health, his very life to the physician.

I became a murderer, because as a result of wrong treatment I, together with Dr. Levin, hastened Menzhinsky's death. At the present moment I shudder picturing to myself the entire gravity of the crime which I committed, the more so that Menzhinsky had full confidence in me as a physician.

I came to commit this crime as a result of direct personal instructions on the part of Yagoda as the first assistant chairman of the O.G.P.U. who intimidated me with threats, and, as a result, I carried out his will and committed this appalling crime.

I am asking myself: could I not at that time deceive Yagoda

677

and pretend that I was carrying out his instructions for bringing about Menzhinsky's death? Ostensibly I could have done so, because I wielded a method of treatment which at that time was not sufficiently widespread and known. But Citizens Judges, it was more than difficult to do—I might say, it was impossible, because I was under control, control exercised by Dr. Levin, the direct executor of the crime, of Yagoda's criminal will. I was bent with the fear which Yagoda instilled in me by his threats and constant surveillance, in addition—the exhaustion of the reserve of strength of Menzhinsky' heart and the death which was bound to follow owing to the methods of treatment which Levin and I applied. Levin exercised the main control over me.

Now, when I stand before you, Citizens Judges, as the murderer of Menzhinsky, I cannot help shuddering and being overcome with horror when I think of the despicable crime into which I was dragged. Not for a minute do I want to disclaim the blame for this crime. On the contrary I want to repent of this crime to the end and rid myself of this nightmare.

But I cannot escape a feeling of hatred, of repugnance which I entertain for Yagoda. I curse this man—this monster, this tyrant, who by means of threats and intimidation, by basely taking advantage of my cowardice, by taking advantage of the high position he occupied, for monstrously vicious purposes, tore me away from the orbit of the honest scientific activity of an honest worker and physician, dragged me into a crime of immeasurable gravity, made a criminal of me in the great land of Soviets where the work of a physician is raised to such a high honourable position, where the government accorded me and my scentific activity exceptional attention and solicitude.

I must say here that all my life, before this crime and during the four years following it, I honestly and consistently carried on scientific clinical work, desiring to bring some little benefit to the land of the Soviets and its working people. I showed a sincere and careful attitude to every patient, trying to the utmost to restore his health.

Four years weigh heavily on me with the nightmare of the crimes which I committed, and by this sincere repentance I want to rid myself of this nightmare. I ask the Court to believe the depth and sincerity of my repentance. I never thought that I would become a criminal. I always strove only to engage in scientific work from which I have now been torn away owing to this nightmare. Four years of this nightmare weigh heavily on me. I tried to rid myself of this nightmare by work. During the four years which passed after this ghastly crime, I made about forty scientific researches. But this did not rid me of its weight, it brought me no comfort, it gave me no joy.

678

I deserve the severest punishment and, if the Court will so decide, I shall accept this decision as deserved. But should I be given the opportunity to work, I will in the course of my further life do everything to wash off this shame which covers me and to atone for my crime by honest and persistent labour, by giving all my strength and all my knowledge to our great country.

THE PRESIDENT: The accused Maximov-Dikovsky may make his last plea.

MAXIMOV-DIKOVSKY: Citizens Judges, when I testified in the Court I was guided by only one consideration: to repent, to tell everything and to accept my deserved punishment.

It was not at once that I entered on the path of crime. I do not belong to those who started to fight the Party from the very beginning of their Party activity. I do not belong to those who joined the Party, carrying with them the load of alien political views. Since 1919, at the age of 18, I firmly entered the road of struggle for the consolidation and defence of the Soviet power. I arrested Whiteguards, I was imprisoned by the Whites, I was in the Red Army and fought at the fronts. I carried on Party work after the demobilization and for three years I conducted mass Party work in a factory.

Those nine years were the years when, under the leadership of the Central Committee, I fought selflessly for the interests of the Party, for the interests of the country, and only later, when I got mixed up with the Rights, I betrayed the interests of the Party, I betrayed the interests of my country. I became just as much a criminal as those who persuaded me to commit this crime.

In the criminal environment of the Right conspirators I sank so low that on the demand of the centre (and the instructions of the centre were quite concrete) I became an accomplice in the organization of one of the terrorist acts. I committed a grave crime, I inflicted great harm on the Party and the country.

The crime which I committed was for me the limit beyond which I did not go. Since 1935 I severed organizational connections with the conspirators and during the last few years have had nothing in common with them, which fact is fully corroborated by the materials of the investigation.

However, since I lacked courage to expose their crimes, to expose myself, I thereby covered up these crimes, and, consequently, objectively continued on the enemy positions. When I was arrested, I immediately confessed and did not deny anything even for a day. I had nothing in common with these old, alien connections. Neither did I have anything in common with them in connection with the practical work which I carried on during the last years in the sphere of railway transport where I had the opportunity to see with my own eyes how great are the successes of the land of the Soviets which no conspirators can turn from its path.

679

I gave testimony about all the counter-revolutionary work of which I knew, I fully disarmed myself, without holding back any secrets and without assuming any disguise. The more reason why the casuistic somersaults of Bukharin during the trial appeared alien to me.

Much of what I learnt during the trial, I had not known before. This is comprehensible, considering the role I played among the conspirators. I could not and was not supposed to know everything. But this does not lessen my guilt because even what I knew and, primarily, the fact that I committed a grave crime are sufficient for me to be tried as a state offender.

At the same time I want to say that the trial has shown with utter clarity what was meant by the so-called restoration of capitalism. The trial showed me that it meant such dismemberment of the country when it would be reduced to semi-colonial dependence on fascist states.

Had these criminal designs been consummated the country would have been drenched in the blood of scores of thousands of its best sons, more cruelly than it was done by Denikin and Wrangel. It would have meant that the country would have been thrown back scores of years in its development, it would have meant that the international struggle of the proletariat would have also been impeded.

I want to say that the trial showed me quite clearly that Hitler, Trotsky and Bukharin are as one in their frenzied struggle against our country. In the light of the picture of the crimes which was unfolded here in Court I cannot but add my voice to the estimation which was given here by the State Prosecutor: a gang of traitors and spies, of diversionists and betrayers, provocateurs and murderers. These are grave, sinister words, but the criminal deeds committed by us are even more grave, the people who committed these deeds are even more despicable. And how can I refrain from calling these crimes by their proper names if I want to repent fully, without in any way minimizing my guilt, without exonerating myself in anything. I declare here firmly: "For several years I was in the camp of the enemies, but I am no longer an enemy. I ask you to believe me that I am not incorrigible and that should I be given the opportunity to work I should be able to prove in any sphere, in any kind of work, that I would not remain in the rear.

THE PRESIDENT: The Court retires for deliberation.

(At 9:25 p.m. on March 12, the Military Collegium of the Supreme Court of the U.S.S.R. retired to the conference room to deliberate on the verdict. Deliberation was completed at 4 a.m. on March 13.)

*   *   *

COMMANDANT OF THE COURT: The Court is coming, please rise.

THE PRESIDENT: The session is resumed. I will announce the verdict of the Military Collegium of the Supreme Court of the U.S.S.R.

THE VERDICT

In the name of the Union of Soviet Socialist Republics the Military Collegium of the Supreme Court of the U.S.S.R., consisting of:

PRESIDENT: Army Military Jurist, V. V. Ulrich, President of the Military Collegium of the Supreme Court of the U.S.S.R.;

MEMBERS: Army Corps Military Jurist, I. O. Matulevich, Vice-President of the Military Collegium of the Supreme Court of the U.S.S.R., and Divisional Military Jurist, B. I. Yevlev, Member of the Military Collegium of the Supreme Court of the U.S.S.R.;

SECRETARY: Military Jurist First Rank A. A. Batner, with the participation of the State Prosecutor, A. Y. Vyshinsky, Procurator of the U.S.S.R., and I. D. Braude and N. V. Kommodov, Members of the Moscow Collegium of Counsel for Defence, in an open Court session, in the City of Moscow, on March 2-13, 1938, heard the case against:

1. BUKHARIN, Nikolai Ivanovich, born 1888;
2. RYKOV, Alexei Ivanovich, born 1881;
3. YAGODA, Genrikh Grigorievich, born 1891;
4. KRESTINSKY, Nikolai Nikolayevich, born 1883;
5. RAKOVSKY, Khristian Georgievich, born 1873;
6. ROSENGOLTZ, Arkady Pavlovich, born 1889;
7. IVANOV, Vladimir Ivanovich, born 1893;
8. CHERNOV, Mikhail Alexandrovich, born 1891;
9. GRINKO, Grigori Fedorovich, born 1890;
10. ZELENSKY, Isaac Abramovich, born 1890;
11. BESSONOV, Sergei Alexeyevich, born 1892;
12. IKRAMOV, Akmal, born 1898;
13. KHODJAYEV, Faizulla, born 1896;
14. SHARANGOVICH, Vasily Fomich, born 1897;
15. ZUBAREV, Prokopy Timofeyevich, born 1886;
16. BULANOV, Pavel Petrovich, born 1895;
17. LEVIN, Lev Grigorievich, born 1870;
18. PLETNEV, Dmitry Dmitrievich, born 1872;
19. KAZAKOV, Ignaty Nikolayevich, born 1891·
20. MAXIMOV-DIKOVSKY, Venyamin Adamovich (Abramovich), born 1900, and

21. KRYUCHKOV, Pyotr Petrovich, born 1889—all charged with having committed crimes covered by Articles 58[1a], 58[2], 58[7], 58[8], 58[9] and 58[11] of the Criminal Code of the R.S.F.S.R., and Ivanov, Zelensky and Zubarev, in addition, with having committed crimes covered by Article 58[13] of the Criminal Code of the R.S.F.S.R.

The preliminary and Court investigations have established:

The accused Bukharin, Rykov, Yagoda, Krestinsky, Rosengoltz, Grinko, Sharangovich, Khodjayev, Ikramov, Ivanov, Zubarev, Zelensky and Chernov, being irreconcilable enemies of the Soviet power, on the instructions of the intelligence services of foreign states hostile to the U.S.S.R., in 1932-33 organized a conspiratorial group known as the "bloc of Rights and Trotskyites," which united underground anti-Soviet groups of Trotskyites, Rights, Zinovievites, Mensheviks, Socialist-Revolutionaries and bourgeois-nationalists of the Ukraine, Byelorussia, Georgia, Armenia, Azerbaijan and the Central Asiatic Republics.

The "bloc of Rights and Trotskyites" set itself the aim of overthrowing the Socialist social and state system existing in the U.S.S.R., restoring capitalism and the power of the bourgeoisie in the U.S.S.R. by means of diversive, wrecking, terrorist, espionage and treasonable activities directed to undermine the economic might and defensive power of the Soviet Union and to assist foreign aggressors in defeating and dismembering the U.S.S.R.

Bereft of all support within the U.S.S.R., the leaders of the "bloc of Rights and Trotskyites," with the object of carrying out their criminal designs, concluded through enemy of the people L. Trotsky and through individual participants in the anti-Soviet "bloc of Rights and Trotskyites," an agreement with representatives of certain foreign states on armed assistance in overthrowing the Soviet power in the U.S.S.R., on condition of its dismemberment and the severance from the U.S.S.R. of the Ukraine, Byelorussia, the Maritime Region, and the Central Asiatic and Transcaucasian Republics for the benefit of the aforementioned foreign states.

The conclusion of this treasonable agreement of the "bloc of Rights and Trotskyites" with representatives of foreign states was facilitated by the fact that leading participants in the anti-Soviet conspiracy were direct agents of foreign intelligence services and for many years carried on espionage activities for these intelligence services.

Krestinsky, on the direct instructions of enemy of the people L. Trotsky, agent of the German and British intelligence services, entered into treasonable connections with the German Reichswehr in 1921 and was a German spy until the day of his arrest in 1937, receiving in return for his espionage work and for the use of the criminal activities of the Trotsky... 250,000 German gold marks per annum.

Rosengoltz began espionage work for the German Ge... in 1923 and for the British Intelligence Service in 1926.

Rakovsky was an agent of the British Intelligence S... since 1924 and a Japanese spy since 1934.

Chernov began his espionage work for Germany in 1928, having formed connections with the German intelligence service with the aid of the notorious Menshevik and émigré, Dan.

Sharangovich was recruited and sent by the Polish intelligence service to carry on espionage work in the U.S.S.R. in 1921 and was a Polish spy to the day of his arrest.

Grinko was a German and Polish spy since 1932.

On the instructions of enemy of the people L. Trotsky, and of leading participants in the "bloc of Rights and Trotskyites"—Bukharin, Rykov and Yagoda—members of the "bloc of Rights and Trotskyites," Rosengoltz, Krestinsky, Rakovsky, Grinko, and Bessonov, with obviously treasonable purposes, entered into direct relations with representatives of foreign states hostile to the U.S.S.R. and negotiated with them regarding the forms of assistance to be given to foreign aggressors in the event of their attack upon the Soviet Union (organization of terrorist, diversive and wrecking acts and espionage).

The leaders of the "bloc of Rights and Trotskyites," Rykov, Bukharin and Yagoda among their number, were not only fully informed of the espionage activities of their accomplices, but in every way encouraged the extension of espionage connections, and themselves gave instructions to the participants in the "bloc of Rights and Trotskyites" when they conducted their treasonable negotiations with representatives of foreign states, thus expediting preparations for foreign intervention.

On the direct instructions of foreign intelligence services, the participants in the "bloc of Rights and Trotskyites" organized diversive and wrecking groups in a number of industrial, transport, agricultural and trading enterprises and carried on destructive activities, their purpose being to paralyse the economic life of the country and to weaken the defensive power of the Soviet Union.

On the instructions of the Japanese intelligence service, participants in the "bloc of Rights and Trotskyites" organized in the Far Eastern Territory the wrecking of a train carrying military material at the Volochayevka Station and of train No. 501 on the Khor-Dormidontovka section, and also committed several diversive acts in the Suchan mines. All these diversive acts were accompanied by loss of human life.

Rosengoltz, on the directions of enemy of the people L. Trot-

s of an agreement with representatives of
on wrecking work within the People's Com-
'rade designed to assist Germany and Japan
conomic damage to the U.S.S.R. In addition,
.ically financed Trotsky by means of various
operations.

che instructions of the German intelligence service
, of Rykov, took advantage of his important official
ne agricultural organs of the U.S.S.R. for the purpose
ng, through his confederates, a number of major diver-
wrecking acts designed to lower the harvest yield of agricultural crops, damage mobilization reserves of agricultural
produce and reduce the number of horses and cattle, in
particular, by artificially spreading epizoötic diseases, as a result
of which about 25,000 horses perished in 1936 in Eastern
Siberia alone.

Grinko, on the instructions of the leaders of the "bloc of
Rights and Trotskyites" and of the German intelligence service,
systematically carried on extensive wrecking activities in the
system of the People's Commissariat of Finance, with the object
of causing dissatisfaction among the population and thereby
making it easier to recruit his followers. This found expression in
delays in payment of wages, bad service by the savings banks to
the population, the unlawful levying of certain taxes on the
peasants, and other wrecking measures.

Sharangovich, one of the leaders of the Byelorussian national-
fascist organization, on the instructions of the organs of the Polish
intelligence service and of leaders of the "bloc of Rights and
Trotskyites"—Rykov and others—organized on a large scale
diversive and wrecking activities in agriculture, stockbreeding
and industry in Byelorussia, thereby facilitating the task of
aggressors if they launched an armed attack on the Byelorussian
Soviet Socialist Republic.

Ikramov and Khodjayev, on the instructions of Bukharin,
developed extensive diversive and wrecking activities in the
various branches of the national economy of Uzbekistan with the
object of causing discontent among the population and thus
creating favourable conditions for the preparation of armed
actions against the Soviet power at the time of foreign intervention.

Zelensky organized wrecking groups in the Centrosoyuz and
in the consumers' co-operatives, and with the help of these groups,
with the object of causing discontent among the population,
muddled the planning of goods, delayed their dispatch to the rural
districts, caused damage to and decay of foodstuffs, mixed glass

and nails into foodstuffs, and deliberately disorgani of consumers' goods to the primary co-operative store

Ivanov, on the instructions of Bukharin, carried on and diversive activities in forestry and the timber industry Northern Territory.

Zubarev, an active participant in the underground organizati of the Rights, on the instructions of Rykov carried on wrecking activities in agriculture in a number of regions of the R.S.F.S.R.

In addition to intensive diversive and wrecking activities, the participants in the "bloc of Rights and Trotskyites," on the instructions of the German, Japanese and Polish intelligence services, under the direct guidance of Rykov and Bukharin and with the active participation of Ivanov, Khodjayev, Ikramov, Zubarev, Sharangovich, Grinko and Zelensky, mustered bandit insurrectionary kulak cadres in Siberia, the North Caucasus, the Ukraine, Byelorussia, Uzbekistan and a number of other parts of the Soviet Union for the purpose of organizing armed actions in the rear of the Red Army, timed for the beginning of intervention against the Soviet Union.

In order to extend the bandit insurrectionary kulak base, and in accordance with a decision of the leaders of the "bloc of Rights and Trotskyites," Bukharin established organizational connections with the undergound Central Committee of the Socialist-Revolutionary organization then active in the U.S.S.R., as well as with the Central Committee of the Socialist-Revolutionaries abroad.

In accordance with a direct agreement with foreign intelligence services, and on the instructions of enemy of the people L. Trotsky, the "bloc of Rights and Trotskyites" organized a number of terrorist acts against the leaders of the C.P.S.U.(Bolsheviks) and the Soviet government.

In 1934, Rykov, one of the leading participants in the "bloc of Rights and Trotskyites," personally formed a terrorist group for the preparation and commission of terrorist acts against Comrades Stalin, Molotov, Kaganovich and Voroshilov.

In August 1937, Rosengoltz personally attempted to commit a terrorist act against Comrade Stalin, for which purpose he repeatedly tried to secure an interview with him.

As the preliminary investigation and the Court proceedings in the present case have established, the dastardly assassination of S. M. Kirov on December 1, 1934, by the Leningrad Trotskyite-Zinovievite terrorist centre was organized in accordance with a decision of the "bloc of Rights and Trotskyites." A direct part in the organization of this terrorist act was taken by the accused Yagoda, who gave special instructions to his accomplices working in the Leningrad Administration of the People's Commissariat

...t to hinder the perpetration of this crime.

...s of enemy of the people L. Trotsky, the ...of Rights and Trotskyites" in 1934 adopted ...sinate the great proletarian writer, Maxim ...zation of this monstrous terrorist act was en- ...a, who initiated Dr. Levin, M. Gorky's family ...physician Pletnev into the purposes of the con- ...structed them to bring about the death of M. Gorky ...methods of treatment; which was done, Dr. Levin ...yed the leading part in this criminal act. An active part ...illainous deed was taken by Kryuchkov, former secretary of M. Gorky, and Bulanov, former secretary of the People's Commissariat of Internal Affairs, participants in the "bloc of Rights and Trotskyites."

In accordance with a decision of the leaders of the "bloc of Rights and Trotskyites," Yagoda, by means of wrecking methods of treatment, organized the murder of V. R. Menzhinsky, Chairman of the O.G.P.U., and of V. V. Kuibyshev, Vice-Chairman of the Council of People's Commissars of the U.S.S.R. A direct part in the perpetration of the terrorist act against Comrade Kuibyshev was taken by Levin and Maximov-Dikovsky, former secretary of Kuibyshev and a participant in the secret organization of the Rights since 1928; while a direct part in the perpetration of the terrorist act against V. R. Menzhinsky was taken by Bulanov and by the physician Kazakov, who had been enlisted in the conspiratorial group by Yagoda and Levin.

It has further been established that Levin and Kryuchkov, on the direct instructions of Yagoda, caused the death of M. A. Peshkov, the son of A. M. Gorky, by means of wrecking methods of treatment.

In connection with the appointment in September 1936 of Comrade N. I. Yezhov to the post of People's Commissar of Internal Affairs of the U.S.S.R., the "bloc of Rights and Trotskyites," fearing the complete exposure and rout of the anti-Soviet cadres, instructed Yagoda to commit a terrorist act against Comrade N. I. Yezhov.

In pursuance of these dastardly instructions, Yagoda, with the direct assistance of Bulanov, in the autumn of 1936 made an attempt upon the life of Comrade N. I. Yezhov, gradually poisoning him by means of a poison specially prepared for the purpose, as a result of which the health of N. I. Yezhov was seriously impaired.

It has been further established that in accordance with a decision of the anti-Soviet organization of the Rights, Bukharin, as early as 1930, arranged with Semyonov, a Socialist-Revolutionary terrorist, organizer of the assassination of Comrade Volodarsky and the attempt on the life of V. I. Lenin in 1918, fo[...] tion by Semyonov of a number of terrorist groups [...] object of preparing and committing terrorist acts against [...] of the C.P.S.U. and the Soviet government.

It has also been established that in 1918 Bukharin, and t[...] group of "Left Communists" headed by him, in conjunction with Trotsky and the "Left" Socialist-Revolutionaries, hatched a plot against the Soviet government.

The aim of Bukharin and his fellow-conspirators was to thwart the Treaty of Brest-Litovsk, to overthrow the Soviet government, to arrest and assassinate V. I. Lenin, J. V. Stalin and J. M. Sverdlov and to form a new government consisting of Bukharinites, Trotskyites and "Left" Socialist-Revolutionaries.

In executing the plan of the conspiracy, the "Left" Socialist-Revolutionaries in July 1918, with the knowledge and consent of Bukharin, raised a revolt in Moscow with the object of overthrowing the Soviet government; it has been further established that the attempt on the life of V. I. Lenin committed by the Socialist-Revolutionary Kaplan on August 30, 1918, was the direct result of the criminal designs of the "Left Communists," headed by Bukharin, and of their confederates, the "Left" and Right Socialist-Revolutionaries.

The preliminary and Court investigations have established the fact that Zelensky, Ivanov and Zubarev, accused in the present ease, had already entered the path of struggle against the revolutionary movement of the working class in the days of tsardom.

Zelensky was an agent-provocateur employed by the Samara Gendarmerie headquarters from 1911 to 1913.

Ivanov was an agent-provocateur of the Okhrana and the Gendarmerie headquarters in Moscow and other cities from 1911 to 1916.

Zubarev, recruited as an agent-provocateur in the city of Kotelnich in 1908, engaged in provocateur activities until 1917.

Thus, the Military Collegium of the Supreme Court of the U.S.S.R. has established the guilt of (1) N. I. Bukharin, (2) A. I. Rykov, (3) G. G. Yagoda, (4) N. N. Krestinsky, (5) K. G. Rakovsky, (6) A. P. Rosengoltz, (7) V. I. Ivanov, (8) M. A. Chernov, (9) G. F. Grinko, (10) I. A. Zelensky, (11) S. A. Bessonov, (12) A. Ikramov, (13) F. Khodjayev, (14) V. F. Sharangovich, (15) P. T. Zubarev, (16) P. P. Bulanov, (17) L. G. Levin, (18) D. D. Pletnev, (19) I. N. Kazakov, (20) V. A. Maximov-Dikovsky and (21) P. P. Kryuchkov, in that, being active participants in a conspiratorial group known as the "bloc of Rights and Trotskyites," which acted under the direct instructions of the intelligence services of foreign states, they carried on treasonable, espionage, diversive, wrecking and terrorist activities, provoking an armed attack by these states on the

rpose of bringing about the defeat and dis-
pviet Union and the severance from it of the
, the Central Asiatic republics, Georgia,
and the Maritime Region in the Far East
states hostile to the U.S.S.R., their ultimate
row of the Socialist social and state system
.S.S.R. and the restoration of capitalism and
ne bourgeoisie in the U.S.S.R.—i.e., of having
mely grave state offences covered by Articles 58^{1a},
58^9 and 58^{11} of the Criminal Code of the R.S.F.S.R.,
Zelensky and Zubarev, in addition, of having committed crimes covered by Article 58^{13} of the Criminal Code of
the R.S.F.S.R.

On the basis of the aforesaid, and guided by Articles 319 and
320 of the Code of Criminal Procedure of the R.S.F.S.R.,

*The Military Collegium of the Supreme Court of the U.S.S.R.
Sentences:*

1. BUKHARIN, Nikolai Ivanovich,
2. RYKOV, Alexei Ivanovich,
3. YAGODA, Genrikh Grigorievich,
4. KRESTINSKY, Nikolai Nikolayevich,
5. ROSENGOLTZ, Arkady Pavlovich,
6. IVANOV, Vladimir Ivanovich,
7. CHERNOV, Mikhail Alexandrovich,
8. GRINKO, Grigori Fedorovich,
9. ZELENSKY, Isaac Abramovich,
10. IKRAMOV, Akmal,
11. KHODJAYEV, Faizulla,
12. SHARANGOVICH, Vasily Fomich,
13. ZUBAREV, Prokopy Timofeyevich,
14. BULANOV, Pavel Petrovich,
15. LEVIN, Lev Grigorievich,
16. KAZAKOV, Ignaty Nikolayevich,
17. MAXIMOV-DIKOVSKY, Venyamin Adamovich (Abramovich), and
18. KRYUCHKOV, Pyotr Petrovich

to the supreme penalty—to be shot, with the confiscation of all
their personal property.

19. PLETNEV, Dmitry Dmitrievich, as not having directly
taken an active part in the causing of death of Comrades V. V.
Kuibyshev and A. M. Gorky, although he was an accessory to this
crime—to imprisonment for the term of twenty-five years, with
deprivation of political rights for a period of five years after

expiration of his prison term and with the confiscation of all his personal property.

20. RAKOVSKY, Khristian Georgievich, and

21. BESSONOV, Sergei Alexeyevich, as not having taken a direct part in the organization of terrorist, diversive and wrecking activities—to imprisonment: Rakovsky for the term of twenty years and Bessonov for the term of fifteen years, each with deprivation of political rights for a period of five years after expiration of his prison term and with the confiscation of all his personal property.

The terms of imprisonment of Pletnev, Rakovsky and Bessonov shall be counted from the day of their arrest.

[*Signed*] PRESIDENT: V. ULRICH
Army Military Jurist
President of the Military Collegium of the Supreme Court of the U.S.S.R.

MEMBERS OF THE COURT:
[*Signed*] I. MATULEVICH
Army Corps Military Jurist
Vice-President of the Military Collegium of the Supreme Court of the U.S.S.R.

B. YEVLEV
Divisional Military Jurist
Member of the Military Collegium of the Supreme Court of the U.S.S.R.

THE PRESIDENT: I declare the Court Session of the Military Collegium of the Supreme Court of the U.S.S.R. closed.

[*Signed*] PRESIDENT: V. ULRICH
Army Military Jurist
President of the Military Collegium of the Supreme Court of the U.S.S.R.

SECRETARY: A. BATNER
Military Jurist First Rank

NOTES

BIOGRAPHICAL NOTES

READINGS

NOTES

Morning Session

MARCH 2

(Pages 1-66)

1. In his famous secret speech of 1956, Khrushchev declared that during the purge era "brutal acts of violations of socialist legality" were committed. He cited a secret directive issued at Stalin's initiative instructing investigative agencies and judicial organs to speed up cases of accused terrorists and to execute death sentences immediately upon sentencing. Petitions for pardon were no longer possible. The directive was signed on December 1, 1934, the day of Kirov's assassination. See Nikita S. Khrushchev, *The Crimes of the Stalin Era* (Special Report to the 20th Congress of the Communist Party of the Soviet Union, annotated by Boris I. Nicolaevsky; New York: *The New Leader*, 1956), pp. S21-S22.

2. The doctors — Levin, Pletnev, and Kazakov — were represented by defense counsels.

3. Grigori E. Zinoviev, one of Lenin's closest associates, member of the Politburo, and head of the Communist International, was a leader of the United Opposition during the twenties. He was expelled from the Party in 1927, later readmitted, and then, tried and sentenced to death in the 1936 Moscow Trial. See *The Case of the Trotskyite-Zinovievite Terrorist Centre* (Report of Court Proceedings Heard before the Military Collegium of the Supreme Court of the U.S.S.R., Moscow, August 19-24, 1936; Moscow: People's Commissariat of Justice of the U.S.S.R., 1936).

4. The Mensheviks and the Socialist Revolutionaries were important pre-Revolutionary parties. The former, a moderate Marxist movement, opposed the October uprising on the grounds that Russia required a period of democratic bourgeois rule before a genuine proletarian revolution was possible. The peasant-oriented Socialist Revolutionaries split in 1917; the Left SRs supported and participated in the new Soviet government for several months. With the introduction of the New Economic Policy in 1921, a considerable number of Menshevik and SR intellectuals

who had not emigrated were able to resume their work under the new regime. Many former Mensheviks worked in the industrial and economic planning agencies, while the agricultural institutions utilized the talents of former SRs. These so-called "non-party specialists" continued to contribute to the economic advances of Soviet Russia until the introduction of the first Five-Year Plan and the fall of Bukharin and Rykov, who had actively sought their cooperation. After 1928-1929, they came under increasing attack and in many instances were tried for wrecking. For example, see *The Menshevik Trial: The Text of the Indictment of the Counter-Revolutionary Menshevik Organization* (New York: Workers' Library Publishers, n.d.

5. Marshal M. N. Tukhachevsky, Commander-in-Chief of the Soviet Army, was arrested and executed in 1937. No details of a trial have ever been published, although he was accused of espionage and plotting a *coup d'état* and the dismemberment of the U.S.S.R. The purges hit the army particularly hard. One estimate places those purged at half the total officer corps. (Leonard Schapiro, *The Communist Party of the Soviet Union.* New York: Random House, 1959, p. 420.) The purge of the military leadership was among the first to be attributed to the "personality cult of Stalin," and since 1956 Tukhachevsky and the other executed officers have been officially rehabilitated. For a discussion of the rehabilitation process since Stalin's death, see Leopold Labedz, "Resurrection — and Perdition," *Problems of Communism,* March-April 1963, pp. 48-59.

6. Budu Mdivani, a prominent Georgian Bolshevik, was arrested and executed in 1937. It is possible that Mdivani's downfall was related to an incident that occurred fifteen years earlier. In 1922, as a leader of the Georgian Communist Party, he had appealed to Lenin in an effort to counteract a campaign conducted by Stalin designed to increase central control over the Trans-Caucasian Republics. At first Lenin supported Stalin's policy; but by early 1923, having learned of Stalin's harsh purge of the rebellious Georgian leadership, he concluded in a Postscript to his famous Testament: "Stalin is too rude ... Therefore I propose to the comrades to find a way to remove Stalin from that position [General Secretary of the Party] and appoint to it another man who in all respects differs from Stalin in one superiority — namely, that he be more tolerant, more loyal, more polite and more considerate to comrades, less capricious, etc." (The five other Party leaders — Trotsky, Zinoviev, Kamenev, Bukharin, and Piatikov — mentioned favorably by Lenin in his Testament, in comparison with his remarks on Stalin, were eventually, directly or indirectly, executed by Stalin.) The Testament is translated in Bertram D. Wolfe, *Khrushchev and Stalin's Ghost* (New York: Praeger, 1957), pp. 260-263. The affair was apparently exacerbated by Stalin's rude conduct toward Lenin's wife during this period; it led Lenin to threaten to break off personal relations with Stalin. The denouement was avoided when, in March 1923, Lenin suffered his third and, as it

turned out, final stroke. The nationality controversy of 1922-1923 and the relationship between Lenin and Stalin are discussed in Robert V. Daniels, *The Conscience of the Revolution: Communist Opposition in Soviet Russia* (Cambridge: Harvard University Press, 1960), pp. 176-187. For relations between Stalin and Lenin, see also Louis Fischer, *The Life of Lenin* (New York: Harper & Row, 1964), pp. 597-671.

7. For the published record of these trials, see *The Case of the Trotskyite-Zinovievite Terrorist Centre* and *The Case of the Anti-Soviet Trotskyite Centre* (Report of Court Proceedings Heard before the Military Collegium of the Supreme Court of the U.S.S.R., Moscow, January 23-30, 1937; Moscow: People's Commissariat of Justice of the U.S.S.R., 1937). The charges brought against Trotsky in the Moscow Trials were examined by a Joint Commission of Inquiry headed by the American philosopher John Dewey. The Commission's findings were published in *Not Guilty* (New York: Harper, 1938). For Trotsky's activities during the thirties and his reaction to the trials, see Isaac Deutscher, *The Prophet Outcast. Trotsky: 1929-1940* (London and New York: Oxford University Press, 1963).

8. Theodore I. Dan, a prominent Menshevik leader, left Russia in the early twenties. He died in New York in 1947. Bukharin is reported to have told Dan, in Paris in 1936, that "we know with certainty that he [Stalin] will devour us [the old Bolsheviks] . . . he is only waiting for the opportune moment." See *Dissent*, Summer 1963, p. 267.

9. Transcripts of the pre-trial examinations have not been published.

10. Grigori L. Piatakov, an old Bolshevik and close associate of Lenin, was a member of Trotsky's Opposition until the late twenties. Having broken off relations with Trotsky's group, he remained on the Party's Central Committee and during the first two Five-Year Plans exercised considerable influence as Deputy Commissar of Heavy Industry. Although there is no evidence that he resumed opposition activity, he was arrested and tried at the second Moscow Trial. He confessed to charges of treason, espionage, terrorism, and wrecking, and was executed. See *The Case of the Anti-Soviet Trotskyite Centre*. For a discussion of the 1937 trial, see David J. Dallin, *From Purge to Coexistence: Essays on Stalin's and Khrushchev's Russia* (Chicago: Regnery, 1964), Chapters 1-9. A recent unconfirmed report from Moscow has suggested that the criminal charges against Piatakov, Bukharin, and others have been quashed. See *The New York Times*, October 19, 1962.

11. Centrosoyuz = Central Union of Consumers' Cooperatives.

12. Leon Sedov, Trotsky's eldest son, died mysteriously in Paris in 1938 while undergoing an operation. For an account of his activities during Trotsky's years in exile, see Deutscher, *The Prophet Outcast*.

13. In Soviet usage, a kulak was a wealthy ("exploiter") peasant.

14. Native discontent in Turkestan during the early years of Soviet rule resulted in a resistance movement known as *Basmachestvo,* and its

members as *Basmachis.* This episode in Soviet history is related in Richard Pipes, *The Formation of the Soviet Union: Communism and Nationalism 1917-1923* (Cambridge: Harvard University Press, 1954), pp. 176-180, 255-260.

15. Shortly after the assassination of Kirov, a number of "White Guards" (anti-Communists) were arrested and accused of terrorism. Later it was charged that they had joined with "Zinovievites" in anti-Soviet activity. An account of the experiences of a person arrested as a member of the former group is given in Elizabeth Lermolo, *Face of a Victim* (New York: Harper, 1955).

16. The accusation that Yagoda, in collusion with the main defendants and the doctors, had brought about the deaths of Menzhinsky, Kuibyshev, and Gorky was the novel charge at the 1938 trial. (M. A. Peshkov, Gorky's son, was also listed as one of their victims.) This charge was not mentioned at the trials of 1936 and 1937. Further, at the time of death of each of these men, the official obituary cited natural causes and gave corroborating medical testimony: Menzhinsky, head of the OGPU, died in 1934; Kuibyshev, a member of the Politburo, Deputy Chairman of the Council of People's Commissars, and Chairman of the State Planning Commission, died in January 1935; Gorky, the famous author, died in 1936. Kirov, head of the Leningrad Party organization and a member of the Politburo, was shot by Leonid V. Nikolayev, a discontented Party member, on December 1, 1934. Various groups and persons were officially linked with the assassination and the crime figured in each of the Moscow Trials. Subsequent information, especially statements by Khrushchev in his secret speech to the Twentieth Party Congress and in his concluding public speech to the Twenty-second Party Congress, reinforces earlier speculation that Stalin actually arranged the murder of Kirov in order to eliminate a potential rival and, above all, to create a pretext for carrying out a reign of terror in the Party by means of the Great Purge. For an analysis of the Kirov affair see Boris I. Nicolaevsky, *Bolsheviks and Bureaucrats* (New York: Praeger, 1965); see also *Letter of an Old Bolshevik* (New York: Rand School Press, 1937), Lermolo, *Face of a Victim,* and Alexander Orlov, *The Secret History of Stalin's Crimes* (New York: Random House, 1953), pp. 3-24. For an opposing theory see Alexander Uralov, *The Reign of Stalin* (London: Bodley Head, 1953), pp. 20-28. There is no satisfactory evidence to indicate that Kuibyshev or Menzhinsky died by other than natural causes, and recent Soviet accounts have disregarded the murder charges. For example, see the article on Menzhinsky in *Voprosy istorii KPSS,* No. 9, 1964, p. 99. The case of Gorky is less certain. There is reason to suspect that both Gorky and Kuibyshev opposed Stalin's attempts to use terror against former opposition leaders, and the possibility has been raised that Stalin was responsible for Gorky's death. For Gorky see Orlov, pp. 261-276; for Kuiby- hev see Nicolaevsky, *op. cit.*

17. Communist Party of the Soviet Union.

18. V. I. Molotov, L. M. Kaganovich, and K. E. Voroshilov were members of the Politburo throughout the purge era. All three were involved in the power struggle following Stalin's death and lost their influence and positions with the victory of Khrushchev. Molotov and Kaganovich were expelled from the Party in the spring of 1964. Khrushchev suggested that Voroshilov be given special consideration but repeatedly implicated Molotov and Kaganovich in the crimes of the thirties. Several speakers at the Twenty-second Party Congress charged that Molotov, Kaganovich, and Voroshilov took part in the events leading to the execution of a number of purge victims, including the military leadership. In particular, see the speeches of Podgorny, Shelepin, and Khrushchev in *Current Soviet Policies IV: The Documentary Record of the 22nd Congress of the Communist Party of the Soviet Union* (New York: Columbia University Press, 1962).

19. Abel S. Yenukidze, an old Georgian Bolshevik and Secretary of the Central Executive Committee of the U.S.S.R., was expelled from the Party in 1935 and shot in 1937. The fall of Yenukidze, once a close friend of Stalin, is discussed in Orlov, *The Secret History of Stalin's Crimes,* pp. 304-313. He has been rehabilitated.

20. At the time of Kirov's assassination, Ivan Zaporozhets was Deputy Director of the Leningrad NKVD (People's Commissariat of Internal Affairs). According to the account of an NKVD defector, Zaporozhets arranged the murder of Kirov on Stalin's orders. See Orlov, *The Secret History of Stalin's Crimes,* pp. 10-24. This version was given at least partial confirmation by Khrushchev in his secret speech: "There are reasons for the suspicion that the killer of Kirov, Nikolayev, was assisted by someone from among the people whose duty it was to protect the person of Kirov." See *The Crimes of the Stalin Era,* p. S22.

21. Lev B. Kamenev, an old Bolshevik and member of the Politburo from 1919 to 1926, held several important Party and state positions during the twenties. With the defeat of the United Opposition in 1927, he was expelled from the Party, was later readmitted, only to be expelled again. Kamenev and Zinoviev were sentenced to ten years' imprisonment for terrorism at a secret trial in 1935, then tried again in 1936 at the first of the three public trials. Kamenev confessed and was executed. See *The Case of the Trotskyite-Zinovievite Terrorist Centre.*

22. Mikhail P. Tomsky, an old Bolshevik, member of the Politburo, and head of the trade unions during the twenties, was one of the leaders (with Bukharin and Rykov) of the Right Opposition. He was removed from his posts after Stalin's victory in 1929 and committed suicide in 1936.

23. General State Political Administration (the political police).

24. On September 26, 1936, Nikolai I. Yezhov replaced Yagoda as

People's Commissar of Internal Affairs. The appointment marked the beginning of the bloodiest period of the purges, and the ensuing era of terror is often referred to as *Yezhovshchina.* In December 1938 Yezhov was replaced by Lavrenti Beria and later disappeared.

25. The Treaty of Brest-Litovsk, signed by the new Soviet government and Germany in March 1918, ended Russia's participation in World War I. By the terms of the agreement, Russia lost a considerable part of her population, sown area, industry, and railways; in return, the new regime— faced by military danger on several fronts as well as internal opposition — obtained a crucial breathing spell. The treaty represented not only a personal triumph for Lenin, who, realizing that another German advance might topple the regime, brought to bear all of his prestige and persuasive powers, but also a major defeat for the Left Communists headed by Bukharin. Despite the imminent danger posed by the possibility of a new German attack on the disintegrated Russian Army, Bukharin and his followers denounced the proposed treaty, regarding it as a debasement of socialist ideals and as a compromise with imperialism. In its place, they advocated a policy of "revolutionary war" which by its idealism would set an example for the European proletariat.

This episode in Soviet history is important because the issues involved transcended the question of the peace treaty and revealed the uneasy balance between political expediency and ideological conviction that would continue to divide the Party leadership. Vyshinsky's account of these events is only partially correct, as indeed Bukharin tried to demonstrate. The best account of the Brest-Litovsk Treaty, Left Communism, and the role of the Left SRs is Leonard Schapiro, *The Origin of the Communist Autocracy. Political Opposition in the Soviet State: First Phase 1917-1922* (Cambridge: Harvard University Press, 1956), Chapters 6-8.

26. Sverdlov, a member of the Politburo, head of the Party apparatus, and Chairman of the Central Executive Committee, died in March 1919.

27. Karelin, Boris Kamkov, and P. P. Proshyan were prominent Left SRs. Proshyan died in the early twenties. It was thought that Kamkov and Karelin, as leaders of former political parties, had long since perished. Their appearance as witnesses at the trial was something of a surprise.

28. Count W. von Mirbach, the German Ambassador to Soviet Russia, was assassinated on July 6, 1918, by a Left SR. The act, which coincided with small revolts in Moscow and Petrograd, grew out of the Left SRs' dissatisfaction with the peace treaty. There is no evidence that the Left Communists were connected with the events of July 1918. See Schapiro, *The Origin of the Communist Autocracy,* p. 142.

29. Ossinsky continued to play an important role in Party affairs during the twenties as head of the Democratic Centralists. In 1929 he was attacked as a Rightist. He perished during the purges.

30. The trial of the Socialist Revolutionaries was held in Moscow during June and July 1922. Bukharin conducted the defense for one group of the accused. For his speech at the trial see *Protsess eserov. Rechi zashchitnikov i obviniaemykh (Trial of the SRs: Speeches of the Counsels for Defense and the Accused)* (Moscow: 1922), pp. 109-144.

31. I. N. Stukov was a member of the Moscow Party Regional Bureau in 1918 and a prominent Left Communist.

32. There is no record of such a trial.

33. The reference is to *Biulletin oppozitsii (Bulletin of the Opposition)*, published in Paris between 1929 and 1940 by the Trotskyites.

34. On July 11, 1928, Bukharin secretly met with Kamenev in search of allies in his struggle against Stalin's abrupt turn to the left. A partial record of their conversation has been preserved. Bukharin said of Stalin: "He has made concessions so that he can cut our throats. We understand this, but he maneuvers so as to make us appear to be the schismatics." A partial English translation is available in Robert V. Daniels, *A Documentary History of Communism* (New York: Vintage Books, 1962), Vol. I, pp. 308-309.

35. Trotsky's daughter, Zinaida Volkov, committed suicide in Berlin in January 1933. The children of the exiled leader suffered for his political opposition and their fate was no less tragic. Trotsky's family life during this period is discussed in Deutscher, *The Prophet Outcast*.

36. The Fifteenth Party Congress met in December 1927. It marked the final defeat of the Left Opposition and the expulsion of many of its members from the Party.

37. Leonid P. Serebriakov, a former Secretary of the Party's Central Committee and a follower of Trotsky, was Deputy People's Commissar of Transport at the time of his arrest. He appeared as a main defendant in the 1937 Moscow Trial and was sentenced to death. See *The Case of the Anti-Soviet Trotskyite Centre*.

38. The Russian word *valiuta* means "currency"; "valuta funds" probably refers to foreign currencies.

39. Krestinsky's statement is interesting in the light of Khrushchev's revelations in 1956 concerning pre-trial investigative methods. A number of old Bolsheviks, having signed false confessions after prolonged physical torture, addressed letters to Stalin and other leaders "calling to you for help from a gloomy cell." Apparently some victims of the purges refused to believe that the leadership was party to the crimes of the NKVD interrogators. See *The Crimes of the Stalin Era*, pp. S28-S29, S52-S53.

40. General I. P. Uborevich, commander of the Byelorussian Military District, was executed in June 1937. He has since been rehabilitated. See Khrushchev's speech in *Current Soviet Policies IV*, pp. 197-198.

Evening Session
MARCH 2
(Pages 67-109)

1. For a study of Borotbism see Iwan Majstrenko, *Borotbism: A Chapter in the History of Ukrainian Communism* (New York: Research Program on the U.S.S.R., 1954).

2. The New Economic Policy (NEP) was introduced in 1921. Designed as a series of concessions to a war-weary and recalcitrant population, it inaugurated a period of peaceful reconstruction after the more militant policies of War Communism. An uneasy balance between private and state ownership was established in industry, agriculture, and trade. The great debates of the twenties centered on whether the evolutionary policies of NEP represented Russia's road to socialism or whether NEP was in fact a tactical retreat that must yield to the more revolutionary and coercive measures of the earlier period. Stalin's final turn to the left in 1928-1929 ended the NEP era. For an account of this period in Soviet history see E. H. Carr, *The Bolshevik Revolution 1917-1923* (Vols. I-III), *The Interregnum 1923-1924,* and *Socialism in One Country 1924-1926* (Vols. I-III) (New York: Macmillan, 1951-1964). An interesting personal memoir describing the views of Rykov and Bukharin on the policies of NEP is William Reswick's *I Dreamt Revolution* (Chicago: Regnery, 1952).

3. Y. A. Yakovlev, a prominent Ukrainian Bolshevik and People's Commissar of Agriculture, disappeared during the thirties along with most of the former Ukrainian leadership.

4. Yan B. Gamarnik, head of the Political Directorate of the army from 1929 to 1937 and Deputy People's Commissar of Defense, was reported to have committed suicide in May 1937 to avoid arrest. He has since been rehabilitated.

5. General N. Z. Yakir, a military-district commander and a member of the Central Committee, was executed in 1937 with Tukhachevsky. Both Khrushchev and Shelepin discussed the case of Yakir at the Twenty-second Party Congress, citing him as an innocent victim of the purges. See *Current Soviet Policies IV,* pp. 181, 197-198.

6. N. K. Antipov, Deputy Chairman of the Council of People's Commissars and member of the Central Committee, disappeared during the purges. He appears to have been a loyal Stalinist throughout the struggle against the various oppositions. Antipov has been rehabilitated.

7. Yan E. Rudzutak, a prominent Party figure and former member of the Politburo, appears to be an example of the Stalinist who resisted Stalin's earlier efforts to inaugurate a blood purge only to be purged him-

self in 1938. See *Letter of an Old Bolshevik*, pp. 12-14. According to Khrushchev, Rudzutak denied all the charges at his secret trial and has been rehabilitated posthumously. See *The Crimes of the Stalin Era*, pp. S29-S30.

8. I. M. Vareikis, a supporter of Bukharin in the mid-twenties, was a member of the Central Committee and a regional Party Secretary until his arrest in 1937. He died in 1939. His downfall is officially attributed to the fact that he questioned Stalin about the arrest of several Party members. He has been rehabilitated. See *Pravda*, September 18, 1964.

9. In a famous 1928 article entitled *"Zametki ekonomista"* ("Notes of an Economist"), Bukharin argued that an exaggerated rate of industrial growth would create a demand for industrial goods that industry would be unable to satisfy. The resulting shortage would produce critical bottlenecks and disproportions in the economy which would limit the rate of industrial expansion. The article represented Bukharin's most complete economic argument against a policy of "super-industrialization." For a condensed translation see Wolfe, *Khrushchev and Stalin's Ghost*, pp. 295-315. Bukharin's economic theory is discussed in Alexander Erlich, *The Soviet Industrialization Debate 1924-1928* (Cambridge: Harvard University Press, 1960).

10. This curious reference by Rykov recalls Trotsky's famous suggestion during the war scare of 1927 that in the event of war the Opposition would emulate Clemenceau and continue to oppose the present incompetent leadership. See Isaac Deutscher, *The Prophet Unarmed. Trotsky: 1921-1929* (London and New York: Oxford University Press, 1959), pp. 349-351, 354-355.

11. A Russian *pood* is equal to 36.113 pounds.

12. A Treaty of Mutual Assistance was signed on May 2, 1935. Directed against Nazi Germany, it stipulated that if either country became the object "of an unprovoked attack on the part of a European State, the U.S.S.R., and, reciprocally, France, shall immediately give each other aid and assistance."

13. The Soviet Union sold its interest in the Chinese Eastern Railway to Japan on March 23, 1935.

14. A grain crisis precipitated by poor harvests and low grain collections in the winter of 1927-1928 provoked a clash between the emerging Right Opposition, led by Bukharin, Rykov, and Tomsky, and the supporters of Stalin. Chernov's account of his views in 1928 is similar to that given by Bukharin at a Central Committee plenum on July 10, 1928. At issue was the new policy of coercive measures introduced to increase grain collections. For a partial record of Bukharin's speech opposing such measures see Daniels, *A Documentary History of Communism*, Vol. I, pp. 306-308.

15. Anastas I. Mikoyan, a Politburo member under Stalin and Khrushchev, is now President of the Soviet Union (Chairman of the Presidium of the Supreme Soviet).

16. Rykov and Bukharin argued in 1928 that repressive measures threatened the alliance between the middle peasantry and the proletariat on which the Soviet government was based. For a discussion of Rykov's and Bukharin's response to the grain crisis of 1928 see Daniels, *The Conscience of the Revolution*, pp. 322-333.

17. *The Socialist Courier*, a journal published from 1921 to 1964 by the Menshevik Party in exile.

18. Boris I. Nicolaevsky, the well-known Menshevik historian and journalist, was related to Rykov by marriage. For Nicolaevsky's recollections of his remarkable conversations with Bukharin in Paris in 1936 and his views concerning the purges see his *Bolsheviks and Bureaucrats*.

19. The reference is probably to I. Y. Liubimov, a member of the Central Committee, who disappeared during the purges.

Morning Session
MARCH 3
(Pages 110-151)

1. The Tsarist political police.

2. As early as 1925, Zinoviev noted that "around Bukharin there is now forming an entire school [*shkola*]." Bukharin's influence among young Party writers and academicians during the twenties was considerable; his prominence as the Party's foremost theoretician, his status in the Institute of Red Professors and his seminars at Sverdlov University, and his many editorial positions brought him a great number of disciples. This "Bukharin school" was under constant attack, first by the followers of Trotsky, Zinoviev, and Kamenev, and after 1927 by the Stalinists. With the defeat of the Right Opposition in 1929 most of these young intellectuals were removed from their positions and subsequently perished during the purges. Some information concerning the followers of Bukharin is contained in Abdurakhman Avtorkhanov, *Stalin and the Soviet Communist Party: A Study in the Technology of Power* (New York: Praeger, 1959).

3. Until 1928, Bukharin's prolific and often original writings on imperialism and contemporary capitalism reflected official Party policy. For a discussion of this body of work see Sidney Heitman, "Between Lenin and Stalin: Nikolai Bukharin," in Leopold Labedz (ed.), *Revisionism: Essays on the History of Marxist Ideas* (New York: Praeger, 1962), pp. 77-90.

4. Probably S. S. Lobov, a member of the Central Committee and Deputy Chairman of the Supreme Council of National Economy of the U.S.S.R., who disappeared during the purges. Lobov has been rehabilitated.

5. Although this famous program has never been published or openly circulated, there are reliable accounts of its contents. Written in 1930 by M. N. Riutin, a former Party Secretary of a Moscow district and a supporter of the Right Opposition, it has been described as "remarkable chiefly for its *severe criticism* of Stalin" (see *Letter of an Old Bolshevik*, pp. 11-15). The clandestine manuscript portrayed Stalin as the "evil genius" of the Revolution and called for his removal and an end to super-industrialization and compulsory collectivization. Stalin became familiar with Riutin's program in 1932 and demanded the author's execution. Apparently Stalin was outvoted in the Politburo and was unable at that time to invoke the death penalty against former Party leaders.

6. A. P. Smirnov, an old Bolshevik and People's Commissar of Agriculture during NEP, was closely associated with Bukharin's school of thought, particularly on the peasant question. He was removed from his post in 1928 and expelled from the Central Committee in 1933 for his participation in a new opposition group. (See *Pravda*, January 13, 1933.) Smirnov disappeared during the purges.

7. A form of local government in pre-Revolutionary Russia.

Evening Session
MARCH 3
(Pages 152-199)

1. I. A. Antonov-Ovseyenko, a famous military leader of the Civil War period, was a supporter of Trotsky until 1928. He later served as Ambassador to Czechoslovakia and as a Soviet agent in Spain during the Spanish Civil War. He was charged with wrecking and treason and secretly executed in 1938. He was rehabilitated in 1956.

2. N. A. Uglanov, head of the important Moscow Party organization and a candidate member of the Politburo, supported the Right Opposition. His defeat in 1928 deprived Bukharin and his followers of an influential organizational base. Uglanov was arrested during the Riutin affair in 1932 and disappeared during the purges.

3. The defeat of Tomsky and his supporters at the Eighth Trade Union Congress in December 1928 eliminated the last organizational base of the Right Opposition.

4. Published in *Pravda*, November 26, 1929; an English translation is given in Daniels, *The Conscience of the Revolution*, p. 369.

5. V. V. Shmidt, former People's Commissar of Labor, member of the Central Committee, and a candidate member of the Party's Organization Bureau, was a close associate of Tomsky and a supporter of the Right Opposition. He perished during the purges. Shmidt seems to be one of the few former Rights to have been officially rehabilitated as of this time. See *The New York Times,* November 23, 1958.

6. V. V. Eismont, an associate of Rykov and a supporter of the Right Opposition, was expelled from the Party in 1933 for his participation in a new opposition group. He disappeared during the purges.

7. Alexander N. Slepkov was one of Bukharin's best-known disciples. A young "Red Professor" and Party activist, he expounded Bukharin's views on the editorial boards of *Bolshevik* (the Party's official theoretical journal) and *Pravda* until his removal in the late twenties. Slepkov participated in Riutin's group in 1932 and perished during the purges.

8. In March 1921 a rebellion broke out at the naval base at Kronstadt, a Bolshevik stronghold in 1917. Although the revolt was suppressed, the dissatisfaction with the economic policies of War Communism expressed by the insurgent peasant-sailors hastened the introduction of the more lenient policies of NEP. During the twenties the leaders of the Right constantly cited the Kronstadt uprising as an example of the consequences of a coercive policy in the countryside.

9. V. A. Kotov, a leader of the Moscow Party Committee, member of the Central Committee, and a supporter of the Right Opposition, disappeared during the purges.

10. A. G. Beloborodov, a former member of Trotsky's Opposition, disappeared during the purges.

11. See note 30, Morning Session, March 2.

12. Lev Karakhan, a famous Soviet diplomat, was tried secretly for treason, espionage, and terrorism, and executed in 1937. He has been rehabilitated.

13. Marshal Joseph Pilsudski headed the Polish government between 1926 and 1935.

Evening Session

MARCH 4

(Pages 202-250)

1. The trade-union controversy which divided the Party leadership in 1920-1921 concerned the role of the trade unions in the new Soviet order. Particularly at issue was the relationship between the state and

the trade-union organizations. Trotsky and his supporters of the Left, who for a brief period advocated the "militarization of labor," were defeated by a group headed by Lenin. For a full discussion of this controversy see Daniels, *The Conscience of the Revolution*, pp. 119-136.

2. Known as the Declaration of the Forty-six, this document was submitted to the Politburo in October 1923. It severely criticized the Party's economic policies and the absence of intra-party democracy. Although Trotsky did not sign the document, the Declaration's criticisms closely paralleled his own statements and most of its signers later participated in his Opposition. An English translation is given in Carr, *The Interregnum*, pp. 367-373.

3. During the debates of the twenties, Trotsky's theory of "permanent revolution" and the emerging official doctrine of "socialism in one country" came to symbolize the ideologies of the Left and the Right. For a discussion of Trotsky's theory see Isaac Deutscher, *The Prophet Armed. Trotsky: 1879-1921* (New York and London. Oxford University Press, 1954), pp. 149-162. For Bukharin's criticism of the theory see "Teoriia permanentnoi revoliutsii" ("The Theory of Permanent Revolution") in *Za leninizm: Sbornik statei* (*For Leninism: A Collection of Articles*) (Moscow: 1925), pp. 332-373.

4. Trotsky was exiled from Moscow to Alma-Ata in January 1928, and deported from the Soviet Union in February 1929.

5. A prominent member of Trotsky's Opposition during the twenties, I. N. Smirnov was tried at the 1936 Moscow Trial and executed. See *The Case of the Trotskyite-Zinovievite Terrorist Centre.*

6. In 1921 the open economic negotiations between the Soviet Union and Germany were accompanied by secret political and military talks. A frequent German representative at the latter negotiations was General von Seeckt, a Reichswehr staff officer and advocate of closer economic and military relations between Soviet Russia and Germany. See Carr, *The Bolshevik Revolution*, Vol. III, pp. 305-338.

7. Michael Farbman, author of several books on Soviet Russia.

8. E. A. Preobrazhensky, a gifted Bolshevik economist, was the main architect of the Left Opposition's economic theories during the twenties. He disappeared during the purges. For a discussion of Preobrazhensky's economic theories see Erlich, *The Soviet Industrialization Debate 1924-1928.*

9. Probably Arkadii Maslow, the left-wing leader of the German Communist Party until 1926 and a supporter of Zinoviev, who joined Trotsky's exiled Opposition in the early thirties.

10. Alfred Rosmer and Madeleine Paz, former delegates to the Communist International, were among Trotsky's closest friends and supporters before and during his exile, Rosmer died on May 6, 1964; see Gustave Stern, "In Memoriam — Alfred Rosmer" in *Survey*, October 1964, pp. 98-106.

11. General V. K. Putna, former military attaché in London, was charged with treason and espionage, and executed in May 1937. He has since been rehabilitated.

12. Grigori Y. Sokolnikov, an old Bolshevik and former candidate member of the Politburo, was People's Commissar of Finance from 1922 to 1926. Although he participated in the Left oppositions of the twenties, he withdrew from the factional struggles and served as Ambassador to Great Britain between 1929 and 1932 and later as Deputy People's Commissar of Foreign Affairs. Sokolnikov was a leading defendant at the 1937 Moscow Trial; he confessed and was sentenced to ten years' imprisonment. He is said to have died in 1939. See *The Case of the Anti-Soviet Trotskyite Centre*.

13. Sergei V. Mrachkovsky, a military hero of the Civil War and a supporter of Trotsky in the twenties, was a defendant at the 1936 Moscow Trial. He confessed to charges of wrecking and terrorism and was executed. See *The Case of the Trotskyite-Zinovievite Terrorist Centre*. Mrachkovsky is reported to have withstood torture and refused to sign a confession until he was finally persuaded that his confession was in the interest of the Revolution. See W. G. Krivitsky, *In Stalin's Secret Service* (New York: Harper, 1939), pp. 198-204.

14. Muralov, an old Bolshevik and one of the organizers of the Red Army during the Civil War, was a supporter of Trotsky. He was tried and sentenced to death at the 1937 Moscow Trial. See *The Case of the Anti-Soviet Trotskyite Centre*.

15. Rakovsky was one of the last major leaders of the Left Opposition to capitulate and his defection in 1934 caused Trotsky great despair: "Rakovsky was virtually my last contact with the old revolutionary generation. After his capitulation there is nobody left..." Quoted in Deutscher, *The Prophet Outcast*, p. 278.

Morning Session
MARCH 5
(Pages 251-296)

1. L. C. Sosnovsky, a well-known Soviet journalist and supporter of Trotsky, disappeared during the purges.

2. Laval arrived in Moscow on May 13, 1935, shortly after the signing of the Franco-Soviet Treaty of Mutual Assistance.

3. The Lausanne Conference took place during the winter of 1922-1923.

4. Max Eastman, the American author, was a supporter of Trotsky and his translator. For Eastman's reaction to the Moscow Trials see his *Stalin's Russia and the Crisis in Socialism* (New York; Norton, 1940), pp. 52-80.

5. In 1925 the Soviet Union signed an agreement with the Lena Goldfields Company, a former British property owner in Tsarist Russia, granting to it important mining concessions in Siberia.

6. On May 12, 1927, Arcos (the official Soviet trading company in London) was raided by British authorities. Although no subversive documents were produced, two weeks later the British government broke off official relations with the Soviet Union.

7. The new Soviet constitution was introduced in 1936 and immediately became known as the "Stalin Constitution." There is a certain irony in the fact that this constitution, heralded as " the most democratic in the world," coincided with the beginning of the *Yezhovshchina;* moreover, there is evidence to suggest that Bukharin was responsible for the original draft. See Schapiro, *The Communist Party of the Soviet Union,* p. 406, note 2.

8. Maxim Litvinov, an old Bolshevik and famous diplomat, was People's Commissar of Foreign Affairs from 1930 to 1939, when he was replaced by Molotov. Litvinov died in 1951.

9. The First Soviet Writers' Congress was held in Moscow in August 1934. For Bukharin's speech to the Congress see *Problems of Soviet Literature* (Reports and Speeches at the First Soviet Writers' Congress; New York: International Publishers, n.d.), pp. 185-258.

10. The Constitutional Democratic Party (Cadet) sought to establish a parliament along English lines.

11. Admiral Alexander Kolchak led the White armies during 1918-1919.

Evening Session
MARCH 5
(Pages 297-350)

1. In a still unpublished platform presented to the Politburo on February 9, 1929, Bukharin, Rykov, and Tomsky described Stalin's collectivization drive as "a policy of military-feudal exploitation of the peasantry." The only account of this platform is J. V. Stalin, *Works* (Moscow: Foreign Language Publishing House, 1955), Vol. XII, pp. 1-113.

2. A system of utilizing forced labor for the construction of roads in eighteenth-century France.

3. Khodjayev testified that he organized the "Group of the Eighteen" in 1918 to take advantage of nationalist dissatisfaction.

4. The Central Asian equivalent of a Kulak.

5. A Crimean Tartar Constituent Assembly established by nationalist groups after the Revolution.

6. An account of Enver Pasha's relations with the Soviet government after his fall from power in Turkey, and his eventual leadership of the rebellious *Basmachi*, is given in Louis Fischer, *The Soviets in World Affairs* (New York: Vintage Books, 1960), pp. 280-290.

7. Felix E. Dzerzhinsky, an old Bolshevik and the first head of the political police, died in 1926.

8. For an example of Bukharin's thinking on the collective farms in the mid-twenties, see his speech to the Fourteenth Party Conference: *Chetyrnadtsataia Konferentsiia Rossiiskoi Kommunisticheskoi Partii (bol'shevikov)*. *Stenograficheskii otchet (The Fourteenth Conference of the Russian Communist Party [Bolshevik]. Stenographic Report)* (Moscow: 1925), pp. 181-189.

9. Although Bukharin had repeatedly objected to Lenin's definition of the early Soviet economy as "state capitalism," there is little doubt that here he is advocating an NEP-type economy. For the controversy over "state capitalism" see Carr, *Socialism in One Country,* Vol. II, pp. 68-75.

10. A peasant.

11. See note 2, Morning Session, March 3; support for Bukharin's policies at Sverdlov University was probably considerable. M. N. Liadov, head of the University from 1923 to 1929, supported the Right Opposition.

12. There is no record of this "memorandum" to which Bukharin refers; it is possible that it concerned the emerging factional struggle against Trotsky and was later developed into a series of unsigned articles entitled *Doloi fraktsionnost' (Down with Factionalism)* which appeared in *Pravda* on December 28, 29, 30, 1923, and January 1, 4, 1924. Bukharin definitely was the author; the articles were included in a later collection of his writings, *K voprosu o trotskizme (On the Question of Trotskyism)* (Moscow: 1925), pp. 7-43.

13. See Note 14, Evening Session, March 2.

14. For a summary of the Right Opposition's platforms of 1928-1929 see Avtorkhanov, *Stalin and the Soviet Communist Party,* pp. 84, 85, 116-118.

Morning Session

MARCH 7

(Pages 351-410)

1. Generals A. I. Kork and M. V. Primakov were executed in June 1937. In 1961 Khrushchev described Kork as an outstanding commander who "fell victim to the mass repressions." See *Current Soviet Policies IV,* p. 197.

2. As Commissar of War and President of the Supreme War Council, Trotsky commanded the Bolshevik forces during the Civil War. His train, which served as a mobile headquarters, became something of a legend.

3. The Seventeenth Party Congress met in Moscow between January 26 and February 10, 1934. Known as the "Congress of Victors," the gathering celebrated the complete defeat of the former oppositions. Nonetheless, according to Khrushchev's secret speech, 70 per cent of the Central Committee elected at the Congress "were arrested and shot (mostly in 1937-1938)." Of 1,966 delegates to the Congress, 1,108 were subsequently arrested. *The Crimes of the Stalin Era,* pp. S20-S21.

4. See note 18, Evening Session, March 2; Nicolaevsky's famous *Letter of an Old Bolshevik* was based partially on this meeting with Bukharin. According to Nicolaevsky, this passage in Bukharin's testimony was intended to confirm the account of Party events given in the *Letter.* See "An Interview with Nicolaevsky" in Nicolaevsky, *Bolsheviks and Bureaucrats.*

5. Bukharin was a member of a Soviet delegation sent to negotiate with Nicolaevsky for the purchase of Karl Marx's manuscripts.

6. Elections to the Constituent Assembly took place in November-December 1917, shortly after the October seizure of power. The Bolsheviks received approximately 25 per cent of the votes and forcibly dispersed the Assembly the day after it opened in January 1918. It did not meet again.

7. In 1938 Trotsky was living in Mexico.

8. The Treaty of Mutual Assistance signed with Czechoslovakia on May 16, 1935.

9. Trotsky formally joined the Party in August 1917, even though he and Lenin had reached agreement as early as July. See Schapiro, *The Communist Party of the Soviet Union,* p. 169.

10. Zinoviev and Kamenev had opposed Lenin's views on insurrection in 1917.

709

Evening Session

1. See Bukharin's letter to the editor in *Pravda,* January 3, 1924.
2. E. M. Yaroslavsky was a well-known Bolshevik historian and journalist; all three were known as "Stalinists." Kuibyshev and Menzhinsky died before the trial began, Yaroslavsky in 1943. For Yaroslavsky's justification of the 1938 Moscow Trial, see his *The Meaning of the Soviet Trials* (New York: Workers' Library Publishers, 1938).
3. As People's Commisar of Foreign Affairs, Trotsky played an important role in the treaty negotiations. See Schapiro, *The Origin of the Communist Autocracy,* pp. 89-110.
4. The original Soviet political police.
5. See note 1, this session.
6. See note 28, Morning Session, March 2.
7. M. A. Natanson, a famous Russian revolutionary, helped found the first Russian revolutionary party, Land and Liberty, in 1876.
8. This important statement of Lenin's views on the organization and aims of the new regime is included in V. I. Lenin, *Selected Works* (Moscow: Foreign Language Publishing House, 1947), Vol. II, pp. 312-341.
9. Lenin was shot and wounded by Dora Kaplan, who was linked with the SR's. Schapiro calls it "free lance activity" and finds no evidence linking the attempt with any party or group. *The Origin of the Communist Autocracy,* p. 153.
10. The Democratic Centralists, comprised mainly of former Left Communists, opposed the growth of bureaucracy and the increasing centralization of the Party apparatus. Their opposition continued in various forms until 1927, when their leaders were expelled from the Party.
11. Bela Kun, head of the short-lived Hungarian Communist government in 1919 and a prominent figure in the Communist International, perished during the purges. He has since been rehabilitated.
12. For the alleged killing of Gorky, Kuibyshev, Menzhinsky, and Peshkov, see note 16, Morning Session, March 2.

Evening Session

1. E. A. Dreitzer, a former supporter of Trotsky, was sentenced to death in the 1936 Zinoviev-Kamenev trial. See *The Case of the Trotsky-ite-Zinovievite Terrorist Centre.*

2. There is some evidence that Yagoda may have favored the Right Opposition in 1928-1929, but it is inconclusive and makes it difficult (though not impossible) to explain how he managed to retain his post as head of the NKVD until 1936. The available evidence concerning this obscure relationship is analyzed in Simon Wolin and Robert M. Slusser (eds.), *The Soviet Secret Police* (New York: Praeger, 1957), pp. 43-46.

3. See note 3, Morning Session, March 7.

4. The appointment was announced in *Pravda*, September 27, 1936.

Morning Session
MARCH 11
(Pages 514-586)

1. At the Shakhty trials of 1928, forty nine non-Communist engineers working in the Donets Basin were found guilty of counter-revolutionary wrecking. There is little doubt that Stalin was using this "plot" to discredit the Bukharin-Rykov policy of fostering cooperation between the Party and non-Party specialists. By representing the affair as evidence of the intensification of the class struggle, he was directly attacking Bukharin's argument that cooperation between all segments of the population would guarantee civil peace. For Bukharin's subtle but effective rebuttal, see his *Uroki khlebozagotovok, shakhtinskogo dela, i zadachi partii* (*Lessons of Grain Collection, the Shakhty Affair, and the Tasks of the Party*)(Moscow: 1928).

2. The trials of the so-called Industrial Party took place in November 1930. Once again a number of former economic specialists confessed to charges of wrecking and sabotage. For a discussion of this "purge of the technical *intelligentsia*" see Raphael R. Abramovitch, *The Soviet Revolution 1917-1939* (New York: International University Press, 1962), pp. 380-382.

3. During the twenties Bukharin argued that hostile segments of the population would eventually elect a form of socialist ownership and hence "peacefully grow into Socialism." Thinking first of the recalcitrant countryside, he advocated policies and institutions designed to re-educate the peasantry; persuasion should now replace former coercive forms of the class struggle. His most complete statement of this program is *Put' k sotsializmu i raboche-krest'ianskii soiuz* (The Way to Socialism and the Worker-Peasant Alliance) (Moscow: 1925).

4. In 1929 Rykov proposed a Two-Year Plan for agriculture to be effected within the context of the Five-Year Plan and designed to maintain the balance between agriculture and industry.

5. In 1928 Bukharin told Kamenev that Stalin's new drive against the individual peasant landholder would lead to "famine and ruin. . . .

711

Stalin's policy is leading to civil war. He will be forced to drown the rebellions in blood." Quoted in Boris Souvarine, *Stalin: A Critical Survey of Bolshevism* (New York: Alliance Book Corporation, 1939), p. 485.

6. The reference is to a crucial date in the French Revolution — the 9th of Thermidor (July 27, 1794) — when moderate forces overthrew Robespierre and his followers. The Bolsheviks, and particularly Trotsky, often thought in terms of historical parallels. Thermidor represented a danger to their rule and was something to be guarded against. Trotsky's later thinking on Thermidor and developments in the Soviet Union is stated in his *The Revolution Betrayed* (New York: Pioneer Press, 1945).

7. The *otzovists* (recallists) opposed Bolshevik participation in the Tsarist Duma (parliament).

8. During the war years, the Bolshevik Party in exile was split over programmatic and ideological questions. Central to the controversy was the future role of national groups and of the state in the transition to socialism. Lenin urged that the immediate aim of the Party should be the defeat of the Tsarist government and the transformation of the present war into a civil war. In this context, he advanced a slogan supporting the right of self-determination for every Russian nation. A Left group within the Party, of which Bukharin emerged as the leading spokesman, opposed Lenin's slogan on the grounds that the impending revolution would be international in scope and would consequently render national lines obsolete. Therefore the slogan was meaningless and served only to divert the world proletariat from its main task. In addition to this matter, the two factions advocated different attitudes toward the future role of the state. Lenin was convinced that during the transition period following the revolution the victorious proletariat would have to utilize the existing state to defeat its enemies. In his view, this was "the dictatorship of the proletariat." Bukharin, relying on a rather literal interpretation of the writings of Engels concerning "the withering away of the state," argued that the existing imperialist state, since it was an instrument for the exploitation of the proletariat, would disappear immediately.

The disputes of the war period are important because they involved fundamental differences — a national emphasis as opposed to radical internationalism and pragmatism versus ideological purity — that appeared again in 1918-1919. The war period is treated fully in Olga Hess Gankin and H. H. Fisher, *The Bolsheviks and the World War: The Origin of the Third International* (Stanford: Stanford University Press, 1940).

9. Published under the pseudonym "Note Bene" in *Jugendinternationale*, No. 6, 1916; Bukharin's early articles stressed the Marxist belief that the proletarian revolution must destroy the existing state. His best-known elaboration of this thesis was written in 1916, but was not published until 1925. See his "K teorii imperialisticheskogo gosudarstva"

712

("On the Theory of the Imperialist State") in *Revoliutsiia prava. Sbornik pervyi* (The Revolution in Law. Collection One) (Moscow: Communist Academy, 1925), pp. 5-32.

10. *Kommunist,* Nos. 1-2, 1915, pp. 4-44; an enlarged version of this article later appeared as *Imperialism and World Economy* (New York: International Publishers, 1929).

11. It is often argued that by 1917 Lenin had come to accept Bukharin's early views on the state. Bukharin quoted a statement by Lenin's wife to this effect. See "K teorii imperialisticheskogo gosudarstya," *op. cit.,* p. 5, note 1; see also note 8, this session.

12. Certain that an international revolution would soon bring about a union of all proletarians, Bukharin continued to argue, as he had during the war years, that national slogans were obsolete. The controversy of 1919 is discussed in Daniels, *The Conscience of the Revolution,* pp. 95-97.

13. During the trade-union controversy of 1921, Bukharin and several other Party leaders occupied a position between that of Lenin and that of Trotsky; hence, they were known as the "buffer."

14. See note 12, Evening Session, March 5.

15. At a Party meeting in April 1925 Bukharin said, "To the peasants, to all the peasants, we must say — Enrich yourselves, develop your farms, and do not fear that constraint will be put on you." Quoted and discussed in Carr, *Socialism in One Country,* Vol. I, pp. 258-261.

16. *Tsesarizm pod maskoi revoliutsii. Po povodu knigi prof. N. Ustrialova "Pod znakom revoliutsii"* (*Caesarism under the Mask of Revolution. In Regard to the Book of Prof. N. Ustrialov* "Under the Sign of Revolution") (Moscow: 1925).

17. See note 9, Evening Session, March 2.

18. This declaration was signed jointly by Bukharin, Rykov, and Tomsky; see note 4, Evening Session, March 3.

19. On November 7, the anniversary of the Revolution, Trotsky, Zinoviev, and the other leaders of the Opposition attempted to appeal to the rank-and-file members in Moscow and Leningrad. The street demonstrations were easily dispersed. For a participant's account of the Leningrad demonstration, see Victor Serge, *Memoirs of a Revolutionary 1901-1941* (London: Oxford University Press, 1963), pp. 226-227.

20. Oblomov, the hero of Goncharov's novel, came to symbolize traits of laziness, ineffective daydreaming, and sloth. Early Bolshevik leaders often cited "Oblomovism" as an obstacle to the transformation of backward Russia. Bukharin was editor of *Izvestia* at the time his article appeared. See *Izvestia,* January 27, 1936.

21. T. V. Sapronov, a leader of the Democratic Centralists, opposed Lenin's plan for restoring individual authority in the administration of industry. He perished during the purges.

22. The State Commission for the Electrification of Russia (GOELRO), the first attempt at a state plan for economic development, was established in 1920.

23. Shuisky was Tsar of Russia from 1606 to 1610. Dramatized versions of the life of Boris Godunov often depict Shuisky as a Judas figure.

24. In August 1917 P. P. Ryabushinsky, a well-known industrialist, suggested that the revolutionary disorders would be checked by the "bony hand of hunger," which "would grasp by the throat the members of the different committees and Soviets." Quoted in William Henry Chamberlin, *The Russian Revolution 1917-1921* (New York: Macmillan, 1960), Vol. I, pp. 267-268.

Evening Session

MARCH 11

(Pages 587-614)

1. Probably a reference to the directive issued on the day of Kirov's assassination. See note 1, Morning Session, March 2.

2. See note 2, Evening Session, March 2.

Morning Session

MARCH 12

(Pages 615-655)

1. Krupskaya, Lenin's wife and a prominent Bolshevik, died in 1939.

2. Kalinin, an old Bolshevik, member of the Politburo, a Chairman of the Central Executive Comittee, was President of the Soviet Union from 1938 until his death in 1946.

3. In August 1920 Trotsky dismissed the railway-union heads and set up in their place the Central Comittee for Transport (*Tsektran*). The institution reflected Trotsky's idea of the merger of the trade unions and governmental apparatus.

4. M. S. Boguslavsky and Y. N. Drobnis appeared as defendants at the 1937 Moscow Trial. Both were executed. See *The Case of the Anti-Soviet Trotskyite Centre*.

5. The Stakhanovite campaign, designed to encourage workers to overfill production norms, was initiated in 1935.

6. N. S. Chkheidze, a prominent Menshevik and the first Chairman of the Petrograd Soviet, emigrated from the Soviet Union in 1921. He committed suicide in 1926.

7. General Yudenich led a White advance against Petrograd in June 1919.

Evening Session

MARCH 12

(Pages 656-680)

1. Lion Feuchtwanger, *Moscow 1937: My Visit Described for My Friends* (London: Gollancz, 1937). The author was present at the 1937 trial.

The Defendants: Biographical Notes

BESSONOV, S. A. (1892-?) — was a member of the Socialist Revolutionary Party between 1912 and 1918. He became a Bolshevik in 1920. There is no reliable information concerning the details of his career during the twenties or early thirties. The memoirs of Alexander Uralov (see list of Readings) contain a reference to a Professor Bessonov who was a follower of Bukharin in the mid-twenties. According to Bessonov's testimony at the trial, he was director of the Commercial Policy Department of the Berlin Trade Representation of the U.S.S.R. in 1931; shortly afterward he became counselor of the Berlin Embassy, where he remained until he returned to the Soviet Union in 1937. Bessonov was brought before a pre-trial *in camera* hearing in August 1937.

BUKHARIN, N. I. (1888-1938) — joined the Party in 1906. He spent the six years preceding the February Revolution in exile in Western Europe and the United States. After returning to Russia, in 1917, he became a member of the Central Committee. (He remained a full member until 1934, when he was demoted to candidacy.) Until his arrest in 1937, Bukharin's official positions were many and varied: candidate and full member of the Politburo from 1919 to 1929; editor of *Pravda*, 1918-1929; editor of *Bolshevik*, 1924-1929; member of the Executive Committee of the Communist International from 1919 to 1929, and Chairman between 1926 and 1929; member of the Collegium of the People's Commissariat of Heavy Industry, 1933, and later President of the Association of Research Institutes and member of the Academy of Sciences; editor of *Izvestia*, 1934-1937. Bukharin's writings, dating from before the Revolution, include many books and hundreds of articles ranging from economic theory to literary criticism. Until 1921 Bukharin stood on the left wing of the Bolshevik Party and in 1918-1919 he was the leader of the Left Communists. But during the ensuing years his views underwent a radical transformation; in 1924, after the death of Lenin, he emerged as the leading spokesman of the moderate, or right, wing of the Party and as the official Soviet theoretician. In this capacity he played a major

717

role in the struggle against the new Left Opposition headed by Trotsky. After the defeat of the Left, Bukharin's continued defense of the policies of NEP and his opposition to compulsory collectivization and super-industrialization brought him into conflict with Stalin, who in 1928-1929 moved to adopt the program of the defeated Left Opposition. This led to Bukharin's political defeat in 1929 as a leader of the newly formed Right Opposition. In 1937 he was expelled from the Party and arrested. Despite the fact that his views have long been considered anathema in the Soviet Union, Bukharin's theoretical writings have earned him a prominent place in the history of Marxist ideas.

CHERNOV, M. A. (1891-1938) — joined the Menshevik Party in 1916 but became a Bolshevik in January 1920. By 1928 he was People's Commissar of Trade of the Ukrainian S.S.R. (Republic) and in charge of grain collection. In this capacity Chernov played an important role in the 1929 collectivization campaign in the Ukraine. He was appointed Deputy People's Commissar of Trade of the U.S.S.R. in 1930, moved to the Commissariat of Agriculture shortly thereafter, and in the mid-thirties became People's Commissar of Agriculture of the U.S.S.R. He was made a full member of the Central Committee in 1934.

GRINKO, G. F. (1889 or 1890-1938) — joined the Party in 1919. Until 1926 he served in the Ukrainian S.S.R. in a number of positions, including member of the Central Committee, People's Commissar of Education, Chairman of the State Planning Commission, and Deputy Chairman of the Council of People's Commissars. Between 1926 and 1929 Grinko was Deputy Chairman of the State Planning Commission of the U.S.S.R., and in 1929 became Deputy People's Commissar of Agriculture of the U.S.S.R. Elected a candidate member of the Central Committee in 1934, he was People's Commissar of Finance of the U.S.S.R. from 1930 until his arrest in 1937. He has since been rehabilitated.

IKRAMOV, A. (1898-1938)—joined the Party in Tashkent in 1918 and carried on Party work until 1922, when he entered Sverdlov University. He was appointed Secretary of the Tashkent Party organization in 1925 and in 1929 Secretary of the Uzbek Central Committee, a post he retained until his arrest in 1937. A candidate member of the All-Union Central Committee since 1925, in 1931 Ikramov was appointed Secretary of its Central Asian Bureau and in 1934 was promoted to full membership in the Central Committee. During the thirties he also served on the Central Executive Committee of the U.S.S.R. and was a candidate member of its Presidium. In 1957 Ikramov became the first defendant in the 1938 Moscow Trial to be rehabilitated.

IVANOV, V. I. (1893-1938) — joined the Party in 1915. In October 1917 he served on a regional Military Revolutionary Committee and in 1917-1918 carried on Party and state work in Moscow. He then became

Secretary of the Yaroslavsky provincial Party organization and in 1924 was appointed Secretary of the Uzbek Central Committee. Ivanov later served as Secretary of the North Caucasus Party organization and beginning in 1931 as Secretary of the Northern Territory Party Committee. A candidate member of the Central Committee since 1927, he was promoted to full membership in 1934. At the time of his arrest in 1937, Ivanov was People's Commissar of the Timber Industry of the U.S.S.R. Although there has been no official statement, recent Soviet sources indicate that the rehabilitation of Ivanov is under way.

KHODJAYEV, F. (1896-1938) — was a prominent figure in nationalist-revolutionary movements in Central Asia before joining the Party in 1920. Between 1920 and 1924 he was Chairman of the Council of People's Nazirs of the People's Republic of Bokhara and a member of the Central Committee of Bokhara. From 1925 until his arrest Khodjayev was Chairman of the Council of People's Commissars of Uzbekistan and a member of the Uzbek Central Committee. A member of the Central Asian Bureau of the All-Union Central Committee since 1922, and, briefly, Chairman of the Central Executive Committee of the U.S.S.R., Khodjayev was the most prominent Uzbek leader of his time.

KRESTINSKY, N. N. (1883-1938) — joined the Party in 1903. From 1917 to 1921 he held a number of important state and Party positions: member of the Central Committee, 1917-1921; People's Commissar of Justice, 1917; People's Commissar of Finance, 1918-1921; Secretary of the Central Committee and member of the Politburo, 1919-1921. Because of his intransigent views during the trade-union controversy of 1921, he was removed from his posts that year and appointed Ambassador to Germany, where he remained until 1930. Although Krestinsky supported Trotsky in the Party disputes of the twenties, after his recantation in 1928 he became a member of the Central Executive Committee and served as Deputy People's Commissar of Foreign Affairs from 1930 until his expulsion from the Party in 1937. Recent praise of Krestinsky in the memoirs of I. M. Maisky (see *Izvestia,* November 27, 1963) makes it clear that he has now been rehabilitated.

RAKOVSKY, K. G. (1873-1941) — was a prominent figure in the social-democratic movements of Rumania, Bulgaria, Switzerland, and France before the Revolution. He joined the Russian Bolshevik Party in 1917 and in 1918 became Chairman of the Council of People's Commissars of the Ukraine. Between 1923 and 1927 Rakovsky served as Ambassador to Great Britain and then as Ambassador to France. A member of the Central Committee from 1919 to 1927, he was one of Trotsky's best-known supporters and a participant in the Left Opposition. He was expelled from the Party in 1927 and exiled from Moscow. In 1934 he finally renounced his former views and was reinstated, but was expelled again in 1938.

ROSENGOLTZ, A. P. (1889-1938) — joined the Party in 1905. A member of the Moscow Soviet's Presidium and of the Military Revolutionary Committee in October 1917, Rosengoltz served as political commissar of several Soviet armies during the Civil War. In 1922 he was appointed to the Collegium of the People's Commissariat of Finance and in 1923-1924 served on the Revolutionary War Council of the Republic. Along with several other of Trotsky's supporters, Rosengoltz was removed from his posts in 1925; he was given a diplomatic position in London, where he remained until 1927. In 1928 he was appointed to the Party's Central Control Commission and to the Collegium of the People's Commissariat of Workers' and Peasants' Inspection, where he later became Deputy Commissar. Rosengoltz was People's Commissar of Foreign Trade from 1930 until his expulsion from the Party in 1937; he was elected a candidate member of the Central Committee in 1934.

RYKOV, A. I. (1881-1938) — joined the Party in 1899. He became a member of the Central Committee in 1906 and served on the Presidium of the Moscow Soviet in 1917. In the first Soviet government, Rykov was People's Commissar of the Interior, and in 1918 became Chairman of the Supreme Council of National Economy. A full member of the Politburo since 1922, successor to Lenin as Chairman of the Council of People's Commissars of the U.S.S.R. (Premier) and of the Russian S.S.R., and a member of the Presidium of the Central Executive Committee — Rykov was one of the most important Soviet leaders of the twenties. A firm supporter of the policies of NEP, he joined Bukharin and Tomsky to form the leadership of the Right Opposition in 1928-1929. After the victory of Stalin in 1929, Rykov was removed from his posts and expelled from the Party. He was readmitted in 1931 and served as People's Commissar of Communications between 1931 and 1936. He was expelled again from the Party in 1937.

SHARANGOVICH, V. F. (1897-1938) — joined the Party in 1917. Other than the fact that he was a delegate from Byelorussia to the Seventeenth Party Congress in 1934, there is no reliable information concerning his career. According to his testimony at the trial, he returned from a Polish prisoner-of-war camp in 1921, and in 1923-1924 was senior assistant to the Procurator of the Byelorussian S.S.R. In 1924 he transferred to trade-union work and in 1926 had similar duties in Siberia. He became Second Secretary of the Byelorussian Central Committee in the late twenties or early thirties, and was First Secretary at the time of his arrest.

YAGODA, G. G. (1891-1938) — joined the Party in 1907. During the Civil War he headed a department of the Supreme Military Inspectorate and in 1919 became a member of the Collegium of the People's Commissariat of Foreign Trade. His career in the political police began in 1920, when he was appointed to the Presidium of the Cheka. Yagoda served as Dep-

720

uty Chairman of the OGPU from 1924 to 1934 and in 1930 became head of the growing system of labor camps and a candidate member of the Central Committee. He succeeded Menzhinsky as head of the NKVD in 1934 and became a full member of the Central Committee. Later he was appointed to the Central Executive Committee of the U.S.S.R. Yagoda's role in the preparation of the first Moscow Trial was considerable, but he was replaced as head of the NKVD by Yezhov in 1936 and demoted to People's Commissar of Communications. He was arrested in 1937.

ZELENSKY, I. A. (1890-1938) — joined the Party in 1906. A member of the Presidium of the Moscow Soviet in 1917, after the Revolution he served on the Collegium of the People's Commissariat of Supply and as head of the Moscow Supply Department. Between 1922 and 1925 Zelensky occupied an important position in the Party apparatus as Secretary of the powerful Moscow Party organization (1922-1924) and as a member of the Party's Secretariat (1923-1925) and its Organization Bureau (1924-1925). His removal from these positions by 1925 apparently resulted from his support of Kamenev and Zinoviev. A candidate and full member of the Central Committee from 1922 to 1937 and Secretary of the Central Asian Bureau of the Central Committee between 1924 and 1931, Zelensky became Chairman of the Central Union of Consumers' Cooperatives in 1931, a post he held until his arrest in 1937. Although there has been no official statement, recent Soviet sources indicate that Zelensky has been rehabilitated.

ZUBAREV, P. T. (1886-1938) — was apparently an agricultural specialist but there is nothing definitely known about his career. According to his testimony at the trial, he was engaged in Party agricultural work in the Urals until 1931, when he was transferred to Moscow. In 1933-1934 he worked in the seed-cultivation department of the People's Commissariat of Agriculture of the U.S.S.R., and in 1934 was transferred to the Commissariat of Agriculture of the Russian S.S.R.

KAZAKOV, I. N. (1891-1938), LEVIN, L. G. (1870-1938), PLETNEV, D. D. (1872 - ?) — were well-known physicians who had previously treated a number of prominent Soviet figures. Levin, a Kremlin doctor, had attended Lenin and was Stalin's physician; Pletnev, a medical professor, was accused of attacking a woman patient in June 1937 and publicly denounced. Previous to that there was no indication that the doctors were involved in any controversy.

BULANOV, P. P. (1895-1938), KRYUCHKOV, P. P. (1889-1938), MAXIMOV-DIKOVSKY, V. A. (1900-1938) — secretaries of Yagoda, Gorky, and Kuibyshev, respectively, played no important role in Party affairs. Bulanov's role at the trial involved furnishing firsthand evidence of Yagoda's alleged crimes. Maximov and Kryuchkov were portrayed as accomplices in the alleged murders of Kuibyshev and Gorky.

Readings on the Moscow Trials and the Purge Era*

ARMSTRONG, JOHN A., *The Politics of Totalitarianism: The Communist Party of the Soviet Union from 1934 to the Present.* New York: Random House, 1961. Chapters 1-5.

AVTORKHANOV, ABDURAKHMAN, *Stalin and the Soviet Communist Party: A Study in the Technology of Power.* New York: Praeger, 1959. Chapters 27-28.

BARMINE, ALEXANDER, *One Who Survived: The Life of a Russian under the Soviets.* New York: Putnam, 1945.

BECK, F., and W. GODIN, *Russian Purge and the Extraction of Confession.* New York: Viking Press, 1951.

BRZEZINSKI, ZBIGNIEW K., *The Permanent Purge: Politics in Soviet Totalitarianism.* Cambridge: Harvard University Press, 1956.

The Case of Leon Trotsky. Report of Hearings before the Dewey Commission. New York: Harper, 1937.

The Case of the Anti-Soviet Trotskyite Centre. Report of Court Proceedings Heard before the Military Collegium of the Supreme Court of the U.S.S.R., Moscow, January 23-30, 1937. Moscow: People's Commissariat of Justice of the U.S.S.R., 1937.

The Case of the Trotskyite-Zinovievite Terrorist Centre. Report of Court Proceedings Heard before the Military Collegium of the Supreme Court of the U.S.S.R., Moscow, August 19-24, 1936. Moscow: People's Commissariat of Justice of the U.S.S.R., 1936.

Current Soviet Policies II: The Documentary Record of the 20th Communist Party Congress and Its Aftermath. New York: Praeger, 1957.

---

* This list of readings has been limited to books dealing, wholly or in part, with the period between 1934 and the end of the great purges. Literature on aspects of earlier Party history relevant to the 1938 trial is cited in the notes. For a bibliography of Bukharin's published works between 1912 and 1936, see Sidney Heitman and Peter Knirsch, *N. I. Bucharin* (Berlin: East Europe Institute of the Free University of Berlin, 1959).

Current Soviet Policies IV: The Documentary Record of the 22nd Congress of the Communist Party of the Soviet Union. New York: Columbia University Press, 1962.

DALLIN, DAVID J., *From Purge to Coexistence: Essays on Stalin's and Khrushchev's Russia.* Chicago: Regnery, 1964. Chapters 1-9.

DANIELS, ROBERT V., *The Conscience of the Revolution: Communist Opposition in Soviet Russia.* Cambridge: Harvard University Press, 1960. Chapter 14.

DAVIES, JOSEPH E., *Mission to Moscow.* New York: Simon and Schuster, 1941. Part 5.

DEUTSCHER, ISAAC, *The Prophet Outcast. Trotsky: 1929-1940.* London and New York: Oxford University Press, 1963. Chapters 4-5.

———, *Stalin: A Political Biography.* New York: Vintage Books, 1960. Chapter 9.

DEWAR, HUGO, *The Modern Inquisition.* London: Allan Wingate, 1953.

———, "How They Saw the Moscow Trials." *Survey,* April 1962, pp. 87-95.

EHRENBURG, ILYA, *Memoirs: 1921-1941.* Cleveland and New York: World Publishing Co., 1964.

GORBATOV, ALEXANDER V., *Years Off My Life.* New York: Norton, 1964.

KENNAN, GEORGE F., *Russia and the West Under Lenin and Stalin.* Boston: Little, Brown and Company, 1960. Chapters 20 and 21.

KHRUSHCHEV, NIKITA S., *The Crimes of the Stalin Era.* Special Report to the 20th Congress of the Communist Party of the Soviet Union, annotated by Boris I. Nicolaevsky. New York: *The New Leader,* 1956.

KIRCHHEIMER, OTTO, *Political Justice: The Use of Legal Procedures for Political Ends.* Princeton: Princeton University Press, 1961.

KOESTLER, ARTHUR, *Darkness at Noon.* New York: Macmillan, 1948.

———, "Darkness at Noon Again. An Interview with Arthur Koestler." *Survey,* July 1963, pp. 173-175.

———, *The Invisible Writing. An Autobiography.* Boston: Beacon Press, 1955. Chapter 37.

KRIVITSKY, W. G., *In Stalin's Secret Service.* New York: Harper, 1939.

LEITES, NATHAN, and E. BERNAUT, *Ritual of Liquidation: The Case of the Moscow Trials.* Glencoe: Free Press, 1954.

LERMOLO, ELIZABETH, *Face of a Victim.* New York: Harper, 1955.

Letter of an Old Bolshevik. New York: Rand School Press, 1937.

MacLean, Fitzroy, *Escape to Adventure.* Boston: Little, Brown, 1950. Chapter 5.

Merleau-Ponty, M., *Humanisme et Terreur.* Paris: Librairie Gallimard, 1947.

Nicolaevsky, Boris I., *Bolsheviks and Bureaucrats.* Essays by Boris I. Nicolaevsky. New York: Praeger, 1965.

Not Guilty. Report of the Dewey Commission of Inquiry into the Charges Made Against Leon Trotsky in the Moscow Trials. New York: Harper, 1938.

Orlov, Alexander, *The Secret History of Stalin's Crimes.* New York: Random House, 1953.

Schapiro, Leonard, *The Communist Party of the Soviet Union.* New York: Random House, 1959. Chapters 22-23.

————, "The Great Purge." In B. H. Liddell Hart (ed.), *The Soviet Army.* London: Weidenfeld and Nicolson, 1956. Pp. 65-72.

Serge, Victor, *The Case of Comrade Tulayev.* New York: Anchor Books, 1963.

Souvarine, Boris, *Stalin: A Critical Survey of Bolshevism.* New York: Alliance Book Corporation, 1939. Postscript.

Uralov, Alexander (Avtorkhanov), *The Reign of Stalin.* London: Bodley Head, 1953.

Weissberg, Alexander, *The Accused.* New York: Simon and Schuster, 1951.

THE EDITORS

ROBERT C. TUCKER is Professor of Politics and Director of the Program in Russian Studies at Princeton University. He has also taught at Indiana University and was attaché of the United States Embassy in Moscow, where he spent nine years. Among his recent works are: *The Soviet Political Mind* (1963) and *Philosophy and Myth in Karl Marx* (1961).

STEPHEN F. COHEN was educated at Indiana University, the University of Birmingham (England), and Columbia University and is currently connected with the Russian Institute at Columbia. At present he is working on a study of Bukharin and his political thought.